THE HOLOCAUST

EUROPE, THE WORLD, AND THE JEWS
1918–1945

Norman J. W. Goda

University of Florida

Routledge
Taylor & Francis Group

LONDON AND NEW YORK

First published 2013 by Pearson Education, Inc.

Published 2016 by Routledge
2 Park Square, Milton Park, Abingdon, Oxon OX14 4RN
711 Third Avenue, New York, NY 10017, USA

Routledge is an imprint of the Taylor & Francis Group, an informa business

Copyright © 2013 by Taylor & Francis.

Cover Designer: Suzanne Duda
Image Permission Coordinator: Stephan Merland
Cover Photo: Jack Kugelmass, Director, Center for Jewish Studies, University of Florida

Library of Congress Cataloging-in-Publication Data

Goda, Norman J. W.
  The Holocaust : Europe, the world, and the Jews 1918-1945 / Norman J.W. Goda.
    p. cm.
  Includes bibliographical references and index.
  ISBN-13: 978-0-205-56841-3
  ISBN-10: 0-205-56841-6
  1. Holocaust, Jewish (1939–1945) 2. World War, 1939–1945—Jews.
3. Germany—History—1933–1945. I. Title.
  D804.3G62 2013
  940.53'18—dc23

                                    2012036298

ISBN13:978-0-205-56841-3 (pbk)

To my sons

Grant Alexander Goda

Lucas Harrison Goda

CONTENTS

MAPS

PREFACE

The term *holocaust* derives from the ancient Greek translation of the word *olah* in Hebrew scripture. The religious term referred to a sacrifice consumed wholly by fire. But in the secular context of the modern world, the English word *holocaust* referred to large-scale destruction of human life in a manmade or natural disaster. During and after World War II, the term *holocaust*, along with other expressions, came to denote the murder of nearly 6 million European Jews by Nazi Germany and its allies. At the same time, Jewish writers in Palestine (Israel after 1948) used specific secular terms—the Hebrew word *Shoah* ("catastrophe") and the Yiddish word *Churbn* ("destruction")—to describe the annihilation of Europe's Jews. The use of precise terms, combined with steadily growing interest beyond Israel, helped to solidify the use of the word *Holocaust* (now with a capital *H*) in the English-speaking world and elsewhere by the 1970s. In recent years, some have sought to (re)expand the meaning of the term to include other human tragedies. In this book, however, the term *Holocaust* refers to the unparalleled Jewish catastrophe.[1]

This particular history of the Holocaust has two goals. One is to provide instructors and their undergraduate students with a readable text containing sufficient but manageable detail. The book is arranged chronologically and geographically to reflect how persecution, experience, and choices varied over different periods and places throughout Europe and beyond, depending on the progress of World War II and depending on local circumstances. As historian Dan Stone has recently noted, there were multiple histories of the Holocaust that depended on these and other factors.[2]

One can also employ a more thematic approach with this book. The chapters have distinct sections on German decisions, Jewish responses, bystander reactions, and other themes. Instructors can assign sections across chapters as they prefer. Weekly assignments in either case would be brief enough so that instructors can also assign additional readings for deeper discussion on a variety of topics, including the mentality of German killers, Jewish leaders and resistors, European citizens' attitudes during deportations, the degradation of humanity in ghettos and camps, the Vatican's silence regarding the destruction of the Jews, the possibilities of Allied actions to stem the killing process, and many more. English-speaking students should find the footnotes and the "Starting Points for Further Reading" at the end of the book to be helpful guides for further reading and paper assignments.

My second goal is to provide a somewhat broader set of perspectives than is often the case in undergraduate texts. Many narratives of the Holocaust proceed from the German vantage point, beginning with the rise of Adolf Hitler and the Nazi Party. Through the rubric of Nazi racism and brutality, they follow German state policies toward Germany's Jews, then toward Jews in Poland, France, the USSR, and elsewhere, who fell under Nazi control. These narratives also show how the Nazis killed substantial numbers of other social and racial enemies. These other victims included communists, homosexuals, Jehovah's Witnesses, the disabled, Roma, African and Soviet prisoners of war, and millions of civilians in the Nazi-occupied territories that were declared suitable for settlement by Germans only. This approach makes sense. The Nazis gave

---

[1]On etymology, see Dalia Ofer, "Linguistic Conceptualization of the Holocaust in Palestine and Israel, 1942–53," *Journal of Contemporary History*, 31, no. 3 (July 1996), pp. 567–95, and Jon Petrie, "The Secular Word 'Holocaust': Scholarly Myths, History, and Twentieth Century Meanings," *Journal of Genocide Research*, 2, no. 1 (March 2000), pp. 31–63.

[2]Dan Stone, *Histories of the Holocaust* (New York, 2010).

the world its first government that placed race at the center of its worldview. How they made and implemented their murderous decisions regarding Jews and their other victims is crucial.

But the Holocaust is also a chapter in Jewish and even world history. The very title of historian Lucy S. Dawidowicz's pioneering 1975 study, *The War Against the Jews*, notes the absolute centrality of the Jews to Nazi thinking.[3] The Jews were the Nazis' primary "racial" enemy. It was the Jews—from Jewish leaders to Jewish infants—who were slated for complete and swift annihilation in areas where the Germans wished to settle and also in areas where they did not. The Jews were also an imagined geopolitical enemy. The Nazis believed that world Jewry was united in a formidable and diabolical global conspiracy against which Germany waged a life-or-death struggle. Berlin Jews were supposedly behind Germany's collapse in 1918, Minsk Jews were supposedly behind the Soviet partisan movement in 1942, New York Jews were supposedly behind the bombing of German cities in 1943, Budapest Jews were supposedly behind the cracks in the Axis alliance in 1944, and so on.

The scope of Nazi thinking about the Jews had a long, international development. More than a century before the Nazis climbed to power, Jews and non-Jews throughout Europe wrestled with what social commentators called the "Jewish question." In forging modern national citizenries, what was to be done with Jewish populations that were never accepted as truly European and were believed to have an alien and, for some, even a malevolent character? Should Jews be forced to acculturate? What if they did not? What if Jews acculturated and still retained their supposed alien characteristics? What if canards about existential dangers of Jews were believed by a critical mass of people? The Jewish question dated from the dawn of modernity, but the political, financial, and social turmoil in Europe during and after World War I triggered dangerously escalating passions toward the Jews, who, according to many, were at the root of the disorder. Despite hard-won Jewish rights in most European countries, many Europeans saw Jews as more foreign and more malignant than ever.

Jews themselves had no common answer. Should they continue to fight for full acceptance? Should they adopt the idea of a national homeland in Palestine? What if these solutions, handled incorrectly, exacerbated matters? The world at large also lacked answers. Several states aimed to disenfranchise, terrorize, or even expel their Jews after World War I. Few, however, wanted to take them. Thus, the Jewish question remained dangerously open when Adolf Hitler came to power in the middle of a global depression in 1933. The Nazis made political and economic war on Jews from the start, and they encouraged their allies and even their enemies to do likewise. Beginning in 1939, they terrorized Jews in the lands they occupied. And in 1941, the Nazis adopted what they called the Final Solution to the Jewish Question in Europe—the murder of every Jew they could reach, mostly by shooting and poison gas. Of a prewar European Jewish population of about 9 million, some two-thirds perished during the war. In areas where the Nazi occupation was strongest, nearly all Jews were murdered.

Jewish reactions to the onslaught varied. Over 500,000 Jews left Europe while there was time, fleeing to places as diverse as the United States, Palestine, Argentina, and even China. Others were trapped because of tightening immigration restrictions during the global economic depression of the 1930s. Even the Jewish national home in Palestine, promised by Great Britain during World War I, faced restrictions thanks to violent Arab objections. After 1939, Jews caught in Nazi-occupied Europe tried to cope, struggling against German policies of terror, plunder, ghettoization, and starvation. They hoped to outlast the Nazis, keep their families together, help their stricken

---

[3]Lucy S. Dawidowicz, *The War Against the Jews 1933–1945* (New York, 1975).

communities, and write down everything they saw of history's greatest crime. Once it was clear that the Nazis were intent on mass murder, some Jews denied the inconceivable truth, others tried to hold on against all odds, some tried to alert the world, and others turned to armed resistance.

Jews abroad, from Palestine to the United States, also reacted. They collected information on Hitler's Final Solution, placed it before Allied leaders, and attempted to move Allied governments to undertake rescue operations, ranging from eleventh-hour immigration efforts to mass ransom schemes. But whether they were in Warsaw or Washington, Jews never had the power to halt the Final Solution. In Europe, their responses were local, confined to isolated communities stretching from France to Ukraine. Battered, terrorized, disoriented, isolated, often unable to comprehend the truth and practically unarmed when they did, Jews could rarely counter state-directed extermination efforts. Jews abroad, meanwhile, were small minorities. They had no state and no army. They could appeal to the moral sense of Allied governments and nothing more.

Might others have done better? The Holocaust was an international catastrophe emerging from the international Jewish question. Peoples occupied, threatened, or aligned with Nazi Germany, whether they lived in Poland, France, the Netherlands, Denmark, Ukraine, Italy, Romania, Hungary, or even the Middle East and Japan, had to decide whether they would collaborate in Hitler's war against the Jews, stand aside, or try and help the victims as best they could. Heartening tales of bravery and rescue come from all European countries, from Sweden in the north to Italy in the south. So do nauseating tales of French collaborators, Polish villagers-turned-murderers, Ukrainian police battalions, Romanian and Hungarian murder campaigns, and silent church officials. Centuries of European ambivalence toward Jews turned to humanity and inhumanity alike under the Nazi whirlwind.

The nations fighting the Germans also had choices. All understood Nazi brutality before the war. Although none envisioned mass murder at that time, all might have taken in more Jews. In 1941, information on mass shootings of Jews reached Germany's enemies. In 1942, more intelligence concerning comprehensive German extermination efforts arrived. In 1944 came detailed eyewitness reporting from within the Auschwitz death camp itself. What would be done with the information? The terrible speed of the Final Solution confounded the issue. The killing was at its height in 1942, when Nazi Germany was at the peak of its military power. But could the Allies have published the information that they had? Could they have attempted rescue operations as their fortunes changed and Germany was on the retreat? Might they have ransomed Jews from the Nazis? Might they have bombed the death camp at Auschwitz in 1944 as they bombed nearby targets?

Ultimately Allied and Soviet leaders understood the war as a struggle for survival. Their aim was to destroy a terrible enemy as quickly as possible. They did not see the conflict as a humanitarian mission for the sake of foreigners, and they surely never understood the war to be for the sake of Europe's Jews, particularly because grand rescue missions could potentially draw away from the fight against Germany itself. The Allies and Soviets crushed Nazi Germany in 1945. Had they not done so, or if they had done so later, far more Jews would have perished. As it was, however, the numbers of Jewish dead were unimaginable.

This book thus attempts to integrate local, national, and global narratives of the Holocaust. But it also seeks to weave together its diverse voices. They include those of state leaders from Adolf Hitler to Franklin Roosevelt. They include those of German perpetrators, from Adolf Eichmann to Aloïs Brunner, and those of collaborators, from Pierre Laval in France to László Endre in Hungary. They include the indifferent, from US Assistant Secretary of State Breckinridge Long to Vatican Secretary of State Cardinal Luigi Maglione. The voices also include those of Jewish leaders, from Adam Czerniaków in Warsaw to David Ben-Gurion in Jerusalem, and those of Jewish resistors of different types, from Abba Kovner in Vilna to Rachel Auerbach in Warsaw, to Tuvia Bielski in the forests of Belarus. They include those of Jews who survived and Jews who did not—from Rudolf Vrba and Ada Lichtman to Raymond-Raoul Lambert and Etty Hillesum. And they include voices of rescuers, from the diplomat Raoul Wallenberg to the cleric Father Pierre-Marie Benoît, to ordinary but unusually brave bystanders like Francisca Halamajowa, who somehow hid half of her town's Jewish survivors.

In part, my aim is to get out of their way and allow them to speak. Together, they remind us of humanity lost and humanity found while teaching us of the horror but also the complexity of the war against the Jews. They remind us how the Holocaust stretched from paranoid fantasies to government bureaucracies, to strategic relations, to domestic politics, to family relationships, to individual consciences. Humanity's greatest crime defies a single book, especially because the floodgates of Holocaust scholarship in the past twenty-five years have produced libraries of international scholarship. This modest attempt, based mostly on scholarship that I admire deeply, aims at least to convey a sense of the Holocaust's many moving parts. I hope that it will raise many more questions than answers.

ACKNOWLEDGMENTS

For their invaluable support for teaching and scholarship in Holocaust Studies at the University of Florida, I thank Norman and Irma Braman, I further thank the Center of Jewish Studies at the University of Florida and its director, Jack Kugelmass, a colleague and friend since my arrival in Gainesville in 2009. I could not have written this book without the Isser and Rae Price Library of Judaica at the University of Florida, headed by its fine librarian, Rebecca Jefferson. I have also been honored to know other friends and supporters of Jewish and Holocaust Studies at the University of Florida, including Gary and Niety Gerson and Nan and David Rich.

My friend Gerhard L. Weinberg taught me the profession of historical scholarship twenty-five years ago at the University of North Carolina at Chapel Hill, and he continues to do so to this day. My friend Carole Fink of Ohio State University encouraged me to undertake this project and had faith in me and my ability to complete it. My friend Richard Breitman of American University read the entire manuscript while working on one of his own, and made many valuable recommendations. Rob DeGeorge, my project editor at Pearson, and Marianne L'Abbate, my copy editor, had faith in this project and put up with me through the production process. Mohinder Singh, my project manager at Aptara, was extremely patient and careful during the final printing. Matt Mingus of the University of Florida located the maps for this book and was instrumental in the painstaking work of adaptation.

The following reviewers read the initial proposal and the finished manuscript, and made many helpful suggestions: William Drumright, Monroe Community College; Myrna Goodman, Sonoma State University; Peter Hayes, Northwestern University; Michael R. Hayse, The Richard Stockton College; Severin Hochberg, George Washington University; Randall Kaufman, Miami Dade College–Homestead Campus; Nameeta Mathur, Saginaw Valley State University; Gary Miller, Southern Oregon University; Jan-Ruth Mills, Pima Community College; Daniel E. Rogers, University of South Alabama; David Scrase, University of Vermont; Nathan Stoltzfus, Florida State University; and David Tompkins, Carleton College.

My family is my greatest gift. I thank my father Herbert L. Goda, my late mother Lilyan Z. Goda, my sisters, Saralee Hillman and Esther Goda, and other family members who have taken interest in this work, including Thelma and Melvin Lenkin. And for their extraordinary patience and unending support—for they had to live with me through this project—I thank my terrific boys Grant and Lucas, and my wonderful wife and best friend Gwyneth.

Norman J. W. Goda
Gainesville, Florida

A NOTE ON PLACE NAMES

Cities and towns in eastern Europe have different names depending on the language: Russian, Ukrainian, Polish, Lithuanian, German, or Yiddish. I have used Anglicized names where these are common in English-language literature, for example, Warsaw, Bucharest, and Prague. For most, I have used the official names used on the eve of World War II in the language of the country to which a given city or town belonged. Exceptions are a few cities whose Russian names are very common in Holocaust studies. Thus, in Lithuania, I use the names Kovno and Vilna rather than the present Lithuanian names of Kaunas and Vilnius. In Ukraine, I use the Russian Lvov rather than the Polish Lwów or the Ukrainian L'viv; in Bessarabia, I use the Russian Kishinev instead of the Romanian Chişinău.

The Jewish Question
to Modern Times

What modern writers called "the Jewish question" was more than a century old when Adolf Hitler came to power in 1933. It rested on Jewish distinctiveness, asking how—or whether—Jews should fit into the broader European world. In the premodern age, Jews were eternal outsiders, believed to engage in wicked anti-Christian acts ranging from the murder of Christian children to ruinous usury. In times of crisis, Jewish communities were subject to violence and expulsion.

Jewish emancipation in the nineteenth century offered Jews citizenship and legal equality, triggering the modern Jewish question. Proponents of emancipation believed that Jews would abandon their "objectionable" traits. But modern Jew-hatred, or antisemitism, held that emancipation was a mistake. Antisemites argued that Jews were an alien element destroying European society through modern means, namely, their alleged control of money, politics, and mass opinion. As the twentieth century dawned, many feared Jews as well as despising them.

Jews had their own answers. While some argued that emancipation meant diluting a distinct religion and culture, others argued that the tradeoff, which meant acceptance, was desirable. Still others, appalled with antisemitic displays, argued that Jews should form their own state. On the eve of the twentieth century, the Jewish question generated many responses—some reasonable, some fanciful, and some hopeful, and some violent.

1.1 JEWS AND CHRISTIANS IN THE ANCIENT WORLD

Ancient Beginnings

What we know of the earliest Hebrews comes from the Hebrew Bible, which provides history of belief rather than history itself. The Hebrews developed the notion of a single, beneficent God when other ancient peoples believed in many deities that tended toward spite and vengefulness. They believed in a covenant with their God symbolized by the ritual of circumcision. They believed they were the people of Israel, the name God gave to Jacob, whose twelve sons formed twelve tribes. They believed God led them from slavery in Egypt in a series of miracles known as the Exodus and that he provided them with a land of their own in Canaan. They believed God gave them laws regulating everything from worship to ethics, to honoring the seventh day on which God rested, to dietary laws that prohibit some foods while describing proper preparation of others.

The Hebrew kingdom, centered on the city of Jerusalem in the tenth century BCE, split after the death of King Solomon. Hereafter, other ancient texts provide more definitive information. The Assyrians conquered the northern kingdom, named Israel, in 722 BCE. The southern kingdom, Judah (from which the word *Jew* comes), became the center of the developing Jewish religion. It focused on the magnificent temple built to God by Solomon in Jerusalem. In 586 BCE the Babylonians conquered Judah, destroyed the temple, and took its leaders to Babylon. The Persians under King Cyrus conquered the entire Near East and allowed Hebrew leaders to return to Jerusalem in 538 BCE.

Exile and eventual return to their land are recurring themes in Jewish belief and history. Prophets understood the Babylonian exile as God's punishment for straying from the law. Under high priests, Jews rebuilt their temple. They placed the Torah—the scrolls with the first five books of the Hebrew Bible containing Jewish law—at the heart of Jewish belief. They rededicated themselves to ritual. Separateness from other peoples became a powerful trend to the point where marriage to foreigners was forbidden. Thus, the Jews became a more distinct religious and cultural community. As they spread into other parts of the Mediterranean world, Jews remained bound to their traditions.

Alexander the Great of Macedonia conquered the Persian Empire, including what the Greeks and Romans called Judea in the 330s BCE, beginning a period of Greek dynastic rule in the Near East. In 63 BCE, the Romans conquered Judea and established their own imperial rule. Neither the Greeks nor the Romans knew what to make of the Jews, who stubbornly rejected Greco-Roman gods and maintained their customs. In 167 BCE, King Antiochus IV tried to eliminate circumcision and force sacrifices to Greek gods in the temple. He triggered a revolt in Judea that was ultimately successful. But in 70 CE, the Romans suppressed a bitter Jewish rebellion, captured Jerusalem, and demolished the second temple. They depleted the Jewish population and reordered the province, renaming it Palæstina (after the Philistines), thus ending Jerusalem's centrality in the Jewish world in all but Jewish collective consciousness.

Thus began another period of exile that lasted nearly two millennia, known as the Diaspora, or dispersion. Jewish tradition and learning practiced in prayer houses known as synagogues replaced the geographic locus of Jerusalem. Learning centered on the Torah and also the Talmud, some five centuries' worth of Biblical commentary by rabbis—scholars who replaced the temple priests as learned sages of Jewish law. As Jews moved to different cities and engaged in trade and crafts, Hebrew remained the language of study and prayer. Jewish culture emphasized education as the means to understand God, who would always protect his people. It was another characteristic shared by Jews wherever they lived.

Early Christianity and the Jews

Christianity began as a Jewish sect. Jesus of Nazareth called for a benevolent kingdom of God on earth while preaching God's unconditional love for all believers, both powerful and weak. In Christian tradition, he is the Messiah, the Son of God, whose death was followed by resurrection and the promise of eternal life for the faithful. The teachings eventually appealed to Roman citizens, whose state gods promised no such thing. Christianity spread, becoming the dominant religion under the Emperor Constantine (312–324 CE), who legalized Christianity. Emperor Theodosius (379–395 CE) made Christianity Rome's sole legal religion.

Early Christian teaching held a toxic view of Jews. Jesus' egalitarian message ran afoul of both Jerusalem's Temple aristocracy and the Roman state. The former handed him over to Rome's prefect in Judea, Pontius Pilate, who had Jesus executed by the Roman method of crucifixion.

The New Testament Gospels, written decades after the crucifixion and edited by the early Church, blamed the Jews—*all* Jews—for Jesus' suffering and death. In the Gospel of Matthew, Pilate is a reluctant figure pressured by the bloodthirsty Jewish multitude. Pilate protests, "I am innocent of this man's blood; see to it yourselves," to which the Jewish rabble responds, "His blood be on us and on our children! [Matthew 27:24–25]."[1] The Jews' guilt for the crucifixion is thus eternal through generations. In fact, Roman prefects did not take orders from local mobs. Roman texts suggest that Pilate ruled forcefully and cared little for Jewish sensibilities. But the early church aimed to separate itself from those who clung to older Jewish ritual. It also existed within Rome's empire. To blame Rome for the crucifixion would have hindered Christianity's spread.[2]

Early Christian writers debated God's judgment on the Jews. Origen of Alexandria (d. 254) argued that the "real cause" for Jerusalem's destruction and the Jews' exile lay in "the plot against Jesus." St. Augustine of Hippo (d. 430), the greatest of early church scholars, agreed, but posited that the Jews still served God's plan. "Dispersed among all nations," he wrote, Jews bore the mark of Cain as "an example of how God uses evil for the improvement of the good." They should not be slain, he said, but they should suffer in exile as "witnesses to the prophecies given beforehand by Christ."[3] Rome's relationship with Jews in its imperial twilight was ambivalent, a mix of declining forbearance and intermittent violence.

The Roman Empire crumbled in the fifth century under the invasions of Germanic tribes and split into a volatile Roman Catholic West and a more stable Greek Orthodox East. Jews tended to move into the more tolerant Persian orbit in the Near East. In the seventh century, when Arab conquerors spread Islam across the Near East, North Africa, and Spain, Jews still viewed Muslim rule as preferable. For centuries, most Jews remained in the Islamic world, paying additional taxes but benefiting from the more advanced civilization that spanned from Baghdad to Cordoba. They engaged in learning, professions, trade, crafts, and agriculture, maintaining tradition as before.

1.2 ASHKENAZIC JEWRY IN THE MIDDLE AGES

Ashkenazic Jewry

Five centuries after the Roman Empire collapsed, decentralized feudal kingdoms emerged in northern Europe. They were based mostly on agriculture but partly on developing commercial towns. In the tenth century, local rulers in western Europe—kings, dukes, counts, and bishops—invited Jews to settle. With their literacy, craft skills, and willingness to risk long-distance trade in spices, fruits, livestock, and other items, Jews spurred growth. In return, Jewish communities received freedom of worship, tax exemptions, and self-governance. By the end of the eleventh century, northern European—Ashkenazic—Jewish communities (as opposed to Sephardic Jews in Spain) took root in French, English, and German towns.

They remained foreign and insular. As a small minority in a Christian world, Jews had more in common with Jewish communities in the Islamic world than with their Christian neighbors. Because landholding demanded a Christian oath, Jews could not engage in agriculture, as did most Europeans. Yiddish, based on Germanic and later Slavic languages but written in

---

[1]Michael D. Coogan, ed. *The New Oxford Annotated Bible*, 3rd ed. (New York, 2001), New Testament, p. 52.

[2]See John Dominic Crossan, *Who Killed Jesus? Exposing the Roots of Anti-Semitism in the Gospel Story of the Death of Jesus* (San Francisco, 1995), pp. 147–52; John T. Carroll and Joel B. Green, *The Death of Jesus in Early Christianity* (Peabody, MA, 1995), pp. 182–205.

[3]Quotes in Paula Fredriksen, *Augustine and the Jews: A Christian Defense of Jews and Judaism* (New York, 2008), pp. 326–8, 348.

Hebrew characters, emerged as their spoken language and also set them apart. Jewish quarters in European towns were built around the local synagogue, religious schools, and kosher slaughterers, and were thus self-contained as well.

The return of economic stability to northern Europe in the eleventh century brought consistency to Christian practice and deeper religiosity. Jesus' martyrdom became a motif for the common man, who also accepted the Gospels' depiction of Jewish guilt. At the same time, the establishment of Christian merchants and craftsmen brought economic resentment of Jews owing to their superior trade connections and their exemptions from membership and production rules by which closed Christian merchant and craft guilds functioned.

Christian Violence

Mob violence against Jews was sporadic. But it was based on the notion that Jews were a hostile and even demonic element. The first major outbreak came with the First Crusade (1096–99), wherein lesser European knights and thousands of commoners journeyed east to reclaim Jerusalem from the Muslims. The crusade unleashed a violent mix of religious fervor and temporal greed. Undisciplined armies killed Jews as a holy act. Jews in the Rhineland—the German region where Jews first settled in the eleventh century—suffered the worst. A Hebrew chronicle from Worms describes how crusaders and locals proclaimed, "Behold the time has come to avenge Him who was crucified, whom their ancestors slew. Now not let a remnant or a residue escape, even an infant or a suckling in the cradle." Many Christians sheltered Jews, but perhaps three thousand were killed in Cologne, Mainz, and Worms alone.[4]

By the late twelfth century, intermittent allegations emerged that Jews celebrated Jesus' death through the ritual murder of Christian children at Easter. The first known charge concerned twelve-year-old William of Norwich in England in 1144. Local Jews were accused of kidnapping William, gagging him, forcing a crown of thorns on his head, fastening him to a cross, and stabbing his side. Jews' consumption of victims' blood entered these accusations in the thirteenth century. Jews also purportedly stabbed the host—the wafer through which Christians accept Christ's body—in order to rob it of its saving power. Riots, torture to extract confessions, and executions often resulted from such claims. Accusations continued into the twentieth century.[5]

The profession of usury—lending of money at high interest—augmented anti-Jewish hostility. In the absence of modern banking, moneylending maintained economic growth. The Roman Catholic Church prohibited Christians from the practice, but Jewish law permitted it, so the field was left mostly to Jews. The business was risky. Because borrowers often defaulted, they had to post collateral. By the twelfth century, kings and local lords taxed Jews without warning, forcing Jewish moneylenders to call back loans whether borrowers could pay or not. Thus was born the stereotype of the greedy Jewish moneylender, though few Jews engaged in the business.[6] The image of the Jews' control of Christian society through their supposed control of money survived into modern times. From the killing of Christ to devilish rituals, to the ubiquitous moneybag, the Jew became a mix of pernicious images.

---

[4]Quote and figure in Robert Chazan, *European Jewry and the First Crusade* (Berkeley, CA, 1987), p. 57.

[5]Summary in Hillel J. Kieval, "Blood Libels and Host Desecration Accusations," in Gershon D. Hundert, ed., *The YIVO Encyclopedia of Jews in Eastern Europe* (New Haven, CT, 2008), vol. 1, pp. 195–200. On William, see Gavin I. Langmuir, "Thomas of Monmouth: Detector of Ritual Murder," in *The Blood Libel Legend: A Casebook in Anti-Semitic Folklore*, ed. Alan Dundes (Madison, WI, 1991), pp. 3–40. On host desecration, see Miri Rubin, *Gentile Tales: The Narrative Assault on Late Medieval Jews* (New Haven, CT, 1999).

[6]Robert Chazan, *Medieval Stereotypes and Modern Antisemitism* (Berkeley, CA, 1997).

Expulsion and Segregation

Pope Innocent III, Europe's most powerful figure in the early thirteenth century, agreed with St. Augustine's dictum that Jews served God's purpose as a foil for Christianity. But he was also convinced of Jewish malevolence. His letters accuse the Jews of mocking Christ, robbing widows and orphans, and defrauding churches through "their vicious usury."[7] In the Fourth Lateran Council of 1215, he prohibited Jews from appearing in public during the three days before Easter and decreed that Jews wear distinctive clothing so that they could be identified.[8] Markings varied from yellow collars, to yellow circles sewn onto coats, to the oft-pointed "Jew Hat" seen in most medieval representations of Jews.

As royal power grew and expenses increased in the thirteenth century, monarchs expelled Jews from royal domains, auctioned Jewish property, and assumed ownership of their loans. King Edward I of England helped finance numerous wars by expelling England's Jews in 1290. King Philip IV of France did the same in 1306. After completing the Catholic reconquest of Spain in 1492, King Ferdinand and Queen Isabella expelled all Jews (and Muslims) who would not convert. Most Sephardic Jews, used to living under Muslim rule, migrated to cities in the Turkish-ruled Ottoman Empire in North Africa, Greece, the Balkan region, and Anatolia. Many Ashkenazic Jews who were expelled from towns in northern Europe migrated to the German principalities of the Holy Roman Empire.

In the mid-1300s, Jews in German towns were attacked for crimes ranging from ritual murder to host desecration, to responsibility for the spread of devastating fourteenth-century plagues. Of the 1,038 Jewish settlements in German cities and towns, more than 400 experienced massacres or expulsions from 1350 to 1550. Centers of Jewish culture were erased from Trier (1418), Vienna (1420), Cologne (1424), Augsburg (1438), Breslau (1453), Magdeburg (1493), Nuremberg (1499), Regensburg (1519), and elsewhere. Townspeople built chapels atop synagogue ruins. They used Jewish gravestones for construction and commemorated expulsions with pilgrimages, religious festivals, and special masses.[9]

Jews remaining in German states could settle outside towns in return for protection taxes. They continued to live in some towns such as Frankfurt and Prague, but they were confined to closed ghettos, which initially emerged in Italy in 1519. Some ghettos were walled, gated sections in flood-prone areas that Jews could leave only during the day, excluding Sundays and Christian holidays. Others were simply town districts beyond which Jews were not allowed to reside. All ghettos were heavily taxed. Jewish cultural life thrived nonetheless because of the humanistic influence of the Italian Renaissance, the first mechanical printing of Hebrew books, and the construction of new synagogues.

The Protestant Reformation of the sixteenth century triggered a break with the Catholic Church in many regions of northern Europe, as well as a century of bloody Protestant-Catholic religious wars. Though Catholics and Protestants eventually made uneasy peace with one another, Jews were another matter. The German reformer Martin Luther, whose protests against the pope triggered the Reformation in 1517, initially condemned Catholic treatment of Jews. Jesus and the

---

[7]Pope Innocent III to King Philip II of France (1205), in *Church, State, and Jew in the Middle Ages*, ed. Robert Chazan (Berkeley, CA, 1979), p. 172.

[8]Relevant decrees of the Fourth Lateran Council in Jacob Rader Marcus, ed., *The Jew in the Medieval World: A Sourcebook 315–1791* (Cincinnati, OH, 1999), pp. 153–7.

[9]Helmut Walser Smith, *The Continuities of German History: Nation, Religion, and Race Across the Long Nineteenth Century* (New York: 2008), p. 75ff.

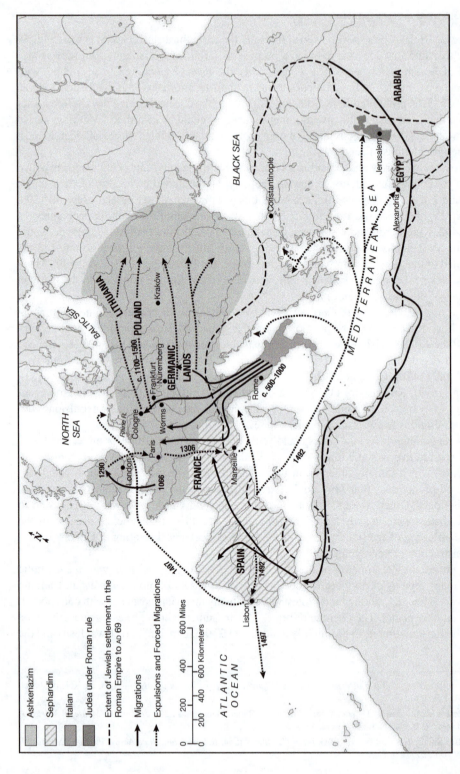

MAP 1.1 Major Jewish migrations, 70–1500 CE *Source: Roger Kean "The Dispersion of the Jews from AD 70 to 1500," from Angus Konstam, Atlas of Medieval Europe* (New York: Checkmark Books, 2000), p. 81.

apostles, Luther reminded his readers in 1523, were Jews. But he soured on learning that Jews would not become Protestants. His pamphlet "On the Jews and Their Lies" (1543) praised previous expulsions, urged destruction of synagogues, called for confiscation of Jewish property, and said Jews should "be driven like mad dogs out of the land."[10]

Catholic monarchs were no more forgiving. As late as 1745, Holy Roman Empress Maria Theresa expelled most of Prague's 11,000 Jews. Locals looted their property and destroyed their synagogues. "It was a terrible sight," said a Catholic university rector, "to see these people, with their children and their sick, depart from the city in the biting cold. . . ."[11] The empress readmitted the Jews three years later owing to Prague's subsequent economic downturn.

1.3 EMANCIPATION AND ACCULTURATION IN WESTERN EUROPE

The Idea of Emancipation

Jewish Emancipation meant that Jews became legally equal citizens in their countries of residence with freedom to live as they wished. The impetus was the Enlightenment, an intellectual movement of the eighteenth century, the aim of which was to bring reason to European society. Enlightenment philosophers rejected religion, which they viewed as superstition, as a basis for social relationships. Natural Law, a system of empirical logic, was to govern. The centerpiece of Natural Law was that men were created equal in rights. Yet emancipation had a price: Jews had to acculturate to European society.

By now resentment of Jews was more cultural than religious. In the seventeenth and eighteenth centuries, a small number of Jewish community leaders rose to positions of court Jews who, through financial and trade connections, procured credit so that their sovereigns could build everything from armies to grand palaces. Some court Jews used their capital for large-scale trade in commodities such as cloth, tobacco, and precious metals and stones. As wealthy outsiders using mysterious methods, they were despised. Hated even more were the majority of poorer Jews who turned to itinerant peddling of used items and to small-scale loans. Because they drove hard bargains and did not "make" anything, they were seen as greedy, haggling bottom-feeders. But there were few options. Jews were barred from most crafts, from selling new goods, and from even establishing residency without paying exorbitant fees. Most turned to what was left.

Voltaire, the French philosopher who embodied the Enlightenment and touted equality, argued nonetheless that Jews were "vagrants or robbers . . . united in the most sordid avarice."[12] Could Jews change? The problem of making Jews "acceptable" to European society triggered debate. In his treatise *On the Civil Improvement of the Jews* (1781), Prussian jurist Christian Wilhelm Dohm argued that Judaism itself was not hostile to Christian society. Objectionable Jewish behavior, he said, owed to poor treatment. The "spirit of ceremonies and pettiness," he noted, "which has now crept into the Jewish religion, will certainly disappear again as soon as Jews obtain a greater sphere of activity, and, admitted as members of political society, are allowed to make its interests their own."[13]

---

[10]Quoted in Klaus P. Fischer, *The History of an Obsession: German Judeophobia and the Holocaust* (New York, 1998), pp. 38–9.

[11]Wilma Abeles Iggers, ed., *The Jews of Bohemia and Moravia: A Historical Reader* (Detroit, MI, 1992), p. 34.

[12]Quoted in Paul Mendes-Flohr and Jehuda Reinharz, eds., *The Jew in the Modern World: A Documentary History*, 3rd ed. (New York, 2011), p. 279.

[13]Quoted in Edward Breuer, "Politics, Tradition History: Rabbinic Judaism and the Eighteenth-Century Struggle for Civil Equality," *The Harvard Theological Review* 18, no. 3 (1992), p. 365.

Jewish philosophers also struggled with the idea of secularism, modernization, and integration. Could Jews embrace these trends and remain Jews? The leading figure of the Jewish Enlightenment (the *Haskalah*), Moses Mendelssohn of Berlin, argued that they could. Jews' gentile critics exasperated him. "They bind our hands," he said, "and then complain that we do not make use of them."[14] Still, Mendelssohn called for Jews to integrate into their surroundings while holding to Judaism's traditions. "Adapt yourselves to the morals and constitution of the land to which you have been removed," Mendelssohn told Jews, "but hold fast to the religion of your fathers too. Bear both burdens as well as you can!"[15] Mendelssohn won praise from Berlin's leading Jews and from the Prussian elite. New Jewish schools teaching modern languages and science opened in Berlin and elsewhere after the 1770s.

Self-styled "enlightened" monarchs remained suspicious. In 1750, King Frederick the Great of Prussia (1740–1786) issued a "Charter for the Jews" that categorized them for residency purposes. "Generally Privileged Jews" were engaged in large enterprises and held the same privileges as Christians, thanks to their economic utility. They numbered but twenty in Berlin. "Protected Jews" were more numerous, but they could not work in occupations represented by craft guilds. This left lesser trades such as engraving, lens polishing, the sale of used goods, and moneylending. They could not choose residence, and only the eldest son could inherit protected status. "Tolerated Jews," such as domestic servants, needed the patronage of a protected Jew. "Begging Jews" with no visible means of support were subject to expulsion. Jews in Prussia paid numerous special taxes, and half made ends meet thanks to charity. For all of Mendelssohn's loyalty, Frederick categorized him as a Protected Jew. And in 1772, when the King annexed the Netze district of Poland (West Prussia), 4,000 poor Jews were expelled.[16]

The Holy Roman Emperor Joseph II (1765–1790) was similarly hesitant. His "Edict of Tolerance" in 1782 aimed to make Austria's Jews "useful and serviceable to the State . . . through better education." Jews were allowed to learn any occupation. But craftsmen were not forced to take on Jewish apprentices; Jews could not hold government positions; and the monarchy tried to break Jewish identity through required instruction in German, a ban on Hebrew and Yiddish in legal documents, compulsory adoption of German surnames such as Weiss ("white"), Schwarz ("black"), Gross ("large"), and Klein ("small"); and special taxes on kosher meat and religious candles. "Tolerated Jews" with permanent residency in Vienna remained limited to roughly 30 wealthy merchants. "We have no intention," Joseph's initial edict read, "to increase the number of the members of the Jewish religion in Vienna in general or elsewhere in Our states."[17]

Emancipation's Early Limits

Legal emancipation arrived with the French Revolution in 1789, which sought to recast society based on the equality of men. But even here resistance was strong. Half of France's Jews (roughly 20,000) lived in the eastern province of Alsace, spoke Yiddish, and engaged in petty trade and moneylending. The French National Assembly debated in 1789 whether they could

---

[14]Quoted in Jacob Katz, *Out of the Ghetto: The Social Background of Jewish Emancipation, 1770–1870* (Cambridge, MA, 1973), p. 61.

[15]Quoted in Breuer, "Politics, Tradition, History," p. 387.

[16]Charter in Marcus, ed., *The Jew in the Medieval World*, pp. 97–110. Figures in Raphael Mahler, *A History of Modern Jewry 1780–1815* (London, 1971), pp. 131, 314.

[17]Edict in Mendes-Flohr and Reinharz, eds., *The Jew in the Modern World*, pp. 42–6. See also Mahler, *Modern Jewry*, 229–33; Stanisław Grodziski, "The Jewish Question in Galicia and the Reforms of Maria Theresa and Joseph II, 1772–1790," *Polin: Studies in Polish Jewry*, 12 (1999), pp. 61–72.

ever become truly French. Even the greatest proponent of Jewish equality, Count Stanislas de Clermont-Tonnerre, made citizenship conditional on amalgamation. "The Jews," he said, "should be denied everything as a nation, but granted everything as individuals. They must be citizens. . . . If they do not want this . . . we shall then be compelled to expel them. The existence of a nation within a nation is unacceptable. . . .[18]

Citizenship was granted in 1791. Jewish advocates of emancipation were ecstatic. Berr Isaac Berr, a Jewish manufacturer from Nancy, thanked God and the French nation for ending Jewish humiliation. He called on Jews in France to embrace citizenship and its duties, including military service and French as the mother tongue. French leaders were less enthused. In 1808, Napoleon Bonaparte, now emperor of France, issued what Jews called the "Infamous Decree." It forgave debts to Jews, limited usury, required Jews to purchase annual business licenses, prohibited Hebrew and Yiddish in trade, required French surnames, and limited additional Jewish settlement. Full emancipation was not restored until 1831. Jews in Alsace endured sporadic local rioting for decades.[19]

Nor was even limited Jewish freedom popular elsewhere. French military dominance in western and central Europe under Napoleon meant elimination of anti-Jewish restrictions. But it also triggered conservative rejection of French liberal ascendancy and the awakening of nationalist sentiments that condemned Jews as foreigners. The Saxon philosopher Johann Gottlieb Fichte declared that the Jews were a hostile entity within the German nation. "I see no other means of giving them civil rights," Fichte declared in 1793, "than to chop off their heads in one night and replace them with new ones that contain not even one Jewish idea. In order to protect ourselves from them, I also see no other means than to conquer their promised land and send them all there."[20]

Napoleon's defeat by a coalition of monarchies left the Jewish question unanswered. By 1815, the Congress of Vienna liquidated Napoleon's wars. In central Europe, it created a new Germanic Confederation of thirty-nine German states while voiding French-imposed laws. Each state handled its own Jewish question. The trading cities of Bremen and Lübeck expelled their Jews the following year. Frankfurt reinstated restrictions on Jews dating from 1616. In 1819, anti-Jewish rioting in Würzburg spread to other western German towns in an effort to turn the clock back to an earlier age. Rioters attacked Jews with residency permits and also attacked Jewish shops. Eventually subdued by local troops, the rioters chanted, "Hep! Hep! Jud' verreck!" (Hep! Hep! Jews drop dead!).[21]

Acculturation in Western and Central Europe

Europe continued to wrestle with the Jewish question. In the German states alone, some 2,500 books and pamphlets appeared on the subject from 1815 to 1850. Those against emancipation sometimes stood on religious grounds, arguing that Jews could become citizens upon conversion; others emphasized the Jews' tendency to act as "vermin feeding on the [German] nation."[22] The desire for access to European society triggered conversions among a small percentage of Jews,

---

[18]Mendes-Flohr and Reinharz, eds., *The Jew in the Modern World*, pp. 123–4.

[19]Paula E. Hyman, *The Emancipation of the Jews of Alsace: Acculturation and Tradition in the Nineteenth Century* (New Haven, CT, 1991), pp. 24–5.

[20]Quoted in, Michael A. Meyer, gen. ed., *German-Jewish History in Modern Times*, vol. 2 (New York, 1997), p. 21.

[21]Smith, *Continuities*, pp. 123–8.

[22]Jakob Friedrich Fries, quoted in Meyer, gen. ed., *German-Jewish History in Modern Times*, vol. 2, p. 32.

perhaps 11,000 in the German states between 1800 and 1870. Converts ironically included the descendants of Moses Mendelssohn.[23]

Most Jews retained their Jewish identity, acculturated as best they could, and pressed for equality as loyal citizens. Over the nineteenth century, western and central European governments finally granted emancipation—sometime generously, sometimes grudgingly—as liberalism, the French Revolution's indelible notion of man's basic freedoms, gained ground. In England, barriers to Jewish commerce and education fell between 1830 and 1871. Italian and German principalities followed suit, mostly after 1848, so that by the time Italy and Germany were unified states in 1870 and 1871, Jews in each country were emancipated. Austria-Hungary recognized Jewish rights in 1867. Switzerland, under pressure from the United States and the Netherlands, granted Jewish citizenship in 1874. Romania, Spain, and Russia rejected Jewish legal equality until the early twentieth century.

With residency restrictions removed, Jews migrated to urban centers and made the most of the burgeoning urban industrial economy of the nineteenth century. Thanks to Jewish culture's emphasis on education and Jewish history's reliance on commerce, they succeeded spectacularly. Germany provides a case in point. Jews were but 1.25 percent of Germany's population in 1872 but made up 10 percent of university students in Prussia, Germany's largest state. They entered the liberal professions, then fully open to Jews, so that, in 1881, 8 percent of Berlin's journalists and 12 percent of its physicians were Jews.

Thanks to unprecedented need for large-scale credit, for everything from railroads to shipyards, Jewish banking families such as the Rothschilds in Frankfurt, Vienna, Paris, and London were synonymous with high finance. In 1870, 23 percent of Berlin's 580 banks were exclusively Jewish-owned.[24] But selling goods was more typical. The movement of rural workers to cities for factory jobs meant expanding markets for everything from furniture to shoes. Jews went into business to provide these items. In 1881, Jews made up 46 percent of Berlin's wholesalers, retailers, and shippers. In 1750, more than half of German Jews were destitute. Perhaps 2 percent were wealthy. By 1871, 80 percent of German Jewish men were successful businessmen or professionals. Sixty percent were in the middle and top tax brackets.[25]

Most Jews in western and central Europe retained their Jewish identity as a matter of pride. Prominent Jews built great synagogues in European capitals, from Amsterdam to Berlin, to Rome. They tried to aid oppressed Jews abroad. Jewish wives maintained Friday night Sabbath rituals. At the same time, they did what detractors long demanded: They surrendered outward signs of separateness. They took Christian names. They abandoned Yiddish. Synagogues introduced vernacular prayers, secular sermons, and pipe organs to appease modern sensibilities. They took immense pride in their French, German, Austrian, Italian, or British nation's history, culture, and power. French Jews in particular viewed themselves as heirs to the French revolutionary ideals of equality and fraternity. They served the French state as commissioned military officers, university professors, and higher civil servants. Benjamin Disraeli, who converted from Judaism to the Anglican Church, became Great Britain's prime minister in 1868 and again in 1874.

---

[23]The global conversion estimate is 200,000, including 13,000 in North America and 84,000 mostly coerced conversions in the Russian Empire. For closer analysis, see Todd E. Endelman, ed., *Jewish Apostasy in the Modern World* (New York, 1987).

[24]Figures from Meyer, gen. ed., *German-Jewish History in Modern Times*, vol. 2, pp. 302–3.

[25]Figures from David Sorkin, *The Transformation of German Jewry* (New York, 1987), p. 109; Fritz Stern, *Gold and Iron: Bismarck, Bleichröder, and the Building of the German Empire* (New York, 1977), pp. 498–9.

But ambivalence toward Jews remained. Amid the anti-Jewish barbs of his enemies, even Disraeli confided to a young Jewish friend that "[y]ou and I belong to a race which can do everything but fail."[26] And in caste-conscious Germany and Austria-Hungary, Jewish army officers, senior state officials, or university professors were practically unheard of. Gerson von Bleichröder was personal banker to German chancellor Otto von Bismarck and might have been Berlin's wealthiest citizen. Yet despite lavish parties, enviable contacts, and fervent German patriotism, he remained first and foremost a Jew. Bleichröder, said one contemporary, "is one of the most intelligent men of our time. . . . And still, he does not have the necessary moral strength to dominate one weakness: his wish at any price to play another role in high society than that of a moneybag."[27]

1.4 JEWS IN POLAND AND THE PALE OF SETTLEMENT

The number of Jews in Europe grew tremendously from about 2.7 million in 1825 to roughly 8.7 million in 1900.[28] But acculturated Jews in western Europe were the minority. The vast majority in 1900 were less acculturated Jews in eastern Europe, more than 5 million of whom lived in the western portions of the Russian Empire, which included most of present-day Poland, the Baltic regions, Belarus, and western Ukraine. For these Jews, life was far more tenuous than it was in western Europe.

Jews in the Kingdom of Poland

Owing to persecution in German-speaking areas in the later Middle Ages, Ashkenazic Jews migrated to the Kingdom of Poland. In return for the economic boost that Jews brought to cities like Kraków and Warsaw, Polish kings and nobles allowed self-government and greater freedoms. Jews in Poland worked as merchants, moneylenders, and craftsmen. They also managed noble estates, collecting taxes and tolls from villages and towns. Life in Poland was comparatively stable, and thanks to a growing Jewish population and contributions by wealthier Jews to synagogues, community buildings, and schools, Jewish culture flourished. In the 1550s, the renowned Rabbi Moses Isserles wrote from Kraków to a former student in Germany: "In this country there is no fierce hatred of us as in Germany. . . . You will be better off in this country. . . . You have here peace of mind."[29]

New opportunities came after 1569 when the Polish monarchy absorbed the Grand Duchy of Lithuania. The new Polish-Lithuanian commonwealth included much of modern Poland, Lithuania, Belarus, Ukraine, and parts of Russia. The new lands were underdeveloped. On the encouragement of Polish nobles who carved out large estates, Jews moved east. Some managed whole noble estates and some worked as minor tax and toll collectors for mills and ponds. Others became innkeepers who bought agricultural products, timber, and wax from peasants and exported them for the lord. Others leased taverns where they distilled and sold beer and whiskey under the lord's liquor monopoly. The Polish kingdom had the world's largest Jewish population, having grown from perhaps 15,000 Jews in 1500 to some 750,000 in 1765. Jewish settlers in Ukraine alone grew from 4,000 to well over 50,000 between 1569 and 1648.[30]

---

[26]Quoted in Fritz Stern, "Reflection: Lessons from German History," *Foreign Affairs* (May/June 2005).

[27]Quoted in Stern, *Blood and Iron*, p. 477.

[28]Mendes-Flohr and Reinharz, eds., *The Jew in the Modern World*, p. 882.

[29]Quoted in Bernard D. Weinryb, *The Jews of Poland: A Social and Economic History of the Jewish Community in Poland from 1100 to 1800* (Philadelphia, PA, 1973), p. 166.

[30]Figures in Antony Polonsky, *The Jews in Poland and Russia*, vol. 1 (Portland, OR, 2010), pp. 9–17.

MAP 1.2   Polish-Lithuanian Commonwealth in 1569.   *Source:* "The Union of Lublin (1569) to 1667" from Harold D. Nelson, ed., *Poland: A Country Study* (Washington, DC: Government Printing Office, 1984), p. 20.

But Jews were not beloved. Lesser nobles and burghers who defaulted on Jewish loans resented them. Polish merchants and craftsmen bristled at Jewish competition. Peasants hated Jews as tax collectors and believed religious anti-Jewish canards. Catholic clerics in Poland called for ghettos. Ritual murder and host desecration accusations emerged in the mid-sixteenth century. So did sporadic anti-Jewish riots known as pogroms that included the destruction of synagogues and homes as well as beatings and killings. A dozen recorded pogroms occurred in Kraków between 1557 and 1682. Lvov (Lwów in Polish, now L'viv in Ukrainian) experienced sixteen pogroms between 1572 and 1664.[31] The Polish monarchy protected Jews, but the monarchy became weaker during the seventeenth century.

The revolt in Ukraine against Polish rule led in 1648 by Cossack leader Bohdan Khmelnytsky triggered the worst series of Jewish massacres to date, melding as it did a Ukrainian Orthodox revolt against Polish Catholic rule with Ukrainian peasant bitterness against Jews as Polish agents. Of the 40,000 Jews that might have lived in Ukraine in 1648, perhaps 22,000 survived. Many died horrifically. Jewish chronicles describe frightful scenes of flaying, dismemberment, and live burials; the victims included women and children.[32] Worse, the destabilization from Khmelnytsky's revolt lasted nearly twenty years and drew in Poland's enemies, Sweden and Russia, each of which hoped to seize Polish territory. Many towns expelled their Jewish populations, allegedly

---

[31]Figures in Weinryb, *Jews of Poland*, p. 156.

[32]Figures in Shaul Stempfer, "What Actually Happened to the Jews of Ukraine in 1648?" *Jewish History*, 17, no. 2, pp. 207–27.

for helping the invaders. Those that allowed Jews to stay imposed special taxes and economic disabilities, which meant that Jewish leaders borrowed increasingly from the church.

The increasing weakness of royal power in Poland meant that in 1772, 1793, and 1795, Poland was partitioned among its stronger neighbors: Prussia, Austria, and Russia. Further redistribution at the 1815 Congress of Vienna left Prussia with Poland's western areas; the Austrian Empire with Galicia (including Kraków and Lvov); and the Russian Empire with most of old Poland, including the heart of Polish territory now known as Congress Poland.

Under the Tsars

Few Jews lived in Russia before the partitions of Poland. But Russia's acquisition of Lithuanian, Belarusian, Ukrainian, and Polish territory brought into the Russian Empire most of eastern Europe's Jews. Neither the Russian Orthodox Church nor Russian merchants wanted Jews in Russia itself. In response, Tsarina Catherine the Great (1762–1796) issued decrees in the 1790s that initiated what became the Pale of Settlement, a region in the western empire eventually consisting of lands taken from Poland. Jews could remain in the Pale, and in Congress Poland, which was administratively separate, but they could not move east and they faced far heavier taxes than their Christian neighbors.[33]

Catherine's successors tried to turn Russia's Jews into Russians rather than improving their lot as Jews. Tsar Nicholas I (1825–1855) tried forced conversion of Jewish boys by conscripting them for twenty-five-year hitches in the army. Tsar Alexander II (1855–1881) offered settlement in Russian provinces to "deserving" Jews such as prominent merchants, university graduates, and a limited number of tradesmen. Some of the beneficiaries entered professions such as medicine and law and succeeded in finance and industry. But these reforms benefitted a tiny minority of Jews. Two percent lived in Russian provinces in 1884.[34] The removal of certain occupational and economic restrictions on Jews in Congress Poland, which the tsar promulgated in 1862 as a way to win Poland's Jews away from the Polish independence movement, was more significant.[35]

In the meantime, the Jewish population in the empire grew from about 1 million in 1800 to roughly 5 million in 1900 thanks to early marriage, a high birthrate, and relatively low infant mortality.[36] Many Jews migrated to growing cities in Congress Poland such as Warsaw and Łódź or the Black Sea port city of Odessa in search of better lives. Warsaw became Europe's largest Jewish city after 1860. A small percentage of Jews there became important bankers and industrialists and acculturated to Polish society. Odessa became a magnet for Jewish adventurers and fortune seekers. Both became centers of modern Yiddish culture.[37]

But most urban Jews supported themselves in small-scale commerce, in workshops engaged in the expanding textile and tailoring trade, or by begging. Rural Jews remained in *shtetls*—small market towns where inhabitants carved out a living, sometimes good and sometimes bad, as tavern keepers, small-scale merchants, moneylenders, or peddlers. By 1900, most Jews in the Russian Empire had no fixed occupation; one-third lived on some form of relief. Rough conditions also affected women. Two-thirds of Warsaw's registered prostitutes in 1874 were Jewish.[38]

---

[33]John D. Klier, *Russia Gathers Her Jews: The Origins of the "Jewish Question" in Russia 1772–1825* (DeKalb, IL, 1986), pp. 75–8.

[34]Figure in Antony Polonsky, *The Jews in Poland and Russia*, vol. 2 (Portland, OR, 2010), p. 11

[35]Artur Eisenbach, *The Emancipation of the Jews in Poland, 1780–1870* (Cambridge, MA, 1991), pp. 448–70.

[36]ChaeRan Y. Freeze, *Jewish Marriage and Divorce in Imperial Russia* (Hanover, NH, 2002), pp. 58–62.

[37]Jarrod Tanny, *City of Rogues and Schnorrers: Russia's Jews and the Myth of Old Odessa* (Bloomington, IN, 2011).

[38]Polonsky, *Jews in Poland and Russia*, vol. 2, pp. 93–4.

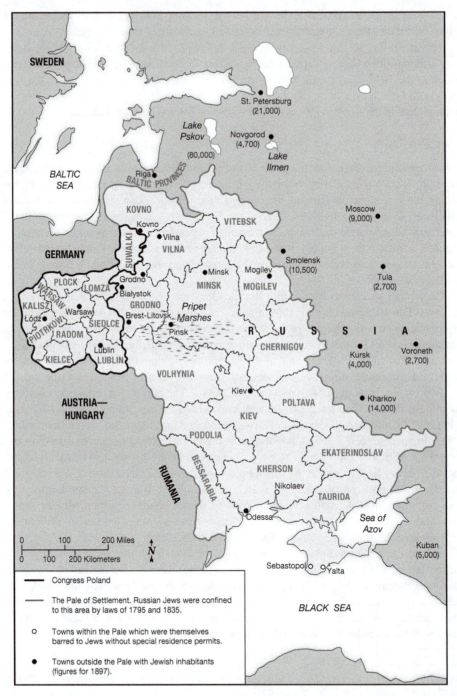

MAP 1.3 Pale of Settlement and Congress Poland, 1835–1917. *Source:* From Martin Gilbert, *The Routledge Atlas of Jewish History* (Routledge, 2006), reproduced by permission of Taylor & Francis Books UK; and John Efron et al., *The Jews: A History* (Pearson, 2009), p. 297.

Jewish market stalls in the shtetl of Łuków, eastern Poland, 1926.   *Source:* Photo courtesy of Menachem Kipnis/Forward Association.

Regardless, Russian nationalists saw Jews as an existential threat. The Russian press argued—despite the high Jewish poverty rate—that Jewish financial exploitation and vodka sales caused the suffering of the peasantry. "I am fully unable to believe," wrote renowned Russian writer Fyodor Dostoyevsky in 1877, "in the screams of the Jews that they are so downtrodden . . . . [How] would it be if in Russia there were not three million Jews but three million Russians, and there were eighty million Jews . . . .? Wouldn't they convert them into slaves? . . . Wouldn't they skin them altogether? Wouldn't they slaughter them to the last man, to the point of extermination?"[39] A year later he added that Jews were behind growing revolutionary activity against the tsarist regime. "Odessa, the city of Yids," he proclaimed, "is the center of our rampant socialism."[40]

Such sentiments contributed to the worst violence Jewish communities had seen in modern times. In 1881, a yearlong wave of pogroms erupted and spread to more than 200 towns and villages in the Pale, resulting in perhaps forty killed, hundreds of women raped, and thousands left homeless. The immediate cause was the rumor that Jews were behind the assassination of Tsar Alexander II that year. But centuries of popular hostility contributed. A "Christmas pogrom" erupted in Warsaw, where the tsar was hardly beloved. Alexander III (1881–1894), the son of the late tsar, blanched at the disorder but blamed the victims. "These Jews," he said, "make themselves too repulsive to Russians and as long as they continue to exploit Christians this hatred will not diminish."[41]

A host of anti-Jewish laws followed, including ceiling quotas on Jews in Russian schools, prohibition of Jewish business on Sundays (thus forcing Jews to close their businesses for

---

[39]Quoted in Mendes-Flohr and Reinharz, eds., *The Jew in the Modern World*, pp. 313–14.

[40]Quoted in John D. Klier, *Imperial Russia's Jewish Question, 1855–1881* (New York, 1995), p. 398.

[41]Quoted in Michael Aronsen, "The Attitudes of Russian Officials in the 1880s Toward Jewish Assimilation and Emigration," *Slavic Review* 34, no. 1 (March 1975): 1–18.

two days), and the expulsion of Jews from Moscow. Jews could avoid these disabilities only through baptism or by leaving, either for Congress Poland, where the laws did not apply, or for other parts of the world. Russia's last tsar, Nicholas II (1894–1917), was more openly hostile. Associating Jews with the growing revolutionary movement, he allowed a new wave of bloodier pogroms. Following an Easter ritual murder charge in 1903, fifty-one Jews were killed in the Bessarabian city of Kishinev (now Chişinău in Moldova). In 1905, the violence spread throughout 300 locales. Some 400 Jews were killed in Odessa alone.[42]

Jewish Responses

The dreadful treatment of Jews in the Pale had disparate results. One was dogged commitment to Jewish religious and community tradition. Orthodox Jewish practice, which strictly observes Jewish law, grew and thrived in the Pale. Many also followed Hasidism, a mid-eighteenth-century variant centering on intense emotional spirituality. Hasidic Jews draw on ritualized song, storytelling, and dance to emphasize joy in the relationship with God, especially in times of despair. Ironically this rejection of modernity emerged just as western and central European Jews embraced the *Haskalah*. Yekhezkel Kotik from Kamenets-Podolsky in Ukraine received slaps from his Hasidic father for learning Russian during the reign of Alexander II. "We have gotten along, thank God, all this time without knowing Russian," the father shouted. "And now you want to learn that language! Under no circumstances will I allow you to do that!"[43]

Jewish community leaders maintained synagogues, cemeteries, and religious schools that all boys and girls could attend. They also ran charitable organizations, from orphanages to clinics, to nursing homes, and provided financial help, including burial fees, for the indigent. Younger Jews, meanwhile, developed the complex world of secular Jewish politics. Working-class Jews flocked to the Bund—the General Federation of Jewish Workers—formed in 1897 as a specifically Jewish socialist party. Like other socialists, Bundists called for economic justice. But they also called for Jewish political autonomy and the legitimacy of Yiddish language and culture. The Bund also formed self-defense groups to combat pogroms. A smaller number of more radical Jewish intellectuals, including Lev Bronshtein—the future Leon Trotsky—abandoned Jewish identity and embraced the multinational cause of revolutionary socialism to destroy the old political-economic order entirely.[44]

In the meantime, a tremendous number of Jews simply left, either physically or emotionally. Between 1881 and 1914, some 2 million Jews emigrated from the Russian Empire. Nearly 1.6 million of them went to the United States, 180,000 to England, and 35,000 to France. Others chose Argentina, Canada, and even Palestine.[45] Others still turned to Zionism—the belief in an entirely separate Jewish nation. The first important Zionist text was *Auto-Emancipation* (1882) by Leon Pinsker, a physician in Poland who believed in assimilation until the 1881 pogroms. Now Pinsker argued that Jews formed a distinct nationality dulled over eighteen centuries by

---

[42]Figures in Shlomo Lambroza, "The Pogroms of 1903–1906," in *Pogroms: Anti-Jewish Violence in Modern Russian History,* eds. John D. Klier and Shlomo Lambroza (New York, 1992), p. 200; Robert Weinberg, "The Pogrom of 1905 in Odessa," in *Pogroms,* eds. Klier and Lambroza, p. 248; Edward H. Judge, *Easter in Kishinev: Anatomy of a Pogrom* (New York, 1992).

[43]David Assaf, ed., *Journey to a Nineteenth Century Shtetl: The Memoirs of Yekhezkel Kotik* (Detroit, 2002), pp. 386–7.

[44]Explanations in Jonathan Frankel, *Prophecy and Politics: Socialism, Nationalism and the Russian Jews, 1862–1917* (New York, 1981).

[45]Figures in Wlad W. Kaplun-Kogan, *Die jüdischen Wanderbewegungen in der neuesten Zeit (1880–1914)* (Bonn, 1914), p. 19.

anti-Jewish tropes and Jews' own delusion that they could be accepted. Jews, he said, must emancipate *themselves* from Europe through a separate homeland and a national renaissance. "Judeophobia," Pinsker concluded in medical terms, "is a psychic aberration. As a psychic aberration it is hereditary; as a disease transmitted for two thousand years it is incurable."[46]

1.5 MODERN ANTISEMITISM

The New Antisemites

The acculturation of much smaller Jewish populations in western and central Europe was exactly what Judeophobes there feared most. Modern antisemitism never fully abandoned premodern Christian tropes. But it also plumbed the Enlightenment's dark side—the notion of man's perfectibility, which spawned modern racial thinking. Nineteenth-century racial theorists understood race as a quasi-mystical bond. Pan-Germans, pan-Slavs, and others believed in a racial essence that reached back to a heroic past and would culminate in redemption in a united racial community. Racial theorists also embraced the quasi-science of Social Darwinism, a bastardization of Charles Darwin's theory of evolution. It argued that racial groups used distinct biological qualities in a struggle for supremacy. By such thinking, Jews comprised a foreign racial—not religious—group characterized by a base "Jewish spirit" of pure materialism and the biological characteristics of deception and exploitation.

Yet modern antisemitism went beyond racism. Arguing that emancipated Jews were the prime agents and beneficiaries of modernization, it also explained the century's painful economic and social upheavals. It could appeal to those parts of society, such as craftsmen and small shopkeepers, who could not compete with mass factory production and sales. It also appealed to traditional religious and monarchial elements that rejected the new secular urban society and feared the urban mass. If Jews created and maintained the dislocations of modern society, then surely they were a dangerous cancer despite their small numbers. Antisemitic writers in the nineteenth century prescribed a rollback of emancipation. Politically speaking, they failed. Culturally, however, modern antisemitism had an impact. Its rhetoric was legitimized by the ambivalence of national leaders and broader populations. Antisemitism thus festered until the social catastrophe of World War I, which made its basest assumptions seemingly more plausible.[47]

The German pamphleteer Wilhelm Marr popularized the term *antisemitism* in his 1879 treatise *The Victory of Judaism over Germandom*. Marr [wrongly] labeled Jews as the "Semitic race" from the near east, characterized them as having "aversion to honest labor," and claimed they had a "legally prescribed enmity towards all non-Jews." The ancient Romans, Marr argued, erred terribly by scattering these people. The Germans furthered the mistake with emancipation. Now Jews dominated German society thanks to their traits of "cunning," "slyness," and "huckstering." Honest, trusting Germans were easy prey. "Without striking a blow," Marr concluded, "Jewry today has become the socio-political dictator of Germany."[48] In fact, Germany's half million Jews constituted just over 1 percent of Germany's population. Their "dominance" was illusory. But Jewish overrepresentation in commerce and the professions helped Marr gain traction. His pamphlet had thirteen printings in its first year.

---

[46]Quoted in Steven Aschheim, *The East European Jew in German and German-Jewish Consciousness, 1800–1923* (Madison, WI, 1982), pp. 81–2.

[47]George Mosse, *Toward the Final Solution: A History of European Racism* (New York, 1985).

[48]Quoted in Richard S. Levy, ed., *Antisemitism in the Modern World: An Anthology of Texts* (Lexington, MA, 1990), pp. 84, 89.

Marr's output was tiny compared to French agitator Édouard Drumont. A failed politician, Drumont became a polemicist who combined Catholic conservatism, French nationalism, and economic populism by blaming Jews for what ailed France. It was a potent argument in a country smarting from a humiliating military defeat by the Germans (1871), the establishment of a secular republic (1875), and the social upheavals that came with industrial development. Drumont's two-volume *La France Juive* (*Jewish France* 1886) went through 114 printings and his daily newspaper *La Libre Parole* (*The Free Word*), which first appeared in 1892, reached a daily audience of roughly 200,000 with caricatures of hooked-nosed, thick-jowled Jews toting moneybags. Frenchmen, Drumont argued, were descendants of Germanic Gauls. They were hardworking, honorable, and trusting—no match for the sneaky, predatory Jew, who had enslaved France through his control of business and capital. "No one can deny," wrote Drumont, "that Jewish wealth has . . . a special character. It is essentially parasitic and usurious. It is not the husbanded fruit of the labor of innumerable generations. Rather, it is the result of speculation and fraud. It was not created by labor, but extracted with remarkable cleverness from the pocket of real workers. . . ."[49]

Marr, Drumont, and others were not mainstream writers, but their influence helped to make antisemitism into a political agenda. Marr's pamphlet was one of the factors behind the Berlin "Anti-Semites' Petition" of 1880–1881. The petition received over 250,000 signatures. It decried Jewish economic and intellectual dominance of "our national way of life" while calling for renewed restrictions on Jews. The petition was dropped in the Reichstag—Germany's elected parliamentary body—but not before it was discussed. In France, the Dreyfus Affair of 1894, in which army captain Alfred Dreyfus (France's only Jewish general staff officer) was convicted of selling secrets to the Germans, confirmed for many on the French right that the Jews—who numbered but 68,000 in France—were a foreign, disloyal, dangerous element. Overwhelming evidence of Dreyfus's innocence was dismissed as a Jewish ploy to divide the French nation. "Death to the Jews" became the French right's battle cry. Dreyfus was not exonerated until 1906.

Antisemitism for some was the key to political success. Hermann Ahlwardt, a German school principal who was caught embezzling his own school's funds, discovered a second career through antisemitism. In 1892, he published a pamphlet accusing the Jewish-owned armament firm Ludwig Löwe of disloyalty by selling defective rifles to the Prussian army. The following year Ahlwardt (who had once said, "when I cannot prove something, I assert it anyway") was found guilty of libel, but not before he was elected to the Reichstag from a conservative peasant district in a year when overtly antisemitic candidates garnered 342,425 votes—4.4 percent of the total.[50] In 1895, Ahlwardt promoted a bill to keep Jews leaving the Russian Empire from passing through Germany. All Jews, he warned, were a biological danger:

> If one says that we antisemites oppose the Jews because of their religion, then I say [that] we do not oppose anyone politically based on their religion. We hold that the Jews constitute another race [with] completely different characteristics. . . . Gentlemen, we Germans stand upon the culture of work. . . . The Jews are different. . . . [They] do not want to create [but] want to appropriate [that] which others have created. . . . The Jews have been with us for 700, 800 years. Have they become German? Have they accepted the culture of work? They have never considered this. . . . [They] began swindling when they came and have been swindling as long as they have been in Germany. [Reichstag Deputy Heinrich Rickert has said] that it would be disgraceful for a nation

[49]Quoted in Mendes-Flohr and Reinharz, eds., *The Jew in the Modern World*, pp. 315–6.

[50]Figures in Richard S. Levy, *The Downfall of the Anti-Semitic Political Parties in Imperial Germany* (New Haven, CT, 1975).

Jewish world dominance as portrayed in Édouard Drumont's *La Libre Parole*, 1893.   *Source:* Lorraine Beitler Collection of the Dreyfus Affair, University of Pennsylvania Libraries.

of 50 million people to be afraid of a few Jews. Indeed [he] would be correct if it were a matter of fighting an honorable enemy. . . . But with the Jews, who work as parasites, it is different. Mr. Rickert, who is as tall as I am, is afraid of a single cholera bacterium, and gentlemen, the Jews are cholera bacteria.[51]

Ahlwardt's motion was defeated and his political career ended in 1902. His demagoguery made him a caricature. But he touched a nerve. Traditional German conservatives had raised the 1895 motion in the first place owing to their ambivalence toward Jews and the expectation that such a law could be politically useful.

Antisemitism was more politically beneficial in Austria-Hungary, where Jewish "dominance" in Vienna was a greater worry. By 1890, Jews made up 8.7 percent of Vienna's population thanks to arrivals from Bohemia, Hungary, and Galicia. Jews were overrepresented at

---

[51]Germany, Reichstag, *Stenographische Berichte über die Verhandlungen des deutschen Reichstags*, 53rd session, March 6, 1895, vol. 160 (Berlin, 1895), p. 1296ff.

the University of Vienna (30 percent of the student body), in the professions (half of Vienna's doctors were Jews), and in the press (most liberal newspapers were edited or owned by Jews).[52] Anti-Jewish resentment brought repeated election of Karl Lueger as mayor of Vienna from 1897 to 1910. A traditional Catholic monarchist, Lueger was also a modern populist who claimed to defend the squeezed lower middle class. He railed against Jewish harm to Christian tradesmen; Jewish pollution of medicine through vivisection of Christian bodies; the unintelligible "Jewish-German" dialect; ritual murder by Jews (Austria-Hungary had twelve ritual murder trials between 1867 and 1914), and the Jewish liberal press, which Lueger described as, "the ally and accomplice of all robberies and thefts that have been committed against the Christian people."[53]

Lueger maintained relationships with Jewish financiers in Vienna and did not advocate anti-Jewish violence. But he gave official imprimatur to open, modern antisemitism. It was because of Lueger's antisemitism, not in spite of it, that his face adorned souvenir beer mugs and postcards. On his death in 1910, the Vienna daily *Die neue Zeitung* gushed, "Vienna and the Reich have truly lost their greatest and most noble son."[54] Among the mourners was a twenty-year-old vagabond named Adolf Hitler.

Theodor Herzl and Political Zionism

Another of Lueger's contemporaries was Theodor Herzl, a Hungarian-born, German-speaking Jew who studied law in Vienna before becoming a journalist and playwright. In 1891, Herzl became a Paris correspondent for Vienna's *Neue Freie Presse* before returning to Vienna as the paper's literary editor. His keen observance of European politics, the ferocity of the Dreyfus Affair in Paris, and the antisemitism of Lueger's Vienna molded Herzl into a Zionist. In 1896, Herzl published the booklet *Der Judenstaat* (The Jewish State), which he described as "An Attempt at a Modern Solution to the Jewish Question." "I do not remember," he later said, "ever having written anything in such an exalted state of mind."[55] It was quickly translated into ten languages.

Historic oppression of the Jews, Herzl argued, had turned them into grotesque figures in gentile eyes. Emancipation was an illusion owing to continued antisemitism wherever Jews lived in appreciable numbers. Even in the United States, Herzl said, the arrival of Jews from the Russian Empire triggered a rise in Jew-hatred. The Jewish question was a national question in that Jews, unable to find acceptance in the countries in which they lived, formed their own distinct nation. For Herzl, the solution was the creation of a sovereign Jewish state built on Jewish toil.

But the Jewish question for Herzl was also global in that it would take a broad effort—political, financial, and social—to create a Jewish state. Herzl viewed Argentina as a possibility due to its fertile soil and to Argentine willingness—at that time—to accept Jewish immigrants. But Palestine, he said, "is our unforgettable historic home." Later, he agreed with earlier Zionists that Hebrew should be revived as the national language of the new state.

Reactions were mixed. Many acculturated Jews believed that Herzl provided more grist for antisemitic mills by arguing that Jews were indeed foreign nationals. Religious Jews argued that the return to Jerusalem was for God, not man, to determine. Others found it impractical. Palestine was part of the Turkish-governed Ottoman Empire, and the sultan would not part with what he viewed as Muslim land even for rich payment.

---

[52]Steven Beller, *Vienna and the Jews, 1867–1938: A Cultural History* (New York, 1991), pp. 33–43.

[53]Quoted in Richard S. Geehr, ed., *"I Decide Who Is a Jew!" The Papers of Dr. Karl Lueger* (Lanham, MD, 1982), p. 325.

[54]*Die neue Zeitung*, no. 69 (March 11, 1910), p. 1.

[55]Quoted in Israel Cohen, *Theodor Herzl: Founder of Political Zionism* (New York, 1959), p. 73.

But Zionists looked to Herzl as the leader of a national dream, and Herzl worked tirelessly to promote his idea with potential Jewish donors and key European political figures. In 1897, he convened the first Zionist Congress in Basel—the first international Jewish congress ever—to help organize the idea. Herzl noted privately that the congress was a dance upon invisible eggs—an effort to further political Zionism without offending the sensibilities of any Jewish group, while also not offending the Turkish or Russian governments, whose support was needed. The congress, which attracted 204 delegates, established a unified Zionist program; provided for future congresses; and established an international Zionist Organization, which Herzl headed until his death in 1904.

The "Jewish Conspiracy"

As Herzl's efforts slowly progressed, a more insidious antisemitic claim emerged. It argued that Jews, through their hidden influence in all states, were engaged in a vast, centrally directed secret plot to wreck European society so that they could rule the entire world. The idea of a global Jewish machination based on Jews' control of finance, industry, and the press remains the ultimate conspiracy theory. That such nonsense was believed owed partly to "authentic texts" of the conspiracy, allegedly of Jewish authorship, which "fortunately" fell into the right hands. These texts supposedly revealed a window into Jewish plots.

In his novel *To Sedan* (1868), the Prussian pulp writer Hermann Goedsche included a (plagiarized) chapter titled "In the Jewish Cemetery in Prague," which told of a secret nocturnal meeting between Israel's twelve tribal leaders and the Devil himself. Antisemitic publicists distilled Goedsche's cemetery chapter into a single "Rabbi's Speech," which witnesses allegedly overheard. By the late 1880s, the "speech" was printed in Russia, Germany, Austria, France, and elsewhere as an authentic document revealing the interconnectedness of Jewish actions and the "real" reasons behind modernity's traumas.

"Eighteen centuries," proclaims the mysterious rabbi, "have belonged to our enemies. This century and the following must belong to us." Finance was key. "Not once during the past centuries," the rabbi says, "did our forefathers succeed in concentrating in our hands such an enormous quantity of gold . . . as the nineteenth century has given us." Jews now controlled government debt, stock exchanges, and industry, but they also used their money to infiltrate other facets of European life. They controlled universities, crippling Christian belief with academic rationalism. They controlled the press, moving mass opinion to revolutionary violence. They controlled the medical and legal professions, learning the intimate secrets of Christian families. And if Jewish actions were revealed, Jews used their influence to attack the credibility of the whistle-blowers. In the meantime, the wreckage of Christian civilization, the Rabbi said, "brings us . . . nearer our goal—to reign over the entire world—as was promised by our father Abraham."

The most infamous and widespread conspiracy text was *The Protocols of the Elders of Zion*. The *Protocols* were ostensibly stolen minutes of twenty-four monologues presented within a secret cabal of Jewish leaders (presumably at the First Zionist Congress at Basel). It was truly an international document. Originally written in the late 1890s and published in 1903 by secret police serving Tsar Nicholas II, the *Protocols* borrowed from antisemitic conspiracy theories throughout Europe, even lifting whole sections of the "Rabbi's Speech." To the tsar's subordinates, the *Protocols* justified the sclerotic regime's repressive policies by blaming progressive and revolutionary activities on Jews.

The *Protocols* had a limited effect until after the cataclysms brought by World War I, after which they were translated into every European language and adapted to various national audiences. The Jews, according to the tale of the *Protocols'* origins, had tried to recover and destroy the *Protocols* before their dissemination. Antisemites explained the subsequent debunking of the *Protocols* as a Jewish plot to hide now-revealed Jewish plans. By this time, the "revelation" that the Jews were behind the chaos brought by the war—the collapse of monarchies, Communist revolution, financial inflation, and social permissiveness—was all too believable to those predisposed to hear them. The following excerpts are representative:

> [W]e have deployed all [political] forces in directions opposite to one another. To this end we have encouraged every enterprise, we have supplied all parties with weapons, we have turned the ruling power into everyone's target. We have turned countries into arenas for inter-party strife. Now in but a short time disorder and collapse will occur everywhere. . . .
>
> We will make ourselves appear to the worker as the liberator from his oppression [and] we will suggest to him that he enter into the ranks of our armies of socialists, anarchists, and communists. We always promote these groups, thus creating the illusion that we want to help the worker out of feelings of fraternity and humanity. . . .
>
> Our power is based on the lasting hunger and the weakness of the worker because through these he bows to our will and he will have neither the strength nor the energy to resist our will. . . .
>
> Remember the French Revolution. . . . The secrets of its preparation are well known to us, because it was our handiwork. Since that time we have led the people from one disappointment to the next so that they have devoted themselves to a King, who we hold in readiness for the world, who will come forth from the blood of Zion.
>
> We will increase wages without bringing any advantages to the worker because at the same time we will raise prices on all everyday goods. As a cause for this we will blame the decline of agriculture and livestock. . . .
>
> Our newspapers will represent the most disparate directions—there will be aristocratic, republican, and even anarchist newspapers. . . . [The] newspapers will have a hundred hands each with a feel of the changing pulse of public opinion. . . . These idiots who believe they are stating the opinions of their newspaper will in fact only represent our view or one that is suitable to us.
>
> So as not to allow the masses the ability to think clearly, we will divert them with amusements, games, entertainment and pastimes. Interest for these things will serve as diversions from the questions over which we are fighting. As the people little by little surrender independent thought, they will finally speak entirely in the sense of our ideas because we will be the only ones producing new directions of thinking, though of course only through such personalities who are not suspected of agreeing with us.
>
> We shall erase from peoples' consciousness all events of previous centuries that do not suit us. . . . [We] shall extinguish the last ray of independence of thought. . . .[56]

***

Hatred of Jews has a long, diverse international pedigree, stretching from one end of Europe to the other. The religious aspects of Jew hatred did not vanish in the modern world. But they were supplemented by the notion that Jews were a distinctly inferior race that posed a dire threat owing to their exceptional cleverness. Such antisemitism before World War I was often the province of political failures or opportunists. But it entered the mainstream of European societies through mass publications, government discourse, and even university lectures. That antisemitism was not more vigorously quashed by those who knew better allowed its pernicious themes to live and grow into the twentieth century. And the Jewish question that it helped to spawn still had no definitive answers.

---

[56]Quotes from "In the Jewish Cemetery" and "The Rabbi's Speech" from Herman Bernstein, *The Truth about "The Protocols of the Elders of Zion": A Complete Exposure* (New York, 1935), pp. 265–92.

2

A People Apart
World War I and Its Aftermath

The overwhelming majority of Jews killed in the Holocaust came from eastern Europe. The Jewish place in eastern Europe became more tenuous after World War I. Part of the reason was the war itself, which brought mass violence against national and political enemies. On the Eastern Front, Jews suffered brutality under the Russian military. After the war, they suffered violence and discrimination amid the wreckage of the Russian and Austro-Hungarian empires, particularly in Ukraine, Poland, and Romania. In Germany, Jews were not persecuted but they were held in deep suspicion by right-wing groups, which blamed them for the defeat.

The 1920s contained no sign that Europe's Jews would be subject to mass murder. But the Jewish question became more pressing, and the world's nations were unwilling to grasp it fully. Zionists turned toward Palestine, and other Jews turned to emigration elsewhere. Others still tried to wrest the full benefits of citizenship. None of these options could solve the Jewish question entirely. It remained unsolved when the Great Depression hit the world and helped bring Adolf Hitler to power.

2.1 THE EMBRACE OF MASS VIOLENCE

Mass Killing

World War I began in August 1914, when the central powers of Germany and Austria-Hungary went to war against the "Entente" powers of France, Great Britain, and the Russian Empire. Promises of territorial reward brought in more belligerents. Italy, Romania, and Japan entered the war on the side of the Entente. Turkey and Bulgaria joined the central powers. The United States entered the war in 1917 for more complex reasons. The Germans in 1914 quickly occupied neutral Belgium and much of northeastern France, the Austrians attacked Serbia, and the Russians invaded German and Austrian territory only to be thrown back. The war was mostly a bloody stalemate until the Russian, Austrian, and German empires collapsed in 1918.

The war's casualties still astonish. Of the 65 million men mobilized for the war, 8.5 million were confirmed killed and over 21 million were wounded. The continental states suffered the worst. Roughly 1.77 million Germans, 1.7 million Russians, and 1.37 million French troops were killed. On average 1,400 Russians, 1,300 Germans, and 900 French soldiers died each day of the war.[1]

---

[1] Averages from Stéphane Audoin-Rouzeau and Annette Becker, *14–18: Understanding the Great War* (New York, 2002), pp. 21–2.

Death in the new mechanized warfare that pitted flesh against steel was ghastly. Mounted machine guns riddled victims with bullets. Flying shards from exploding shells sliced through bodies. Poison gas seared internal organs. The worst battles saw bodies pile up more quickly than they could be buried.

The war affected civilians from the start, suggesting a military culture of total destruction. In the first two months of the war, the German army, following an ethic that tolerated no resistance, killed 6,500 civilians and destroyed perhaps 20,000 buildings in occupied Belgium and France as reprisals for oft-imagined acts of resistance. "Our method in Belgium is certainly brutal," said Prussian Army Chief of Staff Helmuth von Moltke, "but for us it is a matter of life and death, and anybody who gets in our way has to take the consequences."[2] Austro-Hungarian behavior in occupied Serbia, long characterized as a nation of thieves, was worse. One observer estimated that between 3,000 and 4,000 Serb civilians perished in October 1914 alone. "All humanity and all kindness," read one Austrian order, "are out of place; they are even harmful: . . ."[3]

How one saw the violence depended on vantage point. Governments publicly denied crimes against civilians. In a wave of pacifist literature that included Erich Maria Remarque's novel *All Quiet on the Western Front* (1929), the front generation lamented the death of their innocence amidst the war's horrors. But many troops fed on the violence. In his novel *Fire and Blood*, German writer Ernst Jünger proclaimed: "We have appeared here as the God of War himself and as the German appears at times in the course of history, with that Germanic rage against which there is no resistance."[4]

The Armenian Genocide

The war also unleashed ethnic violence within states. The Turkish government's massacre of the Christian Armenian population in eastern Anatolia was the worst case. The "Young Turk" party, which pursued nationalist Turkish policies on coming to power in 1908, viewed Turkey's 2 million Armenian Christians as a disloyal, alien element. Turkish entry into the war triggered a solution of the Armenian problem. Systematic extermination of Armenian men, women, and children began in 1915 when government and army officials deported victims to remote areas in Syria and Mesopotamia on the pretext of resettlement.

More than 1 million Armenians were killed by 1923 through shooting, stabbing, drowning, beating, starvation, and exposure. Tens of thousands of Armenian women were raped. Eyewitness reports emerged as the genocide was happening. "It was a real extermination and slaughter of the innocents, an unheard of thing," said an Italian consul general in eastern Anatolia in August 1915. "There were about 14,000 Armenians in Trebizond [on June 24, 1915]. When I left [on July 23] not a hundred of them remained."[5] To this day, the Turkish government has not acknowledged the Armenian Genocide. The world's forgetfulness encouraged Adolf Hitler on the eve of World War II. "Who, after all," he asked, "still speaks today of the extermination of the Armenians?"[6]

---

[2]Quoted in Isabel V. Hull, *Absolute Destruction: Military Culture and the Practices of War in Imperial Germany* (Ithaca, NY, 2005), p. 208.

[3]Quoted in R. A. Reiss, *How Austria-Hungary Waged War in Serbia: Personal Investigations of a Neutral* (Paris, 1915), p. 46.

[4]Ernst Jünger, *Feuer und Blut: Ein kleiner Auschnitt aus einer grossen Schlacht*, 4th ed. (Berlin, 1929), p. 156.

[5]"Trebizond: Extracts from an Interview with Comm. G. Gorrini," in James Viscount Bryce, ed., *The Treatment of the Armenians in the Ottoman Empire, 1915–1916*, 2nd ed. (Beirut, 1972), p. 291.

[6]Germany, Auswärtiges Amt, *Akten zur deutschen Auswartigen Politik 1918–1945*, series D, vol. 7 (Baden-Baden, 1956), pp. 171–72.

Jews in the Russian Empire

Some 500,000 Jews served in the tsar's armies during World War I. But Russian authorities treated Jews as a disloyal, subversive element that helped the enemy. Locals egged on Russian officers. An elderly Polish maid in Warsaw claimed Jews spotted targets for German artillery and then protected themselves with a magic ointment. "It's obvious," said one Russian officer, "that the Jews have a huge espionage network."[7]

From the war's early stages, Russian troops rounded up and deported between 500,000 and 1 million Jews from Russia's Polish and Baltic provinces to overcrowded eastern provinces in the Pale. Troops and locals engaged in pogroms during deportations. The violence also affected Jews in briefly held enemy territories.[8] Yitzhak Rosenberg of the East Galician town of Józefów recalled that the Russians started beating or killing any Jew they could lay their hands on when they captured the town from the Austrians in August 1914. Polish peasants joined the violence and looting. On the first of September, said Rosenberg, "the entire Jewish population tearfully left our desolate, gutted town."[9]

The worst violence came with the Bolshevik Revolution in November 1917. Born of defeat and deprivation during three miserable years of war, the communist revolution in Russia was the first true class war wherein the oppressed mass was to slaughter its propertied masters and establish a proletarian dictatorship. Vladimir Ilyich Lenin, who led the Bolsheviks (the word refers to the "majority" Lenin's followers held in a 1903 meeting), made peace with the Germans in March 1918. They then launched a brutal civil war to fulfill Karl Marx's vision of a communist utopia. Bloody fighting in what became the Soviet Union continued for three years. Brutality by all armies, combined with the murder of civilians plus famine and disease, might have claimed 7 to 10 million lives.[10]

The civil war in Ukraine triggered horrendous anti-Jewish violence. By 1921, Lenin's Red Army reconquered Ukraine, which had enjoyed brief independence under German tutelage in 1918. In the interim, Ukrainian nationalist fighters under Semyon Petlyura tried to preserve Ukraine's independence, while Russian tsarist troops under General Anton Denikin tried to keep Ukraine within a tsarist empire. Both tsarists and Ukrainian nationalists viewed Jews as Bolsheviks, exploiters, and traitors, and were determined to settle long-standing scores. Peasants, believing old religious canards about Jews and hoping to enrich themselves with Jewish property, often joined in the violence.

Between 1918 and 1921, pogroms occurred in some 700 communities in Ukraine, killing between 50,000 and 60,000 Jews. Another 200,000 Jews were maimed or died of their wounds. Perhaps 1 million more were left homeless. In orgies of violence, Jews were flayed and burned alive, and had their skulls smashed. "It is a pity that pogroms take place," said Petlyura, "but they uphold discipline within the army." "We have come," said one of Denikin's officers, "not to fight the Bolsheviks but to make war on the Jews."[11] Out of necessity, the Jews in the new Soviet

---

[7]Quoted in S. Ansky, *The Enemy at His Pleasure: A Journey Through the Jewish Pale of Settlement During World War I* (New York, 2002), p. 58.

[8]Figures and description in Eric Lohr, *Nationalizing the Russian Empire: The Campaign Against Enemy Aliens During World War I* (Cambridge, MA, 2003), pp. 137–50.

[9]Quoted in Ansky, *Enemy at His Pleasure*, pp. 26–31.

[10]Rough figures in Ewan Mawdsley, *The Russian Civil War* (New York, 2007), p. 287.

[11]Quotes and figures in Nora Levin, *The Jews in the Soviet Union Since 1917: Paradox of Survival*, vol. 1 (New York, 1988), pp. 42–3; Peter Kenez, "Pogroms and White Ideology in the Russian Civil War," in *Pogroms: Anti-Jewish Violence in Modern Russian History*, eds. John Klier and Shlomo Lambroza (New York, 1992), pp. 293–314.

Union looked for protection to the Bolsheviks, who officially rejected antisemitism as a remnant of the bourgeois nationalism of a bygone age.

2.2 GERMANY'S DEFEAT AND THE EARLY WEIMAR REPUBLIC

The German Home Front

Throughout World War I, the German imperial monarchy demanded increased sacrifice from troops and civilians. The officer corps was one of the regime's chief supports and, in 1916, the Supreme Army Command under Generals Paul von Hindenburg and Erich Ludendorff established a quasi-dictatorship to win the war and preserve imperial governance. But the lengthening war meant greater hardships for frontline troops; longer hours for factory workers; and—thanks to the British naval blockade and inefficient rationing—food, coal, and clothing shortages. By the end of the war, 750,000 Germans died of malnutrition-related illnesses. Neither Hindenburg nor Ludendorff showed much sympathy. Their solution was complete victory. The German people would have to endure.

Protests grew louder by 1917. Middle-class liberals within the German Progressive Party and the Catholic Center Party pressed for change, as did the largest party in the Reichstag, the Social Democratic Party of Germany (SPD), which represented the working class. Though nationalistic, these groups wanted a compromise peace and political reform that would turn Imperial Germany into a more constitutional state in which elected representatives would share in policymaking. Introduced by Matthias Erzberger, a one-time annexationist who represented the Catholic Center Party and who had lost faith in Germany's ability to win total victory, the Peace Resolution passed the Reichstag easily in July 1917. In the meantime, the radical left wing of the SPD, which opposed the war from the start, became more vocal. Emboldened by the collapse of the Russian monarchy in 1917, it called for an immediate end to hostilities and for labor strikes.

The army censored opposition and arrested radicals. Hindenburg and Ludendorff gambled everything on complete victory in the field that would justify the hardships and preserve the monarchy intact. If it failed, said Ludendorff privately, then "Germany must just go under."[12] But victory was a mirage. In March 1918, Germany signed the Peace of Brest-Litovsk with Lenin's new Bolshevik regime in Russia. Lenin ended the war to consolidate his revolution at home. The peace detached the western portions of Russia's empire and left Germany, temporarily, as the master of eastern Europe. Now Ludendorff launched a massive spring offensive in France and hoped that Germany could smash its way to victory before the United States (which entered the war in 1917 thanks to Germany's decision to sink US vessels bound for England) could become a decisive factor.

The offensive stalled. Allied counterattacks in the summer of 1918 sent the German army into retreat. Morale collapsed. Troops deserted. Naval crews mutinied rather than embark on suicide missions. After four years of immense strain, few supported the monarchy when news of the impending defeat became public. Kaiser Wilhelm II's abdication was announced on November 9, and two days later a German delegation made up of democratic reformers signed a cease-fire, thus paying the price for the imperial regime's disastrous miscalculations.

---

[12]Quoted in A. J. Ryder, *The German Revolution of 1918: A Study of German Socialism in War and Revolt* (New York, 1967), p. 120.

The Chaos of Defeat

Sudden defeat combined with governmental collapse brought pandemonium. Angry civilians took to the streets as winter shortages loomed. Workers', soldiers', and sailors' councils took control of numerous cities. In Berlin, German communists hoped to follow the Bolshevik example and bring complete revolution. Lesser monarchies in southern Germany collapsed. Kurt Eisner, a socialist who organized a munitions strike in Munich during the war, now declared the former Kingdom of Bavaria an independent republic with himself as president. Germany's political future was up for grabs.

Temporary power in Berlin fell to a provisional coalition government led by Friedrich Ebert, the head of the SPD. Ebert and his associates were practical men. Germany faced shortages of everything, from food to fuel, to clothing. Millions of troops returned home and needed jobs at industrial concerns that needed to produce for civilian needs. Even had the SPD wanted to launch a political revolution, now was not the time. In January 1919, Ebert called elections for a National Assembly that would draft a constitution for a parliamentary republic based on universal suffrage.

The assembly met in Weimar and established what became known as the Weimar Republic. In the meantime, private property remained private, monarchist judges remained on the bench, and Ebert struck a deal with Ludendorff's successor General Wilhelm Groener: The army would protect the government from communists in return for officers' retention of authority with the troops. In fact most Germans—returning troops included—were no friends of the extreme left. Thousands of demobilized former officers, noncommissioned officers (NCOs), and enlisted men joined freebooting formations such as the *Freikorps* (Free Corps) to defend Germany's frontiers while crushing communism.

But both sides were willing to fight. In January 1919, members of the Communist Party of Germany (KPD) under Karl Liebknecht and Rosa Luxemburg attempted a coup in Berlin, seizing government buildings and press offices. To regain control of the city, the SPD-led government employed *Freikorps* units, whose subsequent atrocities included the brutal murders of Liebknecht and Luxemburg. Anger triggered another Berlin communist rising in March, which *Freikorps* and regular troops suppressed in bloodier fashion, killing perhaps 1,200.

The counterrevolutionary "white" terror spread to Munich. Leftist outrage over the murder of Kurt Eisner in February 1919 by a right-wing reserve officer led to the formation of a soviet republic in Bavaria that tried to arm the workers and seize everything, from banks to food supplies. Army and *Freikorps* units retook Munich in May, killing perhaps 600 and legitimizing violent right-wing sentiment there. Communist risings in the Ruhr in 1921 and in Hamburg and Saxony in 1923 were suppressed in short order. Thanks to judges' sympathies, right-wing killings of leftists were lightly punished, if at all.

The Peace of Versailles

But the new parliamentary government also had enemies on the right. In June 1919, it signed the Treaty of Versailles, which formally ended the war. Most Germans viewed the treaty as a humiliation. Germany surrendered several territories. In the east, a reconstituted Poland acquired the Polish Corridor, a strip of territory through eastern Prussia that linked Poland with the Baltic Sea, as well as the industrial region of East Upper Silesia. Roughly 1.4 million Germans found themselves in the new Polish state, and nearly 600,000 soon left for Germany, partly induced by Polish government policies.[13]

---

[13]Figures in Winson Chu, *The German Minority in Interwar Poland* (New York, 2012), pp. 54, 63–7.

In the west, the main territorial provision was a guarantee of French and Belgian security through permanent demilitarization of the Rhineland and the occupation of the Rhine's left bank by French and Belgian troops for up to fifteen years. The French deployed colonial African soldiers for the task, upsetting many Germans all the more. "A civilized nation," pleaded the Women's League of the Rhineland, "is being suppressed and violated by human beings of a far lower order. . . ."[14]

Germany further had to limit its army to 100,000 men, with no tanks or heavy artillery; its navy was limited to a small coastal defense force, with no submarines or battleships; and it could have no air force at all. Finally, Germany was to pay reparations to the nations it damaged on the principle, embodied in the treaty, that Germany and its allies started the war. Reparations were later set at 132 billion *Reichsmarks*.

Successive cabinets were determined to evade as much of the treaty as possible, but the republic never erased the stigma of signing it in the first place. Some senior officials paid with their lives. Matthias Erzberger was murdered in August 1921 while taking a walk. A one-time annexationist who became a cabinet official after the war, his sin was the Peace Resolution and the signing of the cease-fire. In 1922, right-wing extremists murdered Walther Rathenau in Berlin. The Jewish chairman of the electrical firm AEG, Rathenau in 1914 recommended large annexations and worked to organize raw materials for a long war. As foreign minister in 1922—the first Jew to hold this position—he tried to convince the Allies that the financial parts of the peace were unworkable. Neither Erzberger nor Rathenau was a radical leftist. Both were well-to-do liberals and nationalists. Their murders represented the German right's blind anger.

If political terror was not enough, Germany's economy was a mess. The imperial government financed much of the war by selling bonds while raising wages in strategic industries to protect against strikes. To meet its obligations, it printed more money, thus inflating the currency. By 1919 and 1920, food shortages, high prices, and the inability of wages to keep up with consumer needs led to thousands of strikes and decreased production, all in an atmosphere of government reluctance to meet reparations payments.

French and Belgian frustration with their inability to collect reparations led to their occupation of the coal- and steel-producing Ruhr valley in January 1923. They hoped to take what they needed to rebuild their countries. The German government called for passive resistance in the Ruhr while rapidly inflating the currency. In 1914, the ratio between the *Reichsmark* and the US dollar was 4.2 to 1. By December 1923, it was 4.2 trillion to 1. The hyperinflation convinced American and British observers that Germany could not afford reparations, but it also caused deep national trauma. It destroyed middle-class savings, caused skyrocketing food prices, and triggered endemic robbery of basic goods.

The Stab-in-the-Back and the Jews

The so-called Stab-in-the-Back myth, a passing of blame for Germany's defeat in the war, further poisoned the German political atmosphere. The army, so the argument went, was never defeated. Rather, it was stabbed in the back by disloyal elements at home that included pacifists, democrats, socialists, and Bolsheviks—and the Jews, who somehow controlled them all. They planted the knife just as victory was within reach.

Those promulgating the myth truly believed it. Realizing impending defeat in October 1918, Ludendorff called for a new broad-based government to make peace and assume blame.

---

[14]Rhenish Women's League, *Coloured Troops of the Rhine*, 4th ed. (Leipzig, 1922), p. 1.

MAP 2.1   The peace settlements of 1919.   *Source:* Cartography C Philip's. Used with permission.

"They can now," he bitterly remarked, "eat the soup that they have landed us in."[15] During a 1919 parliamentary inquiry on the causes of the defeat, Hindenburg gave public imprimatur to the myth, which the nationalist press further supplemented. Democrats and socialists left holding the bag in November 1918 became known as "November Criminals," whose defeatism besmirched German honor. It was the most enduring narrative of the interwar period, crippling the new republican government from its inception.

The Jewish element to the myth was critical. On the eve of the war, Jewish shipping magnate Albert Ballin, a friend of the kaiser himself, wrote that "[t]here is no official antisemitism here in Hamburg, but a lot of hidden antisemitic feelings."[16] As the war progressed, these feelings emerged, especially among right-wing organizations, which labeled young Jews as shirkers who avoided military duty, Jewish businessmen such as Walther Rathenau as profiteers in German blood, and Jewish leftists as Bolshevik agents.

---

[15]Quoted in Gerald D. Feldman, *Army, Industry and Labor in Germany, 1914–1916* (Princeton, NJ, 1966), p. 516.

[16]Quoted in Saul Friedländer, "Die politische Veränderung der Kriegszeit und ihre Auswirkungen auf die Judenfrage," in *Deutsches Judentum in Krieg und Revolution 1916–1923*, ed. Werner E. Mosse (Tübingen, 1971), p. 28.

In 1916, the army conducted a "Jew Census" to determine whether Jews were draft dodgers. In fact, 17.3 percent of all German Jews served in the army, more than 77 percent of the Jews in uniform served at the front, over 35 percent of Jewish soldiers were decorated, and over 11 percent of those serving were killed. The numbers were comparable to non-Jews.[17] Jewish businessmen, meanwhile, were important in the war economy but were neither dominant nor subversive. The banking house of M. M. Warburg remained annexationist to the end. Ballin committed suicide after the kaiser's fall. And though there were prominent Jewish liberals and journalists who called for a compromise peace, prominent Jewish leftists such as Kurt Eisner and Rosa Luxemburg who called for revolution, and Jews at the head of some soldiers' councils in 1919, they were all heavily outnumbered by non-Jews.

The suspicion of Jews as a disloyal element exploded on the political right with Germany's defeat. "The Jews," as one newspaper put it, "blocked our path to victory and swindled us out of its fruits. The Jews took an axe to the throne and smashed the monarchy into pieces. The Jews wore down the front from within and without. The Jews have destroyed our middle class, spread usury like a plague, and have incited the cities against the countryside and the workers against the Fatherland. The Jews have brought us Revolution, and if we are to lose the peace even after the lost war, Judah is guilty for the wreckage. Thus, German Volk—free yourselves from the dominance of the Jews. . . ."[18] From his exile in the Netherlands, Kaiser Wilhelm chimed in. The republic, he wrote in 1925, was "prepared by the *Jews*, made by the *Jews*, [and] maintained by *Jewish* pay."[19]

The *Protocols of the Elders of Zion* became central. When the *Protocols* were first published in Russia in 1903, they had limited effect. The cataclysms of World War I brought antisemites to examine them anew. The war destroyed the German, Austrian, and Russian monarchies; caused structural financial damages; and brought sociocultural rebellion in the form of pacifism, artistic expressionism, sexual freedom, and, not least, communist revolution. Suddenly the central prophecy of the *Protocols*, that Jews would wreck the old order and assume global control via their influence of governments, finances, culture, and mass opinion, seemed plausible to those predisposed to believe in Jewish conspiracies.

The *Protocols* moved west with the Russian Revolution. Fleeing tsarist émigrés claimed to have escaped Russia with copies of the document. By 1920, the *Protocols* appeared in German, British, American, French, and Polish editions. Italian, Arabic, Portuguese, and Spanish editions soon followed. The German version, edited by Gottfried zur Beek, immediately found an audience on the German right. Although both were murdered in 1919, Jewish communists Kurt Eisner and Rosa Luxemburg represented the link between Jews and Bolshevism. Rathenau, a Jewish capitalist, became a symbol for Jewish capitalist exploitation; the humiliation of Versailles; and the unstable Weimar Republic, which in 1922—when Rathenau was foreign minister—suspiciously recognized the Soviet Union. Rathenau's killers actually insisted that he was one of the Elders of Zion who aimed to bring Bolshevism to Germany.[20]

The Weimar Republic stabilized in 1924, and German Jews had less reason for concern. Germany's small, acculturated Jewish population of 525,000 flourished in the more open

---

[17]Figures in Friedländer, "Judenfrage," pp. 36–8, n. 28.

[18]Quoted in Friedländer, "Judenfrage," p. 53.

[19]Quoted in Lamar Cecil, *Wilhelm II: Emperor and Exile, 1900–1941* (Chapel Hill, NC, 1996), p. 311.

[20]Martin Sabrow, *Der Rathenaumord: Rekonstruktion einer Verschwörung gegen die Republic von Weimar* (Munich, 1994), p. 114.

republican years, particularly in journalism, literature, drama, film, and higher education. These were the years of physicist Albert Einstein and critical theorist Walter Benjamin. But the early republican years set an ominous tone on the German right. "Never," concluded historian Golo Mann, "was the antisemitic fervor in Germany more fierce than from 1919 to 1923."[21]

The 1924 annual report of the American Jewish Committee, which studied worldwide conditions for Jews, said that antisemitism in Germany "is the handmaiden of the broken remnants of militarism . . . and of those forces which are bent on overthrowing the Republic and of combating free and liberal government." The report continued: "It would be a confession of the bankruptcy of civilization if these manifestations of barbarism and stupidity were to prevail for any length of time. Good sense and the plainest dictates of humanity and decency are certain to triumph."[22] Time would tell.

2.3 JEWS IN POSTWAR POLAND AND ROMANIA

Poland Reborn and the Lvov Pogrom

Most European Jews did not live in Germany but in the states that emerged from the wreckage of the Russian, Austrian, and German empires in eastern Europe. Poland was the largest. It included much of the territory lost in the eighteenth-century partitions, including Congress Poland; Austrian Galicia; eastern German territories; and western Lithuanian, Belarusian, and Ukrainian territories that Polish forces conquered in 1919 and 1920 in a war with the Bolsheviks. Although overwhelmingly Polish and Catholic, Poland also had many ethnic minorities ranging from Germans to Ukrainians. But it also had the largest Jewish population of any new state. As opposed to Germany, which had just over a half million Jews in 1933, 3.1 million Jews lived in Poland in 1939, comprising 10 percent of the population.

Polish antisemitism retained a partly religious character. Catholic priests still taught children that the Jews killed Jesus and that they practiced ritual murder. Long-suffering Polish nationalists saw Jews as disloyal aliens. Although some Jews in the new state acculturated and spoke Polish as a first language, most maintained Yiddish as their primary tongue. Orthodox religious traditions remained common. Even left-wing Zionists, many of whom had entered Congress Poland from the Pale after 1881, were more likely to speak Russian than Polish while insisting on the rebirth of Hebrew as everyday language. Jews were not considered loyal Polish citizens. Worse, their commercial place in Polish cities and towns, however modest, was resented.

As Polish forces began carving out their new country after 1918, anti-Jewish riots erupted in numerous locales. The most infamous was in the eastern Galician city of Lvov, a city with a mixed Polish, Ukrainian, and Jewish population. Polish forces captured Lvov from Ukrainian nationalists in November. The city's Jews stayed out of the conflict and guarded the Jewish quarter. Polish troops and civilians, who viewed the Jews' stance as treacherous, attacked the Jewish quarter afterward. "It's right, what's happening to you," explained one Polish officer as black smoke billowed from the Jewish quarter. "People have to rob the Jews. You Jews robbed long enough, now it's time you were plundered."[23]

---

[21]Quoted in Friedländer, "Judenfrage," p. 49.

[22]American Jewish Committee. *American Jewish Yearbook* (hereafter *AJC Yearbook*) (Philadelphia, PA, 1923), vol. 25, pp. 384–5.

[23]Quoted in William W. Hagen, "The Moral Economy of Popular Violence: The Pogrom in Lwów, November 1918," in *Antisemitism and Its Opponents in Modern Poland*, ed. Robert Blobaum (Ithaca, NY, 2005), p. 140.

Israel Cohen was a Zionist journalist in Great Britain who traveled to Poland to investigate anti-Jewish violence there. "The excesses," Cohen wrote, "have been far more numerous than I had believed. . . .There were not fewer than 130 towns, townlets and villages in which anti-Jewish measures had occurred. . . ." Cohen described the violence in Lvov, based on eyewitness accounts:

> One shop after another was forcibly entered, the iron shutters were broken open by means of guns or hand-grenades, and the windows were smashed. . . . Private dwellings were also raided by armed bands of civilians and soldiers, often led by officers. All who resisted were brutally assaulted or shot, and many women and girls were outraged. The orgy of plunder and massacre continued throughout the 22nd and 23rd [of] November, culminating in the setting fire to several blocks of houses and some synagogues. Those who tried to escape from the burning houses were hurled back again into the flames or shot. I found that all that remains of 49 large many-storied houses in two or three neighboring streets are charred, crumbling walls. One ancient synagogue was completely burned to the ground, with all its valuable and historic contents. . . . The acts of vandalism committed during those two days were numerous enough to fill a volume. The casualties . . . amounted to 73 persons killed and over 250 injured. . . . Over 500 families are homeless, over 2,000 families have been totally ruined, and another 4,000 families have sustained considerable loss.

"When I spoke with various members of the Government," Cohen continued, "I was told that [the violence was] the outcome . . . of the hostility of the people, who had been incensed against the Jews for having been pro-German and having profiteered in the war. . . ."[24]

The Minorities Treaty

The Lvov pogrom was a relatively small event against the larger backdrop of anti-Jewish violence in Ukraine. But the Allies had no control over events in the future Soviet Union. Poland, however, needed the Allies' blessing if it was to survive between an angry Germany and a revolutionary Russia. Disappointed with Lvov and facing widespread Jewish protests as far away as the United States, the Allies obliged Poland to sign the so-called Minorities Protection Treaty as part of the Paris peace settlement. It called for equal treatment for national, linguistic, and religious minorities; freedom for minorities to use their languages and establish their own schools; limited state recognition of the Jewish Sabbath; and enforcement by the new League of Nations, the international body created after the war to promote international peace. Seven more states, including Romania, were obliged to sign similar agreements as part of the peace settlements.

The terms, watered down from their original form, were not onerous. But Poles across the political spectrum, rather than expressing regret at the pogroms, complained that the Jews had exaggerated the violence and that the treaty was an intrusion on Poland's sovereignty. For anti-semites, the Minorities Treaty confirmed the existence of a hostile international Jewish network working against Polish independence for its own ends. Because the League of Nations lacked any means of enforcement, life for Jews in Poland would not be protected.[25]

Jews and Their Enemies in Poland

The main political force behind anti-Jewish efforts in Poland was the National Democratic Party (abbreviated as *Endecja* from its initials ND). It represented the Polish middle class, including tradesmen, white-collar workers, professionals, and university students. In a multiparty state, the

---

[24]Israel Cohen, *A Report on the Pogroms in Poland* (London, 1919).

[25]On the Lvov pogrom, Minorities Treaties, and problems of enforcement, see Carole Fink, *Defending the Rights of Others: The Great Powers, the Jews, and International Minority Protection, 1878–1938* (New York, 2004), pp. 101–294.

Endecja could not rule Poland alone. But it exerted influence on successive governments, particularly before and after the military dictatorship of Marshal Józef Piłsudski (1926–1935), the Polish war hero and socialist who had little use for antisemitism.

Roman Dmowski, a bitter rival of Piłsudski, led the *Endecja*. He advocated an ethnically homogenous, economically modernized, fervently Catholic Poland. He was obsessed with Jewish malevolence. "My religion," he proclaimed in England while lobbying for Polish independence, "came from Jesus Christ, who was murdered by the Jews."[26] David Lloyd George, the British prime minister who limited Poland's territorial aims and insisted on the Minorities Treaty in 1919, was, in Dmowski's eyes, a Jewish agent. The *Endecja* made no secret of its solution to Poland's Jewish question: mass Jewish emigration.

Antisemitic politicians targeted Jewish economic security owing to a popular notion of Jewish economic dominance as well as the belief that it stunted the growth of a Polish middle class. Was it true? Poland's larger cities like Warsaw, Łódź, and Lublin were one-third Jewish. Smaller eastern cities like Pinsk in western Belarus had higher Jewish percentages. By the 1920s, over 40 percent of Poland's Jews were engaged in commerce, and in the eastern areas nearly 90 percent were so employed. There were a handful of wealthy Jewish entrepreneurs. But small shops and market-day stalls were far more typical. Meanwhile more than one-third of Jews in Poland worked in handicrafts, from tailoring to shoemaking, to baking, and Jewish unemployment in the 1920s hovered around 10 percent. Jews were also seen as overrepresented in professions because they were more than half of Poland's 4,500 private medical practitioners. But only 1 percent of Jews were professionals.[27]

Jews, meanwhile, had little political power despite their numbers. They were politically active. But the Jewish question in Poland generated many Jewish answers. Poland had twenty-five Yiddish-language daily newspapers. Jews were divided on the issues of religion versus secularism, socialism versus capitalism, distinction versus assimilation, and improving conditions in Poland versus the idea of mass emigration. Thus, an array of Jewish political parties competed for Jewish votes. Even Jewish workers' votes were split among the Bund (which preached Jewish rights and Yiddish identity in Poland); a variety of labor-oriented Zionist parties; and the Polish Socialist Party, which was not Jewish at all. Because of these divisions, Jewish deputies in the *Sejm*—Poland's parliament—were fewer in number than they might have otherwise been, and they could not block antisemitic legislation.

Jews thus paid a disproportionate share of state taxes owing to the government's policy of protecting peasants, landowners, and merchants by taxing traders and artisans. Although 10 percent of the population, Jews in Poland paid 40 percent of the taxes. Local tax officials also overvalued Jewish property and confiscated it if Jews could not meet tax assessments. In 1919, the *Sejm* outlawed Sunday business over Jewish objections. The law hurt Jewish retailers who observed the Sabbath on Saturday. A 1927 law requiring licenses for craftsmen, attainable through a fee and demonstrated knowledge of Polish history and language, drove thousands of Yiddish-speaking artisans out of business.

Meanwhile the state did not hire Jews in government-monopoly industries like tobacco and alcohol or for civil service jobs in transportation, public schools, or the post office (one Jew in old Congress Poland had a postal job).[28] University-educated Jews depended on independent

---

[26]Quoted in Margaret MacMillan, *Paris 1919: Six Months That Changed the World* (New York, 2003), p. 212.

[27]Figures in Ezra Mendelsohn, *The Jews of East Central Europe Between the World Wars* (Bloomington, IN, 1983), pp. 23–8.

[28]Figures in Yehuda Bauer, *My Brother's Keeper: A History of the American Joint Distribution Committee 1929–1939* (Philadelphia, PA, 1974), pp. 31–2

professions such as medicine and law, but beginning in 1924, universities restricted Jewish matriculation so that Jews, who made up 25 percent of all university students in 1921, were reduced to 8 percent by 1938. Jewish rights as guaranteed by the Minorities Treaty were ignored. Up to 30 percent of Jews in Poland survived at subsistence level. The arrival of the Great Depression made matters far worse.

Romania and Its Jews

"It is hardly an exaggeration," wrote the German-Jewish philosopher Hannah Arendt, "to say that Rumania was the most anti-Semitic country in [interwar] Europe." Historians of Romania do not dispute the assessment.[29] Before World War I, Romania treated its Jews miserably owing to a right-wing Romanian intelligentsia that saw Jews as malicious foreigners who controlled the country, the Romanian Orthodox Church that saw them as incorrigible heretics, and a peasantry that believed it all. Despite international pressure, the government denied citizenship to most Jews and in the years before World War I, it passed over 200 discriminatory laws. Local expulsions and pogroms were common. Accusations of espionage during the World War I resulted in more expulsions and even executions, despite the fact that 825 Jewish soldiers were decorated for bravery.

Romania fought on the Allied side in World War I and expanded its borders. It added the once Hungarian-held region of Transylvania, the once Austrian-held province of Bukovina, and the once Russian-held territory of Bessarabia. Jews numbered 230,000 in 1916, but in the expanded state they numbered 757,000, forming east central Europe's second largest Jewish population. They were mostly urban, numbering over half the population of some towns. In old Romania (known as the Regat), most of the roughly 2,000 Jews who had procured citizenship were acculturated and engaged in commerce, manufacturing, and the professions. But most Jews spoke Yiddish and worked as merchants or in the urban trades. Jews in Bessarabia, who outnumbered those in the Regat, overwhelmingly spoke Yiddish and maintained traditional *shtetl* culture.

After the war, the Allies insisted that Romania emancipate all Jews within its new borders. Romania signed a minorities treaty similar to that signed by the Poles but seethed afterward. Although Romanian Jews were eager to become part of the Romanian polity, Romanian nationalists argued that Jews, especially in the new lands, were hostile aliens. An army brochure charged, "Jews who have sold Christ, Bolshevik pagans, bloodthirsty executioners, who drink Christian blood, unbaptized barbarians, offspring of filthy Israel, until when will you pauperize the Christians and suck the marrow out of their bones?" Others insisted that 1 million Jews "invaded" from Poland and Russia, settling in places where they could get rich or act as communist agents. In fact, 50,000 Jewish refugees came to Bessarabia to escape Ukrainian pogroms and returned thereafter.[30]

Romanian Students

Romanian universities were incubators of antisemitism in the 1920s. "Antisemitism in Romania," wrote Wilhelm Filderman, Romania's most tireless Jewish rights advocate, "has always been

---

[29]Quote in Hannah Arendt, *Eichmann in Jerusalem: A Report on the Banality of Evil*, rev. ed. (New York, 1965), p. 190. Assessment in William Oldson, *A Providential Anti-Semitism: Nationalism and Polity in Nineteenth Century Romania* (Philadelphia, PA, 1991).

[30]Quote and figures in Jean Ancel, ed., *Wilhelm Filderman: Memoirs and Diaries*, vol. 1. (Philadelphia, PA, 2004), pp. 149, 161.

the disease of idle semi-intellectuals."[31] The most prominent of these was Alexandru C. Cuza, self-proclaimed theologian, professor at the University of Iaşi, parliamentary deputy, confirmed plagiarist, and prolific antisemitic writer. "Jesus," he once proclaimed, "fought the Jews until the day of his death. It is why they crucified him. . . . Easter is the call to war against satanic Judaism."[32]

In 1923, Cuza founded the League of National Christian Defense, the platform of which was, "the sole possible solution to the Kike problem is the elimination of Kikes."[33] Naturally he opposed Jewish citizenship and favored expulsion. "The mission of the new generation," he wrote in 1924, "is to reconstruct the Romanian nation. . . . Something that cannot be realized without the elimination of the Jews. On this there can be no discussion and no dispute. The elimination of the Jews is the historical exigency of our day."[34] Cuza and his ilk had an impact on Romanian university students, who were willing to use violence. Indeed Jews were generally denied entrance to universities, and those who managed to enroll endured harassment and risked severe beatings.

The following example is instructive. Rigged admissions tests in 1925 for the University of Cernăuţi in Bukovina resulted in all Romanians being admitted and 85 percent of Jews being rejected. A group of protesting Jewish students were arrested for "attacking" Christian professors and put on trial in 1926, whereupon David Falik, the leader of the accused Jews, was shot in the courtroom by a Romanian student named Nicolae Totu, an admirer of Cuza from Iaşi. Totu then turned to a policeman and said, "Take the revolver. I have had my pleasure." A jury acquitted Totu of murder after ten minutes' deliberation. Cuza defended Totu as "our beloved boy."[35]

The Legion of St. Michael

In 1927, a Cuza protégé named Corneliu Codreanu formed the Legion of the Archangel Michael. Codreanu viewed himself as a Christian mystic heading a violent, youthful movement of national and spiritual renewal that was antimonarchist, anti-republican, fascist in nature, and violently antisemitic. The Legion espoused everything from pogroms to assassination of government officials, and in 1930, it established a paramilitary arm called the Iron Guard. In December 1927, the Legion provoked rioting in Oradea Mare, a city in Transylvania where Jews had participated in Hungarian as well as a rich Jewish culture. Students burned five synagogues, desecrated Torah scrolls, smashed businesses and homes, and beat all Jews they could find. The violence spread to other towns, most notably Cluj, where eight more synagogues were destroyed.

Jews worldwide were dismayed. Already in January 1927, the American Jewish Congress, an American Zionist association under Rabbi Stephen Wise, pressed Secretary of State Frank Kellogg to protest. Kellogg reluctantly did so, prompting the comment from Romanian Ambassador Gheorghe Cretziano that "reports concerning Romanian Jews had been greatly exaggerated in this country."[36] Concerned in this instance that the students were truly out of control, the Romanian government suspended 380, imprisoned thirty more, and paid a token

---

[31]Ancel, ed., *Wilhelm Filderman*, p. 158.

[32]Quoted in Ancel, ed., *Wilhelm Filderman*, p. 176.

[33]Quoted in International Commission on the Holocaust in Romania, *Final Report of the International Commission on the Holocaust in Romania* (Bucharest, 2004), p. 34.

[34]Quoted in Ancel, ed., *Wilhelm Filderman*, p. 283.

[35]Quoted in I. C. Butnaru, *The Silent Holocaust: Romania and Its Jews* (Westport, CT, 1992), pp. 41–2.

[36]United States, Department of State, *Foreign Relations of the United States, 1927*, vol. 3 (Washington, DC, 1942), p. 640.

sum for damages. Yet the government was also convinced that international Jews sought to destroy Romania's standing. "Jews who recognized the value of speaking with moderation," said Cretziano, "are convinced that the majority of Rumanians are entirely free from anti-Semitism."[37] Sporadic student rioting against Jews continued in the years ahead, often spurred by the Iron Guard; it involved everything from the desecration of Jewish cemeteries to occasional murders. The government did nothing.

2.4 THE ZIONIST SOLUTION

Zionism and the Balfour Declaration

Theodor Herzl's call for a Jewish state at the First Zionist Congress in Basel in 1897 brought the formation of the permanent Zionist Organization, which served as an umbrella organization for Zionist political parties. But internal squabbling concerning the practicality of a Jewish state in Ottoman Palestine weakened the Zionist movement in the years before World War I. Herzl at one point considered a plan for a Jewish state in Britain's East African colony of Uganda, which caused the breakup of the Sixth Zionist Congress in 1903. Before World War I, the most dynamic Jewish political party in eastern Europe was the Bund, which was not Zionist at all. The Bund remained a force in the interwar period for Jews in Poland who were determined to remain in Europe. But Zionism also entered a new phase.

Chaim Weizmann was an accomplished chemist, born near Pinsk in 1874 and educated in Germany and Switzerland. He taught at the University of Manchester and became Britain's leading Zionist, lobbying Arthur James Balfour, Manchester's parliamentary representative, for a Jewish home in Palestine and not in Uganda, as Balfour suggested. "We had Jerusalem," Weizmann insisted, "when London was a marsh."[38] During World War I, Balfour served as foreign secretary. He was sympathetic to Zionism already. London also hoped to stem French ambitions in Palestine while finding political cover to offset the terrible treatment of Jews by Russia, then Britain's ally. Britain's military campaign against the Turks in the Middle East in 1917 provided multiple opportunities.

On November 2, Balfour issued the now-famous sixty-seven-word declaration, which stated,

> His Majesty's Government view with favor the establishment in Palestine of a national home for the Jewish people, and will use their best endeavors to facilitate the achievement of this object, it being clearly understood that nothing shall be done which may prejudice the civil and religious rights of existing non-Jewish communities in Palestine, or the rights and political status enjoyed by Jews in any other country.[39]

London remained careful. Balfour mentioned Palestine as *a* national home, not *the* Jewish national home, as Zionists wanted. And in 1922 when the League of Nations awarded Britain Palestine to rule as a mandate—meaning that Britain was to develop the region for eventual self-rule—it was up to London to determine what the Jewish national home meant.

London worried about an Arab backlash in Palestine, which was foreshadowed by Arab riots in Jerusalem in 1920, as well as anger in the broader Arab world. The Suez Canal in

---

[37]*AJC Yearbook*, vol. 31, p. 363ff.

[38]Walter Laqueur, *The History of Zionism: From the French Revolution to the Establishment of the State of Israel* (New York, 2003), p. 188.

[39]Itamar Rabinovitch and Jehuda Reinharz, eds., *Israel and the Middle East: Documents and Readings on Society, Politics, and Foreign Relations, Pre-1948 to the Present*, 2nd ed. (Lebanon, NH, 2008), p. 29.

neighboring Egypt, also under British protection, was the lifeline to Britain's imperial holdings in East Africa, India, and the Far East. Thus, there could be no talk of a Jewish state in Palestine. As Colonial Secretary Winston Churchill described Britain's duties in a 1922 policy paper, Palestine's purpose was to become "a center in which the Jewish people as a whole may take, on grounds of religion and race, an interest and a pride."[40] Immigration was part of this equation, but it could not harm Arab rights nor could it exceed Palestine's economic capacity to absorb new arrivals.

Zionist Parties and Youth Groups

Persecution in eastern Europe and the Balfour Declaration energized the Zionist movement. The interwar period saw the emergence of an array of Zionist parties, ranging from middle-class General Zionists to no fewer than six labor-oriented Zionist parties. Generally these Zionist parties accepted Churchill's idea of a limited Jewish national home, believing that some Jews would always live in Europe. They hoped that a national home in Palestine alongside Arabs would provide fulfillment to settlers while helping Jews in Europe to develop a new identity.

Not all agreed. The slowness of settlement in Palestine combined with persecution in eastern Europe led to the development of the Union of Zionist Revisionists under Ze'ev Jabotinsky, a Jewish journalist originally from Odessa, who advocated Jewish military training as well as immediate mass Jewish settlement on both sides of the Jordan River with or without Arab cooperation. More traditional Zionists worried that Jabotinsky's rhetoric of mass emigration could endanger existing Jewish settlements in Palestine as well as existing stability for Jews remaining in eastern Europe.

Zionism's greatest energy lay with its many youth groups, which attracted young men and women alike. Zionist youth groups aimed to create a new self-reliant, independent Jew. They advocated the learning of Hebrew as the everyday language while training young Jews to return to the ancestral land as laboring pioneers. Physical and spiritual renewal on communal, self-sufficient kibbutzim was to replace the subservient Diaspora existence.

Hashomer Hatza'ir ("The Young Guard") was formed as a middle-class pioneer movement in Galicia in 1916. Its members were among the first to settle in Palestine after World War I, and by 1939, it had 70,000 members in Palestine and Europe. *He-halutz* ("The Pioneer") was a working-class group founded in Russia in 1917. It reached 100,000 members by 1935. *Betar*, founded in 1923, was the youth movement of Jabotinsky's Revisionists and advocated greater militancy. As the situation of Jews in Europe became more desperate in 1930, *Betar* grew to 90,000 members. During the Holocaust, the youth groups formed the most important Jewish resistance movements in eastern Europe.

Initial Postwar Settlement

London installed a High Commissioner in Jerusalem to govern Palestine in consultation with Arab and Jewish Leaders. To create economic balance, the British developed eleven immigrant categories, ranging from capitalists to workers, from rabbis to relatives, from orphans to artisans. The Jewish leadership body in Jerusalem, approved by the Zionist Organization, was eventually called the Jewish Agency Executive (JAE) for Palestine. Twice annually it submitted estimates of immigration potential, and the British made adjustments. The JAE also steered Jewish settlement

---

[40]Rabinovitch and Reinharz, eds., *Israel and the Middle East*, p. 34.

Portrait of Hashomer Hatza'ir members in Kobryn, Poland, 1926.   *Source:* United States Holocaust Memorial Museum.

and economic development for the *Yishuv*, the Jewish community in Palestine. By 1935, the JAE chairman was David Ben-Gurion, a labor-oriented Zionist from Poland who arrived in 1905 and later became Israel's first prime minister.

From 1922 to 1932, *net* immigration of Jews to Palestine (arrivals minus departures) was 66,353. Initial immigrants tended to be young pioneers who had trained for life in Palestine and established kibbutzim. Middle-class immigrants joined them in the mid-1920s. They developed the city of Tel Aviv, which grew from 2,000 inhabitants in 1920 to 46,607 by 1931. By that year, 175,006 Jews lived in Palestine out of a total population of 1.035 million. Jews owned 275,000 acres of land and created 2,500 industrial enterprises. Most came from Poland and Romania, 40 percent from Poland alone. Fewer than 2,500 in this period came from Germany, where Jews were established and had little desire to start over.[41]

But Palestine could not solve the Jewish problem. Owing to British immigration restrictions, 60,000 Jews in youth groups in Poland were still waiting to emigrate by 1930. Large numbers of settlers left Palestine (27,809 between 1922 and 1931), suggesting to the JAE that only the hardiest and most committed should come.[42] Relations with Arabs also portended future problems. In August 1929, religious disputes at the Western Wall in Jerusalem (the last remnant of the second temple) between Jews and Arabs led to a week of rioting. Haj Amin al-Husseini, the Grand Mufti of Jerusalem, whose title made him responsible for Islamic holy sites there, fanned the fire by arguing that the Jews' intent was to take over Jerusalem's al-Aqsa Mosque, built on the rock where the Prophet Mohammed is said to have ascended to heaven. Arab rioting killed seventeen Jews in Jerusalem and sixty-seven more in Hebron.

---

[41]Figures in *AJC Yearbook*, vols. 24–36.

[42]*AJC Yearbook*, vol. 37, pp. 362, 381–2.

Undermanned British authorities could do little. Firing into the Arab crowd, they worried, would redirect violence at them. A parliamentary inquiry established that, while nothing justified the Arab riots, which were based on the Arabs' "racial animosity" toward Jewish immigrants, Arab anger was based on "the disappointment of [Arab] political and national aspirations and fear for their economic future."[43] To forestall future violence, the inquiry recommended a reconsideration of Jewish immigration to Palestine and of land sales to Jews.

2.5 OTHER DESTINATIONS: THE AMERICAS AND EUROPE

Other emigration alternatives for east European Jews were closing in the 1920s. Between 1881 and 1914, over 3 million Jews left Europe, 2.58 million for the Americas.[44] After the war, more wanted to leave. Politically, they were a diverse group. Although many held Zionist sentiments, not all had interest in pioneering or in learning Hebrew. Others were not Zionists at all. Before World War I, Jews could come to the Americas with nothing more than money for ship passage. Now matters became more difficult.

The United States

Over 2.3 million Jews arrived in the United States between 1881 and 1924, an average of more than 20,000 per year. Most were Yiddish speakers from eastern Europe. Jewish immigrants comprised almost 12 percent of the US immigrant total from 1899 to 1909.[45] Most entered through the ports of New York, Philadelphia, and Baltimore and began work in trades and in commerce.

The United States was built on freedom of worship but was not immune to antisemitism, particularly as more Jews arrived. *McClure's Magazine* spoke in 1913 of "The Jewish Invasion of America," and argued that avaricious, aggressive, unassimilable Jews would wrest control of the United States from the proper Anglo-Saxons who built it. Business firms, private clubs, and vacation resorts excluded even assimilated "uptown" Jews whose families arrived from central Europe in the mid-nineteenth century. Harvard led US universities in limiting the number of Jewish students in order to protect "its character."[46]

Fear of communism after the war led to new diatribes, the most infamous coming from automobile mogul Henry Ford, whose ghostwritten articles were combined into a set of books titled *The International Jew*. It sold 500,000 copies and was translated into sixteen languages. Ford linked Jews to control of US finance, US entrance into World War I, international Bolshevism, and US cultural decline. "Do you know," Ford asked an acquaintance in 1931, "that the world war was caused simply by the desire of the Jews to get control of everything in Germany?" He continued that Jews also caused the Bolshevik revolution. "I have," he said, "the documents to prove it."[47]

---

[43]Great Britain, Parliament, *Report of the Commission on the Palestine Disturbances of August 1929*, cmd. 3530 (London, 1930).

[44]Wlad W. Kaplun-Kogon, *Die jüdische Wanderbewegungen in der neuesten Zeit* (1880–1914) (Bonn, 1914), pp. 18–19.

[45]Figures in *AJC Yearbook*, vol. 27, p. 398.

[46]Leonard Dinnerstein, *Antisemitism in America* (New York, 1994), pp. 61, 84–93.

[47]Quoted in Richard Breitman, Barbara McDonald Stewart, and Severin Hochberg, eds., *Refugees and Rescue: The Diaries and Papers of James G. McDonald 1935–1945* (Bloomington, IN, 2009), p. 114.

The Johnson-Reed Act

After the war, US politics took an increasingly nativist turn that aimed to stifle recent immigration trends associated with cultural subversion and political radicalism. In 1924, by a Senate vote of 62 to 6, Congress passed the National Origins Immigration Act, also known as the Johnson-Reed Act. It limited annual immigration of any national group to 2 percent of its US population total, using 1890 as a base year—that is, before masses of Italians, Slavs, and Jews entered the United States (Asians were banned altogether). The yearly quota from Great Britain was 65,721, and for Germany it was 25,957. But the quotas for Poland and Romania were 8,254 and 377, respectively. Already excluded in accordance with earlier laws were "persons likely to become a public charge," a vague construction initially meant to bar the mentally disabled. Total immigration per year could not exceed 153,774.[48]

Consular officials abroad now assumed authority to issue entrance and residence visas without which prospective immigrants could not enter or stay. To procure visas, applicants had to present broad documentation including a passport; two certified copies of birth certificates; two copies of a police report affirming good conduct; financial records demonstrating self-sufficiency; and an affidavit from a sponsor in the United States, often a relative or prospective employer, listing his own financial worth and the degree to which the sponsor could support the immigrant if need be. Consuls were responsible for keeping undesirables out. The burden of proof was on the applicant to show that he or she was not undesirable.

Founded in 1906 by conservative, acculturated Jewish leaders, the American Jewish Committee (AJC) fought antisemitism and spoke for oppressed Jews around the world. Understanding the number of Jews who wished to leave eastern Europe, it lobbied against the Johnson-Reed Act, estimating that it would cut Jewish emigration by 90 percent. The prediction was correct. In 1921, three years before the Johnson-Reed Act, 119,036 Jews immigrated to the United States. In 1924, when the act went into effect, thousands of Jews were left stranded in European ports, now forced to attain visas in their home countries. By 1927, Jewish immigration to the United States was cut to 11,483.[49]

Argentina

With possibilities in the United States waning, eastern European Jews looked elsewhere in the western hemisphere, primarily to Argentina. In the late nineteenth century, the Argentine government's desire to populate the country's interior prompted a liberal immigration policy. Over 2 million immigrants arrived between 1892 and 1914. Jews were also welcome, and their desire to leave the Russian Empire after 1881 even prompted Argentine consuls and immigration agents in Europe to place immigration advertisements in Yiddish newspapers. Argentina's remoteness was unattractive at first, but Jews began migrating from the Russian Empire to Argentina in 1890, and by 1919, Jews in Argentina numbered some 130,000.

In the early 1920s, Jews in Poland who could not immigrate to the United States looked to Argentina. In the mid-1920s, Argentina curtailed immigration partly owing to economic downturn, partly owing to suspicion of Bolsheviks, indigents, and the like. No new laws were passed, but consuls granting visas were told to insist on documents from the applicant's country of origin. For eastern European Jews who had reached western Europe, this was not possible. The 1923 Jewish immigration number of nearly 14,000 dropped to an average of 6,500 per year for the remainder

---

[48]For quotas, see appendixes to "Myron C. Taylor to Secretary of State, June 29, 1938," in *The Holocaust: Selected Documents in Eighteen Volumes*, eds. John Mendelsohn and Donald Detwiler, vol. 5 (New York, 1982), 228ff.

[49]Figures in *AJC Yearbook*, vol. 31, p. 66; vol. 33, pp. 294–5.

of the decade. Still, from 1920 to 1930, 74,607 Jews officially entered Argentina and stayed. By 1930, nearly 200,000 Jews lived there; more than 80 percent of them were from Poland, Russia, and Romania, and half of these lived in the multinational capital city of Buenos Aires.

They ranged from religious Jews to Bundists, to Zionists; they worked as factory workers, craftsmen, and merchants; and most spoke and continued to debate politics in Yiddish. Jewish leaders in Buenos Aires also worked in the 1920s to liberalize Argentine immigration laws for other Jews in eastern Europe, arguing, in the words of Aaron Benjamin of the Hebrew Immigrant Aid Society, that "South America could absorb 20,000 Jewish immigrants per year," with Argentina alone absorbing two-thirds.[50] In fact, Brazil, which hoped to augment its population after the war, became the western hemisphere's third most promising destination for eastern European Jews. Numbering perhaps 6,100 persons in 1920, Jews in Brazil numbered 40,000 by 1933.[51]

But the days of safe haven in Latin America were numbered. Catholic Church complaints about the Jews became more shrill over the course of the 1920s. Aside from the linkage of Jews to the increase of strikes, anarchist attacks, and communism in Argentina over the course of the decade, church writers returned to old religious saws, including Jews as the killers of Christ. The Great Depression of 1929 and the subsequent economic collapse triggered a military coup that would nearly end Jewish immigration to Argentina.

Central and Western Europe

The democratic and cosmopolitan atmosphere of central and western European cities in the 1920s was a magnet to émigrés from Eastern Europe, including Jews, particularly if they could not go elsewhere. Important destinations included Berlin, Vienna, Rome, Paris, Brussels, and Amsterdam. In Belgium alone, 85 percent of the 65,000 to 75,000 Jews in 1939 arrived between 1918 and 1930.[52] Most Jewish immigrants to western Europe retained Yiddish culture, continued their occupational traditions, and were sympathetic or fully engaged in left-wing politics. Native populations and even some assimilated western European Jews viewed them with extreme ambivalence. Two examples, Germany and France, follow.

During World War I, over 100,000 Jews made their way from Poland to Germany in search of safety. By 1925, eastern European Jews there numbered over 85,000 (nearly 60 percent of whom came from Poland). The greatest concentrations were in Berlin and the coal- and steel-producing Ruhr valley. Unlike German Jews, they tended to work in trades, including tailoring, and in heavy industry.[53] As Jews and aliens besides, they were targets for antisemites and hooligans. In 1923, eastern Eurpean Jews were actually expelled from Munich, and in the same year, hooligans systematically attacked their shops and stalls.

Many young German-speaking Jewish intellectuals viewed the eastern European Jew, or *Ostjude*, as more authentically Jewish while lamenting their own lost heritage. Writer Franz Kafka suddenly saw German-Jewish culture as having a "Christian coldness." German Jews also protected *Ostjuden* from violence, either through protests to the government or through direct action on the streets. Other German Jews worried that these "alien" unassimilated elements would intensify the recent spike in antisemitism toward all Jews. A few even tried to deflect these

---

[50]Quote and figures for Argentina in Victor A. Mirelman, *Jewish Buenos Aires, 1890–1930: In Search of an Identity* (Detroit, MI, 1990), pp. 14–34; *AJC Yearbook*, vol. 36, p. 377.

[51]Figures in *AJC Yearbook*, vol. 36, p. 377.

[52]Figures in Rudi van Doorslaer, "Jewish Immigration and Communism in Belgium, 1925–1939," in *Belgium and the Holocaust: Jews, Belgians, Germans*, ed., Dan Michman (Jerusalem, 1998), pp. 63–82.

[53]Figures in Trude Maurer, *Ostjuden in Deutschland, 1918–1933* (Hamburg, 1986), pp. 65–6, 72–6, 91.

sentiments toward *Ostjuden* specifically. "Everywhere we look into their strange eyes," wrote Jewish Socialist Franz Neumann in 1922, "everywhere we hear the coarse noises of their excited conversation. . . . Whatever is worth money becomes for them only an object, for buying and selling." This German-Jewish identity crisis ultimately helped neither group.[54]

France was more hospitable. Between 1906 and 1939, up to 170,000 eastern European Jews arrived in France, some 90,000 settling permanently in Paris. They were roughly double the number of native French Jews in France and in Paris itself. Most were part of a general wave of refugees that arrived in Paris after World War I, thanks to France's long republican and cosmopolitan reputation. In some ways, the French government did not disappoint. Having lost nearly 1.4 million men in the war and conscious of its demographic inferiority to Germany, the government relaxed citizenship laws in 1927 so that some 50,000 eastern European Jews became French citizens between 1927 and 1940.[55]

But with the advent of the Great Depression, ambivalence toward foreigners was in the air, even among native French Jews. Those whose families had been in France since emancipation in 1791 were by now fully assimilated and believed that the Dreyfus Affair was behind them. Calling themselves *Israélites Françaises* rather than *Juifs*, a pejorative used for eastern European Jews or by antisemites, they viewed themselves as French citizens first.[56] They tended toward university education, large businesses, professions, and government careers. Their Jewishness was not false. They belonged to synagogues governed by the *Consistoire Israélite*, a state-supervised institution created by Napoleon in 1808 to guarantee Jewish loyalty. They were also historically interested in the welfare of Jews outside France, particularly Jewish children.

But they had little in common with the new arrivals, who settled in poorer neighborhoods; set up their own synagogues independent of the *Consistoire*; spoke Yiddish; kept to working-class trades; and veered toward the political left, including communism. As Baron Robert de Rothschild put it in 1934, "The immigrants who arrive among us with their memories and habits of Poland, Romania, and elsewhere retard the assimilation process and help create xenophobic feelings among Frenchmen." Though the eastern European Jews made up the bulk of Jewish resistors in France during World War II, such attitudes doomed tens of thousands. "We were great snobs toward the East European Jews in those days," remembered Jacques Trèves, "They did not seem to fit into our tradition, and for us they were a plain and simple embarrassment."[57]

****

On the eve of the Nazi takeover in Germany, the Jewish problem had been inflamed but not solved. East European countries that emerged from the war were openly antisemitic, while others, such as Germany, had strong antisemitic tendencies. Minority protection had been established in principle, but enforcement by the League of Nations or by Jewish groups was not possible. Thousands of Jews were able to move to better situations in other geographic areas, but many were only seemingly safe. Most, meanwhile, were not able to go anywhere. On the Jewish question, the world was not ready to confront Adolf Hitler.

[54]Quotes in Steven E. Aschheim, *Brothers and Strangers: The East European Jew in German and German Jewish Consciousness, 1800–1923* (Madison, WI, 1982), pp. 204, 221.

[55]Figures in David H. Weinberg, *A Community on Trial: The Jews of Paris in the 1930s* (Chicago, 1977), pp. 3-7; Renée Poznanski, *Jews in France During World War II* (Hanover, NH, 2001), pp. 1–7.

[56]Distinction explained in Phyllis Cohen Albert, "Israelite and Jew: How Do Nineteenth Century Jews Understand Assimilation?" in *Assimilation and Community: The Jews in Nineteenth Century Europe*, eds. Jonathan Frankel and Stephen J. Zipperstein (New York, 1992), pp. 88–109.

[57]Quotes in Howard Morley Sachar, *Diaspora: An Inquiry into the Jewish Contemporary World* (New York, 1985), pp. 89–92. In general see Paula E. Hyman, *From Dreyfus to Vichy: The Remaking of French Jewry, 1906–1939* (New York, 1979).

3

Adolf Hitler, the Nazi Party, and the Jews

Mistreatment and suspicion of Jews in some states combined with reluctance in others to solve the Jewish question were serious problems. But they do not alone explain the looming Jewish catastrophe. The rise of the Nazi Party in Germany was at the eye of the impending storm. Adolf Hitler was the first national leader who placed antisemitism at the very center of his world-view and of his nation's politics. Hitler did not invent antisemitism or its more noxious variants regarding Jewish racial characteristics or grand conspiracies. Rather, he swallowed these ideas and gave them fanatic urgency.

Hitler was a minor politician until 1930. The Great Depression combined with disastrous political decisions in Germany helped bring him to power in 1933. The world now had a leader who embraced the violence of the World War I era and who was convinced that he was at war with a malevolent global Jewish conspiracy. If Hitler could not be understood or stopped by more traditional politicians, then Jews would suffer as never before, first in Germany and then in the countries that Germany conquered.

3.1 ADOLF HITLER'S EARLY YEARS

A Shiftless Existence

Nothing in Hitler's early life suggested that he would amount to anything. He was born in April 1889 in the Austrian town of Braunau am Inn to Alois Hitler, a customs official, and his third wife Klara Pölzl. Much of Hitler's childhood was spent in the area of Linz, where the family moved in 1898. Hitler encountered problems in secondary school due to his father's insistence that he become a civil servant. The young Hitler resisted, showing aptitude for drawing and for daydreaming.

Alois died in 1903. In 1905, at age sixteen, Adolf quit school. He spent his remaining teen-age years without direction. His indulgent mother allowed him to live on money left by his father until her own death in 1907, at which point Hitler lived on an orphan's pension. He became passionate about German composer Richard Wagner's operas, which hearkened to an imagined, heroic German past. Increasingly he occupied a make-believe world where he styled himself an authority on various subjects but rejected learning a profession or trade with which to support himself. As his biographer Ian Kershaw writes, ". . . the young, dandified Hitler scorned the notion of working to earn one's daily bread."[1]

Hitler moved to Vienna in 1908, intending to study at the Academy of Fine Arts and become a renowned artist. He remained until 1913. The glittering capital of the multinational Austro-Hungarian Empire pulsed with ethnic and economic tensions that resulted from rapid growth. Vienna's staunch bourgeois German population felt besieged by the rising tide of socialism and by the large number of Slavic peoples—Czechs, Slovaks, Croatians, Serbs, as well as Hungarians and Jews—who arrived from the empire's provinces. As much as Vienna was the city of the aging Emperor Franz Joseph, it was also the city of Karl Lueger, the populist mayor who appealed to ethnic Germans' economic and cultural insecurities through antisemitic rhetoric. Pan-Germanism, the notion that ethnic Germans in Austria and Germany should form their own expanded polity, was also in the wind. Cheap racist publications that pilloried Slavic and Jewish elements supported it all.[2]

Hitler later described his time in Vienna as formative. We have but scattered, problematic accounts of these years; the best known comes from Hitler's one-time roommate August Kubizek.[3] Surely Vienna's tensions influenced Hitler, a youthful ne'er-do-well dilettante, whose days and nights mixed soaring fantasy with abject failure. His rejection by the Academy of Fine Arts left him seething at faceless enemies who he imagined worked against him. Meanwhile, he slept late and spent afternoons reading, drawing, and dreaming fantastic projects—all quickly dropped—from heroic operas to urban redesign. Meanwhile he held no job, supplementing his orphan's pension early on with a "loan" from his maternal aunt.

Fortunately his tastes were ascetic. He lived in modest lodgings and ate little. His one indulgence was Wagner's operas, for which he purchased standing room tickets. He neither drank nor smoked, and he steered clear of women, determined, he said, to protect his "flame of life" for something grand. Yet he still ran short of money. By 1909, he lived in a men's hostel, barely making ends meet with his mediocre drawings and paintings, which were hawked cheaply. In the meantime, he read Vienna's gutter press. He formed increasingly strident political views, which embraced pan-Germanism and condemned socialism but had not yet, despite his later statements, fully developed regarding the Jewish peril.[4]

Possibly owing to its turbulent political and ethnic undercurrents, Hitler never felt loyalty toward the Austro-Hungarian Empire. He never registered for compulsory military service, and the possibility of arrest prompted him to leave Vienna for Germany in 1913 at age twenty-four. By now Hitler was also eligible to receive his share of his father's inheritance. He continued to avoid work. He settled in Munich where, as in Vienna, he read a lot, sold cheap paintings, and idled in cafés while dreaming of a new career as an urban planner.

Defeat, Anger, and the Nazi Party

The outbreak of war finally gave Hitler, now age twenty-five, some purpose. Like most of his generation, he absorbed the "spirit of 1914" for its promise of camaraderie, glory, and renewal in a monotonous modern world. He volunteered for the Bavarian army and served in the List Regiment, named for its first commander Colonel Julius von List. He initially saw combat at the

---

[1] Ian Kershaw, *Hitler 1889–1936: Hubris* (New York, 1998), p. 22.

[2] Brigitte Hamann, *Hitler's Vienna: A Dictator's Apprenticeship* (New York, 2000).

[3] August Kubizek, *The Young Hitler I Knew: The Definitive Inside Look at the Artist Who Became a Monster* (New York, 2011).

[4] A careful account of Hitler's early years is in Kershaw, *Hitler 1889–1936*, pp. 3–67.

first Battle of Ypres in Belgium against British forces in October 1914. There the poorly trained regiment suffered 75 percent casualties.

Because of the heavy losses, Hitler was promoted to corporal. He also received an Iron Cross Second Class for bravery. By December 1914, he served as a dispatch runner. He fulfilled his duties and was actually wounded by a shell fragment at the Battle of the Somme in 1916. But he spent much of his time at regimental headquarters in relative comfort among officers rather than on the battlefields of Belgium and France. The lack of consistently hazardous combat duty explains why he was not promoted further, and perhaps why he received the Iron Cross First Class in 1918. He had simply put in the time at regimental headquarters.

It also explains his dogged optimism despite continued enemy shelling of the troops, wretched conditions in the trenches, and deflated morale of frontline soldiers. "We shall hang on until Hindenburg has softened Russia up," he wrote in 1915. "Then comes the day of retribution!" Indeed Hitler envisioned that the war, when won, would create a better Germany—"a purer place," as he put it in 1915, "less riddled with foreign influences." The war, he continued, "will not only help to smash Germany's foes outside but . . . our inner internationalism, too, will collapse." Defeatism infuriated him. In down moments he withdrew. As a nonsmoking, nondrinking, nonphilandering loner, he read, drew sketches, and trained the regimental dog, to which he was closer than his comrades at regimental headquarters.[5]

Hitler was angry and disoriented after learning of Germany's defeat in November 1918, in a military hospital in Pasewalk, where he was treated for poison gas inhalation. Aside from his bitterness at the shock of defeat, he had neither a family nor any occupation to which to return. He avoided discharge by performing political work for the army in the political melee of Munich in the aftermath of the brief soviet republic there. Hitler gave anticommunist lectures to army personnel and discovered an immense talent for passionate and angry speaking. He came to despise and fear Bolshevism, and became one of millions of Germans who swallowed the stab-in-the-back myth. He connected the Jews to both and began to speak of them as a decrepit race, a "leech upon the peoples of the world."[6]

Populist *völkisch* political groups flourished in the counterrevolutionary atmosphere of Munich. Fervently nationalist in character, they believed in biological German superiority and an eternal, almost mystical heroic German spirit. Wary of domestic subversion, they also espoused antisemitism. Part of Hitler's job was to report on Munich's political groups, one of which was the small *völkisch* German Workers' Party. Hitler joined it in September 1919 as member number 555. In March 1920, the army discharged Hitler and he became a full-time political activist. His passion, anger, thunderous speaking abilities, and simple explanations of complex problems struck a chord, drew crowds in the thousands, and made him the small party's main attraction.

By July 1921, Hitler assumed leadership of the party, now renamed the National Socialist German Workers' Party (NSDAP). Propaganda was his early trademark, and he borrowed much from the political left that he loathed. He designed the Nazi flag with the runic, *völkisch* symbol of the swastika on a bold red background. He encouraged the party to purchase the newspaper *Völkischer Beobachter* ("People's Observer") to carry its message. He supported the reshaping of the party's disorderly army-veteran beer hall enforcers into a somewhat disciplined, paramilitary, street-fighting force known as the SA (*Sturmabteilung* ["Storm Detachment"]) to crack leftist heads. And he insisted that politics be a raucous, violent business with more passion than debate.

---

[5]Quotes from Thomas Weber, *Hitler's First War: Adolf Hitler, the Men of the List Regiment, and the First World War* (New York, 2010), pp. 69, 70. For Hitler's day-to-day experience and his Iron Cross First Class, see pp. 92–140, 214–16.

[6]Quoted in Weber, *Hitler's First War*, p. 255.

Adolf Hitler in 1923.   *Source:*
Pictorial Press Ltd/Alamy.

The Beer Hall Putsch

Increasingly Hitler saw himself as a messiah sent to rescue Germany from decrepitude, particularly by 1923, a year that saw the French occupation of the Ruhr, hyperinflation, and a communist coup attempt in Hamburg. To Hitler, internal enemies were to blame. He spent much of the year railing to packed houses in Munich's massive beer halls against the November Criminals in Berlin and the Jews, who he was now convinced stood behind them.

Inspired by Benito Mussolini's October 1922 fascist coup in Italy, Hitler concluded that the hour had come for the Nazis to seize power in Germany, starting in Munich. On the night of November 8–9 he launched the so-called Beer Hall *Putsch*. Armed with a pistol, Hitler entered the *Bürgerbräukeller*; disrupted a meeting led by the head of the Bavarian State, Gustav Ritter von Kahr; and announced that the national revolution against the "Berlin Jew government and the November criminals of 1918" had begun.[7] Hitler would be the new head of government, and Erich Ludendorff, whom the Nazis had co-opted, would be the new army chief.

Yet the Nazis never gained control of the army or police barracks in Munich. Hitler led a column of 2,000 Nazis through Munich in the hope of winning the masses, but his following was no match for fully armed police. After a brief gun battle, the *Putsch* collapsed. Its leaders were arrested and, from February through April 1924, Hitler along with six others stood trial in Munich for treason. A sympathetic court refused to find Ludendorff guilty of anything, and thus it allowed Hitler a wide berth as well.

Hitler grabbed the stage at his trial. In a four-hour opening statement, he wove a past of self-sacrifice and intense political awakening while seizing the mantle of opposition to the republic. "As young man of 16½," he testified, "I was forced to earn my own daily bread. . . ." "I went to Vienna a cosmopolitan," he continued, "and left as an absolute antisemite." He claimed to tell his fellow soldiers during the war that, "[I]f the problem of Marxism is not solved, then

---

[7]Quoted Kershaw, *Hitler 1889–1936: Hubris*, p. 207.

Germany cannot be victorious." He turned the high treason charge inside out. The surrender of 1918, he said, was "a stab in the back against the army that fought heroically, against the German *Volk*, German freedom and the German nation. As such it can never be legalized. . . ." "If we created a new movement," he continued, "then such happened in the hope that one day, even in the twelfth hour, we would be able to turn around Germany's fate."[8]

The trial became a national media event. Left-wing newspapers were outraged. Right-wing newspapers were sympathetic. "All the accused of the trial," said one, "shared a common, great idealist objective: to save Germany from her great misfortune."[9] The court pronounced an astonishingly lenient sentence of five years. Hitler's comfortable confinement in Landsberg Prison, where he received flowers, visitors, letters, and soft treatment by guards, was not even that long. He was released in December 1924 for good behavior. Having served just over eight months, he was able to play the martyr without, as in the war, any real suffering.

3.2 HITLER AND THE JEWISH ENEMY

Germans and Jews

Hitler used the time to dictate the first part of his infamous book, *Mein Kampf* ("My Struggle"). It was published in 1925, with a second volume appearing the following year. In part *Mein Kampf* is a political testament that unveils a worldview borrowed from mystical pan-German nationalism, Social Darwinism, antisemitism, and seething postwar anger, all crystallized in 1924. Yet *Mein Kampf's* other fundamental aspect is its urgency. A prophet on a mission with no time to lose, Hitler claimed to understand a terrible, impending threat to which everyone else was blind—the international Jewish plot to destroy Germany and dominate the world.

For Hitler, the world was a jungle in which races struggled with one another for survival. Racial conflict was the motor that drove history and explained all major events. Because all races had certain biological and spiritual traits, they were fundamentally unequal. And because they evolved like all living things, their traits sharpened over time as the weaker members died off, or they became blunted if members of a racial community bred with members of a lesser race. Nature, if left to itself, would ensure the dominance of the strong over the weak.

Atop Hitler's racial hierarchy was the northern European Aryan man. "All human culture," he insisted, "all the results of art, science, and technology that we see before us today, are almost exclusively the creative product of the Aryan. He is the Prometheus of mankind from whose bright forehead the divine spark of genius has sprung at all times. . . ."[10] If the Aryan were to die out, Hitler warned, "the dark veils of an age without culture will again descend on the globe."[11]

Other races were able at most to copy Aryan achievements. But at humanity's very bottom were the Jews. Hitler now claimed that, during his years in Vienna, he was made "sick to [his] stomach" by the dirty physical appearance and the smells of caftan-wearing eastern Jews. Their very presence destroyed the Austro-Hungarian Empire, Hitler said, like "a maggot in a rotting body."[12]

---

[8]Lothar Gruchmann and Reinhard Weber, eds., *Der Hitler-Prozess 1924: Wortlaut der Hauptverhandlung vor dem Volksgericht München*, vol. 1 (Munich, 1997), pp. 20–7.

[9]Bernhard Fulda, *Press and Politics in the Weimar Republic* (New York, 2009), p. 70.

[10]Adolf Hitler, *Mein Kampf*, trans. Ralph Mannheim (Boston, MA: Houghton Mifflin, 1971) p. 290.

[11]*Mein Kampf*, p. 383.

[12]*Mein Kampf*, pp. 56–7.

Since the dawn of time, Hitler said, the Jews created nothing. They lived off the work of others, using their traits of lying, swindling, and manipulating. The Jews' religion and language were covers for their wretched activities and their *Talmud* was nothing more than an instruction book for exploitation. "He is," said Hitler referring to the typical Jew, "a parasite [who] like noxious bacillus keeps spreading as soon as a favorable medium invites him. And . . . wherever he appears, the host people dies out."[13] "If the Jews were alone in this world," said Hitler, "they would stifle in filth and shit," for with no one else to exploit, they would turn like vermin on one another.[14]

Despite their inferiority, the Jews to Hitler were "the mightiest counterpart to the Aryan" because of their sinister adaptability. They survived popular violence in the Middle Ages by latching onto local rulers for protection. They survived in the Enlightenment by learning the languages and customs of their host societies. In this disguise, they propagated nature's greatest lie—that all men were equal. "All at once," Hitler said, "the Jew becomes a liberal and begins to rave about the necessary progress of mankind."[15]

From this point, a broader Jewish takeover began. Jews used the press to tear down the legal barriers that had restrained them. They wormed their way into the industrial economy through banking and stock markets. They eliminated small craftsmen and merchants, replacing them with impersonal factories that could leech labor from millions of workers at a time though long, dehumanizing hours. The "Jewification" of German life, Hitler said, transformed respect for manual work into contempt for the physical laborer.

The Jewish Conspiracy

The Jews, Hitler said, next reached for political control. It was here that his reading of the *Protocols of the Elders of Zion* emerged. "[With] terrifying certainty," he said, the *Protocols* "reveal the nature and activity of the Jewish people and expose their . . . ultimate final aims."[16] Jews brought down monarchies and created parliamentary democracies, replacing strong rulers with jabbering political parties stuffed with mediocrities but dominated by "Jews and only Jews."[17]

Worse, Jews deployed their chief weapon—Marxism—the diabolical coup-de-grace that mobilized and manipulated the unthinking mass in the name of social justice in order to take over the world outright. "Karl Marx," said Hitler, "was the *one* among millions who, with the sure eye of the prophet, recognized in the morass of a slowly decomposing world the most essential poisons, extracted them, and, like a wizard, prepared them into a concentrated solution for the swifter annihilation of the independent existence of free nations of this earth . . . all in the service of his race." "Marxism," Hitler said, "systematically plans to hand the world over to the Jews."[18]

World War I was to Hitler the climax of the struggle between Aryan creativity and Jewish manipulation—the "last flicker of national self-preservation in face of the progressing pacifist-Marxist paralysis of our national body."[19] The Jews, by propagating socialist and pacifist rhetoric on the home front, sapped the German will to fight, stabbing their hosts in the back. The surrender by the November Criminals was a defeat years in the making.

---

[13]*Mein Kampf*, p. 305.

[14]*Mein Kampf*, p. 302.

[15]*Mein Kampf*, p. 315.

[16]*Mein Kampf*, p. 308.

[17]*Mein Kampf*, p. 442.

[18]*Mein Kampf*, p. 382.

[19]*Mein Kampf*, p. 329.

But it might have been worse. Bolshevik takeover through use of the masses occurred in Russia. The Bolsheviks would have succeeded in Germany too had German troops not returned home and forced the SPD to adopt a more moderate, parliamentary government. But the Jews had not given up. The Jew, Hitler said, continued his strategy of "sneaking in among the nations and boring from within, [fighting] with lies and slander, poison and corruption, intensifying the struggle to the point of bloodily exterminating his hated foes. *In Russian Bolshevism we must see the attempt undertaken by the Jews in the twentieth century to achieve world domination. . . .* Germany is today the next great war aim of Bolshevism."[20]

The Weimar Republic, meanwhile, was defined by relentless Jewish erosion of Germany's remaining strength. "The Jew today," Hitler said, "is the great agitator for the complete destruction of Germany."[21] Through agents such as "the international Jew Kurt Eisner," they attempted to fracture German unity. Through the Treaty of Versailles, Jews removed Germany's weapons. Through the League of Nations, Jews preached pacifism, thus removing the racial instinct of self-preservation. Through expressionist art, jazz, and antiwar literature, the Jew dragged heroic German art "down into the sphere of his own base nature."[22]

And most diabolically, Jews attacked German blood. France, which in Hitler's mind was controlled by an alliance of Jewish financiers and French nationalists, deliberately stationed African troops in the Rhineland to defile German blood. France, raved Hitler, *"more and more negrified, constitutes in its tie with the aims of Jewish world domination an enduring danger for the existence of the white race in Europe."*[23] Jews also polluted German blood themselves. "With Satanic joy in his face," said Hitler, "the black-haired Jewish youth lurks in wait for the unsuspecting girl whom he defiles with his blood, thus stealing her from her people."[24] "Bear in mind," Hitler warned, "how racial disintegration drags down and often destroys the last Aryan values of our German people. . . . The contamination of our blood, blindly ignored by hundreds of thousands of our people, is carried on systematically by the Jew today."[25] Jews were behind the selling of birth control products to healthy German parents while advocating humanitarian arguments that allowed "every degenerate the possibility of propagating."[26]

For Hitler, the Jewish danger was an impending catastrophe. The German people, he said, stood "at the edge of an abyss."[27] "[The] development we are going through today if continued unobstructed," he warned, "would fulfill the Jewish prophecy—the Jew would really devour the peoples of the earth [and] would become their master."[28] The answer was to fight back. And because the Nazis understood the nature of the Jewish threat, the task was up to them. The SA would break Marxist skulls because mastery of the streets would yield mastery of the state. On coming to power the Nazis would "judge and execute some ten thousand of the . . . criminals [responsible] for the November betrayal and everything that goes with it."[29]

---

[20]*Mein Kampf*, pp. 661–2. Italics in original.

[21]*Mein Kampf*, p. 623.

[22]*Mein Kampf*, p. 326.

[23]*Mein Kampf*, p. 624. Italics in original.

[24]*Mein Kampf*, p. 325.

[25]*Mein Kampf*, p. 562.

[26]*Mein Kampf*, p. 402.

[27]*Mein Kampf*, p. 385.

[28]*Mein Kampf*, p. 452.

[29]*Mein Kampf*, p. 545.

But the Nazi state would not be a throwback to the imperial monarchy that had tolerated parliamentarians, socialists, and Jews in the first place. Nazism was a young, spiritual movement with a window into Jewish destructiveness and a will to destroy it. German consciousness would be reawakened. German unity would be forged. German blood would be protected. In short, "The *völkisch* state must make up for what everyone else today has neglected in this field. *It must set race at the center of all life.*"[30]

To ensure the proper path, there would be but one leader—Hitler himself. And he would be ruthless. "The nationalization of our masses will succeed only when, aside from all the positive struggle for the soul of our people, their international poisoners are exterminated."[31] Whether Hitler in 1924 was already thinking in terms of systematically murdering Germany's Jews is not clear. Yet Hitler's embrace of terrible violence should be obvious to any reader.

Lebensraum and War

So that Germans could propagate over the following centuries, Germany had to expand its borders through rearmament and war. Hitler spoke to this issue more in an unpublished second book manuscript of 1928 than in *Mein Kampf*, but in both books he differed sharply with traditional nationalist parties who focused solely on territories lost in 1919.

To Hitler, Germany's 1914 borders were "a political absurdity"—they never provided the land necessary for German self-sufficiency and never sustained real population growth. On the contrary, limited borders encouraged birth control and emigration, both of which cost Germany some of its best racial elements. Because a new war would sacrifice thousands of German lives anyway, the new borders should be worth the blood. They should encompass a tremendous living space—or *Lebensraum*—that would feed Germans for centuries while sustaining growth.

Germany had to crush France because the Jewish-led plutocracy there would never allow Germany to expand. But the real living space that Germany needed lay to the East. "If we speak of soil in Europe today," Hitler said in *Mein Kampf*, "we can primarily have in mind only Russia and her vassal border states."[32] Fortunately, he continued, the Bolsheviks had killed off the anti-semitic Germanic leadership that had led the Slavs of the Russian Empire since the time of Peter the Great. It was now a Jewish-led state made up of inferior peoples from top to bottom. Conquest would be easy. Germany would gain its living space while striking world Bolshevism at its heart. Once this task was completed, German survival and dominance in Europe would be guaranteed for a millennium. A revived German society could even confront the United States for global supremacy.

The implications of *Mein Kampf* were clear for the millions of people already living in Germany's future living space. The lesser Slavic peoples to the east could not be Germanized simply through teaching them the German language. "Race," Hitler said, "does not happen to lie in language but in the blood." And blood could not be changed.[33] The land, not the people, was to be Germanized. "The way to do this," Hitler said, "is above all for the state not to leave settlement of newly acquired territories to chance, but to subject it to special norms."[34]

---

[30]*Mein Kampf*, p. 404. Italics in original.

[31]*Mein Kampf*, p. 338.

[32]*Mein Kampf*, p. 649ff.

[33]*Mein Kampf*, p. 389.

[34]*Mein Kampf*, p. 405.

In his unpublished second book, Hitler was more specific when discussing the Poles—Germany, he said, "could under absolutely no circumstances annex Poles with the intention of turning them into Germans. It would instead have to decide either to isolate these alien racial elements in order to prevent the repeated contamination . . . or it would have to remove them entirely. . . ."[35] But for the millions of Jews living in Poland and in the Soviet Union, who were an aggressive threat rather than simply racial flotsam, these words were even more dire.

3.3 HOW HITLER CAME TO POWER

Weimar's Stabilization and Erosion

When Hitler was paroled from prison in December 1924, he had determined that an armed coup would not win power. The Nazis would take control of the state through the ballot box. Yet he was as far from victory as he could be. State authorities had banned both the Nazi Party and the SA, and they had prohibited Hitler from public speaking.

The Weimar Republic, had stabilized thanks to its greatest politician, the pragmatic nationalist Gustav Stresemann, who served as foreign minister from 1925 to his death in 1929. Stresemann restored confidence in the German currency, secured loans from US bankers to stabilize the German economy, forged new deals over reparations and normalized relations with the Allies, brought Germany into the League of Nations as a permanent member of the League Council in 1926, convinced the French to withdraw their troops from the Rhineland earlier than the Versailles Treaty had stipulated, all without ever formally recognizing Germany's borders with Czechoslovakia and Poland and without admitting clandestine violations of Germany's disarmament obligations.

But Stresemann's measures were never good enough for the political right. Their continued ambivalence toward the republic was manifested in the 1925 election of Paul von Hindenburg as the republic's new president. That one of the monarchy's most conspicuous military figures could win the republic's highest office was a bad sign, especially since the president could invoke emergency powers through the invocation of Article 48 of the Weimar constitution, through which he could make law without Reichstag approval. On the other hand, Hindenburg represented a traditional conservatism that rejected the *völkisch*, populist right as well as the socialist left. As long as politics within the republic remained steady, Hindenburg was not a danger.

But as Stresemann warned before his death, German economic solvency was a "dance on a volcano." With the recession of the late 1920s and the crash of the US stock market in October 1929, the German economy tumbled over the edge. New American loans dried up and old ones were called back so that German firms were left undercapitalized, underproductive, and unable to maintain their white- and blue-collar workforces. Small businesses, from shops to restaurants, slumped too because consumers had less to spend.

The agricultural sector, already wobbly before 1929, collapsed next. Banks called in loans to farmers, resulting in layoffs of agricultural workers and decreased farm production. To make matters worse, declining tax revenue obliged the government to lay off hundreds of thousands of government officials and state workers, such as railway and postal employees. By early 1932, perhaps 6 million Germans were unemployed. Counting their dependants, 13 million Germans, about one-fifth of the population, were without a source of income. Those who retained their jobs were often obliged to take pay cuts.

---

[35]Gerhard L. Weinberg, ed., *Hitler's Second Book* (New York, 2003), p. 53.

Successive cabinets appointed by Hindenburg deliberately excluded the political left that he mistrusted, but Hindenburg's choices had no answer for the crisis either. No state in the 1930s had the broad social safety net programs associated with the post-1945 world. The wisdom of the day favored deflationary policies in which government spending would shrink, the budget would be balanced, and economic confidence would be restored.

Those in distress resented cuts in already limited government spending. Those with income resented the idea of taxation to balance the national budget. The result in Germany from 1930 to 1932 was government deadlock between Hindenburg's chancellor, the conservative Catholic monarchist Heinrich Brüning, and the Reichstag, which refused to pass his austere measures. The government enacted laws through emergency decree, which eroded the democratic process and failed to alleviate the economic crisis. Worse, the ongoing depression led to alarming voting patterns, with the industrial working class swinging to the extreme left and the middle class to the extreme right.

The Republic's Collapse

The initial fire bell came in the elections of September 1930, which Brüning called in the expectation that they would result in a more cooperative Reichstag. He miscalculated badly. The Social Democrats (SPD) remained the largest party but lost ten seats, dropping from 153 to 143 out of a total of 577. The Communist Party of Germany (KPD) won 13.1 percent of the vote, and their number of seats jumped from 54 to 77. The Nazis, though, were the true winners. In 1928, they had won just 2.6 percent of the vote, 810,000 votes in all, earning a paltry twelve seats. Now they won 6.4 million votes and 107 seats in the Reichstag, becoming the second largest party. The government became dysfunctional as Nazi deputies, who entered the Reichstag in SA uniforms, disrupted debate.

In May 1932, Hindenburg hoped that a cabinet of old-line aristocrats from a world that had since passed might be able to rule with popular confidence. But the new chancellor, Franz von Papen, though a confidante of Hindenburg, had no popular support. Von Papen's call for new elections in July resulted in greater disaster: The Nazis won 13.7 million votes—37.4 percent of those cast—and jumped from 107 to 230 seats Reichstag seats out of 608. They were now the Reichstag's largest party.

Despite the fact that the Nazi vote had grown to formidable proportions, Hindenburg, an aristocrat and former field marshal, held Hitler in contempt. He consistently refused to make him chancellor. Hitler, determined to gain absolute power, would accept nothing less. A new election in November 1932 lessened the Nazi vote to 33.1 percent of the total. They were still the largest party, with 196 Reichstag seats, but they had peaked. In December, Hindenburg appointed his minister of defense, General Kurt von Schleicher, as chancellor based on Schleicher's hope that he could institute programs that would garner support from the political center and left while further weakening the Nazis. Von Schleicher failed, and von Papen, who had been ousted as chancellor by von Schleicher, aimed to get even. He adopted a disastrous scheme whereby he attempted to co-opt the Nazis for traditional conservative aims.

In January 1933, von Papen proposed to Hindenburg that Hitler become chancellor. The new cabinet would have popular support without the inclusion of the political left. The Hitler cabinet would have but two other Nazis. The bulk of the cabinet would be traditional conservatives, including von Papen as vice chancellor. The cabinet was supposed to follow von Papen's lead rather than that of the unaccomplished army corporal and former beer hall speaker. On the fateful day of January 30, 1933, Hitler became chancellor. Von Papen was sure that his scheme would work. "We have him hemmed in," he said privately. "In two months we'll have pushed Hitler so far into a corner that he'll squeal."[36] History proved von Papen wrong within weeks.

Party Organization and Propaganda

How had the Nazis, led by a delusional antisemite who had been in jail eight years earlier, achieve power in a literate, developed state? Who supported them? Did voters approve of the Nazis' millenarian antisemitism? Or was it all a tragically misplaced protest against the traditional parties' inability to solve the depression?

Hitler understood in 1925 that, to achieve power, the Nazis had to become a mass national movement rather than a traditional German party that appealed to a specific class, region, or confession. To win members and votes beyond *völkisch* groups in Bavaria, he expanded the Nazi administrative apparatus and divided Germany into party districts, each known as a *Gau*. Each *Gau* had a party *Gauleiter* who would implement orders from party headquarters in Munich on propaganda, fundraising, membership drives, SA recruitment, and election strategy. The party used the media of speech, print, posters, and films, and eventually tried to appeal to everyone, even workers in what was then known as "Red Berlin."

Joseph Goebbels was a disillusioned, club-footed intellectual from the Rhineland who followed Hitler's trial in 1924. He was completely smitten. "Let us thank Fate," he wrote in October 1924, "for giving us this man, our helmsman in need, our apostle of truth, our leader to freedom, our fanatic of love, our voice in battle, our hero of loyalty. . . ."[37] In April 1925, he met Hitler personally and became completely devoted to his new Führer. "I love him," Goebbels confessed to his diary.[38] In 1926, Hitler rewarded Goebbels, a gifted speaker, fulminous writer, and tireless organizer, by naming him *Gauleiter* of Berlin, the left-leaning capital where the Nazis were especially weak. Goebbels accepted the challenge to win workers away from the political left.

Goebbels worked constantly and spoke often. He developed a Berlin party newspaper, *Der Angriff* ("The Attack"), which relentlessly blamed Jewish conspiracies for class conflict. "The Jew," he wrote in 1928, "is the cause and beneficiary of our enslavement. He exploited the social distress of the masses to deepen the fatal split between Right and Left within our people. . . ."[39] He ceaselessly attacked Berlin's Jewish deputy police chief Bernhard Weiss, referred to in *Der Angriff* as "Isadore." Goebbels provoked brawls with communist paramilitaries by marching the Berlin SA into working-class neighborhoods. From 1924 to 1929, twenty-nine Nazis and ninety-two communists were killed and thousands injured in the fighting.[40] In the years ahead, Goebbels added many more titles. But he remained *Gauleiter* of Berlin until the day he died.

Despite their efforts, Nazi gains in the 1920s were limited. They recruited most successfully among young men in their twenties and thirties from the lower middle class, which included artisans, small retailers, white-collar workers, and civil servants, as well as upper middle-class university students. It was a restless, dynamic group—old enough to be embittered by 1918 if not to have fought in the war; fearful of large capitalist concerns on the one hand and Marxism on the other; yearning for mystical unity among Germans; susceptible to xenophobia and antisemitism;

---

[36]Quoted in Henry Ashby Turner, *Hitler's Thirty Days to Power: January 1933* (New York, 1996), p. 148.

[37]Quoted in Ralf Georg Reuth, *Goebbels* (New York, 1990), p. 60.

[38]Quoted in Kershaw, *Hitler 1889–1936: Hubris*, p. 277.

[39]Quoted Reuth, *Goebbels*, p. 91.

[40]Figures in Richard Evans, *The Coming of the Third Reich* (New York, 2004), p. 269.

Joseph Goebbels in 1934.
Source: United States Holocaust
Memorial Museum.

and accepting of political violence. Still, in April 1928, the party numbered but 80,000 members and could not manage even 1 million votes out of nearly 31 million votes cast.

The electoral success after 1928 and the growth in party membership to 450,000 by late 1932 came from several factors connected with the deepening depression. The Nazis also increased their use of street violence. During the bloody summer of 1932, 105 were killed in street clashes between Nazi and communist forces.[41] Hitler characterized the head-cracking SA, which now numbered 400,000, as liberators fighting Marxism for a restored, united German *Volk*.

The Nazis' best electoral results still came from the lower middle class. But aided by Hitler's charisma and a cadre of youthful activists, the Nazis broadened their appeal. They polled well with anxious middle- to upper-class voters fed up with the republic's inability to solve its crises and worried by the communists' growing popularity with unemployed industrial workers. The traditional conservative and liberal parties, from which the Nazis took many older voters, could not match the Nazis' raucous campaigning, angry nationalism, and violent anti-Marxism. Within their bloc, the Nazis also polled well among women who traditionally stayed away from the polls at election time. They also attracted a significant percentage of workers, particularly from the more conservative countryside, with promises of economic security and social harmony rather than class conflict.[42]

German Voters and the Jews

In many speaking venues from 1930 to 1932, the Nazis toned down their antisemitism. In the feverish election campaigns of those years, Hitler and his followers pointed to the symptoms of the Jewish threat rather than to the Jews themselves. Hitler ranted against fractured democratic

---

[41]Figure in Dirk Schumann, *Political Violence in the Weimar Republic 1918–1933: Fight for the Streets and Fear of Civil War* (New York, 2009), pp. 261–2.

[42]See the essays in Conan Fischer, ed., *The Rise of National Socialism and the Working Classes in Weimar Germany* (Providence, RI, 1996).

rule, the shameful defeat of 1918, the republic's weak foreign policy, and the need of the Germans to act as a single *Volk*.[43]

Although Jews were mentioned less than usual in Hitler's speeches, antisemitism was part of the Nazi vocabulary from the start and was still apparent for anyone who wished to look. In a speech before the September 1930 election that was printed in *Völkischer Beobachter*, Hitler insisted that the Jew, who used the bourgeoisie and liberalism in the French Revolution to attain equality, now used the German worker and communism to gain supremacy. "We harbor no hatred toward the communist," said Hitler, "for he does not see who stands behind him."[44] In other pre-election speeches, he continued to blame the Jews for the defeat of 1918, for the party politics of the republic, and for the growth of communism, and he warned that this foreign race would dominate Germany.[45]

More insightful foreigners sensed trouble as the Nazis' popularity grew. In September 1932, James G. McDonald, then the head of the Foreign Policy Association in the United States, lunched with Ernst Hanfstaengl, a close supporter of Hitler from the early 1920s. McDonald heard Hitler speak the previous evening to 25,000 people at Berlin's Sport Palace. "His reception," wrote McDonald in his diary, "was the most extraordinary I have ever seen given a public man." Now McDonald asked Hanfstaengl about Nazism and the Jews. Hanfstaengl acted as Hitler's press liaison. He knew that his answer would not be kept confidential. Nonetheless, as McDonald wrote in his diary:

> Immediately his eyes lighted up, took a fanatical look, and he launched into a tirade against the Jews. He would not admit that any Jew could be a good patriot in Germany. He attributed to them the fact that Germany was forced to sign the peace treaty and charged that Jewish bankers were profiting from Germany's reparations payments. I tried to argue with him . . . but made no progress at all. It was clear that he and, I presume, many of the other leaders of the Nazis really believe all these charges against the Jews.[46]

If millions of traditionally conservative Germans voted for the Nazis for reasons other than antisemitism, they were at the very least in passive agreement or indifferent to what was at the very heart of the Nazi movement.

And indeed, suspicion toward German Jews during the republic was evident even with non-Nazis, who believed that "Jewish influences" during the 1920s had grown alarmingly. Were their fears justified? In 1933, Germany's roughly 525,000 Jews comprised 0.76 percent of the German population. They comprised 4.7 percent of university students, 10.9 percent of doctors, 16.3 percent of lawyers, 2.8 percent of judges and district attorneys, 2.6 percent of professors, 2 percent of musicians, 5.1 percent of editors and writers, 5.6 percent of film producers, and 14 of the 608 Reichstag deputies elected in July 1932. Three-fourths of all German Jews made their living in smaller commercial enterprises. And in Berlin, which had Germany's largest Jewish population, Jews made up over one-third of the physicians and almost half of the lawyers.[47]

---

[43]Christian Hartmann, ed., *Hitler: Reden—Shriften—Anordnungen, Februar 1925 bis Januar 1933*, vol. 3, part 3 (Munich, 1995), pp. 420–30.

[44]Hartmann, ed., *Hitler: Reden—Schriften—Anordnungen*, vol. 3, pt. 3, p. 371.

[45]Hartmann, ed., *Hitler: Reden—Schriften—Anordnungen*, vol. 3, pt. 3, p. 390.

[46]Original diary entries of September 1 and 2, 1933, in United States Holocaust Memorial Museum, James G. McDonald Papers, Box 3, Folder 9.

[47]Figures in Jeffrey Herf, *The Jewish Enemy: Nazi Propaganda During World War II and the Holocaust* (Cambridge, MA, 2006), pp. 3–37.

German Jews, generally committed to equality, also tended to back more democratic parties and issues. They supported the German Democratic Party (known as the "Jew Party" by its right-wing opponents) and the much stronger Social Democratic Party. Both parties had Jews in key positions, including Reichstag deputies and even government officials.[48] Jews also held important positions in the German press, editing major liberal papers like the *Berliner Tageblatt* and writing for many others. University posts were opened so that, of the nine Nobel prizes won by German academics during the Weimar period, five went to German Jews. Jews were important in Weimar theater, cinema, visual arts, music, and literature, much of which challenged conservative mores. Jewish intellectuals, meanwhile, tended to support the day's progressive causes, from pacifism to women's rights.

It is true that Jews were overrepresented in certain professions and certain political parties. It is nonsensical to believe that they dominated either. And no one saw themselves as more German than German Jews. Regardless, the Jewish presence rankled even non-Nazis. In September 1933, Hitler's foreign minister, Konstantin von Neurath—a landed aristocrat in the cabinet designed by Franz von Papen to box Hitler in—publicly defended Nazi anti-Jewish policies, arguing that they brought a "necessary cleaning up of public life." Even when put on trial by the Allies after the war, von Neurath maintained this stance: "In view of the [Jewish] domination of public life in Germany which occurred after the last war, I thought it absolutely right. . . . That is still my view today."[49]

Some middle-class Germans were more vocal, at least in private. On a train in Switzerland in April 1933, James McDonald spoke with a non-Nazi German businessman. When McDonald asked if the man thought Nazi policy toward Jews (which to this point had just begun) was unfair, the man said,

> No! We must remember . . . that the Jew is the bacillus corrupting the German blood and race, and that once a Jew, always a Jew. He cannot pass from one kind of animal to another. The Jews are but 1 percent of the German population, but they have dominated our culture. They cannot be tolerated.[50]

3.4 THE NAZI POLICE STATE

Co-opting the Police

On the night of January 30, 1933, the Nazis celebrated Hitler's chancellorship with torchlight parades through Germany's cities. It was the crowning moment of a fourteen-year struggle. Yet there was no guarantee that Hitler would last. The Nazi vote had dropped between July and November of 1932 and though Hitler was chancellor, his cabinet contained three Nazis balanced against eight traditional conservatives who intended to use Hitler's popularity and then replace him. Parties to the left of the Nazis, such as the Catholic Center, the SPD and the KPD, also remained strong. Hitler's first task—even before any systematized measures against Jews—was the neutralization of political enemies, the elimination of the constitution, and the establishment

---

[48]Bruce B. Frye, "The German Democratic Party and the 'Jewish Problem' in the Weimar Republic," *Leo Baeck Institute Yearbook* 21 (1976): 143ff.

[49]*Völkischer Beobachter*, September 17, 1933; International Military Tribunal, *Trial of the Major War Criminals Before the International Military Tribunal, Nuremberg, 14 November 1945–1 October 1946* (hereafter *TMWC*), (Nuremberg, 1949), vol. 17, June 25, 1946, p. 166.

[50]Original diary entry of April 9, 1933, in United States Holocaust Memorial Museum, James G. McDonald Papers, Box 3, Folder 8.

of a firm dictatorship. It was accomplished with dizzying speed accompanied by violence. Within months, the Nazis had no real opposition.

Hitler insisted that Nazis hold two key cabinet positions. One was the Ministry of the Interior, which directed the national police apparatus. The post went to Wilhelm Frick, a Bavarian police official during World War I who had winked at *Freikorps* excesses in 1919 and who had since been associated with Hitler. The other was Hermann Göring, a gregarious former flying ace who joined the Nazi Party in 1922 and who served as Reichstag president after the Nazi electoral victory of July 1932. Göring became a minister without portfolio, but also the minister-president for Prussia, which gave him police powers in Germany's largest state.

Göring speedily removed twenty-two of thirty-two police chiefs in Prussia (many of whom were from opposition parties such as the SPD) and replaced them with Nazis. He also expanded the police force in Prussia by 50,000 auxiliaries, mostly from the SA. The police became a hammer for eliminating political enemies, especially with Göring's order of February 17 encouraging the police to shoot leftist opponents:

> The activities of subversive organizations are to be combated with the most drastic methods. Communist terrorist acts and attacks are to be proceeded against with all severity, and weapons must be ruthlessly used when necessary. Police officers who in the execution of this duty use their firearms will be supported by me without regard to the effect of their shots; on the other hand, officers who fail from a false sense of consideration may expect disciplinary measures. . . .[51]

Nazi police also infiltrated communist meetings and networks, tortured detainees for additional names, and used seized documents to make more arrests. By July 1933, more than 25,000 state enemies had been placed in "protective custody," a euphemistic expression suggesting that arrest was for the detainee's own safety.[52]

Ending the Republic

The Nazis also moved to dismantle the constitution. The key event was the Reichstag Fire on the night of February 27, 1933. The alleged arsonist, a slow-witted Dutch communist named Marinus van der Lubbe, was arrested on the scene. Whether van der Lubbe set the fire or whether he was a patsy was irrelevant. The same night Göring insisted that the fire signaled the start of a communist rising and documents were fabricated to prove it. Hitler promised revenge. "Every communist official," shouted Hitler, "will be shot where he is found."[53] Four thousand communists were arrested that night.

The morning after the blaze, Hitler convinced President von Hindenburg to sign an emergency decree, drafted by Frick, suspending constitutionally guaranteed civil liberties. Freedom of the press, freedom of assembly, privacy of mail and telephone communication, and freedom from arbitrary search and arrest were suspended for the duration of the emergency of an impending communist coup. The emergency, of course, never subsided, and the Nazis used the decree to amass advantage in the Reichstag election of March 5, 1933.

Hitler called the March 1933 election the moment he took power with the expectation that the Nazis could secure the votes needed to legislate the constitution out of existence. When it

---

[51]Quoted in Jeremy Noakes and Geoffrey Pridham, eds. *Nazism 1919–1945: A Documentary Reader*, vol. 2, new ed. (Exeter, 1998), p. 136.

[52]Figures in Richard Evans, *The Third Reich in Power* (New York, 2005), pp. 60–6.

[53]Quoted in Noakes and Pridham, eds., *Nazism 1919–1945*, vol. 1, p. 140.

was held, the Nazis increased their seats in the Reichstag from 196 to 288, winning 43.9 percent of the vote. Given Nazi terror against other parties, SA toughs at polling stations, and the constitutional requirement of a two-thirds vote in the Reichstag to alter the constitution, the March election was but a limited success. Over half the voters chose other parties. The SPD maintained 120 seats, the KPD 81, and the Catholic Center Party 73.

When the new Reichstag met on March 24 at the Kroll Opera House, however, the Enabling Act, which allowed the chancellor to make law without the consent of the Reichstag or the president, passed by 444 to 94 votes. The German National People's Party (DNVP), long-time conservative enemies of the constitution, voted with the Nazis, as did the Catholic Center Party on Hitler's dubious assurance that he would respect Catholic interests. Hitler's threats from the podium against anyone who voted against the act and the SA thugs who menacingly walked up and down the aisles intimidated numerous deputies into either voting for the act or not showing up at all. The eighty-one communist deputies were arrested earlier, as were a handful of SPD delegates.

The ninety-four votes against the Enabling Act all came from the brave delegation of the SPD. Party chair Otto Wels made the following statement. "No enabling law," he said, "can give you the power to destroy ideas that are eternal and indestructible." Turning toward Hitler, he warned, "You can take our lives and our freedom, but not our honor." Wels ultimately fled the country and died in Paris in 1939. Joseph Goebbels, now a cabinet official with the new title of Minister of Propaganda and Enlightenment, described the new reality. "No more voting," he wrote in his diary, "The Führer decides."[54] By mid-July, all parties save the Nazis had been outlawed.

Heinrich Himmler, the SS, and the Police

To keep opposition from rising again, the Nazis systematized a permanent police apparatus. Though Frick and Göring were the top police officials in the regime's early days, the chief authority for police matters would be Heinrich Himmler, the chief of the SS (*Schutzstaffel* ["Protection Corps"]). He was one of Nazi Germany's most sinister figures thanks to an absolute devotion to Hitler, a talent for administration and bureaucratic infighting, and fanatic antisemitism.[55]

Heinrich Himmler was born in October 1900 in Munich to a middle-class family. Barely too young to have fought in the war, Himmler nonetheless fought against the communists in Munich in 1919 in a *Freikorps* regiment. He joined the Nazi Party in 1923. After Hitler's release from prison, he worked his way up the party ladder, earning the title *Reichsführer SS* in 1929. At the time, the SS was a corps of bodyguards for Hitler and numbered 280 men. Himmler built it into an elite party force numbering 2,700 by 1930 and 50,000 by 1932.

Himmler expected that the black-uniformed SS would form an Aryan vanguard. A new aristocracy united by proper birth and mystical bonds of racial brotherhood, they would lead the struggle for German blood and spirit. SS members were recruited with greater care than the thugs that made up the SA; they were thoroughly indoctrinated about what they represented, they learned the details of the Jewish danger, and they swore loyalty to Hitler himself. There was little doubt as to their mission. "We shall take care," Himmler wrote in 1936, "that never again in Germany, the heart of Europe, will the Jewish-Bolshevistic revolution of subhumans be sparked either from within or through emissaries from without. . . . We will be a merciless sword of justice."[56]

---

[54]Elke Fröhlich, ed. *Die Tagebücher von Joseph Goebbels*, Teil I: *Sämtliche Fragmente*, vol. 2 (Munich, 1989), April 22, 1933.

[55]The most comprehensive biography is Peter Longerich, *Heinrich Himmler: A Life* (New York, 2012).

[56]Heinrich Himmler, "The SS as an Anti-Bolshevist Fighting Organization," *TMWC*, Document 1851-PS, vol. 29, pp. 13–15.

Heinrich Himmler in 1938.
Source: INTERFOTO/Alamy.

SS ascendancy in the Nazi state was assured on the "Night of the Long Knives," on June 30, 1934. The night brought the decapitation of the SA, which had grown to 4 million men, many of whom were uncontrollably violent lower-class thugs. The problem was not SA violence as such but rather the tenuous state control over SA excesses directed not only against leftists and Jews but also against passersby and even police officers. Worse, the SA leader Ernst Röhm, a cigar-chomping, beer-guzzling soldier of fortune, called for the SA to become the new German army. Fearing reaction by the army itself, Hitler struck, using the SS. Eighty-five were rousted from bed and murdered, including Röhm, his immediate SA subordinates, and even some of Hitler's old conservative enemies who were not SA members at all. The SA was finished as a political factor, and the SS, led by men more educated, disciplined, and loyal, came of age. Violence remained Nazi Germany's trademark, but the bloodletting would be more deliberate.

The rise of the SS was more ominous because Himmler also assembled an extensive police empire. In March 1933, he became police president in Munich and, with the elimination of local state governments, Himmler assumed police functions in most other German states. By outmaneuvering Göring and Frick, Himmler in June 1936 assumed the title "*Reichsführer SS* and Chief of German Police" at Hitler's order. Theoretically he answered to Frick, but in truth he answered to Hitler alone.

Himmler's power lay in his control of increasingly dangerous police organs. One was the SD (*Sicherheitsdienst* ["Security Service"]). A subsidiary organization of the SS, the SD served as a party intelligence service aimed at opposition groups as well as opponents within the Nazi party itself. It was headed by Himmler's protégé Reinhard Heydrich, a cultured yet cold-blooded former naval officer who was discharged in 1931 for womanizing and who joined the SS that year. Four years Himmler's junior, Heydrich demonstrated his ruthlessness by orchestrating the Night of the Long Knives. The other organization—also controlled by Heydrich—was the Security Police (*Sicherheitspolizei*, or *Sipo*). It contained two branches. One was the Criminal Police (*Kriminalpolizei*, or *Kripo*), and the other was Secret State Police (*Geheime Staatspolizei*, or *Gestapo*), a proactive police organ aimed at proactively rooting out political enemies.

Because Himmler headed the SS and the police, the two were intertwined. SS officers became police officers, and German police officers became members of the SS. The entire apparatus was an entity unto itself. The Gestapo, for example, followed its own laws, held suspects without trial, and used "intensified interrogations" that left subjects injured or dead. Hamburg Gestapo chief Bruno Streckenbach arranged to have dead prisoners cremated so that autopsies would not reveal evidence of torture.[57] Heydrich's legal adviser, Werner Best, popularized new police methods, omitting the gory details, through his magazine *Die deutsche Polizei* ("The German Police"). The police, Best said, acted as surgeons, proactively removing diseased organs from the body of the *Volk*.[58]

The Concentration Camps

The crown jewels of SS police methods were the concentration camps. Not to be confused with later extermination camps in Poland, concentration camps, first constructed near major German cities, initially contained political enemies, including communists, liberals, and trade unionists who spilled over from German prisons. By 1937, the camps also became holding areas for elements deemed asocial or degenerate, such as habitual criminals, the work-shy, alcoholics, homosexuals, prostitutes, and Roma.

Himmler established the infamous camp at Dachau outside Munich in March 1933. Sachsenhausen, north of Berlin, was built in 1936; Buchenwald, near Weimar, followed in 1937; Flossenburg near Bayreuth was established in 1938; Mauthausen, near Linz in Austria, came in 1938 (after Germany's annexation of Austria in March of that year); and Ravensbrück, a camp for women prisoners, was built near Berlin in the same year. Most of these camps replaced more numerous ad hoc camps developed in the wake of the Reichstag Fire. The main camps developed systems of subsidiary camps over the course of the 1930s so that they represented a unified system.

Initially, undisciplined guards inflicted random violence and even murder. Deaths were explained to state courts as prisoners shot "while trying to escape." In May 1933, a guard at Dachau named Johann Kantschuster killed thirty-year-old lawyer named Alfred Strauss, a Jew who was arrested as a political enemy. Kantschuster claimed that Strauss had made a break for it. Forensics revealed open wounds, contusions, and two close-range pistol shots to the back of Strauss's head.[59]

Aside from the embarrassment they caused, ad hoc killings ran counter to Himmler's desire for order. In June 1933, he appointed Theodor Eicke as the Commandant of Dachau, and in July 1934, Eicke became Himmler's Inspector of Concentration Camps. A Bavarian war veteran and police officer who joined the SS in 1931, Eicke believed equally in comradeship and brutality. He developed tightly knit, fastidious SS guard details, aptly known as "Death's Head Units." Camp violence continued. But it became more structured. "Punishment," ordered Eicke, "will be mercilessly dispensed whenever it appears necessary in the interests of the Fatherland."[60]

Prisoners were soon used for routinized slave labor, beginning with full days of digging ditches. By 1937, the SS had gone into actual business. Amid a wide collection of enterprises ranging from textile mills to agricultural establishments, the SS also acquired brickworks and stone quarries near Sachsenhausen, Flossenburg, and Mauthausen. The infusion of new prisoners

[57]Michael Wildt, "Der Hamburger Gestapochef Bruno Streckenbach," in *Hamburg in der NS Zeit: Ergebnisse neuerer Forschung*, eds., Frank Bajohr and Joachim Szodrzynski (Hamburg 1995).

[58]Ulrich Herbert, *Best: Biographische Studien über Radicalismus, Weltanschauung und Vernunft 1903–1989* (Bonn, 1996), pp. 163–4.

[59]*TMWC*, vol. 26, Document 641-PS, pp. 171–2.

[60]*TMWC*, vol. 26, Document 778-PS, pp. 291–6.

from various asocial categories—there were some 24,000 camp inmates by November 1938—meant an expanded slave labor force for various projects with which the SS could help build the new Reich and turn a profit.

From the start, the German press publicized concentration camps as facilities of temporary detention that created badly needed law and order while teaching what Himmler in 1939 called "hard, new values, created through work, a regulated daily routine [and] a strict but fair handling."[61] In fact, Death's Head guards' handling of camp laborers was brutal and inefficient to the point where poorly nourished, badly beaten, and overworked prisoners could never be as productive as German publications claimed.[62] The war made matters more terrible. Germany needed more slave labor, and with the expanded pool of potential political prisoners from occupied countries, some 700,000 prisoners labored under the SS whip by 1944.

*****

When the Nazis came to power in 1933, they focused on the neutralization of political enemies and the retention of power. As long as Germany remained economically and militarily weak, they were more careful in their handling of German Jews. They believed that the supposedly Jewish-controlled governments in Europe and the United States backed Jews in Germany. But over the course of the 1930s, Nazi Germany prepared for war in terms of economic development, armament, and strategic advantage. Increasingly the regime became less restrained regarding what it saw as its primary enemy.

---

[61]Quoted in Robert Gellately, *Backing Hitler: Consent and Coercion in Nazi Germany* (New York, 2001), p. 66.

[62]On SS use of slave labor, see Michael Thad Allen, *The Business of Genocide: The SS, Slave Labor, and the Concentration Camps* (Chapel Hill, NC, 2002); Paul B. Jaskot, *The Architecture of Oppression: The SS, Forced Labor, and the Nazi Monumental Building Economy* (London, 2000).

4

The Tide of Persecution, 1933–1939

When Hitler took power in 1933, Germany was economically and militarily weak. The Nazis were also convinced that they were dealing, not with a small population of German Jews but with a large, powerful Jewish conspiracy of which German Jews were but a part. Therefore, initial steps against German Jews were conditioned by what was—for the Nazis—moderation. As the state became more economically and militarily secure, it ratcheted up anti-Jewish measures. Physical annihilation was not yet state policy.

Initially the state aimed to educate Germans about the Jewish threat while removing Jews from positions of governmental and cultural influence. The hope was that Jews would emigrate from Germany while leaving their property and their savings. By 1938, measures became more brutal, initially in German-annexed Austria where Jews were stripped of their property and forced out. Eastern Europe's more antisemitic governments took their cue from Hitler and also aimed to force a mass Jewish exit. In November, the dam of antisemitic sentiment broke throughout Germany with the *Kristallnacht* pogrom, signaling that Germany was no longer bound by legality or world opinion.

4.1 PROPAGANDA: THE NAZI REPRESENTATION OF JEWS

The Nazis sought to create a unified *Volk* to confront the Jewish world danger. Many Germans shared this view by the time the Nazis came to power. But many Germans' antisemitism was more moderate; others had not thought much about Jews at all. The Nazis aimed to bring everyone to their own level of understanding. Nazi information campaigns were fabrications, but one should not minimize their conviction. The name of Joseph Goebbels's new Ministry—Propaganda and Enlightenment—makes this trend clear. And if state-sponsored "enlightenment" did not turn all Germans into fanatic antisemites, it helped most to remain indifferent to the Jews' fate.

The Press

The press was the central medium in an age when most still read newspapers. Under Goebbels's Ministry of Propaganda, democratic and leftist newspapers were closed and their writers, Jewish or not, were arrested or driven abroad. Old prestigious newspapers were taken over, and Nazi Party newspapers circulated more broadly. Goebbels never pretended objectivity, nor did his press chief Otto Dietrich, a war veteran who earned a doctorate in political science and who joined the Nazi Party in 1929 and the SS in 1932. A press adviser to Hitler, Dietrich in 1933 centralized "reporting" with daily press directives reflecting Hitler's views. National and local papers praised the aim of a united *Volk* and carried antisemitic polemics emphasizing Jewry's global conspiracy against Germany.

Nazi Germany's most pernicious newspaper was *Der Stürmer*, edited by Julius Streicher, a Bavarian war veteran who founded his own antisemitic party in 1919 and joined the Nazis in 1922. Begun in 1923, *Der Stürmer* was a weekly dedicated to the "struggle for the truth." Aside from drawings of hook-nosed, thick-lipped, money-grabbing, Talmud-reading, maiden-defiling Jews, the newspaper constantly emphasized the state of the Jewish conspiracy against Germany while tossing in medieval-style stories of present-day ritual killings of young Germans, thus amalgamating two millenia of antisemitic mythology.

Der Sturmer had a circulation of nearly 500,000 per week by 1938 but was also displayed and read at kiosks at street corners, squares, and bus stops. It received enthusiastic letters to the editor. *Reichsführer-SS* Heinrich Himmler praised it as one of Germany's most important journalistic sources.[1] At the trial of Nazi leaders at Nuremberg in 1946 (after which he was hanged), Streicher was proud that his was the most prominent of thousands of Nazi antisemitic publications. He defended his intention "to inform the public. . . . I did not intend to agitate or inflame but to enlighten."[2]

Education

Dressed up as an educational curriculum, Nazi propaganda targeted children especially. In 1933, Jewish and leftist teachers were dismissed, and teaching came under the Ministry of Education, headed after 1934 by long-time Nazi and once-fired teacher Bernhard Rust, who ordered teachers to "raise and educate the ethnically aware German."[3] The most benign teaching materials praised Hitler as a thoughtful, selfless father figure devoted to his *Volk*. The worst emphasized the Jewish danger. They included lessons on Jewish racial inferiority, Jewish physical characteristics, and Jewish responsibility for everything from the crucifixion to communism, complete with illustrated books and wall charts.

For small children, Streicher's publishing house created books like *The Poison Mushroom* (1938)—a collection of seventeen antisemitic fairy tales with illustrations that contained the following moral: "Like a single poisonous mushroom that can kill a whole family, so also a solitary Jew can destroy a whole village, a whole city, even an entire *Volk*."[4] Jewish schoolchildren, few though they were, were excluded from field trips and class ceremonies recognizing academic achievement. Although some teachers quietly took pity on Jewish children, others humiliated them before the rest of the class.

It had its effect. Irmgard Paul was nine when she read *The Poison Mushroom*. Even as an adult she remembered. "I was horrified," she recalled, "by the crimes Jewish people were being

---

[1] Himmler to Streicher, January 19, 1937, International Military Tribunal, *Trial of the Major War Criminals Before the International Military Tribunal, Nuremberg, 14 November 1945–1 October 1946* (hereafter *TMWC*), (Nuremberg 1949), vol. 31, p. 80.

[2] *TMWC*, April 29, 1946, vol. 12, pp. 317–18.

[3] Quoted in Claudia Koonz, *The Nazi Conscience* (Cambridge, MA, 2003), p. 137.

[4] Quoted in Gregory Paul Wegner, *Anti-Semitism and Schooling Under the Third Reich* (New York, 2002), p. 160.

accused of—killing babies, loan-sharking . . . and conspiring to destroy Germany and the rest of the world. The description of the Jewish people would convince any child that these were monsters." Disapproving of the book but afraid to say so openly, Irmgard's mother had her return the book to its owner.[5] Others were less charitable. Louis Lochner, the Associated Press representative in Berlin, relayed accounts of German children stoning Jewish children arriving from the countryside.[6]

Research

Most "knowledge" about Jews came from specially funded academic institutes that studied Jews and underpinned Nazi antisemitism with pseudoscience. The first Nazi "think tank" was the Institute for the History of the New Germany. Its specialized branch, the Research Department for the Jewish Question, was founded in 1936 by Walter Frank, a prolific historian and long-time Nazi who, crushed by Hitler's suicide in 1945, took his own life as well.

The institute funded research projects while sponsoring academic conferences, journals, and public lectures. Supposedly based on sound research, the work drew substantial general interest. The Research Department's first lecture series in 1937 coincided with a museum exhibit in Munich called "The Eternal Jew," itself a jaundiced look at Jewish perfidy through the ages, that drew 400,000 visitors. A lecture series in Berlin in January 1939 had listeners sitting in the aisles just weeks after the brutal *Kristallnacht* pogrom.

Frank's Institute and other state agencies encouraged scholars at once-prestigious institutions such as the Kaiser-Wilhelm-Institute and at centuries-old German universities to research the Jewish question. Such scholars, some already in their academic posts and some appointed after Jewish scholars were fired, applied their disciplines from anthropology to biology, to archaeology, to history, to theology. They published "findings" on racial differences between more noble ancient Israelites and more corrupt modern Jews, on the genetic origins of Jews' aversion to military service and physical labor, on the consequences of racial mixing for the spread of disease, on mental illness resulting from Jews, on the predisposition of Jews to crime, on the Talmud as a Jewish manual for power, and so on.

All findings confirmed the immutability of racial characteristics. Walter Dornfeld, a schoolteacher who completed a doctorate in anthropology, took skull measurements between 1932 and 1934 of more than 2,000 Berlin Jews, many of them children in his own classes, to show continuity of racial characteristics of children born to Jews from Poland. Findings like this filtered down through the Propaganda Ministry to more popular venues, including newspapers, magazines, pamphlets, and schoolbooks. They also gave legitimacy to Nazi anti-Jewish laws, whose exclusionary and ultimately murderous nature was supposedly based on science rather than paranoia.[7]

4.2 ANTI-JEWISH MEASURES, 1933–1935

Ad Hoc Violence in 1933

Most early state-sponsored action was aimed at communists because the Nazis saw them as the main obstacle to absolute power. The American Jewish Committee (AJC) characterized Hitler's first five weeks as "a cautious policy with regard to the Jews. . . ."[8] Once the Nazis neared absolute

---

[5]Irmgard A. Hunt, *On Hitler's Mountain: Overcoming the Legacy of a Nazi Childhood* (New York, 2005), pp. 157, 162.

[6]Richard Breitman, Barbara McDonald Stewart, and Severin Hochberg, eds., *Refugees and Rescue: The Diaries and Papers of James G. McDonald, 1935–1945* (Bloomington, IN, 2009), August 22, 1935.

[7]Alan E. Steinweis, *Studying the Jew: Scholarly Antisemitism in Nazi Germany* (Cambridge, MA, 2006).

[8]*American Jewish Yearbook* (hereafter *AJC Yearbook*), vol. 35, pp. 26, 27, 29.

power after the March 5, 1933, election, however, wanton violence against Jews erupted. SA thugs targeted synagogues, stores, and homes as well as Jewish doctors, lawyers, judges, teachers, and professors. There were also occasional murders. "Many Jews," reported the *Manchester Guardian*, "were beaten by the brown shirts until blood ran down their heads and faces. Many were . . . left to die in the streets, until they were picked up by friends or passersby and brought to hospitals."[9] Victor Klemperer, a Jewish professor of Romance languages in Dresden, kept a diary that provides a singular look at Nazi policies. "Everything I considered un-German," he wrote, "brutality, injustice, hypocrisy . . . all of it flourishes here."[10]

International press coverage of Nazi excesses triggered Jewish and even interdenominational protest meetings in Britain, the Netherlands, Belgium, France, Turkey, Mexico, Brazil, Argentina, and Australia. Over seventy protest meetings occurred in US cities. Leading Jewish groups, although alarmed, were divided on how to proceed. The conservative American Jewish Committee preferred written statements and quiet lobbying. Open protest, it feared, would worsen matters for German Jews. The American Jewish Congress, a Zionist organization, insisted that, "nothing . . . exempts us as Jews from the solemn obligation of standing up as a people . . . and protesting against the horror and the shame of the Hitler war against the Jewish people."[11]

For the Nazis, any foreign reaction confirmed the existence of a global Jewish conspiracy. German radio claimed the Jews abroad invented atrocity stories to disgrace Germany. Hitler called for law and order only insofar as undirected violence caused "possibly embarrassing international incidents." Göring complained, "I refuse to turn the police into a guard for Jewish stores."[12] Klemperer noted in his diary that Berlin was "constantly issuing official denials [but] openly threatens to proceed against the German Jews if the mischief making by 'World Jewry' does not stop."[13] Hitler was, in fact, furious. Beating his fists, he privately fumed, "[W]e shall show that we are not afraid of international Jewry. The Jews must be crushed. Their fellows abroad have played into our hands."[14]

The April Boycott

Because the German economy remained vulnerable, retaliation was limited. The choice was a national economic boycott on German Jews, slated for April 1, 1933. Joseph Goebbels called it a defensive measure—a warning to world Jewry. Officially it would last but a day if the world's Jews backed down. On April 1, the SA was orderly, at least by its standards, blocking Jewish professionals from their offices while jeering at Germans that entered Jewish businesses.

In some ways, the 1933 boycott failed. Many Germans shopped in Jewish stores, and not all Jewish stores were identified as such. The German economy in 1933 could not risk the collapse of Jewish businesses, the largest of which employed thousands of Germans. Hitler actually approved a loan to a major Jewish-owned department store chain so that 14,000 Germans could keep their jobs.[15] But the violent mood was not tamed. In Kiel, a young Jewish man who surrendered to the

---

[9]Quoted in Michael Wildt, "Violence Against Jews in Germany," in *Probing the Depths of Nazi Antisemitism: German Society and the Persecution of the Jews, 1933–1941*, ed. David Banker (Jerusalem, 2000), pp. 181–212.

[10]Victor Klemperer, *I Will Bear Witness: A Diary of the Nazi Years, 1933–1941* (New York, 1998), April 3, 1933.

[11]Quotes and discussions in *AJC Yearbook*, vol. 35, pp. 40, 55.

[12]*AJC Yearbook*, vol. 35, pp. 30, 32.

[13]Klemperer, *I Will Bear Witness, 1933–1941*, March 27, 1933.

[14]Richard Breitman, Barbara McDonald Stewart, and Severin Hochberg, *Advocate for the Doomed: The Diaries and Papers of James G. McDonald, 1932–1935* (Bloomington, IN, 2007), March 29, 1933.

[15]Figures in Karl Schleunes, *The Twisted Road to Auschwitz: Nazi Policy Toward German Jews, 1933–1939* (Urbana, IL, 1970), pp. 93–4.

A crowd of Germans gathered in front of a Jewish-owned department store in Berlin on the first day of the boycott. Signs exhorting Germans not to buy from Jews are posted on the storefront. *Source:* National Archives and Records Administration, courtesy of the United States Holocaust Memorial Museum.

police after shooting an SS man was shot thirty times by a mob in his holding cell.[16] And the message was sent. James G. McDonald, a US foreign policy scholar then in Berlin, saw the frightening implications. "Jewish trade," he wrote, "could be completely stifled." Worse, "[n]o hand was raised against the SA." Days afterward, leading Nazis and conservatives lectured McDonald on the international Jewish danger. "The casual expressions used [in] speaking of the Jews" he wrote, "make one cringe . . . one would not speak so of even a most degenerate people."[17]

"And we young Jews," remembered forty-three-year-old Edwin Landau, a decorated German-Jewish war veteran, "had once stood in the trenches for this people in the cold and rain and spilled our blood to defend our nation from its enemies." Landau, who had a plumbing business, was defiant at first. "I took my war decorations, put them on, went into the street, and visited Jewish shops. . . ." Yet he quickly became disgusted and turned to Zionism. The following year, he left for Palestine. He never returned to Germany.[18]

Anti-Jewish Legislation in 1933

Shortly after the April 1 boycott, the Nazis implemented laws to remove Jews, initially described as "non-Aryans," from crucial state and professional positions. The first law, enacted April 7, 1933,

[16]Wildt, "Violence Against Jews in Germany, 1933–1939," pp. 187–8.

[17]Breitman et al., eds., *Advocate for the Doomed, 1933–1935*, April 1, 1933, April 3, 1933, April 4, 1933.

[18]Monika Richarz, ed. *Jewish Life in Germany: Memoirs from Three Centuries* (Bloomington, IN, 1991), p. 311; Margarete Limberg and Hubert Rübsaat, eds., *Germans No More: Accounts of Jewish Everyday Life, 1933–1938* (New York, 2006), pp. 9, 185.

and signed by Hitler and Interior Minister Wilhelm Frick, was the Law for the Restoration of the Professional Civil Service. The title suggested routine administrative streamlining. In truth, the law aimed to fire Jews and other political enemies from government posts including ministries, courts, and universities. On the same day, the Law on Admission to the Legal Profession focused on disbarring all non-Aryan jurists, including private attorneys. An additional law of April 22 excluded non-Aryan healthcare professionals, from surgeons to dental technicians, from German health insurance groups, for which one needed a license.[19]

At the behest of German university students, the regime on April 25 enacted the Law against Crowding in Schools and Institutions of Higher Learning. The number of new non-Aryan students could not exceed 1.5 percent of the student body. In the summer and fall of 1933, the state further legislated non-Aryans out of the arts and journalism. This was primarily the work of Goebbels, who in September formed within the Propaganda Ministry various Reich Chambers of Culture, which oversaw music, theater and cinema, and the press. One now needed membership in the relevant chamber to continue working. Thousands of Jewish editors, journalists, writers, artists, and performers were expelled from German intellectual and cultural life.[20]

An April 11 supplement to the civil service law defined "non-Aryan" as anyone "descended from non-Aryan, particularly Jewish, parents or grandparents." One Jewish grandparent classified one as "non-Aryan." The definition reflected the Nazi insistence that biology, not faith, determined Jewishness. Officials immediately worried that Jews might change their names to assume new Aryan identities. Later in 1938, the state required Jews without clearly recognizable Jewish names (provided on an official list) to legally add the names "Israel" or "Sarah" and to use these names in all official correspondence. In the meantime, the initial laws spawned a new genealogical research industry to prove Aryan descent.[21]

The Hindenburg Exceptions

For the moment, the 1933 laws carried exceptions. Those affecting Jewish civil servants, lawyers, doctors, and students did not apply to Jews who held their positions before World War I, who fought at the front during the war, or whose fathers or sons were killed in the war. The exceptions came at the insistence of the venerated President von Hindenburg, whom Hitler could not ignore. Roughly 1,200 Jewish university professors who attained their posts after the war were dismissed in 1933 (with virtually no protests from their colleagues). But 336 Jewish state jurists out of 717 could keep their jobs for the moment, as could 70 percent of Jewish lawyers in all.[22] Jewish doctors' names were published so that German patients would know whom to boycott, but up to 75 percent fell under the Hindenburg exception and thousands of Germans continued to visit them, especially since smaller towns lacked many alternatives.[23]

---

[19]For the laws, see Schleunes, *The Twisted Road to Auschwitz*, pp. 92–131; Diemut Majer, *"Non-Germans" Under the Third Reich* (Baltimore, MD, 2003), pp. 79–141.

[20]Alan E. Steinweis, *Art, Ideology and Economics in Nazi Germany: The Reich Chambers of Music, Theater, and the Visual Arts* (Chapel Hill, NC, 1993), pp. 103–26.

[21]April 11 supplement quoted in Saul Friedländer, *Nazi Germany and the Jews: The Years of Persecution, 1933–1939* (New York, 1998); see also Raul Hilberg, *The Destruction of the European Jews*, 3rd ed. (New Haven, CT, 2003), vol. 1, pp. 64–72; Jeremy Noakes and Geoffrey Pridham, eds., *Nazism 1919–1945: A Documentary Reader*, vol. 2, new ed. (Exeter, 2001), pp. 332–3.

[22]Figures in Schleunes, *The Twisted Road to Auschwitz*, p. 109.

[23]Michael Kater, *Doctors Under Hitler* (Chapel Hill, NC, 1989), pp. 185–90.

Hindenburg's exceptions were not principled. In the spirit of the 1916 Jew Census, Jews had to have "fought at the front" to keep their jobs, or had to have been killed in the war for their sons to keep theirs. One Jewish surgeon who had lost his arm at a field hospital during the 1916 Battle of Verdun was declared in 1933 not to have been a frontline soldier.[24] Hitler viewed the exceptions as temporary anyway. On April 7, he met with James G. McDonald and insisted that Germany was on the right path. "I will do the thing that the rest of the world would like to do," he said. "It doesn't know how to get rid of the Jews. I will show them."[25] Hitler, McDonald wrote, was "absolutely irreconcilable" on the Jewish question. "The Chancellor insists," McDonald noted, "that no matter what the cost, the Third Reich must be built on the basis of an Aryan race unimpeded by the foreign influence of Jews in governmental, cultural, or high professional and financial posts."[26]

Municipalities and nongovernmental bodies meanwhile acted against Jews on their own initiative, knowing that their actions would receive approval in Berlin. In Munich, the mayor forbade city contracts to Jewish firms. In Breslau, city contracts with Jewish firms were cancelled. Company boards dismissed Jewish members to avoid endangering future business with government entities. The German Red Cross banned Jewish nurses. Cities banned Jews from public places such as swimming pools. Municipalities posted signs clearly announcing that "Jews Are Not Wanted Here."

And random violence still occurred. Jewish gynecologists, for instance, were arrested or beaten on occasion by local toughs who imagined that they despoiled their female Aryan patients or that they performed secret abortions of Aryan infants.[27] *Commonweal*, the American Catholic weekly, saw that "[t]he situation of the Jews in Germany is deplorable beyond words."[28] Victor Klemperer kept his academic post thanks to his frontline service, which he had to prove despite his medals. "For the moment I am still safe," he wrote, "but as someone on the gallows, who has the rope around his neck, is safe. At any moment a new 'law' can kick away the steps. . . ."[29]

The Nuremberg Laws

The stairs were kicked away two years later. Hindenburg died in August 1934. Hitler consolidated the offices of chancellor and president. The army, which some hoped would overthrow Hitler, swore personal allegiance to him instead, partly because his rearmament aims corresponded with theirs. Germany left the League of Nations over the rearmament issue in October 1933. In March 1935, Hitler announced not only that Germany was conscripting an army of 550,000 men, but that it was also building an air force, both open violations of the Treaty of Versailles. But slowing German exports and the resulting shortage in foreign currency needed to buy strategic materials threatened rearmament.

In 1935, local violence against Jews resumed after the previous year's lull. The violence was launched by the Nazi base who thought measures against Jews proceeded too slowly. In August, Hitler's conservative Minister of Economics, Hjalmar Schacht, argued that the excesses

---

[24]Breitman et al., eds., *Advocate for the Doomed, 1933–1935*, August 10, 1933.

[25]Quoted in Breitman et al., eds., *Advocate for the Doomed, 1933–1935*, p. 48.

[26]McDonald to Mildred Wertheimer, August 22, 1933, quoted in Breitman et al., eds., *Advocate for the Doomed, 1933–1935*, pp. 85–6.

[27]Kater, *Doctors Under Hitler*, pp. 192–3.

[28]Quoted in *AJC Yearbook*, vol. 35, p. 38.

[29]Klemperer, *I Will Bear Witness, 1933–1941*, April 12, 1933.

were "putting the economic basis of rearmament at risk."[30] Indeed, pressure from American Zionists in 1934 prompted major US retailers like Sears and Roebuck to stop selling German-made goods. Boycott advocates tried to coordinate international efforts, including a boycott of the upcoming Olympic Games to be held in Germany in 1936.[31]

These problems resulted in the Nuremberg Laws of September 1935. On the one hand, they legally separated Jews from Germans while eliminating the Hindenburg exceptions in order to appease the Nazi base. On the other, they ostensibly showed the world that Jews in Germany had a defined legal status that would be honored, at least for the moment. The most important was the Reich Citizenship Law, which distinguished between citizens, who enjoyed "full political rights," and subjects, who received state protection in return for "particular obligations." Only Germans could be citizens, and a supplementary decree in November defined who was a Jew more concretely than had the 1933 definition. Full Jews had four or three Jewish grandparents, or two Jewish grandparents *if* such a half-Jew was also married to a Jew or practiced Judaism. Others with two Jewish grandparents were first-degree *Mischlinge* (mixed bloods), and those with one Jewish grandparent were second-degree *Mischlinge*.

Whether *Mischlinge* should be classified as full Jews was debated. Some party officials wanted to categorize even those with one Jewish *great*-grandparent as full Jews. More practical state officials who drafted the law insisted that the narrow definition was simpler. It placed disabilities on fewer people, avoided confusion between courts about how to treat those with one or two Jewish grandparents, and sidestepped protests from family members who might defend one-half or one-quarter Jews. Jewish civil servants meanwhile, were fired within weeks. "A Jew," read the first supplementary decree to the law, "cannot be a citizen of the Reich. He has no right to vote in political affairs and he cannot hold public office."[32]

The second of the Nuremberg Laws—the Law for the Protection of German Blood and Honor—was more straightforward. Reflecting Nazi phobia of blood poisoning, it prohibited marriage or even sex between Aryans and Jews. In keeping with the stereotype of the lecherous Jew and the naïve German maiden, Jews were forbidden from hiring German females younger than forty-five as maids, nurses, secretaries, and so on. To keep them from disguising themselves to their neighbors, Jews could not display the German flag. Punishments for "racial defilement" stopped short of the death penalty but remained severe. Nearly 2,000 Jews and Aryans were convicted in the next five years, most denounced by prurient busybodies to the Gestapo. Mostly males were put on trial owing to contemporary belief in female passivity.[33]

To add popular imprimatur, the Reichstag unanimously approved the new laws in a special session convened at the Nazi Party rally in Nuremberg. Afterward, Hitler proclaimed the significance. Jews worldwide would see that Jews in Germany now had their own properly circumscribed cultural space. Yet the laws had a millennial significance too. As Hitler told the Reichstag: "You have now approved of a law, the impact of which will only become evident . . . after many centuries have passed"[34] The Third Reich, now in its third year, had only begun to rebuild the Aryan race.

---

[30]Quoted in Donald McKale, *Hitler's Shadow War: The Holocaust and World War II* (New York, 2002), p. 72.

[31]R. A. Hawkins, "Hitler's Bitterest Foe: Samuel Untermyer and the Boycott of Nazi Germany, 1933–1938," *American Jewish History*, 93, no. 1 (March 2007), pp. 21–50.

[32]Quoted in Noakes and Pridham, eds., *Nazism 1919–1945,* vol. 2, pp. 342–5.

[33]Figures in Patricia Szobar, "Telling Sexual Stories in Nazi Courts of Law: Race Defilement in Germany, 1933 to 1945," in *Sexuality and German Fascism,* ed. Dagmar Herzog (New York, 2005), pp. 131–163.

[34]Max Domarus, ed., *Hitler: Speeches and Proclamations,* vol. 2, *The Years 1935–1936* (Wauconda, IL, 1997), p. 707.

Some German Jews hoped the Nuremberg Laws would normalize their status as subjects. But the government only feigned civility during the 1936 Winter and Summer Olympics to avoid international boycott. In the Bavarian village of Garmisch-Partenkirchen, site of the winter games, the locals removed anti-Jewish signs and *Der Stürmer* kiosks and stopped harassing Jews only after repeated government efforts.[35] Hitler, convinced that international Jewry was conspiring to ruin the new Germany, resented even these small steps. The Olympics, meanwhile, presented a grand illusion that Nazi Germany was a lawful and even peaceful state.

4.3 READYING FOR WAR

Rearmament and Expansion

Meanwhile Germany prepared for war. In March 1936, German forces occupied the demilitarized Rhineland. With this step, Germany violated not only the Treaty of Versailles, which the Germans signed involuntarily in 1919. It also violated the 1925 Locarno Accords, by which the republican government willingly honored Germany's western border and the Rhineland's permanent demilitarization in return for the early removal of French occupation troops. The balance of power now shifted dramatically because any French invasion of Germany through a fortified Rhineland would be a bloody affair, which the French public desperately wished to avoid. The last war had cost too many lives.

In July 1936, Germany intervened in the Spanish Civil War on the side of Francisco Franco, an army general determined to eradicate Spanish democrats, communists, and anarchists. Primarily, the Germans provided air support. Franco did not win until May 1939, but in the meantime the war in Spain kept the western democracies off balance while ensuring that Mussolini's Italy, which committed far more resources and manpower to Franco than had Germany, was firmly aligned with Berlin.

To make Germany less dependent on imported strategic materials and more prepared for war, Hitler also created the Four-Year Plan in August 1936. He named Hermann Göring, already serving as air force commander-in-chief, as the Four-Year Plan's commissioner. At home, Göring assumed greater influence over the German economy through Four-Year Plan offices, which worked to steer industrial production. Abroad, Göring worked to gain greater control of strategic materials, for instance, the rich tungsten ore deposits in Spain, which Germany needed for armor plating and shells.

By November 1937, German rearmament had proceeded to the point where Hitler assembled his armed service chiefs and told them that the consolidation of territory in central Europe would begin forthwith. Austria and its German-speaking population would be annexed. Czechoslovakia, which pressed into Germany's midsection, would be destroyed. Hitler expected that Great Britain and France would stand clear. Afterward Germany had to conquer its broader continental living space by 1945 lest it lose its lead in weapons and technology. Hitler's obsession with his own death, particularly after a throat cancer scare in 1938, only made him more determined to conquer sooner rather than later. He was sure that any successor would lack the nerve.

Germany annexed Austria in March 1938, establishing the so-called *Anschluss* between the two states. In September, Hitler tried to start a war with Czechoslovakia using as his pretext the alleged Czech mistreatment of the 3 million ethnic Germans in the Sudetenland, the

---

[35]David Clay Large, *Nazi Games: The Olympics of 1936* (New York, 2006), pp. 117–18.

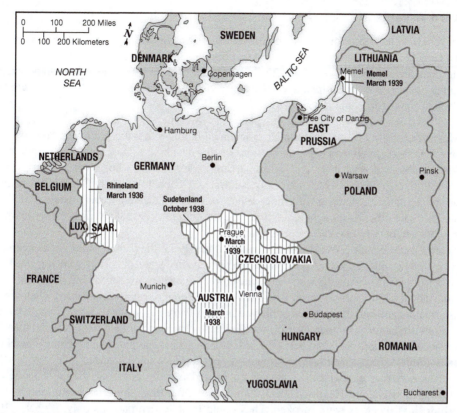

MAP 4.1   German Aggression, 1936–1939   *Source:* Map courtesy of the Department of History, United States Military Academy.

mountainous ring of territory that once belonged to the Austro-Hungarian Empire. Following an international crisis that nearly led to a general war, Germany annexed the Sudetenland amidst sighs of relief in European capitals. Yet war could not be postponed indefinitely. Despite Hitler's promises to preserve the integrity of the remaining Czechoslovak state, German forces occupied Prague in March 1939. Berlin created a "Protectorate of Bohemia and Moravia" within the greater German Reich while leaving a nominally independent Slovakia under German influence.

By the summer of 1939, Hitler was ready to go to war with Poland. He hoped that Britain and France would again stand aside so that Germany could attack them later. On August 23, 1939, nine days before the attack on Poland, Germany concluded a nonaggression pact with the Soviet Union, the blood enemy of Nazism, to give London and Paris pause. Unlike in World War I, there would be no Russian Empire to aid Britain and France. Soviet leader Joseph Stalin was content to let the capitalist powers destroy one another, and Hitler promised him eastern Poland in return. But if the western democracies went to war anyway, Germany would fight them too. And the pact with Moscow would be honored only as long as Hitler found it convenient.[36]

---

[36]On German foreign policy leading to war, see Gerhard L. Weinberg, *Hitler's Foreign Policy, 1933–1939: The Road to World War II* (New York, 2005).

Toward Aryanization

The feverish preparations for war meant that the Nazi government augmented its obsession with Jewry. Convinced that Germany lost the last war because Jews manipulated enemy governments, certain that Jews in Germany stabbed the army in the back in 1918 and would do so again if given the chance, and determined to confiscate Jewish assets in Germany, the Nazis were fully resolved to run the Jews out of Germany.

Official language was clear on this point. In November 1935, just after the enactment of the Nuremberg Laws, Heinrich Himmler proclaimed publicly that the Jews were "composed of the waste products of all the people and nations on this planet. . . ." They were "the people whose goal is the domination of the world, whose breath is destruction, whose will is extermination, whose religion is atheism, whose idea is Bolshevism." Goebbels concurred. "This Jewish pestilence," he wrote in his diary in November 1936, "must be eradicated. Totally. None of it should remain."[37] State officials thought emigration was the solution. To make German Jews leave, the state tightened the screws on Jewish livelihoods.

Jewish physicians provide a case in point. After 1935, they found it harder to keep their practices. They could not keep Aryan nurses under forty-five years old. They were removed from private insurance lists. Patients who were state employees were threatened with dismissal if they did not find Aryan doctors. Patients who were not state employees were harassed when visiting Jewish doctors and had their names published in Nazi Party newspapers. Young female patients sent to Jewish doctors as undercover plants filed false charges that the doctor seduced them and performed secret abortions. Otto Schwabe, a doctor so accused as part of a neighbor's blackmail scheme, jumped from a fourth-floor window during a police interrogation.[38] In regions where physicians were scarce, Jewish doctors were not treated as badly, but the writing was on the wall. In April 1937, Reinhard Heydrich's SD started a list of Jewish physicians, and in July 1938, Jewish doctors' licenses were revoked. They could treat Jewish patients only. By early 1939, only 285 Jewish doctors practiced in Germany.[39]

Jewish businesses were more important than professional practices because they contained assets and productive capacity that could be steered toward rearmament. Small Jewish businessmen in Germany saw their stores, workshops, and property Aryanized—purchased by German buyers at prices far below value. Until November 1938, this process was voluntary only insofar as no law made it mandatory. But small Jewish retailers were increasingly pressured by local boycotts, harassment of potential customers, and refusal by suppliers to sell to Jews.

German banks especially benefited from Aryanization. They searched for Jewish businesses that might be for sale, matched them with German buyers, took a commission for the service, and extended loans to buyers. Berlin in 1933 had about 6,000 small Jewish businesses. By April 1938, the number was cut in half. Some small Jewish merchants returned to the degrading medieval business of peddling.[40]

Larger Jewish businesses held out because of their financial strength, their ability to sell shares abroad, and the paucity of buyers for larger enterprises. But the tide was against them. As chief of the Four-Year Plan, Göring defined Jewish firms as those with even a single Jew in a governing position. He limited the amount of raw materials and foreign exchange such firms

---

[37]Quoted in Friedländer, *Years of Persecution,* pp. 182–4.

[38]Richarz, ed. *Jewish Life in Germany,* p. 331.

[39]Figures in Kater, *Doctors Under Hitler,* pp. 194–220.

[40]Hilberg, *Destruction,* vol. 1, pp. 98–100; Friedländer, *Years of Persecution,* pp. 234, 317.

could have, and he forbade the awarding of public contracts to Jewish firms. In April 1938, after the *Anschluss* with Austria, he ordered all Jewish property in Germany registered and appraised.

4.4 THE NAZI EFFECT IN EASTERN EUROPE

Germany was Europe's fulcrum. It sat on the League Council until 1933, its rearmament changed Europe's strategic balance, and it had Europe's most powerful economy thanks to armament and construction. The Nazis' stance toward the Jewish question triggered revulsion in democratic states, but it brought no serious repercussions. Meanwhile in eastern Europe, antisemitic statesmen understood that they could intensify their own anti-Jewish policies. They tried to do so through legal, organized expulsion that they hoped would outflank more rabid antisemites who threatened not only Jews, but also state authority. The Jewish question thus became more internationalized as more states raced to expel their Jewish populations. The confluence triggered terrible violence on the eve of World War II.

Poland and Jewish Expulsion

"The Nazi movement," noted an admiring *Endecja* student newspaper in 1934, "fascinates by its . . . ruthless fight against Jews."[41] Marshal Józef Piłsudski's dictatorship acted as a brake on antisemitic violence, but his sudden death in 1935 opened the floodgates, starting in universities against Jewish students who refused to sit on designated "ghetto benches" in lecture halls. "Wherever you see a Jew," read one 1937 *Endecja* pamphlet, "knock out his teeth. Don't waver even if it is a woman. The only thing to be regretted is that you did not hit hard enough."[42] Jewish students were often beaten unconscious. Two at the University of Lvov were stabbed to death.[43]

Endecja gangs and Polish merchant groups also launched anti-Jewish boycotts, smashing Jewish market stalls and using everything from pickets to crowbars to intimidate Polish consumers. By 1937, local authorities even outlawed kosher butchering, which affected thousands of families in the meat industry. Full-scale pogroms also erupted, often in response to Jewish defiance. In May 1937, in Brezść, a thirty-hour-long pogrom broke out after a Jewish butcher stabbed a police officer who confiscated his stock. The pogrom killed or wounded 200 Jews and caused, said the American Jewish Committee, "almost complete destruction of the business and domestic property of close to 25,000 Jews of the town."[44] In 1937 alone, 400 violent attacks against Jews were reported from seventy-nine different locales. From 1935 to 1939, perhaps 350 Jews in Poland were killed.[45]

Piłsudski's successors provided little comfort. By 1937, Poland's government was dominated by a promilitary group of conservative parties called the Camp of National Unity. The camp condemned wanton violence against Jews: Violence threatened order and made Poland look bad internationally. But the Camp agreed that Jews were a foreign element that hindered Polish development. Its 1938 official statement on the Jewish question called for "large scale reduction in the number of Jews in Poland." In January 1937, Foreign Minister Józef Beck

---

[41]Quoted Pawel Korzek, "Antisemitism in Poland as an Intellectual, Social and Political Movement," in *Studies on Polish Jewry, 1919–1939*, ed. Joshua A. Fishman (New York, 1974), p 82.

[42]Quoted in Sander L. Gilman, *Jurek Becker: A Life in Five Worlds* (Chicago, 2003), p. 9.

[43]Incidents in Emanuel Melzer, *No Way Out: The Politics of Polish Jewry 1935–1939* (Cincinnati, OH, 1997), pp. 71–80.

[44]*AJC Yearbook*, vol. 39, p. 231.

[45]Figures in Leonard Rowe, "Jewish Self-Defense: A Response to Violence," *Fishman, ed., Studies on Polish Jewry*, p. 118; William H. Hagen, "Before the 'Final Solution': Toward a Comparative Analysis of Political Anti-Semitism in Interwar Germany and Poland," *Journal of Modern History*, 68, no. 2 (June 1996), p. 371.

announced to the *Sejm* that Poland had room for 500,000 Jews. The other 3 million had to go. He later spoke of 80,000 to 100,000 leaving per year for the next thirty years.[46]

The Catholic Church in Poland thought that the Camp of National Unity was too timid. In 1936, Poland's chief cleric, Cardinal August Hlond, issued a statement titled "The Catholic Moral Principles," which denounced hatred and violence but justified boycotts because Jews were enemies of the Catholic Church; the vanguard of Bolshevism; and the purveyors of immorality, from atheism to pornography. Churches served as meeting places for *Endecja* groups, church periodicals criticized the Camp for not forcing emigration quickly enough, and local priests supported anti-Jewish boycotts.

With obvious destinations such as Palestine and the United States restricted, the government became interested in Madagascar, a French possession since 1896. Antisemites since the late nineteenth century saw Madagascar, an island plagued by malaria, as a solution to the Jewish question. In 1937, Beck tried to lease 450,000 hectares of land there, hoping in five years to resettle 500,000 Jews. Polish newspapers enthusiastically backed the idea. But the French government balked. Colonial Minister George Mandel, himself Jewish, noted in 1938 that "[w]e would appear to be adopting the point of view of foreign governments that consider the Jews not as citizens but as outsiders. . . . We would thus risk encouraging the very persecutions and harsh measures that have helped provoke the exodus of Jewish populations."[47]

Meanwhile the Great Depression combined with anti-Jewish actions drove more of Poland's Jews into misery. Even in 1934, it was reported that one-quarter of Warsaw's Jews were malnourished. By 1939, nearly one-fifth of Poland's Jews lived completely on charitable aid and nearly two-fifths lived partly on charity. Seven of ten Jewish families in Łódź lived in a single room. Child mortality rose, as did diseases like tuberculosis. Neville Laski, a British Jewish leader touring Poland in 1934, said of Warsaw's Jewish quarter: "I have never seen such poverty, squalor, and filth. It made me despair of civilization."[48] Jewish writer Sholem Asch relayed that "[e]very second person was undernourished, skeletons of skin and bones, crippled, candidates for the grave."[49] "The Jewish situation became worse than ever," remembered Chaya Finkielsztajn, who lived in the small town of Radziłów in eastern Poland. "A large part of the Jewish population collapsed under the heavy burden. . . . Anyone who had the smallest possibility to do so left."[50] The government's answer was to get them to leave more quickly.

Romania, Jewish Citizenship, and Expulsion

In 1935, a delegation of British Jews visited Romania to investigate recent Romanian violence against their Jewish brethren. They met with Miron Cristea, the patriarch of the Romanian Orthodox Church. The patriarch argued that Jews in Romania "appropriate all the riches of the country. . . . They cultivate and encourage all social plagues. Where is it written that we have no right to defend ourselves against this danger as against any other parasite?" The Jews, argued Romania's most senior church official, should leave for another part of the world.[51]

---

[46]The Camp's official "theses" on the Jewish question is quoted in Melzer, *No Way Out*, pp. 29–30. On economic discrimination, see pp. 39–52.

[47]Quoted in Michael R. Marrus and Robert O. Paxton, *Vichy France and the Jews*, (New York, 1981), p. 62.

[48]Quoted in Hagen, "Before the Final Solution," p. 354.

[49]Yehuda Bauer, *My Brother's Keeper: A History of the American Jewish Joint Distribution Committee*, 1929–1939 (Philadelphia, PA, 1974), p. 189.

[50]Yad Vashem Recorded Testimony of Chaya and Yisroel Finkielsztajn, http://radzilow.com/yadchaya.htm.

[51]Jean Ancel, ed., *Wilhelm Filderman: Memoirs and Diaries*, vol. 1: *1900–1940* (Jerusalem, 2004), p. 488.

For King Carol II, a monarch of authoritarian temperament and marginal ability, such "respectable" antisemites were preferable to the overtly fascist and violent Legion of the Archangel Michael under Corneliu Codreanu and its paramilitary Iron Guard. After Hitler's rise to power, Iron Guard violence affected the government as well as Jews. Codreanu openly endorsed Hitler despite Romania's security arrangements with France, which existed to protect Romania's territorial gains from World War I. In December 1933, the government banned the Iron Guard and killed several of its leaders. The Iron Guard assassinated Prime Minister Ion Duca the same month. Regardless, votes for the Legion in parliamentary elections increased. In April 1938, government police arrested Codreanu, later murdering him and thirteen other Iron Guard leaders in prison.

The king chose governing cabinets based on their loyalty to the crown and their pursuit of lawful rather than lawless antisemitism. Legislative anti-Jewish measures resulted. In 1934, the government passed the Law for the Use of Romanian Personnel in Enterprises, whereby at least 80 percent of the personnel in any enterprise had to be ethnic Romanian in origin. Jews were henceforth limited in all enterprises ranging from the post office to factories to universities. Businesses were fined for having too many Jews on their payrolls. Jews were dismissed from the bar association and from medical school and other faculties. Tens of thousands of Jews fell into unemployment, although qualified non-Jewish replacements could not easily be found.[52]

From December 1937 to February 1938, a brief six-week government under long-time antisemitic charlatans Octavian Goga and Alexandru Cuza brought the harshest prewar measures. "Goga and I," Cuza announced, "have taken an oath, in church before God, to return Romania to the Romanians."[53] The government fired Jewish employees, closed Jewish newspapers, and revoked Jewish liquor licenses. Most notably, Decree No. 169 called for a review of Jewish naturalizations. By September 1939, 225,000 Jews lost their citizenship and in many cases their livelihood because they could not produce the necessary documents or because of minor inconsistencies.[54]

Goga and Cuza also pressed for "a radical and early solution to the Jewish question in Romania by means of internationally assisted migration."[55] Goga hoped at one point that an international flotilla of warships might move 500,000 Jews. The government encouraged illegal Jewish immigration to Palestine and latched onto Poland's scheme to resettle Jews in Madagascar. Cuza told the Nazi newspaper *Völkischer Beobachter* that Madagascar must solve the Jewish problem. The western powers, he said, must "either develop new areas for Jewish immigration or . . . take into account a forceful solution."[56]

Goga and Cuza were not in power for long. Increased agitation by the Iron Guard prompted the king to dissolve all political parties and establish a royal dictatorship. But previous antisemitic measures remained, and the king and future ministers continued to call for Jewish emigration. The first prime minister under the royal dictatorship was in fact the aforementioned patriarch, Miron Cristea. King Carol, meanwhile, told British representatives in Bucharest that he envisioned the departure of 200,000 Jews from Romania.

---

[52]Summary in Ancel, ed., *Wilhelm Filderman*, vol. 1, pp. 463–87.

[53]Quoted in Ancel, ed., *Wilhelm Filderman*, vol. 1, p. 492.

[54]Note on the Jewish Situation in Romania, June 16, 1938, Jean Ancel, ed., *Documents Concerning the Fate of Romanian Jewry During the Holocaust* (Jerusalem, 1984), vol. 1, p. 230. International Commission on the Holocaust in Romania, *Final Report of the International Commission on the Holocaust in Romania* (Bucharest, 2004), p. 41.

[55]Michael R. Marrus, *The Unwanted: European Refugees from the First World War Through the Cold War* (Philadelphia, PA, 2002), p. 143.

[56]Quoted in Magnus Brechtken, *Madagascar für die Juden: Antisemetische Idee und politische Praxis* (Munich, 1997), pp. 141–2.

Austria's Jews, Austrian Nazis, and Adolf Eichmann

In Austria, pan-Germans yearned to join the German Reich even before World War I in order to create an ethnically based greater German state. These sentiments heightened after 1933, particularly as the depression worsened in Austria. Hitler created jobs, order, and national vigor in Germany, and he was Austrian by birth. Among antisemites in Vienna, where most Jews in Austria lived, Hitler's Jewish policies were his strongest point. The Nazi Party in Austria grew despite being banned in 1934.

The *Anschluss* with Austria in March 1938 brought 206,000 more Jews into the Reich. During the crisis that resulted in the annexation, Austrian Jews optimistically hoped that an independent Austria would survive. They were thus caught unprepared. Anti-Jewish rioting, looting, and humiliations erupted in Vienna on March 11, 1938, the night before German troops entered the country. With the occupation, Jewish women were forced to scrub sidewalks in their finest clothes and Jewish children were forced to write antisemitic slogans on their fathers' shop windows. Eastern European Jews from Galicia were pulled around by their beards and forced to eat grass in Vienna's parks.

The legislative isolation of Jews that took five years in Germany hit Austria's Jews overnight because German laws applied to Austria almost immediately with the *Anschluss*. Jewish civil servants were fired, Jewish lawyers and doctors lost their gentile clients, Jewish artists were prohibited from performing, Jewish students were limited to tiny quotas, and Jews were prohibited from public places such as parks and sporting events. Ordinary Austrians boycotted Jewish businesses and excluded Jews from gentile businesses such as cinemas, restaurants, and coffeehouses. In a surreal decision, some wealthier Viennese Jews took hotel rooms in Berlin because Jews were safer there.[57]

Jewish property, from furs to jewelry, to furniture, to automobiles, to cash, was simply plundered by Austrian citizens and German troops alike. "Austrian Nazis," said one refugee, "immediately started a mad scramble to obtain . . . possession and/or control of businesses belonging to Jews. . . ."[58] Jewish apartments were Aryanized to solve Vienna's chronic housing shortage. By July 1938, more than 1,900 leading Jews were sent to Dachau in order to convince them to sell. It was all too much for many. In March 1938, 213 Austrian Jews committed suicide, and over 140 more took their own lives each month from April through July. The SS magazine *Das schwarze Korps* jealously noted that the Jewish problem in Austria was being solved far more speedily than in Germany.[59] Berlin's aim was to force Austria's Jews to leave. Vienna, Göring said in March 1938, was to be a German city again—free of Jews by 1942.[60]

It was in Vienna where the infamous SS officer Adolf Eichmann first attained importance. Eichmann was born in Germany in 1906 and raised in Austria in a middle-class household. He joined the Nazi Party and the SS in 1932, working his way through small jobs until finding a place in the Jewish department of Heydrich's SD, where he was assigned the task of studying Zionism. Eichmann read Zionist texts, spoke with Zionist agents, and in 1937 even tried to visit Palestine. He failed to get in and gathered information from Egypt instead. He became convinced

---

[57]Bruce Pauley, *From Prejudice to Persecution: A History of Austrian Antisemitism* (Chapel Hill, NC, 1992), p. 280.

[58]Survey of Foreign Experts, #N81, March 27, 1943, National Archives and Records Administration, College Park, Maryland, Record Group 226, Entry 25, Box 2, Folder #291–300.

[59]Figures in Jonny Moser, "Österreich," in *Dimension des Völkermords: Die Zahl der jüdischen Opfer des Nationalsozialismus*, ed. Wolfgang Benz (Munich, 1991), p. 88; Pauley, *Austrian Antisemitism*, pp. 283–5, 289–91.

[60]Moser, "Österreich," p. 68.

that Jews were a nation united by money, that they were an existential threat, that they would leave Germany once their economic position was destroyed, and that they should go to undeveloped areas of the world where they would not be dangerous.

Eichmann's importance grew with the *Anschluss*. He arrived in Vienna in March 1938 and soon created the Central Agency for Jewish Emigration—in a palace seized from the Rothschild family—to streamline Jewish expulsion. The process was brutal. Eichmann used the assets of wealthy Vienna Jews and relief contributions from Jewish organizations abroad to fund emigration more generally, including that of poor Galician Jews, for whom the Nazis held special contempt. Currency exchange rates between Austrian schillings and German marks were rigged, as were tax assessments, so that most Jewish funds went into state coffers. Regardless, Austria's Jews left as quickly as they could. By May 1939, more than half had fled the country. By September 1939, two-thirds had left. Of the 206,000 Jews who lived in Austria in March 1938, 77,000 remained.[61]

Ludwig Klausner was the principal stockholder of the Delka, a shoe manufacturer that he founded in 1907 with ten retail stores in Vienna. In April, the Gestapo arrested him and sent him to Dachau, where he was repeatedly beaten. In September, he was sent back to Vienna to sell his property. "The firm," Klausner later told US intelligence officials, "was appraised at one million marks by the Nazis." Klausner, who owned two-thirds of the shares, received but 96,000 marks. He was then forced to pay state transfer taxes based on the full value of his shares and the full value of his real estate holdings in Vienna. The Nazi attorney who arranged the sale of Klausner's property received Klausner's house in Vienna as his fee. Klausner reported to the Americans that he "succeeded in getting 10,000 marks . . . part of which was used to help some of his relatives."[62] He went to Switzerland in 1938 and to the United States in 1940. His wife Ella, for whom the Delka was named, killed herself in a concentration camp.

4.5 *KRISTALLNACHT*

Germany and Its Eastern European Jews

By 1938, about 130,000 Jews—25 percent of German Jews as defined by the Reich Citizenship Law—had left Germany.[63] Many Jews remaining in Germany in 1938 were *Ostjuden*—east European Jews, many of whom had sought refuge in Germany during and after World War I and who now worked in small trades such as tailoring. The Nazis compared them to locusts and vermin. It was a measure of conditions for Jews elsewhere that even in mid-1933, some 88,000 *Ostjuden* remained in Germany (over 56,000 from Poland) and by 1938, 40 percent of all *Ostjuden* in Germany had been born there.[64]

The fear that Polish and Romanian Jews living in Austria in 1938 might flee back to their countries of origin after the *Anschluss* prompted preventive action. The Polish government, on March 31, 1938, enacted a law revoking the citizenship of anyone who had spent five years out of the country. Their Polish papers would be voided on October 31 if not renewed in person.

[61]Jonny Moser, *Demographie der jüdischen Bevölkerung Österreichs 1938–1945* (Vienna, 1999), pp. 29, 37.

[62]Survey of Foreign Experts, #N1186, March 20, 1943, National Archives and Records Administration, College Park, Maryland, RG 226, Entry 25, Box 2, Folder #291–300.

[63]Herbert A. Strauss, "Jewish Emigration from Germany: Nazi Policies and Jewish Response (I)," *Leo Baeck Institute Year Book*, vol. XXV (1980), pp. 313–62.

[64]Figures in Trude Maurer, *Ostjuden in Deutschland, 1918–1933* (Hamburg, 1986); Jerzy Tomaszewski, *Auftakt zur Vernichtung. Die Vertreibung polnischer Juden aus Deutschland im Jahre 1938* (Munich, 2002).

Herschel Grynszpan on His
Arrest by French Police,
November 1938   *Source:* United
States Holocaust Memorial Museum.

In April and June 1938, Romania's government simply voided the citizenship of those living abroad. Thus, as Germany geared for war, it ran the risk that it would be stuck with tens of thousands of *Ostjuden*.

Days before the Polish deadline, police across Germany arrested over 18,000 Polish Jews. From Leipzig, the US consulate reported that police "combed schools, homes, shops, and even an old ladies home for Polish Jews."[65] Once arrested, they were given minutes to pack, then loaded onto railcars, taken to the Polish border, and dumped there. It was Germany's first forced deportation. Eight thousand Jews were pushed off the trains at the border town of Zbąszyń. Polish authorities tried forcing them back, and the refugees, including elderly and children, stood for days in inclement weather on the train platform or in crowded waiting areas with no food or water. Many collapsed. Some went mad. Five committed suicide.

Under German pressure, Poland eventually accepted the deported Jews, but state authorities provided nothing. Jewish organizations in Poland brought food, bedding, and medicine. Emanuel Ringelblum, a left-wing Zionist who later became the archivist of the Warsaw ghetto, came to Zbąszyń to help. He stayed for five weeks. "I have neither the strength nor the patience," he wrote to a friend, "to describe everything we went through in Zbąszyń. . . . I do not think any Jewish community has ever experienced so cruel and merciless an expulsion as this one."[66]

A Murder in Paris

Among those expelled penniless from Germany to Poland was the family of Herschel Grynszpan, a seventeen-year-old living a subsistence life with an uncle in Paris. Feeling he must take some action, Grynszpan went to the German embassy in Paris on November 7. There he shot a minor

---

[65]Quoted in Sybil Milton, "The Expulsion of Polish Jews from Germany October 1938 to July 1939: A Documentation," *Leo Baeck Institute Yearbook*, 24 (1984): pp. 181, 186.

[66]Quoted in Milton, "The Expulsion of Polish Jews," p. 190.

official, Ernst vom Rath, who died on November 9 at 5:30 p.m. "It is not, after all, a crime to be Jewish," Grynszpan said when French police arrested him. "I am not a dog. . . . My people have a right to exist on this earth."[67]

The murder was the pretext for the *Kristallnacht* pogrom—the Night of Broken Glass—across the German Reich. Senior Nazis were sure that Grynszpan was part of a larger Jewish conspiracy. But the death of a minor diplomat was not decisive in itself. In 1936, David Frankfurter, a Jewish medical student, killed the head of the Swiss Nazi Party, Wilhelm Gustloff. The government did nothing because that murder occurred on the eve of the Olympics. But now on the eve of war, it was time to bring the hammer to Germany's Jews. Grynszpan provided the reason.

Unlike pogroms in eastern Europe, *Kristallnacht* was no spontaneous riot started by hooligans, nor did it spread like a half-aimless fire. When vom Rath died on the evening of November 9, Hitler and the party leaders were in Munich commemorating the Beer Hall Putsch. Violence had already begun in isolated areas. The question now was whether to turn it into a national pogrom. Goebbels thought the time fortuitous. Hitler agreed and, on his approval, Goebbels passed orders to the Nazi Party district leaders, who passed them on to SA detachments throughout the country. *Kristallnacht* was not planned so much as loosely coordinated. "For once," Goebbels said in his diary, "the Jews should get the feel of popular anger. . . ."[68]

Kristallnacht

Historian Saul Friedländer describes *Kristallnacht* as "an explosion of sadism [that] burst through on all levels [from] the highest leadership [to] the lowliest party members." "The only immediate aim," he says, "was to hurt the Jews as badly as the circumstances allowed . . . to hurt them and humiliate them."[69] On the night of November 9, SA detachments in Berlin, Munich, Hamburg, Breslau, Vienna, and smaller locales throughout Germany attacked synagogues, businesses, dwellings, old-age facilities, and even orphanages. Over 1,000 synagogues were plundered and torched. German firefighters manned the roofs of neighboring buildings to protect them from spreading flames. Seventy-five hundred Jewish businesses were destroyed, beginning with the smashing of their glass windows. Jewish homes were ransacked. Everything, from furniture to pianos, to picture frames, was smashed into splinters.

After midnight on the night of November 9 and 10, Security Police Chief Reinhard Heydrich ordered police supervision and prohibited looting and killing. Police were to arrest healthier well-to-do Jews and take them to concentration camps.[70] Ideally their release was to be granted on their promise to emigrate, and their wealth was to finance more emigration, as in Austria. But the SA could not be controlled entirely. Ninety-one murders occurred. Victims included an eighty-one-year-old Jewish woman who an SA leader shot once in the chest and twice through the head when she refused to leave her home, as well as a seventy-eight-year-old physician and his wife, who were shot multiple times.[71]

Other Jews were subjected to severe beating and humiliation. One SA detachment rousted elderly Jews from their nursing home in the middle of the night and made them do calisthenics

---

[67]Quoted in Alan E. Steinweis, *Kristallnacht 1938* (Cambridge, MA, 2009), p. 17.

[68]Quoted in Friedländer, *Years of Persecution*, p. 272. The sequence of decisions appears in Steinweis, *Kristallnacht*, pp. 22–54.

[69]Friedländer, *Years of Persecution*, p. 277.

[70]Heydrich to State Police HQ and Branch Offices, November 10, 1938, 0120 Hrs; *TMWC*, vol. 31, Document 3051-PS, pp. 516–18.

[71]Friedländer, *Years of Persecution*, p. 269; Steinweis, *Kristallnacht*, p. 66.

in front of a burning synagogue. Another detachment forced children from an orphanage as they demolished it.[72] About 31,000 Jews were arrested and sent to Dachau, Sachsenhausen, and Buchenwald, which quickly became overcrowded. Many were old men. Others were schoolchildren. Hundreds of Jews died from mistreatment by guards or committed suicide.[73]

Goebbels was delighted. As the night of November 9 and 10 progressed, he noted that "[f]rom all over the Reich, information is now flowing in: 50, then 70 synagogues are burning. . . . Bravo! Bravo! The synagogues burn like big old cabins." His entry on November 11 noted that, in Berlin, "all proceeded fantastically. One fire after another. . . . In the whole country synagogues have burned down. I report to the Führer. . . . He agrees with everything. His views are totally radical and aggressive."[74] The point made, Goebbels ordered a halt to the pogrom on the afternoon of November 10. But it was not so easy. The violence dragged on through the next day.

How ordinary Germans saw these events varied. Many joined in. On a ship bound for Havana in 1939, Else Gerstel met a distinguished Jewish family whose home in a smaller German town was ransacked. "Each piece in the apartment was smashed, each glass, cup, plate, piece of furniture. . . . We asked, 'Who were the destroyers? In such a small town people know each other.' 'Yes, they were all acquaintances, teachers, assistant principals and superintendents of schools, finance officials, shopkeepers, many people in uniform.'"[75]

Postwar Jewish philosopher Emil Fackenheim, who was twenty-two in 1938, remembered that on Berlin's fashionable Kurfürstendamm, "well-dressed men and women . . . stepped over all that broken glass into Jewish stores . . . to help themselves to coats, shoes, gloves, and whatever else struck their fancy."[76] Teenagers, encouraged by their teachers, joined in vandalism and beatings. Smartly dressed women cheered during rampages. Others watched in embarrassed silence, perhaps afraid to speak. Others still voiced condemnation to friends and neighbors. A very few protected Jews. Meanwhile the state punished no German for murder or assault after the pogrom. And the churches said next to nothing.[77]

To combat whatever uneasiness there was, the Ministry of Propaganda undertook a press, lecture, and museum campaign described by Goebbels as an "antisemitic crusade." It included the long history of Jewish viciousness and subversion, including ritual murders, manipulative seventeenth-century court Jews, modern Jewish physician poisoners, and contemporary communists. Vom Rath's murder was the latest in a long line of crimes. Germany, Goebbels argued, had no choice but to fight back. Other countries, he continued, felt the same way about Jews. Otherwise they would accept more Jewish immigrants.[78]

Global Reactions

Whether ready to accept more immigrants or not, international opinion was appalled. Germany, unlike Poland and Romania, was a highly developed, seemingly advanced country. And *Kristallnacht*

---

[72]Incidents in Steinweis, *Kristallnacht 1938*, p. 74.

[73]Details in Steinweis, *Kristallnacht*, pp. 107–113.

[74]Quoted Friedländer, *Years of Persecution*, pp. 272–3.

[75]Andreas Lixl-Purcell, *Women in Exile: German-Jewish Autobiographies Since 1933* (Westport, CT, 1988), p. 194.

[76]Emil Fackenheim, *An Epitaph for German Judaism: From Halle to Jerusalem* (Madison, WI, 2007), p. 62.

[77]Steinweis *Kristallnacht*, pp. 82–91, 115–27; Martin Gilbert, *Kristallnacht: Prelude to Destruction* (New York, 2007), pp. 33, 46–7, 52; Gellately, *Backing Hitler*, p. 130.

[78]Herbert Obenhaus, "The Germans: 'An Antisemitic People': The Press Campaign After 9 November 1938," in Bankier, ed, *Probing the Depths of German Antisemitism*, pp. 147–80.

was no expression of frustration. It occurred amid full employment and German foreign policy victories in Austria and Czechoslovakia. The illusion from the Berlin Olympics that Nazi Germany was a respectable state ended. "I have seen several anti-Jewish outbreaks in Germany," wrote Hugh Carleton Greene for *The Daily Telegraph*, "but never anything as nauseating as this."[79] Amid near-unanimous US condemnation, President Franklin Roosevelt summoned Ambassador Hugh Wilson back to Washington. Not until 1955 was there another US ambassador in Germany.

Berlin assuaged world opinion only to the point that its own aims were served. In the weeks after the pogrom, Heydrich ordered concentration camps to release Jews who intended to surrender their property, Jews with emigration papers or steamship tickets, Jews over fifty and under eighteen, and Jewish frontline soldiers from World War I. All were ordered to reveal nothing of their camp experiences.[80] And there was no mistaking that the government wanted Jews out of the country after they left their assets behind. Goebbels noted that "[t]he Führer wants to take very sharp measures against the Jews. They must themselves put their businesses back in order again. The insurance companies will not pay them a thing. Then the Führer wants a gradual expropriation of Jewish businesses."[81]

Kristallnacht's Aftermath

In fact, expropriation was not gradual. On November 12, with synagogues still smoldering and the streets littered with glass, Göring, in his capacity of Four-Year Plan chief, hosted a meeting of top government officials. "Gentlemen," he said, "today's meeting is of decisive importance. I have received a letter . . . written on the Führer's orders according to which the Jewish question now be solved decisively one way or another." The long meeting that followed concerned the liquidation of Jewish assets prior to mass emigration.[82]

Göring decried the previous days' destruction, not for its violence but because Jewish property destroyed was Jewish property lost. Aryan property was also destroyed. Aryan landlords who rented space to Jewish businesses suffered damages. German owners of former Jewish business who had not yet changed the business names also suffered losses, as did German suppliers, whose goods were destroyed in Jewish stores. "I would rather," Göring remarked, "that you had killed 200 Jews and had not destroyed such amounts." Ordinary Germans, meanwhile, had looted Jewish jewelry stores, furriers, and other businesses. Heydrich, who attended the November 12 meeting, estimated 800 cases of plunder but said that the police were arresting looters.

Göring insisted to Eduard Hilgard—who represented the German insurance industry—that insurance companies would have to pay Aryan policyholders for their losses. Payoffs on Jewish-held policies would, Göring said, go to the state. Hilgard argued that the extent of the damage, calculated later at 49.1 million marks, made full payment impossible. Aryan losses were indeed made good, but of the 46.1 million marks in estimated Jewish damages, German insurance companies paid the state but 1.3 million. Thus, Jews were assessed an additional state fine of 1 billion marks because of their "provocation" of the violence. What was left of Jewish property would therefore be plundered as Jews left the country.[83]

[79]Quoted in McKale, *Hitler's Shadow War*, p. 110.

[80]Steinweis, *Kristallnacht*, pp. 112–14.

[81]Quoted in Friedländer, *Years of Persecution*, p. 273.

[82]All in *TMWC*, vol. 28, document 1816-PS, pp. 499–540.

[83]Financial figures in Gerald D. Feldman, *Allianz and the German Insurance Business, 1933–1945* (New York, 2001), pp. 221–2.

After the pogrom, the Germans made Jewish life impossible in every way imaginable. Göring's decree of November 12 formally expelled Jews from the economy. With very few exceptions, Jewish doctors, dentists, pharmacists, veterinarians, and even hairdressers were forbidden to practice. Remaining Jewish businesses, from factories to shops, were Aryanized, as were Jewish homes. Valuables, from jewelry to rugs, to artworks, were auctioned, and ordinary Germans purchased the discounted belongings. Jews' savings accounts were blocked so that they could withdraw but small amounts after petitioning to do so. Jewish unemployment soared. Many sold remaining household goods from vases to furniture, to old children's clothing, to survive.

The state also moved to protect the German people from even occasional contact with Jews. "A further item," Goebbels insisted to Göring in the November 12 meeting, "is that the Jews not be allowed to sit around in German parks. Take the whisper propaganda by Jewish women in the park areas at Fehrbelliner Platz [in Berlin]. There are Jews that really do not look all that Jewish. They sit with German mothers who have children and start complaining and agitating. I see an especially big danger with this. I think it is necessary that certain parks be placed at the disposal of the Jews—not the nicest—and tell them, 'Jews can sit only on these benches. These are designated specially: For Jews only!' Otherwise they have no business in German parks."[84]

Such paranoia—which viewed even terrified Jewish mothers as a national threat—triggered a devastating barrage of laws over the following days. Jews remaining in German schools and German universities were expelled. Jews were banned from public places, including movie houses, playhouses, museums, libraries, zoos, ice skating rinks, swimming pools, parks, and benches. The mania that Jews would still have secret means of communication led to the confiscation of Jewish communal and synagogue records, the cancellation of Jewish driver's licenses, and even a prohibition against Jews owning carrier pigeons.

*****

"There was nothing else to do but emigrate," remembered Hertha Beuthner after the war. But there were very great difficulties. . . . [We] were allowed only ten German marks to take on the journey. In spite of all that, everyone tried to leave this hostile land as quickly as possible."[85] From 1933 to 1938, about 130,000 Jews left Germany. In 1938 and 1939 alone, 118,000 emigrated from within Germany's 1937 borders.[86] Of Germany's 525,000 Jews in January 1933, 185,000 remained when the war broke out in September 1939. Of 206,000 Jews in Austria in March 1938, 77,000 remained when the war began.[87] And of the 118,000 Jews living in Bohemia and Moravia before Germany declared the Protectorate in March 1939, some 103,000 remained when Hitler went to war.[88]

By 1939, 77 percent of Jews remaining in Germany were over forty. Two-thirds were over sixty-five.[89] With their jobs taken, their businesses ruined, and their property Aryanized, they became an increasingly miserable minority. The Nazis hoped to push them out as soon as possible. Convinced that even this miserable remnant represented a powerful threat, they were dismayed at the immigration restrictions abroad that prevented them from doing so. Indeed as war clouds gathered in 1938 and 1939, the question bearing on Jews concerned where they might possibly go.

---

[84]*TMWC*, vol. 28, document 1816-PS, pp. 499–540.

[85]Lixl-Purcell, *Women in Exile:* p. 57.

[86]Figures in Strauss, "Jewish Emigration (I)," pp. 317–28.

[87]Figures in Moser, *Demographie*, pp. 29, 37.

[88]Figures in Ilsemarie Walter, *Das Protektorat Böhmen und Mähren: Sozialgeschichtliche Aspekte* (Norderstedt, 2000), p. 26.

[89]Figure in Francis R. Nicosia, *Zionism and Anti-Semitism in Nazi Germany* (New York, 2008), p. 159.

5

No Safe Haven
The World and the Jewish Question, 1933–1939

Germany's policies toward its Jews became progressively more brutal between 1933 and 1939 in the hope that Jews would emigrate. The response in Poland and Romania was to treat their Jewish populations worse than before so that they too would leave. The Jewish question thus entered a more urgent, global phase. Could the democratic states and Jewish groups abroad improve life for Jews in Germany or eastern Europe? Would they provide refuge for Jews who wished desperately to emigrate?

The world was not prepared to answer. Few wanted to press Hitler on the Jewish question because maintenance of the European peace was paramount. Meanwhile, the world depression combined with latent antisemitism meant that the need to emigrate outstripped capacity or the desire to help. Few politicians saw the Jewish question in comprehensive terms, and Hitler's timetable for war was shorter than anyone imagined, leaving little time to solve the crisis. Many Jews could leave Europe. More, however, could not. They stood in the Nazis' path when war erupted in 1939.

5.1 JEWISH RESPONSES TO PERSECUTION

German Jews: Fatalism Versus Hope

"I am a Jew and a socialist," lamented distinguished economist Otto Nathan in March 1933. "There is no place for me in Germany."[1] Nobel Prize–winning physicist Albert Einstein similarly had no illusion about the Nazis or Germans' willingness to halt them. Both accepted academic appointments in the United States, Nathan at Princeton and Einstein at the nearby Institute for Advanced Study.

About 1,200 Jewish academics in Germany learned with the enactment of the April 1933 civil service law that their careers there were over. But they carried their livelihoods in their heads, and because their expertise was desirable abroad, nearly half emigrated that year.[2] Most

---

[1] Richard Breitman et al., eds., *Advocate for the Doomed: The Diaries and Papers of James G. McDonald 1932–1935* (Bloomington, IN, 2007), March 31, 1933.

[2] Doron Niederland, "The Emigration of Jewish Academics and Professionals from Germany in the First Years of Nazi Rule," *Leo Baeck Institute Yearbook*, vol. 33 (1988), p. 291.

Jewish professionals and businessmen had a harder decision. They knew one language. Leaving meant starting over without one's savings. The German state in 1931 prohibited taking liquid assets from the country to prevent a currency drain. The Nazis would not repeal the law, maintaining that Jews has swindled their assets in the first place.

Meanwhile, many Jews insisted that Germany was still their country while hoping that human decency would prevail if they could hold out. Often the argument divided along gender lines. "He was wrong," the men argued in a Dortmund synagogue after a physician from their congregation emigrated in 1935. "It indicates a lack of courage to leave the country now when we should stay together, firm against all hatred." "It takes more courage to leave," the women replied. "What good is it to stay and to wait for the slowly coming ruin? Is it not far better to go and to build up a new existence somewhere else in the world, before our strength is crippled by the everlasting strain on our nerves, on our souls? Is not our children's future more important than holding out against Nazi cruelties and prejudices?"[3] Rare, given gender relations of the day, was the case of Liselotte Müller, whose husband said, "If you decide you would like to live in Palestine, I will like it too."[4]

Indeed, many Jewish women understood that life in Germany meant emotional as well as financial hardship and that their children got the worst of it. By law, children under age fourteen had to attend school and there were not enough Jewish schools to accommodate the growing demand. Jewish children endured daily misery from classmates' jeers to teachers' scorn. They lost what friends they had because of societal pressures, which proscribed being seen with a Jewish child. One child who finally convinced his father to remove him from school, confessed, "Father . . . had you continued to force me to go to a [German] school, I would have thrown myself under a train."[5]

Jewish organizations in Germany tried to ease matters. In 1933, German Jewish leaders formed the Reich Representation of German Jews (*Reichsvertretung der deutschen Juden*). Chaired by Berlin Rabbi Leo Baeck and financed by Jewish contributions, it coordinated smaller Jewish organizations in self-help efforts that included financial aid for Jews suddenly without jobs, healthcare for Jews who could not afford it, retraining for Jews who needed it, Jewish schools, and emigration. It also maintained contact with Jewish organizations abroad and tried negotiating with the Nazi authorities for what it called a "tolerable relationship" after the Nuremberg Laws. Baeck did not understand that the battle could not be won.

Jewish emigration from Germany before *Kristallnacht* was a steady stream if not a flood. Thirty-seven thousand Jews left Germany in 1933. No fewer than 20,000 left each year thereafter. Jews planned for life elsewhere, learning skills from carpentry to cooking. But the tightening of immigration restrictions abroad through the 1930s meant that most could not say where, if anyplace, they would go. To the oft-asked question, "What language are you learning?" came the gallows-answer: "The wrong one."

Zionism and German Jews

Zionism had not been popular with acculturated German Jews. The Nazis made it more attractive, particularly for young Jews who now had no prospects. The Zionist Federation for Germany had over 23,000 active members in 205 local branches by 1936. *He-halutz* grew

---

[3]Monika Richarz, ed., *Jewish Life in Germany: Memoirs from Three Centuries* (Bloomington, IN, 1991), p. 356.

[4]Quoted in Marion A. Kaplan, *Between Dignity and Despair: Jewish Life in Nazi Germany* (New York, 1998), p. 60.

[5]Quoted in Kaplan, *Between Dignity and Despair*, p. 102.

from 500 members in Germany in 1933 to 14,000 in 1935. Hebrew courses were in demand. By 1937, Zionists had twenty-four language programs in the Berlin area alone.[6] Other emigration training areas were established for German Jews living in Holland, Czechoslovakia, France, Denmark, Italy, and Luxemburg. They retrained Jews in agriculture, carpentry, plumbing, metallurgy, and electrical work.

Initially the Nazis were not sure what to think of Zionism. On the one hand, it rejected Jewish assimilation and called for emigration. Nazi theorist Alfred Rosenberg, a Baltic German who had early influence on Hitler and who swallowed whole the *Protocols of the Elders of Zion*, wrote in 1919 that "Zionism must be vigorously supported in order to encourage a significant number of Jews to leave. . . ." Ranting in a beer hall in 1920, Hitler said that the Jew "should look for his human rights where he belongs—in his own state of Palestine."[7]

On the other hand, Zionism promoted the imagined Jewish conspiracy from a center in Palestine. The Nazis dissolved Zionist organizations in Germany after *Kristallnacht*. But they used Zionism when they could. In August 1933, the German government concluded the *Ha'avara* (Transfer) Agreement with the Jewish Agency Executive (JAE) for Palestine. The Germans released the blocked assets of Jews who wished to go there. The JAE returned a portion of the money to the immigrants so they could meet British financial requirements and begin life anew. Importers in Palestine used immigrants' remaining assets in Germany to purchase needed industrial goods. For Germany, the *Ha'avara* agreement allowed increased exports and buildup of cash at a time when businesses in other parts of the world boycotted German goods.

For the Jewish Agency, the *Ha'avara* Agreement allowed the use of Jewish funds that would have been lost anyway, 100 million marks' worth of needed equipment, and the arrival of 60,000 talented German Jews by September 1939. The unfortunate by-product was a further rift in global Jewish strategy. While the JAE felt that the Jews' place in Germany was over anyway, boycott advocates abroad argued that the JAE encouraged escalated violence against German Jews so that they would leave sooner. And not all German Jews could go to Palestine.

Emigration and Eastern Europe

Because Polish and Romanian Jews were less acculturated and because their condition had been miserable for longer, their responses to persecution were different. From 1921 to 1931, 395,223 Jews emigrated from Poland. But emigrants did not offset natural increase—3.1 million Jews still lived in Poland in 1931. And immigration restrictions elsewhere in the 1930s shrunk the number of Jews who could leave just as the Polish and Romanian governments forced the issue. In 1937, just 717 Jews from Poland and 148 from Romania immigrated to the United States.[8] "All the Jews endlessly chew over the one preoccupation: leaving Romania," wrote Emil Dorian, a Jewish physician and writer in Bucharest in May 1938. "But this is merely . . . a neurotic symptom of powerlessness and despair. . . . Nobody moves since there is nowhere to go. . . . There is no way out."[9]

Zionism was more popular among Jews in Poland and Romania than elsewhere. But immigration to Palestine became more difficult with time because of British restrictions and increased

---

[6]Figures in Francis R. Nicosia, "German Zionism and Jewish Life in Nazi Berlin," in *Jewish Life in Nazi Germany: Dilemmas and Responses*, eds. Francis R. Nicosia and David Scrase (New York, 2010), pp. 89–116.

[7]Quoted in Francis R. Nicosia, *The Third Reich and the Palestine Question* (London, 1985), pp. 24, 25, 28.

[8]*American Jewish Yearbook* (hereafter *AJC Yearbook*), vol. 40, pp. 559, 574. Figures for the United States are for the fiscal year ending June 30, 1937.

[9]Marguerite Dorian, ed., *The Quality of Witness: A Romanian Diary 1937–1944* (Philadelphia, PA, 1982), May 6, 1938; July 2, 1940.

demand from Germany. From 1919 to 1942, only 136,756 Jews from Poland immigrated there— .04 percent of Poland's Jewish population.[10] In 1936, Revisionist Zionist leader Ze'ev Jabotinsky called for 1.5 million east European Jews to move *en masse* to Palestine and blaze a trail for more immigrants. His popularity grew, as did the membership of the Revisionist youth group *Betar*. Meanwhile tens of thousands of young traditional Zionist pioneers clung to their youth groups in Poland, as one young Jew said, "like a drowning person to a board."[11]

The Polish government pressed after 1937 to move hundreds of thousands of Jews to Madagascar amid economic boycotts and pogroms. Voluntary emigration to a better life was one thing; being dumped on a malarial island was another. "We will not leave," announced Arieh Tartakower, a Jewish academic and labor Zionist, "because Poland is our country."[12] The American Jewish Committee concurred. "The solution of the problem of Jewish relations," they wrote Foreign Minister Józef Beck, "can be found only on Polish soil."[13]

The socialist-oriented Bund indeed pressed for Jewish security within Poland. It launched a general strike in 1936 to protest antisemitic violence; advocated self-defense; supported Yiddish schools; and provided an array of services to the poor, from soup kitchens to hospitals. It became the most popular Jewish urban party over the 1930s. With fewer Jews able to leave, the alternative of staying and improving living conditions was all that was left.

Yet conditions did not improve and Jewish politics remained splintered. The Bund, a working-class party, distrusted even labor Zionist parties, to say nothing of middle-class, religious, or revisionist Zionists. Agudas Yisroel ("Union of Israel"), the Orthodox religious party that hoped to work through the government to secure religious freedoms and recognized only the rabbinate as a legitimate Jewish authority, thought little of democratic socialism or Zionism. All attempts at unity failed as Jewish leaders blamed each other. As historian Ezra Mendelsohn puts it, the Jewish population in Poland was "divided, demoralized, and impoverished" as it entered its most terrible period.[14]

5.2 PALESTINE, THE ARAB REVOLT, AND THE WHITE PAPER

Immigration and the Rise of Hitler

"The Jew who comes to Palestine," said Chaim Weizmann, who headed the international Zionist Organization after 1935, "comes not as a refugee but as of right. He is not just tolerated here but received with open arms into his national home."[15] But Great Britain held the League of Nations Mandate for Palestine, and London never saw solving the Jewish question as part of its charge. Dependent on its global empire, it blanched at anything in Palestine threatening economic stability and regional peace. Thus, Jewish immigration was limited. By 1931, 175,006 Jews lived in Palestine out of a total population of 1.035 million persons.[16]

Hitler's rise to power caused a jump in immigration demand, and initially Britain allowed more Jews to enter. The apex came in 1935, when 61,854 Jews immigrated to Palestine.

---

[10]Figure in Ezra Mendelsohn, *The Jews of East Central Europe Between the Wars* (Bloomington, IN, 1983), p. 79.

[11]Quoted in Mendelsohn, *The Jews of East Central Europe*, p. 78.

[12]Quoted in Vicki Caron, *Uneasy Asylum: France and the Jewish Refugee Crisis, 1933–1942* (Stanford, CA, 1999), p. 153.

[13]*AJC Yearbook*, vol. 39, p. 228.

[14]Mendelsohn, *Jews of East Central Europe*, p. 81.

[15]*Jewish Telegraphic Agency News Bulletin*, May 25, 1933.

[16]*AJC Yearbook*, vol. 37, p. 362.

By then, 375,000 Jews lived there, comprising nearly 30 percent of the population.[17] With fewer than 5,000 Jews admitted to the United States and 624 to Canada that year, it is no wonder that many viewed Palestine as a solution. Arthur Ruppin, a German Jew who moved to Palestine in 1908 and who helped direct kibbutz settlement there, saw a miracle. "Every child," he said, "who has been snatched from the inferno of hatred which Germany has become for the Jews, has been saved and restored to life."[18]

But British policy had not changed fundamentally. The immigration jump was conditioned less by the Jews' plight than by a rise in Jewish capital investment in Palestine, which created more jobs. Jewish land purchases increased by 73 percent from 1933 to 1934, and capital investment in new companies rose 304 percent. Relative to opportunity, Jewish immigration did not increase as much as it might have. There was actually a Jewish labor shortage in the second quarter of 1934, triggering migration from farms to cities where wages were higher.[19]

British authorities feared recession once temporary and seasonal jobs, such as urban construction or farm labor, disappeared. London thus rejected Jewish Agency requests for higher immigration, suggesting that Jewish enterprises hire Arab workers. JAE representatives were livid. Jewish capital, they argued, should hire Jewish immigrants.[20] In fact, the British economic predictions were correct. A severe recession beginning in 1937 triggered rising Jewish unemployment in Palestine until mid-1941.

The Arab Revolt and the White Paper

Meanwhile the political situation came unhinged. In 1936, the Grand Mufti of Jerusalem, Haj Amin al-Husseini, called for an Arab general strike to protest Jewish immigration. Sporadic violence, which might have included 10,000 Arab fighters (including volunteers from Syria and Iraq), erupted against Jewish settlements, British railways, and the new oil pipeline running from Iraq through Palestine's port city of Haifa.

The British lost control of large areas. They increased their military presence by 20,000 men, enlisted the Jewish defense militia (the Hagana), and resorted to counterinsurgency tactics, including collective punishment of villages, dynamiting of city blocks, and torture—"a disgrace to the British name" according to one British police investigator. By the end of the revolt in March 1939, the Mufti's followers outside the German consulate in Jerusalem chanted, "We want Hitler!"[21]

The death toll included up to 6,000 Arabs, many of whom were clan enemies of the Grand Mufti and murdered by his followers. Four hundred Jews and 200 British troops were also killed. The Mufti fled to Iraq to avoid arrest. But Jews in Europe also felt the impact. Recession and revolt meant a decline in immigration certificates. The 1936 immigration figure (27,910) was

---

[17]*AJC Yearbook*, vol. 36, p. 403; vol. 37, p. 385; vol. 37, pp. 562, 585.

[18]Quoted in Debórah Dwork and Robert Jan Van Pelt, *Flight from the Reich: Refugee Jews, 1933–1946* (New York, 2009), p. 47.

[19]Great Britain, Colonial Office. *Report by His Majesty's Government in the United Kingdom of Great Britain and Northern Ireland to the Council of the League of Nations on the Administration of Palestine and Transjordan for the Year 1933* (London, 1934), pp. 97, 202.

[20]Interview among Arthur Wauchope, David Ben-Gurion, Moshe Shertok, October 20, 1933, Great Britain, Colonial Office, *British Colonial Office Palestine Correspondence, 1931–1934* (Wilmington, DE, 1979), Class No. 733, vol. 236, file 17313, part 3, roll 10.

[21]Quoted in Matthew Hughes, "The Banality of Brutality: British Armed Forces and the Repression of the Arab Revolt in Palestine, 1936–1939," *English Historical Review* 124, no. 507 (April 2009), pp. 313–54.

half that of 1935. The 1937 figure (9,855) was one-third that of 1936. Certificates increased slightly in 1938 (11,441) and 1939 (13,914), and for the first time in 1938 the majority of immigrants came from Germany and Austria.[22] By the end of 1939, 424,373 registered Jews lived in Palestine. But the figure fell far short of Jewish needs and expectations.[23]

The British, meanwhile, rethought their obligations in Palestine as a whole. As war clouds gathered in Europe and East Asia in 1939, policymakers in London under Prime Minister Neville Chamberlain understood that the Middle East, with the Suez Canal, Iraqi oil, and the British naval base at Alexandria, was key to all potential war theaters. Unrest in Palestine and spreading Arab anger in the Middle East could trigger geopolitical disaster.

A White Paper (policy statement) of May 1939 thus assured the Arabs that "His Majesty's Government . . . declare unequivocally that it is not a part of their policy that Palestine should become a Jewish State. They would indeed regard it as contrary to their obligations to the Arabs . . . that the Arab population of Palestine should be made the subjects of a Jewish State against their will." Jewish immigration, the statement continued, would not continue indefinitely, nor would Jews ever outnumber Arabs. It would be limited to 10,000 immigrants each year over the next five years, plus 25,000 refugees *if* they could be absorbed economically. Thus, 75,000 more Jews at most could go to Palestine, and the Jewish population there would not exceed one-third of the total.

Zionist leaders angrily rejected the White Paper as an illegal deviation from the League of Nations mandate for a Jewish national home, which, they said, was more urgent than ever. When British Colonial Secretary Malcolm MacDonald told Weizmann that the Jews too had made mistakes in Palestine, Weizmann countered, "Oh yes, certainly we have made mistakes; our chief mistake is that we exist at all." McDonald blandly noted, "We have some interests of our own in Palestine."[24] In the end, Palestine took roughly 60,000 German-speaking Jews between 1933 and 1939. Over 30,000 more than that went to the United States by 1939. The British accepted 86,705 Polish Jews into Palestine from 1933 to 1939, a relatively small number given the demand.[25] Only after the Holocaust did Palestine become a solution to the Jewish question in Europe.

5.3 THE JEWISH QUESTION ON THE WORLD STAGE

Western Europe

In the 1920s, western Europe was a preferred haven for Jewish refugees. It was easily reached and liberal in nature, with a history of granting asylum. But the depression made western European countries less hospitable after 1933, just as German Jews and more from eastern Europe sought safety. In Belgium, the signals were especially clear. Most of Belgium's 65,000 to 75,000 Jews arrived from eastern Europe between 1925 and 1931. Antisemitic sentiment in Belgium ran high afterward, culminating in right-wing electoral gains in 1936, manhunts for illegal German Jewish immigrants in 1937, and anti-Jewish rioting in Antwerp in August 1939.[26]

---

[22]Immigration figures from *AJC Yearbook*, vol. 41, p. 613.

[23]*AJC Yearbook*, vol. 42, p. 604.

[24]Quoted in Bernard Wasserstein, *Britain and the Jews of Europe, 1933–1945* (New York, 1979), pp. 21, 22.

[25]German figures in *AJC Yearbook*, vol. 42, p. 596. Polish figures in Mendelsohn, *Jews of East Central Europe*, pp. 77–79.

[26]Lieven Saerens, "Antwerp's Attitude Toward the Jews from 1918 to 1940 and Its Implications for the Period of Occupation," in *Belgium and the Holocaust: Jews, Belgians, Germans*, ed. Dan Michman (Jerusalem, 1998), pp. 117–58.

France, meanwhile, displayed growing ambivalence toward Jewish refugees. "These undesirable elements," grumbled Metz's Chamber of Commerce in 1933, referring to incoming German Jews, "will become a veritable plague for honest French merchants." The Strasbourg Chamber of Commerce insisted that Jews from Germany remained fundamentally German and thus ready to "commit treason against the country that had so generously offered them hospitality." Even Jacques Heilbronner, the vice president of the *Consistoire Israélite*, complained in 1934 that more Jewish refugees "would only create an atmosphere of hostility . . . that could degenerate into a more or less blatant antisemitism."[27]

The French government tightened visa regulations but without success. Some 15,000 east European Jews entered France illegally during the 1937 World's Fair. Thousands of German-speaking Jews did the same in 1938 and 1939. French authorities began jailing illegal immigrants as a deterrent, but arrestees preferred jail to a return to their former homes. By 1939, some 60,000 recently arrived central and east European Jewish refugees lived in France, perhaps two-thirds of them illegally.[28]

The Netherlands held perhaps 20,000 Jewish refugees when the war broke out but with similar reticence, even from native Jews. The Committee for Jewish Refugees in the Netherlands raised funds for Jewish arrivals. But it did not press for more liberal asylum policies for fear of the accusation that it favored Jewish refugees over Dutch workers amid 30 percent unemployment. The Netherlands accepted 7,000 Jews from Germany after 1938 only on the condition that they live in refugee camps. By May 1939, there were twelve camps in the Netherlands as well as twenty-four institutions for Jewish refugee children. On the eve of the German invasion in 1940, Dutch authorities created a central Jewish refugee camp in a bleak area known as Westerbork near the German border. The Germans occupied it on the first day of the invasion.[29]

The Western Hemisphere

In the United States, the 1924 Johnson-Reed Act restricted immigration based on national quotas. The annual visa quota for Germany was 25,957. For Poland, it was 8,524 and for Romania, 377. The depression tightened matters. In 1930, President Herbert Hoover ordered strict interpretation of the "public charge" criteria. Initially intended to bar the mentally disabled, it now applied to anyone consular officials deemed unable to support him- or herself financially, often regardless of affidavits of support from relatives in the United States. Only 4,134 Jews from all countries (1,786 from Germany, 672 from Poland, and 98 from Romania) were allowed to immigrate in the fiscal year ending June 30, 1934, a number far under available quotas. By 1937, State Department officials congratulated themselves for keeping 1 million poor aliens from swelling the ranks of the unemployed.[30]

President Franklin D. Roosevelt took office in 1933. He was sensitive to the Jewish question, but he also understood political realities. As late as April 1939, 83 percent of Americans polled believed immigration quotas should not be raised.[31] Roosevelt could not launch a fight with

[27]Quotes in Caron, *Uneasy Asylum*, pp. 23, 25, 103, 132, 136.

[28]Figures in Caron, *Uneasy Asylum*, pp. 2, 164, 210.

[29]Bob Moore, *Victims and Survivors: The Nazi Persecution of the Jews in the Netherlands 1940–1945* (New York, 1997), pp. 32–4.

[30]On the public charge criteria, see Bat-Ami Zucker, *In Search of Refuge: Jews and US Consuls in Nazi Germany 1933–1941* (London, 2001), pp. 40–5, 86–97, 143–4.

[31]Richard Breitman and Alan Kraut, *American Refugee Policy and European Jewry, 1933–1945* (Bloomington, IN, 1987), p. 73.

Congress that he was sure to lose. Instead he worked quietly within existing laws and their loopholes. After he won a second term in 1936, consular officials received new instructions, likely at his insistence, that they should only reject visa applicants who were *probably*—not *possibly*—going to become public charges. After the *Anschluss*, Roosevelt added the defunct Austrian immigration quota to Germany's, thus creating a combined German quota of 27,370. After *Kristallnacht*, he indefinitely extended thousands of visitors' visas so that German Jews would not be deported. "I cannot, in any decent humanity," Roosevelt said at a press conference, "throw them out."[32]

The United States admitted 11,000 Jews in fiscal year 1937; over 19,000 in 1938; and over 43,000 in 1939, the only year in which the State Department filled its own quotas. From 1933 to 1939, the United States took over 92,000 Jews—far more than any other country. Unlike other states, US immigration figures for Jews rose rather than contracted as the 1930s progressed. Yet they tell only a partial story. Despite surging demand, the law itself had not changed. And though 92,000 Jews from the Reich reached the United States by 1939, fully 300,000 had sought entry. In Europe, the waiting list for quota slots by 1939 stretched eleven years into the future.[33]

Canada, meanwhile, provided almost no help. In 1931, Jews numbered 155,614—1.5 percent of the Canadian population. Most—primarily east European working-class Jews—arrived early in the century, and most settled in major cities such as Toronto and Montreal. The depression triggered restrictions. Orders-in-Council of 1930 and 1931—executive orders from the cabinet—banned immigrants who did not have enough money to establish themselves in farming. Only 3,421 Jews (2,234 from Poland) were admitted in 1931 out of a total immigrant population of 88,223.

Hitler's rise to power tightened restrictions further. The French-Catholic province of Quebec was especially opposed to new Jewish immigrants. In September 1933, Catholic workers petitioned Prime Minister R. B. Bennett to prohibit the immigration of German Jews, and in October, the Quebec City Council resolved that German Jews were not assimilable and should not enter the country. French Canadian newspapers and provincial Quebec politicians maintained the drumbeat. When asked if Canada might serve as a refuge to some German Jews in 1934, Bennett said that, at most, "there might be a place for a few ladies' tailors or for butchers."[34]

The ascent of the Liberal Party of William Mackenzie King in 1935 changed nothing. Frederick Charles Blair, a narrow-minded, inflexible bureaucrat with a fetish for regulations, became the director of the government's Immigration Branch. Blair was an antisemite who in 1938 scrutinized each application personally. He warned of Canada being "flooded with [unassimilable] Jewish people" while complaining that Canadian Jews were "utterly selfish in their attempts to force through a permit for the admission of relatives and friends." He noted with pride that he had kept the doors closed. Jews, he added, should ask themselves "why they are so unpopular almost everywhere."[35] In 1938, Canada allowed but 584 Jews into the country, 379 coming from the United States. Twenty-three came from Germany and Austria.[36]

Similar problems characterized South America. Jewish populations, mostly from eastern Europe, had grown quickly over the past four decades in Argentina, which had 251,000 Jewish citizens, and in Brazil, which had 40,000. In 1934, both countries adopted requirements for an array of documents required to obtain visas, ranging from birth certificates to police reports. Local

---

[32]On these steps, see Richard Breitman and Alan Lichtman, *FDR and the Jews* (Cambridge, MA, 2013), Chapter 6.

[33]Figures in *AJC Yearbook*, vol. 43, pp. 681–84. See also Breitman and Lichtman, *FDR and the Jews*, Chapter 6.

[34]Breitman et al., eds., *Advocate for the Doomed*, September 19, 1934.

[35]Quoted in Irving Abella and Harold Troper, *None Is Too Many: Canada and the Jews of Europe, 1933–1948* (New York, 1982), pp. 8–9.

[36]Immigration numbers in *AJC Yearbook*, vol. 41, pp. 598–604.

Catholic publications trumpeted the connection between Jews and labor unrest. "The source of the hatred of Christ," said one in Argentina, "may be found in Judeo-Communist ideals."[37] Brazil's Foreign Ministry instructed consulates in 1937 to deny visas to persons of "Semitic origin."[38]

Jews who could profess a desire to create farms and those with family members already in residence could still enter, as could those who successfully bribed consular officials. But procedures were tightened in 1938 because of the expected influx from Austria. From 1934 to 1937, at least 13,800 Jews reached Argentina.[39] In 1938, just 1,050 Jews entered the country. Brazil denied entrance even to American Jews with tourist visas and even planned to deport 2,000 German Jews living on expired tourist documents. US pressure induced President Gétulio Vargas to rescind this order. But only 530 Jewish refugees reached Brazil in 1938.[40]

The League of Nations and the Jews

In theory, the League of Nations guaranteed the Minorities Treaties signed with Poland, Romania, and five other states. In truth, the League had no method of enforcement. The problem became worse when Germany, a League Council member since 1926 that had never signed a minorities' treaty, began terrorizing its own Jews in 1933.

Hitler pulled Germany from the League in October 1933 over rearmament. The League was more interested in resuming disarmament discussions than it was in German Jews, especially because Hitler was unyielding on the Jewish question. Joseph Avenol, the French secretary-general of the League, further worried that if the League intervened for German Jews, Hitler might call its bluff and insist that the League take responsibility for them.

Poland took advantage of the uncertainty. In September 1934, Foreign Minister Beck, speaking before the League Assembly, renounced the Minorities Treaty that his country signed in 1919. Jews in Poland knew better than to take their case to the League, and the League had no plan to act lest Poland leave the League entirely. Beck's announcement was met with "glacial silence," but the League did not even censure the Polish government.[41]

If the League could not enforce minority protection, then perhaps it could help with the growing refugee problem. On the urging of the Dutch government, which complained about the expense of refugees (there were 3,682 in the Netherlands in 1933), the League created a High Commission for Refugees (Jewish and Other) Coming from Germany.[42] The High Commissioner from 1933 to 1935 was James G. McDonald, scholar and president of the US Foreign Policy Association, who was deeply sympathetic to the Jewish plight. Fifteen other countries were represented. The commission's name showed that the Jewish problem in Germany was prioritized. No one wished to grasp the more massive problem of eastern Europe's Jews.

McDonald hoped to create a giant fund of up to $50 million to finance emigration and new starts for German Jews in countries around the world. He did not get close. The League, for fear of offending Germany, did not even cover the High Commission's administrative costs, much less create a fund for Jews. As Avenol put it, "[I]t is dangerous to assume that governments are vitally interested

---

[37]Quoted in Graciela Ben-Dror, *The Catholic Church and the Jews in Argentina, 1933–1945* (Lincoln, NE, 2008), p. 125.

[38]Quoted in Jeffrey Lesser, *Welcoming the Undesirables: Brazil and the Jewish Question* (Berkeley, CA, 1995), p. 92.

[39]Figure in Haim Avni, *Argentina and the Jews: A History of Jewish Immigration* (Tuscaloosa, AL, 1991), p. 141.

[40]Figures in *AJC Yearbook*, vol. 42, pp. 625–6. Avni, *Argentina and the Jews*, p. 141.

[41]Quoted and described in Carole Fink, *Defending the Rights of Others: The Great Powers, the Jews, and International Minority Protection, 1878–1938* (New York, 2004), pp. 338–42.

[42]Figure in Yehuda Bauer, *My Brother's Keeper: A History of the American Jewish Joint Distribution Committee 1929–1939* (Philadelphia, PA, 1974), p. 170.

in the success of the High Commission."[43] Individual states also balked. England and France provided nothing. Germany would not free Jewish assets to help with emigration unless it was part of an arrangement like the *Ha'avara* agreement. Many influential gentiles also failed to help. "Isn't it true," asked the Archbishop of Canterbury in 1934, "that the excesses of the Jews themselves under the [Weimar] Republic are responsible for the excesses of the Nazis, at least in part?"[44]

Nor could McDonald alter immigration laws. The British government insisted that Palestine was not within the High Commission's purview. He got nowhere with State Department officials in charge of visas. He could not convince the Canadian government to liberalize. The French government refused to issue work permits to the 10,000 German-Jewish refugees living in France in 1934, and it sheltered them in awful facilities.[45] McDonald spent four months in South America in 1935, talking with Brazilian, Argentine, and Paraguayan officials, and left with nothing concrete. He resigned in protest at the end of the year. *The Nation* described his mission as "an honorable failure."[46]

Jewish Charities

The chief American Jewish fund-raising organ in the United States was the American Jewish Joint Distribution Committee (JDC), founded in 1914 to dispense charitable aid collected from across the American Jewish spectrum through its agents in Europe to Jews during World War I. Its scope was massive. From 1914 to 1929, the JDC collected $78.5 million, most of which went to help east European Jews via subsidized health organizations, facilities for needy children, and interest-free loans. But the JDC budget contracted after 1929. The depression shrank Jewish contributions just when more money was needed. Annual JDC income from 1933 to 1937 never topped $3 million.

The JDC, led by German American Jewish banker Felix Warburg until his death in 1937, did what it could for Jews in Germany, helping to finance Jewish schools, retraining for young adults, and welfare. It also helped German Jewish refugees in other states. As late as 1937 and 1938, one-third of JDC aid went to Poland, where daily conditions of violence, starvation, and disease were at their worst. In 1939, in the wake of *Kristallnacht*, the JDC raised $8.1 million. But the need simply outstripped the means.[47]

The chief Anglo-Jewish fund-raising organ, the Central British Fund (CBF) for German Jewry, was a latecomer to such work, depending more on ad hoc appeals than systematic annual fund-raising. Income fell short of targets despite the generosity of leading British Jews such as Anthony de Rothschild and Simon Marks. "The response of the Anglo-Jewish community has been remarkable in the extreme," read the 1936 appeal, but nearly 400,000 pounds still remain to be found."[48] And if the JDC was too hopeful in thinking that its programs could make life bearable for Jews in Europe, the more Zionist CBF was impractical in its schemes to retrain and move all German Jewish youth to Palestine while ignoring the policies of its own government. American and British Jews thus disagreed on the nature of the Jewish question in Europe and on the nature of its solution.

---

[43]Breitman et al., eds., *Advocate for the Doomed*, August 23, 1934.

[44]Breitman et al., eds., *Advocate for the Doomed*, October 14, 1934.

[45]Bauer, *My Brother's Keeper*, pp. 150–2.

[46]Richard Breitman et al., eds., *Refugees and Rescue: The Diaries and Papers of James G. McDonald 1935–1945* (Bloomington, IN, 2009), p. 104.

[47]Figures in Yehuda Bauer, *American Jewry and the Holocaust: The American Joint Distribution Committee, 1939–1945* (Detroit, MI, 1981), pp. 17–31.

[48]Quoted in Amy Zahl Gottlieb, *Men of Vision: Anglo-Jewry's Aid to Victims of the Nazi Regime 1933–1945* (London, 1998), p. 206.

Still, most of the money for McDonald's work in resettling Jewish refugees came from private sources. When he resigned as High Commissioner in December 1935, he reported that, of the 80,000 Jews who left Germany up to that time, two-thirds had been resettled, half in Palestine, the rest back in their countries of origin. "The accomplishment," he said, "has been primarily the work of the refugees themselves and of the philanthropic organizations—Jewish and Christian. . . ." Yet the Nuremberg Laws were just months old. McDonald feared worse to come. German Jews, he said, "are being driven to the point where, in utter anguish and despair, they may burst the frontiers in fresh waves of refugees."[49]

The World Jewish Congress

In 1936, after extensive preparation, Jewish leaders from thirty-two states (minus Germany and the USSR) established the World Jewish Congress (WJC), headquartered in Paris. It was a permanent body of elected delegates claiming to represent the welfare of the world's Jews, religious and secular, socialist and conservative, Zionist and non-Zionist. Jewish advocacy groups in different countries had pressed for Jewish rights since the nineteenth century. But not until the Nazi onslaught did they create a permanent international structure. International Zionist congresses had met since Theodor Herzl's day and the international Zionist Organization had existed since that time. But in the 1930s, it was mostly occupied with Palestine-related issues.

The WJC's chief officers were Rabbi Stephen Wise, a golden-tongued American Zionist leader, and Nahum Goldmann, a German Jewish scholar of Belarusian origin who fled Germany and settled in the United States. In his initial address to the WJC, Wise explained the global urgency of the Jewish question. The world's Jews, he said, shared an "essential oneness." Germany's war, he argued, was acting against "the Jewish totality, including all of us." Goldmann followed. Minority guarantees from the League of Nations, he said, "hardly amount to anything now. . . . The Jewish problem in Europe is becoming ever more a question of physical survival in the most elementary sense of the word."

But what could the WJC do? Goldmann noted that there could be no compromise with antisemitic regimes, but he also noted that Jews were a small minority everywhere and could hardly steer the policies of governments. "The world," he said, "is not eager to hear us talk of our sufferings. . . ."[50] The answer lay in rhetorically linking the Jewish fate with that of humanity. Both, WJC leaders insisted, were under threat. WJC representatives collected and disseminated information from all over Europe to Jewish groups and national governments. The WJC Executive made public declarations countering everything from antisemitic violence in Poland to Nazi statements on global Jewish conspiracies. WJC members also met with League of Nations officials; foreign policy leaders; and leading politicians, including Roosevelt himself, who Rabbi Wise knew well.

These steps were of moral import. They kept the Jewish question visible and reminded politicians and populations that they could not ignore it without defying their own conscience. They were also not without practical effect. Protests to Romania in 1938 spurred by the WJC might have protected the citizenship of the majority of Romania's Jews. But as a congress with no state attached, neither the WJC nor its affiliates could force governments to act against their political interests. Meanwhile, to the Nazis, the WJC simply confirmed the existence of a secret Jewish government that influenced Germany's enemies.

---

[49]Letter of Resignation of James G. McDonald, December 27, 1935, in Norman Bentwich, *The Refugees from Germany, April 1933 to December 1935* (London, 1936), pp. 221, 223.

[50]Quotes above in World Jewish Congress, *Unity in Dispersion: A History of the World Jewish Congress* (New York, 1949), pp. 48–50.

Jews in Vienna wait for exit visas at Margarethen District Police Station, 1938 *Source:* Austrian Society of Contemporary History, courtesy of the United States Holocaust Memorial Museum.

5.4 DESPERATION: THE ÉVIAN CONFERENCE AND AFTER

The Emigration Crush

The year 1938 brought a full-blown refugee crisis, beginning with the German annexation of Austria. "The misery that has overtaken Vienna's Jewish population," reported French officials, "is indescribable."[51] "There are," reported the US consulate in Vienna in June, "innumerable cases where individuals are given the choice between leaving Austria within a given period . . . or of being sent to Dachau."[52] After *Kristallnacht* and Germany's assumption of control in Czechoslovakia, consulates were further choked with terrified Jews. Hundreds of thousands sought refuge abroad.

---

[51]Quoted in Caron, *Uneasy Asylum*, p. 172.

[52]John C. Wiley (US Consul General Vienna) to Secretary of State, June 13, 1938, *The Holocaust: Selected Documents in Eighteen Volumes*, vol. 5, eds. John Mendelsohn and Donald S. Detwiler (New York, 1982), p. 222ff.

Life became a maelstrom of forms, papers, and timing. Jews leaving the German Reich needed an exit visa, which could only be attained with a tax clearance form. Those without entry visas for destination countries had to go through increasingly complex application processes regardless of destination. If they planned to travel via third countries they needed transit visas for them as well. Certain consulates, such as that of the United States in Vienna, were sympathetic. But they could not help beyond the limits of the law. Others, such as the US consulate in Stuttgart, were notorious for rejecting applications or for repeatedly asking for new documentation.

Even ad hoc flight to neighboring states became harder. In 1933, Switzerland allowed 10,000 German Jews into the country on the correct assumption that most would not stay indefinitely. In April 1938, as thousands of Austrian Jews fled for Switzerland, the Swiss government instituted visa requirements for those with Austrian passports. In August, Swiss authorities sealed the border entirely to stem a "refugee invasion." Several thousand Jews entered Switzerland through secret crossings with the help of sympathetic border guards. Paul Grüninger, a police captain in St. Gallen, lost his job for helping perhaps a thousand desperate Jews. He was pardoned posthumously only in 2003.[53]

President Roosevelt was one of the few who grasped the Jewish question's urgency. He also thought in terms of a coordinated global solution. In January, he told Rabbi Wise that "if we can stave off war for another two years or three at most," undeveloped areas for Jewish resettlement might be found in order to supplement Palestine. After the *Anschluss*, he asked a trusted US diplomat: "Why not get the democracies to unite to share the burden? After all, they own most of the free land in the world, and there are only, what would you say, fourteen, sixteen million Jews in the whole world, of whom about half [sic] are already in the United States. If we could divide up the remainder . . . there wouldn't be any Jewish problem in three or four generations."[54]

The Évian Conference

Could such coordination be achieved? In March 1938, the president bypassed the League of Nations and his own State Department, and invited thirty-three nations to attend a conference on refugees. Twenty-nine accepted. South Africa, Italy, Iceland, and El Salvador declined. The conference was held in July at the French spa town of Évian-les-Bains. The Évian Conference created an Inter-Governmental Committee on Refugees that began meeting in London in August 1938. It was to work with governments to coordinate orderly emigration from Germany to various points on the globe. Washington indicated it would maintain its own quotas so that 140,000 Reich Jews could come to the United States over the next five years, and indeed the US quota was filled in 1939.

Few countries were willing to follow Roosevelt's lead. Switzerland, which housed the League of Nations, refused even to host the refugee conference. Poland and Romania, meanwhile, hoped to use Évian to solve their own Jewish problems, a measure that no one else would consider. In May 1938, shortly after Roosevelt's invitation to Évian, Britain instituted new visa requirements for German passport holders. "The last thing we wanted here," explained Home Secretary Samuel Hoare, "was the creation of a Jewish problem."[55] Britain hoped to relieve pressure on Palestine by finding alternate refuge in its colonies, but administrators in Kenya, Rhodesia, and elsewhere refused to take large numbers of Jews.

---

[53]Quote and figures in Regula Ludi, "Dwindling Options: Seeking Asylum in Switzerland, 1933–1939," in *Refugees from Nazi Germany and the Liberal European States*, eds. Frank Caestecker and Bob Moore (New York, 2010), pp. 82–93.

[54]Breitman et al., eds., *Refugees and Rescue*, pp. 125–6.

[55]Quoted in Dwork and Van Pelt, *Flight from the Reich*, p. 148.

President Roosevelt's representative, Myron Taylor, addresses the Évian Conference. James G. McDonald sits to his right. *Source:* United States Holocaust Memorial Museum.

Argentina and Brazil had already sliced immigration. Two weeks after the Évian Conference, on July 28, the Argentines added a new requirement on top of a visa—a landing permit issued not by Argentine consulates but by a special committee in Buenos Aires. The orders were to "give priority to immigration [of those] with the greatest capacity for assimilation in order to meet our social, cultural, and economic needs."[56] The law was to go into effect on October 1. The impending deadline caused a crush of requests for visas at Argentine consulates in Europe to beat the date. Nearly all were rejected. In addition, some 2,000 Argentine visas issued between July and October were reviewed and cancelled.[57]

The Germans, meanwhile, refused serious cooperation. In August, German Jews had their passports stamped with the letter *J* (for *Jude*). Berlin took the measure at the behest of Switzerland to help Swiss border guards distinguish between German business travelers and Jewish refugees. In October, British and US representatives asked if Germany would "assist other governments upon which [the refugee] problem has been forced by relaxing the pressure upon people who desire to leave [and] to permit the arrangement of an orderly emigration and by permitting them to take with them a reasonable percentage of their property."[58] Berlin would not consider it. Instead *Kristallnacht* was launched the following month, adding more despairing Jews to the problem.

Britain and the Kindertransport

Britain's visa requirement for German passports in May 1938 ensured that the number of German Jewish refugees there remained small. But *Kristallnacht* triggered pressure on the government from Jewish and Gentile leaders alike. Prime Minister Chamberlain was ambivalent. "No doubt," he wrote privately, "the Jews [aren't] a lovable people; I don't care for them myself; but that

[56]Quoted in Avni, *Argentina and the Jews*, p. 141.

[57]Leonardo Senkman, "Argentina's Immigration Policy During the Holocaust (1938–1945)" *Yad Vashem Studies*, 21 (1991), p. 164.

[58]Memorandum, British Embassy, Berlin, October 17, 1938, *The Holocaust*, eds. Mendelsohn and Detwiler, vol. 5, d. 10.

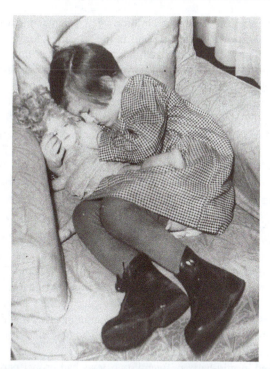

An arrival from the second *Kindertransport*, December 1938.   *Source:* United States Holocaust Memorial Museum.

is not sufficient to explain the pogrom."[59] On November 21, London announced streamlined British visa procedures for Jews with advance means of support as well as the rescue of Jewish children as long as they were supported with charitable rather than public funds.

Of the 60,000 to 70,000 Jewish refugees in England in September 1939, all but about 6,000 arrived the year before the war.[60] More than 20,000 German Jewish refugees, mostly women, came as domestic servants in England. Although they had no experience in such work, it offered the best chance of employment and thus asylum.[61] On arrival, many adjusted for class-conscious British employers for whom they were merely the help, entitled to little more than a cold room and leftover food. "I had to work very hard as a chambermaid," remembered Nelly Hewspear, "and once I was told off for reading a copy of [Rainer Maria] Rilke's poems. . . ."[62] But it was better than Germany.

More admirable were the British volunteers who worked with Jewish leaders in the Reich to find desperate parents ready to send their children to safety. From December 1, 1938, until

---

[59]Quoted in Louise London, *Whitehall and the Jews 1933–1948: British Immigration Policy and the Holocaust* (New York, 2000), p. 106.

[60]Figure in London, *Whitehall and the Jews*, pp. 103, 131.

[61]Tony Kuscher, "An Alien Occupation: Jewish Refugees and Domestic Service in Britain, 1933–1948," in *Second Chance: Two Centuries of German-Speaking Jews in the United Kingdom*, eds. Julius Carlebach et al. (Tübingen, 1991), p. 570.

[62]Zöe Josephs, ed., *Survivors: Jewish Refugees in Birmingham 1933–1945* (Warley, 1988), p. 140.

the outbreak of war, nearly 10,000 Jewish children aged seventeen and under (out of roughly 60,000) were moved from Germany to England in the so-called *Kindertransport* ("Children's Transport"). Supported by charities, they lived in hostels and foster homes. Parting scenes were traumatic. "My parents ran alongside the train on the platform," remembered Hedy Epstein, "tears were streaming down their faces."[63]

There were limits to London's generosity. Chamberlain rejected Jewish Agency requests to send Jewish children to Palestine over and above the immigration quota. Indeed Britain issued the White Paper in May 1939. Of the British dominions, only Australia followed London's example. It offered to take 15,000 refugees over the next three years, and 7,200 reached Australia by the outbreak of war.[64]

The Voyage of the *St. Louis*

Most states remained less forthcoming. The voyage of the German liner *St. Louis* is an infamous example. After *Kristallnacht*, elements of Cuba's government cooperated with Roosevelt's Évian initiative. Refugees could purchase tourists visas, come to Cuba, and wait for their US quota numbers to come up. Between December 1938 and May 1939, about 2,000 Jews with tourist visas arrived and lived with JDC help. The *St. Louis* left Hamburg on May 13. It carried 937 passengers, mostly Jews with Cuban tourist visas. A week earlier the Cuban government, responding to antisemitic protests, required arrivals to obtain landing permits, which, like those required by Argentina, were only issued from the capital. When the *St. Louis* reached Havana harbor on May 27, Cuban authorities would not allow it to dock.

The ship anchored in mid-harbor. Twenty-two Jews had proper permits and disembarked. One passenger who did not committed suicide. From June 2 to 6, the ship steamed between Cuba and Florida while the JDC negotiated with Cuban president Federico Laredo Brú. On the night of June 4, Laredo Brú demanded some $600,000 in sureties to ensure that the Jews would not become public charges. His deadline of June 6 suggests that he simply did not want the Jews to disembark. The *St. Louis* turned back for Germany before the JDC was able to convey its agreement.[65]

"What started as a voyage of freedom," passenger Josef Joseph wrote in his diary, "is now a voyage of doom."[66] Passengers held suicide watches as the press followed the *St. Louis* drama. Meanwhile the JDC, State Department, and Inter-Governmental Committee on Refugees feverishly negotiated for what were then safe havens. Captain Gustav Schröder, an anti-Nazi, would not return to Germany until they were found. By June 14, Britain, France, Belgium, and the Netherlands agreed to take the passengers. The JDC facilitated the landings by providing a $500 surety bond for each refugee. "Eighty percent of us, remembered passenger George Axelsson, "would have jumped overboard had the ship put back to Hamburg."[67] Of the 620 *St. Louis* passengers placed on the European continent, 365 survived the war.[68]

---

[63]Mark Jonathan Harris and Deborah Oppenheimer, eds., *Into the Arms of Strangers: Stories of the Kindertransport* (London, 2000), p. 111.

[64]Figures in Michael Blakeney, *Australia and the Jewish Refugees, 1933–1948* (Sidney, 1985).

[65]Newest details in C. Paul Vincent, "The Voyage of the *St. Louis* Revisited," *Holocaust and Genocide Studies*, 25, no. 2 (Fall 2011), pp. 252–289.

[66]Quoted in Sarah A. Ogilvie and Scott Miller, *Refuge Denied: The* St. Louis *Passengers and the Holocaust* (Madison, WI, 2006), p. 23.

[67]Quoted in Vincent, "Voyage of the *St. Louis*," p. 272.

[68]Ogilvie and Miller, *Refuge Denied*, p. 175.

Ships with fewer refugees were turned away in Uruguay, Brazil, Panama, and Venezuela. But Argentina turned away the most. After *Kristallnacht*, Jews in Buenos Aires protested Argentine immigration laws with a business strike. Argentine socialists hoped to open immigration to Jewish children at least. Timely interventions and bribes sometimes brought leniency from government officials (4,373 Jews entered Argentine legally and illegally in 1939). Meanwhile nationalist newspapers like *La Fronda* proclaimed, "The Semitic invasion must be opposed."[69] Those lacking landing permits were generally turned away, including sixty-eight Jewish refugees on the *SS Conde Grande* in February 1939; they were sent back to Europe as their relatives watched from the harbor. Argentine authorities turned away Jewish refugees on twenty-three vessels between December 1938 and December 1939.[70]

American Efforts

As indicated, the United States maintained its quota so that 43,000 Jews entered in 1939. But US lawmakers did not follow Britain's *Kindertransport* example. A bill introduced by Senator Robert Wagner and Representative Edith Rogers to accept 20,000 German Jewish refugee children over the quota died in congressional committee between February and June 1939. As Washington socialite Laura Delano, a cousin of Roosevelt's, warned at cocktail parties, "[Twenty thousand] charming children would all too soon grow up to be 20,000 ugly adults."[71] Political observers noted that Congress was more likely to cut the quota than raise it.

Roosevelt, meanwhile, looked for alternatives. He proposed that world governments provide $400 million for resettlement, $150 million to come from the United States. He pressed Chamberlain's government to allow more Jews into Palestine and Transjordan. He suggested that the colonies Britain and France took from Germany after World War I, including the Cameroons and Tanganyika, might also be used for Jewish settlement. None of these ideas succeeded.

Latin American countries that wanted goodwill in Washington were more promising. In 1939, Brazil amended earlier restrictions and at least allowed 4,600 Jews to enter.[72] Bolivia was willing to accept settlers in the underdeveloped Chaco region, over which it had just fought a war with Paraguay. Over 20,000 Jews, including many from Poland, received visas and reached Bolivia between 1938 and 1944. Though many immediately left for Argentina and others resorted to peddling in La Paz—provoking antisemitic discourse there—Bolivia accepted more Jews than any other Latin American state after 1933. The JDC provided part of the settlement costs, as did Mauricio Hochschild, a Bolivian mining tycoon of German Jewish origin who was instrumental in the settlement scheme.

Roosevelt placed substantial hopes in the Caribbean nation of the Dominican Republic, where General Rafael Trujillo expressed willingness to accept up to 100,000 refugees. A corrupt and bloody dictator, Trujillo wanted more whites in the country as well as substantial payment (he offered to take the *St. Louis* passengers for $500 apiece). Through the State Department, Roosevelt pressured Trujillo to create humane settlement conditions. A US mission studied sites, and the JDC and individual Jewish donors helped with costs. But the inchoate project took too

---

[69]Figures and quotes above from Avni, *Argentina and the Jews*, pp. 143–6.

[70]Avni, *Argentina and the Jews*, p. 148.

[71]Quoted in Barbara McDonald Stewart, *United States Government Policy on Refugees from Nazism, 1933–1940* (New York, 1982), p. 532.

[72]*AJC Yearbook*, vol. 43, p. 691.

long. Trujillo granted 5,000 visas and made land available, but by then it was 1940. Only 757 Jews reached the country. Most left after the war.[73]

Shanghai: The Unlikely Refuge

As war drew closer, the surest haven for those lacking visas was the Chinese port city of Shanghai. Following the Opium War between China and Britain (1839–1842), Shanghai was one of five Chinese ports opened for international trade. Within the city, the British developed a self-governing district called the International Settlement where foreign business could function under European laws. About 1,000 Middle Eastern Jews and 5,000 from the Russian Empire moved to Shanghai thereafter and engaged in large business and small trade.

War between Imperial Japan and China erupted in full in July 1937. After heavy bombardment, Japanese troops in December occupied Chinese Shanghai, but not the International Settlement. Chinese officials could not exercise immigration control in Shanghai and, for the moment, neither passports nor visas were required to enter. German Jews could get there directly on liners, primarily from Italy.

The very name *Shanghai* was synonymous with overcrowding, disease, and crime. Indeed 1.5 million desperate Chinese refugees fled the countryside for Shanghai by late 1938. Michael Blumenthal, whose family escaped Berlin after *Kristallnacht*, remembered that, compared with other destinations, Shanghai was "the worst place to go. . . . A very frightening prospect."[74] Passage was also prohibitively expensive, and German swindlers played on Jews' desperation. Many Jews preferred to remain in Germany and wait for passage elsewhere.

Ernest Heppner's parents decided on Shanghai after *Kristallnacht* and after learning of the wait for entry into the United States. The family could purchase but two tickets. Ernest and his mother left his father and older sister and boarded a train for Genoa. They were allowed to take 10 marks each. German officials strip-searched them at the Italian border for additional cash and jewelry. From Genoa, they reached Shanghai. "It was difficult to believe," Heppner remembered, "that no one asked us for our papers as we passed through the customs house. . . . Hundreds of thousands of Jews in Europe were trying to find a country permitting them entry, and here Jews could just walk ashore!"[75]

International Settlement leaders in Shanghai protested the influx because most Jewish refugees settled in that part of the city. But Japanese officials did not create serious obstacles before the war. They imagined that supposed Jewish power might aid Japan's war effort, and that help for Jewish refugees would win friends in Washington, whose acquiescence Tokyo wanted for Japan's expansion in the Far East.[76]

Some 17,000 German-speaking Jewish refugees lived in Shanghai by May 1940 Initial arrivals benefited from the help of the local Jewish community. Some—perhaps 10 percent—quickly supported themselves in business and professions. Shanghai soon had nearly a dozen German-Jewish newspapers, including medical journals. More lived a tenuous existence, often in group dormitories in the International Settlement's overcrowded Hongkou district, supported by

---

[73]On Bolivia and the Dominican Republic, see Breitman et al., eds. *Refugees and Rescue*, pp. 264–91; Allen Wells, *Tropical Zion: General Trujillo, FDR, and the Jews of Sosúa* (Durham, NC, 2009).

[74]Quoted in Steve Hochstadt, "Flucht ins Ungewisse: Die jüdische Emigration nach Shanghai," in *Exile Shanghai, 1938–1941*, eds. Georg Armbrüster et al. (Teetz, 2000), p. 29.

[75]Ernest Heppner, *Shanghai Refuge: A Memoir of the World War II Jewish Ghetto* (Lincoln, NE, 1993), p. 40.

[76]Gao Bei, *Shanghai Sanctuary: Chinese and Japanese Policy Toward European Refugees During World War II* (New York, 2012).

additional funds from financially established refugees and from the JDC.[77] Heppner remembered "the sight of these new arrivals, dressed in their heavy European clothing . . . waiting in line with tin pots in hand for their next meal."[78]

5.5 THE VATICAN AND THE JEWISH QUESTION

The Church and Antisemitism After World War I

For Catholics and non-Catholics in the western world, the Vatican served as a moral guide. It might have spoken forcefully against Nazi antisemitism, pressed Catholic Poland to halt abuses of Jews, and pressed Latin American governments to shelter more Jewish refugees. But it failed to speak forcefully in the 1930s. Partly, the church had not abandoned doctrines that blamed Jews for the crucifixion. Partly, the church feared that open protest might endanger its ability to administer pastoral care to Catholics in Germany.

There were elements in the Catholic Church who, by the 1920s, acknowledged the dangers of antisemitism. In the 1920s, a movement emerged called *Amici Israel* ("Friends of Israel") consisting of nineteen cardinals, 278 bishops, and about 3,000 priests. *Amici Israel* tried to alter the venomous language of the Good Friday liturgy, "Let us pray for the perfidous Jews. . . ." In 1928, *Amici Israel* noted to Pope Pius XI that "whenever Christians seek arguments for anti-Semitism they always cite this formulation." A less "corrosive" prayer for the Jews might lead to reconciliation and even Jewish conversions.

The proposal failed. Traditionalists surrounding the pope argued that the Good Friday prayer was based on Holy Scripture, particularly the Gospel of Matthew wherein the Jews say, "His blood be upon us and our children." The prayer, they said, suitably expressed "abhorrence for the rebellion and treachery of the chosen, disloyal, and deicidal people." Given this, reconciliation between Catholics and Jews could only come with the baptism of the latter, for which the church would still pray. The pope insisted that *Amici Israel* leaders retract their arguments, that *Amici Israel* be dissolved, and that its literature be destroyed.

Jewish publications viewed the dissolution ruefully. On March 22, 1928, Pope Pius XI approved a Vatican statement that condemned "the hatred against the people formerly chosen by God, the hatred that today customarily goes by the name antisemitism." This very general statement against blind hatred of Jews was designed to protect the Vatican against charges that *Amici Israel*'s dissolution was itself antisemitic. Later Catholic publications that year distinguished between unchristian, biological antisemitism and a more Christian "evaluation of the danger emanating from Jews," which included modern financial power on the one hand and revolution on the other.

How well readers understood this fine distinction is not clear. As historian Hubert Wolf puts it, "Pius XI wasted his big chance. It took decades and more than six million murdered Jews for the Church to summon the courage to cleanse its relationship with Jews of anti-Semitism."[79] Pope Benedict XVI altered the Good Friday prayer eighty years later: in 2008.

---

[77]In general, see the summary in Irene Eber, *Voices from Shanghai: Jewish Exiles in Wartime China* (Chicago, IL, 2008), pp. 1–27.

[78]Ernest Heppner, "The Relations Between the Western European Refugees and the Shanghai Resident Jews: A Personal Memoir," in *The Jews of China*, vol. 2, ed. Jonathan Goldstein (Armonk, NY, 2000), p. 59.

[79]Quotes about *Amici Israel* in Hubert Wolf, *Pope and Devil: The Vatican's Archives and the Third Reich* (Cambridge, MA, 2010), pp. 94, 105, 116, 121.

The Pope's Diplomat

Born in 1876, Eugenio Pacelli rose through the church hierarchy as a conservative cleric and trained diplomat. He served as papal nuncio in Germany from 1917 to 1929 and as Vatican secretary of state until 1939, when he succeeded Pope Pius XI as Pope Pius XII. In the 1930s, Pacelli had decisive influence on Pius XI and determined Vatican foreign policy.

Although he shared the religious antisemitism of fellow conservative clerics, including those in Germany, he also deplored the Nazi violence against Jews that erupted with Hitler's chancellorship and he looked dimly on Nazism's glorification of race. Nazism, he reported, was "perhaps the most dangerous heresy of our time."[80] But to Pacelli, the Vatican's primary mission was pastoral care of Catholics and he understood that Hitler could close churches in Germany. And like all Vatican officials, Pacelli was anticommunist because of communism's violent atheism, which defaced churches and killed priests in the USSR and in Spain's civil war from 1936 to 1939. If nothing else, the Nazis were anticommunists.

Pacelli thus made the best of a weak hand. In July 1933, he negotiated the Concordat between the Holy See and the German Reich. The concordat was to secure the religious prerogatives of the Catholic Church in Germany, but the guarantees were shaky. By 1936, the Nazis closed Catholic schools and dissolved Catholic youth groups while placing Catholic priests on trial on trumped up homosexuality charges. The Vatican sent numerous complaints to Berlin concerning breaches of the concordat, and in 1937, Pius XI issued an encyclical entitled "With Burning Anxiety," which protested the violations to no avail. But for the moment, the churches in Germany remained open and the sacraments were administered.

Pius XI and the Speech Not Given

As Nazi steps against Jews progressed, Pope Pius XI received countless letters from Jews and Catholics alike urging him to speak. Edith Stein, a Jewish convert to Catholicism and now a Carmelite nun in Cologne, brought an especially impassioned appeal. Jews and Catholics both, she said in 1933, "have been waiting and hoping for the Church of Christ to raise its voice to put a stop to this abuse of Christ's name." "Why," added Martin Gillet, the Master General of the Dominican Order in 1938, "is no voice raised?"[81]

No statement came. The Vatican feared that Hitler would retaliate with stronger measures against the church in Germany. "The battle against the Jews," said Cardinal Michael von Faulhaber, the Archbishop of Munich, "would then . . . become the struggle against the Catholics." Faulhaber, in any event, was most distressed that "even those [Jews] who have been baptized for ten or twenty years and are good Catholics . . . are legally still considered Jews."[82]

In 1938, Pius XI reached a breaking point. A series of antisemitic laws enacted by Mussolini in Italy starting in September (the pope's native land that, until now had no such legislation) might have been decisive. The laws barred Italian Jews from various professions and public education, prohibited foreign Jews from entering the country, retracted citizenship from Jews naturalized since 1919, and banned marriage between Jews and non-Jews. "I am ashamed to be an Italian," he said to his liaison to Mussolini, "and I want you, Father, to tell that to Mussolini!"[83]

[80]Wolf, *Pope and Devil*, p. 135.

[81]Wolf, *Pope and Devil*, pp. 185, 205.

[82]Saul Friedländer, *Nazi Germany and the Jews: The Years of Persecution, 1933–1939* (New York, 1997), p. 43.

[83]Wolf, *Pope and Devil*, p. 207.

Following *Kristallnacht*, Pius XI had Pacelli order Vatican representatives in the Americas and Australia ask whether these countries might take more Jewish refugees. Like Roosevelt, the pope misjudged how little time remained, and the Vatican received little cooperation in any event. The pope also planned a major speech for February 11, 1939, which was to attack Germany's treatment of Jews. But Pius XI's poor health betrayed him. He died the day before the speech. Pacelli ordered all printed copies and even the master plates in the Vatican printing office destroyed.[84]

We cannot know what might have happened had Pius XI acted sooner. An early energetic rejection of antisemitism in all of its forms, a condemnation of anti-Jewish legislation and violence in Europe, and pressure on Catholic states such as Argentina and Brazil to accept more Jews might have provided additional relief to Europe's Jews. As it was, Pacelli was now elected Pope Pius XII.

*****

In a lengthy speech to the Reichstag on January 30, 1939, commemorating the anniversary of his chancellorship, Adolf Hitler addressed the Jewish question. Either the Jews—all of them—would be accepted elsewhere, or they would be left to their fate. And should the world's Jews in Paris, London, and elsewhere start a new war, he warned, the reckoning would come.

> I would like to say the following on the Jewish question: It is truly a shaming display when we see today the entire democratic world filled with tears of pity at the plight of the poor, tortured Jewish people while remaining heard-hearted and obstinate in view of what is therefore its obvious duty: to help. . . .
>
> We are determined to undercut the efforts of a certain foreign people to nest here. . . . We will banish this people. . . . Should not the outside world be most grateful to us for setting free these glorious bearers of culture and placing them at its disposal?
>
> I believe the earlier this problem is resolved, the better. For Europe cannot find peace before it has dealt properly with the Jewish question. . . . There is more than enough room for settlement on this earth. . . . Either the Jews will have to adjust to constructive, respectable activities . . . or, sooner or later, they will succumb to a crisis of yet inconceivable proportions.
>
> And there is yet one more topic on which I would like to speak on this day, perhaps not only memorable for us Germans: I have been a prophet very often in my lifetime, and this earned me mostly ridicule. In the time of my struggle for power, it was primarily the Jewish people who mocked my prophecy that, one day, I would assume leadership of this Germany, of this State, of the entire *Volk*, and that I would press for a resolution of the Jewish question. . . . The resounding laughter of the Jews in Germany . . . may well be stuck in their throats today. . . .
>
> Once again I will be a prophet: should the international Jewry of finance succeed, both within and beyond Europe, in plunging mankind into another world war, then the result will be not a Bolshevization of the earth and the victory of Jewry, but the annihilation of the Jewish race in Europe.[85]

Emigration was still Germany's preferred solution. But the language of extermination now entered the public vocabulary.

---

[84]Wolf, *Pope and Devil*, p. 210.

[85]Max Domarus, ed., *Hitler: Speeches and Proclamations*, vol. 3 (Wauconda, IL, 1997) pp. 1146–49.

6

The Assault on Poland's Jews, 1939–1941

When Germany conquered Poland in September 1939, 2 million additional Jews suddenly came under German control. Most were Yiddish-speaking and unassimilated. On touring Poland in November, Joseph Goebbels referred to them as "animals"—a collective "waste product"—but also as "predators with a cold intellect, which have to be rendered harmless."[1] But how would this be done?

The systematic annihilation of Poland's entire Jewish population did not develop until late 1941. But Nazi policy toward Poland's Jews was genocidal even in 1939. Hitler spoke in apocalyptic terms about the fate of Europe's Jews should war come. Now their lives were utterly without value. Tens of thousands of Jews in Poland were killed from 1939 to 1941 through deliberately imposed terror, exposure, disease, and starvation.

Many Jews fled. Many of those who did not flee worked to preserve their families and communities, some wondering what the Jewish future in Europe might be. Survival until Hitler's defeat was everyone's aim. Yet Germany's enemies were divided and unprepared for war. Its downfall was years, not months, in the future.

6.1 THE NAZI ASSAULT ON POLAND

Terror

At 6:00 a.m. on September 1, 1939, German forces attacked Poland. The diplomatic path was clear. Days before the attack, the Germans concluded a nonaggression pact with Joseph Stalin's Soviet Union. If Great Britain and France wished to fight over Poland's fate, they would do so alone. On September 3, London and Paris declared war on Germany, but German forces overran Poland in two weeks. The Soviet Union cooperated with Germany. Secret provisions of the German-Soviet nonaggression pact divided eastern Europe into spheres of influence. On September 17, the Red Army attacked Poland from the east, incorporating territories lost after

---

[1]Quotes in Saul Friedländer, *Nazi Germany and the Jews, 1939–1945: The Years of Extermination* (New York, 2007), pp. 17, 21.

World War I. The new German-Soviet border in what had been Poland was set on September 28 along the Bug River.

Hitler's war in Poland was criminal from the start. It aimed not at the recovery of the Polish Corridor, but rather, as Hitler told his army officers, at living space for the German people and the reduction of Poles to a state of slavery. By the end of the war, 3 million Poles had died from combat operations, bombing, shooting, slave labor, and Nazi reprisals. The initial campaign aimed to terrorize Poland into surrender. In repeated sorties over Warsaw in September 1939, German aircraft killed 30,000 people, mostly civilians, possibly more than the Allies killed during their controversial firebombing of Dresden in February 1945. The Germans also bombed 158 other cities and towns.[2]

Another immediate aim was to eliminate Poland's national leadership in a campaign code-named Operation Tannenberg. "Only a nation whose upper ranks are destroyed," Hitler said, "can be pushed into the ranks of slavery."[3] Atrocities were carried out by the regular armed forces; three SS-Death's Head Regiments; seven mobile police task forces known as *Einsatzgruppen*, which were created from Gestapo and SD officers by Himmler's Security Police Chief Reinhard Heydrich; five battalions of uniformed Order Police; and ethnic Germans who had chafed under Polish rule and itched to settle scores. They targeted Catholic priests, aristocrats, civil servants, and teachers. By the end of October, 16,000 Poles were executed by firing squad. By the end of the year, the Germans had murdered some 50,000 civilians.[4]

Poland's Jews, from leaders to the impoverished, formed another kind of target. From west to east, they suffered a massive, sustained pogrom for which even the past two decades had not prepared them. Synagogues were torched and Torah scrolls desecrated. The Germans burned the famous 400,000-book Talmudic Library in the Jewish Theological Seminary in Lublin. The fire blazed for twenty hours. The Germans struck up a military band to drown out Jewish cries. "For us," remembered one of the burners, "it was a matter of special pride to destroy the Talmudic Academy which had been known as the greatest in Poland."[5]

Jews also suffered shocking loss of life, disproportionately making up 15 percent of civilians killed in Poland in 1939.[6] In September, on the High Holy Days of Rosh Hashanah and Yom Kippur, German bombers and artillery targeted Warsaw's Jewish quarter. Roughly 5,000 Jews there were killed and 20,000 Jewish apartments destroyed.[7] Jews elsewhere were horse-whipped, tortured, and shot. Women were gang-raped. Religious men's beards were cut off with bayonets or set on fire. From September to December 1939, in the town of Bydgoszcz in the Polish Corridor, German police simply killed or expelled all Jews. "The Jewish problem," reported a police unit, "no longer exists in Bydgoszcz."[8]

Individual memories are searing. Jacob Wolhendler was a child when German troops took Zawiercie, a city in western Poland with 7,000 Jews. "Toward the evening the soldiers burst into the house and ordered all outside. . . . I was near my father. Suddenly my father fell to the ground;

---

[2]Figure in Timothy Snyder, *Bloodlands: Europe Between Hitler and Stalin* (New York, 2010), p. 119.

[3]Quoted in Snyder, *Bloodlands*, p. 126.

[4]Alexander B. Rossino, *Hitler Strikes Poland: Blitzkrieg, Ideology, and Atrocity* (Lawrence, KS, 2003), pp. 29–87, 234.

[5]Quoted in Steven J. Whitfield, "Where They Burn Books," *Modern Judaism*, vol. 22, no. 3 (October 2002), pp. 213–33.

[6]Rossino, *Hitler Strikes Poland*, p. 234.

[7]Figure in Martin Dean, *Robbing the Jews: The Confiscation of Jewish Property in the Holocaust, 1933–1945* (New York, 2008), p. 178.

[8]Quoted in Central Commission for the Investigation of German Crimes in Poland, *German Crimes in Poland* (Warsaw, 1946), p. 143.

German soldiers and Polish civilians watch as one Jewish man is forced to shave the beard of another in Tomaszów Mazowiecki in western Poland, September 1939. *Source:* Instytut Pamieci Narodowe, courtesy of the United States Holocaust Memorial Museum.

he had been shot by one of the soldiers. I fell on him and saw the blood bursting out from my father's body. He was dead in the next few minutes. I had to leave him there. . . ."[9] In the eastern Polish town of Włodawa, German officers ordered the Hasidic Reb Avrom Mordkhe Maroco to destroy his Torah scrolls or be burned alive. He refused. They doused him in gasoline and set him alight, throwing the Torah on the fire.[10]

Perhaps 300,000 Jews fled over the Soviet border before the Soviets sealed it in December. But German army and police units drove other Jews across the Polish border whether bridges existed or not. The Germans herded the Jews from the border *shtetl* of Dubiecko to the San River. "[The] Germans," says the Dubiecko memorial book, "pushed them into the river water and some of them drowned during the crossing. . . . [On] the Soviet side of the San River . . . Ukrainian peasants robbed them of the rest of their belongings."[11] Army officers occasionally protested the violence. Hitler angrily dismissed the complaints and then removed Poland from the army's jurisdiction in October, handing security tasks over to SS and Police Chief Heinrich Himmler.

Jews who fled to the USSR became refugees. Over 33,000 fled to Białystok. "At first, they slept in fields and forests," remembered Felicja Nowak, who reached Białystok from Warsaw. "Afterwards they found temporary shelter in railway stations, empty trucks . . . synagogues, schools and pioneer collectives. Here they lived for months like herds of animals, hungry and

---

[9]Jacob Wolhendler, "The Beginning and the End," in *Flares of Memory: Stories of Childhood During the Holocaust*, ed. Anita Brostoff (New York, 2001), pp. 32–33.

[10]Samuel D. Kassow, *Who Will Write Our History? Emanuel Ringelblum, the Warsaw Ghetto, and the Oyneg Shabes Archive* (Bloomington, IN, 2007), p. 168.

[11]Abraham Wein and Aharon Weiss, eds. *Encyclopedia of Jewish Communities in Poland*, vol. 3 (Jerusalem, 1984), pp. 103–5.

unwashed."[12] Some 20,000 reached Vilna, a center of Jewish culture now in still-independent Lithuania. "Thus they trudged over the streets of Vilna," wrote diarist Hermann Kruk, "refugees from all over Poland . . . searching for an open door, some water to wash with, a board to lie down on. . . ."[13]

Expulsion

Germany divided its part of Poland into two major sections. The first comprised Poland's western territories, including the old Polish Corridor regions of Danzig, West Prussia, Posen, and East Upper Silesia. It had a prewar population of 8.9 million ethnic Poles and between 550,000 and 600,000 Jews. Germany annexed these lands to the Reich, just as it annexed Austria in 1938. Hitler wanted the region fully Germanized and entrusted the task to Himmler, who assumed the additional title Reich Commissioner for Strengthening of Germandom. Imagining the new lands populated with hearty German farmers, Himmler went to work instantly.

Over 1 million ethnic German settlers were to come from areas under Soviet control, including the former Polish-ruled areas of eastern Galicia and Volhynia (now part of the Soviet Ukraine), the Baltic States and Romanian areas soon to be taken by the Soviets, and from South Tyrol in northern Italy. The center of German resettlement was to be the *Warthegau*—the largest district in the newly annexed lands. Settlers began arriving immediately and by mid-1941, 300,000 ethnic Germans lived in the district. Answering "the call of the Führer" to come "home to the Reich," they expected homes and employment.[14]

Poles and Jews living in the newly annexed lands were to be moved forcibly into the other major German-controlled territory in what had been Poland. This was the General Government—the rump region of Poland established in October 1939 that now formed a buffer between Germany and the Soviet Union. It included the cities of Warsaw, Kraków, Radom, and Lublin, and had a population of about 12 million, including nearly half—perhaps 1.4 million—of Poland's prewar Jewish population. Refugees from the Reich territories were dumped there with next to nothing. The General Government became a colony of misery.

The top civilian official in the General Government was the General Governor, Hans Frank, a long-standing Hitler crony and Nazi Party lawyer. His governing bureaucracy was in Kraków, and he answered to Hitler alone. Frank could entertain guests by playing Chopin's piano nocturnes (he had some admiration for Polish culture) while remaining indifferent to mass suffering. In the meantime he aimed to make the General Government into a productive industrial region. But Frank had a rival in Himmler, who saw the General Government as a racial dung heap.

Because Himmler controlled the police apparatus, he ultimately won the arguments. On September 27, 1939, Himmler restructured most of Germany's police network into an umbrella agency called the Reich Security Main Office (RSHA) under Reinhard Heydrich. The RSHA was responsible for combating enemies at home and in occupied territories. Himmler also had a network of personal subordinates, titled Higher SS and Police Leaders, who, along with their own subordinates, held broad police powers in occupied regions and overruled German civilian authorities.

---

[12]Sara Bender, *The Jews of Białystok During World War II and the Holocaust* (Lebanon, NH, 208), p. 53.

[13]Hermann Kruk, *The Last Days of the Jerusalem of Lithuania: Chronicles from the Vilna Ghetto and the Camps, 1939–1944* (New Haven, CT, 2002), p. 29.

[14]Rainer Schulze, "'Der Führer ruft!' Zur Rückholung der Volksdeutschen aus dem Osten" in, eds., Jerzy Kochanowski and Maike Sach *Die "Volksdeutschen" in Polen, Frankreich, Ungarn und der Tschechoslowakei: Mythos und Realität* (Osnabrück, 2006), pp. 183–204.

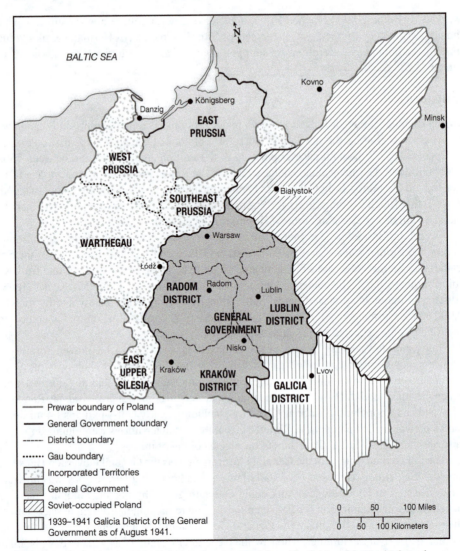

MAP 6.1 Occupied Poland, 1939–1941. *Source:* Reprinted from *The Origins of the Final Solution* by Christopher R. Browning, by permission of the University of Nebraska Press. Copyright 2004 by Yad Vasham, the Holocaust Martyrs and Heroes' Remembrance Authority, Jerusalem, Israel.

Mass expulsions from annexed lands to the General Government began quickly. In October 1939, Himmler ordered that, by February 1940, all Jews (then estimated at 550,000) would leave the annexed lands for the General Government, as would all politically suspect Poles (perhaps 450,000): 1 million deportees in four months. But deportations could not proceed as planned. Jews in the annexed territories lived in urban centers such as Łódź. Most arriving ethnic Germans were farmers, not businessmen. They had to displace rural Poles rather than urban Jews, and they were to receive generous plots of land.

Meanwhile the railways were overtaxed. Aside from resettlements, the army needed the rails to move troops west in 1939 and then east again in 1941. The rails could not accommodate

Himmler's timetables. Frank, meanwhile, increasingly complained about the number of refugees dumped into the General Government. After a series of plans and targets, the RSHA issued a stop order in March 1941. By that time, perhaps 47,000 Jews and 370,000 Poles were removed from the annexed lands either in systematic or spontaneous, "wild" actions. Over 250,000 angry ethnic Germans still waited in temporary camps in the *Warthegau* for their new stolen homes.[15]

But the disappointing pace of deportation did not make the process less brutal. German police rousted deportees from their homes, gave them an hour or less to pack, and allowed them to take but 200 złoty in cash (Jews could take 50 złoty). Valuables and the keys to their homes were left behind and bank accounts were surrendered. Deportees were moved to transit camps, body-searched for valuables, then placed on trains to various points in the General Government. "One could see entire families," remembered Yehoshua Eibeshitz of Kalish, "pushing and dragging baby carriages filled with linens, clothes, and books. The Germans inspected the contents . . . to make sure they weren't 'smuggling' anything."[16] Deportees spent days in overcrowded freight or open flatbed cars with no food or blankets in severe cold waiting for tracks to open up. Trains arrived in the winter of 1939–1940 with men, women, and children frozen to death. "It's just the climate there," Himmler shrugged. "I consider it wrong to moan and groan about it now."[17]

Jews in the annexed lands who were not deported were further terrorized. Most notable was Łódź, a textile city on the edge of the *Warthegau*, which the Germans in 1939 renamed Litzmannstadt after the German general who conquered it in World War I. It was redesigned with new parks, boulevards, and even lakes. A third of the population was Jewish, but Jews could not be moved immediately because Łódź was a railroad chokepoint. Łódź district governor Friedrich Übelhör ordered in November 1939 that all Jews wear stars colored "Jew-Yellow," on pain of death, to distinguish them from Poles.[18] Jewish businesses were to be marked with yellow signs, with the word "*Jude*" so that they could be identified. Remaining synagogues were destroyed. Łódź Jews were driven in February and March 1940 into a sealed ghetto in the city's most primitive neighborhoods. "The final goal," said Übelhör, "must be that we completely burn out this pestilence."[19] Long processions of Jews accompanied by their children, carrying what little they still had, entered the ghetto amid catcalls from German police and Polish civilians.

Expropriation

The plunder of Jewish property in Poland began with the invasion. In a nationwide spree, German soldiers, police officers, administrators, and local ethnic Germans helped themselves to Jewish property, ranging from silverware to furniture, to bolts of cloth, in both homes and businesses. In September 1939, the army declared Jewish bank accounts and safety deposit boxes blocked.

---

[15]Figures on Jews and Poles in Christopher R. Browning, *The Origins of the Final Solution: The Evolution of Nazi Jewish Policy, September 1939–March 1942* (Lincoln, NE, 2004), pp. 43–44, 99, 109. German figures in Götz Aly, *Final Solution: Nazi Population Policy and the Murder of Europe's Jews* (London, 1999), p. 149.

[16]Yehoshua Eibeshitz, *The Uprooted: A Survivor's Autobiography* (Haifa, 2002), p. 273.

[17]Quoted in Philip Rutherford, *Prelude to the Final Solution: The Nazi Program for Deporting Ethnic Poles, 1939–1941* (Lawrence, KS, 2007), p. 102.

[18]Quoted in Philip Friedman, *Roads to Extinction: Essays on the Holocaust* (New York, 1980), p. 12.

[19]Isaiah Trunk, ed., *Łódź Ghetto: A History* (Bloomington, IN, 2006), doc. 4.

Jews could hold but 2,000 złoty at one time, take but 250 złoty weekly from their accounts, and receive in payment for services or goods no more than 500 złoty. Such restrictions placed a near-freeze on any Jewish commerce on all but the smallest-scale enterprises.

More systematic, "legalized" confiscations in Poland followed. In his first public speech as general governor, Hans Frank promised that Poles in his region could live through their labors. But there was "no place for agitators, profiteers, or Jewish parasites."[20] In September 1939, Hermann Göring, as head of the Four-Year Plan, made all Jewish property in German-occupied Poland subject to confiscation through trusteeship. By mid-1940, nearly 200,000 large and small Jewish businesses in the annexed lands were appropriated, some 75 percent of all Jewish businesses in Warsaw were liquidated, and 20,000 railroad cars packed with stolen stocks chugged into Germany.[21]

Some materials essential for the war effort, such as cloth, went right to the army. Others, such as furs, were sold to countries such as Sweden to pay for strategic materials such as iron ore. Former Jewish businesses such as factories were sold to German buyers, the latter using easy credit provided by German banks. And though such plunder was made legal by official decree, there was plenty of high- and low-level corruption. Rivers of stolen property ran through Hans Frank's administration in Kraków. His four opulent residences in the General Government were stocked with everything from fine art to furs, to jewelry. Jews, meanwhile, were left with next to nothing.

Forced Labor

Jewish forced labor was another form of plunder. Starting with the occupation, German police and army authorities seized Jewish men off the streets for day labor, for everything from local road construction to unloading trucks to snow removal. In October 1939, Frank proclaimed all Jews subject to forced labor, the details to be left to Friedrich-Wilhelm Krüger, Himmler's Higher SS and Police Leader in the General Government. Jewish leaders in Warsaw and then elsewhere began to raise labor battalions for the Germans. It was preferable to Jews being seized without warning. In Warsaw alone, the Germans used 8,000 to 9,000 Jews per day by May 1940. Frank's offices made efforts to organize Jewish labor by having card files for Jewish workers broken down by craft. In fact, Jewish workers were driven like animals.

From summer to fall 1940, the Germans created over fifty labor camps in the General Government with some 30,000 Jews. Most were in the General Government's easternmost Lublin district under the Higher SS and Police Leader there, Odilo Globocnik, a brutal Austrian Nazi. Jews dug antitank ditches on the Soviet border, built roadbeds, and dug canals. Horrid camp conditions included death from starvation, disease, overwork, and sadism by guards. Even small camps of 400 to 500 Jews had a dozen fatalities a day. Many Jews never returned to their families, and those who did were ruined men. Because labor was free, lives were cheap. In the end, just thirteen miles of antitank ditches were dug: The construction of the camps cost more than the amount of labor squeezed from the Jews who were living in them.[22]

---

[20]Quoted in Yisrael Gutman, *The Jews of Warsaw, 1939–1943: Ghetto, Underground, Revolt* (Bloomington, IN, 1982), p. 15.

[21]Figures in Isaiah Trunk, *Judenrat: The Jewish Councils of Eastern Europe Under Nazi Occupation* (Lincoln, NE, 1972), p. 64; Martin Dean, *Robbing the Jews*, p. 177ff.

[22]Figures in Raul Hilberg, *The Destruction of the European Jews*, 3rd ed., vol. 1 (New Haven, CT, 2003), pp. 252, 258–59. See also Christopher Browning, *Nazi Policy, Jewish Workers, German Killers* (New York, 2000), pp. 60–4.

6.2 SCHEMES FOR JEWISH COLONIZATION

Hitler's speech of January 1939, wherein he prophesized the extermination of Europe's Jews, might have revealed his ultimate intentions; however, it did not reveal methods. At the start of the occupation, the Germans worked on plans of mass Jewish migration to closed reservations where Jews would be permanently segregated from the rest of Europe. These schemes never got off the ground, and historians are divided as to how seriously the Germans took them. Nonetheless their genocidal nature provides a clue toward German thinking between emigration and mass murder.

The Lublin Reservation

In negotiating the new border with the Soviet Union in September 1939, the Germans gave the Soviets influence over Lithuania in return for an additional slice of Polish territory between the Vistula and the Bug Rivers. Centered on the city of Lublin, it became the easternmost region of the General Government. On September 29, the day after the agreement with Moscow, Hitler told Alfred Rosenberg, an old fighter of the Nazi movement and one of its chief ideologues, that all Jews in the Reich and in Poland would be moved to a reservation in this area, separated from the rest of Reich territory by a giant barrier on the Vistula River. The same day, Heydrich mentioned the impending Reich ghetto in the Lublin area to his RSHA division heads.[23]

The Lublin reservation was a genocidal solution to the Jewish question. On November 20, Hans Frank's district governor of Lublin, Friedrich Schmidt, told Frank's visiting delegation that "[t]his area with its very swampy character . . . could very well serve as a Jewish reservation," adding that it "could lead to strong decimation of the Jews."[24] Frank concurred when addressing German officials at Radom on November 25. Noting that the impending winter would be severe, Frank noted that "[w]e won't waste much time on the Jews. . . . The more that die the better. . . . We want to put ½ to ¾ of all Jews east of the Vistula. We will crush the Jews wherever we can. Everything is at stake. Get the Jews out of the Reich, Vienna, everywhere."[25]

The Lublin scheme was no secret. The international press discussed its deadly nature. The London *Times* posited that "[t]o thrust 3,000,000 Jews, relatively few of whom are agriculturalists, into the Lublin region . . . would doom them to famine. . . . That, perhaps, is the intention."[26] By the end of the year, the progressive US periodical *The Nation* commented that nearly 2 million Jews crammed into an area of eighty by a hundred kilometers and unable to trade with neighboring areas could not create a viable community: "One cannot imagine," it said, "that they will survive until the first harvest."[27]

The first shipments of Jews to the Lublin Reservation came from the Reich itself—Germany, Austria, and the Protectorate of Bohemia and Moravia—where there were still 365,000 Jews in September 1939 that Nazi leaders itched to expel. Adolf Eichmann, the head of the Central Office for Jewish Emigration, rose to even greater importance. After the formation of the

[23]Hans Seraphim, ed., *Das politische Tagebuch Alfred Rosenbergs aus den Jahren 1934/35 und 1939/40: Nach der photographischen Wiedergabe der Handschrift aus den Nürnberger Akten* (Göttingen, 1956), p. 98.

[24]International Military Tribunal, *Trial of the Major War Criminals Before the International Military Tribunal, Nuremberg, 14 November 1945–1 October 1946* (herafter *TMWC*), vol. 30 (Nuremberg, 1949), Document PS-2278, p. 95.

[25]Jeremy Noakes and Geoffrey Pridham, eds., *Nazism 1919–1945: A Documentary Reader*, vol. 3, new ed. (Exeter, 2001), p. 447.

[26]Quoted in Aly, *Final Solution*, pp. 17–18.

[27]Quoted in Jonny Moser, "Nisko: The First Experiment in Deportation, *Simon Wiesenthal Center Annual*, 2 (1985), pp. 1–30.

RSHA, Eichmann also became chief of the Gestapo's new department for Jewish affairs, eventually designated RSHA Office IV [Gestapo] B [Sects] 4 [Jews]. On October 15, 1939, Eichmann chose Nisko, a swampy area on the eastern border of the Lublin district on the San River, as the dumping point. The first Jews to go to Nisko were men, mainly engineers and builders, who could build barracks and make the region somewhat habitable.

Many Jews volunteered, hoping for sustenance in a new place. The first transports on October 18 and 20 included 912 Jews from Vienna, 901 from Moravian Ostrau in the Protectorate, and another 875 from Katowice in the annexed area of East Upper Silesia, plus building materials. Fewer were willing to go on the second transport. Leaving from Vienna on October 26, it included Jewish men conscripted from asylums and nursing homes. Eichmann met the first transport at Nisko. "The Führer has promised the Jews a new homeland," he proclaimed. "If you carry out the construction you will have a roof over your head. There is no water. Wells in the whole area are infested; cholera, dysentery, and typhoid are rampant. If you start digging and find water, then you will have water."[28]

Altogether Eichmann deported some 5,000 Reich Jews to the Nisko region before the idea collided with the aforementioned problems regarding the need to move Poles, Jews, and ethnic Germans in and out of the annexed lands by rail when the army also needed the trains. Meanwhile Jews from the annexed lands and from elsewhere in the General Government were driven into the Lublin district. By November 1941, some 65,000 Jewish refugees with no money and nothing to sell pushed the distressed Jewish population in the district to over 300,000. Some made their way into the Soviet Union, some to Globocnik's work camps in search of some shelter and food, some to Lublin itself.[29]

"Lublin," wrote a Jewish journalist, "is a vale of sorrow. . . . All are phantoms, shadows, haunting a world that is no longer in existence. Nobody speaks in Lublin. . . . They have even ceased to weep. . . . Men die like flies in the thoroughfares, their bodies strewn on the roadway like old cinders. . . . The devil himself could not have devised such hell."[30] Globocnik was indifferent. "The evacuated Jews," he said, "should feed themselves and be supported by their countrymen. . . . If this did not succeed, one should let them starve."[31]

The Madagascar Scheme

The other Jewish reservation scheme involved Madagascar. The Polish and Romanian governments pressed the French for permission to send their Jews to Madagascar in the 1930s. After *Kristallnacht*, Hitler mentioned the idea to Göring, and the Germans also raised the idea with the French government.[32] Germany's conquest of France in June 1940 and the expected British surrender (discussed in the next chapter) seemed to put French Africa at Germany's disposal for the 3.2 million Jews now under its control. Hitler mentioned Madagascar twice that summer, once to Mussolini and once to Erich Raeder, Germany's naval commander-in-chief.

[28]Figures in Moser; "Nisko: The First Experiment." Quote in David Cesarani, *Becoming Eichmann: Rethinking the Life, Crimes, and Trial of a "Desk Murderer"* (Cambridge, MA, 2004), pp. 79–80.

[29]Figures in Bogdan Musial, *Deutsche Zivilverwaltung und Judenverfolgung im Generalgouvernement: Eine Fallstudie zum Distrikt Lublin 1939–1941* (Wiesbaden, 1999), pp. 102, 157–159.

[30]S. Moldawer quoted in Jacob Apenszlak, gen. ed., *The Black Book of Polish Jewry: An Account of the Martyrdom of Polish Jewry Under the Nazi Occupation* (New York, 1943), pp. 93–94.

[31]Quoted in Dieter Pohl, *Von der "Judenpolitik" zum "Judenmord:" Der Distrikt Lublin des Generalgouvernements, 1939–1944* (Frankfurt am Main, 1993), p. 52.

[32]*TMWC*, vol. 28, Document 1816-PS, p. 539.

German Foreign Ministry officials planned to include the cession of Madagascar in the peace treaty with France, as well as the demand that the 25,000 French settlers leave the island. Eichmann's office thought that twenty ships with 1,500 Jews each could move 4 million Jews to Madagascar in four years.[33] Hans Frank's subordinates in the General Government, who complained about train-loads of Poles and Jews moving into their bailiwick, were thrilled. As early as January 1940, Frank had mentioned sending several million Jews to Madagascar. Now he hoped that the 250,000 Jews in the *Warthegau* (including Łódź, where local officials had been trying to move Jews into the General Government) would be the first to go. In July, Frank even halted the plans to construct a ghetto in Warsaw on the expectation that Jews there would also go to Madagascar.[34]

None of this materialized. The British did not surrender, the Germans never controlled the necessary ships or sea-lanes, and the anticipated peace conference with the French never occurred. But Madagascar, like Lublin, was a genocidal solution. Rail transports to the General Government provide an idea of what Jewish transports in cargo holds might have been like. And everyone knew the island's interior was malarial. In 1938, the former French governor of Madagascar, Marcel Oliver, assumed that Madagascar as a solution to the Jewish question involved decimation rather than settlement.[35]

Himmler was already thinking of more drastic solutions. In May 1940, he wrote a memo for Hitler that stated, "I hope to see the term 'Jews' fully eradicated through . . . a great emigration of all Jews to Africa. . . ."[36] But by July, he changed his mind. He ominously mentioned that "the other half," meaning Polish Jews, must remain in Europe. As Eichmann explained later, the biological foundations of Jewry lay with the eastern Jews, not the assimilated Jews of western Europe, whose birthrates were lower.[37] In 1940, they were viewed as hostages to ensure the good behavior of the Jews who supposedly controlled the US government, which seemed to be moving toward war. By 1941, Berlin determined that they would simply be murdered.

6.3 GHETTOIZATION IN POLAND

Organizing Poland's Jews

As the Germans tried to devise resettlement options, they worked to bring Poland's Jewish population under some sort of administrative order. The first step was a September 21, 1939, directive from Heydrich to his security police chiefs. For now, Heydrich ordered, Jews in Poland were to be moved from small towns to urban centers. "Jewish communities of fewer than 500 persons," he said, "are to be dissolved and to be transferred to the nearest city of concentration." This step, Heydrich continued, would "facilitate subsequent measures."[38] He did not commit to paper what these measures were.

---

[33]*TMWC*, vol. 26, Document 661-PS, pp. 207–39; analyses in Richard Breitman, *The Architect of Genocide: Himmler and the Final Solution* (New York, 1991), pp. 130–31; Browning, *Origins*, pp. 81–89.

[34]Diary of Hans Frank, National Archives and Records Administration, College Park, Maryland, (hereafter NARA), Microcopy Publication T-992, roll 2, July 3, 1940.

[35]Eric T. Jennings, "Writing Madagascar Back into the Madagascar Plan," *Holocaust and Genocide Studies*, vol. 21, no. 2 (2007): 187–217.

[36]Helmut Krausnick, ed., "Denkschrift Himmlers über die Behandlung der Fremdvölkischen im Osten, Mai 1940," *Vierteljahrshefte für Zeitgeschichte*, 5, no. 2, (1957), p. 197.

[37]Breitman, *Architect of Genocide*, pp. 125–26.

[38]Yitzhak Arad, Israel Gutman, and Abraham Margaliot, eds., *Documents on the Holocaust: Selected Sources on the Destruction of the Jews of Germany and Austria, Poland and the Soviet Union*, 8th ed. (Lincoln, NE, 1999), doc. 73.

Smaller Jewish communities that had existed for centuries were now expelled at gunpoint and streamed into the larger population centers with nothing. "There were no exceptions," said a one-time bookkeeper from Pułtusk, a town north of Warsaw with some 960 Jewish families. "Even old men with canes and sick people on the point of death were exiled." Polish villagers, he added, "attacked the rabbi, beat him up, and stole his last few pennies."[39]

Urban Jewish communities were also thrown into flux as the Germans worked to segregate Jews from Poles. During the invasion, Poles and Jews often cooperated against the common enemy. In Warsaw, they fought fires jointly as German aircraft dropped bombs and strafed civilians, and they built barricades to defend the city. Their welfare organizations coordinated and shared resources to help refugees.[40] The Germans wanted to end whatever camaraderie that existed. After October 1939, Hans Frank prohibited Polish welfare organizations from aiding Jews.[41] In November, he ordered that all Jews over ten years old in the General Government wear identifying armbands "at least 10 cm wide, with the Star of David on it," on pain of imprisonment.[42] He imposed curfews and prohibited rail travel by Jews. Local German administrators banned Jews from streetcars, restaurants, public parks, and promenades. Jewish doctors and dentists could not treat non-Jews. Jewish lawyers were disbarred altogether. Although Polish elementary and vocational schools were reopened in December 1939, all Jewish schools remained closed.

The Germans sponsored widespread Polish-language antisemitic print and radio propaganda. In Warsaw, diarist Chaim Kaplan noted its gist: "All your lives you have fought against the Jewish plague and you have accomplished nothing. We will show you the way."[43] Some Poles helped Jews regardless. In Kraków, Polish pharmacist Tadeusz Pankiewicz famously maintained his business in the ghetto after the ghetto was established in March 1941; he provided Jews with medicines as well as a place to relay information. A few helped Jews procure false Polish identity papers. Local hooligans, however, picked up where they left off before the war. They pointed out Jews, their businesses, and their apartments for the Germans to plunder, and they happily participated in humiliations, beatings, and robberies, even raiding peddlers of their last wares.

In March 1940, hundreds of young Polish toughs armed with crowbars launched a pogrom in Warsaw to coincide with Passover. They looted what they could still find from Jewish stores and homes, beating Jews as they went, while howling, "We want a Poland without Jews." Polish police officers watched. German observers snapped pictures. Young Bundists fighting back with pipes seem to have stopped this particular pogrom. But Kaplan noted the terrible irony. "The accursed youth," he wrote, "walking on the ruins of their homeland, organize demonstrations in honor of the Führer."[44]

The Making of Ghettos

Heydrich was ambivalent about closed Jewish ghettos, believing medieval ghettos to have been unsupervised hubs of Jewish power. He refused to create ghettos in Germany, and his September 1939

---

[39]Abraham I. Katsch, ed., *Scroll of Agony: The Warsaw Diary of Chaim Kaplan* (hereafter *Kaplan Diary*) (New York, 1965), October 26, 1939.

[40]Emanuel Ringelblum, *Polish-Jewish Relations During the Second World War* (Evanston, IL, 1992), pp. 23–36.

[41]Barbara Engelking and Jacek Leociak, *The Warsaw Ghetto: A Guide to the Perished City* (New Haven, CT, 2009), p. 296.

[42]Arad et al., eds, *Documents on the Holocaust*, doc. 74.

[43] *Kaplan Diary*, February 1, 1940. On propaganda, see Lucjan Dobroszycki, *Reptile Journalism: The Official Polish Language Press Under the Nazis, 1939–1945* (New Haven, CT, 1994).

[44] *Kaplan Diary*, March 28, 1940.

concentration order for Poland noted only that security requirements in Polish cities could necessitate prohibitions on Jews leaving their own neighborhoods. Ultimately local administrators decided the issue of individual ghettos, which emerged in the annexed territories and General Government between 1939 and 1942.[45] Of the more than 400 ghettos that came and went there, (and the eventual 1,150 in that the Germans set up in Poland and the USSR as a whole), no two were alike either in the circumstances of their establishment, their economies, or their size.[46] But the process was brutal everywhere.

German administrators delineated the worst urban neighborhoods for ghettos, excluded valuable enterprises from ghetto areas, and forced Jews into ghettos with short deadlines and terror. In Łódź, Jews were ordered into the ghetto on February 8, 1940. When they moved too slowly, German police shot roughly 200 to speed the process. "It is impossible to describe the hellish scenes," remembered Bernard Goldstein of the Bund when describing movement into the Warsaw ghetto in November. "Everywhere there was a wild panic, unashamed hysterical terror. The multitude filled the streets. . . . Long, long rows of little carts and all sorts of makeshift vehicles heaped with household possessions, wailing children, the old, the sick, the half dead . . . pulled or led by the stronger and healthier, who plodded along, tearful, despairing, bewildered."[47]

Jews already living in designated ghettos areas might at least have started with a dwelling. Jews from other parts of town or refugees from other towns entirely began with no more than they could carry. The abandonment of their furniture, the last property many poor Jews had, caused greater trauma than one imagines today. "Jewish housewives," wrote Josef Zelkowicz of Łódź, "have an umbilical relationship with their furniture. . . . This is because only they know how much agony and blood each saved penny cost, how many family quarrels erupted and how frequently, over every chair, every pot. Therefore, they moistened with their tears every item of furniture that they had to leave behind, parting from it like mothers forced to abandon and forsake their children."[48]

Poland's largest ghettos were terribly overcrowded. With insufficient sewage facilities, they became breeding grounds for typhus. The Warsaw ghetto, sealed in November 1940 by a ten-foot concrete wall, was by far Europe's largest. In March 1941, it had a population of 460,000 because of its large prewar Jewish population and the 90,000 Jewish refugees driven toward Warsaw by that time. German administrators and Polish residents, including Catholic clergy, were determined that the Jews receive as few blocks as possible, even in Warsaw's old Jewish quarter. Thus, Warsaw's Jews—30 percent of the city's population—were forced into 2.4 percent of Warsaw's space. The ratio of persons to rooms was 9.2 to 1. The ghetto in Łódź was Europe's second largest. According to a ghetto census of June 1940, 160,423 Jews were confined to a wretched space containing but 3,361 buildings. Forty-nine ghetto dwellings in Łódź had bathrooms.[49]

Other ghettos were less crowded. Kraków was the capital of the General Government and army officers there complained of seeing Jews in their apartment buildings. Thus, Hans Frank decreed in 1940 that Kraków would be the region's "most Jew-free city."[50] He provided

---

[45]Dan Michman, *The Emergence of Jewish Ghettos During the Holocaust* (New York, 2011).

[46]All described in Geoffrey P. Megargee and Martin Dean, eds., *The United States Holocaust Memorial Museum Encyclopedia of Camps and Ghettos, 1939–1945*, vol. 2 (Bloomington, IN, 2012).

[47]Bernard Goldstein, *The Stars Bear Witness* (London, 1950), p. 64.

[48]Josef Zelkowicz, *In Those Terrible Days: Writings from the Łódź Ghetto* (Jerusalem, 2002), p. 58.

[49]Figures in Engelking and Leociak, *Warsaw* Ghetto, p. 49; Gutman, *Jews of Warsaw*, p. 60; Trunk, ed., *Łódź Ghetto*, pp. 13–16, 46.

[50]Diary of Hans Frank, Abteilungsleitersitzungen, April 12, 1940, NARA, RG 238, entry 7C, box 1, vol. 2.

incentives for Jews to leave by allowing them to transport their property, but this ploy did not clear Jews from the city. The Germans established the ghetto in March 1941 outside the city limits in the Podgórze suburb across the Vistula River, where 24,000 Jews lived in 320 buildings. Despite the lesser numbers, Mieczysław Staner, a Jewish teenager at the time, remembered that Jews in Kraków lived "in sanitary conditions far below anybody's imagination."[51]

Survival in Ghettos

Food in ghettos was never sufficient thanks to wartime shortages and the Germans' determination that Jews receive the most meager provisions. For the Warsaw ghetto in 1941, local German administrators allowed an average equivalent of about 253 calories per day, per inhabitant.[52] Quality was poor. The Łódź ghetto chronicle from July 1942 reads, "Yesterday a shipment of 800 kilograms of meat in a state of advanced decay arrived. . . . There were green, yellow [and] white pieces. . . . Not long ago we wrote about the arrival of 10,000 kilograms of butter. It was completely rancid and black. . . . After repeated washing, the Milk Department managed to remove the bitterness and derive a product that was relatively clean and digestible for the ghetto's residents' stomachs that are used to everything."[53] Loaves of bread that were to last a week and thin soup made from potato peels were staples for most.

Smuggling became a question of life and death. It was easier in some ghettos. The ghetto in Lublin, with its 40,000 Jews, was not sealed, and residents could procure food from local Poles via black market connections. The Warsaw ghetto procured 80 to 97.5 percent of its food through smuggling.[54] Child smugglers there sneaked through gaps in the wall to help their families. Sometimes German policemen did not shoot at them; sometimes they did. Jewish underworld elements in Warsaw who understood the smuggling business maintained outside contacts to import goods, snuck into the ghetto via Polish contractors. Some smugglers became relatively rich, frequenting incongruous ghetto restaurants and cabarets. Łódź had almost no smuggling. Embedded within a Germanized city, the ghetto was tightly sealed, and its currency was not Polish złoty but special ghetto marks, valueless outside the ghetto.

Ghetto existence revolved around food. Josef Zelkowicz described a Jewish housewife's day in Łódź:

> At 6:00 a.m. she has to line up for bread. At 8:00 a.m. they open the milk cooperative where she has to grab a place in line to get a quarter liter of milk for her youngest son, who is a toddler. Later on, she will go from door to door to sell the milk to the affluent for thirty pfennigs, so she can redeem coupons for soup at the public kitchen. . . . To accomplish that, she has to stand in one line for coupons and in another for soup. Then, after gulping down the lunch she got at the kitchen, she circulates desperately among neighbors so she can prepare the dish that she will cook: a few groats here, some beets there, a little oil somewhere else—she promises to return it after the next distribution—and a bit of borrowed salt elsewhere. One neighbor gives her, a tablet of saccharine; another neighbor a match. . . . When all the ingredients are ready, she'll have to spend several hours at the stove, blowing on the fire so the soup in the pot will cook. As that happens, night falls. . . .[55]

---

[51]Mieczysław Staner, *The Eyewitness* (Krakow, 1999), p. 7.

[52]Figure in Engelking and Leociak, *Warsaw Ghetto*, p. 417.

[53]Trunk, ed., *Łódź Ghetto*, doc. 74.

[54]Figure in Engelking and Leociak, *Warsaw Ghetto*, p. 458.

[55]Zelkowicz, *In Those Terrible Days*, p. 58.

Fuel was also in short supply. The Germans did not supply coal, which left ghetto residents scrambling to burn anything in the winter months. In the winter of 1940–1941, Łódź Jews dismantled fences and old buildings for fuel. They burned their furniture, their floorboards, their wall supports, their doors, and finally their bedding to keep warm. Children, known colloquially as "coal miners," searched garbage for anything flammable. Most inhabitants had no heavy clothing. The Germans had confiscated it.

Work was essential. Employment meant pay, and pay—however insufficient—meant food, particularly once possessions were sold. Some inhabitants could leave the ghetto by day if they had skilled jobs outside in essential industries. Specially issued work permits allowed them to come and go through guarded ghetto gates. Most were trapped, and with their livelihoods already taken, many had no means of support. "People who were engineers yesterday," wrote Henryk Brysker of the Warsaw ghetto, "are happy to get a job as a doorman today; a lawyer—a peddler of candies; one who was a rich merchant a little while ago stands in line to receive a free portion of soup from the low-class charity kitchen; a professor of music plays in the streets. . . ."[56]

Production or Attrition?

By late 1940, German ghetto managers understood that ghettos could produce goods inexpensively for the army or domestic markets. Hans Biebow, who oversaw the Łódź ghetto with its textile workshops, called for more sewing machines and for slightly higher rations for working Jews. By summer 1941, 40,000 Jews worked in the Łódź ghetto compared to only 5,000 in October 1940. German firms also began setting up workshops in the Warsaw ghetto to produce everything from brushes to shoes, to metal goods, at minimal cost. By June 1942, because of the lengthening war, these workshops employed up to 25,000 workers. Over the same period, Jewish authorities set up training programs that accommodated 20,000.[57]

But whatever the benefits of Jewish war production, ideology trumped pragmatism, particularly in regard to a despised population amid general shortages. The Germans never increased food deliveries to any effect. Thus, in the Warsaw ghetto, writer Stefan Ernst guessed that perhaps 20,000 Jews were "properly nourished," 200,000 made do "more or less . . . their bodies not swollen by hunger," and 250,000 were beggars attempting "to postpone the hour of death from starvation."[58] Between 1940 and 1942, up to 100,000 Jews starved to death in Warsaw—43,000 in 1941 alone. In Łódź, 11,437 Jews perished the same year. Bodies, including those of children, simply lay in the street, in corridors, or in refugee shelters until they could be moved.[59]

If German authorities were bothered, it was aesthetically, because as one administrator put it, "There are only two ways. We sentence the Jews in the ghetto to death by hunger or we shoot them. . . . We have one and only one responsibility, that the German people are not infected and endangered by these parasites."[60] In April 1940, Ingrid Greiser—the *Warthegau* district chief's daughter—toured the Łódź ghetto. Blaming the victims for their squalor, she wrote

---

[56]Quoted in Gutman, *Jews of Warsaw*, p. 77.

[57]See Browning, *Origins*, pp. 151–168, for the debate between "productionists" and "attritionists" and above figures. On training, see Trunk, *Judenrat*, p. 87. The survey of shops can be found in Engelking and Leociak, *Warsaw Ghetto*, pp. 396–405, 481–89.

[58]Quoted in Gutman, *Jews of Warsaw*, p. 77.

[59]Figures in Gutman, *Jews of Warsaw*, pp. 64–65; Kassow, *Who Will Write Our History?* p. 92; Trunk, ed., *Łódź Ghetto*, p. 208.

[60]Quoted in Browning, *Origins*, p. 161.

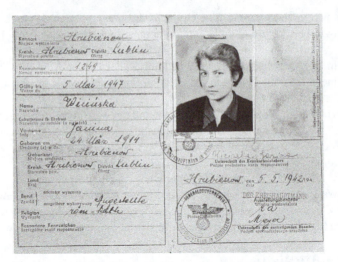

The false identification papers of Zivia Lubetkin (using the false name Janina Wiecinska), who became a leader of the Warsaw ghetto uprising in 1943.   *Source:* Beit Lohamei Haghetaot.

her fiancée that "[y]ou know, one can't have any sympathy for these people."[61] In May 1941, Warsaw District Governor Ludwig Fischer complained that "corpses in the streets create a very bad impression."[62] And when considering the fortuitous typhus epidemic in Warsaw, Heydrich suggested that perhaps worse epidemics might be introduced.[63]

Leaving the Ghetto

Before the deportations of 1942, most Jews remained in ghettos as the best of many bad alternatives. The penalty for leaving without authorization was death. The penalty for Poles sheltering Jews was death. Jews also had family members to protect, and many believed further that Jews generally should support one another in their hour of need. Some managed to procure "Aryan" papers from Polish contacts—fake birth certificates or passports proving that the bearer was Polish or Ukrainian. Aryan papers allowed Jews to live outside the ghetto. But they were expensive and they could not save those who had overtly "Jewish" features. One needed what were called "good looks," as well as accent-free Polish or Ukrainian.

Jewish men were more easily caught partly because of circumcision but also because of greater difficulty in blending. "People were less suspicious of women," remembered Alexandra Gutter. "A woman could dye her hair. Dressed up, she looked more like a Polish woman." "Because he looked very Jewish," remembered Ania Rud of her brother, "he stayed in the ghetto longer than I. . . . He once tried to leave. He grew a moustache but it was very dangerous for him; everybody looked at him. So, he went back to the ghetto."[64]

---

[61]Quoted in Catherine Epstein, *Model Nazi: Arthur Greiser and the Occupation of Western Poland* (New York, 2010), 169–70.

[62]Raul Hilberg et al., eds., *The Warsaw Diary of Adam Czerniaków: Prelude to Doom* (hereafter *Czerniaków Diary*) (New York, 1999), May 25, 1941.

[63]Breitman, *Architect of Genocide*, p. 139.

[64]Nechama Tec, "Hiding and Passing on the Aryan Side," in *Contested Memories: Poles and Jews During the Holocaust and Its Aftermath*, ed., Jonathan Zimmerman (New Brunswick, NJ, 2003), pp. 196, 198.

6.4 JEWISH COUNCILS

Origin and Early Functions

Heydrich's September 1939 concentration order called for Jewish Councils of Elders to govern Jewish communities. They would, he said, be *"fully responsible . . . for the exact and prompt implementation of directives already issued or to be issued in the future."* These bodies were known as Jewish Councils (*Judenräte*) or Councils of Elders (*Ältestenräte*). Council members were chosen haphazardly. Often the Germans corralled prominent Jewish leaders and ordered them to present suitable names. Most council members came from the professions and the merchant class, most had held mid-level community leadership positions before the war, and most had families with children and were thus vulnerable. Among their first tasks were to provide the Germans with Jewish censuses. None understood the significance at the time.

Might Jewish leaders have refused to work under the German occupiers? Many senior Jewish leaders fled when the Germans attacked, and many of those remaining were unsure. Most had no ambition other than to help their communities. In Lublin, Marek Alten, a Jewish lawyer and World War I veteran who became a senior member of the Jewish Council, related that "in tragic times like these there could be no excuse for deserting the people who had given . . . a vote of confidence before the war." Furthermore, should those chosen decline to serve, "nobody could predict who the Nazis would put in charge instead."[65]

Yet Jewish leaders were unprepared for the task that lay ahead. With Jewish property plundered, livelihoods wrecked, and everything from food to coal, to clothing, to living quarters in short supply, Jewish Councils immediately faced a massive humanitarian crisis under a hostile and ruthless occupier. Worse, they had nothing to bargain with. German police immediately raided community treasuries of emergency funds and demanded further "contributions" in cash, jewelry, and other goods, sometimes taking hostages as collateral. They overcharged for food deliveries and underpaid for what the ghetto produced. Council members, meanwhile, operated under two false assumptions because they could not imagine otherwise—that some Germans could be negotiated with and that there would be some sort of Jewish future after the war.

As executive bodies, Jewish Councils soon presided over large ghetto bureaucracies that included departments of housing, health, statistics, food, social welfare, and burial, all aimed at providing ghetto inhabitants with dwellings, sustenance, medical care, education, and basic order. Jewish Councils maintained soup kitchens, hospitals, homeless shelters, orphanages, and even schools, which were allowed to reopen in October 1941. The Warsaw ghetto counted 6,000 official Jewish employees by 1942, and Łódź counted 12,880. These numbers did not include Jewish ghetto police—the so-called Order Service—armed with truncheons and made up of apolitical men who needed jobs. Those from leftist parties refused to apply. "The Bund leaders were unanimous in their opinion," remembered Bernard Goldstein, "that the police could only be tools, willing or unwilling, of Nazi policy toward Jews."[66] But 9,000 others from Warsaw applied, paying a five-złoty application fee in hope of securing steady work.

Despite the size of the Jewish bureaucracy, services could never match the need. Worse, the salaries of council members and police as well as costs for social services were financed the only way possible—through taxes, including head taxes, taxes on food ration cards, and burial fees. Theoretically, taxes on all meant that all were treated equally. In truth, equal taxes fell disproportionately on the poorest. Forced labor was another source of anger. The only way Jewish

---

[65]Quoted in Trunk, *Judenrat*, pp. 18–19.

[66]Goldstein, *The Stars Bear Witness*, p. 68. On applications, see *Kaplan Diary*, November 10, 1940.

Councils could stop the Germans from seizing men off the street was to provide workers' battalions. Councils paid forced laborers a small wage funded partly by Jews who could pay a fee to avoid labor service. But why should the poor bear the terror? Nor were Jewish Councils ever successful in wresting more space, food, coal, or medicines from the Germans. On the contrary, Jewish policemen were ordered to protect what resources there were from theft while collecting taxes and rounding up forced laborers. The fact that Jewish policemen could be bribed only added to the hatred many felt for them.

Might Jewish Councils have defied the Germans? Death was the price of doing so. The Gestapo murdered twenty members of the Łódź Council of Elders as soon as it was formed in October 1939 to create a pliant atmosphere. They also murdered hostages if ransoms were paid late or only in part. In Warsaw, the Gestapo entered the ghetto and killed nearly fifty underground ghetto writers in April 1942. Jewish policemen were shot for questioning German decisions and orders. The Germans met defiance with bullets.

Czerniaków and Rumkowski

Council chairmen reacted to these pressures differently. Adam Czerniaków, the chairman of the Jewish Council in Warsaw, was an engineer by profession—a good but mediocre man who tried to navigate a calamity for which none could be prepared. He repeatedly interceded with German authorities for everything from increased space to food rations, to the release of Jewish prisoners. He rarely got anywhere, and in two cases the Germans beat him severely. Nor could he curb corruption in the ghetto bureaucracy or properly tax wealthier residents. He lived with sleeplessness and migraine headaches, occasionally confiding his helplessness to his diary. "All [these] Jewish complaints," he lamented, "[they] keep demanding that I intervene. . . . And when my efforts fail . . . they blame me without end as if the outcome depended on me."[67]

In November 1941, Czerniaków launched a fund-raising effort—The Month of the Child—with the slogan "Our Children Must Live: The Child Is the Holiest Resource!" Public contributions were significant but fell far short. Street children froze to death in stairwells, their bodies ironically covered by "Month of the Child" posters.[68] Czerniaków pressed on. In a speech of January 31, 1942, given for the opening of a new orphanage, he promised "severe sanctions against the rich who refuse to contribute their share to help the poor."[69] In April and May, he had police raid stores and restaurants with luxury foods and distributed the items to children. Yet other council members rejected increased taxation or forced contributions. Henryk Rozen of the Jewish Council expressed the day's cruel realism. "I see it," he said, "as a positive sign that people . . . have become so toughened, so hard-hearted, that they pass by the dead and keep fighting for life."[70]

Mordechai Chaim Rumkowski, the Elder of the Łódź ghetto, was more authoritarian. Thinking that production for the German economy would see the ghetto through the war, the onetime insurance salesman told the Germans that Łódź, a textile city, was a gold mine that could serve their needs. Rumkowski ruthlessly turned the ghetto into a centrally coordinated production facility with 117 workshops by 1943. Germans authorities purchased finished goods at low prices and sold provisions to the ghetto at high prices while skimming profits off the top. Ghetto revenue combined with taxes enabled Rumkowski to provide hospitals, orphanages, soup kitchens, and schools while

---

[67]*Czerniaków Diary*, July 9, 1940.

[68]*Czerniaków Diary*, October 5, 1941, November 16, 1941; Kassow, *Who Will Write Our History?* p. 261.

[69]*Czerniaków Diary*, January 31, 1942.

[70]Quoted in Kassow, *Who Will Write Our History?* p. 237.

Destitute children of the Warsaw ghetto in 1940 or 1941.
Source: Instytut Pamieci Narodowej, courtesy of the United States
Holocaust Memorial Museum.

promoting Yiddish culture. It was still not enough. Food remained in short supply and of poor quality; most workers could not pay their rent; and small infractions, for example, missing work or forging ration cards, carried heavy council-imposed punishments such as harder labor.

"With your help," Rumkowski told the Łódź population, "I shall be able to fulfill my mission and create the conditions that will make it possible to survive this period, stay alive, and sustain the health of large segments of the ghetto population and the young generations within it."[71] But most knew megalomania when they saw it. Hunger demonstrations broke out as early as August 1940. Ghetto inmates bitterly referred to Rumkowski as "King Chaim." Czerniaków, who met Rumkowski in 1941, noted that "The individual does not exist for him . . . [he is] conceited . . . dangerous . . . too, since he keeps telling the authorities that all is well in his preserve."[72] In the end, both Czerniaków and Rumkowski lived under the illusion that their ghettos were sustainable. Neither could preserve his ghetto once the Germans turned to mass murder in 1942.

6.5 JEWISH SELF-HELP, THE JDC, AND THE UNDERGROUND

Aleynhilf

Jewish Councils, which were often led by men of the political center and right, were not the only form of leadership. The Jewish left had a strong prewar tradition of communal charity owing to prewar Poland's high Jewish poverty rate. By January 1940, Jewish welfare and charitable associations were joined into a general organization initially called Jewish Social Self Help (ŻSS) or, as it was known in Yiddish, *Aleynhilf*. Its general headquarters were in Kraków, but by far the largest ŻSS section was in Warsaw. It acted as a counterorganization to the Jewish Council there.

Emanuel Ringelblum was the most dynamic figure in the Warsaw *Aleynhilf*. A trained academic, left-wing Zionist, and a believer in the Jewish national home in Palestine, Ringelblum was

---

[71]Quoted in Trunk, ed., *Łódź Ghetto*, p. xxxviii.

[72]*Czerniaków Diary*, May 17, 1941.

Emanuel Ringelblum, in the
mid-1920s. *Source:* Yad Vashem.

also a skilled social organizer and a lover of Yiddish working-class culture—part of the Jewish
heritage that he treasured. We last saw Ringelblum in Zbąsyń in 1938 aiding Jews expelled from
Germany. Urged by friends in 1939 to flee as the Germans approached Warsaw, he remained to
help. He distrusted the Jewish Council, which he viewed as too assimilated, too authoritarian,
too corrupt, and—because of its forced labor and tax policies—too deaf to working-class needs.

Under Ringelblum, *Aleynhilf* in Warsaw aimed at self-sufficiency and charity. At its heart
were some 2,000 house committees. They were elected leadership boards for crowded apartment houses. They looked after everything from coal provisions to clothing needs, communal
kitchens, sanitation, childcare, schools, and burial of the dead. They collected monthly dues and
voluntary donations from tenants to help finance their activities. They also put on theatrical per-
formances and even gambling nights to raise more money.

Ringelblum insisted that Jewish committees were tied together and that a greater Jewish
self-consciousness must emerge. "Each house committee," he said, "has to remember that it is a
member of a large family, a part of one large whole. The house committee gives direct help to the
[tenants of the house]. . . . But it becomes harmful when the house forgets about the destitution
that is spreading beyond its walls. . . . There are houses where practically everyone is poor. Who
will help them? There are orphanages, refugee centers, soup kitchens. . . . These institutions do
not have house committees."[73]

But could *Aleynhilf* work over a long-term emergency? Rachel Auerbach, a close associate of
Ringelblum, ran an *Aleynhilf* soup kitchen. "On our first day," she remembered, "we handed out fifty
portions. We served our last two thousand bowls of soup at the time of the liquidations at the end of
July 1942."[74] She came to know some of the men and women who frequented her kitchen. Some
confided to her their past lives. Adolf Bund, a refugee from Vienna whose parents moved there from
East Galicia after World War I, spoke of his jewelry store. When he came to Warsaw, he sold his
last possession, a gold pocket watch, for food. Despite Auerbach's best efforts, Bund, like so many,
developed signs of starvation—swollen fingers and skin that did not bounce back when pressed.

---

[73]Quoted in Kassow, *Who Will Write Our History?* p. 125.

[74]Seymour Levitan and Rachel Auerbach, "A Soup Kitchen in the Warsaw Ghetto: From the Memoirs of Rachel
Auerbach," *Bridges*, 13, no. 2 (Autumn 2008), p. 100.

"The whole balance of this self-help activity," Auerbach wrote in despair in February 1942, "is simply that people die more slowly. . . . I have not been able to rescue anybody."[75] Ringelblum dejectedly agreed. He wrote in May 1941 of the Jewish cemetery outside the ghetto walls, where each night, Jews were dumped into mass graves. "Various groups of [German] excursionists," he wrote, "military men—private visitors, keep visiting the graveyard. Most of them show no sympathy at all for the Jews. On the contrary some of them maintain that the mortality rate among the Jews is too low."[76]

Help from Jews Abroad

Jews in the United States were informed of conditions in Poland. Jewish newspapers gave a clear rendering of massacres, the lethal nature of the Lublin reservation, and conditions in the ghettos. The American Jewish Committee stated in early 1940 that "there is little doubt that the ultimate aim of the Nazi government is to eliminate the Jews as quickly as possible in any way short of direct mass execution." Nahum Goldmann of the World Jewish Congress predicted in February 1940 the death of up to 1 million Jews in Poland should the war continue for another year.[77]

The best option in 1940 and 1941 was financial help. US charitable aid came, as it had since 1914, from the American Jewish Joint Distribution Committee (JDC). With the German conquests of western Europe in 1940, JDC headquarters in Europe moved from Paris to the Portuguese capital of Lisbon. "Ours," said JDC European chief Morris Troper in September 1940, "is the sacred task of keeping our brethren alive; if not all, then at least some. . . ." Yet the JDC budget was tight. It was hard to raise money in the depressed US economy and, by previous agreement, the JDC had to share Jewish monetary gifts with the United Palestine Appeal. The JDC budget was already at a deficit in 1939. All JDC projects in Europe received $660,000 in January and February 1940 and then $440,000 in March.[78]

Emigration for central and west European Jews able to leave formed a primary JDC effort. Meeting with JDC officials in Lisbon in January 1941, Josef Löwenherz, the head of Vienna's Jewish community, argued that "the solution of the Jewish problem in Vienna can be met only through emigration, prompt and in substantial numbers."[79] Even those with US visas or Palestine immigration certificates needed cash for transit visas and passage. Shanghai, where one needed no visa at all, remained an expensive journey. The JDC helped 81,000 Jews maintain themselves and then emigrate from Europe between 1939 and 1944.[80]

Maintenance and travel were expensive. The thousands of Jewish refugees who reached Portugal in 1941 and 1942 cost the JDC over $545,000. The JDC spent over $262,000 to maintain roughly 3,000 Jews who reached Japan as they waited for passage elsewhere.[81] The JDC also spent money on programs in the USSR. As we will see in Chapter 9, Joseph Stalin deported over 200,000 Jews from the regions he occupied from 1939 to 1941 to the Soviet interior. The

---

[75]Quoted in Kassow, *Who Will Write Our History?* p. 142.

[76]Jacob Sloan, ed., *Notes from the Warsaw Ghetto: The Journal of Emanuel Ringelblum* (New York, 1958), May 20, 1941.

[77]Quoted in Alex Grobman, "What Did They Know? The American Jewish Press and the Holocaust, 1 September 1939–17 December 1942," *American Jewish History*, vol. 63, no. 8 (March 1979), pp. 327–52.

[78]Quotes and figures in Yehuda Bauer, *American Jewry and the Holocaust: The American Jewish Joint Distribution Committee, 1939–1945* (Detroit, MI, 1981), pp. 39, 40.

[79]Quoted in Bauer, *American Jewry and the Holocaust*, p. 61.

[80]Figure in Moses A. Leavit, *The JDC Story: Highlights of JDC Activities 1914–1952* (New York, 1953), p. 13.

[81]Figures in Bauer, *American Jewry and the Holocaust*, pp. 125, 207.

JDC created 250,000 parcels of food, clothing, and blankets, then paid exorbitant Persian and Soviet duties to send them.[82]

A sizable portion of the JDC budget went to Poland. Until the United States entered the war in December 1941, Warsaw actually had a JDC office. Some money funded projects for vocational training so that Jews could learn new crafts to support themselves. JDC money also went to Jewish Council and *Aleynhilf* charity projects, including soup kitchens, children's aid, and help for Jews in labor camps. The JDC also shipped supplies directly. During Passover in the spring of 1940, JDC representatives in neutral countries arranged for 137 railroad wagons of food—1,000 tons in all—to arrive in Poland (nearly half in Warsaw) through Romania, Yugoslavia, and Lithuania. Perhaps 560,000 adults and 75,000 children benefited. It is a measure of Jewish misery in Poland that the Passover shipment—a one-time gift—was such a sensation.

The gift was not repeated. The New York JDC office balked at further food shipments to Nazi-occupied Europe, arguing to a furious Lisbon office that shipments relieved the Germans of their obligation to feed the Jewish population. The frustrations of the New York office were understandable. Dollars and goods could be transferred to occupied Europe only through complicated transfer agreements, and the Germans converted US currency at exceptionally poor rates—złoty were sold to the JDC at no more than 20 percent of the official exchange rate.[83] The New York office did not comprehend that the Germans had no intention of changing their policies.

Might the JDC have done more? More money would have meant more visas, rail tickets, ship berths, food, clothing, and medicines. But saving Jews also depended on issues beyond the JDC's control. The most important factor was time. The Nazis were uninterested in saving Jewish lives; for them, Jews could not die quickly enough. And by the fall of 1941, Hitler was no longer interested in emigration or in allowing help for the Jews under his control. No number of care packages would change the fundamental course of events.

The Jewish Underground

The Germans prohibited Jewish political parties and youth organizations, but in many ghettos such groups were able to meet secretly in soup kitchens, publish news on mimeograph sheets, and have a political and social impact. The Bund, for example, maintained its central committee, its party discipline, and its contacts with the Polish Socialist Party outside ghettos. In Łódź, it was behind opposition to Rumkowski and strikes that broke out in 1940 and 1941 for better working conditions. In Warsaw, it remained the largest political party.

Zionist youth groups also remained especially active, maintaining their political and social ideals while recruiting new members. Their headquarters were in refugee centers and kitchens, and they received funds from both the JDC and *Aleynhilf*. "I went today to a *Hashomer Hatza'ir* meeting," wrote Ringelblum in November 1941. "In the room there were nearly 500 young people of both sexes. . . . A new group of members was ceremonially accepted into *Hashomer Hatza'ir*."[84] Zionist youth groups provided training, self-help, and a warm atmosphere amid despair while preparing for what they thought would be the postwar world.

With the help of false identification papers and couriers, parties and youth groups communicated with one another between ghettos. Many ghettos in Poland were not hermetically sealed and some were not as closely guarded as others. Most were surrounded with barbed wire. Warsaw and Kraków were the only ghettos with walls. Young women often served as couriers

---

[82]Herbert Agar, *The Saving Remnant: An Account of Jewish Survival* (New York, 1960), p. 122.

[83]Bauer, *American Jewry and the Holocaust*, pp. 95–98.

[84]Quoted Engelking and Leociak, *Warsaw Ghetto*, p. 675.

because they passed as Poles more easily. For now, they simply relayed information. But the youth groups that spread the word of mass murder when it began in the USSR in 1941 also coalesced into fighting groups in numerous ghettos on understanding the terrible truth.

Oyneg Shabes

One of the most important underground movements was not a fighting group. In November 1940, with the formation of the Warsaw ghetto, Ringelblum put together a team of forty to fifty male and female writers to document life in the ghetto. The group was named *Oyneg Shabes* (Sabbath Joy) because its members met secretly on Saturdays. *Oyneg Shabes* chronicled everyday life in the ghetto through the collection of ghetto publications and diaries, essays, letters, and targeted research studies that involved interviews of ordinary Jews. *Oyneg Shabes* studied everything from religious life to social welfare, from the pulse of the ghetto street to Jews' hopes and fears, from the changing roles of women to the tragic deaths of children.

   Oyneg Shabes buried their archive in milk cans and metal boxes so that they might be preserved. Only two members, Rachel Auerbach and Hersch Wasser, survived the war. The others were deported in 1942 or, like Ringelblum, killed afterward. After the war, Auerbach and Wasser located much of the hidden archive under the rubble of what was once the Warsaw ghetto. The scope of the 35,000 items is breathtaking, ranging from religious opinions on Jewish Gestapo informants ("The Talmud permits the killing of informers") to the last letter of a young man condemned to death for leaving the ghetto illegally ("If I have done any wrong to my parents, may they forgive me"), to reflections on escaping the ghetto to avoid deportation ("What will happen to those who have no way of getting out?")

   But the helpless accounts of starving children still wrench the soul. "The most terrible thing," Ringelblum wrote in November 1941, "is to look at the freezing children, children with bare feet, bare knees, and tattered clothes, who stand mutely in the streets and cry." In her essay, "Scenes from a Children's Hospital," Dora Wajnerman described a scene from her overcrowded facility, which struggled to save the dying:

> A swollen five-year old is lying in the corridor. He is dying of hunger. He came to the hospital yesterday. Two swollen eyes, hands and feet like little pumpkins. We did all the tests. . . . The child barely moves his lips and asks for a piece of bread. I give him something to eat. Maybe he'll swallow? But no, his throat is swollen, nothing goes down, it's too late. . . .[85]

The carefully compiled and miraculously preserved archive is at once an anguished cry from the grave and a defiant seizure of historical narrative from the murderers, who hoped to hide their crimes forever.

*****

   Caught in an unprecedented maw of malice, Jewish reactions in Poland could never have been sufficient. Day-to-day perseverance and hope for Germany's defeat was the logical path many chose. In an optimistic moment, Abraham Lewin, teacher, activist, and member of *Oyneg Shabes*, wrote, "I consider it a certainty that the Anglo-American invasion of Europe will come to fruition in the near future. . . . This huge army will hit the continent like an avalanche and strike a death-blow at the enemy of humanity."[86] It was May 26, 1942. The Allies did not land in France for more than two years, and the Soviets did not take Warsaw for two and a half. Deportations from Warsaw to the gas chambers in Treblinka, however, began just two months after Abraham Levin's entry.

---

[85]All quoted from Kassow, *Who Will Write Our History?* pp. 141–142, 158, 167, 169, 261, 265.

[86]Abraham Lewin, *A Cup of Tears: A Diary of the Warsaw Ghetto* (Cambridge, MA, 1989), May 26, 1942.

7

Western Europe, the War, and the Jews, 1939–1942

In 1940, Hitler turned west. In April, his forces occupied Denmark and Norway to protect Germany's northern approaches. In May, they overran the Netherlands, Belgium, and Luxemburg. Germany's defeat of France in May and June was a terrible shock. Most expected a long stalemate as in World War I. Mussolini's Italy, which hoped to acquire numerous Mediterranean territories, joined Hitler's war on June 10, attacking France and later Egypt and Greece. Britain, under Winston Churchill after April 1940, fought alone, enduring German air attacks and the threat of invasion.

In the east, the Soviets continued to benefit from German success. In November 1939, they attacked Finland, forcing its surrender of strategic territories in March 1940. In June and July, they annexed the Baltic States of Lithuania, Latvia, and Estonia and took Bessarabia and northern Bukovina from Romania. The British briefly regained some initiative by attacking the Italians in Libya and Greece. But in February 1941, the German Afrika Korps bolstered Italian forces in Libya and drove toward the Suez Canal. In April and May 1941, the Germans pushed the British from mainland Greece and from Crete. The series of German victories stunned Jewish observers who prayed for Hitler's defeat.

In western Europe, Jews were a smaller percentage of the population than in Poland, and they were more assimilated into their communities. The Germans, with smaller occupation forces than in Poland, needed to act with greater care. Yet Jewish circumstances became more brutal with time, and the help offered by the rest of the world was not sufficient to help more Jews escape.

7.1 GERMAN JEWS IN WARTIME

Jewish Existence in Wartime Germany

The German government never created ghettos in German cities, but it drove German Jews further into poverty and isolation. Already in 1939 Jews were banned from most public places and removed from the German economy. On the war's first day, the state subjected them to curfews. A week later, the Gestapo arrested the 11,500 *Ostjuden* still living in the Reich and sent them to concentration camps as enemy aliens. Aryanization of Jewish-owned homes was already under-way, and as of April 1939, German landlords were permitted to evict Jewish tenants. In the months that followed, whole urban districts were cleared of Jews. Party officials and ordinary Germans claimed Jewish homes.

Evicted Jews were given days to move into "Jew Houses" (*Judenhäuser*). These ranged from remaining Jewish-owned houses to Jewish nursing homes, funeral parlors, synagogues, and even dilapidated buildings. Finding a dwelling quickly was difficult. Elisabeth Freund, who sent her children abroad in the *Kindertransport*, noted in 1941 that "[t]he atmosphere in our circle is terrible. Some have found rooms . . . most of them found very poor housing. All the women are very depressed. They have to sell furniture once again, and the prices they get are ridiculous. . . ."[1]

Judenhäuser were overcrowded. In Hannover, more than 100 Jews lived in a single house, and 150 others shared a Jewish funeral home.[2] Jews in Ulm shared a decaying castle outside town. Mattresses filled rooms and hallways. Privacy vanished, hygiene declined. "Lack of space," Victor Klemperer confided to his diary, ". . . promiscuity, chaos . . . never ending washing up made utterly difficult. . . . Every day the same wretchedness. . . . Every day a torment."[3] Nor could Jews find peace outdoors. Banned from squares, parks, and forests, they turned to Jewish cemeteries for fresh air and greenery. Cemeteries, wrote Freund, "are not only the last quiet set-tings for the old people; they are also the only place Jewish children can play."[4]

To eat, German Jews had to work. The state conscripted Jewish men and women—including the elderly—for labor in sectors such as sewage removal and road construction, but also in armaments. By October 1941, 32,000 Jews in Berlin alone, half of whom were women, worked ten-hour days for low wages in munitions factories.[5] Theoretically they could buy essentials despite wartime rationing. But Jews could shop only at certain markets at certain hours, for instance, between 4 and 5 p.m. in Berlin. By 1941, Jewish ration cards, marked with a *J*, disal-lowed purchase of meat, fish, poultry, fruits, vegetables and legumes, canned foods, coffee, tea, milk, white bread, butter, and candy. Stocks of permitted food like potatoes were often depleted.

Some feared starvation. Even care packages from abroad were deducted from approved rations. German neighbors or shopkeepers sometimes took pity. "Occasionally," remembered Rabbi Leo Baeck, "I found a bag of fruit at my apartment door left by an anonymous donor."[6] But this generosity was not normal. Many Germans complained about what Jews could still purchase.

Clothing was another difficulty. After January 1940, German Jews did not receive coupons for clothes or the materials needed to repair them. Clothing became threadbare. Because Jews could not use public transport, their shoes wore out from long walks to work and stores. Because of small or nonexistent coal rations, Jewish dwellings were cold in the winter. Even information was in short supply. In the fall of 1939—on Yom Kippur no less—the state confiscated Jews'

---

[1]Excerpt from testimony of Elisabeth Freund, Yad Vashem Archive, 033/2202.

[2]Figure in Konrad Kwiet, "Without Neighbors: Daily Living in *Judenhäuser*," in *Jewish Life in Nazi Germany: Dilemmas and Responses*, Francis R. Nicosia and David Scrase, eds. (New York, 2010), pp. 131, 138.

[3]Victor Klemperer, *I Will Bear Witness: A Diary of the Nazi Years, 1933–1941* (New York, 1998), June 6, 1940.

[4]Quoted in Wolfgang Benz, ed., *Die Juden in Deutschland 1933–1945: Leben unter nationalsozialistischer Herrschaft* (Munich, 1989), p. 605.

[5]Figure in Benz, ed. *Die Juden in Deutschland*, p. 576.

[6]Leo Baeck, "A People Stands Before Its God," in *We Survived: The Stories of the Hidden and Hunted of Nazi Germany*, ed. Eric H. Boehm (New Haven, CT, 1949), p. 288.

radios. In mid-1940, it took private telephones. By late 1941, Jews could not use public telephones, and in 1942, they were prohibited from buying unauthorized periodicals. Police searches of *Judenhäuser* for contraband turned brutal. Police stole money, destroyed belongings, and beat residents, even old women, when the mood struck them.

The discovery of forbidden items was serious. Per a Himmler order of October 1939, offenders would be placed in a concentration camp for the war's duration. Many Germans, denounced Jews and anyone who helped them to the Gestapo.[7] Thus, while some risked arrest, most German Jews managed as best they could. *Judenhäuser*, despite crowding, arguing, and even occasional stealing, sometimes became cooperatives in which Jews bartered food and clothing and gave moral support. Many German Jews rediscovered Judaism with regular prayer services. But the quiet hope that Hitler would meet defeat was disappointed. "I cannot imagine how [Hitler] can succeed," lamented Klemperer after the French campaign. "But so far he has succeeded with everything."[8]

Elisabeth Freund lamented in 1941 that "[t]he worst is that the hopelessness of our situation is becoming increasingly clear to everybody . . . I have lost my nerve. I don't know how I am going to survive." Yet she found inspiration in others. "When I see these women work," she wrote, "how they have to wake their children before 5 am [to] bring them to day care; how in the evenings and then on Sundays they wash and sew and keep everything orderly in one room that most often serves the entire family; how they manage to acquire a few groceries by waiting endlessly in shops; how they magically create a new child's dress out of an old curtain; how they work themselves to death and how each woman bears her individual fortune—it is admirable."[9]

German Jewish Leadership

German Jews' welfare was left to the *Reichsvereinigung der Juden in Deutschland* ("Reich Union of Jews in Germany"), an organization created by the state in July 1939 and kept under the supervision of Reinhard Heydrich's Reich Security Main Office (RSHA). The Reich Union replaced the more independent Reich Representation of German Jews, which had tried to defend Jewish interests until the state dissolved it in February. Rabbi Leo Baeck and Dr. Otto Hirsch, former leaders of the Reich Representation, now led the Reich Union. Its job was to provide help to German Jews and, like Jewish Councils in Poland, to relay state decrees. Most important, it was charged with speeding emigration.

Emigration was also a Jewish preoccupation. "The emigration problem demanded our greatest labors," remembered Alfred Schwerin, whose daughter left with the *Kindertransport* in 1939. "We registered children and adults with the emigration aid agencies, filled out endless questionnaires, wrote testimonials, and took care of providing funds for the journey. . . ."[10]

The Nazis' assumption that Jews' global connections would result in mass flight was disappointed. Their impatience resulted in expulsions. The deportations to Nisko in October 1939 have been mentioned. In February and March 1940, 1,800 more Jews from the Pomeranian cities of Stettin and Schneidemühl—including octogenarians from nursing homes—were rounded up

---

[7]Robert Gellately, *The Gestapo and German Society: Enforcing Racial Policy, 1933–1945* (New York, 1992), pp. 160–64, 192–96.

[8]Klemperer, *I Will Bear Witness 1933–1941*, July 18, 1940.

[9]Testimony of Elisabeth Friend, Yad Vachem Archive, 033/2202; Marion A. Kaplan, *Between Dignity and Despair: Jewish Life in Nazi Germany* (New York, 1999), p. 176.

[10]Monika Richarz, ed., *Jewish Life in Germany: Memoirs from Three Centuries* (Bloomington, IN, 1991), p. 402.

and sent to Lublin. Seventy froze to death. Others found shelter in the primitive homes of poor local Jews and received aid from the Reich Union. On Hitler's personal order, 7,663 more Jews from the western German regions of Baden and the Saar-Palatinate were dumped into France in October 1940. Eighteen-year old Miriam Sondheimer's family was awoken at 7:30 a.m. on October 22. "You are to be at the station within an hour!" shouted the police. Allowed one suitcase each and "paralyzed with fear," they were expelled over the French border. One deportee was ninety-seven.[11]

The Reich Union protested these deportations and leaked the news abroad. It also called for a day of fasting as a sign of mourning, rabbinical sermons throughout Germany, and cancellation of Jewish cultural activities for a week. This was too much. The RSHA prohibited the fast day, and the Gestapo arrested Dr. Julius Seligsohn, the member of the Reich Union Executive Board who issued the circular. He was imprisoned in Oranienburg concentration camp and died there in 1942. In 1938, Seligsohn was in the United States trying to arrange emigration for more German Jews. "It would have been easy," remembered Rabbi Baeck after the war, "for him to have stayed in the USA, but his strong sense of duty brought him back to Germany."[12] The Nazis' willingness to murder prominent German Jewish leaders that they themselves had appointed ended any hope at overt Jewish resistance.

Over the course of 1941, the Nazi government decided on the murder of all European Jews. The result in Germany was more overt isolation. On September 1, 1941, on Hitler's order, the state decreed that Jews over age six wear a yellow Star of David in public, tightly sewn on all outerwear. Failure to wear the properly affixed star—or hiding it—was punishable. The star ended anonymity and thus a final shred of dignity. "I had a raving fit of despair," Klemperer wrote, when his wife sewed the star to his coat.[13] Some Germans expressed private sympathy, some avoided Jews like poison, some tormented even Jewish children. Others were surprised that so many Jews were left in Germany. "When Jews were forced to wear the yellow star," remembered one German, "only then did it occur to us at all how many there were."[14]

Back on October 25, 1940, the RSHA prohibited the emigration of Jews from the General Government so that Jews from Germany could procure emigration visas first. A year later, on October 23, 1941, Himmler issued a new decree for German Jews. "Permission for the emigration of individual Jews," read the order, "can only be approved *in single very special cases*; for instance, in the event of a genuine interest on the part of the Reich. . . ."[15] Even if some German Jews could find refuge abroad, it was now too late for most.

7.2 GERMANY AND THE JEWS OF THE NETHERLANDS, 1940–1942

The Holocaust in Western Europe

The Holocaust in Belgium, the Netherlands, and France varied widely once the Germans began to deport western Europe's Jews to Auschwitz in 1942. One-quarter of the Jews in France were

---

[11]Richarz, ed., *Jewish Life in Germany*, p. 425.

[12]Leo Baeck, "In Memory of Our Two Dead," *Leo Baeck Institute Year Book*, 1 (1956), p. 56.

[13]Klemperer, *I Will Bear Witness, 1933–1941*, September 20, 1941.

[14]Quoted in Eric Johnson and Karl-Heinz Reuband, eds., *What We Knew: Terror, Mass Murder, and Everyday Life in Nazi Germany—An Oral History* (New York, 2005), p. 362.

[15]Himmler order in Yitzhak Arad et al., eds., *Documents on the Holocaust: Selected Sources on the Destruction of the Jews of Germany and Austria, Poland and the Soviet Union*, 8th ed. (Lincoln, NE, 1999), doc. 68.

murdered. The Germans killed 44 percent of Jews registered in Belgium.[16] They killed 73 percent of the Jews registered in the Netherlands.[17] How to account for the differences?

As Chapter 12 will show, much depended on geography. German police could cover more of the Netherlands than they could of France. The timing of Allied liberation also mattered. Drancy, the chief transit camp in France, was liberated in August 1944. Westerbork, the Netherlands' main transport camp, was not captured until April 1945. Also crucial were measures of assistance the Germans received from local police and the degree of help local bystanders provided to Jews.

But Jewish responses also mattered. In the Netherlands, 85 percent of all Jews were Dutch citizens. Acculturated with deep roots in a country known for religious tolerance, they had no reason to distrust their state. They followed Dutch orders after the occupation, reluctant to break the law, unable to imagine that the orders would lead to their murders. In France and Belgium, most Jews came from eastern Europe in the prewar decades, and many also belonged to the political left. They distrusted their surroundings and were more given to hiding, protest, and resistance. These responses make the experience of the Dutch Jews all the more tragic.

Incremental Measures

The Germans invaded the Netherlands on May 10, 1940. Queen Wilhelmina and the Dutch cabinet fled to England. Dutch forces surrendered in five days. Many Dutch Jews tried unsuccessfully to flee the German advance by sea or automobile. But on returning to their homes, they discovered that German occupation forces, unlike in Poland, behaved correctly. "Nothing happened," remembered one survivor. "No pogrom and no persecutions. . . . People made the best of it and went back to work."[18] The 16,000 German Jewish refugees in the Netherlands had reason for fear. But Dutch Jews became more hopeful.

Though the Dutch cabinet fled, the civil service remained, including the College of Secretaries-General, the executive body presiding over the different government ministries. The Dutch police also remained intact. The government-in-exile ordered the Secretaries-General to protect the Dutch constitution, which guaranteed complete civic equality. Generally, however, Dutch leaders took a path of less resistance to maintain normality. Dutch industry, for instance, filled German contracts to keep Dutch workers employed. As long as the Germans acted with reasonable care, the Dutch state would not protect Jews any more than it protected Dutch honor.

Arthur Seyss-Inquart, an Austrian Nazi who was Hans Frank's deputy in Poland, became the Reich Commissioner in the Netherlands. He expected to rule through the Dutch civil service but understood the realities of the Jewish question. Most Dutch, save for the small Dutch National Socialist Movement, were not sympathetic to Nazism. Thus, in his initial speech of May 29, 1940, Seyss-Inquart did not mention Jews. An early German assessment noted that "[t]he Jewish question must be treated with great care." "The simple fact" wrote Professor Paul Scholten, who led an academics' petition to the Germans in September 1940, "[is] that there is no Jewish question in the Netherlands."[19]

---

[16]Figure in Maxime Steinberg, "The *Judenpolitik* in Belgium Within the West European Context: Comparative Observations," in *Belgium and the Holocaust: Jews, Belgians, Germans*, ed. Dan Michman (Jerusalem, 1998), p. 203, n. 10.

[17]Figure in Bob Moore, *Victims and Survivors: The Nazi Persecution of the Jews in the Netherlands 1940–1945* (New York, 1997), pp. 2, 259–60.

[18]Quoted in Moore, *Victims and Survivors*, p. 51.

[19]Quoted in Jacob Presser, *The Destruction of the Dutch Jews* (New York, 1969), pp. 12, 20–1.

Germany's first anti-Jewish steps were thus incremental and carried exceptions to help mute Dutch reaction. The Secretaries-General never knew where to draw the line and, as a result, never drew it. Decrees concerning the civil service are prime examples. If the Germans were to rule through the Dutch civil service, then it could have no Jews. But the initial German order of August 28, 1940, banned Jews only from *new* civil service appointments. The Secretaries-General pointed out that even this decree violated the constitution. On the other hand, no Jews lost their jobs. The Secretaries-General thus accepted the order, with the caveat that "we are forced to comply, but . . . do so most reluctantly."[20]

In October, the Germans insisted that Dutch civil servants complete racial background forms. Aryans completed Form A. Jews completed Form B, which defined Jews according to the Nuremberg Laws' formulas. Proper Dutch leadership might have called for a boycott. But 98 percent of Dutch civil servants—including Jews—completed the forms. "None of us really knew what we were doing," recalled Abel Herzberg, who eventually survived the war. "Each signed his own death warrant, though a few appreciated this at the time."[21]

The following month, the Germans ordered the dismissal of all Jewish civil servants. The Secretaries-General sought middle ground. Perhaps the dismissals could be changed to "temporary suspensions," to make the decree more constitutional. It mattered not to Seyss-Inquart. Jews would never be reinstated and the change in language turned vocal Dutch opposition into mere discomfort. "Once again," remembered Benno Gitter, an Amsterdam Jew who survived the war, "the optimists around us found some consolation. . . . 'These are harmless, temporary regulations—just until the war is over.'" Indeed they affected but 2,000 of 200,000 civil servants.[22]

The most notable "temporary" dismissal was Lodewijk E. Visser, the chief justice of the Dutch High Court and a Dutch Jewish leader. His colleagues, judges no less, failed to take a stand. Despite the violation of the law they were pledged to uphold, they remained on the bench, arguing that mass judicial resignations would cause chaos. But if the High Court would not protect its own chief justice, what would others do for ordinary Jews?

What protests occurred were limited, compromised, and met with deadly force. Dutch university professors and students—unlike their German colleagues—protested the suspension of Jewish academics. Leo Polak, a noted philosophy professor at the University of Groningen, continued to lecture despite his suspension, referring to the Germans as "the enemy." His own rector denounced him to the German police. He was sent to Sachsenhausen in May 1941 and was dead by the end of the year.

General registration affecting all Jews in the Netherlands followed civil service dismissals. An October 1940 German decree announcing registration of Jewish businesses threatened heavy fines and confiscation for noncompliance. A January 1941 decree for a Jewish census threatened five years' imprisonment and the loss of all property for those not registering. A tiny number of Jews refused to register. But most did so by late August 1941. Dutch census offices kept extended hours so they could register. On a Jewish woman's question whether her children had to register, a Dutch census official smiled, "Even if they're just one hour old, madam."[23]

[20]Quoted in Presser, *Destruction*, p. 16.

[21]Quoted in Presser, *Destruction*, p. 19.

[22]Quote in Benno Gitter, *The Story of My Life* (London, 1999), p. 56. Figure in Moore, *Victims and Survivors*, p. 58.

[23]Klaas A. D. Smelik, ed., *Etty: The Letters and Diaries of Etty Hillesum* (New York, 1983), March 19, 1941.

The Joodse Raad

After February 1941, the Germans became more violent. An attempted pogrom by Dutch National Socialists in Amsterdam's working-class Jewish quarter triggered reaction by Jews and non-Jews. A Dutch storm trooper was killed in the fighting. Dr. Hans Böhmcker, the German commandant for Amsterdam, insisted that Jewish leaders form a Jewish Council to keep order in Amsterdam, where more than half of Dutch Jews lived and where most Jewish organizations were located.

The council—eventually known as the *Joodse Raad*—was led by Abraham Asscher, a diamond merchant, and David Cohen, a professor of ancient history. Both were respected figures. Asscher headed Amsterdam's chamber of commerce and was president of the Netherlands Israelite Congregation. Cohen, a follower of Chaim Weizmann's general Zionism, was active in prewar Jewish refugee affairs. The council proclaimed in its first meeting that it would not accept "orders that are dishonorable to the Jews."[24] But Asscher, according to historian Joseph Michman, was "an incurable optimist," and Cohen was a compromiser who "disliked fighting over principles."[25] German demands, moreover, came with threats of extreme violence.

Böhmcker's first order was the handover of all Jewish weapons. Otherwise, he said, 500 Jews would be shot. On Asscher's appeal, Jews surrendered their weapons. No firearms were among them. Arrests of young Jewish men followed. Between February and October 1941, the Germans arrested 900, shipping them to Buchenwald and Mauthausen, where most were killed. The initial wave of 425 arrests on February 19 triggered a communist-led Dutch general strike in Amsterdam on February 25 and 26. "For once," wrote Jacob Presser, a Dutch Jewish survivor, "[Dutch Jews] did not feel that their Dutch compatriots were leaving them in the lurch."[26] Convinced that the Jews were behind the strike, the Germans threatened to shoot 500 Jews if it did not end immediately. Paralyzed into compliance, Asscher begged Dutch leaders to end the strike.

In the year and a half between February 1941 and July 1942, the Germans issued a steady stream of decrees aimed at complete segregation and impoverishment. Jews were banned from parks, swimming pools, spas, hotels, boarding houses, public markets, restaurants, museums, libraries, concerts, and art exhibitions. They were prohibited from owning radios and carrier pigeons. Jewish children were expelled from public schools. Jewish property and bank accounts were taken under trusteeship and valuable artworks were confiscated. Jews were eventually allowed but 250 guilders per family, and they were banned from working as manicurists, pedicurists, masseurs, and hairdressers. Over 5,000 unemployed Jews were used for forced labor in the Netherlands. Jews had to surrender their bicycles—the primary mode of transportation in Amsterdam—plus spare tires and tubes. The list of items that they could keep included wedding rings, four pieces of flatware per person, pocket watches, and their own gold teeth.[27]

In October 1941, the *Joodse Raad* was made responsible for all Dutch Jews, who in the first half of 1942 were ordered to move to Amsterdam with no more than they could carry. In May 1942, the Germans decreed that Jews would wear yellow stars in public, marked with the word *Jood*. Noncompliance carried a six-month prison sentence. Average Dutch citizens showed

---

[24]Quoted in Presser, *Destruction*, p. 48.

[25]Joseph Michman, "The Controversial Stand of the *Joodse Raad* in the Netherlands: Lodewijk E. Visser's Struggle," in *The Nazi Holocaust: Historical Articles on the Destruction of the European Jews*, ed., Michael R. Marrus (Westport, CT, 1989), vol. 6, part 2, p. 855.

[26]Presser, *Destruction*, pp. 56–7.

[27]Listed in Moore, *Victims and Survivors*, pp. 79–90.

solidarity. One Dutch underground newspaper printed 300,000 stars for its readers to wear, proclaiming that "Jews and non-Jews are one."[28] Yet moral demonstrations did not alter German policy any more in 1942 than they did in 1940.

And the *Joodse Raad*, terrified by the killing of nearly 1,000 young Jewish men in Mauthausen in 1941, could effect no change. "We live in an occupied country," explained David Cohen, "where the occupier has his own way. We, for our part, can only try to obtain some concessions on certain points which would not be granted without our intervention." Yet the Germans rejected even small mitigation requests, such as that of a Jewish father to keep a long-trusted Dutch caregiver for his mentally disabled daughter. Former Supreme Court justice Lodewijk E. Visser, who bravely intervened on his own for the Mauthausen prisoners, pointed out the problem. "The attitude of the Jewish Council," he wrote Cohen in November 1941, "is to oblige the occupier . . . hoping thereby 'to prevent worse to come.' . . . It is possible that in the end, the occupier will achieve his goal concerning us, but it is our duty as Dutchmen and as Jews to do everything to hamper him. . . . That is not what you are doing." Visser died of a heart attack in March 1942. His son, who was in the Jewish underground, was sent to Mauthausen.[29]

Amsterdam's Jews, meanwhile, fought to keep up their spirits, convinced that decency would prevail. In her diary entry for June 20, 1942, Etty Hillesum, a twenty-eight-year-old intellectual, wrote as perhaps only a young adult could:

> Humiliation always involves two. The one who does the humiliating, and the one who allows himself to be humiliated. If the second is missing . . . then the humiliation vanishes into thin air. All that remains are vexatious measures that interfere with daily life but are not humiliations that weigh heavily on the soul. We Jews should remember that.
>
> They can't do anything to us, they really can't. They can harass us, they can rob us of our material goods, of our freedom of movement, but we ourselves forfeit our greatest assets by our misguided compliance. By our feelings of being persecuted, humiliated, and oppressed. . . . We may of course be sad and depressed by what has been done to us; that is only human and understandable. However our greatest injury is one we inflict upon ourselves."[30]

She was murdered in Auschwitz with her family in 1943.

7.3 VICHY FRANCE, THE GERMANS, AND THE JEWS, 1940–1942

The Jews in France in 1940

Germany's cease-fire agreement with France on June 22, 1940, divided France into two zones. The German army occupied the northern three-fifths of France, including Paris, for continued operations against Britain. The southern two-fifths was a free zone under a new French government, located in the spa town of Vichy. The Vichy government, under eighty-four-year-old World War I hero Marshal Henri-Philippe Pétain, thought the war almost over. Pétain hoped to extricate France from the war as inexpensively as possible. But Vichy was also an authoritarian regime, determined to reverse what it saw as years of republican decadence and to promote conservative Catholic tradition that would restore France after its catastrophic defeat.

---

[28]Quoted in Presser, *Destruction*, p. 125.

[29]Cohen to L. E. Visser, November 13, 1941, and L. E. Visser to Cohen, November 18, 1941, printed in Joseph Michman, "The Controversial Stand of the *Joodse Raad*," pp. 889–97.

[30]Smelik, ed., *Etty*, June 20, 1942.

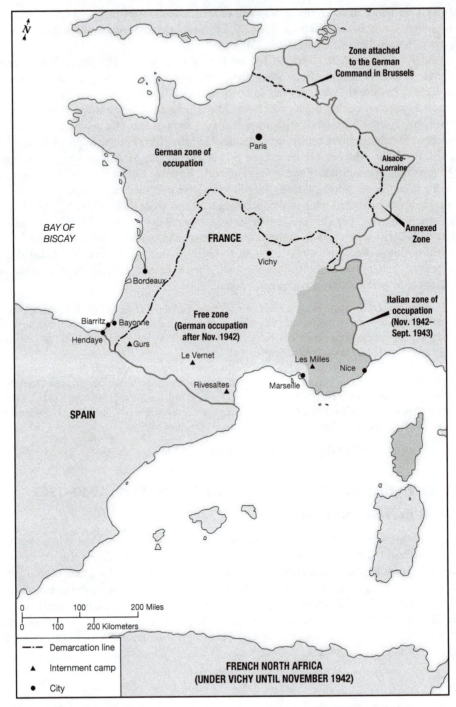

MAP 7.1 Occupied France, 1940–1942. *Source:* Adapted courtesy of Serge Klarsfeld.

This reversal included recasting the place of Jews, whom many on the French right equated with republican decline. By the time of France's surrender, there were between 300,000 and 330,000 Jews in France, two-thirds living in Paris. Ninety thousand were *Israélites Françaises*—long-established and acculturated professionals, businessmen, and public servants. They viewed themselves as French patriots. There were at least 170,000 Jews of east European origin, not including the most recent arrivals, who entered and stayed illegally. They ranged from shopkeepers to workers, from Zionists to communists. Perhaps 50,000 east European Jews became French citizens in the 1920s and 1930s, but they were more openly Jewish in culture. There were also roughly 30,000 German and Austrian Jewish refugees in 1939, with more arriving as Hitler's armies advanced through western Europe.[31]

French antisemites especially viewed eastern Jews as perpetual foreigners and German Jews as enemy agents. Even the *Israélites Françaises*, who feared the growth of antisemitism before the war, were ambivalent toward foreign Jews. With the outbreak of war, French police arrested and interned some 15,000 German and Austrian Jewish refugees as enemy aliens (the British government carried out a similar policy) even though few hoped more fervently for Hitler's defeat. Meanwhile up to 60,000 foreign Jews volunteered to fight the Germans—the largest contingent of foreigners to do so. Certain foreign combat units were perhaps 30 percent Polish Jews.[32] It mattered not. The French right claimed that France had a Jewish question, and in 1940, they had a government willing to solve it.

Vichy's Internment Camps

The initial problem for Vichy in the unoccupied zone concerned millions of refugees who fled to southern France to outrun the German advance. The refugees included 165,000 to 210,000 Jews, mostly from Paris but also 10,000 who fled from Belgium, the Netherlands, Luxembourg, and the border region of Alsace-Lorraine, which Germany re-annexed after having lost it in 1919.[33] Perhaps 30,000 Jews returned to Paris after the cease-fire. Their homes were still there, and German occupation authorities in Paris behaved correctly. "Life in Paris seemed normal," wrote the Jewish historian Léon Poliakov. "One was not even alarmed for the Jews. . . . There were no massacres and no pogroms."[34]

The Jewish return to Paris, however, prompted a German military decree on September 27, 1940, whereby no more Jews could return to the occupied zone. Germany instead dumped more of its own Jews into the unoccupied zone, including the 4,000 Jews remaining in Alsace-Lorraine and 7,663 Jews from Baden and the Saar-Palatinate. The Vichy government protested unsuccessfully. Before the war, perhaps 5,000 Jews lived in the area of France's unoccupied zone. By spring 1941, there were perhaps 150,000, most of whom were foreigners.[35]

---

[31]Figures in Renée Poznanski, *Jews in France During World War II* (Hanover, NH, 2001), pp. 2–18; Vicki Caron, *Uneasy Asylum: France and the Jewish Refugee Crisis, 1933–1942* (Stanford, CA, 1999), pp. 2, 210; Susan Zuccotti, *The Holocaust, the French and the Jews* (New York, 1993), p. 19.

[32]Figures in Richard I. Cohen, *The Burden of Conscience: French Jewish Leadership During the Holocaust* (Bloomington, IN, 1987), pp. 15–16; Douglas Porch, *The French Foreign Legion: The Complete History of the Legendary Fighting Force* (New York, 1991), pp. 451–7, 462–3.

[33]Figures in Caron, *Uneasy Asylum*, p. 330.

[34]Figure and quote from Cohen, *Burden of Conscience*, p. 18.

[35]Figures in Michael R. Marrus and Robert O. Paxton, *Vichy France and the Jews* (New York, 1981), p. 103; Caron, *Uneasy Asylum*, p. 332.

Women prisoners at Gurs cook soup in Îlot ("Bloc") 12. This photograph was shot secretly by Alice Rensch-Synnestvedt during her stay at Gurs in 1942 as a delegate of the American Friends Service Committee. *Source:* United States Holocaust Memorial Museum.

Vichy's initial solution was to intern aliens in a series of desolate detention camps in the unoccupied zone. Jews arriving from Germany in October 1940 were interned immediately. By January 1941, prisoners in these camps numbered 51,439. Two-thirds were Jews, including children, pregnant women, the elderly, and the sick. Conditions included exposure to harsh weather, hunger, disease, overcrowding, rats, lice, and cruelty from guards.

The most infamous detention camp in the unoccupied zone was at Gurs near the Pyrenees border with Spain. Built for 15,000 alien detainees in 1939, it eventually held 29,000. "Lice were everywhere," remembered Frederick Raymes, who was expelled from western Germany as a child. "There were frequent outbreaks of diphtheria, typhoid fever, dysentery, and other infectious diseases. . . . We can't remember receiving solid food. We were given watery soup in which a few cabbage leaves floated."[36] One Jewish physician at Gurs remembered an intestinal epidemic toward the end of 1940. "Over six hundred men and women," he said, "perished in those three months."[37]

Religious organizations such as the Quakers delivered food. The Joint Distribution Committee (JDC) provided funds. The *Oeuvre des Secours aux Enfants* ("French Children's Aid Society"), a Jewish children's welfare organization, moved many of the children to about a dozen orphanages in the unoccupied zone. The children received proper care, but most never saw their parents again. By November 1943, 1,038 people died at Gurs alone and 3,900 foreign Jews were shipped from Gurs to Auschwitz.[38] Jewish refugees in the Vichy zone who could support

---

[36]Frederick Raymes and Menachem Mayer, *Are the Trees in Bloom Over There? Thoughts and Memories of Two Brothers* (Jerusalem, 2002), pp. 75–76.

[37]Bella Gutterman and Naomi Morgenstern, eds., *The Gurs Haggadah: Passover in Perdition* (Jerusalem, 2003), p. 22

[38]Figures in Donna F. Ryan, *The Holocaust and the Jews of Marseille: The Enforcement of Anti-Semitic Policies in Vichy France* (Urbana, IL, 1996), p. 89.

themselves financially were not interned. But they lived under police surveillance in rural areas where, as foreigners competing for food and as Jews besides, they were hardly beloved.

Initial Anti-Jewish Legislation

In the aftermath of defeat, the Vichy government addressed many pressing issues: from the welfare of its prisoners of war (POWs) to meeting larcenous German occupation costs, to protecting its overseas empire. But it addressed the Jewish question from the start, and it did so—significantly—without any German prompting. Initially, the government targeted foreign Jews and Jews overseas. A law of July 22, 1940, just weeks after the cease-fire, called for the review of all naturalizations since 1927 (when citizenship was liberalized) and the stripping of citizenship from "undesirables." Six thousand eastern Jews instantly lost their citizenship.[39] A decree in October repealed French citizenship from some 40,000 Jews in Algeria, the North African colony with large cities like Algiers, which, with 1 million Europeans, was administratively part of France.

How did native French Jews react? The defeat shocked them, as it did everyone else. Their main concerns were not with Jews that they regarded as foreigners, particularly German ones. They were uneasy with the repeal of Algerian Jewish citizenship. But the severe blow came with Vichy's October 3, 1940, promulgation of the *Statut des Juifs*—the "Jewish Law"—that was applicable in both French zones. It defined Jews as having two Jewish grandparents (Germany's Nuremberg Laws used three), whether they were east Europeans or assimilated French. The *Statut* further excluded all Jews, including French Jews, from positions in the civil service, army, and any profession that influenced public opinion including the press, radio, film, and education.

Raymond-Raoul Lambert was a forty-six-year-old French Jewish liberal who had been involved in Jewish refugee affairs in the 1930s. He was a decorated soldier in World War I and an officer in World War II. He found the law so repugnant that he could only assume it came on Hitler's order, not from his own government. "What a boundless disgrace!" he wrote in his diary. "This cannot last, it's not possible. I shall never leave this country for which I risked my life, but can my sons live here if they are not allowed to choose freely what career to follow? Because of my blood I am no longer allowed to write, I am no longer an officer in the army. . . . I cannot believe it yet. . . ."[40]

A few openly protested. Lucien Vidal-Naquet of the law faculty at the University of Marseille protested before the Palace of Justice before losing his job.[41] Most *Israélites Françaises* adopted a quieter stance. Amidst Vichy propaganda blaming Jews for everything, from war profiteering to the malaise of the defunct republic, to the defeat itself, they emphasized their loyalty to France and the bravery of their sons, fathers, and grandfathers on battlefields past and present. But they remained stunned in disbelief. "Yesterday evening," Lambert wrote in mid-October, "I wept, like a man who is suddenly abandoned by the wife who has been the love of his life. . . ." In December he still insisted that "I am French in my culture, in my blood, and by inclination."[42]

Many eastern European Jews knew better. Bundist and Zionist organizations in Paris, together with their youth groups, immediately organized joint cooperatives to distribute necessities, establish clinics, and share news. Their canteens dispensed tens of thousands of meals.

---

[39]Figure in Caron, *Uneasy Asylum*, p. 325.

[40]Richard I. Cohen, ed., *Diary of a Witness 1940–1943* (hereafter *Lambert Diary*) (Chicago, IL, 2007), October 19, 1940.

[41]Ryan, *The Holocaust and the Jews of Marseille*, p. 25,

[42]*Lambert Diary*, October 19, 1940, December 20, 1940.

Jewish communists went underground immediately, perhaps less as Jews than as communists, and in June 1940, they began an underground Yiddish newspaper, *Unser Vort* ("*Our Word*") calling for resistance.[43] Jewish divisions contained seeds of tragedy. Wealthy French Jews, for instance, provided little aid to east European Jewish efforts. More money came from the JDC and Quaker organizations. French Jews' disinterest toward east European immigrants was difficult to overcome. As Frenchmen jilted by their own state, most were concerned with recovering their prewar status.

Xavier Vallat and the Commissariat for Jewish Affairs

Xavier Vallat was a fifty-year-old conservative Catholic politician who lost a leg and an eye in World War I. In March 1941, he became Vichy's first General Commissioner for Jewish Affairs. An open antisemite, Vallat blamed Jews for Christ's crucifixion and warned of their harmful economic and cultural influence. "The Jew," said Vallat, "is not only an unassimilable foreigner whose implantation leads to form a state within the state. He is also, by tempera-ment, a foreigner who wants to dominate."[44] A second *Statute des Juifs* enacted by Vallat on June 2, 1941, extended exclusions to the legal, medical, and architectural professions, as well as crafts and commerce. Two percent limits were later allowed for doctors, lawyers, and uni-versity students.

Vallat rejected lawless violence and subservience to the Germans. He expected Jews, par-ticularly foreign ones, to emigrate after the war. In deference to French liberal traditions—what Vallat called French sentimentality—his Jewish Statute also provided limited exemptions for those who had rendered "exceptional service" to France and those whose family trees in France stretched five generations—that is, a very select group of *Israélites Françaises*. These conces-sions, he thought, would make antisemitism go down more easily in France while avoiding obse-quiousness to the Germans.

French Jews scoured local archives to reconstruct their family trees and they retrieved evidence of service. But the state recognized almost no exemptions. French Jews who cited war records, medals, or wounds received replies such as "All French families have done what your family has done." René Guastalla, an academic and combat veteran, simply refused to submit a petition. To do so, he said, would be "to recognize the legitimacy of the law."[45] Thousands of Jewish civil servants—including teachers, judges, army officers, and eighteen Jewish parliamentarians—were dismissed throughout France and its empire.

In the summer of 1941, the Vichy government compiled a detailed Jewish census in the unoccupied zone that also inventoried Jewish property. As in the Netherlands, Jews were obliged to appear at police stations and fill out detailed census forms. French Jews, meanwhile, addressed pleading and even angry letters to the government. "On behalf of my child," wrote Madame René Lipmann to Marshall Pétain, "who has died as a hero [as a soldier in 1940] for our beloved France. . . . I dare demand justice for all." Perhaps 15 percent of Jews in the unoccupied zone, likely east Europeans, refused to complete census forms, a higher percentage than in the Netherlands.[46]

---

[43]Jacques Adler, *The Jews of Paris and the Final Solution: Communal Responses and Internal Conflicts, 1940–44* (New York, 1987), pp. 37, 166–7.

[44]Quoted in Marrus and Paxton, *Vichy France and the Jews*, p. 88.

[45]Quoted in Poznanski, *Jews in France*, pp. 108–09.

[46]Quote and figure in Poznanski, *Jews in France*, pp. 98, 101.

The transfer of Jewish property in the unoccupied zone to French owners in cities, from Marseille to Toulouse, soon followed in accordance with a law of July 22, 1941, which aimed at the elimination of "all Jewish influence from the national economy."[47] Nearly 2,000 Jewish properties, ranging from department stores to tailor shops, were transferred in the unoccupied zone alone.[48] And when Jewish businesses were aryanized, their Jewish employees were fired. Vallat assumed the French, not the Germans, would be the beneficiary of this measure. Indeed there was no shortage of French buyers.

The Germans and the *Union Générale des Israélites de France (UGIF)*

But did Vichy go far enough for the Germans? At first, German authorities were pleased enough to push Jews into the unoccupied zone. In September 1940, the Germans ordered a census of Jews in the occupied zone, including Paris, which revealed, even accounting for Jews who did not fill out the forms, that 75 percent of the Jews in Paris were foreigners and that half of the foreigners were from Poland.[49] The Germans also confiscated Jewish enterprises in the occupied zone and sold them to new French owners, while also plundering Jewish-owned artworks.

But this was not sufficient. Vichy interned thousands of foreign Jews and drove many more, foreign and French alike, into increasing poverty. But they had not fully segregated Jews, as was the case elsewhere. Despite antisemitic incidents, many French Jews interacted with neighbors. Jews could still congregate and communicate in synagogues and canteens. There were no curfews. Some French Jews lived on their cash reserves, while charities kept foreign Jews fed. And because of a loophole in the cease-fire agreement with France, German ordinances, which came from the army, applied to the occupied zone only.

The RSHA insisted on a more comprehensive Jewish policy, particularly once the war in the USSR began in June 1941. It was driven after August 1941 by Theodor Dannecker—Adolf Eichmann's representative in Paris from RSHA Office IV-B-4. Just twenty-eight years old, Dannecker aimed to implement his superiors' wishes for a complete solution to the Jewish question in Europe. Subtleties in French policy regarding exemptions and differences between eastern and French Jews did not interest him. He turned to Vallat, demanding the creation of a comprehensive Jewish organization for France as existed in Germany to implement German orders.

Vallat chafed at German meddling, but he approached established French Jewish leaders in the occupied and unoccupied zones, telling them that the Germans demanded such a body, that it could coordinate Jewish charities, and that it was better to work autonomously under Vichy's Commissariat for Jewish Affairs than under the Gestapo. Vallat's talks with Raymond-Raoul Lambert bore fruit. Lambert spoke for those French Jews who viewed a general responsibility to all Jews in France, both French and foreign. Vallat, Lambert wrote in his diary, "has the idea of creating a unified Jewish Community. Thus our charitable work in the [unoccupied] zone can continue . . . if, as he is planning to do, he gives us money to aid the poor . . . out of confiscated Jewish funds. . . . [We] cannot refuse since the important thing is for the social workers to carry on." In November 1941, the *Union Générale des Israélites de France* (UGIF) was established in both zones. Lambert became its leading figure. "I am pursuing my course," he wrote, "with a clear conscience and the clear desire to remain both an excellent Jew and an excellent Frenchman."[50]

---

[47]Quoted in Marrus and Paxton, *Vichy France and the Jews*, p. 152.

[48]Figure in Poznanski, *Jews in France*, p. 116.

[49]Figures in Adler, *The Jews of Paris*, pp. 8–9

[50]*Lambert Diary*, October 3, 1941, November 30, 1941.

The Germans took advantage immediately. Even in May 1941, the Germans ordered the arrest of nearly 4,000 foreign Jews in Paris for underground activity. Most were interned in a makeshift camp in Drancy near the city. With the German invasion of the USSR, the Jewish communist press in Paris called for greater resistance. Jewish women from various groups demonstrated openly for the release of the internees. In August, Dannecker ordered the arrest of over 4,000 more Jews in Paris. In November, the World Jewish Congress, now headquartered in Geneva, relayed a report that the 8,000 Jews sent to Drancy "have been condemned to slow death by starvation, cold [and] the lack of the most primitive hygiene requirements."[51] In October, Jewish communists initiated strikes in the Paris glove and woolen industries, which supplied German troops on the Eastern Front. Bund and Zionist groups joined in.[52]

But with the formation of the UGIF, Dannecker could act against all Jews in France. On December 6, 1941, the Germans fined the UGIF 1 billion francs. It was an enormous sum that came from blocked Jewish accounts and from loans that the UGIF had to procure from the Bank of France. On December 12, the Gestapo arrested and detained 743 well-known Parisian Jews, including doctors, professors, and writers. Vallat, who believed that Jewish affairs in France were his own prerogative, protested the highhandedness. "I have been an antisemite far longer than you," he chided Dannecker in February 1942. "What's more, I am old enough to be your father."[53] Dannecker did not have to listen. On March 27, 1942, 558 of the prisoners arrested in December were deported. It was the first train from western Europe to Auschwitz.[54] Vallat was dismissed the following month.

7.4 WAS ESCAPE STILL POSSIBLE?—*ALIYAH BET*

How *Aliyah Bet* Worked

According to the 1939 White Paper, the British were to issue 10,000 immigration certificates for Palestine each year for the next five years. But the war made Middle Eastern stability all the more crucial and changed London's thinking. The authorities issued no certificates from October 1939 through March 1940 and 9,050 from April 1940 through March 1941. And a certificate did not guarantee one's ability to reach Palestine in wartime. In 1940, only 4,547 legal immigrants made it there, and in 1941, the number was 3,647.[55]

Illegal immigration to Palestine, what Zionists called *Aliyah Bet* ("Plan B" immigration) had existed since 1934. In 1939, it became more urgent. It was simple in theory. Embarking in Vienna, groups of Jewish refugees could be ferried down the Danube River, which winds through Hungary, Yugoslavia, and Romania, and spills into the Black Sea. An international waterway, the Danube obviated the need for multiple transit visas, save for Romania, which sold transit visas in limited numbers to Jews after 1938. From Romania, another ship could take refugees down the Black Sea coast, through the Turkish Straits and the Aegean to Palestine, where launches could carry the refugees ashore, hopefully without detection.

---

[51]Henry Friedlander and Sybil Milton, gen. eds., *Archives of the Holocaust: An International Collection of Selected Documents*, vol. 8, doc. 46.

[52]Figures in Adler, *The Jews of Paris*, pp. 175–86.

[53]Quoted in Marrus and Paxton, *Vichy France*, pp. 110–9.

[54]Susan Zuccotti, *The Holocaust, the French, and the Jews*, pp. 88–9.

[55]Figures in Dalia Ofer, *Escaping the Holocaust: Illegal Immigration to the Land of Israel, 1939–1944* (New York, 1990), p. 320.

In reality, the plan was harder to put into motion. The only ships available once war broke out were in disrepair. Shipping agents charged at least double the usual prices for chartered ships. Fearing arrest by the British and seizure of their vessels, most captains and crews shied away from smuggling immigrants. Those who risked it were unsavory characters, who also overcharged. Jewish money deposited for illegal charters was lost when deals fell through. Delays in procuring and repairing ships meant that groups of refugees were stranded for months in hostile areas.

Various groups organized *Aliyah Bet*. They ranged from the Mossad (the intelligence arm of the Hagana, the Palestine Jewish militia) and the Revisionist Zionists (who called for a flood of illegal immigrants to Palestine), both of which preferred to take young Zionists who were trained for life in Palestine. Individual Jewish businessmen in Europe who understood the shipping trade and who could pull together partial financing also arranged transports and did not limit themselves to Zionist passengers. Ironically, the Gestapo supported ad hoc smuggling in 1939 and 1940 because of Berlin's aim of expelling Jews from the Reich any way it could. The Germans extended travel visas for Mossad agents trying to arrange illegal immigration and interceded with German shipping lines to facilitate Danube transports.

British Officials and Zionist Leaders

Jewish leaders in Palestine viewed *Aliyah Bet* as a moral absolute. "Anyone," said Hagana leader Aaron Zisling, "who calls for a halt in immigration at a time [like this] negates our very right to stand on this soil." Jewish Agency Executive chairman David Ben-Gurion was more careful. The British were fighting the Nazis, and a rupture with London could make the Jewish plight even worse. "We must," he said on September 12, 1939, "aid the [British] army as if there were no White Paper, and fight the White Paper as if there were no war."[56] Zionist leaders pressed London only so far while winking at illegal immigration.

Between September and December 1939, 3,880 illegal immigrants reached Palestine on five transports.[57] British colonial officials suspected the worst from Zionist leaders. "The Jews," said Colonial Office Undersecretary Sir John Shuckburgh in February 1940, "are all out to defeat the White Paper policy. . . . [The] obvious means is to pour . . . illegals into the country as rapidly as possible. Every Arab . . . will be convinced that . . . we have surrendered to Jewish pressure. . . ."[58] British officials also thought the Gestapo used Jewish transports to send German agents to Palestine. No such agents were ever discovered.

Meanwhile the British tried to scotch *Aliyah Bet*. On the prompting of Sir Harold MacMichael, the British high commissioner in Palestine, London pressured the Romanian, Bulgarian, Greek, and Turkish governments to prevent the use of their ships for refugee smuggling. The British also impounded ships, arrested crews, and interned Jewish refugees who arrived illegally, eventually releasing them but counting their numbers against pending immigration certificates. It seemed the only option. No one in Europe would take the refugees back. Prime Minister Winston Churchill was sympathetic to the refugees. "I should be glad to know," he wrote Colonial Secretary Malcolm MacDonald, "how you propose to treat these wretched people when they have been rounded up."[59] But Churchill would not overrule his officials either.

---

[56]Quoted in Ofer, *Escaping the Holocaust*, pp. 19–26.

[57]Figures in Ofer, *Escaping the Holocaust*, pp. 323–34.

[58]Quoted in Michael J. Cohen, *Churchill and the Jews* (London, 1985), p. 278.

[59]Quoted in Bernard Wasserstein, *Great Britain and the Jews of Europe, 1939–1945* (London, 1979), p. 55.

British soldiers stand guard on a beach in Tel Aviv to detain Jewish refugees landing from the ship *Parita*, in August 1939. *Source:* Central Zionist Archives.

The *Atlantic* Tragedy

Matters came to a head in 1940 when Adolf Eichmann pressed for more Jews to sail for Palestine. He used Bernhard Storfer, a Jewish businessman in Vienna with international shipping links, to speed arrangements. Storfer had long experience with *Aliyah Bet*, connections to German Jewish communities, and access to the JDC. After difficult preparations, he arranged for a large group of 3,500 Jews from throughout the Reich to sail via Tulcia, Romania. The diverse group included young Zionists, more than 500 persons over sixty-five years old, and a number of Jews recently freed from Buchenwald.

The ships Storfer hired, the *Atlantic* (1,829 passengers), the *Pacific* (1,061 passengers), and the *Milos* (702 passengers), left Tulcia between October 7 and 11, 1940. British naval patrols, tipped by British intelligence, intercepted all three and detained the passengers in Haifa. Conditions on board shocked the authorities. All three ships were short on food and fuel. The overcrowded *Atlantic* had no lifeboats or life preservers, and for air in the hold, passengers cut holes in the hull near the waterline. Yet by now MacMichael was completely frustrated. Intending to placate the Arabs while dissuading further smuggling, he planned to deport the new arrivals to Mauritius, an island in the Indian Ocean. He arranged to use the *Patria*, a commandeered French liner. The Hagana planted a bomb on the *Patria* simply to sabotage it and thwart the deportation, but the plan went awry on November 25. The *Pacific* and *Milos* passengers boarded. Then as the *Atlantic's* passengers climbed aboard the bomb tore through the *Patria's* hull. It sank in minutes, killing 267.

MacMichael insisted on seeing the deportation to Mauritius through. But the global reach of the story, intervention of US Jewish leaders, and Churchill's sympathy for the refugees induced compromise. The *Patria's* survivors remained in Palestine. The remaining passengers of the *Atlantic*—1,580 in all, including 621 women and 116 children—went to Mauritius. These deportations were carried out as a military operation. British authorities dragged the passengers from their barracks, beating many, then transported them to the harbor on roads that they sealed off in advance. Forty-one passengers died of typhus en route to Mauritius.[60]

Disasters at Sea

Aliyah Bet continued under more difficult circumstances. Baruch Konfino, a Jewish doctor in Bulgaria, had arranged four successful voyages on the seaworthy *Rudnitchar* in 1939. In early 1940, the Bulgarian government, perhaps under British pressure, told Konfino that he could no longer use the ship. He found other vessels of poorer quality, including the *Salvador*, a rotten wooden ship with nonfunctioning engines, that was towed to sea and put under sail in December 1940. The overcrowded boat hit a storm, split in two, and sank. There were eighty lifejackets on board. Most of the 350 passengers drowned. The British broadcast the news to southeast Europe to dissuade further voyages. "There could have been no more opportune disaster," said a British Foreign Office official, "from the point of view of stopping the [illegal] traffic." Most of the *Salvador*'s survivors were deported back to Bulgaria.[61]

   Aliyah Bet might have saved more Jews. From September 1939 to March 1941, fifteen ships left Europe with 12,863 Jewish refugees bound for Palestine. Yet it could not solve the Jewish plight. The months that it took to arrange single voyages, some with only several dozen passengers, did not accord with Hitler's timetable. In 1939 and 1940, the Germans were pleased enough to push for speedier emigration. The prohibition on Jewish emigration from the Reich, decreed in October 1941, ended such possibilities. For the remainder of the war, eighteen ships left Romanian ports with 5,703 passengers. In February 1942, a Soviet submarine mistakenly sunk the first of these, the *Struma*, after the British authorities refused to let it proceed to Palestine after it received repairs in Turkey. All but one of the 769 aboard drowned.[62]

7.5 OTHER ESCAPE ROUTES: THE AMERICAS AND ASIA

Breckinridge Long and US Immigration Policy

The United States first filled its visa quota for German Jews in 1939. It was also the last time the quota was filled. Jews entering the United States in fiscal year 1940 from all countries numbered 36,945, with 19,880 declaring Germany their last country of residence. In fiscal year 1941, overall Jewish immigration dropped to 23,737, with 3,793 declaring Germany their last country of residence. In the same year, just 404 arriving Jews declared Poland and Romania as last countries of residence. The numbers dropped precipitously thereafter: 10,608 Jews arrived in fiscal year 1942, and just 4,705 in fiscal year 1943.[63]

   What had happened? It is true that antisemitic voices in the United States became louder when the war broke out. Speakers such as Father Charles Coughlin and Charles Lindbergh warned receptive audiences in 1939 and 1940 that Jews were trying to push the United States into war. But growing fear of communist and Nazi infiltration with the outbreak of war also had a Jewish aspect. Eastern Jews were suspected communists and German Jews possible Nazi agents.

---

[60]Story in Ofer, *Escaping the Holocaust*, pp. 38–39, 98–127.

[61]Figures and quote in Wasserstein, *Britain and the Jews of Europe*, pp. 76–77.

[62]Figures above and *Struma* affair in Ofer, *Escaping the Holocaust*, pp. 147–166, 326–27.

[63]Figures in *American Jewish Yearbook*, vol. 43, pp. 681–2; vol. 44, pp. 589–90.

Even Roosevelt noted in June 1940 that "the refugee has got to be checked. . . ." The Nazis, he said, could force Jews to spy by threatening their families. Such cases, Roosevelt said, were "a very, very small percentage," but "it is something that we have to watch."[64]

In the spring of 1940, Roosevelt appointed Breckinridge Long, a loyal political supporter, as Assistant Secretary of State for Special War Problems—a new division that included the visa section. A stickler for rules, a bare-knuckled political infighter, and a genteel southern antisemite who found Hitler's equation of Jews with Bolshevism "eloquent," Long became America's gatekeeper.[65] Primarily, he viewed himself as a guardian against foreign agents. "Among the refugees," he repeatedly warned, "are many agents of the German Government."[66] Long's infamous memorandum of June 1940 recommended barring suspicious aliens even if their paperwork seemed in order:

> We can delay and effectively stop for a temporary period of indefinite length the number of immigrants . . . by simply advising our consuls to put every obstacle in the way and to require additional evidence and to resort to administrative devices, which would postpone and postpone and postpone the granting of visas.[67]

In 1941, Long added more bureaucratic hurdles. He told consuls to reject applicants even from neutral or occupied states who had close family members in German-controlled territory. He instituted new, longer visa forms that were now reviewed by consuls *and* three separate committees in Washington that included FBI and army intelligence personnel. Even if approved, a visa was valid only for the fiscal year in which it was granted. Roosevelt meanwhile gave Long the benefit of the doubt, signing in June 1941 the Bloom-Van Nuys Bill, which required consuls to consider public safety when reviewing visas forms.

Jewish leaders accused the State Department of using security as a cover for antisemitism. American rabbis visited Long personally with thousands of names of Jews to save. They were generally unsuccessful.[68] And in June 1941, the Germans insisted that the United States close its consulates in German-occupied Europe. The Americans, Berlin said, were spying. As already stated, Himmler prohibited Jewish emigration from the Reich altogether in October 1941.

US immigration numbers still compared well for the western hemisphere. Canada allowed 626 Jewish immigrants in fiscal year 1941, more than half of whom came from the United States. In August 1941, Argentina refused a British request to take twenty Jewish children with relatives in Buenos Aires. There were "already too many Jews in the Argentine," said Ambassador Tomás Le Breton. Perhaps, he suggested, British doctors could sterilize the children first. Up to 2,200 Jews reached Argentina in 1941, usually after family members in Argentina paid bribes of up to $5,000 to Argentine officials.[69] Cuba expected $2,800 in surety bonds per head.[70] Bolivia and the Dominican Republic accepted Jews owing to US efforts. But tens of thousands more could have been rescued.

---

[64]Quoted in Richard Breitman and Alan Kraut, *American Refugee Policy and European Jewry, 1933–1945* (Bloomington, IN, 1988), p. 121.

[65]Quoted in Henry Feingold, *The Politics of Rescue: The Roosevelt Administration and the Holocaust, 1938–1945* (New Brunswick, NJ, 1970), p. 135.

[66]Quoted in Bat-Ami Zucker, *In Search of Refuge* (London, 2001), pp. 99–101.

[67]Quoted in Zucker, *In Search of Refuge*, p. 41.

[68]Breitman and Kraut, *American Refugee Policy*, pp. 135–6.

[69] *AJC Yearbook*, vols. 43, 44; Haim Avni, *Argentina and the Jews: A History of Jewish Immigration* (Tuscaloosa, AL, 2002) p. 157; conversation with Tomás Le Breton, August 5, 1941, Great Britain, National Archives, FO/371/29210. I am grateful to Richard McGaha for the National Archives reference.

[70]Yehuda Bauer, *American Jewry and the Holocaust: The American Jewish Joint Distribution Committee, 1939–1945* (Detroit, MI, 1981), p. 60.

Diplomatic Rescuers: Aristides de Sousa Mendes

Even with a visa for the Americas, how could one arrange transport in relative safety? Germany's conquest of the Low Countries and France, plus Italy's entrance into the war, made it nearly impossible to sail from those countries' ports. The best remaining prospect in western Europe was neutral Portugal. Even here, however, the situation was difficult. The authoritarian government under Antonio Oliveira de Salazar did not want Portugal overrun with refugees. In November 1939, the Portuguese foreign ministry issued a consular directive—Circular 14—according to which various categories of peoples, including most Jews, were not to receive visas of any kind without prior foreign ministry approval.

The matter became urgent in the spring of 1940, when Germany's western offensive drove throngs of refugees into southern France. In mid-June, Bordeaux became the temporary seat of the French republican government, which had fled Paris. It was in chaos. State officials commandeered hotels. Ambassadors slept in cars. Crowds of refugees, 30,000 of who might have been Jews, lined up at consulates hoping to get visas for anywhere before the Germans arrived. "My father," remembered Regina Weiss, whose family fled from Cologne to Amsterdam, to Paris, to Bordeaux, "went to every consulate and tried to get every visa he could possibly get."[71]

Portugal's consul in Bordeaux was Aristides de Sousa Mendes, a fifty-five-year-old career diplomat. While away from his consulate building, de Sousa met Chaim Kruger, a rabbi in Antwerp's Orthodox community who had fled south with his wife and five children. Kruger had no money or shelter. De Sousa took the Krugers and other families in. The Portuguese consulate and even de Sousa's private apartment were filled with refugees. There were, according to de Sousa's nephew, "dozens of them . . . and mainly old and sick people. They slept on chairs, on the floor, on the rugs. . . . Most of them had nothing but the clothes they were wearing."[72]

But what they most needed were transit visas. De Sousa asked Lisbon for guidance. He was ordered to follow Circular 14. Wedged between his conscience and his orders, de Sousa retired to his bedroom for three tortured days. He emerged on June 16 with a decision, which he claimed came from God: "I'm giving everyone visas," he said.[73] Rarely stopping, de Sousa began signing visas and waiving fees. Rabbi Kruger helped by gathering passports from the crowd outside and returning them with signed Portuguese transit visas inside. "Jews!" Kruger called into the crowd. "Give me your passports! I will get you visas!"[74]

Ignoring orders from Lisbon that he cease, de Sousa next traveled to the border towns of Bayonne, Hendaye, and Biarritz, signing more visas and ordering subordinates to sign them too. His superiors were furious, ordering him back to Lisbon on June 24. The Germans entered Bordeaux six days later. It is not clear how many visas were issued to Jewish refugees thanks to de Sousa—perhaps around 6,500.[75] They were lifesavers. With the visas, the refugees could cross Spain into Portugal.

---

[71]Regina Weiss interview, January 22, 1998, University of Southern California, Shoah Foundation Institute.

[72]Quoted in Avraham Milgram, "Portugal, the Consuls and the Jewish Refugees, 1938–1941," *Yad Vashem Studies*, 27 (1999), pp. 123–55.

[73]Quoted in José-Alain Fralon, *A Good Man in Evil Times: The Story of Aristides de Sousa Mendes* (London, 2000), p. 60.

[74]Remembered by Rabbi Jacob Kruger, Interview of 1992, Museo Virtual Aristides de Sousa Mendes, http://mvasm. sapo.pt.

[75]For the estimate, see Milgram, "Portugal, the Consuls and Jewish Refugees."

Ironically, by the end of 1940, the Portuguese government liberalized its policy, allowing and even extending transit visas for Jews as long as their maintenance and transportation costs out of Portugal were paid. Trains ran regularly from Berlin, Vienna, and Prague to Lisbon carrying Jews who had arranged visas and travel. Jewish organizations, including the JDC, helped arrange travel and covered most costs. Perhaps 25,000 Jews in all escaped to Lisbon between 1940 and 1942.[76] De Sousa, meanwhile, was fired for disobedience. As Rabbi Kruger's son Jacob remembered years later "[h]e was willing to sacrifice everything he had."[77] De Souza died in 1954 owning nothing more than his burial plot.

Diplomatic Rescuers: Sugihara Chiune

A similar story involved Lithuania, a haven for Jews fleeing Poland in 1939. Vilna, a historic center of Jewish culture and Zionist politics (now Vilnius as the Lithuanian capital) belonged to Poland between the wars. In September 1939, the Soviets occupied the city, then transferred it to Lithuania as part of the arrangement by which Germany received the future Lublin district and Stalin could occupy an enlarged Lithuania at his discretion. Before the Soviets closed the border with Poland in December 1939, some 15,000 Jewish refugees fled Poland for Vilna, including religious and political leaders. Lithuanian independence ended when the Soviets occupied the Baltic States in June 1940.

Jewish refugee leaders in Vilna feared the Soviets would arrest them as state enemies. But where could they go? Europe to the west was German-controlled. One could reach the United States by heading east. But the US ambassador in Moscow, Laurence Steinhardt, America's only senior Jewish diplomat in Europe, would not help. An "uptown" descendant of German Jews who placed security and career concerns first, Steinhardt reported that Zionist and Bundist leaders were "professional political agitators," not fit to become US citizens.[78] A somewhat fictional possibility was the Dutch Caribbean colony of Curaçao. One needed the Dutch governor's permission to disembark on arrival there, but Jan Zwartendijk, who represented the Dutch government-in-exile in Lithuania, was willing to stamp passports that "entry to Curaçao does not require a visa." This "official" stamp made it theoretically possible to procure a transit visa for Japan, which was the logical stopover en route. Word spread among Jewish refugees in Vilna, who appeared at Japan's consulate in Lithuania's capital of Kovno.

Sugihara Chiune was the Japanese consul. As he shut down the consulate—Moscow ordered foreign consulates in Lithuania closed by August 31, 1940—he wired for instructions. Tokyo agreed with transit visas as long as the holders had money to support themselves and permission to enter a third country. Interpreting these instructions liberally, Sugihara issued 2,132 transit visas, some for whole families, some for Jews lacking Zwartendijk's Curaçao stamp. Visa holders still needed Soviet exit visas, rail passage to the Soviet port of Vladivostok, and ship passage to Japan. But with help from the JDC, some 3,044 Jews reached Japan before the Germans invaded the USSR in June 1941. They stayed in the coastal Japanese town of Kobe, from which a small number reached Palestine, others reached the western hemisphere, and over 1,000 were sent to Shanghai by September 1941.[79]

---

[76]Bauer, *American Jewry and the Holocaust*, p. 48.

[77]Rabbi Jacob Kruger, Interview of 1992, Museo Virtual Aristides de Sousa Mendes, http://mvasm.sapo.pt.

[78]Quoted in Barry Rubin, "Ambassador Laurence A. Steinhardt: The Perils of a Jewish Diplomat, 1940–1945," *American Jewish History*, 7, no. 3 (March 1981), p. 334.

[79]Figures in Gao Bei, *Shanghai Sanctuary: Chinese and Japanese Policy Toward European Jewish Refugees During World War II* (New York, 2012), Chapters 3, 4; Pamela Rotner Sakamoto, *Japanese Diplomats and Jewish Refugees: A World War II Dilemma* (Westport, CT, 1998), pp. 101–32.

Why did Imperial Japan, hardly a humanitarian state, accept Jewish refugees? Japanese leaders had hoped since the 1930s that imagined Jewish power could help in Japan's quest for expansion. Inuzuka Koreshige, a naval captain and one of Japan's "Jewish experts," had likened Jews to the Fugu, a seafood delicacy, that "may prove fatal," but could be delightful if "one knows well how to prepare [it] properly. . . ." For this reason, German Jews were permitted to enter Shanghai in 1939. By September 1940, Japan had signed a defense pact with Germany, and Foreign Minister Matsuoka Yōsuke was reluctant to accept refugees in Japan. But he still hoped that aid for Jews might improve relations with Washington. Tokyo had yet to decide on war with the United States. Years later, the head of the Jewish community in Kobe remembered Matsuoka's "great scheme in dealing with the Jewish power."[80] Sugihara, meanwhile, spent the rest of the war in Japan's embassy in Bucharest. He explained his own, simpler thinking five decades later. "There is nothing wrong," he said, "in saving many people's lives."[81]

---

[80]Quotes in David Kranzler, "The Japanese Ideology of Antisemitism and the Holocaust," *Contemporary Views on the Holocaust*, ed. Randolph Braham (Dordrecht, 1983), pp. 79–102.

[81]Quoted in Hillel Levine, *In Search of Sugihara: The Elusive Japanese Diplomat Who Risked His Life to Rescue 10,000 Jews from the Holocaust* (New York, 1996), p. 259.

8

Other Enemies
Steps Toward Mass Murder

In 1941 and 1942, the persecution of Europe's Jews turned to mass murder. The Final Solution to the Jewish Question in Europe, as the Nazis called it, envisioned the killing of every Jew in Germany's reach. Even before this shift, the Nazis adopted more organized maltreatment and even murder of other political and biological enemies. Victims ranged from disabled Germans to French African prisoners of war (POWs). At the same time Germany approved of murderous policies by their allies in southeast Europe, Romania, and Croatia. When Berlin reached the decision to murder Europe's Jews, the Nazi state had already espoused mass murder as a desirable policy.

8.1 THE AD-HOC KILLING OF SOCIAL OUTSIDERS

Nazi Germany persecuted and often killed social outsiders. By 1937, those in German concentration camps were denoted by colored cloth triangles sewn upside down onto their uniforms. Red triangles signified political prisoners such as communists. Green denoted career and habitual criminals. Asocials, a broad category that included Roma ("Gypsies"), alcoholics, and prostitutes, wore black triangles. Jehovah's Witnesses bore purple triangles and homosexuals pink ones. A yellow triangle sewn right side up under the other made a Star of David and identified the inmate as a Jew in one of the aforementioned categories. Not all of Germany's social outsiders were marked for death. The state allowed for the possibility that homosexuals and Jehovah's Witnesses would "reform." Large numbers of others, however, such as Roma and habitual criminals, were deliberately murdered along with the Jews after the decision to kill the Jews was reached.

Homosexuals

Nazism frowned on homosexual men in Germany, where, according to a 1933 estimate, they numbered at least 2 million.[1] Homosexuality supposedly reflected republican decadence. It also

---

[1] Geoffrey J. Giles, "The Institutionalization of Homosexual Panic in the Third Reich," in *Social Outsiders in Nazi Germany*, eds. Robert Gellately and Nathan Stoltzfus (Princeton, NJ, 2001), p. 243.

slowed racial propagation and subverted "manliness" needed for conquest. But to the Nazis, homosexuality was at least partly "correctable." The state punished homosexual acts and murdered homosexuals, but never tried to exterminate homosexuals entirely.

In 1933, the Nazis saw themselves as applying earlier laws from 1871 prohibiting "unnatural indecency" between males. Thus, Hermann Göring's police in Prussia closed homosexuals' bars and banned their literature. Heinrich Himmler, who obsessed over homosexuality and believed it contagious, was more aggressive after becoming Chief of German Police in 1936. More systematic police arrests began, especially in the permissive port city of Hamburg.

The press meanwhile represented homosexuals as effeminate seducers prowling for young boys. It portrayed Adolf Seefeld, an actual sexual predator prosecuted and hanged in 1936 for raping and killing twelve boys, as typical. "Germany," said one Hamburg newspaper, "has no use for criminals and weaklings, perverts and inverts, but requires instead straightforward and sincere manly souls."[2]

Some 50,000 homosexual men were arrested between 1933 and 1945, most after denunciation by neighbors, coworkers, landlords, hotel managers, or friends, the last under police interrogation.[3] Himmler hoped that proper punishment (time in prison or a concentration camp) would deter homosexual behavior. Those seduced, he was sure, could return to the straight and narrow. But those repeatedly arrested were deemed incorrigible. Per a Himmler order of 1940, they were sent to concentration camps, even after completing prison sentences. In an effort to scotch homosexual acts in the SS, Himmler in 1941 also prescribed the death penalty for SS men who engaged in these acts. Detailed investigations took place until the last weeks of the war.[4]

Up to 10,000 homosexuals spent time in concentration camps from 1933 to 1945. Their pink triangles meant torment not only at the hands of the SS, who killed them for sport or assigned them the hardest jobs, but also from fellow inmates. During the war, the medical staff at Buchenwald performed often fatal medical experiments on homosexuals involving hormonal injections into testicles. Himmler thought they would find a "cure" for homosexuality.[5] Thirteen percent of homosexual concentration camp inmates were released. Sixty percent died. "The inmates with the pink triangle," said one witness, "never lived long."[6]

Jehovah's Witnesses

Jehovah's Witnesses are a small religious denomination that emerged in the 1870s from independent Bible study groups in the United States. By the 1930s, they espoused the conviction that the Bible was literal truth, that 1914 marked the start of humanity's final phase, and that believers would survive Armageddon to live in an earthly paradise. Witnesses preach door to door and distribute their publication, *The Watchtower*. They reject worldly associations, refuse to salute

---

[2]Quoted in Stefan Micheler, "Homophobic Propaganda and the Denunciation of Same-Sex-Desiring Men Under National Socialism," in *Sexuality and German Fascism*, ed. Dagmar Herzog (New York, 2005), pp. 115–6.

[3]Figure in Micheler, "Homophobic Propaganda," 117–30.

[4]Geoffrey Giles, "The Denial of Homosexuality: Same Sex Incidents in Himmler's SS and Police," *Journal of the History of Sexuality*, 11, no. 1 (January/April 2002), pp. 256–90.

[5]Documents in Günther Grau, ed., *Homosexualität in der NS-Zeit: Dokumente einer Diskriminierung und Verfolgung* (Frankfurt, 1993), pp. 347–58.

[6]Figures and quote in Rüdiger Lautmann, "The Pink Triangle: Homosexuals as 'Enemies of the State,'" in *The Holocaust: The Known, the Unknown, the Disputed and the Reexamined*, eds. Michael Berenbaum and Abraham J. Peck (Bloomington, IN, 1996), pp. 343–57.

national flags, and refuse military service. As one scholar puts it, "Jehovah's Witnesses see them-selves as citizens of another state and members of another army."[7]

Jehovah's Witnesses arrived in Germany in the 1890s. There were 25,000 when Hitler came to power. They were no threat to anyone, but they represented a rival ideology based (seemingly) on Judaism and were international in scope. Unlike German Catholics and Protestants, they would neither join Nazi Party organizations nor serve in the army. Their children refused to sing national songs or give the Hitler salute in school. Harassment and arrests of Jehovah's Witnesses began in 1933, and in 1935, the state officially banned the sect. Jehovah's Witnesses tried convincing the government through petitions, declarations, and leaflets that they were politically neutral.

Regardless, from 1933 to 1945, police arrested some 10,000 Jehovah's Witnesses. Two thousand went to concentration camps. At certain times female Witnesses—including seventy-year-old grandmothers—made up the highest percentage of prisoners in some women's camps. The state took children from parents and placed them in reformatories, where they were beaten for recalcitrance. Nazi administrators in prisons, camps, and reformatories tried to force Jehovah's Witnesses to sign preprinted declarations renouncing their faith. A few signed and gained release, but most refused despite threats of worse treatment. Jehovah's Witnesses not arrested continued to operate, either underground in Germany or in exile where their publications exposed Nazi violence. The Nazis strengthened their resolve.

Persecution turned more deadly with the war. Military courts sentenced some 250 male Jehovah's Witnesses to death by firing squad or guillotine for refusing military service. Jehovah's Witnesses were the largest group executed for this offense. "As a true Christian," said thirty-one-year-old Franz Zeiner before his court martial in 1940, he "could not and would not bear arms. God," he insisted, "prohibited killing." The court ruled that Zeiner's "implacable opposition to military service is dangerous propaganda [that] can undermine the willingness of others for military service. Therefore the death penalty must be implemented."[8] Up to eighty female Jehovah's Witnesses were similarly executed for refusing to do war-related work or for repeated arrests.

Jehovah's Witnesses sustained each other in camps. They shared their food, prayed before they ate, and offered each other spiritual comfort. They endured taunts of SS guards and helped one another through hard labor. They maintained Bible study, although Bibles were prohibited. "No one understands how they can stand it," remembered one Jewish survivor from the Neuengamme camp near Hamburg. "They say that Jehovah gives them the strength for this."[9] Regardless roughly 1,200 Jehovah's Witnesses died as a result of Nazi persecution, 60 percent of the number of Witnesses remanded to camps.[10]

Habitual Criminals

In November 1933, the Nazi state enacted the Law Against Dangerous Habitual Criminals, which allowed courts to assign "security confinement"—indefinite prison terms in separate prison blocks—for incorrigible offenders. The criterion was three criminal acts. By October 1942, more

---

[7]Christine King, "Jehovah's Witnesses Under Nazism," in *A Mosaic of Victims: Non-Jews Persecuted by the Nazis*, ed. Michael Berenbaum (New York, 1990), p. 188.

[8]Case in Sybil Milton, "Jehovah's Witnesses: A Documentation," in *Persecution and Resistance of Jehovah's Witnesses During the Nazi Regime, 1933–1945*, ed. Hans Hesse (Bremen, 2001), pp. 161–4.

[9]Quoted in Christoph Daxelmüller, "Solidarity and the Will to Survive: Religious and Social Behavior of Jehovah's Witnesses in Concentration Camps," in Hesse, ed., *Persecution and Resistance of Jehovah's Witnesses*, p. 25.

[10]Figure for arrests and deaths in Hesse, ed., *Persecution and Resistance of Jehovah's Witnesses*, pp. 12, 32. See also Detlef Garbe, *Between Resistance and Martyrdom: Jehovah's Witnesses in the Third Reich* (Madison, WN, 2008).

than 14,000 Germans were in security confinement.[11] Relatively few were the violent, hardened criminals who became sadistic block leaders, or *Kapos*, in concentration camps. Most were poorly educated urban males, often with alcohol problems, who engaged in small-time stealing. Before 1933, police arrested hundreds of them, but prisons provided no rehabilitation. The Nazis saw them as a biologically flawed part of the *Volk* to be weeded out.

After the law's enactment, repeat offenders received indefinite sentences in security confinement. Numerous habitual criminals already in regular prisons received similar sentences retroactively. Security confinement meant military drill, nine hours of hard labor daily, and sometimes sterilization for the especially incorrigible. Many such inmates sank into poor health from overwork, underfeeding, and the strain of not knowing when sentences would end. One wrote to his sister in 1937, "I have stolen, but I will rather do myself in . . . than be buried alive."[12] One chronic thief, on his arrest for stealing a coat in 1940, dug his eyes out with a pencil to avoid indefinite security confinement.

When the war began in 1939, security-confined prisoners' workday expanded to twelve hours and their food rations shrank. More became ill from malnutrition and unfit for work. By 1941, Hitler and the Justice Ministry lost patience. The death penalty was now applied to multiple offenders who came before the courts and, starting in late 1942, more than 20,000 asocials, including habitual criminals, were moved from prisons to concentration camps where they were systematically annihilated through work and SS barbarity. The shift came from Hitler's phobia that the weak and degenerate were living while the brave died in battle. It was time, he said, to "ruthlessly exterminate the vermin."[13] By mid-February 1944, three-fourths of the more than 10,000 security-confined prisoners transported to Mauthausen in Austria were dead. After Jews, the security-confined were the most likely group to die in Mauthausen in this period.

8.2 FORAY INTO MASS MURDER: KILLING THE DISABLED

Hitler and the Disabled

Disabled Germans were the first victims of comprehensive, state-planned Nazi mass murder. As early as 1929, Hitler proclaimed,

> If Germany were to get a million children a year and were to remove 700–800,000 of the weakest people, then the final result [would] be an increase in strength. . . . As the result of our modern sentimental humanitarianism we are trying to maintain the weak at the expense of the healthy. It goes so far that a sense of charity . . . [ensures] that even cretins are able to procreate while healthy people refrain from doing so.[14]

Hitler drew on a body of German pseudomedical writing that appeared in the lean years after World War I. It called for "merciful" elimination of life rendered "unworthy of life," pointing to the mentally disabled in particular. By 1932, German universities offered over forty courses on "racial hygiene." Theoretically the issue was economic. Patients in state mental asylums

---

[11]Figure in Nikolaus Wachsmann, "'Annihilation Through Labor': The Killing of State Prisoners in the Third Reich," *Journal of Modern History* (September 1999), p. 645.

[12]Quoted in Nikolaus Wachsmann, "From Indefinite Confinement to Extermination: 'Habitual Criminals' in the Third Reich," in *Social Outsiders in Nazi Germany*, p. 174.

[13]Quoted in Wachsmann, Gellately and Stoltzfus, eds., "Annihilation Through Labor," p. 628.

[14]Klaus A. Lenkheit, ed., *Hitler: Reden, Schriften, Anordnungen Februar 1925 bis Januar 1933*, vol. 2, part 2 (Munich, 1994), p. 348.

increased during the Weimar years. Facility budgets did not. Yet contempt was clear. *Morons*, *idiots*, and *imbeciles* were the terms many officials and doctors used to describe the mentally ill.

In 1933, German racial hygienists had a government that spoke their language. The Nazis churned out literature dehumanizing mentally disabled persons, including a 1937 story in *Das Schwarze Korps* entitled "A Courageous Step" about a farmer who shot his retarded son in the middle of the night. Asylums became freak shows. Tours taken by party members viewed what one newspaper called "grinning grotesques who bear scarcely any resemblance to human beings."[15]

Many mental patients were capable of fulfilling lives that included reading, crafts, and drawing. Regardless, the Nazis cut their state funding, which resulted in sharp drops in food and medicine as well as a rise in doctor–patient ratios from, for example, 1 per 162 in 1935, to 1 per 446 in 1938 at the Eichberg psychiatric hospital in Hesse-Nassau. Doctors who were Nazi Party and even SS members were posted to state mental hospitals, as were orderlies who had been SA men. Patients died of neglect, poor diet, disease, and even suicide amid indifferent and cruel staff. "If you have too many patients in your institution," said Fritz Bernotat, the supervisor for mental institutions in Hesse, "just beat them to death and then you will have space."[16]

The Sterilization Law

In July 1933, Hitler's cabinet enacted the Law for the Prevention of Hereditarily Diseased Progeny. It required sterilization for those with disabilities including "feeblemindedness," depression, epilepsy, deafness, blindness, and even harelips. Up to 400,000 Germans were sterilized, most before the war, after rulings by specially created health courts. The courts based decisions on written denunciations, mostly from institutional directors and state doctors. More than 388,000 denunciations in 1934 and 1935 alone created a backlog. Only half of those marked for sterilization in 1934 could be processed that year. Surgeons were paid on a piecework basis and worked quickly—certain hospitals had "sterilization days"—performing up to five female or twelve male sterilizations in a morning.[17]

Denouncers and courts often tossed asocials, including habitual criminals and Roma, into the sterilization pool. Health officials used pseudomedical terminology for Roma, such as "moral" or "disguised" mental retardation. A doctor denounced one Roma who worked as an actor because "his relatives live in a second-rate caravan and are typical Gypsies—work-shy and unreliable." Another denounced a young pregnant Roma because, in addition to convictions for theft and fraud, "she is dirty and a heavy smoker." Roughly 500 Roma were sterilized under criteria such as these by 1939—a figure representing a higher percentage for Roma in Germany than for the German population as a whole.[18]

Sterilization under these conditions was hazardous. Roughly 5,000 women died from surgical carelessness. Physicians blamed the patients for acting obstinately. Postsurgical depression caused perhaps 1,000 more women to commit suicide.[19] But worse was coming. In 1935,

---

[15]Quoted in Michael Burleigh, *Death and Deliverance: "Euthanasia" in Germany c. 1900–1945* (New York, 1995), p. 44.

[16]Figures in Burleigh, *Death and Deliverance*, pp. 44–51. Quote in Henry Friedlander, *The Origins of Nazi Genocide: From Euthanasia to the Final Solution* (Chapel Hill, NC, 1987), p. 62.

[17]Figures in Gisela Bock, *Zwangssterilization im Nationalsozialismus: Studien zur Rassenpolitik und Frauenpolitik* (Opladen, 1986), pp. 231–8.

[18]Quotes and figures from Guenther Lewy, *The Nazi Persecution of the Gypsies* (New York, 2000), pp. 40–1.

[19]Figure in Bock, *Zwangssterilization*, pp. 372–81.

Hitler commented privately that when war began, he would take up the "question of eutha-nasia," a polite expression meaning state killing of disabled persons. War, Hitler understood, heightened secrecy.[20]

The Euthanasia "Law"

No law ever sanctioned the Nazi euthanasia program. Laws had to be published. The unease with which German Catholics and the families of the disabled reacted to sterilization made secrecy desirable. The euthanasia machinery ran through Hitler's private chancellery, a small personal office with reliable cronies. The head of the chancellery was Philipp Bouhler, a long-time Nazi from Munich who joined the party in 1922. Karl Brandt, the head of Hitler's medical escort, assisted Bouhler in guiding policy. Viktor Brack, who ascended within Hitler's chancellery thanks to personal contacts with Himmler, handled day-to-day administration.

Euthanasia operated behind front organizations under the program's code name, T-4, an abbreviation for a formerly Jewish-owned home in Berlin (at the address Tiergartenstrasse 4), which secretly housed the central offices after April 1940. Recruits to T-4, including the physi-cians, nurses, and police, used false names on correspondence. They also received quasi-legal cover through Hitler's signed authorization, typed on personal stationery in October 1939 but backdated to September 1, the day the war began. Though not a law, it read:

> Reichsleiter Bouhler and Dr. med. Brandt are charged with the responsibility to extend the powers of certain doctors, in such a way that, after the most careful assessment of their condition, those suffer-ing from illnesses deemed to be incurable may be granted a mercy death.[21]

On this basis of euphemism, subterfuge, and personal suggestion from Hitler, Nazi Germany targeted a group perceived as defective for complete destruction.

Children's Euthanasia

German children with both mental and physical disabilities were the first targets. Central to the effort was the Reich Committee for the Scientific Registration of Serious Hereditary and Congenital Illnesses, a cover organization through which T-4 in August 1939 ordered local doc-tors and midwives to report—on supplied forms—all children under three years old suffering from "idiocy" (a category that included blindness and deafness), mirocephalus, hydrocephalus, Down's syndrome, and various physical deformities. Medical professionals completing forms received a gratuity of two marks per form. In Berlin, a standing panel of three doctors evaluated the forms. Each doctor placed a + ("plus" sign) or a – ("minus" sign) on each form. Two + des-ignations meant that the child on the form would be transported for death. None of the three ever examined a case in person.

In 1940, T-4 set up special pediatric wards in hospitals throughout Germany. There were about thirty such wards, all run by politically reliable physicians. Children slated for death were transferred to the special wards either by the hospitals where they were already institutionalized or from their own homes. Parents were told that the wards provided better care. Reluctant parents were threatened with the loss of custodial rights because only unfit parents (who, Nazi officials

---

[20]See testimony by Karl Brandt, National Archives and Records Administration, RG 238, Entry 1, Box 5, p. 2482.

[21]Jeremy Noakes and Geoffrey Pridham, eds., *Nazism 1919–1945: A Documentary Reader*, vol. 3, new ed. (Exeter, 2001), p. 413.

suggested, might have hereditary illnesses themselves) would reject sound medical advice. Mothers of disabled children whose husbands were in the army were later conscripted for labor so that they would have no choice but to surrender their children.

Clinical staff then quietly murdered the children. Some children died of slow starvation, some from overdoses of sedatives such as luminal (phenobarbital) provided by police labs. Either method rendered the children susceptible to diseases like pneumonia, enabling doctors to report that children had died naturally. Suspicious and angry parents received no satisfaction either from doctors or from local law enforcement. The children's remains, especially their brains, were often used for research. Many records have disappeared, but between 1940 and 1945, desensitized and even sadistic doctors and nurses murdered between 5,000 and 6,000 children. After the war they remained proud of their work. Four-year-old Richard Jenne was the final victim. He was killed three weeks after Germany's surrender on May 29, 1945.[22]

Adult Euthanasia—the First Gas Chambers

The T-4 program to murder mentally disabled adults, most of whom had already been sterilized, was more expansive. Preparations began in the summer of 1939 with discussions among T-4 physicians on how to kill large numbers of mental patients. They settled on carbon monoxide gas. In October 1939, T-4 officials requisitioned hospitals in remote areas of Germany to serve as killing centers. There were six in all, each with a staff of roughly forty administrators, doctors, nurses, orderlies, and laborers. T-4 recruited staff members based on political reliability and with incentives like higher pay and the chance for advancement. No one joined under duress.

Victims were located as follows. A September 21, 1939, decree ordered local governments to forward the names of all state and private hospitals, sanitaria, and nursing homes in their region. In October, forms went to the institutions—one for each patient—asking for name, age, citizenship, race, next of kin, and (ominously) frequency of visits by relatives. Institutions filled out a form for each patient with schizophrenia, epilepsy, senility, encephalitis, Huntington's disease, and other conditions causing feeblemindedness; anyone institutionalized for five years or more; and Jews, Roma, and those of mixed blood regardless of disease.

The forms were due by November 1, 1939, and contained no room for medical history or evaluation. Two hundred thousand were completed and returned. Three-man panels from a pool of about forty doctors processed them and made perfunctory choices of death (+) and life (−). Financial rewards encouraged speedy evaluations. The notorious physician Hermann Pfannmüller, who was already killing toddlers at his pediatric ward in Bavaria, passed judgment on between 31,000 and 48,000 adult cases between November 1939 and April 1941.[23]

Names of adults selected for death went to another T-4 cover office called the Charitable Foundation for the Transport of Patients. It arranged steady transfer of groups, usually on buses with blacked-out windows, to the killing centers. The key was to prevent suspicion by not taking too many patients from one locality at a time. Institutions were notified days before the pickup date to have the named patients ready to travel with their belongings, including valuables. The transfer, it was said, would free hospital beds for wounded troops. Objections from local doctors

---

[22]Friedlander, *The Origins of Nazi Genocide*, p. 163. On children's euthanasia, see Friedlander, *The Origins of Nazi Genocide*, pp. 36–61; Burleigh, *Death and Deliverance*, pp. 97–111.

[23]Figure in Dick de Mildt, *In the Name of the People: Perpetrators of Genocide in the Reflection of Their Post-War Prosecution in West Germany—The "Euthanasia" and "Aktion Reinhard" Trial Cases* (The Hague, 1996), pp. 57–8.

were ignored. Patients, told that they were going on an outing, boarded the buses. Those who understood the purposes of the transports had to be sedated after boarding.

The first killings were in January 1940 at the Grafeneck asylum in Württemberg, but the process was similar at all centers. A nurse led arriving patients, usually a group from twenty to seventy-five, to a reception area and had them undress. Staff tagged their clothing for the illusion that patients would redress. Patients were measured, weighed, photographed, and examined by a doctor in a show of medical care. They were then led to gas chambers built to look like showers and told that they were to bathe or inhale therapeutic medicine. The doctor then opened the gas valve releasing carbon monoxide through perforated pipes along the floor. Unconsciousness came in five minutes, death in ten. Staff members could view the horrifying process through a window in the chamber door. One staff member at Hadamar, the killing center in Hesse, testified in 1946:

> I looked through the window. . . . I saw about 40 to 45 men pressed against one another in the [chamber] slowly dying. Some lay on the floor, others were down on their knees, many with their mouths open as if they could not get any air. The killing method was so agonizing that one could not speak of a humane death, especially when so many of the murdered might also have had lucid moments. I watched . . . for about 2 to 3 minutes, after which I left because I could not stand the sight any longer and I became ill.[24]

Once the chamber was ventilated, workers designated as stokers (who worked in twelve-hour shifts) disentangled the bodies and dragged them out. They knocked loose gold teeth. Some brains were removed for study. Stokers then burned the bodies in a crematorium two to eight at a time. It took an entire night to incinerate a single transport, the constant burning of fat causing occasional chimney fires. Using mills, the stokers ground remaining bone chips into powder. They scooped ashes from a macabre communal pile and placed them into urns should the family want loved ones' remains. From arrival to disposal, the business was complete in twenty-four hours.

Deceiving victims' families was essential. T-4 staff notified loved ones of initial transfers only after patients had been killed. Ten days later, they sent written death notices with a plausible cause of death (there was a list of sixty "causes" including heart attack, stroke, and pneumonia) and curt words to the effect that death was deliverance from suffering. Concern for epidemics, notices read, necessitated immediate cremation. T-4 postdated deaths by ten days in order to collect ten days of fees for "hospital care" either from the family or from local welfare agencies.

Hitler's "Stop Order"

Despite efforts to camouflage the process, it quickly became an open secret. Those living near killing centers saw buses arrive full and leave empty. They smelled the smoke rising from the crematoria. They overheard boozy conversations of staff members at local inns. T-4 closed the killing centers of Brandenburg and Grafeneck in late 1940 thanks to local hostility but replaced them with two new ones at Bernburg in Saxony and Hadamar in Hesse.

Hitler issued a "stop" order in August 24, 1941, that theoretically halted T-4 operations. Many credit August Graf von Galen, the bishop of Münster, with forcing Hitler's hand. On August 3, von Galen publicly condemned the program in a sermon that traversed the Catholic parts of Germany. Joseph Goebbels mused about having the bishop hanged. But von Galen reflected

---

[24]Ernst Klee, ed., *Dokumente zur Euthanasie* (Frankfurt, 1985), p. 125.

broader antipathy. Though some families were relieved at the passing of a family member whom they saw as a burden, others angrily demanded redress. Open protests were a possibility. The program was even known in other countries by the time of Hitler's "stop" order.

In fact, the regime simply changed tactics. By its own count, T-4 had already killed 70,273 adults between January 1940 and August 1941. After Hitler's "stop" order, it continued to kill in more decentralized, discreet ways known collectively as "wild euthanasia." At Hitler's insistence, the children's program never stopped. It even expanded to older children. Hospitals that housed the children's wards now also accepted adults, who were still selected and transported by T-4 personnel, ostensibly to protect them from air raids. After their arrival in the wards, doctors and nurses murdered them using slower "natural" methods like starvation and overmedication. Hospital routine shrouded murder. And it remained ghastly. Certain wards were notorious for unsanitary conditions; patients begging for food; sadistic staff members; and torturous experiments, from electric shocks to spinal taps.

The Nazis had already been far less discreet in occupied areas. In the German-annexed regions of Poland, SS units killed over 10,000 German, Polish, and Jewish mental patients between October 1939 and April 1940. Some were moved from their hospital beds to the forest and shot. Polish prisoners dug and filled mass graves before German police shot them as well.[25] Police also used carbon monoxide gas in specially built vans. When the Germans invaded the USSR, police units killed local patients with dynamite, shootings, lethal injections, and gas vans. Foreigners used for slave labor in Germany were also euthanized as late as 1944 if they suffered from mental illness, as were infants born to female forced laborers.

Four T-4 killing centers were also still used after Hitler's "stop" order in a program known as Special Treatment 14 f 13 (an administrative code referring to the death of infirm prisoners), whereby the SS thinned the German concentration camp population by over 20,000 after April 1941. Beginning that month, SS camp physicians and roving T-4 personnel selected prisoners for transport and death; 14 f 13 victims included habitual criminals and others defined as lazy, insolent, chronically ill, or otherwise incapable of work. They also included Jewish inmates, whether they had maladies or not.

The full number of victims murdered by various euthanasia programs following Hitler's "stop" order is unknown. Surely it amounted to many tens of thousands. The eastern German hospital at Meseritz-Obrawalde, which was liberated by the Soviet army in January 1945, was symptomatic. Mass graves and death registers confirmed 18,232 deaths there. In 1944 alone, 3,948 patients were admitted and 3,814 died, a mortality rate of 97 percent. Stockrooms held large supplies of syringes and lethal drugs along with thousands of urns. The victims, exhumed from their graves, ranged from age sixty to age two.[26]

8.3 ALIEN ELEMENTS: AFRICANS AND ROMA

"Rhineland Bastards"

Before World War I, the French army recruited troops from France's African colonies. They made up for manpower shortages caused by France's declining birthrate. German commentators were incensed. African troops, they said, were savages who mutilated their victims. France's

---

[25]Figures in Götz Aly, *Final Solution: Nazi Population Policy and the Murder of the European Jews* (New York, 1999), pp. 70–6.

[26]Burleigh, *Death and Deliverance*, pp. 269–70; de Mildt, *In the Name of the People*, pp. 65–7.

use of Africans to occupy the Rhineland in 1919 brought the first African encounter for most Germans, who resented any occupation much less one by black troops.

Some Germans railed against supposedly insatiable African sexual appetites. Overblown rape stories appeared in German pamphlets. Actual fraternization between black soldiers and German women provoked fears of national emasculation and caused, some said, pollution of German blood. Children of such unions carried the label "Rhineland bastards," and personified an imaginary French campaign to "mulattoize" Germany. Hitler's contribution to the discussion was his belief that the Jews were behind it all.

The Nazis never had a "black policy" because Germany had so few black people. But they had not forgotten what one German doctor called the "residual of the black shame on the Rhine that must be eliminated."[27] Martin Bormann, Rudolf Hess's secretary in the Nazi Party chancellery, estimated in 1936 that there were 600 to 800 "Rhineland bastards" born in the early 1920s now sexually mature. They were not disabled so they did not fall under the sterilization law.

In April 1933, Göring had police authorities register mulattoes in the Rhineland. In March 1934, Interior Ministry officials argued that, if Germany were to avoid mongrelization, it had to take action. In 1937, on Hitler's personal order, between 400 and 500 mixed-race teens were sterilized with the help of a special Gestapo office, which provided legal backing and coerced parental consent.[28]

The Murder of African Soldiers

Forty thousand French African troops saw combat during Germany's campaign in France. The German army had no directives concerning black troops, but officers and soldiers often viewed them as animals in uniform. Goebbels fanned the fire. "Today," said one statement in *Völkischer Beobachter*, "France has again let loose the cruel black beasts from the jungle against us, and again they have given free rein to their animalistic instincts."[29]

After tough battles near the Somme and Loire rivers in late May and early June 1940, some German troops showed no quarter, massacring surrendering black troops with bullets, bayonets, and rifle butts. Others were more deliberate, separating white from black prisoners, then shooting the latter in remote areas. In one instance, black prisoners were taken to a field, ordered to run, then machine-gunned and run over by tanks during the "escape attempt." On some marches to prison camps, black POWs were given no food or water and were sometimes shot. In certain POW camps, the Germans denied them shelter or adequate food and used them for reprisal shootings. German perpetrators destroyed the identification tags of murdered black troops and prohibited their burial so there would be no record of their existence. "[An] inferior race," explained one German officer, "does not deserve to do battle with such a civilized race as the Germans."[30]

The spasm of crimes against African troops ended in the summer and fall of 1940, perhaps because of Red Cross inspections of prison camps. It is hard to say how many black troops the Germans murdered. German military records are vague, noting deaths of black troops "in battle" or while "trying to escape." Historian Raffael Scheck counts nearly fifty documented massacres

---

[27]Quoted in Tina Campt, *Other Germans: Black Germans and the Politics of Race* (Ann Arbor, MI, 2004), pp. 73–4.

[28]Figure in Reiner Pommerin, *Sterilisierung der Rheinlandbastarde: das Schicksal einer farbigen deutschen Minderheit, 1918–1937* (Düsseldorf, 1979), pp. 82–4.

[29]Quoted in Raffael Scheck, *Hitler's African Victims: The German Army Massacres of Black French Soldiers in 1940* (New York, 2006), p. 106.

[30]Quoted in Scheck, *Hitler's African Victims*, pp. 30–1.

with at least 3,000 victims and points to suspiciously high black casualty rate in certain battles.[31] Though many German units behaved correctly toward African prisoners, the German treatment of black Africans forms an essential link to greater army atrocities soon to take place in the Soviet Union.

Roma in Germany

Roma, colloquially known as Gypsies, originated in the Punjab region of northern India and migrated to eastern Europe after the eighth century. They appeared in German towns in the fifteenth century. By 1939, there were roughly 1 million Roma in Europe, most living in the southeastern region. Twenty-six thousand lived in Germany and perhaps 11,000 more in Austria.[32]

The English word *Gypsy* is based on a mistaken assumption that Roma originated in Egypt. Germans call them *Zigeuner*, referring to their itinerant tendencies. They worked in trades but also as travelling entertainers, including musicians and fortune-tellers as well as peddlers. Imperial Germany and Austria regarded them as a nuisance, but left it to local police to chase them from one locality to the next.

Nazi theorists in the 1930s regarded Roma as biologically inferior, asocial parasites predisposed to crime. Neurologist Robert Ritter in 1936 described them as "primitive, subversive, and criminal."[33] But Hitler never mentioned the Roma in *Mein Kampf* nor did they occupy a central part of Nazi thinking. Rather they initially fell under eugenic and criminal laws that covered other groups ranging from the disabled to habitual criminals.

Roma were considered a local problem in the Nazi regime's early years. State governments harassed them by raising rents, destroying their camp areas, or forcing local Roma into ad-hoc "Gypsy camps," sometimes fenced in and guarded. In December 1938, Himmler issued a circular, "Combating the Gypsy Plague," which described the "Gypsy problem" as stemming from "the inner characteristics of that race."[34] The criminal police established a special office to register Roma, who they then categorized as pure or mixed. As mentioned, 500 Roma were sterilized on the pretext of mental deficiency by 1939.

In 1938 and 1939, as part of its proactive anticrime measures, the criminal police also arrested 200 "work-shy" males from each German police district and interned them in concentration camps. Up to 2,000 Roma in SS concentration camps were among the work-shy by December 1939.[35] By October, Roma not already in Roma camps or concentration camps were no longer allowed to change their domiciles.

The Roma Question

Germany's conquest of Poland raised the issue of expelling Roma from the Reich to the General Government. The criminal police were more preoccupied with Roma than were other agencies and pressed for their complete expulsion. During the deportations of Jews to Nisko in October 1939, Arthur Nebe, the head of the criminal police, tried to convince Adolf Eichmann to "add

---

[31]Scheck, *Hitler's African Victims*, pp. 53–60.

[32]Figures in Lewy, *The Nazi Persecution of the Gypsies*, pp. 15, 56.

[33]Quoted in Sybil Milton, "Gypsies and the Holocaust," *The History Teacher*, 24, no. 4 (August 1991), pp. 379–80.

[34]Quoted in Michael Zimmermann, "The National Socialist 'Solution of the Gypsy Question'": Central Decisions, Local Initiatives, and Their Interrelation," *Holocaust and Genocide Studies*, 15, no. 3 (Winter 2001), p. 414.

[35]Figures in Zimmermann, "The National Socialist 'Solution of the Gypsy Question,'" pp. 412–4.

three or four train cars of Gypsies," ultimately without success.[36] The army, meanwhile, considered Roma in the Rhineland as spies as it prepared its attack on France. In May 1940, police evacuated 2,330 Roma from western German cities. Again the criminal police hoped for more comprehensive deportations, but train shortages made it impossible.

Roma within the Reich became more isolated regardless. Nebe's criminal police planned to create Roma transit camps while local citizens called for "the rapid transportation of these pests." Police offices promised "a final solution to the Gypsy question," once the war was over.[37] The comprehensive solution never occurred. Senior officials considered Roma to be bandits and spies, but never an existential threat on par with Jews. Himmler even developed a fascination with settled, pure-blooded Roma, believing them to offer clues to Indo-European origins.[38]

Still, the handling of the Jewish problem enabled partial handling of the Roma problem. In all during the war, Germany and its allies killed perhaps 250,000 Roma. German police units killed up to 50,000 in shooting and gassing operations in the USSR and Serbia. Ostensibly these Roma were shot as partisans, but women and children were among the victims. Police organs also deported Roma from the Reich to the east. In Auschwitz, a special "Gypsy camp" held 23,000 men, women, and children. They were not killed on arrival as were most Jews, but some 5,600 were eventually gassed and some 14,000 died from hunger, disease, and medical experiments.[39] Germany's allies, most notably Croatia and Romania, either killed Roma in their territories or deported tens of thousands more to their deaths.

8.4 HITLER'S SOUTHEASTERN ALLIES: ROMANIA

Between Hitler and Stalin

In 1940 and 1941, Germany's war triggered lethal repercussions in southeast Europe. One area of unrest was Romania, where deep antisemitism, geopolitical shifts, and bitter political feuds proved deadly to Jews. By September 1939, successive governments under King Carol II, beginning with the Goga-Cuza government of early 1938, stripped one-third of all Jews in Romania—some 225,000—of their citizenship and livelihoods.[40] The sole consolation was that the king kept the Legionnaires and Iron Guard, who espoused wanton violence, from power. Jews in Romania just hoped to get through it all. "For the moment," wrote Emil Dorian, a Jewish physician and writer in Bucharest, "it seems we have escaped the war. . . . And yet no one knows anything for sure."[41]

Yet Romania was caught between Germany and its brutal ally to the east, the USSR. On June 26, 1940, with the Germans pushing through France, the Soviets demanded from Romania the immediate return of Bessarabia (which Romania received from Russia after World War I) and the transfer of northern Bukovina (which Romania received from Austria-Hungary). The Romanian army withdrew, often in disarray, followed by thousands of Romanian civilians who lived in these disputed regions.

---

[36]Quoted in Milton, "Gypsies and the Holocaust," p. 381.

[37]Quoted in Zimmermann, "The National Socialist 'Solution of the Gypsy Question,'" p. 417.

[38]Lewy, *The Nazi Persecution of the Gypsies*, pp. 135–40.

[39]Figures in Lewy, *The Nazi Persecution of the Gypsies*, pp. 122–32, 157, 166.

[40]Figure in International Commission on the Holocaust in Romania, *Final Report of the International Commission on the Holocaust in Romania* (hereafter *Final Report Romania*) (Bucharest, 2004), p. 81.

[41]Marguerite Dorian, ed., *The Quality of Witness: A Romanian Diary 1937–1944* (hereafter *Dorian Diary*) (Philadelphia, PA, 1982), September 24, 1939.

Many Jews, mainly in Bessarabia, welcomed the Soviets because their arrival signaled an end to Romanian persecution. In the eyes of angry Romanians, Jews were thus to blame for the humiliation. Bitter Romanian army units retreating from the disputed regions engaged in sporadic anti-Jewish violence, including throwing Jews from trains, beating and shooting fellow Jewish soldiers, rampaging through the Jewish sections of Dorohoi (just west of Bukovina), and shooting Jewish refugees at Galaţi (just west of southern Bessarabia). Estimates of Jews killed after the withdrawal range from 136 to several hundred.[42] Romanian refugees arriving from Bessarabia and Bukovina brought tales of Jews stoning retreating Romanian soldiers and killing officers.[43] Determined to prove Jewish loyalty, Romania's chief Jewish leader Wilhelm Filderman insisted that "we are and we shall remain—whatever should happen and whatever we might suffer—loyal to the Roumanian country and people."[44]

Regardless, the state punished Romania's Jews. By decree of June 22, 1940, civil servants had to belong to the Party of the Nation, from which Jews were excluded. In July, government ministries began firing perhaps thousands of Jewish doctors, engineers, teachers and other civil servants with notices that read, "Dismissed on grounds of Jewish ethnic origins and on suspicion of endangering state security." A subsequent law—the Jewish Statute of August 1940—defined Jews by blood and faith more stringently than Germany's Nuremberg Laws. One Jewish parent sufficed, and all Jews so defined, even those whose citizenship extended before 1918, faced disabilities ranging from occupation to property-holding.[45] Acculturated Romanian Jews descended into angry despair. Emil Dorian wrote:

> During this half century, my existence unfolded between the cry of "Down with the kikes," in eighteen-hundred-and-something and that of "Down with the kikes," in 1940. During all that time I gave the best of myself, over and over. . . . I suffered in the belief that everything would be accounted for, paid for. Yet today the balance of this half century closes with new humiliations and new crimes.[46]

Antonescu and the Legionnaires

Aligned with France before the war, Romania moved into Germany's diplomatic orbit in July 1940 to prevent further territorial losses. In return, Germany stationed troops in Romania and received full access to its rich oil reserves. But Hungary, which also lost territory to Romania after World War I and also aligned with Germany, pressed its territorial claims next. The Germans brokered a compromise, called the Second Vienna Award of August 1940, whereby Hungary recovered the northern part of Transylvania, a chunk of territory slicing deep into the heart of Romania. Popular anger at King Carol, which included protests in Bucharest, prompted the king to abdicate in September1940.

Power fell to Lieutenant General Ion Antonescu, a conservative Romanian expansionist who held the army's support. Like Hitler and Mussolini, he took the title of "Leader," or in Romanian, "Conducător." On the Germans' urging, Antonescu ruled in tandem with the

---

[42]*Final Report Romania*, pp. 84–6.

[43]G. H. Bossy and M. H. Bossy, eds., *Recollections of a Romanian Diplomat 1918–1969: Diaries and Memoirs of Raoul V. Bossy*, vol. 2 (Stanford, CA, 2003), June 28, 1940.

[44]Filderman to Charles Sonnenreich, July 15, 1940, Jean Ancel, ed., *Documents Concerning the Fate of Romanian Jewry During the Holocaust* (Jerusalem, 1984), vol. 1, p. 419.

[45]Quote and details in Jean Ancel, *The History of the Holocaust in Romania* (Lincoln, NE, 2012), pp. 78–9, 94–6; *Final Report Romania*, pp. 182–3.

[46]*Dorian Diary*, July 16, 1940.

MAP 8.1   Romanian border changes, 1940.   *Source:* Ioanid, Radu. *The Holocaust in Romania: the Destruction of Jews and Gypsies Under the Antonescu Regime, 1940–1944* (Chicago: Ivan R. Dee, 2000), p. xxvi.

Legionnaires and Iron Guard. Legionnaire chief Horia Sima became deputy prime minister, five other Legionnaires held ministries, and more Legionnaires still held senior government posts. Antonescu's partnership with the Legionnaires lasted four months.

Despite Dorian's comment that "there is little new they can implement," the period brought additional misery for Jews.[47] Antonescu's government initiated a program of "Romanization," whereby the state began legal appropriation of Jewish urban and rural property ranging from oil company shares to chicken coops. Antonescu favored the dispossession of Romania's Jews. On taking power, he insisted that his program was "rooted entirely in the tenets of integral nationalism" and that "the Jews are to a large extent responsible for the calamities that have befallen this country."[48] But he insisted that Romanization proceed in orderly fashion, lest economic collapse result.

The Legionnaires were less patient. They seized Jewish businesses, from sizable stores to peddlers' carts. They confiscated Jewish homes and stole cash, jewelry, furs, radios, and even livestock. They also indulged their violent impulses, beating Jews, shearing their heads, forcing them to perform hard labor, driving them from towns, and occasionally murdering them. Degradation was its own reward. In the city of Călărași, Legionnaires arrested forty-five Jewish men, forced them to lie naked on the floor, then took turns beating them with cords for three days. Călărași's Jews were then ordered to leave town without their property.[49]

Antonescu was equivocal concerning anti-Jewish violence. Wilhelm Filderman forwarded numerous reports to the government, but when he met with Antonescu in October 1940.

---

[47]*Dorian Diary*, September 19, 1940.

[48]Quotes in *Final Report Romania*, p. 181, and Ancel, *The History of the Holocaust in Romania*, p. 96.

[49]Radu Ioanid, *The Holocaust in Romania: The Destruction of Jews and Gypsies Under the Antonescu Regime, 1940–1944* (Chicago, IL, 2000), p. 48.

Antonescu insisted that the Jews had to "understand the circumstances without exaggerating isolated instances of abuse that the government had no intention of tolerating." Jews who lived in Romanian territory only after 1919, he said, would have to emigrate, while the remainder would receive livelihoods in proportion to their numbers. In December 1940, Antonescu was similarly ambivalent. "I do not protect [those] Jews who are primarily guilty of the misfortunes afflicting our nation," he said, "[but] as head of the government, I cannot tolerate acts that compromise the effort to achieve recovery by means of law and order."[50]

The Bucharest Pogrom

As an army officer, Antonescu also worried about the Legionnaires' bloody settling of scores against former royal officials. "What am I supposed to do with the fanatics?" he asked Hitler rhetorically on January 14, 1941. "You have to get rid of them," Hitler said.[51] On January 20, 1941, Antonescu removed the Legionnaires from the government. The Iron Guard exploded into open rebellion the next day. By the January 24, the army suppressed the Iron Guard revolt. In three days' fighting, at least 375 were killed on both sides, and 9,352 Legionnaires were arrested. Hitler and the German government wanted stability in Romania for the sake of its oil. They backed Antonescu. German SD agents in Bucharest, however, backed the Iron Guard and helped several hundred Legionnaires, including Horia Sima, escape to Germany.

For Romanian Jews, the significance of the Iron Guard rebellion was the vicious pogrom launched by the Legionnaires in Bucharest. It was Romania's *Kristallnacht*. Viorel Trifa, the Iron Guard's student leader, fanned the violence. In a rally on the night of January 20, he praised Hitler for confronting the Jewish threat to Europe and posted a manifesto calling for "Death to the Masons and the Jews," whom the Iron Guard blamed for the break with Antonescu.[52] "We know very well who to shoot at," said an Iron Guard leaflet.[53] Legionnaires descended on Bucharest's Jewish quarter, burning, looting, and sadistically killing 125 Jews. "What happened in Văcăreşti, Dudeşti, and the surrounding neighborhoods," wrote Emil Dorian, "is indescribable."

> The fury of the looters has not spared anybody or anything. . . . Here a store littered with watches ground to powder. Next to it, an old woman crying in the middle of a dry goods store, black with soot, empty. . . . The majestic Sephardic synagogue has been completely destroyed. They set it on fire with gasoline . . . and the looters danced by the flames. Countless Jews were taken from their homes by Iron Guard bands and led to several spots in the city where they were slaughtered. . . . Before the victims were killed, their noses were smashed, their tongues cut out, their eyes gouged. . . . Jewish corpses were hung from hooks in the city slaughterhouse or simply dumped in the street. . . . Some were chewed up by dogs. . . . Every day one discovers new corpses of Jews who disappeared in the night when the bells rang, signaling the beginning of the pogrom.[54]

Foreign observers were similarly appalled. "What my eyes have seen," wrote Chile's ambassador Manuel A. Rivera, "should not be passed over in silence. It cries out to heaven!"[55]

---

[50]Quotes from Ioanid, *The Holocaust in Romania*, p. 45, 50.

[51]Quoted in Radu Ioanid, "The Pogrom of Bucharest 21–23 January 1941," *Holocaust and Genocide Studies*, 6, no. 4 (January 1992), p. 376.

[52]Richard Breitman et al., *US Intelligence and the Nazis* (New York, 2005), pp. 237, 240.

[53]Quoted in Ioanid, "The Pogrom of Bucharest," p. 377.

[54]*Dorian Diary*, January 24, 1941, February 5, 1941.

[55]"Blood, Tears and Shame over Roumania," Ancel, ed., *Documents Concerning the Fate of Romanian Jewry*, vol. 3, p. 178.

The Legionnaires were now removed from power. But the Antonescu government continued to press for more orderly Jewish expropriation and exodus. "The Jews must go," reported Hermann Neubacher, Germany's economic envoy to Romania, "but they will be liquidated gradually and according to laws and regulations."[56] Romanian laws in the next six months dismissed more Jews from their jobs, expropriated more Jewish urban and rural property, and increased taxes on Jews. Jews able to emigrate were allowed to take three changes of clothes, a blanket, a pen, a watch, and a wedding ring. The press lauded Antonescu. The newspaper *Curentul* proclaimed, "That which was believed impossible . . . has been realized by the courageous national act of the Leader. . . . There is a feeling of freedom in the country. . . . And the Semitic virus has been eliminated forever."[57]

8.5 HITLER'S SOUTHEASTERN ALLIES: CROATIA

Croatia and the Ustaša

Hitler's bloodiest ally in 1940 and 1941 was the Independent State of Croatia. A mostly Roman Catholic region that had once been part of the Austro-Hungarian Empire, Croatia formed the second largest part of the Yugoslav kingdom born in 1919 and known as the Kingdom of the Serbs, Croats, and Slovenes. The new multiethnic, multireligious state was dominated by Serbia, the orthodox Christian kingdom that gained independence in 1878 and tried afterward to unite the south Slavs. With the collapse of Austria-Hungary in 1918, the Serbs got their chance. But the Serbs never forged political or ethnic consensus in the new kingdom because they insisted on political dominance. In 1929, the Serb monarchy established a dictatorship to hold Yugoslavia together.

The Serbs' most violent opponents were the fervently Catholic Croatian separatists known as the Ustaša ("rebels"), founded by the terrorist Ante Pavelić in 1929 with the slogan, "Knives, revolvers, automatic pistols and time bombs are the bells that ring in the dawn and rebirth of the Croatian state."[58] A violent fringe movement, the Ustaša had little popular support within Croatia, but it received funds and logistical help from Italy and Hungary, each of which had territorial demands in Yugoslavia. In 1940, Italian diplomats schemed with the Ustaša for Yugoslavia's dismemberment—Croatia would become independent and Italy would get long-coveted territories on the Adriatic coast.

The Germans overran Yugoslavia themselves in April 1941 after an anti-German coup there in March threatened Germany's southeastern flank before the impending attack on the USSR. German troops occupied Serbia. Germany's allies—Italy, Bulgaria and Hungary—received chunks of Yugoslavia's corpse. On April 10, before the German campaign was over, Hitler and Mussolini awarded Pavelić and the Ustaša with the new "Independent State of Croatia." Centered in Zagreb and still under German and Italian supervision, the new state comprised Croatia itself as well as the more ethnically mixed region of Bosnia-Herzegovina.

---

[56]Franklin Mott Gunther to Secretary of State, no. 1744, February 10, 1941, Ancel, ed., *Documents Concerning the Fate of Romanian Jewry*, vol. 2, p. 260.

[57]Ancel, ed., *Documents Concerning the Fate of Romanian Jewry*, vol. 3, p. 51.

[58]Quoted in Jonathan E. Gumz, "*Wehrmacht* Perceptions of Mass Violence in Croatia, 1941–1942," *The Historical Journal*, 44, no. 4 (December 2001), pp. 1015–38.

MAP 8.2 Occupied Yugoslavia. *Source: Tomasevich, Jozo, War and Revolution in Yugoslavia, 1941–1945: Occupation and Collaboration* (Palo Alto, CA: Stanford University Press, 2001).

Reactionary in its Catholicism and extremely violent in its methods, the Ustaša held the support of perhaps 10 percent of all Croatians. But the group had Hitler's backing and aimed to purify the new state religiously and ethnically. The Ustaša took aim at Serbs, Jews, and Roma, blaming the former two groups for Croatia's subjugation in the interwar period. "Christ and the Ustaša," proclaimed one Catholic newspaper, "march together through history."[59] From the moment the state was founded, these groups were placed outside the law. The Decree on the Defense of the People and the State proclaimed that anyone who "acts or has acted against the honor and vital interests of the Croatian people in any way . . . even if the act is only attempted . . . commits an act of high treason." The punishment was death.[60]

Ustaša Slaughter of Serbs

"There is no method that we . . . will not use," proclaimed Ustaša leader Milovan Žanić, "to make this land truly Croatian and to cleanse it of Serbs who have endangered us through the centuries. . . . This is not a secret, this is the policy of our state. . . ."[61] Serbs in the new state numbered 1.8 million and comprised 30 percent of the population. They were the Ustaša's chief victims.

---

[59]Quoted in Gumz, "*Wehrmacht* Perceptions of Mass Violence in Croatia," p. 1025.

[60]Quoted in Jozo Tomasevich, *War and Revolution in Yugoslavia, 1941–1945: Occupation and Collaboration* (Stanford, CA, 2001), p. 383.

[61]Quoted in Tomasevich, *War and Revolution*, p. 392.

In the regime's initial months, the Ustaša solution to the Serb question was mass deportation and murder. Local Ustaša militia removed Serb families from their homes, allowing them thirty minutes' notice, fifty kilograms of luggage, and no valuables. They placed them in assembly camps and deported them to German-occupied Serbia. By September 1941, when the Germans insisted on a halt to these deportations, the Germans counted some 118,000 Serb deportees in authorized and unauthorized transports. The Ustaša deported tens of thousands afterward, including children. More Serbs fled voluntarily. By the summer of 1942, Serbia had some 200,000 refugees from Croatia.

To eliminate political enemies and quicken the pace of deportation, the Ustaša also encouraged local massacres of Serbs. The killings were bestial. Victims included everyone from senior Orthodox clergy to Serb children, from larger cities to small villages. Ustaša militia used knives, hammers, pick-axes, and rifle butts to maim, behead, and even impale Serb men, women, children, and infants. Ustaša thugs killed sixty-six-year-old Bishop Platon Jovanović of Banja Luka and threw his mutilated body into the Vrbanja River. He was one of three Orthodox bishops and 154 priests murdered. Orthodox churches, cathedrals, and cemeteries were similarly demolished.[62]

German army officers stationed in Croatia were no strangers to violence against prisoners and civilians. Even so, using terms like *plunder*, *excesses*, *atrocities*, *murder*, and *butchery* in reporting to Berlin, German officers complained that such "inhuman" Ustaša behavior stood "in defiance of all the laws of civilization," and thus increased the likelihood that even harmless Serbs would become resistors. "The hatred between Serbs and Croatians," said one German intelligence officer, "has climbed to an unbearable level."[63]

Hitler, who accepted Pavelić's argument that the Croatians were Aryans descended from Goths, understood his protégé. When the two met in June 1941, Hitler advised Pavelić, "[I]f the Croatian State were to become really stable then a nationally intolerant policy had to be pursued for 50 years, because only damage resulted from too much tolerance in these matters."[64] Pavelić actually stepped up the killing after this meeting. But by August 1941, the Ustaša faced growing resistance in Bosnia, with Serbs making up 90 percent of all resistors in the growing Serb nationalist and Yugoslav communist movements.[65]

The Croatians established a string of concentration camps for their political and racial enemies. Jasenovać, set up in August 1941 south of Zagreb, was the most notorious. With German extermination camps not yet established, it was the prototype for horror. Women were separated from their children with bayonets. Shelter and food were minimal; prisoners ate bits of grass and drank handfuls of rainwater. Sadistic Ustaša guards beat, killed, and mutilated prisoners at random, including children, dumping the bodies into the Sava River.

Pavelić also tried what he thought was moderation, calling in September 1941 for Croatia's Serbs to convert to Roman Catholicism. Perhaps 250,000 did so with varying degrees of sincerity. In April 1942, Pavelić allowed the formation of a Croatian Orthodox Church that would function under state control. But the policy of forced assimilation never worked. Ethnic-cleansing

[62]Figure in Tomasevich, *War and Revolution*, pp. 395–7, 529.

[63]Quoted in Gumz, "*Wehrmacht* Perceptions of Mass Violence in Croatia," pp. 1032–33.

[64]Germany, Auswärtiges Amt, *Akten zur deutschen Auswartigen Politik 1918–1945*, series D, vol. 12 (Baden-Baden, 1956), d. 603.

[65]Marko Attila Hoare, *Genocide and Resistance in Hitler's Bosnia: The Partisans and Chetniks, 1941–1943* (New York, 2006).

operations against Serbs continued in part owing to the growing resistance, and tens of thousands of Serbs were still held in Croatian concentration camps.[66]

Up to 52,000 Serbs died at the Jasenovać complex alone, as did up to 20,000 Jews and perhaps 20,000 Roma. Observers thought they had seen the apocalypse. "Jasenovać," one source reported to Allied intelligence in 1942, "is a real slaughterhouse. You have never read anywhere—not even under the . . . Gestapo . . . of such horrible things as the Ustaša commit there."[67] Death figures for Serbs in wartime Croatia are difficult to gauge because of destruction of records and postwar Croatian-Serb enmity. One sober estimate holds that roughly 334,000 Serbs died within the borders of the wartime Croatian state.[68]

Croatia's Jews and Roma

Unlike Serbs, the new Croatian state's 39,000 Jews and 25,000 Roma had no opportunity for forced assimilation. With a few exceptions, such as army doctors, Croatia's Jews immediately lost their livelihoods and homes, were required to wear yellow stars, and were forced into ghettos and camps. A proclamation from Pavelić himself on June 26, 1941, blamed them for spreading "false reports in order to cause unrest," and economic chaos "to hinder and increase the difficulty of supplying the population." Thus, he said, "the authorities will act against them and beyond criminal legal responsibility."

In October 1941, the Croatian government asked the Germans to take Croatia's Jews. The Germans refused. Thus, most of Croatia's Jews—perhaps 20,000—died in Croatian camps, primarily Jasenovać. Once the Germans had their killing machinery in place in Poland, they insisted on solving Croatia's remaining Jewish question, deporting 9,000 remaining Jews to Auschwitz between August 1942 and May 1943. Some 76 percent of Croatia's Jews were murdered during the war. As discussed in Chapter 13, several thousand fled to Italian-controlled areas and survived there. Others joined the communist partisan resistance. Others still were protected because they were in mixed marriages.

If, according to Ustaša propaganda, Jews were harmful because of whisper propaganda and speculation, then Roma were a danger because they supposedly spread communicable diseases. They were registered in the fall of 1941. The state did not harm the small number of Roman Catholic Roma, but it transferred the majority of Orthodox Roma to Jasenovać in 1942 where they were given the heaviest jobs and the least food. Twenty thousand likely died there.[69]

The Catholic Church and the Croatian State

Because the new Croatian state was openly Roman Catholic, Vatican policy toward the new state is worth discussion. Notable is that the Ustaša regime made no secret of its policies and that, from the start, many extreme Croatian priests collaborated with the Ustaša. One priest served in Pavelić's bodyguard, another ran the camp at Jasenovać, another was a security police chief in Sarajevo, and another claimed publicly in state newspapers that killing seven-year-olds was no longer a sin.[70]

---

[66]Mark Biondich, "'We Were Defending the State:' Nationalism, Myth, and Memory in Twentieth Century Croatia," in *Ideologies and National Identities: The Case of Twentieth Century Southeast Europe*, eds. Mark Mazower and John Lampe (New York, 2004), pp. 54–81.

[67]Figures and quote in Richard Breitman et al., *US Intelligence and the Nazis*, pp. 206–7.

[68]Figures in Tomasevich, *War and Revolution*, p. 738.

[69]Figures in Tomasevich, *War and Revolution*, pp. 592–610.

[70]Michael Phayer, *The Catholic Church and the Holocaust, 1930–1965* (Bloomington, IN, 2001), pp. 34–35.

Vatican officials were dismayed. But despite the suggestion from French cardinal Eugene Tisserant that Pope Pius XII speak out, the Vatican issued no public condemnation of Pavelić or the Ustaša. Hoping to avoid rupture with the new Catholic state and hoping that it might calm down on its own, Vatican officials made gentler, private appeals to Ustaša leaders and suggested to Italian occupation authorities in Croatia in late 1942 that they might shelter fleeing Jews. One of the pope's closest confidantes, Father Domenico Tardini put it this way: "Croatia is a young state. . . . Youngsters often err because of their age."[71]

Croatia's senior bishop was less sure. Alojzije Stepinać became the archbishop of Zagreb in 1937 before he turned forty. Like other Croatian clerics, he applauded the birth of an independent Croatia. Ustaša excesses, however, shocked him. In May 1941, he wrote Interior Minister Andrija Artuković insisting that the application of anti-Serb and anti-Jewish laws "is a question of humanity and morals," and in November he complained to Pavelić about "inhuman and cruel treatment of non-Aryans."[72] In 1942 and 1943, he became bolder. He repeatedly argued in sermons that "it is forbidden to exterminate Gypsies and Jews because they are said to belong to an inferior race" and that "all people and races descend from God."[73] The Croatian government, though Catholic, forbade publication of the archbishop's sermons. Stepinać thus sent reports of Ustaša atrocities as well as copies of his sermons to the Vatican, to the Yugoslav government in exile in London, and to British and US intelligence.

Stepinać quietly arranged work permits for Jews in Zagreb; arranged baptismal certificates for Jews who asked for them; hid Jews on church property; and helped save the lives of hundreds of Jews, including the elderly, children, and Jews in mixed marriages. He maintained a relationship with Miroslav Freiberger, Zagreb's chief rabbi, and with Vatican support he helped Freiberger with the movement of fifty Jewish children to Palestine via Hungary, Romania, and Turkey.

When the Germans cleared Zagreb of its remaining Jews in May 1943, Stepinać urged Freiberger to hide. The rabbi refused, sharing the fate of Zagreb's Jews. After Freiberger's arrest and deportation to Auschwitz, Stepinać intervened, to no avail. Stepinać was heavily criticized during and after the war for not making a stronger public stand against the Ustaša. Telling, however, is that Ustaša members viewed him as a traitor and that the SS in Croatia complained in 1943 that "Archbishop Stepinać is a great friend of the Jews."[74]

****

The period from 1939 to 1941 represented a transitional phase. The elimination of Nazi enemies through attrition was no longer enough. The murder of the disabled, the killing of African troops, and the green light offered to religious fanatics in Romania and Croatia presaged a change in German tactics to be employed against Jews in the USSR. It was here that the Final Solution of the Jewish Question, as the Nazis called the mass murder of Europe's Jews, began.

---

[71]Quoted in Phayer, *The Catholic Church*, p. 37.

[72]Quoted in Esther Gitman, "A Question of Judgment: Dr. Alojzije Stepinać and the Jews," *Review of Croatian History*, 2, no. 1 (2006), pp. 59, 60, 72.

[73]Quoted in Breitman et al., *US Intelligence*, p. 208; Phayer, *The Catholic Church*, p. 38.

[74]Quoted in Gitman, "A Question of Judgment," p. 64.

9

War of Extermination
The Campaign in the USSR, 1941

Hitler's intentions toward Europe's Jews might always have been genocidal. He used apocalyptic language regarding Jews throughout his career, and in 1939 he predicted their annihilation. Although Germany terrorized Jews in 1939 and 1940, it did not turn to mass murder until June 22, 1941, with the attack on the Soviet Union, code-named Operation Barbarossa. With this invasion, the Germans began the systematic murder of Jews in the USSR through mass shootings, first of men, then of women and children.

There is no written Hitler order to murder the Jews of the USSR. The pace of killing fluctuated from region to region. Historians thus debate the decision's timing and its nature. Did Hitler intend to liquidate all Jews in the USSR even before the campaign? Did the targeted killing of Jewish men as a perceived security measure in June and July 1941 expand to women and children afterward because of preconceived planning or to ad hoc radicalization? Or was there no unified policy at all? Did local German officials, understanding their superiors' expectations, direct mass killing depending on particular local circumstances, ranging from the need for workers to the availability of food supplies?[1]

However one answers the question, it is worth remembering that the Jews' fate in the USSR had an internal logic. Germany's living space lay there. Mass German settlement meant elimination of all biological inferiors. Bolshevism, meanwhile, was world Jewry's most lethal weapon, supposedly uniting the subhuman masses. German leaders and subordinates alike agreed that the war had to eliminate the carriers as well as the contagion. Germany's war on Jews in the USSR, meanwhile, received its own brand of international support. The Germans encouraged Lithuanians, Latvians, Poles, Ukrainians, Romanians, and others to settle longstanding scores with Jews. While German killing strove for efficiency, Germany's allies took revenge in the most primitive ways from the start. No methods of killing, however, bothered the Nazi leadership.

It is also worth noting that the Nazis viewed the war against the Jews in global as well as regional terms. Barbarossa aimed to break the imagined alliance between Jewish Bolshevism

---

[1]Alternative interpretations are discussed in Tom Lawson, *Debates on the Holocaust* (Manchester, 2010), pp. 125–92; Dan Stone, *Histories of the Holocaust* (New York, 2010), pp. 64–112.

and Jewish capitalist plutocracy that the Nazis believed united the USSR, Great Britain, and the United States. Britain continued to fight, Hitler thought, because Jewish plutocrats there expected Soviet and US help. Jews in the United States, meanwhile, supposedly pressed a pliant government toward war. Roosevelt's trade of fifty destroyers to Britain for western Atlantic bases in September 1940; his Lend Lease program announced in March 1941, which provided weapons to Germany's enemies; and the Atlantic Charter of August 1941, which called for Nazi Germany's destruction, all confirmed this belief. With the USSR destroyed, Britain would lose its last continental hope, and the United States would have to defend its Pacific interests from Japan, whose expansion was limited by Soviet pressure in the east.

With supposed Jewish centers of power neutralized, there was no reason not to eradicate the Jews. In 1939, Hitler warned that international Jewry hoped to plunge the world into a new global war, and he threatened that this time, it would mean the annihilation of the Jews in Europe. In 1941, his prophecy seemed confirmed. "The Jews wanted their war," wrote Joseph Goebbels in November 1941, "and now they have it."[2]

9.1 PREPARING MASS MURDER

War of Extermination

On July 31, 1940, Hitler told his military chiefs that Germany would attack the USSR the following spring. He signed the military directive for Operation Barbarossa on December 18. The campaign was expected to take two months. The Red Army, after all, comprised supposed racial inferiors and was directed by Jews. But Barbarossa would be a different kind of campaign. Hitler told his senior military officers on March 30, 1941, to put their scruples aside for what he called a "war of extermination."[3]

On May 19, the Armed Forces Supreme Command issued directives for the behavior of German troops in the USSR. "*Bolshevism,*" the order said, "*is the deadly enemy of the National Socialist German people. . . .* This struggle requires ruthless and energetic action against Bolshevik agitators, guerillas, saboteurs, and Jews, and the total elimination of all active or passive resistance." The directive continued that even captured troops, cunning and unfeeling Asiatics that they were, remained dangerous.[4] By June, German soldiers received steady propaganda. "Bestial" and "infernal" Jews, it said, aimed to lead Soviet subhumans into the heart of Europe in their war against "everything that is noble in humanity."[5]

The army targeted prisoners immediately. Issued from Hitler's headquarters before the attack, the Commissar Order of June 6, 1941, ordered commanders to segregate from captured Red Army units the attached communist party functionaries, all of whom were assumed to be Jews. They were then to be shot. Commissars were identified by their badges and killed by the thousands after capture. Afterward, in POW camps, up to 600,000 more prisoners were shot on suspicion of being political agitators.[6]

---

[2]Quoted in Jeffrey Herf, *The Jewish Enemy: Nazi Propaganda During World War II and the Holocaust* (Cambridge, MA, 2006), p. 122.

[3]Hans-Adolf Jacobsen, ed., *Generaloberst Halder: Kriegstagebuch*, vol. 2 (Stuttgart, 1963), March 30, 1941.

[4]Jeremy Noakes and Geoffrey Pridham, ed. *Nazism 1919–1945: A Documentary Reader*, vol. 3, new ed. (Exeter, 1998), p. 486.

[5]Militärgeschichtliches Forschungsamt, gen, eds., *Germany and the Second World War*, vol. 4 (hereafter *Germany and the Second World War*) (New York, 1998), p. 516.

[6]*Germany and the Second World War*, vol. 4 (New York, 1998), pp. 1225–31.

But the Germans treated rank-and-file Soviet POWs similarly. German troops shot Soviet prisoners on forced marches and allowed others to freeze to death on open rail transports. Prison camps for Soviet prisoners had no barracks to protect them from the elements, and the Germans provided almost no food. "Prisoners of war who are not working," ordered Army Quartermaster Edouard Wagner, "are supposed to starve to death." Two million were already dead by February 1942. Other Soviet prisoners were worked to death in SS labor camps and enterprises in Germany. Limited protests from German officers were ineffective. "The issue here," said Field Marshall Wilhelm Keitel, the chief of the Armed Forces Supreme Command, "is the annihilation of a world view!"[7] Of 5.7 million Soviet POWs in German captivity during the war, some 3.3 million perished. After European Jews, they were the Nazis' second largest group of victims.

The Germans also committed appalling crimes against Soviet civilians. Musings by Himmler on January 1941 on long-term demographic aims became more concrete with *Generalplan Ost* ("General Plan East"), a colonization scheme emerging in various drafts between July 1941 and May 1942. Some 10 million ethnic Germans were to settle the vast lands between Germany and the Ural Mountains. Some 31 million Slavs—Poles, Ukrainians, and Belarusians—were to be destroyed. The rest would serve as slave labor, constructing roads, cities, and villages.[8] Hitler lost the war, so *Generalplan Ost*'s full effect was never achieved.

But German policies remained catastrophic. By September 1941, the Germans divided the occupied eastern lands into new administrative commissariats, districts, and subdistricts, with hosts of new civilian administrators. Army, police, and civilian authorities deliberately starved Soviet citizens while diverting grain harvests to the troops and to the German home front. The Germans decreased the flow of food into occupied Kiev so that tens of thousands died in the winter of 1941–1942. Other cities suffered similar disasters. After surrounding Leningrad in September 1941, the Germans allowed 653,000 to starve to death. Hermann Göring estimated in November that "this year between twenty and thirty million people will die in Russia of hunger." Despite the overestimate, he was unbothered. "Perhaps it is well that it should be so," he said, "for certain nations must be decimated."[9]

Army and police formations also killed civilians based on decrees of May 1941 that called for the elimination of guerilla fighters, saboteurs, and agitators as well as reprisals against whole communities. In Belarus alone, special army and police units destroyed 5,000 villages and killed up to 300,000 civilians for (often alleged) partisan activity over the course of the war.[10] By August 1944, another 2.1 million civilian laborers from the Soviet Union, many conscripted through terror methods, worked in Germany to alleviate labor shortages in agriculture and industry. They lived in barbed wire compounds where hunger and typhus were endemic.[11]

---

[7]Quotes in Christian Streit, *Keine Kameraden: Die Wehrmacht und die sowjetischen Kriegsgefangenen* (Bonn, 1997) pp. 157–8, 181.

[8]Adam Tooze, *The Wages of Destruction: The Making and Breaking of the Nazi Economy* (New York, 2006), pp. 466–85.

[9]On Kiev and Göring's quote, see Karel C. Berkhoff, *Harvest of Despair: Life and Death in Ukraine Under Nazi Rule* (Cambridge, MA, 2004), pp. 168–9, 186. On Leningrad, see Tooze, *The Wages of Destruction*, p. 485.

[10]Christian Gerlach, *Kalkulierter Mord: Die deutsche Wirtschafts- und Vernichtungspolitik in Weißussland 1941 bis 1944* (Hamburg, 1999), p. 870.

[11]Figure in Ulrich Herbert, *Hitler's Foreign Workers: Enforced Foreign Labor in Germany Under the Third Reich* (New York, 1997), p. 298.

In all, Soviet population losses during the war were between 26 and 27 million. Of these, about 8.6 million were soldiers. The rest were civilians, who were shot, starved, or worked to death. The Soviet population declined by 13.5 percent as a result of Germany's war.[12] This horrendous figure dwarfs other countries' losses. US deaths on two fronts totaled 418,000, a terrible figure that nevertheless represents but one-third of 1 percent of the US population.

"Special Tasks"

But nearly *all* Jews in the occupied USSR were murdered. To the Nazi leadership, they were subhumans who also represented the nerve center of the Bolshevist system. Army units cooperated and often participated in the killing, but police units carried out much of the dirty work. General orders to murder Jews en masse were never expressed as such. But on March 13, 1941, months before Barbarossa began, Hitler limited army authority as much as possible to front operations. He placed rear areas under police control, entrusting Himmler with *"special tasks,"* related to "the necessity of finally resolving the conflict between two opposing political systems."[13] Hitler did not have to tell Himmler to put scruples aside.

Foremost in carrying out "special tasks" were motorized police units of 600 to 1,000 men each, soon to be assembled by Heydrich and designated *Einsatzgruppen* ("Special Task Forces"). Officers and rank-and-file members came from the Security Police and SD. The units were to follow the army's advance into the Baltic States (*Einsatzgruppe A*), Belarus (*Einsatzgruppe B*), and Ukraine (*Einsatzgruppen C* and *D*). By agreement between Heydrich and the army command on April 28, 1941, the *Einsatzgruppen* were to "carry out special security tasks *outside the ambit* of military forces."[14]

The Germans also deployed twenty-three battalions of so-called Order Police—uniformed police units given more routine tasks in ordinary circumstances. Nearly 12,000 Order Police, generally SS members, were assigned to the aforementioned special tasks.[15] In July, Himmler also deployed a mobile Waffen-SS Cavalry Brigade of over 10,000 men to suppress "criminals" in the Pripyet Marsh region of Belarus.[16] Overall command was divided. Heydrich commanded the *Einsatzgruppen*. Many of the police battalions and the SS cavalry units stood under personal representatives of Himmler called Higher SS and Police Leaders, three of which were appointed for separate zones of the Eastern Front.

The Germans also expected local nationalists in the USSR—Lithuanians, Latvians, Poles, Ukrainians, and others—to help. As the Germans reordered occupied areas, they used new anti-Soviet local mayors, councilmen, and police. Local officials provided information on Jews, from their numbers to their locations, to possible hiding places. By 1943, some 300,000 anticommunist and antisemitic local policemen also stood under Himmler's command.[17] They

---

[12]The figure is the best we have, but it is not without problems. See Michael Ellman and S. Maksudov, "Soviet Deaths in the Great Patriotic War: A Note," *Europe-Asia Studies*, 46, no. 4 (July 1994), pp. 671–81.

[13]Noakes and Pridham, eds., *Nazism 1919–1945*, vol. 3, pp. 484–5.

[14]"On Co-operation with the Security Police and SD in the Eastern War Which Is Envisaged," April 28, 1941, Noakes and Pridham, eds., *Nazism 1919–1945*, vol. 3, p. 485.

[15]Figure in Edward B. Westermann, *Hitler's Police Battalions: Enforcing Racial War in the East* (Lawrence, KS, 2004), p. 163.

[16]Figure in Jürgen Matthäus, "Controlled Escalation: Himmler's Men in the Summer of 1941 and the Holocaust in the Occupied Soviet Territories," *Holocaust and Genocide Studies*, 21, no. 2 (Fall 2007), p. 225.

[17]Figure in Christopher Browning, *The Path to Genocide: Essays on Launching the Final Solution* (New York, 1995), p. 106.

outnumbered German police by ten to one. Without them, the extermination of Jews in the USSR would have been impossible.

Secret Orders

Orders traveled word of mouth by senior officers to preserve secrecy. The earliest *written* order for mass murder in the USSR came from Heydrich on July 2, 1941, confirming what was said at a pre-invasion meeting. Heydrich commanded execution for Communist Party officials and "Jews in Party and State employment." It was an order to kill Jewish men at least, because in the Soviet Union, Jews with any employment worked for the party or the state whether political officers or pharmacists. German police indeed targeted adult Jewish males in the first weeks of the campaign. They moved on to Jewish women and children by August. Perhaps this means that no decision for general mass murder was reached until that time. On the other hand, the killing of women and children might always have been understood. The Germans encouraged locals to attack all Jews from the start.

Senior police officers understood the expectations. SS-General Friedrich Jeckeln, Himmler's Higher SS and Police Leader in Ukraine, boasted to a friend in April 1941 that "I myself will, I have learned secretly, be used in connection with great events, which are to be expected."[18] Walter Blume, commander of an *Einsatzgruppe B* detachment, testified after the war that "[d]uring June we were already being instructed about the tasks of exterminating the Jews. It was stated that Eastern Jewry was the intellectual reservoir of Bolshevism and, therefore, in the Führer's opinion, must be exterminated."[19]

Order Police received fewer details. But on April 15, 1941, at their Vienna headquarters, the men of Police Battalion 322 received word they would act under Himmler's "personal supervision." They were expected to "fulfill their duty" as "racial superiors." One battalion member recalled after the war that "[i]t was preached to us at every instructional period that one needed to exterminate this race. They were responsible for all the evil in the world. . . ."[20]

Hitler knew exactly what he wanted. On January 30, 1941, he spoke at Berlin's *Sportpalast* commemorating his seizure of power. He reviewed the creation of a *völkisch* community from the ruins of 1918. He cursed the British, "dominated by a conglomeration of Jews, their financiers, and profiteers," for continuing the war. He then made a prediction:

> [T]he year 1941 will be . . . the historical year of a great reorganization of Europe. . . . I would not like to forget to repeat the advice that I gave . . . [on January 30, 1939] . . . that should the outside world allow itself to be plunged into a general war by Jewry, then all of Jewry will be finished in Europe. . . . The coming months and years will show that I have foreseen things correctly. . . .[21]

On August 1, 1941, six weeks after the attack on the USSR, Gestapo Chief Heinrich Müller notified *Einsatzgruppen* leaders that Hitler himself expected status reports concerning the "work of the *Einsatzgruppen* in the East."[22]

---

[18]Quoted in Richard Breitman, *Official Secrets: What the Nazis Planned, What the British and Americans Knew* (New York, 1990), p. 39.

[19]Affidavit of Walter Blume, June 29, 1947, *Trials of War Criminals Before the Nuremberg Military Tribunals Under Control Council Law No. 10*, vol. 4 (Washington, DC, 1949), pp. 139–40.

[20]Quoted in Westermann, *Hitler's Police Battalions*, pp. 1–2, 13.

[21]Max Domarus, ed., *Hitler: Speeches and Proclamations*, vol. 4 (Wauconda, IL, 1997), p. 2367.

[22]Peter Klein, ed. *Die Einsatzgruppen in der besetzten Sowjetunion 1941/42: Die Tätigkeits- und Lageberichte des Chefs der Sicherheitspolizei und SD* (Berlin, 1997), p. 342.

9.2 JEWS IN THE USSR ON THE EVE OF BARBAROSSA

Jews in the USSR to 1941

In January 1939, Jews in the USSR numbered 3.028 million: 1.8 percent of the Soviet population.[23] The areas annexed by the Soviet Union in 1939 and 1940, including the Belarusian and Ukrainian parts of Poland, the Baltic States, Bessarabia, and northern Bukovina, had up to 2.15 million additional Jews. With the German invasion, many Jews fled east, but up to 2.74 million remained. Up to 2.62 million of them were murdered, partly because they supposedly embodied the Bolshevist system and the communist manipulation of the masses.[24]

Was it true? Only 5 percent of Lenin's Bolsheviks in 1917 were Jews. As late as 1940, only 4.3 percent of the Communist Party comprised Jews. No Jews were in senior government positions by that time. Jewish communists had more opportunities than under the tsars, and they were overrepresented in certain administrative and professional jobs. But they never dominated. In Ukraine in 1939, where more than half of all Soviet Jews lived, 64,000 Jews held 20 percent of Communist Party and government posts, ranging from judges to plant managers. They also comprised 13.7 percent of the medical profession and 10.9 percent of educational personnel in Ukraine.[25]

Jews who wished to be culturally and politically Jewish faced difficulties. The USSR closed religious schools (Jewish and others) and places of worship (churches and synagogues). It disbanded local Jewish community councils (*Kehillot*), which handled Jewish welfare. It nationalized Jewish businesses, from factories to workshops, to small stores, and punished hundreds of thousands of Jews for employing workers. The Soviets also abolished Jewish political parties such as the Bund and arrested thousands of Zionists. From 1919 to 1936, 32,000 Zionists from the USSR left for Palestine.[26] And after 1936, Jewish Communist Party officers, army officers, and intelligentsia suffered and died in Stalin's purges like Soviets of other nationalities.

When the Red Army occupied eastern Poland in September 1939 and the Baltic and Romanian regions in June 1940, many Jews in these areas openly celebrated. The reasons were clear enough. Polish and Romanian rule ground Jews into hopeless poverty. And in the war's opening weeks, German forces in eastern Poland burned synagogues, destroyed Jewish homes and businesses, and terrorized Jews. During six days of occupation in Białystok in September 1939, the Germans killed over a hundred Jews. The Soviets represented an improvement when they arrived.

Avraham Vered, a teenager in Białystok, remembered that Soviet troops "were bombarded with flowers" on their arrival. "We climbed up on to the tanks. The soldiers hugged us close, and we laughed with joy."[27] When the Soviets entered Lvov, one survivor felt "an immense feeling of relief." Local Ukrainians had been organizing pogroms. Thus in Lvov too, Jews jumped on tanks and cheered.[28] Others were more measured. "I know who the Bolsheviks are," said one

---

[23]Figure in Mordechai Altschuler, *Soviet Jewry on the Eve of the Holocaust: A Social and Demographic Profile* (Jerusalem, 1998), pp. 221, 225.

[24]Figures in Yitzhak Arad, *The Holocaust in the Soviet Union* (Lincoln, NE, 2009), p. 525.

[25]On leadership positions, see Benjamin Pinkus, *The Jews of the Soviet Union: The History of a National Minority* (New York, 1988), pp. 77–83. On professions, see Altschuler, *Soviet Jewry on the Eve of the Holocaust*, pp. 309–10.

[26]Figure in Arad, *The Holocaust in the Soviet Union*, p. 19.

[27]Sara Bender, *The Jews of Białystok*, pp. 50–1.

[28]Eliyahu Yones, *Smoke in the Sand: The Jews of Lvov in the War Years, 1939–1944* (Jerusalem, 2004), p. 42.

Jewish merchant in western Ukraine. "[T]hey'll take my property, but . . . they will leave me with my life." Gershon Adiv, who was visiting Vilna from Palestine, remembered, "Who took stock in those days? At a time when the German axe was raised over their necks, everyone greeted the Russians unanimously as they would the Messiah."[29]

Did Stalin Favor the Jews?

"We do not distinguish between a Pole, a Russian, a Jew, a Ukrainian," proclaimed the Soviets in the new lands.[30] One's politics mattered more. Jews, including Jewish communists, rose to local importance at first. In many smaller communities they became prominent in militias and in local government. This trend was logical. In rural Belarus, East Galicia, and Bessarabia, former municipal officials fled the Soviets, Jews often made up half the population, and the Soviets viewed them as reliable. Many Jews also encountered educational and professional opportunities that they lacked under Polish and Romanian rule. By 1941, 30 to 40 percent of the medical students at the University of Lvov were Jews.[31]

It all rubbed locals badly. What rubbed them worse were waves of mass arrests of Poles, Ukrainians, and others by the NKVD—the Soviet secret police—and subsequent deportation to central Asian camps because of anti-Soviet activity. Nearly 1 million were deported from the eastern Polish lands alone.[32] The final wave of arrests began on June 14, 1941, a week before the Germans invaded. Locals reflexively blamed Jews, especially because some were indeed NKVD informants. "We have to get rid of the fascists," said one Jewish man to his wife. "They are not good for the Jewish people."[33] Lithuanians, Poles, and Ukrainians who chafed at Jewish celebrations, supposed Jewish takeover, and the deportation of friends and relatives developed a slogan: "Death to Bolsheviks and Jews."

In fact, the Soviets hardly favored Jews in the new borderlands. Needing to attract other locals, they soon replaced Jews in key party positions. In Lvov, for example, the Soviets favored Ukrainians in municipal elections so that two Jews served in a municipal assembly of 160, even though Jews comprised one-third of Lvov's population. Despite popular perception, very few Jews served in the NKVD. And Soviet economic policy, which nationalized private concerns, harmed Jews disproportionately. In Lithuania, 83 percent of nationalized enterprises, from banks to factories, to mills, to shops, to homes, were Jewish.[34] Savings in old currency, meanwhile, became worthless.

The Soviets also deported Jews to central Asia along with Poles, Ukrainians, and everyone else. Perhaps 20 percent of those deported from the annexed regions of Poland were Jews.[35] Jewish deportees included community leaders, rabbis, journalists, and Zionists, whom NKVD interrogators accused of being British spies. The Jewish deportees were ironically spared the

---

[29]Quoted in Dov Levin, *The Lesser of Two Evils: Eastern European Jewry Under Soviet Rule* (Philadelphia, PA, 1995), pp. 33, 34.

[30]Quoted in Levin, *The Lesser of Two Evils*, p. 60.

[31]Figure in Yones, *Smoke in the Sand: The Jews of Lvov*, p. 56.

[32]Figures are in dispute. For figures from eastern Poland, see Katherine Jolluck, "Gender and Antisemitism in Wartime Soviet Exile," in *Antisemitism and Its Opponents in Modern Poland*, ed. Robert Blobaum (Ithaca, NY, 2005), p. 212.

[33]John Munro, ed., *Białystok to Birkenau: The Holocaust Journey of Michel Mielnicki* (Vancouver, 2000), p. 84.

[34]Figure in Levin, *The Lesser of Two Evils*, p. 69.

[35]Figure in Zbigniew Siemaszko, "The Mass Deportations of the Polish Population to the USSR, 1940–1941," in *The Soviet Takeover of the Polish Eastern Provinces, 1939–1941*, ed. Keith Sword (London, 1991), p. 231.

horrors of German occupation. But Jews who had once welcomed the Soviets lived in fear of arrest up to the German invasion.

Might Jews have fled the initial German attack? Many did so in the summer and fall of 1941, but one needed luck. Jews who lived near the border with Germany knew of German atrocities in Poland from refugees' stories. Jews further east were not so well informed. Allied with Berlin until June 1941, Moscow reported nothing of German atrocities in Poland. Most Jews who escaped as the Germans advanced left on state orders, either drafted into army units or receiving commands to move east with their factory cohort to resume production.

Avraham Tory of Kovno remembered trains leaving the city packed with military personnel. Some Jews fled on foot. But most Jews, he said, "feared . . . trial later for desertion and treason."[36] Thus, while large percentages of Jews in some cities evacuated, many remained. Of the perhaps 4.32 million Jews who once lived in the regions occupied by the Germans in 1941, up to 2.74 million found themselves under German occupation.[37] They quickly discovered that they were in far greater danger than their brethren in Poland.

9.3 THE ONSLAUGHT: POGROMS

The German Attack

On June 22, 1941, three German army groups of more than 3 million men attacked the USSR. They were quickly joined by 500,000 troops from Romania, Hungary, Slovakia, and Italy. Spanish, Vichy French, Belgian, Croatian, and Scandinavian volunteers also joined the crusade on Bolshevism. Stalin misread innumerable warning signs. The Red Army was caught unprepared by the attack. The morale of Soviet troops dropped immediately. And many subject nationalities from the Baltic States to Ukraine initially welcomed the Germans as liberators from Stalinist oppression.

The Axis advance was relentless at first. In the north, the Germans sliced through the Baltic States and, by September 9, surrounded Leningrad. By September 19, they entered Kiev, which Stalin ordered held at all costs, and by late October they seized most of the Crimean Peninsula. By December, German troops were twenty kilometers from Moscow's suburbs. By year's end, the Soviets lost more than 4 million troops (killed, captured, wounded, or missing)—the strength of its entire peacetime army. Desperate Soviet counteroffensives in freezing temperatures west of Moscow halted German advances in December. But much of the Soviet Union was under German control. The British planned for "the event of a Russian collapse" well into 1942.[38]

Jews, the Germans were sure, orchestrated sabotage and partisan activity behind the swiftly advancing lines. Just days after the invasion, members of *Einsatzgruppe A* together with army personnel killed several hundred Jews, mostly men, along the East Prussian frontier. They were the first such victims.[39] But the Germans also expected local populations in the Baltic States, Belarus, and Ukraine to launch pogroms. On June 17, 1941, Heydrich ordered *Einsatzgruppen*

---

[36]Avraham Tory, *Surviving the Holocaust: The Kovno Ghetto Diary*, ed. Martin Gilbert (Cambridge, MA, 1990), June 22, 1941.

[37]Figures in Arad, *The Holocaust in the Soviet Union*, p. 87.

[38]Quote and figure in Chris Bellamy, *Absolute War: Soviet Russia in the Second World War* (New York, 2007), pp. 5, 279.

[39]Klein, ed. *Die Einsatzgruppen*, p. 31; Christoph Dieckmann, "The War and the Killing of the Lithuanian Jews," in *National Socialist Extermination Policies: Contemporary German Perspectives and Controversies*, ed. Ulrich Herbert (New York, 2000), pp. 242–45.

chiefs to "trigger" and "intensify when necessary" . . . "self-cleansing efforts by anti-communists and anti-Jewish circles in the territories to be newly occupied."[40]

German aircraft dropped propaganda leaflets with proclamations like "we have come to liberate you from [the] Jews of Moses . . . the friends of Roosevelt, Churchill and Stalin who brought Bolshevism, abuse, and exploitation into the world. . . ."[41] Freed from Soviet rule, Lithuanian, Polish, Ukrainian, and Romanian mobs were already vengeful. None limited themselves to killing just men. Pogroms erupted from Lithuania in the north to Romania in the south. Only representative examples will be discussed here.

Kovno

Pogroms throughout Lithuania killed up to 10,000 Jews in the first weeks of the war.[42] As the Red Army withdrew from the Lithuanian capital of Kovno on June 23, Lithuanian nationalist partisans of the Lithuanian Activist Front (LAF) donned white armbands and took to the streets. Nationalist Lithuanian émigrés in Germany broadcast speeches over the radio urging violence against Jews.

Einsatzgruppe A arrived in Kovno on June 24, 1941. Its commander, Dr. Franz Stahlecker, reported that "local anti-Semitic elements were induced to engage in pogroms against the Jews. . . . It was thought a good idea for the security police not to be seen to be involved, at least not immediately. . . . The impression had to be created that the local population itself had taken the first steps on its own. . . . The task of the security police was to set these purges in motion and put them onto the right track. . . ."[43]

As Lithuanian partisans observed the movements of Kovno's Jews, nineteen-year-old Sara Ginaite went to her uncles' apartment for safety. At 6 a.m. on June 25, five Lithuanian partisans broke in. "We tried," she remembered, "to explain that we were not communists and that the Soviets had deported our close relatives . . . just a week earlier. Unmoved, [they] arrested all five Jewish men living in the building including my mother's three brothers. . . . I watched in horror as the five men . . . were shot. . . . Broken hearted, my grandmother Malka Virovichiene died the very next day. . . ."[44]

The pogrom broke out in earnest that night. Stahlecker reported that "1,500 Jews were eliminated by Lithuanian partisans, several synagogues were set on fire or destroyed by other methods, and a Jewish quarter of about sixty houses was burnt down. On the following nights, 2,300 Jews were rendered harmless in the same way. . . ."[45] Stahlecker's polite language omitted the true horror. A German army photographer in Kovno recorded what he saw at a local garage on June 25:

> In the left corner of the courtyard was a group of [Jewish] men between 30 and 50 years old. There must have been between about 40 and 50 [of them]; they had been rounded up and held by some civilians [who were] armed with guns and wore armbands. . . . A young man with rolled up sleeves—he

[40]Heydrich to Einsatzgruppen Chiefs, June 29, 1941, Klein, ed., *Einsatzgruppen*, p. 319.

[41]Quoted in Yaffa Eliach, *There Was Once a World: A Nine Hundred Year Chronicle of the Shtetl of Eishyshok* (Boston, MA, 1998), p. 576.

[42]Figure in Arad, *The Holocaust in the Soviet Union*, pp. 92–3.

[43]Ernst Klee et al., eds., *The Good Old Days: The Holocaust as Seen by Its Perpetrators* (New York, 1988), pp. 24–7.

[44]Sara Ginaite-Rubinson, *Resistance and Survival: The Jewish Community in Kovno, 1941–1944* (New York, 2005), pp. 18–19.

[45]Klee et al., eds., *The Good Old Days*, p. 27.

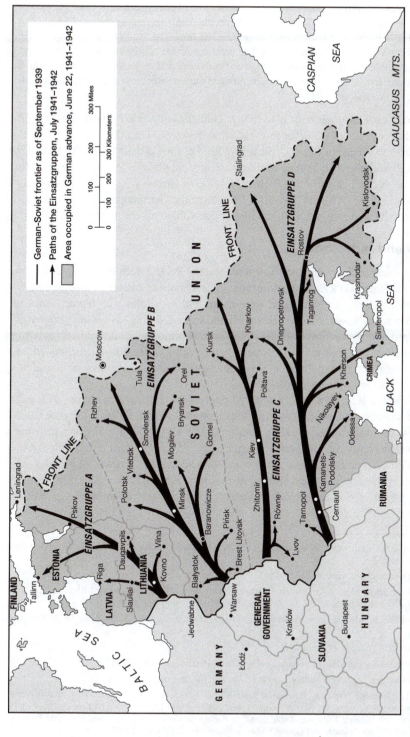

MAP 9.1 German invasion of USSR 1941. *Source: The War Against the Jews 1933–1945*, by Lucy S. Davidowicz. Text copyright © 1975 by Lucy S. Davidowicz, maps by Vincent Kotschar, copyright © 1975 by Henry Holt and Co., Inc

must have been Lithuanian—was armed with a tire iron. He pulled the men one by one from the group, and with one or more blows to the back of the head, struck each dead with the tire iron. In this way he killed the entire group of 45–50 people within three quarters of an hour. . . . After all of them had been beaten to death, the young man laid down the tire iron, picked up an accordion, and played the Lithuanian national hymn. The behavior of the civilians present (women and children) was incredible, for after each killing they began to clap, and they sang and clapped with the start of the national hymn. There were women standing in the very front row with small children, who stayed for the entire affair until the end.[46]

Nor were men the pogrom's only victims. Diarist Avraham Tory wrote that "[w]e feared for the fate of the men . . . but we never imagined that they would murder women, children, and the elderly."[47] Bishop Vincentas Brizgys, the acting head of the Catholic Church in Kovno, answered Jewish appeals with the reply that he could do nothing but pray.[48] "We will," howled one teenage partisan, "slaughter all of you Jews."[49] Nearly 4,000 of Kovno's 36,000 Jews were murdered in the days following the Germans' arrival.[50] Thereafter, the Germans ended the pogrom, disarmed the LAF partisans, and reorganized them into police volunteers for more organized killing.

Radziłów and Jedwabne

Even before the war, Poles in small towns in eastern Poland near Białystok and Łomża tilted toward Roman Dmowski's *Endecja*. After the Soviets annexed eastern Poland, nearly 60 percent of those they deported to central Asia were ethnic Poles.[51] Poles who blamed Jews for Soviet practices were ready to settle scores. Heydrich understood, telling his *Einsatzgruppen* chiefs that anticommunist and antisemitic Poles were of "special importance" not only for intelligence but also for pogroms.[52] At least twenty *shtetlach* in the region of Białystok experienced pogroms at the hands of local and roving Polish mobs encouraged by German security police, although eyewitness accounts vary concerning the details.

The *shtetl* of Radziłów, which suffered pogroms in 1918 and again in 1933, experienced some of the worst violence. The day after the German invasion, Polish hooligans attacked Jews in Radziłów, burning homes, stealing property, and killing with clubs and iron bars. Some children were decapitated; others were buried alive. "Screams were unbearable," remembered Menachem Finkielsztejn, eighteen at the time, who added that "crowds of Polish men, women and children were standing and laughing at the miserable victims. . . ."[53] On July 7, German and Polish police herded Radziłów's Jews into a barn outside town and set it on fire, killing

---

[46]Wilhelm Gunsilius's testimony of November 11, 1958, is in the Bundesarchiv Außenstelle Ludwigsburg, Bestand 162, 5 AR-Z 14/58, pp. 133–9.

[47]Tory, *Kovno Ghetto Diary*, June 23–July 7, 1941.

[48]Sara Schner-Neshamit, "Jewish-Lithuanian Relations During World War II: History and Rhetoric," in *Bitter Legacy: Confronting the Holocaust in the USSR*, ed. Zvi Gittelman (Bloomington, IN, 1997), p. 169.

[49]Quoted in William W. Mishell, *Kaddish for Kovno: Life and Death in a Lithuanian Ghetto 1941–1945* (Chicago, IL, 1988), p. 19.

[50]Figure in Klee et al., eds., *The Good Old Days*, p. 27.

[51]Figure in Siemaszko, "The Mass Deportations of the Polish Population to the USSR," p. 231.

[52]Heydrich to Einsatzgruppen Chiefs, July 1, 1941, Klein, ed., *Einsatzgruppen*, p. 320.

[53]Menachem Finkielsztejn Testimony, translation from Polish, Document 301/974, Jewish Historical Institute, Warsaw. On the pogrom and its sources, see Andrzej Żbikowski, "Pogroms and Massacres During the Summer of 1941 in the Łomza and Białystok District: The Case of Radziłów," in *Facing the Catastrophe: Jews and Non-Jews in Europe During World War II*, eds. Beate Kosmala and Georgi Verbeeck (New York, 2011), pp. 41–72.

everyone inside, hundreds at least. Virtually nothing remained of the five-hundred-year-old Radziłów Jewish community.

Three days later, a similar pogrom occurred in the *shtetl* of Jedwabne, thirty kilometers to the south, where Polish toughs beat Jewish men, women, and children to death, then burned the rest, as in Radziłów, in a kerosene-soaked barn. Estimates of those killed range from 400 to 1,600.[54] Szmul Wasersztajn remembered that "[t]he order was given by the Germans but it was the Polish hooligans who took it up and carried it out. . . ."[55] The Germans, according to another witness, "stood and took pictures" during the massacre.[56] "The screams," Alina Lukowianka remembered years later, "could be heard two kilometers away."[57]

Jews received little assistance. The pogroms pleased many locals while leaving others indifferent. Radziłów's priest, Alexander Dolegowski, waved aside pleas for help. "It is well known," he said, "that every Jew, from the youngest to those sixty years old, are communists."[58] "My family had nothing to do with the slaughter," remembered one Jedwabne resident four decades later. But the Jews, he insisted, "bore their share of the blame. From the start of the war they sided with the Russkies. . . ."[59] The revenge motive notwithstanding, locals scoured the bodies for hidden coins.

Others were horrified, but they were intimidated by the mob as well as the small-town dynamic whereby everyone knows everyone. Decades after the pogrom, some would still not name names. "Let the truth be discovered by those whose duty it is," said an elderly woman in Jedwabne in 2000 as a tear rolled down her face. "I'm scared."[60] Survival in 1941 was thus rare. Menachem Finkelsztejn remembered that no one in or around Radziłów would shelter his family. They hid in a wheat field and then afterward with a series of Poles in return for payment. Pure altruism was scarce. Szmul Wasersztajn survived Jedwabne because a nearby Polish woman hid him in her home. Thirty years later, he viewed her photograph and sobbed: "This woman risked the lives of her own eight children to save my lousy Jewish life."[61]

Lvov

Jews fared no better in East Galicia, a disputed region of mixed Ukrainian and Polish ethnicity that belonged to Poland between the wars and to the Soviets after 1939. Before June 1941, Germany supported a Ukrainian terrorist group from East Galicia called the Organization of Ukrainian Nationalists (OUN) that demanded an independent and ethnically homogeneous Ukraine including East Galicia. Berlin now enlisted their help against the Soviets. For the OUN, Poles in East Galicia had to leave. But Jews were unredeemable. One OUN resolution called

---

[54]The pogrom is recounted in Jan Gross, *Neighbors: The Destruction of the Jewish Community of Jedwabne, Poland* (New York, 2002). On the figure, see Bogdan Musial, "The Pogrom in Jedwabne: Critical Remarks about Jan T. Gross's *Neighbors*," in *The Neighbors Respond: The Controversy over the Jedwabne Massacre in Poland*, eds. Antony Polonsky and Joanna B. Michlic (Princeton, NJ, 2004), pp. 324–5.

[55]Anna Bikont, "We of Jedwabne," in Polonsky and Michlic, eds., *The Neighbors Respond*, p. 270.

[56]Quoted in Gross, *Neighbors*, p. 48.

[57]Bikont, "We of Jedwabne," p. 276.

[58]Quoted in Gross, *Neighbors*, p. 36.

[59]Quoted in Gabriela Szczesna, "The Blood of Jedwabne," in Polonsky and Michlic, eds., *The Neighbors Respond*, p. 62.

[60]Quoted in Maria Kaczyńska, "In Memory and Adminition," in Polonsky and Michlic, eds., *The Neighbors Respond*, p. 65.

[61]Bikont, "We of Jedwabne," p. 277.

Jews "the most reliable props of the Soviet regime and the spearheads of Moscow's imperialism in the Ukraine."[62] Another manifesto warned that the Jews "welcomed Stalin with flowers. We will lay your heads at Hitler's feet. . . ."[63]

As the Soviets evacuated East Galicia, the NKVD murdered thousands of Ukrainian nationalists that it had imprisoned in twenty-two different cities and towns. As Germans troops invaded, Iaroslav Stetsko, a senior OUN official, blamed the Jews, despite the fact that Zionists were also among the dead. "Jews," Stetsko said, "are deliberately causing provocations . . . we are organizing a militia that will help remove Jews and protect the population."[64]

With German and OUN prompting, Ukrainian merchants, professionals, judges, and even priests organized pogroms against local Jews. Peasant mobs, including women, arrived from the countryside to share in the violence and plunder. Jews were blamed for everything, from killing Jesus to the NKVD murders. German army personnel also participated. Perhaps 12,000 Jews died in pogroms in thirty-five Eastern Galician towns and villages.[65]

The Germans, accompanied by OUN leaders and German-trained Ukrainian troops, captured the East Galician capital of Lvov on June 30. Lvov had interwar Poland's third largest Jewish population and was a haven for Jewish refugees fleeing Poland in 1939. Some 230,000 Jews lived there. Flowers and OUN banners now welcomed the German liberators, urging them to "[s]mash the Jews and the Communists."[66] Stetsko publicly proclaimed Ukrainian independence while promising OUN collaboration with Hitler.

A pogrom then erupted in Lvov in retaliation for two years of "Jewish Bolshevik" rule and for the NKVD murder of Ukrainian prisoners the previous day. Ukrainian thugs broke into Jews' homes and attacked men, women, and children with crowbars, axes, and knives. Other Jews were taken to a prison yard and murdered. Jewish women were gang-raped. In 1918, a Polish-led pogrom in Lvov that killed seventy-three Jews received world attention. Now 4,000 Jews were murdered in Lvov in four days of violence.

In smaller towns, a number of local priests saved Jews from the mob. In two townships, they might have prevented pogroms altogether. Meanwhile a monastery in Lvov turned Jews away, the abbot insisting that the pogrom was the will of God. The metropolitan of the Greek Catholic Church in Lvov, Andrei Sheptytsky, reflects this ambivalence. As a Ukrainian, Sheptytsky welcomed the Germans as liberators. He later sent personal congratulations to Hitler when the Germans captured Kiev. At the same time, he was horrified by the pogrom on Lvov and hid a number Jews.

But in a discussion with Rabbi David Kahane during the pogrom, the metropolitan asked, "Have you ever thought about it and asked yourself, what is the source of hatred and savage persecution of the Jewish people from ancient times to the present?" Sheptytsky pointed to the Gospel of Matthew: "It says there," he said, "And the whole people answered and said His blood will be on us and on our children."[67] Regardless of the reasons, the Germans were pleased with

---

[62]Quoted in Yones, *Smoke in the Sand: The Jews of Lvov*, p. 90.

[63]Quoted in Karel C. Berkhoff and Marco Carynnyk, "The Organization of Ukrainian Nationalists and Its Attitude Toward Germans and Jews: Iaroslav Stesko's 1941 *Zhyttiepys*," *Harvard Ukrainian Studies*, 23, no. 3–4 (1999), p. 154.

[64]Quoted in Berkhoff and Carynnyk, "Organization of Ukrainian Nationalists," p. 154.

[65]Figure in Dieter Pohl, *Nationalsozialistische Judenverfolgung in Ostgalizien, 1941–1944: Organisation und Durchführung eines staatlichen Massenverbrechens* (Munich, 1997), p. 67.

[66]Quoted in Yones, *Smoke in the Sand: The Jews of Lvov*, p. 77.

[67]Quoted in John-Paul Himka, "Ukrainian Collaboration in the Extermination of the Jews During the Second World War: Sorting Out the Long-Term and Conjunctural Factors," in *The Fate of the European Jews: Continuity or Contingency?* ed. Jonathan Frankel (New York, 1997), p. 181.

A woman is chased after a sexual assault during the pogrom in Lvov, June 1941.   *Source:* Bildarchiv Preußischer Kulturbesitz.

the result in Lvov. "In the first few hours after the Bolsheviks left," read the Security Police report, "the Ukrainian population embarked on a commendable *Aktion* against the Jews."[68]

9.4 THE ONSLAUGHT: SYSTEMATIC SHOOTING

Perpetrators

As the Germans pushed into the Soviet Union, units of the *Einsatzgruppen* and Order Police followed. Enlisting the help of local police officers, they initiated systematic murder of Jews. The timing of ghettoization and mass killing of Jews varied from place to place. It depended on pressures from the Nazi leadership, regional German police and civilian initiatives, the number of police officers present in different areas, the army's need for skilled labor, perception of Jews'

---

[68]International Military Tribunal, *Trial of the Major War Criminals Before the International Military Tribunal, Nuremberg, 14 November 1945–1 October 1946*, vol. 21 (Nuremberg, 1948), p. 401.

responsibility for Soviet resistance, and a variety of other factors. In the Baltic States and central Ukraine, the killing was terribly swift. In Belarus and the western Ukraine, most killing came later. But killing continued from the time of the invasion in 1941 to German expulsion from the USSR in 1944. It simply never stopped.

The pattern of killing was this: German and local police either abducted Jews off the streets at gunpoint or ordered them to assemble for work or resettlement. Another police detail then moved Jews in groups of several hundred at a time, mostly by foot but sometimes by lorry, to remote spots several miles from town where a ravine, a tank ditch, or large pits dug by prisoners awaited. Other police surrounded this area to prevent escapes and to chase off onlookers. In a holding area where one could not see the pits, Jews surrendered their last possessions—watches, wedding rings, coins, clothes, and even underwear. Police then led their naked victims in smaller groups to the pit, where a final police detail waited. They shot each victim in the back of the neck or head. Bodies tumbled into the pit. Most who tried to escape were shot.

The Germans euphemistically called such a process an *Aktion*. There were thousands of them in the occupied Soviet territories. Local police in the German-occupied USSR were volunteers. German police, however, were under orders. Were they forced to take part in shootings? A tiny minority of German police personnel refused to shoot unarmed civilians. They risked being called cowards but were never punished. "We were just assigned different duties," remembered one from Police Battalion 322, "We were not threatened with any kind of punishment."[69] Others drowned their consciences in alcohol or suffered psychological breakdowns. Many, however, simply became inured to the job or took pride in their work. As SS-Lieutenant Karl Kretschmer put it in a letter to his children, "[I]t is a weakness not to be able to stand the sight of dead people; the best way of overcoming it is to do it more often. . . ."[70] Only examples from the *Aktionen* of 1941 can be recounted here.

Lithuania and the Example of Vilna

Killing operations were frenetic in the Baltic States from the start. *Einsatzgruppen* detachments together with Lithuanian, Latvian, and Estonian auxiliary police were so active that most Baltic Jews were dead just six months after the German invasion. In Latvia alone, 75,000 Jews in June 1941 were reduced to 6,500 by January 1942. In Lithuania, 197,000 Jews were reduced to 35,000, left to work for the German war effort until they too became expendable.

The experience of Vilna, a major center of Jewish culture known as "Jerusalem of Lithuania," with a 40 percent Jewish population, was not atypical. Thanks to the Japanese Consul Sugihara, more than 3,000 Jewish refugees had left Vilna for Japan. The Soviets deported 4,000 more Vilna Jews a week before the invasion. As the Germans bombed the city on June 23, 1941, perhaps 3,000 more managed to flee. When the Germans captured Vilna on June 24, some 57,000 Jews were trapped there.[71] In July and August, German authorities ordered Jews to wear the Star of David, keep off sidewalks, surrender their radios, and assemble a Jewish Council and police force. By August, they ransomed Jewish Council members for suitcases full of jewelry, watches, and money.

Killing began quickly and was relentless. Throughout July, German and Lithuanian police abducted some 5,000 Jewish males off the street and from their homes, ostensibly for labor

---

[69]Klee et al., eds., *The Good Old Days*, p. 77.

[70]Klee et al., eds., *The Good Old Days*, p. 171.

[71]Figure in Arad, *Ghetto in Flames: The Struggle and Destruction of the Jews of Vilna During the Holocaust* (Jerusalem, 1980), pp. 28–35.

details. In theory, they sought Jewish leaders but they seized old men and teenagers too. They soon moved building by building. Women and children wailed as their husbands, fathers, and sons were beaten and torn away. The screams, wrote Herman Kruk, the Vilna ghetto's most important diarist, spread "from neighbor to neighbor and from courtyard to courtyard. . . . It often seems that a whole street screams."[72]

Many Vilna Jews actually labored for the German army, and many more were told to bring towels and soap. An illusion thus existed that arrestees would actually work. Those seized, however, never returned. Police detained them at Vilna's main prison, then took them in smaller groups to a forest clearing in Ponary, eight miles southwest of Vilna. At Ponary, they were shot and dumped into giant pits. The first mass execution at Ponary was on July 4, 1941.

Kazimierz Sakowicz was a Pole living near Ponary. Distressed by what he heard and saw, he kept a diary. He heard Jewish voices cry, "I am not a Communist!" "Where is the work?" "What are you doing?" He heard rifle volleys, day after day in some stretches, and into the night as police hunted escaped Jews. He heard machine guns and even hand grenades "when it's raining or late." He saw ravens circle the murder site. And he saw a "brisk business in clothing" sold by Lithuanian police. "For the Germans," Sakowicz wrote, "300 Jews are 300 enemies of humanity; for the Lithuanians they are 300 pairs of shoes. . . ."[73]

In August, the Germans expanded the killing in Vilna while concentrating the Jews there. The Security Police staged a provocation on August 31 whereby two Jews allegedly shot at German soldiers. About 3,700 Jews from the alleged shooters' neighborhood—mostly women and children—were arrested, robbed, imprisoned, and then shot at Ponary. Ten Jewish Council members were also taken and killed.[74] On German orders, Lithuanian police on September 6 crammed Vilna's remaining Jews into two ghettos located in the neighborhood whose residents had just been murdered. Ghetto 1 was to be a ghetto of workers. Ghetto 2 was not.

Some Christian neighbors offered to hide Jews' property and later entered the ghettos to bring bread and clothes. Kruk wrote that "[t]he sympathy of the Christian population, more precisely of the Polish population, is extraordinary." "Others," he wrote, came "like jackals" to buy Jewish property cheap or simply to steal it.[75] Jews entered the ghettos in terrified confusion with no more than they could carry. Ghetto 1 initially had roughly 28,000 Jews and Ghetto 2 roughly 9,000. Police units killed the rest—3,334—at Ponary.[76]

September 30 was Kol Nidre, the holy eve of Yom Kippur. "The prayer houses," wrote Kruk, "are full to bursting." On Yom Kippur, German and Lithuanian police entered both ghettos to arrest more Jews. Panic erupted. "Jews in prayer shawls ran through the streets," wrote Kruk, "The prayer houses emptied out."[77] Nearly 4,000 were taken from both ghettos and shot at Ponary.[78] By the end of October, police formations liquidated Ghetto 2 in three *Aktionen*, which killed roughly 5,500 (2,000 to 3,000 escaped to Ghetto 1).[79] On October 25, a day Sakowicz

---

[72]Hermann Kruk, *The Last Days of the Jerusalem of Lithuania: Chronicle from the Vilna Ghetto and the Camps, 1939–1944*, ed. Benjamin Harshav (New Haven, CT, 2002), July 4, 1941.

[73]Kazimierz Sakowicz, *Ponary Diary: A Bystander's Account of a Mass Murder*, ed. Yitzhak Arad (New Haven, 2005), July 23, 1941, August 1–2, 1941, August 19 1941.

[74]Arad, *Ghetto in Flames*, pp. 104–5.

[75]Kruk, *The Last Days*, September 6, 8, 1941.

[76]Figures in Arad, *Ghetto in Flames*, pp. 113–6.

[77]Kruk, *The Last Days*, September 30, 1941, October 1, 1941.

[78]Figure in Arad, *Ghetto in Flames*, pp. 136–7.

[79]Figures in Arad, *Ghetto in Flames*, pp. 139–42.

labeled "Terrible Saturday" in his diary, trucks carried 2,578 women with children, including infants, to Ponary. Some of the women begged for their lives. Lithuanian police hit them with rifle butts. "At night they tried to escape," recorded Sakowicz, "Shooting the whole night."[80]

Ghetto 1 now had a population of perhaps 28,000 Jews crammed into a space that once held 4,000. In mid-October, German civilian authorities provided the ghetto with 3,000 work permits, each of which allowed its bearer to protect himself, his wife, and two children under age 16, from arrest. The remainder, some 15,000 were unprotected. During several *Aktionen* in late October and early November, German and Lithuanian police entered the ghetto and combed homes and hiding places for Jews without permits. They arrested and killed nearly 7,000 Jews over this period.[81] The remainder either had permits or hid effectively. At Ponary, during one shooting, Lithuanian police staged a "game hunt" whereby Jewish men were told to run and hide in the forest. It was over in two hours. Two days later the police ran out of bullets. They killed the children with rifle butts.[82]

SS-Colonel Karl Jäger commanded *Einsatzkommando 3*, a detachment of *Einsatzgruppe A*. After July 2, 1941, his unit was charged with killing most Lithuanian Jews, and after August 9, his responsibilities also included Vilna. On December 1, Jäger sent a nine-page report listing 113 separate shooting actions with well over 130,000 Jewish victims involving his unit. For October 1941 alone, he dutifully reported the killing of 10,810 Vilna Jews, 5,424 of whom were women and 2,526 of whom were children. He reported on December 1:

> I can now establish that EK 3 [*Einsatzkommando 3*] has achieved the goal of solving the Jewish problem for Lithuania. In Lithuania there are no more Jews, except for work Jews inclusive of their families. . . . I wanted to bump off these work Jews [and] their families also, which brought me strong objections from the [German] civilian administration and the *Wehrmacht* and triggered the [following] interdiction: These Jews and their families may not be shot!
>
> I consider the Jewish *Aktionen* for EK 3 to be essentially finalized. The residual work Jews and Jewesses are badly needed. . . . I am of the view that, in order to prevent reproduction, sterilization of the male work Jews begin immediately. If a Jewess nonetheless becomes pregnant, she is to be liquidated.[83]

In five months, 57,000 Vilna Jews were reduced to 15,000 "legal" Jews. By now, the German offensive against Moscow had definitively stalled, and the army needed skilled Jewish workers in armament factories. As Jäger reluctantly noted, they would survive for a time.

Ukraine and the Example of Kiev

More than 1.5 million Jews—nearly all the Jews in occupied Ukraine—were murdered over the course of the war.[84] Over 500,000 were killed in the second half of 1941 alone. Especially heavy killing occurred in what the Germans called the Zhitomir General District, which had up to 170,000 Jews when the Germans arrived. Himmler's desire to build the district into a showcase

---

[80]Account in Arad, ed., *Ponary Diary*; figures in "Gesamtaufstellung der im Bereich des EK.3 bis zim 1. Dez. 1941 durchgeführten Executionen" (hereafter Jäger Report), December 1, 1941, printed in Klee, ed., *The Good Old Days*, pp. 46–58.

[81]Figures in Arad, *Ghetto in Flames*, pp. 147–57.

[82]Arad, ed., *Ponary Diary*, November 17, 1941, November 19, 1941.

[83]From the Jäger Report held at the Bundesarchiv Außenstelle Ludwigsburg in Germany.

[84]Figures in Alexander Kruglov, "Jewish Losses in Ukraine, 1941–1944," in *The Shoah in Ukraine: History, Testimony, Memorialization*, eds. Ray Brandon and Wendy Lower (Bloomington, IN, 2008), pp. 272–90.

German police and auxiliaries in civilian clothes look on as a group of Jewish women are forced to undress before their execution (date and place unknown).   *Source:* Instytut Pamieci Narodowe, courtesy of the United States Holocaust Memorial Museum.

colony of German farming settlements added urgency to the killing of Jews. Hitler visited the district on August 6. By late July 1941, German police and army personnel, with help from Ukrainian police, shifted from killing Jewish men to killing all Jews. More police arrived in late August, and the pace of the killing accelerated.

The city of Berdichev within the Zhitomir District was not atypical. Here the Germans established a ghetto on August 25, 1941, for 17,000 Jews, killing 3,000 in the process. On September 15 at 4:00 a.m., German and Ukrainian police broke into the ghetto, shot Jews who could not walk, and rounded up the rest amid terror and chaos. "The terrible wailing of women and the crying of the children," remembered one witness, "woke up the whole city." Twelve thousand were murdered nearby. The loosely covered pits moved afterward, "heaving from the pressure inside." Berdichev's remaining Jews were killed on November 3, save for 150 artisans and their families. German and Ukrainian police, along with their mistresses and girlfriends, looted Jewish homes for everything, from flatware to scarves. By winter, most of the Jews in the Zhitomir District were dead. Only 2 percent survived the war.[85]

Little, however, could compare with Kiev. Ukraine's capital to the east of the Zhitomir district had a prewar population of 230,000 Jews, but its interior location allowed many to flee. Sixty to seventy thousand Jews remained when the Germans entered the city on September 19, 1941, after hard fighting. As the Germans set up in former Soviet administrative buildings, the buildings began to explode. The NKVD rigged the structures before the Soviets evacuated and now the blasts went on for days. "Kiev was on fire," remembered one Jewish survivor. "It felt like

[85]Quotes in Ilya Ehrenburg and Vasily Grossman, eds., *The Complete Black Book of Russian Jewry*, ed. David Patterson (New Brunswick, NJ, 2002), pp. 15–16. For the Zhitomyr district, see Wendy Lower, *Nazi Empire Building and the Holocaust in Ukraine* (Chapel Hill, NC, 2005); Arad, *The Holocaust in the Soviet Union*, pp. 168–71.

MAP 9.2   German administrative districts in the occupied USSR.   *Source:* Timothy Snyder, *Sketches from a Secret War: A Polish Artist's Mission to Liberate Soviet Ukraine* (New Haven, CT: Yale University Press, 2005), p. x.

Judgment Day. . . . Houses were collapsing, burning beams were flying through the air, chunks of stone were raining down . . . glass was showering down from windows like a fine rain."[86]

The Germans blamed Kiev's Jews. A meeting between army and SS officers on September 26 determined that all of them would be eliminated. *Einsatzgruppe C* personnel, Order Police battalions, and Ukrainian police were to carry out the immense task. Ukrainian police posted notices on September 28 for all of Kiev's Jews to report the following morning for relocation with money, valuables, and warm clothing. "Failure to appear," the notices said, "is punishable by death."[87]

Over the next two days, thousands of Kiev's Jews, from noted physicians to housewives, were marched to a ravine at Babi Yar outside the city. "Many of them," survivors remembered,

---

[86]Joshua Rubenstein and Ilya Altman, eds., *The Unknown Black Book: The Holocaust in the German-Occupied Soviet Territories* (Bloomington, IN, 2008), p. 72.

[87]Ehrenberg and Grossman, eds., *The Complete Black Book*, p. 5.

"thought they were being sent to provincial towns. . . . Families baked bread. . . . Old men and women walked along supporting each other. . . . Mothers carried their infants. . . . Children plodded along with their parents.[88]

Dina Pronicheva was one of very few survivors. After the war, she described the massacre many times. As Jews entered the area near the ravine, German police stole their belongings and forced them to run a brutal gauntlet, beating them with truncheons. Terrified Jews trampled others. Ukrainian police then forced Jews to strip (many women resisted) then chased them to the ravine. "Before my very eyes," Pronicheva remembered, "people went insane, they turned gray. . . . All day long there was machine-gun fire. I saw how Germans took children away from their mothers and threw them from the precipice into the ravine." Pronicheva's turn came at dusk. Before she was shot, she jumped into the ravine. She lay motionless until the shooting stopped. She dug her way out and managed to survive the war by staying on the move.[89]

Einsatzgruppe C reported that over the course of two days—September 29 and September 30—German police and their Ukrainian helpers killed 33,771 Jews.[90] Despite the unimaginable number, there was still work to do. Thousands of Kiev's Jews had hidden. German and Ukrainian police hunted them in the following weeks and months, and shot them instantly or took them to Babi Yar. Victims included hospitalized Jews; Jewish Red Army POWs captured near Kiev; and other Jews handed over by their neighbors on police orders, which threatened death for sheltering Jews.

Some neighbors needed but a suggestion. "After this order," remembered Emilia Borisovna, "our neighbors would no longer let me into my apartment; these were people with whom I had lived in the same [building] for eight years in great friendship." One of Borisovna's neighbors, she said, "turned me in and set herself up in my room. She took all my belongings. . . ." Borisovna managed to hide her Jewish identity and trudged 140 kilometers to Zhitomir. She met a Ukrainian man en route. "He told me about how enthusiastically he had taken part in the killings of Jews at Babi Yar. He went to Babi Yar every day to help the Germans and for that the Germans gave him junk belonging to the Jews and food the Jews had left behind in heaps. He had even collected 43,000 rubles in Soviet money. . . . I asked him: 'Are you happy that they killed so many Jews?' He smiled pleasantly and quickly answered: 'I'm very glad about it.'" Borisovna reflected after the war. "No mind," she wrote, "can grasp what happened at Babi Yar."[91]

9.5 ROMANIA'S WAR ON THE JEWS

Romania joined Hitler's war on the USSR from the beginning in order to recover Bessarabia and northern Bukovina, the territories lost to the Soviets in 1940. When Barbarossa began, two Romanian armies advanced with one German army into both lands. Though relatively cautious with Jews in old Romania in 1940, head of state Ion Antonescu was unrestrained with the prospect of new lands in 1941. Over the course of their ill-fated war with the Soviets, the Romanians killed up to 380,000 Jews—a number second only to the Germans themselves.[92] Although the

---

[88]Ehrenburg and Grossman, eds., *The Complete Black Book*, p. 8.

[89]Quote and analysis in Karel C. Berkhoff, "Dina Pronicheva's Story of Surviving the Babi Yar Massacre: German, Jewish, Soviet, Russian, and Ukrainian Records," in Brandon and Lower, eds., *Shoah in Ukraine*, pp. 291–317.

[90]Klein, ed., *Die Einsatzgruppen*, p. 232.

[91]Rubenstein and Altman, eds., *The Unknown Black Book*, pp. 79, 68.

[92]See figures in International Commission on the Holocaust in Romania, *Final Report of the International Commission on the Holocaust in Romania* (hereafter *Final Report Romania*) (Bucharest, 2004), p. 179.

Romanian government reconsidered its path after the massive defeat outside Stalingrad in late 1942, its barbarism in 1941 and 1942 is clear.

The Pogrom in Iaşi

Few pogroms in history compare to that in the Romanian city of Iaşi. With a population of 100,000, Iaşi sat ten miles west of the border with Bessarabia. The city was nearly half-Jewish and a hothouse of Romanian antisemitism. Iaşi spawned Alexandru Cuza's League of National Christian Defense and Corneliu Codreanu's Legionnaire movement. Before the attack on the USSR in June 1941, Romanian head of state Ion Antonescu ordered the expulsion of Jews living near the Soviet border, including Iaşi, as potential security risks. Romanian secret police compiled information on Jewish centers and congregations.

On June 24 and 26, 1941, a few days after the Romanian offensive began, the Soviets attacked Iaşi by air. Romanian officials and citizens alike were convinced that local Jews were spotting for Soviet flight crews, who were also presumed to be Jews. On June 26, German and Romanian troops, police, and Legionnaires searched Jewish homes for evidence such as binoculars and flashlights. They arrested and shot a number of Jews accused of helping the Soviets. Posters then incited Iaşi's citizens to act. "Each kike killed is a dead communist," promised one poster. "The time for revenge is now."[93]

Full-blown massacres began the night of June 28 as the mob joined in. Jews were dragged from houses, sometimes in pajamas, beaten, and shot, their property often plundered. German troops draped a Jewish corpse over a machine gun to prove that Jews fired on Romanians. There were courageous rescuers. Grigore Profir, a cereal mill manager, refused to allow soldiers and police to take roughly one hundred Jewish workers from his mill despite threats to shoot him. A pharmacist named Beceanu saved dozens of Jews the same way. A police inspector named Suvei freed 350 Jews instead of leading them to police headquarters. Railway workers killed a lathe operator named Ion Gheorghiu for trying to save Jews. A priest named Rasmerita was shot dead with the Jews he tried to save, as was an engineering professor named Naum, whose killer yelled, "[D]ie you dog with the kike you are defending."[94]

During the same night, several thousand Jews were arrested and marched to police headquarters as onlookers pelted them—killing some—with rocks, bottles, and iron bars. Some 3,500 arrestees were crammed into the courtyard of police headquarters. On the afternoon of June 29, German and Romanian soldiers and Romanian police opened fire into the courtyard. Jews who escaped were hunted down and killed. Iaşi's streets were littered with Jewish dead by evening, including the elderly, women, and children. Bodies were ransacked for everything from watches to fountain pens. City crews dumped the bodies in garbage heaps and washed blood from Iaşi's streets.

On the same day, June 29, up to 7,700 Jews who had been arrested but not shot were shoved into sealed freight cars on two trains and evacuated for a tortuous six-and-a-half-day journey to a holding center in Călăraşi in southern Romania away from the front. Many were wounded. Despite the summer heat the authorities provided no water. Some Jews went insane. Some drank blood and urine. Others suffocated and died standing. On stops along the way, the dead were pulled from boxcars and dumped in trenches. German and Romanian soldiers threw

---

[93]Quoted in Radu Ioanid, "The Holocaust in Romania: The Iaşi Pogrom of June 1941," *Contemporary European History*, 2, no. 2 (1993): 127–8.

[94]Quoted in I. C. Butnaru, *Waiting for Jerusalem: Surviving the Holocaust in Romania* (Westport, CT, 1993), p. 203. Other instances are in Ioanid, "The Holocaust in Romania," pp. 119–48.

Bodies of a Jewish family killed on Vasile Conta Street during the Iaşi pogram, June 1941.   *Source:* United States Holocaust Memorial Museum.

stones at the living and shot those—even children—trying to escape. Of the perhaps 5,000 Jews who left Iaşi on the first train, 1,011 arrived in Călăraşi alive. The second train, which began with up to 2,700 Jews, arrived with about 700 still living. In all, up to 14,850 Jews were killed in the Iaşi pogrom and its terrible aftermath.[95]

Viorica Agarici was the head of the Red Cross in the town of Roman, southeast of Iaşi. When the first train from Iaşi stopped in Roman she insisted on providing water, food, and first aid to the Jews with Red Cross and Jewish volunteers. She even ordered embarrassed Romanian troops to help. Most Jews who expired on the first train died before Agarici's efforts. For her trouble, Agarici was later shunned and harassed by her local community, despite the fact that her son was a famous Romanian air force pilot. She was forced to resign her Red Cross position and move to Bucharest, where she lived anonymously.

The Recovery of the Lost Lands

When Romania received Bessarabia and Bukovina in 1919, the Allies forced it to grant citizenship to Jews there. When Romanian forces recovered these lost lands from the Soviets in 1941, Antonescu did not intend to repeat the mistake. All Jews in Bessarabia and Bukovina, were to be killed or expelled. "You must be merciless," his vice premier ordered Romanian district authorities on July 8, 1941. "I don't know how many centuries will pass before the Romanian people meet with such total liberty of action. . . . If necessary use your machine guns. . . . I couldn't care less if history will recall us as barbarians. . . ."[96] But unlike the Germans, the Romanians

---

[95]Figures in Ioanid, "The Holocaust in Romania," pp. 84–86; *Final Report Romania*, p. 126.

[96]Figures and quote in *Final Report Romania*, pp. 127–8, 175–6.

had neither the personnel nor the planning for "efficient" killing. The raw primitiveness of their crimes comprised some of the Holocaust's worst horrors.

Romanian troops and police, elements of *Einsatzgruppe D*, Ukrainian gendarmes, and Romanian and Ukrainian peasants "liberated" Bessarabia and Bukovina from Jews. In July and August 1941, up to 60,000 Jewish men, women, and children, including the elderly and infants, were shot, beaten to death, and sometimes mutilated.[97] Yosef Govrin's father was killed in Bessarabia. "For years [after the war]," he remembered, "I sought . . . Bessarabian Christians who saved or even tried to save Jews from massacres. . . . I found none."[98] Indeed some of the very few who aided Jews paid with their lives. On learning that Jews detained in his school were to be shot, Paramon Lozan, the school's principal, released them. He was executed thereafter. Others were simply disgusted. One Romanian priest refused to give mass after Jews were dis-membered in his village. "I am ashamed," he said, "to enter this church."[99]

In August the Romanian government decided to expel the remaining Jews in the recovered lands (and from the Regat's eastern border region) to a dumping ground east of the Dniester River soon dubbed Transnistria. Romanian police moved thousands of Jews at a time, toward the Dniester and beyond, on forced marches of nearly twenty miles a day without food or water. Peasants along the way, remembered one soldier, "waited like crows to steal something," right down to clothing and shoes that Jews wore."[100] Jews who dropped were shot or left to die. Routes were littered with corpses. Jews drowned in the Dniester when crude rafts overturned. Those surviving were herded into overcrowded makeshift camps in Transnistria where they awaited an unspeakable fate. Romania's governor in Bessarabia reported to Antonescu in mid-December that "there are no more Yids [in Bessarabia]."[101] Of the up to 170,000 Jews expelled, between 104,000 and 121,000 died in Transnistria.[102] Officers of *Einsatzgruppe D* applauded the results but not the methods. The Romanians, they complained, did not bury the bodies.

Transnistria and the Kingdom of Death

August 1941 was a grand month for Antonescu. King Michael granted him the title Marshal of Romania and Hitler granted Romania governance over Transnistria, a 40,000-square-kilometer swath of territory between the Dniester and Bug rivers. As mentioned, it became Romania's dumping ground for Jews from the recovered territories. "Govern," commanded Antonescu, "as if Romania will rule these territories for two million years."[103] The Germans had already killed tens of thousands of Jews in Transnistria. Up to 200,000 Jews native to the region remained. Under Romanian administration, up to 180,000 were murdered.[104]

Beginning in September 1941, Jews native to Transnistria and those driven there from Bessarabia and Bukovina, were pushed to the borders of German-controlled territory on the Bug River. There they were to be exterminated. Chaos and sadism reigned en route. Masses of Jews went by foot on muddy routes with no food or shelter. Romanian and Ukrainian police raped

---

[97]Figure in *Final Report Romania*, p. 177.

[98]Yosef Govrin, *In the Shadow of Destruction: Recollections of Transnistria and Illegal Immigration to Eretz Israel, 1941–1947* (London, 2007), p. 26.

[99]Quoted in Radu Ioanid, *The Holocaust in Romania: The Destruction of Jews and Gypsies Under the Antonescu Regime, 1940–1944* (Chicago, 2000), p. 98.

[100]Quoted in Ioanid, *The Holocaust in Romania*, p. 147.

[101]Quoted Jean Ancel, *Transnistria, 1941–1942: The Romanian Mass Murder Campaigns*, vol. 1 (Tel Aviv, 2003), p. 225.

[102]Figures in *Final Report Romania*, pp. 177–8.

[103]Quote in Ancel, *Transnistria*, vol. 1, p. 24.

[104]Figures in Ancel, *Transnistria*, vol. 1, pp. 51–2; *Final Report Romania*, pp. 178–9.

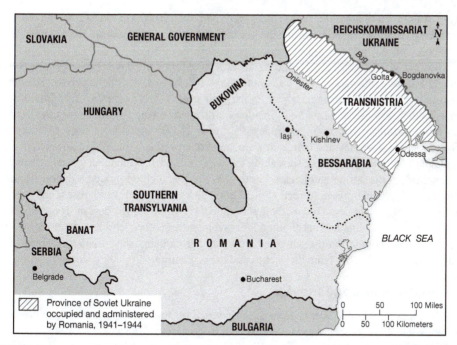

MAP 9.3   Romanian-occupied USSR.   *Source:* Solonari, Vladimir. *Purifying the Nation: Population Exchange and Ethnic Cleansing in NaziAllied Romania.* p. xxx. © 2009 by the Woodrow Wilson International Center for Scholars. Reprinted with permission of Johns Hopkins University Press.

the women, beat the men, and shot those who lagged. Tens of thousands of corpses—from the elderly to children—littered roadsides. Jews were not allowed to stop and bury loved ones. "We could not," remembered one survivor, "even say a mourner's prayer."[105]

Arriving Jews were detained in the primitive Golta district just west of the Bug in a series of makeshift camps. The Golta District, which received 110,000 Jews by March 1942, was soon known as the "Kingdom of Death." Its camps lacked shelter and food and they teemed with typhus.[106] Neglect was Romania's initial extermination method. Antonescu was unmoved. "Everyone must understand," he wrote in September, "that the struggle is not against the Slavs but the Jews—a struggle to the death. Either we will win and the world will be cleansed, or they will win and we will become their slaves. . . . The war in general and the battles in Odessa in particular have proven beyond the shadow of a doubt that the Jew is the Devil."[107]

Odessa

Antonescu's reference to the Black Sea city of Odessa was poignant. It was the main port city in Transnistria. Romanian forces began trying to capture it mid-August. It took three months and cost nearly 100,000 Romanian casualties before the Soviets evacuated all troops by sea to defend the Crimean Peninsula from the Germans. On October 22, five days after Odessa fell, NKVD charges left in a building used by the Romanian command killed several Romanian and German

---

[105]Quoted in Ancel, *Transnistria,* vol. 1, p. 75.

[106]Figure in *Final Report Romania,* p. 146.

[107]Quoted in Ancel, *Transnistria,* vol. 1, pp. 89–90.

officers. Antonescu blamed the Jews—there were perhaps 120,000 in Odessa and its environs—"for making us suffer losses" during the assault and for the explosions. He ordered "drastic punitive measures."[108]

Revenge was horrifying. Five thousand Jews were killed the day following the explosions, hundreds hanged from lampposts, trees, and makeshift beams. As one survivor remembered, "you could see gallows everywhere you turned your eyes. . . . It [was] the city of the hanged." But as another witness remembered "the Jews who died during the first few days . . . were much more fortunate than their comrades."[109] Some 25,000 more Jews from Odessa and its environs, including women and children, were marched in a giant convoy five kilometers west to the village of Dalnik. Many were shot along the way. In Dalnik, Romanian troops ordered them into trenches, fifty at a time and began shooting. When this method proved too slow, Romanian troops, on Antonescu's orders, forced some 22,000 Jews into grain warehouses, and then fired into the openings for hours. This method also failed. At nightfall, Romanian troops soaked the warehouses with gasoline and set them ablaze. Women threw their children from the windows. Jews who climbed out in flames staggered aimlessly before being shot. Even Romanian officers began to break emotionally from the scenes and the screaming.[110]

The Massacres at Bogdanovka

Thirty-five thousand more Odessa Jews were deported on foot 200 kilometers to the Golta district camps. The largest camp was in the village of Bogdanovka. By December 1941, it held more than 55,000 Jews. Conditions were appalling. Shelter from the −35°C temperatures comprised cowsheds and pigpens. Jews lay atop one another. There was no food. Many froze to death. Typhus killed 500 to 700 per day. To prevent the spread of disease and to impress the German authorities across the Bug, Antonescu in mid-December ordered mass executions, which were carried out by Romanian and Ukrainian police.

On December 21, 5,000 of the sickest in Bogdanovka were locked in four cowsheds and burned alive. The rest, about 48,000, were marched to steep ravines in groups of several hundred and shot over the course of two weeks. Gendarmes cut off their fingers to get their rings and knocked out their gold teeth. Meir Feingold, one of very few survivors, had stayed alive in Bogdanovka by trading clothing to Ukrainian women for bread. After one exchange they asked him, "Have you heard they are shooting the Jews? You will not have time to eat the bread." By January 9, most Jews held in Bogdanovka were dead. For two terrible months, the Romanians ordered a detail of some 200 Jews to burn the bodies in order to hide the evidence. "They were piled up to the height of a man," Feingold remembered. "We turned our brethren to ashes, and in the fierce cold we warmed ourselves by the fire."[111]

"Let the Jews of America come and take me to court!" said Marshal Antonescu in private. "We must not pity the Jews, because if they could, they would not pity us. Do not think they will not take revenge when they have the opportunity. However, to ensure that no one will be left to take revenge, I will wipe them out first. . . ."[112] Left to itself for the most part, Romania was Hitler's most enthusiastic ally in the war against the Jews.

---

[108]Quotes and figures in Ioanid, *The Holocaust in Romania*, p. 177; Ancel, Transnistria, vol. 1, p. 187.

[109]Quoted in Ehrenburg and Grossman, eds., *The Complete Black Book*, pp. 57, 58.

[110]Described in Ancel, *Transnistria*, vol. 1, pp. 193–201.

[111]Quotes in Ancel, *Transnistria*, vol. 1, pp. 130, 137.

[112]Quotes in Ancel, *Transnistria*, vol. 1, pp. 137, 209.

10

The Holocaust in the USSR
The Jewish and World Response, 1941–1944

The initial wave of killing in the USSR—from July to the winter of 1941—encompassed Jews in the Baltic States, eastern Belarus, central Ukraine, and the Romanian-occupied territories. Surviving Jews were used for work. A second wave of killing in the spring of 1942 continued until the winter of that year. It included Jews in western Ukraine and Belarus. Partly it was a continuation of earlier operations. Partly it was linked to the German belief that the Jews in these regions aided Soviet partisans. In 1942, the Germans used gas vans in killing operations, and in 1942 and 1943, they shipped Jews from the Białystok region to the Treblinka and Auschwitz extermination camps. East Galicia was joined administratively to the General Government, and 250,000 of its Jews were sent to the extermination camp in Bełżec in 1942. But shooting remained the overwhelming method of killing in the USSR.

From November 1942 to February 1943, Soviet forces turned the tide of the war by destroying the German Sixth Army at Stalingrad as well as Romanian, Hungarian, and Italian units outside the city. The Soviets steadily advanced and the Germans never regained the initiative. Still, a final wave of killing Jews began in the spring of 1943, ending in the summer of 1944 when the German occupation ceased. Most remaining Jews in ghettos and labor camps were killed on the spot. Some were sent to Auschwitz. Those left alive were transported to camps in Germany.

Jews' reactions to mass murder in the USSR were local in nature. Reactions depended on local understanding of German intentions, the nature of Jewish leadership in different localities, the material resources available to Jews, and the level of help Jews received from local populations. Reactions were also characterized by extreme vulnerability. Evident regardless of locality was the desire to preserve life as long as possible, to preserve evidence of Nazi crimes, and to kill Germans and collaborators when possible. Despite immense difficulties, such actions were more common than is appreciated. They are all the more notable in the USSR because Jews received no outside help until the Soviet Red Army liberated their camps and ghettos. In most cases, Jews in the USSR were completely alone.

10.1 JEWISH REACTIONS: RECOGNITION AND SURVIVAL

What Jews Understood

The Germans aimed to keep the mass extermination secret. But Jews who escaped death pits and a few bystanders supplied information to some ghettos. Jews in Lithuania and Latvia were the first subjected to mass killing, and most were killed between July and December 1941. At first, they did not accept the truth. In July 1941, Jewish Council members in Vilna thought news of mass shootings in Ponary was "an unfounded rumor."[1] The same was true in Latvia. "We in Riga didn't believe," remembered survivor Eliezer Karstadt, "that the Jews were taken away and shot. . . ."[2] But additional witnesses forced realization. "We saw it with our own eyes," reported six survivors from Ponary after making it back to Vilna in September. "There were whole mountains of people. . . ." "Is it possible," asked Vilna diarist Herman Kruk, "that all of those taken out of here have been murdered? If heaven is heaven," he wrote, "it should start pouring down lava."[3]

The truth arrived differently elsewhere. In the *shtetl* of Nowogródek in Belarus, large-scale killing did not begin until December 8, 1941, when German and Lithuanian police murdered 4,500 Jewish men, women, and children just a few kilometers from town. Jewish Council members there had already been shot. "Those of us who are still alive," wrote Lyuba Rudnicki, "begin to comprehend that gradually all of us will be killed. . . . [The] Germans promised that the ones who were allowed to live were needed. . . . Despite that, the aspiration for most of us is to get out of the ghetto. But where can we hide?"[4]

Matters were more obvious in Lida in Belarus, where mass killing began on May 8, 1942. German and local police killed more than 5,000 Jews just a short distance from town, tossing hand grenades in a pit with children. Days later police units moved to the nearby *shtetl* of Raduń, shooting Jews just a half-kilometer from the ghetto. "After hearing these shots," remembered Avraham Aviel, "we were in no doubt that this was our last day on earth."[5]

Survival Through Work

Slim chances of survival depended on many factors, most beyond Jewish control. Testimonies reflect raw, overwhelming fear. Ilya Gerber, a teenager in Kovno, recorded how Jews fought for placement in labor brigades that they thought might preserve their families. "Nothing but 'I' existed," he wrote, "'my children, my wife, they are hungry, they ask for food, I must bring them something today.'"[6] In this perverse world, strangers were sometimes protected first. A work permit in Vilna could preserve four lives. "I had permission to register two children," recalled Mark Dworzecki, who had none. "I wasn't able to register my mother and father. . . . I took my sister and recorded her as my daughter. . . . In the midst of the general confusion, I suddenly saw a boy walking along and shouting, 'Who wants to be my father?' and I said, 'I shall be your father.' I gave him the slip. . . . We went as a family on the day of selection—I, my wife, my sister . . . and the boy, whose identity was unknown to me, who had become my son."[7]

Jews who survived as workers depended on Germany's need for them, their own endurance, and luck. The largest German forced labor project in the USSR was *Durchgangsstrasse IV*

---

[1]Hermann Kruk, *The Last Days of the Jerusalem of Lithuania: Chronicle from the Vilna Ghetto and the Camps, 1939–1944*, ed. Benjamin Harshav (New Haven, CT, 2002), July 20, 1941.

[2]State of Israel, Ministry of Justice, *The Trial of Adolf Eichmann: Record of Proceedings in the District Court of Jerusalem* (hereafter *Eichmann Trial*), vol. 1 (Jerusalem, 1992), p. 490.

[3]Kruk, *Last Days*, September 4, 1941.

[4]Jack Kagan, ed., *Novogrudok: The History of a Shtetl* (London, 2006), p. 176.

[5]Avraham Aviel, *A Village Named Dowgalishok: The Massacre at Radun and Eishishok* (London, 2006), p. 106.

[6]Alexandra Zapruder, ed., *Salvaged Pages: Young Writers' Diaries of the Holocaust* (New Haven, CT, 2002), Ilya Gerber, August 26, 1942.

[7]*Eichmann Trial*, vol. 1, p. 451.

(Transit Road 4), a supply highway begun in September 1941 that was to run 2,175 kilometers through Lvov to southeast Ukraine. Crude labor camps dotted the route. The Germans worked prisoners to death, first Soviet POWs and, in 1942, Jews imported from Transnistria (the Germans had already shot most Jews from eastern Ukraine). Arnold Daghani and his wife Anisoara survived for an entire year in the camp at Mikhailovka before escaping in 1943. Daghani was an artist, and the German engineers wanted portraits of themselves. He repeatedly saw German and Lithuanian guards shoot Jewish workers at random. "My mind," Daghani wrote in his diary, "simply refuses to understand all that is going on around me."[8] After their escape, the Daghanis learned that the entire Mikhailovka camp population was murdered over the course of six hours.[9]

Survival Through Hiding

Thousands of Jews trapped in ghettos, especially those without work permits, hid during *Aktionen* in self-built hiding places called *malines*. "An underground town was established," remembered Dworzecki in Vilna. "Every simple house had a built-in hideout—either in the cellars or in the attic walls, or below a well, or beneath a lavatory or under any storeroom."[10] But *malines* hardly guaranteed survival. They had to be used for days at a time. Police searched for them, became increasingly angry as they did so, and shot or threw grenades into possible hiding spaces. "People are usually discovered," remembered one partisan from Minsk, "because of the children. Children cannot sit in complete silence and endure the hunger that lasts for days on end, the unbearably stuffy air, the darkness. They start to get fidgety and cry, which leads to the discovery of the *maline*."[11]

In Kovno, Jewish physicians injected children with sedatives before suspected *Aktionen*, the more mature among the children saying, "Doctor, it isn't necessary, I'll keep quiet, I won't shout."[12] Mothers in rural areas drugged their children with poppy seeds, and children played games based on silence in *malines*. But according to some, "nobody wanted a family with a baby . . . life for those with small children was even more precarious than for everybody else."[13]

During the *Aktion* in Raduń in May 1942, adults hiding in a hayloft surrounded Zipporah Sonenson, whose baby Shaul would not stop whimpering. "He is just a baby," said one. "We are all adults. Because of him we are all going to be murdered."[14] Zipporah watched in horror as the adults smothered the infant. When the *Aktion* was over she catatonically rocked the dead infant. Days later she buried him. Other parents preferred their own deaths. In the Koretz ghetto in Volhynia in western Ukraine, a man strangled a crying infant in front of its mother. She surrendered herself to the Germans. "My conscience," she said to the others, "does not permit me to stay here with you."[15]

---

[8]Deborah Schultz and Edward Timms, eds., *Arnold Daghani's Memories of Mikhailowka: The Illustrated Diary of a Slave Labour Camp Survivor* (London, 2009), November 3, 1942.

[9]In general, see Andrej Angrick, "Annihilation Through Labor: Jews and Thoroughfare IV in Central Ukraine," in *The Shoah in Ukraine: History, Testimony, Memorialization*, eds. Ray Brandon and Wendy Lower (Bloomington, IN, 2008), pp. 190–223.

[10]*Eichmann Trial*, vol. 1, p. 449.

[11]Ilya Ehrenburg and Vasily Grossman, eds., *The Complete Black Book of Russian Jewry*, ed., David Patterson (New Brunswick, NJ, 2002), p. 127.

[12]*Eichmann Trial*, vol. 1, p. 479.

[13]Yaffa Eliach, *There Was Once a World: A Nine Hundred Year Chronicle of the Shtetl of Eishyshok* (Boston, MA, 1998), p. 602.

[14]Quoted in Eliach, *Eishyshok*, p. 605.

[15]Quoted in Yitzhak Arad, *The Holocaust in the Soviet Union* (Lincoln, NE, 2009), p. 455.

Regardless, *malines* increasingly presented difficulties for the Germans and their auxiliaries. Wilhelm Kube, the general commissioner for the Belarus General District, received a report that in Dokshytsy, where the Germans killed 2,652 Jews in May 1942, "Jews in the ghetto had been so good at hiding that it took a full week to find the last of them."[16] The Germans resorted to demolition. With the Soviets approaching Kovno in June 1944, Aharon Peretz remembered that the Germans "blew up the *malines* and following the explosion people emerged . . . wounded and stifled by the smoke. . . . All the remaining bunkers, which they were unable to discover easily, were blown up in the course of time, and then about 1,500 to 2,000 people were killed inside these bunkers. People emerged alive from only two. . . . When we left the ghetto it was all in flames."[17]

Jews could rarely hide with gentiles for long stretches of time. Most Lithuanian, Latvian, Polish, Belarusian, or Ukrainian gentiles were indifferent or hostile to Jews. Some collaborated with the Germans. Some hid Jews as long as Jews could pay and kicked them out afterward. But many inclined to help were simply afraid. Avraham Aviel escaped from Raduń in May 1942 and hid with a Pole named Ancilowicz for several months. "If [the Germans] had found Jews in his house," remembered Aviel, "he would have been killed, destroyed. No trace of him would have remained. . . . Naturally, in such circumstances, people were afraid to take us in."[18]

Jews worried for gentile rescuers. During an *Aktion* in Vilna in October 1941, the Yiddish poet Avrom Sutzkever knocked on a door hoping for a miracle. "A barefoot old woman [named Yanova Bartoshevitch] opened the door," he remembered. "My tongue was paralyzed. . . . She let me in, locked the door behind me, drew the curtain across the window and said, 'Keep calm. I'll hide you. . . . ' She took me down to the cellar. . . ." Yanova's husband, a street sweeper, agreed that "[w]e must help people in trouble." The couple contacted Sutzkever's family in the ghetto and passed them food. Sutzkever worried for his protectors' safety and for his own family. "I couldn't stay there any longer," he remembered, "I returned to the blood-drenched streets of the ghetto."[19] Sutzkever's mother and newborn son were later murdered. He survived the war as a resistor.

One rare tale of long-term assistance involves Francisca Halamajowa, a hard-drinking, tobacco-chewing Polish woman in Sokol—a town in East Galicia with a Ukrainian majority. Thirty of Sokol's 6,000 Jews survived the war. As the Germans sent Sokol's Jews to the Bełżec extermination camp, Halamajowa hid three families, two over her pigsty and one under her kitchen. In September 1942, as gunfire resounded through Sokal's ghetto, Halamajowa was terrified she would be discovered and that her own daughter would be killed. But she did not kick the Jews out. "If the Germans find you," she told the family of Moshe Maltz, "I'll take all the blame for sheltering you and I'll tell the Germans to take me wherever they'll be taking you."[20] Despite further *Aktionen*, suspicious neighbors, murderous Ukrainian gangs, and bouts of debilitating fear, Halamajowa hid the families until the Red Army arrived in July 1944. Knowing the sentiments of her neighbors, Halamajowa asked her charges to keep her deed secret. "The Poles in town," she said, "don't like people who put themselves out to help Jews."[21]

---

[16]Quoted Arad, *The Holocaust in the Soviet Union*, p. 253.

[17]*Eichmann Trial*, vol. 1, p. 482.

[18]*Eichmann Trial*, vol. 1, p. 499.

[19]All quoted from Joseph Leftwich, *Abraham Sutzkever: Partisan Poet* (New York, 1971), pp. 102–4.

[20]Moshe Maltz, *Years of Horror—Glimpse of Hope: The Diary of a Family in Hiding* (New York, 1993), September 1942, p. 41.

[21]Maltz, *Years of Horror*, July 20, 1944.

Amidah

Amidah refers to the central prayer in Judaism whereby one stands facing Jerusalem. For Israeli Holocaust scholar Yehuda Bauer, it also means a type of inner resistance—standing fast, preserving life and culture within a community structure. Emanuel Ringelblum's work in the Warsaw ghetto is an example. But Warsaw was Europe's largest Jewish community, and extermination there did not begin for nearly three years after the Germans took the city.

Could smaller Jewish communities staggered by Soviet policies and suddenly facing mass murder in 1941 carry out *Amidah*? It depended on the place. Jewry in Vilna had a vibrant cultural history, active Zionist youth groups, and numerous cultural treasures. Bundist and Zionist organizations rebuilt school curricula and provided political instruction. Rabbis maintained synagogues and the Jewish faith. Herman Kruk kept a diary and wrote poetry and prose in Vilna and later when he was deported to a work camp in Estonia. "Neighbors in Camp Klooga [in Estonia] often ask me," he wrote in March 1944, "why do you write in such hard times . . . for we won't live to see it anyway. For future generations I leave it as a trace . . . let it show what I could not live to tell."[22] He was killed on September 18, one day before the Soviets liberated his camp.

A telling example of *Amidah* in Vilna was the rescue of Jewish manuscripts. In 1925, the Institute for Jewish Research (YIVO) was founded there as a global repository for Jewish historical, literary, ethnographic, and artistic material. Vilna's Jewish libraries housed even more rare books and manuscripts. Alfred Rosenberg was a Nazi ideologue from Hitler's earliest political days. After 1941, he held the title of Minister for the Occupied Eastern Territories. In 1942, a special detachment under Rosenberg's command arrived in Vilna to seize the more valuable Jewish materials. The Germans ordered a group of Jewish intellectuals to sort. Among them were the aforementioned Kruk and Sutzkever.

The team hid thousands of priceless books, letters, manuscripts, Torah scrolls, and artworks ranging from the fifteenth to the twentieth centuries. They placed the materials in the recesses of YIVO and smuggled them into the Vilna ghetto. "The risk to their life [sic] by taking away any piece of paper is awesome," wrote Kruk, "every scrap of paper endangers your head. Nevertheless these are idealists who do it easily."[23] Although much of what was hidden did not survive the Soviet liberation, priceless treasures were saved. YIVO was moved to New York City after the war.

Such examples were not found everywhere. In poorer regions with weak Jewish leadership, it was impossible. Krzemieniec was a *shtetl* in Volhynia in northwest Ukraine, where the Germans herded 14,000 Jews in 1942. Starvation was rampant and smuggling impossible owing to an unsympathetic Ukrainian population. Yehuda Bauer notes that "[n]o *Amidah* was remotely possible, no educational activities took place, no one cared about orphans, no religious life existed . . . no trace of social welfare activity has been found [and] anything resembling cultural life could not even be dreamt of."[24] Fourteen Jews from Krzemieniec survived. The ghetto in Buczacz, a *shtetl* of 11,000 in East Galicia, was little better. The Jewish Council was corrupt, there were no social welfare efforts, and nothing existed for children beyond private efforts. "A person," said Baruch Milch, one of Buczacz's very few survivors, "ceases to be a human being when the Angel of Death stands at the threshold. . . . Solidarity and communal togetherness dissolved."[25]

---

[22]Kruk, *Last* Days, March 24, 1944.

[23]Kruk, *Last Days*, July 9, 1942; see also October 18, 1942.

[24]Yehuda Bauer, *The Death of the Shtetl* (New Haven, CT, 2009), p. 76.

[25]Quoted in Bauer, *Death of the Shtetl*, p. 78.

Facing Death

Many Jews in the Soviet Union succumbed to death out of despair or resignation. Gutke Kanichowski lived in the Raduń ghetto with her three small children. "If three such beautiful angels have to go to the slaughter," she said, "I don't care to try to survive the war."[26] Avraham Aviel's mother walked with her children to her death, praying and telling her children that "we shall die as Jews. . . ." "She accepted her fate," remembered Aviel, "and did not try to influence it in any way [with a] fervent belief in divine providence. Quite often she had expressed her sorrow at the possibility of one of her children remaining alive among the gentiles. She would rather have the child die as a Jew. . . .[27]

Even Jews resigned to death exhibited uncommon strength, sometimes putting their terror aside for the sake of their children. Hermann Gräbe was a German construction engineer who employed Jewish workers in the Ukraine. He saved many from execution. After the war, he provided an affidavit for the Nuremberg Trials regarding a shooting in Dubno in Volhynia in October 1942. Gräbe remembered:

> Without screaming or weeping, these people undressed, stood around in family groups, kissed each other, said farewells, and waited for a sign from another SS man, who stood near the pit, also with a whip in his hand. During the 15 minutes I stood near, I heard no complaint or plea for mercy. I watched a family of about eight persons, a man and a woman both of about 50, with their children of about 1, 8, and 10, and two grown-up daughters of about 20 to 24. An old woman with snow-white hair was holding a one-year-old child in her arms and singing to it and tickling it. The child was cooing with delight. The parents were looking on with tears in their eyes. The father was holding the hand of a boy about 10 years old and speaking to him softly; the boy was fighting his tears. The father pointed to the sky, stroked his head and seemed to explain something to him. At that moment the SS man at the pit started shouting. . . .[28]

Others, we know not how many, were defiant in the last moments. "Not a drop of blood will be forgotten," yelled an old woman from a Jewish village to her executioners before she was shot. "You will pay for all of this."[29]

10.2 VARIETIES OF JEWISH LEADERSHIP

Jewish Council chairmen in Poland, such as Adam Czerniaków, and Jewish leaders in western Europe, such as Raymond-Raoul Lambert, strove to establish stability in their communities between 1939 and 1942. But Jewish leaders in the Soviet Union faced mass murder almost immediately. Their reactions varied depending on how quickly they apprehended the truth, their backgrounds and temperaments, the locations of their communities, and their assessments of the chances for survival. Most hoped to save what they could of the Jews in their ghettos. All failed to halt German killing operations, and most were themselves murdered.

---

[26]Eliach, *Eishyshok*, p. 601.

[27]Aviel, *A Village Named Dowgalishok*, pp. 105, 109.

[28]International Military Tribunal, *Trial of the Major War Criminals Before the International Military Tribunal, Nuremberg, 14 November 1945–1 October 1946* (Nuremberg, 1946) (hereafter *TMWC*), vol. 19, p. 508.

[29]Ehrenburg and Grossman, eds., *The Complete Black Book*, p. 158.

Elkes in Kovno

The pogroms in Kovno after June 25 killed nearly 4,000 Jews. Afterwards German and Lithuanian police began to hunt, capture, and march Jewish men and women to old tsarist fortresses outside town, where nearly 5,000 were killed by August 18.[30] Over the same period, Kovno's remaining 30,000 Jews were forced into a ghetto, which the Germans sealed off. They demanded that the Jews create a Council of Elders. Elchanan Elkes was a respected physician. Aged 62 and armed with nothing but decency, he agreed on August 4 to head the council at the pleading of local Jewish leaders. "If you believe that by accepting I will render a service to the common good," Elkes said, "then I accept."[31]

By October 4, German and Lithuanian police shot an additional 3,453 Jews, including hospital patients. But on October 28, the Germans conducted a massive selection of all remaining Jews to separate the productive from the nonproductive. By now, rumors of giant grave pits outside town circulated throughout the ghetto. In a town square surrounded by machine gun emplacements, the selection took all day. Avraham Tory wrote in his diary that "Dr. Elkes stood there, his pale face bearing the expression of bottomless grief." Elkes saved hundreds by interceding with the Germans. Regardless, Tory wrote, some 10,000 were marched into a small, separate holding ghetto. "It wasn't worthwhile living for more than sixty years," Elkes said afterward, "in order to witness a day like this. . . . I can't bear it any longer."[32]

And the next morning, the Germans emptied the small ghetto. Elkes again intervened with the SS but saved only a hundred. Entering the small ghetto to try and help Jews in any way he could, he was beaten and knocked unconscious by Lithuanian guards. When he recovered days later, the Germans and Lithuanians had shot 9,200 Jews, 7,193 of whom were women and children.[33]

Elkes hoped that Kovno's remaining Jews would survive by working for the German military. The SS moved perhaps 6,000 Jews from Kovno to other work camps over the course of 1943. In July 1944, as the Red Army neared Kovno, the Germans intended to move the remaining 8,000 Jews to Germany for work. Understanding that evacuation meant death in a war whose result had been decided, Elkes tried an ethical appeal. "You have the ability to save us," he insisted to the Germans, "by not carrying out the order to evacuate the ghetto." His words fell on deaf ears. The Germans set the ghetto ablaze, killing at least 1,500, then sent most of the survivors to concentration camps in Germany. Elkes died in Dachau in October.[34]

Gens in Vilna

Jacob Gens of Vilna was a different type of Jewish leader. He was relatively young at thirty-six and had been an officer in the Lithuanian army. Initially he commanded the ghetto police, but by the spring of 1942, he emerged as Vilna's chief Jewish authority. He appealed to Jews across

---

[30]See Karl Jäger's report of December 1, 1941, in Ernst Klee et al., eds., *The Good Old Days: The Holocaust as Seen by Its Perpetrators* (New York, 1988), pp. 46–58.

[31]Avraham Tory, *Surviving the Holocaust: The Kovno Ghetto Diary*, ed. Martin Gilbert (Cambridge, MA, 1990) (hereafter *Tory Diary*), August 4, 1941.

[32]Quotes in *Tory Diary*, October 28, 1941.

[33]Figure from Jäger Report in Klee, et al., eds., *The Good Old Days*, pp. 46–58.

[34]Quote and figure in Arad, *The Holocaust in the Soviet Union*, p. 330.

the political spectrum and executed Jews who collaborated with the Germans as informants. "We shall," he said, "eliminate them with our own hands."[35]

Gens raised money by taxing Jews who had income from work or business. He staged paid cultural events such as theater and concerts. Revenues procured money to bribe German officials; funds for food, fuel, and medicines from outside the ghetto; and resources for food kitchens, sanitation services, schools, a library, and a hospital with a secret infections disease unit (the Germans burned the infectious disease unit in Kovno with the patients and staff inside).

Herman Kruk wrote that entertainment in the ghetto was "an offense to our feelings. . . . You don't make a theater in a graveyard."[36] Gens argued, however, that theatrical and musical productions aimed "to give man the opportunity to free himself from the ghetto for several hours. . . . Our bodies are in the ghetto, but our spirit has not been enslaved. . . . We must be strong in body and soul. . . ."[37] Indeed the ghetto was miserable. But the Jewish death rate for 1942, though higher than peacetime, was less than 3 percent of the population, with no deaths due to cold or hunger.[38]

Determined to maintain revenue and sure that the Germans would not liquidate a productive ghetto, Gens followed a "work to live" policy. He negotiated with the Germans for more work permits, and by July 1943, 14,000 of 21,000 Vilna Jews were employed. Understanding Nazi ruthlessness and the overall military situation, Gens also sacrificed lives to buy time. In July 1942, the Germans demanded 500 elderly and children. Gens whittled the demand to 100 elderly, but indeed his Jewish police handed them over. His police also helped deliver 406 elderly Jews in nearby Oszmiana in October, less than the 1,500 the Germans demanded, but hundreds nonetheless.

Local rabbis condemned Gens. "Better all be killed than one soul of Israel be surrendered," they argued.[39] But most understood Gens's calculus. In the terrified ghetto, Kruk wrote, "the tragedy is that the public mostly approves of Gens's attitude."[40] "It is incumbent on us," Gens said, "to save the strong and the young . . . I don't know if all will understand and justify it when we come out of the ghetto. But this is the point of view . . . to save what is possible, without regard for our good name."[41]

Gens hoped to maintain the ghetto until the Soviets arrived. But in August 1943, the Germans began to liquidate the ghetto, sending its Jews to work camps in Estonia to build fortifications. In September, the German Security Police arrested and shot Gens, ostensibly for helping Jewish partisans. Warned by associates to flee, Gens thought that running would endanger the ghetto's remaining 11,000 inhabitants.

Chaim Lazar, a Jewish resistor, wrote, "It may be charged that [Gens's] course was harmful, but everyone know he was never a traitor . . . he was convinced to the last moment that he would be able to save the ghetto."[42] A week after his death, German and Ukrainian police liquidated the ghetto. Less than half were taken to work camps in Latvia and Estonia. The rest were murdered, some at Ponary, and some at the death camp at Majdanek in Poland.

[35]Quoted in Yitzhak Arad, *Ghetto in Flames: The Struggle and Destruction of the Jews in Vilna in the Holocaust* (Jerusalem, 1981), p. 293.

[36]Kruk, *Last Days*, January 17, 1942.

[37]Quoted in Arad, *Ghetto in Flames*, p. 323.

[38]Figures in Arad, *Ghetto in Flames*, pp. 314–15, 318.

[39]Quoted in Arad, *Ghetto in Flames*, p. 156.

[40]Kruk, *Last Days*, October 28, 1942.

[41]Quoted in Arad, *The Holocaust in the Soviet Union*, pp. 261–2.

[42]Quoted in Arad, *Ghetto in Flames*, p. 426.

Jewish officials from Vilna seated at a sporting event. Jacob Gens wears a light suit and is seated sixth from the left.   *Source:* United States Holocaust Memorial Museum.

Mushkin and Yoffe in Minsk

Jewish Council chairmen in the Belarusian capital of Minsk were even more different leaders. Jews in Minsk had become assimilated into the Soviet system over the past twenty years. Belarusians there were more pro-Soviet and less antisemitic owing to a less developed nationalism. With Moscow and Leningrad unconquered, the Germans viewed Minsk as a substitute trophy, carrying out savage atrocities against Jews and gentiles alike. Soviet POWs were also marched through Minsk to notorious POW camps near the city. Ethnic Belarusians and Jews in Minsk shared affinity as fellow Soviet citizens oppressed by the invader. And Belarus, because of its thick forests, was the center of the growing partisan war; thus, Minsk became a center of partisan support.

The Germans fenced off the Minsk ghetto in August 1941. By October, it held 100,000 Jews. They appointed Ilya Mushkin as Jewish Council chairman simply because he knew some German. Mushkin was a Soviet state functionary before the war. He quickly recognized German barbarity, which included repeated night raids into the ghetto, the murder of entire Jewish families, and the frequent rape and killing of Jewish women.[43] On November 7, 1941, the anniversary of the Bolshevik Revolution, German police hanged 100 Belarusians throughout the city. They then marched some 13,000 Minsk Jews, including women and children, to nearby Tuchinka, killing all of them. Thousands of Jews killed that day were forced to dress up for the anniversary, carry red flags, and sing Soviet anthems as the Germans filmed them filing past.[44]

---

[43]Ehrenburg and Grossman, eds., *The Complete Black Book*, 115–16.

[44]Figures in Ehrenburg and Grossman, eds., *The Complete Black Book*, p. 118. Description in Timothy Snyder, *Bloodlands: Europe Between Stalin and Hitler* (New York, 2010), p. 226.

The Jewish ghetto underground became part of a larger city underground, which in turn was connected with growing partisan bands in the nearby forests. Mushkin and other Jewish Council members supported underground activity. Feyda Shedletsky, a teenage member of the Jewish resistance, recalled, "I told [Mushkin] that I had come from a partisan unit that needed warm clothes, medicines, and a cooking pot. I was surprised when he agreed to provide all this."[45] The Jewish Council in fact reserved part of Jewish production for the underground, encouraged sabotage among Jewish workers, removed Jewish escapees from housing lists so that the Gestapo could not punish their families, and smuggled hundreds of children to families and orphanages outside the ghetto with the help of Belarusian contacts.

By March 1942, the Germans were resolved to reduce the ghetto as part of the growing partisan war in Belarus. They demanded on March 1 that Mushkin hand over 5,000 Jews the following day. When he did not do so, they entered the ghetto, and killed 3,414 Jews, including children. They then attacked the underground itself, killing 251 members. Over the course of the whole month, they tortured Mushkin for information, finally killing him in April.[46] Throughout the spring, they launched repeated night raids into the ghetto, shooting Jews, burning buildings with Jews inside, and torturing Jews for information about the underground.

The Gestapo replaced Mushkin with his assistant, Moshe Yoffe, a refugee from Vilna who also spoke German. But Yoffe was also connected to the Jewish underground. He took special pains to protect Jewish underground leader Hersh Smolar, whom the Gestapo demanded by threatening the entire Jewish Council with death. Smolar was quickly hidden in the Jewish hospital. Yoffe convinced the Gestapo with fake identity documents bearing Smolar's name and smeared with blood that Smolar was already dead.

In late July 1942, the Germans commanded Minsk's Jews to assemble in Jubilee Square in the ghetto as a prelude to mass gassings in mobile vans. From a podium, Yoffe was to tell the Jews that the trucks were for work transport. Instead he shouted, "Comrades! They are going to kill you!" The Germans pulled Yoffe from the podium and shot him, along with the other members of the Jewish Council. Mass killing of men, women, and children ensured. "The entire square," remembered one witness, "was littered with bodies and flowing with blood."[47] The Germans also bayoneted all of the patients in the ghetto hospital. No council existed thereafter. By August 1942, the Minsk ghetto population was reduced to 12,000.[48]

10.3 JEWISH RESISTANCE IN THE USSR

Spontaneous Resistance

There were many forms of open Jewish resistance, including small, spontaneous acts of defiance. Most resulted in a different kind of death. During the July 1942 *Aktion* in Minsk, a Soviet partisan saw that "[m]others standing in line for the mobile gas units . . . either went insane or attacked the Germans like tigers. They were murdered by machine guns." An artist named Zorov "rushed at the fascists . . . he was knocked unconscious and thrown into a gas truck. . . . Mothers threw themselves on the fascists in fits of rage and then fell dead with their skulls crushed."[49]

---

[45]Quoted in Barbara Epstein, *The Minsk Ghetto 1941–1943: Jewish Resistance and Soviet Internationalism* (Berkeley, CA, 2008), p. 121.

[46]Figure in Snyder, *Bloodlands*, p. 236. On Mushkin, see Ehrenburg and Grossman, eds., *The Complete Black Book*, 121–2.

[47]Ehrenburg and Grossman, eds., *The Complete Black Book*, p. 129.

[48]Figure in Epstein, *Minsk Ghetto*, p. 106.

[49]Ehrenburg and Grossman, eds., *The Complete Black Book*, pp. 129, 130.

In Raduń, 100 men were taken to the cemetery to dig mass graves for themselves and the rest of the ghetto in May 1942. As they prepared to dig, Meier Stoler, a hulking blacksmith, whispered to the others. "It's shovels against automatic weapons . . . David against Goliath."[50] They attacked the police then scattered into the woods. Most were tracked down and killed. At Ponary, in April 1943, a trainload of Jews from the small ghetto at Swieciany (who had been told they were going to Kovno) burst from their wagons, some attacking German and Lithuanian police barehanded and with knives and pistols. The police fired into them, killing most.

Even small acts of resistance often carried a moral conundrum because the Germans took bloody reprisals. In the Białystok ghetto in February 1943, a young Zionist named Yitzhak Malmed threw sulfuric acid in the face of a German police officer who, instantly blinded, fired wildly and killed another German. The Gestapo executed 100 Jews in reprisal and threatened to liquidate the entire ghetto if Malmed did not surrender. He did so. "I regret," said Malmed before he was publicly hanged, "[that] I killed only one."[51]

Rabbi David Kahane remembered another story, this one concerning a young Jewish butcher in Lvov who, awaiting his own shooting in August 1942, incited his fellow Jews to attack. "If I must die," he said, "at least I shall kill some Germans." Others dissuaded him. "There are still several thousand Jews left in town," said one. "Are you prepared to have them on your conscience?" Kahane recounts: "[T]he young man lowered his head, gritted his teeth, and waited patiently for his death. No, this was not an act of cowardice. These were heroic acts."[52]

The Problem of Ghetto Resistance: The FPO

Organized resistance in ghettos was nearly impossible to sustain, whether or not it received support from Jewish Councils. Potential resistors argued as to whether they should defend the ghettos or join Soviet partisan units. Weapons were attainable only with great difficulty. And following the Warsaw ghetto uprising in April 1943 (see Chapter 11), German police doubled efforts to uncover smuggled weapons. Eliezer Karstadt of the Riga ghetto remembered that "an underground movement of sorts was there with us all the time, and little by little weapons would be brought in. . . . The SD got to know of it. Searches began in April 1943. . . . They found all the weapons and, unfortunately, they also found a list of all the members of the underground. They arrested 300 Jews and all of them were killed."[53]

Other organized resistance movements had more success. In a youth leaders' meeting in the Vilna ghetto on January 1, 1942, Abba Kovner, a twenty-three-year-old poet and *Hashomer Hatza'ir* activist, proclaimed that "Hitler has plotted to destroy all the Jews of Europe. The Jews of Lithuania are doomed to be the first in line. . . . *Let us not go as lambs to the slaughter*."[54] Kovner's statement that all of Europe's Jews were slated for destruction was intuitive on his part in early 1942. Regardless, he was adamant that Jewish youth must defend themselves.

---

[50]Quoted in Eliach, *Eishyshok*, p. 602.

[51]Quoted in Rafael Rajzner, "The Action of February 1943," *The Białystoker Memorial Book*, ed. I. Shmulewitz (New York, 1982), pp. 83–7.

[52]David Kahane, *Lvov Ghetto Diary* (Amherst, MA, 1990), p. 74.

[53]*Eichmann Trial*, vol. 1, p. 492.

[54]Full text of the manifesto can be found in Dina Porat, *The Fall of a Sparrow: The Life and Times of Abba Kovner* (Stanford, CA, 2010), p. 71.

Abba Kovner, December 1945,
in Palestine. *Source:* United
States Holocaust Memorial Museum.

The result was the founding of the United Partisans Organization in Vilna (known by its Yiddish initials FPO)—a union of about 300 male and female right- and left-wing youth group activists, from Zionists to communists to Bundists. The FPO's main success in 1942 was to sabotage German weapons and tank motors in Vilna factories. But the FPO also smuggled weapons and prepared for combat in case the ghetto was liquidated.

In 1943, the Gestapo learned of arms smuggling in Vilna. Ghetto leader Jacob Gens had provided funds to the FPO for weapons, but now concluded that "hotheads" endangered the ghetto as a whole. "The situation on all fronts is changing," he insisted to an FPO operative. "It may be that the Germans will . . . retreat and won't have time to liquidate the ghetto. We must not shorten its existence even by one day."[55]

Matters climaxed in July 1943 when the Gestapo demanded the handover of Yitzhak Witenberg, the communist chief of the FPO. Gens called for his surrender, as did terrified ghetto residents lest the Germans destroy the entire ghetto. The FPO would not deliberately provoke a German attack on the ghetto. Witenberg surrendered himself and then ingested cyanide so he would reveal nothing under interrogation. Witenberg's surrender showed the FPO that broad ghetto support for armed uprising was lacking as long as the chance of survival existed. As ghetto inhabitants were sent to work camps in Estonia in September 1943, FPO members left for the forest, joining Soviet partisan groups. Some, including Kovner, returned to Vilna when the Soviets liberated it in July 1944.

The Problem of Ghetto Resistance: Białystok

Vilna demonstrated that the timing of a ghetto revolt was always problematic. A revolt too early would suffer from fewer smuggled weapons while triggering mass destruction. Waiting, meanwhile, meant surrendering lives and risking discovery. Many ghetto revolts, therefore, were spontaneous, desperate acts at the last moment before liquidation. Notable is that Jewish underground

---

[55]Quoted in Arad, *Ghetto in Flames*, p. 383.

groups discussed these issues with Jewish Council leadership. Both understood that, at a certain point, there was nothing to lose.

In cooperation with Jewish Councils and Jewish police, resistors set many ghettos ablaze when the moment of liquidation came in 1942 and 1943. The hope was to allow mass escape through the smoke and flames, and in some cases Jewish fighters engaged the Germans with small arms. As the Germans liquidated small ghettos in the Lida region of Belarus in June 1942, Jews set fire to the ghettos of Disna, Druya, and Sharkovshchina. In July, they set the ghetto at Kletsk ablaze. In September, the Jews of Lakhva did the same. The scene was repeated in dozens of smaller ghettos in western Belarus and Ukraine. Very few escapees survived. German police and Ukrainian guerillas from the Organization of Ukrainian Nationalists (OUN) killed most of the 2,000 Jews who escaped from the Volhyinian *shtetl* of Tuczyn in September 1942. Twenty survived the war, helped by friendlier Ukrainian peasants.[56]

The largest example of this problem is the Białystok ghetto, which housed over 40,000 Jews. It was a productive work ghetto. The Germans did not target it until 1943, when they relocated its production facilities to the west. By 1943, Białystok Jews knew of the slaughters in Vilna and the liquidations of the smaller ghettos around Białystok. They also knew of the mass deportations of 1942 from ghettos in the General Government to extermination camps there. Białystok's Jewish Council chairman Ephraim Barash, an engineer and Zionist, had few illusions about the Germans. But he hoped that production would save the ghetto. "Turn the ghetto," he said, "into an element so beneficial . . . that it would be a shame to destroy it."[57] In the meantime, he kept contact with the underground.

Mordechai Tenenbaum was a member of the *He-halutz* Zionist youth group who migrated from Warsaw to Vilna in September 1939, then back to Warsaw in March 1942. In Warsaw, he warned his comrades of German intentions and later helped organize resistance activity. In November 1942, he made his way to Białystok to organize resistance there. "We have nothing to lose anymore," he said in January 1943. "They will poison us with gas like dogs with rabies and then they will burn us in ovens."[58] But youth factions could not agree on strategy. Communist and even *Hashomer Hatza'ir* youth were leaving the ghetto for partisan groups. And the smuggling and making of weapons were agonizingly slow. "At such a rate," Tenenbaum lamented in his diary, "the Messiah will come first."[59]

Thus, on the eve of the first deportation from Białystok in early February 1943, Tenenbaum was torn. Barash bargained the Germans down from their initial demand of 17,000 Jews to 6,300, and he spread word for Jews to hide. Tenenbaum wanted "to retaliate as soon as the first Jew is led to the slaughter. . . ." But he could not defend the ghetto against German reprisals. "What's so hard to bear," he said, "is the responsibility for the thousands of people who are still alive in the Białystok ghetto. . . ."[60] Together with Barash, Tenenbaum decided, "If the *Aktion* is limited, as promised—we shall not react, but shall sacrifice 6,300 Jews to save the remaining 35,000."[61] That week the Germans captured 10,000 Jews and took them to Treblinka.

[56]Bauer, *The Death of the Shtetl*, pp. 124–5.

[57]Quoted in Gershon David Hundert, ed., *The YIVO Encyclopedia of Jews in Eastern Europe*, vol. 1 (New Haven, CT, 2008), p. 125.

[58]Quoted in Raul Hilberg, *Perpetrators, Victims, Bystanders: The Jewish Catastrophe, 1933–1945* (New York, 1992), p. 182.

[59]Quoted in Sara Bender, *The Jews of Białystok During World War II and the Holocaust* (Lebanon, NH, 2008), p. 204.

[60]Quoted in Bender, *The Jews of Białystok*, p. 193.

[61]Quoted in Bender, *The Jews of Białystok*, p. 196.

On the night of August 15, SS detachments surrounded the ghetto and commanded all Jews to assemble. The underground had 200 fighters, 130 guns, and some homemade bombs. Tenenbaum hoped to create diversions and punch holes in ghetto fences so that Jews might escape. The plan failed. On the morning of August 16, the Jews inflicted casualties but the Germans, having by now experienced the Warsaw ghetto uprising of April 1943 (see Chapter 12), had superior firepower. Most Jewish fighters were killed the first day. In the next week, SS troops conducted mass shootings while evacuating the ghetto. Thirteen thousand Jews were taken to labor camps, primarily Majdanek, where Barash probably died. Twelve thousand went to Treblinka and Auschwitz.[62] Tenenbaum, it is believed, committed suicide in the ghetto.

The Problem of Jewish Partisan Resistance

On July 3, 1941, Joseph Stalin called for Soviet citizens to engage in partisan warfare against the invaders. "In the occupied regions," he commanded, "conditions must be made unbearable for the enemy and his accomplices. They must be hounded and annihilated at every step. . . ."[63] Initially comprised of Red Army troops caught behind enemy lines, the partisan movement grew slowly. But by 1944, the Red Army counted well over 181,000 partisans operating behind German lines under its direction, more than half in the thick forests of eastern Belarus.[64]

It was no easy matter for ghetto Jews to join. Leaving family members to die was an unbearable choice. "I've got to go, Papa," Leibke Kaganowicz told his father in the Raduń ghetto. "I can't wait around to be killed." "You'll have to go without me," his mother replied. "Grandmother could never make the journey. . . . I must stay here to look after her." The family argument lasted four days. Finally, Leibke, his two siblings, and his father left his mother and grandmother behind. "I was torn," remembered Leibke. "A hundred times I told myself to stay. A hundred times my terror forced me to leave behind my adored mother. . . ."[65] Other Jews who fled the ghetto reluctantly placed loved ones at more immediate risk. The Germans, if they could locate them, killed the family members of partisans who left for the forest.

Geography was another problem. In Lithuania and western Belarus, the Polish Home Army (*Armia Krajowa* [AK])—the underground remnant of Poland's wartime forces—fought for resurgence of the old Polish state partly by killing ethnic enemies. It was more likely to kill fleeing Jews than accept them. In the western Ukraine, OUN guerillas killed Soviet partisans, Polish villagers, and Jews in an effort to cleanse the region of their ethnic and political enemies. In Belarus, Jews fleeing ghettos had better survival chances because of the dense forest and swamps, which the Germans could not penetrate. By 1942, Soviet partisan groups there, based on shattered Red Army units, were beginning to coalesce.

But survival odds even in Belarus's forests were slim. Many Jews who fled into the forest found an unforgiving natural environment, particularly in winter, and few peasants willing to help with shelter or food. Many returned to the ghettos. Others were killed or handed over by collaborators. Soviet partisan detachments, meanwhile, wanted no one who could not fight and were wary of ghetto Jews. Most had no military training. Soviet partisans shot some as suspected German spies. Other Soviet partisans disarmed Jews and occasionally killed Jewish fighters.

---

[62]Figure in Bender, *The Jews of Białystok*, p. 266.

[63]Quoted in Kenneth Slepyan, *Stalin's Guerillas: Soviet Partisans in World War II* (Lawrence, KS, 2006), p. 15.

[64]Figure in Slepyan, *Stalin's Guerillas*, p. 51.

[65]Leon Kahn, *No Time to Mourn: The True Story of a Jewish Partisan Fighter* (Vancouver, 2004), pp. 69–73.

Jews only became an integral part of the partisan war at the end of 1942, after most Jews in the German-occupied USSR were dead. Estimates are that about 20,000 Jews joined partisan units in the Soviet Union, and that up to 13,000 more created family camps in the forests in order to survive. Perhaps a third of both groups were killed.[66] Detachments that accepted Jews noted their bravery and thirst for revenge. "There are many Jews in partisan detachments," reported one commander to Moscow, "not a few of them are excellent fighters trying to avenge brutal murdering of Jews by the fascists."[67]

Minsk: A Partisan Ghetto

Minsk had no ghetto revolt. From its creation in September 1941, the Minsk underground worked to aid the Soviet war effort by supporting partisan groups in the forests around the city. The underground's Jewish section was part of this effort. Hersh Smolar, a thirty-six-year-old Jewish communist, led the Jewish underground. "We were an organic part," he remembered, "of a united fighting force."[68] The Jewish section helped supply partisans with food, clothing, valuables for trade, and even ammunition and weapons from factories where Jews worked.

The city underground prioritized sending those into the forest who could fight immediately, meaning escaped Soviet POWs and other young men, preferably with weapons. Four thousand young Jewish men were also moved to the forest by March 1942.[69] Smolar told Minsk's non-Jewish underground leaders that they should help more Jews. Meanwhile, the continual and brutal reduction of the ghetto in 1942 convinced the Jewish underground to send its own groups of Jews into the forest. More Jewish men and women fled and joined partisan detachments. Jewish teens served as forest guides for other fleeing Jews. In October 1942, the Germans liquidated the Minsk ghetto. There was no ghetto uprising. But according to recollections by underground leaders, up to 10,000 Minsk Jews reached partisan groups. Even if this figure exaggerates, it explains that resistance in Minsk was centered in partisan activity rather than ghetto fighting.[70]

The Bielski Partisans

All-Jewish partisan detachments were rare. Moscow did not approve of them, Jews lacked resources to create them, and most Jews under German occupation were dead by the time any partisan detachments achieved success. The combination Jewish partisan detachment and family camp commanded by Tuvia Bielski and his brothers is thus especially noteworthy. It was formed mostly of Jews who fled the western Belarusian *shtetlach* of Nowogródek and Lida as the Germans eliminated those ghettos in 1942 and 1943. A villager from Stankiewicz near Nowogródek, Bielski had served in the Polish army and was intent above all on saving Jews. "I wish," he said repeatedly, "that thousands of Jews would join us . . . we will absorb them all."[71]

The Bielski detachment attacked German logistics and killed local informants. But it also created a forest encampment that included smiths, tailors, doctors, and even kosher butchers. General Vasily Chernyshev, who commanded partisan operations from Moscow, visited the

---

[66]Figures in Yehuda Bauer, *Rethinking the Holocaust* (New Haven, CT, 2001), p. 136; Slepyan, *Stalin's Guerillas*, p. 57; Arad, *The Holocaust in the Soviet Union*, pp. 514–15.

[67]Kagan, ed., *Novogrudok*, p. 183.

[68]Hersh Smolar, *Resistance in Minsk* (Oakland, CA, 1966), p. 23.

[69]Figure in Epstein, *Minsk Ghetto*, p. 192.

[70]Figure in Epstein, *Minsk Ghetto*, p. 191.

[71]Shmuel Amarant, in Kagan, ed., *Novogrudok*, p. 206.

A group of partisans from various fighting units, including the Bielski partisans in the Naliboki Forest, July 1944.   *Source:* United States Holocaust Memorial Museum, courtesy of Moshe Kaganovich.

Bielski camp in December 1943. "The General was astonished," remembered Bielski, "at the industriousness and dedication of the workers."[72] Ultimately the Bielski detachment saved over twelve hundred Jews, even during brutal German anti-partisan operations in 1943 that killed thousands of Belarusian civilians and Soviet partisans alike. Bielski's achievement is especially noteworthy when one remembers that, by some estimates, only 119,000 of the up to 2.74 million Jews who fell under Nazi occupation in the USSR survived the war.[73]

Despite the small number of Jewish partisans, German officials insisted in 1942 and afterward that Jews were behind the entire partisan war. On July 31, 1942, Wilhelm Kube, the general commissioner of the Belarus District, reported from his headquarters in Minsk that "[i]n all the fighting with the partisans in Belarus it has been proved that Jewry . . . is the main bearer of the partisan movement." Kube boasted that just 8,794 Jews remained alive in Minsk (another 3,000 were in hiding), he complained about the army's demand for Jewish labor, and he suggested that "[t]he SD and I would most prefer if Jewry in the General District of Belarus were finally eliminated."[74] Massacres of remaining Jews in Kube's district followed. But Kube himself was killed in September 1943. His housekeeper and mistress, Yelena Mazanik, planted a bomb in his apartment. She was Belarusian.

10.4 THE SOVIETS, THE ALLIES, AND THE HOLOCAUST IN THE USSR

Stalin and the Holocaust

Joseph Stalin's mass collectivization efforts and political purges in the 1920s and 1930s killed tens of millions of Soviet citizens. More deaths in 1941 and 1942 bothered Stalin only insofar

---

[72]Quoted in Kagan, ed., *Novogrudok*, pp. 202–3.

[73]Arad, *The Holocaust in the Soviet Union*, p. 525.

[74]*TMWC*, vol. 12, p. 67, document PS-3428; Epstein, *Minsk Ghetto*, p. 302, n. 49.

as they signaled a losing war effort. Stalin was also extremely suspicious of supposed Jewish nationalism in the USSR. During the period of the nonaggression pact with Germany, the Soviet press reported nothing on German antisemitic policies in Poland or any place else. As late as June 1941, the NKVD arrested Bundist and Zionist leaders for nationalist and foreign-agent activity and deported them to central Asia.

The Soviet government knew early of German mass murders of Jews. Word came to Moscow from fleeing civilians, and the Soviets also left stay-behind agents in occupied cities and parachuted other agents behind German lines. News of Babi Yar and dozens of other sites reached Moscow. The Red Army discovered mass graves teeming with Jewish dead in its winter offensives of 1941. The Soviet state publicly decried the murders, sometimes including estimates of numbers killed.

But Moscow obscured the fact that most mass shooting victims were Jews. Instead they characterized them as Slavic nationals or simply as "Soviet citizens." Part of the reason lay in Stalin's paranoia concerning Jewish nationalism. Part also lay in his realization that if the USSR were to be saved, it would be saved by the Slavic nationalities he now urged to fight to the death.

On November 7, 1941, Stalin gave a celebrated speech commemorating the Bolshevik Revolution and calling all Soviets to arms. The Nazis, Stalin said, "organize medieval pogroms against the Jews as readily as the tsarist regime did." But the real German aim, he said, was "to exterminate the Slavonic nations—the Russians, Poles, Czechs, Slovaks, Bulgarians, Ukrainians [and] Byelorussians."[75] It was Stalin's only public discussion of the Jews the entire war, and it was more a backhanded attack on the tsars than a plea for Jewish citizens. On the same day, the Germans killed some 13,000 Jews in Minsk.

Subsequent official statements continued to obscure the Jews' fate. In 1942, Foreign Minister V. I. Molotov issued a series of international communiqués. The first of January 6 mentioned Jews obliquely, characterizing the victims of Babi Yar as "Ukrainians, Russians and Jews who had shown any devotion to Soviet rule." The third, on April 28, mentioned mass killings at Kerch, Vitebsk, Pinsk, Minsk, and elsewhere but characterized the victims as "[h]undreds of thousands of Ukrainians, Russians, Jews, and Moldavians." Purely domestic reporting often did not mention Jews at all. "Hitler," said the Communist Party newspaper *Pravda* in July 1943, "developed cannibalistic plans to annihilate the Slavs. . . . [D]uring the first months of their rule, they annihilated tens of thousands of peaceful citizens of Kiev, Odessa, Minsk, Vitebsk, Brest-Litovsk, and Lvov. . . ."[76]

Jews, meanwhile, did their part for the eventual Soviet victory. Over 500,000 Jews served in the Red Army during World War II. Nearly half were killed, either on the battlefield or as German prisoners.[77] In the words of one young Jewish officer, they had "a score to settle with Hitler's gang."[78] Jews served as senior officers and were awarded medals in proportions higher than their percentage of the Soviet population. Yet the Soviet press, when reporting decorations by nationality, deliberately omitted Jewish medals.[79] Meanwhile no order to Soviet partisans

---

[75]J. V. Stalin, *On the Great Patriotic War of the Soviet Union* (Moscow, 1946), p. 29.

[76]Quoted in Yitzhak Arad, "The Holocaust as Reflected in the Soviet Russian Language Newspapers in the Years 1941 to 1945," in *Why Didn't the Press Shout? American and International Journalism During the Holocaust*, ed. Robert Moses Shapiro (Jersey City, NJ, 2003) pp. 201–13.

[77]Figure in Yitzhak Arad, *In the Shadow of the Red Banner: Soviet Jews in the War Against Nazi Germany* (New York, 2010), pp. 126–7.

[78]A. E. Gitelman to Mikhoels, April 13, 1944, in *War, Holocaust and Stalinism: A Documented Study of the Jewish Anti-Fascist Committee in the USSR*, ed. Shimon Redlich (Luxembourg, 1995), p. 221.

[79]Figures in Arad, *In the Shadow of the Red Banner*, pp. 115–18.

has even been found directing partisan detachments to rescue Jews or to help Jewish refugees from ghettos. A few partisan detachments saved Jews on their own initiative, but never on orders from Moscow.[80]

The Jewish Anti-Fascist Committee

Stalin's one concession to the truth was the creation of the Jewish Anti-Fascist Committee (JAC) in April 1942. Closely supervised by the state, the JAC was a collection of prominent Soviet Jewish intellectuals. Their task was to ensure the support of Soviet Jews for the war effort while also gaining support abroad. Stalin's policy was cynical. It was based on the notion of a powerful world Jewry that Moscow could tap for funds and political support. The Soviets were especially dependent on material help from the British and US governments.

The problem for Soviet Jewish intellectuals lay in identifying the uniqueness of Hitler's war against the Jews while simultaneously demonstrating their loyalty to the Soviet Union. Their initial meeting in Moscow on August 24, 1941, was broadcast worldwide, but aimed especially at Jews in Britain, Palestine, and the United States. It contained numerous speeches pointing to the extermination of Jews while calling for material aid for the Red Army. The Yiddish theater producer and actor Solomon Mikhoels, who soon became the JAC's chairman, painted a stark portrait:

> Hitler's bloody regime has brutally planned the complete and unconditional annihilation of the Jewish people by all means available to the fascist executioners. . . . The spilled blood demands not fasting and prayers but revenge! It is not by memorial candles but by fire that the murderers of humanity must be destroyed. . . . It's now or never! . . . The brown scourge, which has brought tears and grief, torture and despair to the whole world, must now find itself a grave . . . in the Soviet Union. We note with pride the names of our fellow Jews among those fighting Hitler's bandits in the air, on sea and on land. . . . Fellow Jews the world over! They are fighting for you as well! . . . Work everywhere for solidarity and mobilize effective help for the Soviet Union."[81]

The JAC broadcast further speeches, published documents and pamphlets, and started a Yiddish-language newspaper called *Eynikeit* ("Unity") in June 1942 with some 300 correspondents and numerous stories of anti-Jewish atrocities. The JAC suggested the newspaper because, as Mikhoels said, "there is not one Yiddish newspaper in the entire USSR," and because "a Yiddish newspaper is a vital necessity in order to influence politically the Jewish masses in the USSR and to evoke and strengthen sympathy toward the USSR on the part of the Jewish population abroad, especially in the USA, where Jews play an important role. . . ."[82]

JAC leaders went on a seven-month world tour in 1943, speaking to some 500,000 listeners in forty-six cities, from Argentina to the United States, to Canada, to Britain, including a rally of 50,000 in New York's Polo Grounds. The JAC raised some $10 million in the United States alone throughout the war.[83] Beginning in 1942, the JAC also began work on what was to become *The Black Book*—a documentary volume of German crimes against Jews, assembled from personal

---

[80]Leonid Smilovitsky, "Antisemitism in the Soviet Partisan Movement, 1941–1944: The Case of Belorussia," *Holocaust and Genocide Studies*, 20, no. 2 (Fall 2006), pp. 207–34.

[81]"An Appeal to World Jewry (August 24, 1941)," in Redlich, ed., *War, Holocaust and Stalinism*, pp. 174–7.

[82]Mikhoels et al. to A. S. Shcherbakov, September 14, 1941, and Mikhoels et al. to Shcherbakov, March 4, 1942, in Redlich, ed., *War, Holocaust and Stalinism*, pp. 187, 190.

[83]Figure in Arno Lustiger, *Stalin and the Jews: The Tragedy of the Soviet Jews and the Jewish Anti-Fascist Committee* (New York, 2003), p. 120.

survivor testimonies. Heading the project was the Russian Jewish writer Ilya Ehrenburg, whose Moscow apartment was soon stuffed with written testimonies from Jews, determined that their voices be heard.

But there were limits to how far Stalin would go. In mid-1943, just 2,000 copies of each issue of *Eynikeit* were for sale in the USSR. Most copies were sent abroad.[84] Ehrenburg's *Black Book* was never published in the Soviet Union, and Ehrenburg himself dejectedly noted increased antisemitism among Soviet citizens. And in the years following the war, Jewish Anti-Fascist Committee leaders were secretly tried and executed.

What the British Knew

Scholars now know that the British government was well informed concerning German crimes in the USSR.[85] Himmler insisted that his Higher SS and Police Leaders in the USSR, who oversaw Waffen-SS and Order Police operations, keep him informed on anti-Jewish actions. The primary means of rapid communication was wireless radio. The German encryption system for Order Police radio messages did not use the more advanced Enigma machine used by the German navy; instead, it used a hand-cipher based on an old British system from World War I.

British cryptologists broke Order Police codes in 1941. They did not transcribe everything, but they knew of dozens of massacres by Order Police units. Selections of German police messages were sent to Prime Minister Churchill, who circled the numbers of Jews killed. Between August 23 and 31, 1941, alone, British decoding revealed that the SS and Order Police killed 12,361 Jews. An intelligence summary of September 12 surmised that the number of executions was probably double this number because code breakers decrypted only half of German police communications.

The British understood German aims well enough that intelligence officers commented: "The fact that the Police are killing all Jews that fall into their hands should by now be sufficiently well appreciated. It is not therefore proposed to continue reporting these butcheries specifically, unless so requested."[86] Churchill was sympathetic to Europe's Jews, but his government did little with the information. London never even made it public. The reasons are speculative. In late 1941, the British were on the defensive in the Atlantic and in North Africa, and it seemed unlikely that the USSR would survive the German attack. Survival was the first priority. London shied from extreme atrocity stories out of concern that they could cause skepticism in the United States, where there was no sentiment for entering the war and where even material help for the British was controversial. Stories about German murders of Jews would also not appeal to ordinary Germans, many of whom the British hoped to turn against Hitler through British Broadcasting Corporation (BBC) broadcasts to Germany.

Primarily, London worried about the Middle East, where the German *Afrika Korps* pressed toward the Suez Canal. With the help of Arab sympathizers in Berlin, Germany broadcast radio propaganda to the Middle East. It argued that Britain was fighting for the Jews, having promised them not only Palestine, but also Transjordan, Syria, and Iraq. It was a Muslim's duty, said Radio Berlin in October 1941, to support Germany in "the destruction of Bolshevism [and] Islam's

---

[84]Figures in Dov-Ber Kerler, "The Soviet Yiddish Press During the War, 1942–1945," in Shapiro, ed., *Why Didn't The Press Shout?* p. 223.

[85]In general, see Richard Breitman, *Official Secrets: What the Nazis Planned, What the British and Americans Knew* (New York, 1998), pp. 88–93.

[86]Quotes and figures from Breitman, *Official Secrets*, p. 96.

other two great enemies, Britain and the Jews."[87] Making stories from the USSR public would create greater pressure to revise the 1939 White Paper amid this propaganda.

In short, there was no political advantage and plenty of political detriment. "Horror stuff," said the Ministry of Information, "must be used very sparingly and must deal always with treatment of indisputably innocent people. Not with violent political opponents. And not with Jews."[88] In August 1941, Jewish Agency Executive chairman David Ben-Gurion was in London pressing for the creation of a Jewish army in Palestine. British officials rejected the proposal as too politically explosive. It is likely that they did not inform Ben-Gurion of what they had learned through German radio decoding either.

The US Ambassador in Bucharest

What might have been achieved had the Soviet or British governments acted differently? They might have broadcast accurate information to ghettos that had not been liquidated. This might have coalesced resistance in places where it had not yet developed. But it is unlikely that any government could have deterred the Germans from their chosen course.

Romania offers a case in point. Thanks to Wilhelm Filderman, Romania's chief Jewish leader, news of Romanian atrocities in the USSR immediately reached diplomats in Bucharest. The US ambassador was Franklin Mott Gunther, who kept Washington fully informed. In November 1941, he described the brutal expulsions of Jews from Bessarabia and Bukovina into Transnistria. "It is becoming more and more evident," Gunther reported, "that the Romanians, obviously with the moral support of the Germans, are utilizing the present period for handling the Jewish problem in their own way." Romanian policy, he concluded, "would seem deliberately calculated to serve a program of virtual extermination."

Gunther raised unofficial protests to senior Romanian officials. "I have availed myself of every suitable occasion," he reported, "to intimate to Marshal Antonescu and other Rumanian officials how deeply my government and the people of the United States deplore and abhor the exercise of wanton license in dealing with human lives, even in the liquidation of what this country may consider an internal problem. There is, I feel, no mistaking as to the American view of butchery. . . ." Gunther's protests brought denials. Marshal Antonescu's deputy prime minister told Gunther that the violence was carried out "by subordinate and irresponsible people," and that Marshal Antonescu and his government "regretted what has been done and were doing their utmost to set matters right."

Gunther saw though these statements. Although appalled by the violence, he remained ambivalent. "The fact remains," he reported, "that the lower class Jew who has filtered into Rumania since the war . . . and fastened upon village and small-town life is, by and large, not assimilable. The Rumanian resents his presence. . . ." Could anything be done? "I doubt," said Gunther, "if any public or private condemnation . . . on our part would do any good any more and might make matters worse."

Gunther knew that Washington would not loosen immigration quotas and that London would not revise the White Paper. All that was left was an unnamed territory, perhaps in Africa, where a possible Jewish homeland might be established after the war. This idea, he reported, "would go far to deter this Government from the diabolical measure now being applied to

---

[87]Quoted in Jeffrey Herf, *Nazi Propaganda for the Arab World* (New Haven, CT, 2009), p. 73.

[88]Quoted in Breitman, *Official Secrets*, p. 102.

Jews. . . . I have frequently counseled patience here," he added, "and averred that a world solution of the Jewish problem would be reached at the time of the peace conference."

In the meantime, he became less hopeful. "The program of systematic extermination is continuing," he reported in November, "and I see little hope for the Rumanian Jews as long as the present German-controlled regime is in power." Gunther's superiors in Washington had no answers either. "So far as I know," wrote one State Department official on November 12, "we are not ready to tackle the whole Jewish problem."[89]

*****

If the United States was not ready to tackle the whole Jewish problem, then Hitler surely was. Preparations to murder all of Europe's Jews—not just those of the Soviet Union—had been underway since the fall of 1941. For Hitler, the fundamental correctness of this decision was confirmed by the end of the year. On December 7, Japanese forces attacked the US Pacific fleet at Pearl Harbor and began a massive offensive in the Pacific against US, British, Dutch, and French holdings. Encouraged by Japan's offensive and his own expectation that he could complete the war in the USSR the following spring, Hitler declared war on the United States on December 11. Germany's allies in Europe followed suit. The United States would be an eventual enemy anyway. Now, with the British and Soviets reeling and the United States unprepared, Berlin seized the moment.

Ultimately, the grand coalition of Great Britain, the Soviet Union, and the United States would destroy Nazi Germany through the air, ground, and sea. But victory was more than three and a half years away. For the moment, the Nazis were convinced that the war with world Jewry that Hitler predicted in 1939 had finally arrived. "We know what powers stand behind Roosevelt," Hitler insisted during his Reichstag speech on December 11. "It is the eternal Jew who thinks his time has come. . . ." Goebbels concurred. "Regarding the Jewish question," he wrote in his diary, "the Führer is determined to settle the matter once and for all. He prophesied that if the Jews once again brought about world war, they would experience their extermination. This was not an empty phrase. The world war is here. The extermination of the Jews must be its necessary consequence. . . . the originators of this conflict must pay with their own lives."[90]

---

[89]All quotes from Gunther's correspondence with Washington are in United States, Department of State, *Foreign Relations of the United States: Diplomatic Papers 1941*, vol. 2 (Washington, DC, 1959), pp. 860–79.

[90]Quoted in Herf, *The Jewish Enemy*, pp. 131–2.

11

Aktion Reinhard and the Final Solution in Poland, 1942–1943

In 1941, the Germans decided on the Final Solution of the Jewish Question—the extermination of all Jews in Europe wherever they were. *Aktion Reinhard* was the German code name for the murder of the largest concentration of Jews, those in the General Government. It was named for Reinhard Heydrich, the Chief of the Reich Security Main Office (RSHA) and of the Security Police, who was assassinated by Czech partisans in June 1942. It used carbon monoxide gas in specially built extermination camps. Preparations began in the fall of 1941; operations, the following spring. By the end of 1942, most Jews in the General Government, estimated at 2,284,000 by the Nazis in January, were dead. Some 300,000 were spared for work, and the Germans killed most of them in 1943.

Jews in the General Government's ghettos feared that deportation meant death but often did not learn their exact fate until the last moments. Polish reactions varied. Some helped Jews at great risk. Others collaborated with the Germans. Most remained indifferent. The Allies, despite steady information from Poland, provided nothing beyond threats to the Germans. With little hope of survival or help from the outside, Jewish youth turned to armed resistance to leave a memory of Jewish military honor. Nothing, however, could stop the Final Solution in Poland.

11.1 THE DECISION TO KILL EUROPE'S JEWS

Locating the Decision

Scholars disagree on when the Nazis decided on the Final Solution. One argument is that the fundamental decision to murder all European Jews was part of the decision to murder the Jews of the USSR and that it was made as early as March 1941. Another is that the two decisions were separate, that the basic decision to kill Europe's Jews came in October of 1941 when Kiev had been captured, the road to Moscow seemed open, and victory in the Soviet Union seemed assured. More recent arguments state that killing, even gassing in Poland, was implemented by local initiative only; a central decision to kill *all* European Jews did not come until December 1941 or even afterward, once the machinery of killing was in motion on the local level.[1]

As with the murder of Jews in the USSR, there was no written Hitler order for broader Jewish extermination. Orders were passed word of mouth to ensure secrecy. Directives and discussions used euphemisms such as "resettlement" to denote mass killing. Senior officials knew better than to commit much to paper. "This," Himmler said later in October 1943 to senior SS officers, "is a glorious page in our history and one that . . . can never be written."[2] In following the decision as it emerged in 1941, we are left with cryptic signposts, some ambiguous, some less so, and historians continue to debate about them.

In November 1940, the Reich Security Main Office (RSHA) banned Jewish emigration from the General Government. One reason was to speed Jewish emigration from the Reich. The other was more sinister. "The continued emigration of Jews from Eastern Europe [to the West]," reads the relevant decree, "spells a continued spiritual regeneration of world Jewry. . . . It is the United States in particular which is endeavoring, with the help of newly immigrating Jews, especially from Eastern Europe, to create a new basis from which it intends to force ahead its struggle, particularly against Germany."[3]

In fact, no place, least of all the United States, wanted Poland's Jews. But if the Germans would not allow them to emigrate on principle, then what options were left? Would they remain in Poland? In March 1941, when listening to General Governor Hans Frank complain about renewed expulsions of Reich Jews to the General Government, Hitler promised that the General Government would be the first territory freed of Jews. But where would they go? Official documents spoke of "resettlement in the East," meaning the conquered USSR. But it is unlikely that the Germans would move Poland's Jews to replace the Soviet Jews that they would soon take great pains to kill. As historian Richard Breitman argues, "there was only one way to have a 'final evacuation' of [Reich] Jews to Poland and simultaneously to make Poland free of Jews. . . ."

Nor was German thinking confined to Jews in those areas—the USSR and Poland—where they planned to settle Germans. All Jews *everywhere* were a danger. In May 1941, Himmler's subordinate Walter Schellenberg informed RHSA officials in France and Belgium that they were to prevent Jewish emigration from those countries, "in view of the surely approaching Final Solution of the Jewish question."[4] On July 22, Hitler hosted Slavko Kvaternik, Croatia's war minister. He predicted swift victory in the USSR, then argued that Europe as a whole had to be entirely freed of Jews. "If one state tolerates a Jewish family among it," he said, "this would provide the core bacillus for a new decomposition. If there were no more Jews in Europe, the unity of the European states would no longer be disturbed."[5]

Hitler insisted on solving the Jewish question in Germany first. An RSHA decree of September 1, 1941, forced Germany's Jews to wear the yellow star, a step delayed to this point.

---

[1]Overview of arguments in Christopher R. Browning, *Nazi Policy, Jewish Workers, German Killers* (New York, 2000), pp. 26–57; Dan Stone, *Histories of the Holocaust* (New York, 2010), pp. 64–112.

[2]Quoted in Donald Bloxham, *The Final Solution: A Genocide* (New York: 2009), p. 24.

[3]Yitzhak Arad, Israel Gutman, and Abraham Margaliot, eds., *Documents on the Holocaust: Selected Sources on the Destruction of the Jews of Germany and Austria, Poland, and the Soviet Union*, 8th ed. (Lincoln, NE, 1999), p. 219.

[4]Quotes from Richard Breitman, *The Architect of Genocide: Himmler and the Final Solution* (New York, 1991), pp. 153–9.

[5]Quoted in Ian Kershaw, *Hitler, 1936–1941: Nemesis* (New York, 2000), p. 471.

Reinhard Heydrich in 1940.
Source: DIZ München GmbH,
Süddeutsche Zeitung Photo/Alamy.

On September 18, Himmler informed Arthur Greiser, the Gauleiter of *Warthegau*, of "the Führer's wish" that the Reich and Protectorate "be emptied and liberated from the Jews from west to east as soon as possible."[6] They would go to the Łódź ghetto first, then further east in the spring, not coincidentally where Jews were being systematically shot. On October 15, 1941, the deportation of German Jews to eastern ghettos began. And on October 23, Jewish emigration from Germany abroad was forbidden.

The Wannsee Conference

The fate of Europe's Jews still demanded discussion. On July 31, 1941, Hermann Göring sent an order to Reinhard Heydrich. It charged Heydrich with "making all necessary preparations . . . for the execution of the intended Final Solution of the Jewish question." Heydrich himself solicited this order, which was then sent on Hitler's instructions. It formed the legal basis for his authority over the fate of Europe's Jews. Having come from Göring, who had headed Jewish policy in Germany following *Kristallnacht*, other agencies would understand that whatever character the Final Solution was to take, the RSHA was in charge.[7]

Göring's order eventually became the basis for the Wannsee Conference, named for the Berlin suburb where, in a once-Jewish-owned villa, Heydrich hosted the meeting. Initially scheduled for December 8, 1941, the meeting was delayed because of Japan's attack on Pearl Harbor and Hitler's declaration of war on the United States. On January 20, 1942, Heydrich hosted representatives of relevant agencies: from the Ministry of Justice to the General Government, to the Foreign Ministry, to the Four-Year Plan. Much had happened since Göring's initial order. Heydrich reviewed the failure of emigration efforts. He then announced that "the evacuation of

---

[6]Jeremy Noakes and Geoffrey Pridham, eds., *Nazism 1919–1945: A Documentary Reader*, new ed., vol. 3 (Exeter, 2001), pp. 519–20.

[7]Arad et al., *Documents on the Holocaust*, p. 233; Raul Hilberg, *The Destruction of the European Jews*, 3rd ed., vol. 3 (New Haven, CT, 2003), p. 1062.

Jews to the East has now emerged, with the prior permission of the Führer, as a further possible solution instead of emigration." By now it was clear to all what "evacuation to the East" meant.

Europe, Heydrich said, "will be combed from west to east." A chart breaking down Europe's Jews by country, including neutrals such as Sweden, Switzerland, and Ireland, listed 11 million Jews in all, an overestimate of about 2 million. A small percentage would work before dying. "In the course of the Final Solution," Heydrich said, "Jews fit to work will work their way eastward constructing roads. Doubtless the large majority will be eliminated by natural causes. Any final remnant that survives will doubtless consist of the most resistant element. They will have to be dealt with appropriately because otherwise, by natural selection, they would form the germ cell of a new Jewish revival."[8]

Discussion ensued on the status of *Mischlinge* (half or quarter Jews as defined by the Nuremberg Laws), Jews in mixed marriages, on allies such as Hungary that would be reluctant to hand over Jews, and other details. Noteworthy however, was the statement from Dr. Joseph Bühler, Hans Frank's deputy from the General Government. Bühler relayed Frank's insistence that the Final Solution begin in the General Government because of "epidemics being brought on by Jews [and because] the 2½ million Jews in the region were in any case largely unable to work." The conference, in other words, finished not with a discussion of the principle of killing Europe's Jews—this had been settled—but rather a discussion of which Jews would be killed first.

In his Reichstag speech of January 30, 1942, ten days after the Wannsee Conference, Hitler yet again hearkened to his prophecy of 1939, namely, that if the world's Jews plunged the world into war, "the result of this war will be the annihilation of Jewry. . . . The hour will come when the *most evil enemy of all time at least in the last thousand years* will be finished off."[9] His meaning was clear even beyond Germany. Five months later, Chaim Kaplan noted from the Warsaw ghetto, "The Führer is a man who speaks with assurance; he is not one to . . . make meaningless pronouncements. And he has explicitly stated: Whether the war ends in victory or defeat, the Jews of Europe will be wiped off the face of the earth."[10]

11.2 *AKTION REINHARD* AND POLAND'S JEWS

In Search of Method: Chełmno

On August 15, 1941, Himmler traveled to Minsk and observed an execution of about 100 prisoners. He became uneasy. Some victims, wounded at first, had to be finished with pistol shots to the head. Higher SS and Police Leader Erich von dem Bach-Zelewski explained the permanent effect on the German killers. "Reichsführer," he said, "look at the eyes of the men . . . [they] are finished for the rest of their lives. . . ."[11] Himmler reminded his men that this was a war of self-preservation against dangerous vermin. But at the same time, he was sympathetic to the effects of such bloody work on the killers.

---

[8]Protocol in Mark Roseman, *The Wannsee Conference and the Final Solution: A Reconsideration* (New York, 2002), pp. 157–72.

[9]Quoted in Jeffrey Herf, *The Jewish Enemy: Nazi Propaganda During World War II and the Holocaust* (Cambridge, MA, 2006), p. 144.

[10]Abraham I. Katsch, ed., *Scroll of Agony: The Warsaw Diary of Chaim Kaplan* (hereafter *Kaplan Diary*) (New York, 1965), May 30, 1942.

[11]Quoted in Hilberg, *Destruction*, vol. 1, p. 343.

Mass shootings in the USSR continued. But with Himmler's approval, the SS explored more "humane" killing methods. Arthur Nebe, the commander of *Einsatzgruppe B*, tried dynamiting mental patients in bunkers. But some survived the explosions and body parts had to be collected afterward. Gas vans, which killed victims with carbon monoxide gas routed from the engine into the van's interior, were another alternative. They were tried on Soviet POWs in Sachsenhausen concentration camp in early November 1941, and by the following month several were deployed to supplement shooting operations in the USSR.[12]

The Germans settled on gas vans to kill the Jews of the *Warthegau*, most of whom lived in the Łódź ghetto. SS-Major Rolf-Heinz Höppner, the head of the *Warthegau's* Race and Resettlement office, wrote Adolf Eichmann on July 16, 1941, predicting that many Jews in Łódź would starve during the winter. "It must be seriously considered," he said, "whether a liquidation of all Jews not capable of working, with the aid of a fast working means, would not be more humane. . . ."[13] In October, 20,000 deported German Jews arrived in Łódź, exacerbating the problem. At the end of the month the SS established a camp sixty kilometers away near a remote village named Chełmno, the center of which was an old palace.

Chełmno was the first Nazi death camp, built to kill the Jews of the *Warthegau*. The first killings were on December 8, 1941. Prisoners arrived at the palace courtyard and were told that they were en route to a work camp. In groups of fifty, they were ushered to the palace's ground floor, where they were told they would take disinfectant showers. They surrendered clothing and valuables and were forced to the basement where they were packed into the rear of a gas van. The doors were shut, the motor turned on, and the Jews asphyxiated within ten minutes. The dead were transported to mass graves six kilometers away on the edge of the forest. Between the initial killings in December 1941 and the final killings of July 1944, a minimum of 152,000 Jews from the *Warthegau* were murdered at Chełmno. Six Jews sent to Chełmno survived the war.[14]

The *Reinhard* Camps

The General Government's Jews formed the largest concentration in Europe, far too many for gas vans. Stationary gassing, however, was another matter. Already in early 1940, the T-4 "euthanasia" program shipped disabled German patients to gassing centers in the Reich. In August 1941, Hitler issued a stop order for the T-4 program because of unease on the part of ordinary Germans. But the method itself could be relocated and expanded.

On October 13, 1941, Himmler met with SS-General Odilo Globocnik, the Higher SS and Police Leader for the General Government's Lublin district. Both had been occupied with German settlement in the district and wished to rid it of the roughly 320,000 Jews there.[15] After the meeting, T-4 specialists arrived in Lublin. The construction of a gassing facility in Bełżec, south of Lublin, began in late October 1941. The first such camp in the General Government, Bełżec became operational in March 1942. Sobibór, a second gassing camp in the Lublin district, was begun in March 1942 and was complete by mid-April. Construction at Treblinka, north of Warsaw, began in late April 1942 and killing commenced there in July.

---

[12]Mathias Beer, "Die Entwicklung der Gaswagen beim Mord an den Juden," *Vierteljahrshefte für Zeitgeschichte*, 37, no. 3 (July 1987), pp. 403–17.

[13]Quoted in Isaiah Trunk, ed., *Łódź Ghetto: A History* (Bloomington, IN, 2006), p. 229.

[14]On various estimates, see Patrick Montague, *Chełmno and the Holocaust: A History of Hitler's First Death Camp* (Chapel Hill, NC, 2011), pp. 2–3, 183–8.

[15]Bogdan Musial, "The Origins of 'Operation Reinhard': The Decision-Making Process for the Mass Murder of the Jews in the *Generalgouvernement*," *Yad Vashem Studies*, 28 (2000), pp. 113–53.

Bełżec, Sobibór, and Treblinka were the three *Aktion Reinhard* camps, charged with destroying the Jews of the General Government. All were located in remote forested areas near existing railway lines and camouflaged to the outside world. They were small because of their singular and temporary purpose. Almost all Jews were to be killed on arrival, so there was no need for extensive barracks or workshops. Bełżec's dimensions were but 275 × 265 meters; Sobibór and Treblinka measured 400 × 600 meters each. The far larger Auschwitz complex was part of the broader effort to destroy Europe's Jews beyond Poland while providing endless slave labor. Its narrative is different and it is discussed in detail in Chapter 12.

Himmler entrusted *Aktion Reinhard* to Globocnik, described by contemporaries as "fanatically obsessed with the task . . . a courageous man of action."[16] He and his staff, centered in Lublin, moved quickly, improvising as they went. SS-Major Hermann Höfle, who began working under Globocnik in 1940, coordinated with a small staff the day-to-day operations, from deportations to exterminations. Each *Reinhard* camp had a commandant plus a small staff of twenty to thirty-five SS officers. Most had served in the T-4 program. All were ideologically reliable and sworn to secrecy.[17]

The handling of prisoners was left to police auxiliaries. In July 1941, Heydrich ordered the recruitment of anticommunist Soviet POWs, including ethnic Germans, Lithuanians, and Ukrainians, for police and intelligence functions in the USSR. Miserable POW camp conditions made recruiting easy. The recruits ultimately served *Aktion Reinhard*. By January 1942, up to 1,200 were trained at an SS facility in Trawniki near Lublin. They prepared to help with ghetto roundups and to serve as camp guards, and they shot Jewish prisoners as part of their training. "We were not to give the slightest quarter," remembered one. At any one time, they numbered 90 to 120 in each *Reinhard* camp.[18] The camps also had labor details numbering 700 to 1,000 able-bodied Jewish men and women from transports. They were periodically murdered and replaced by new arrivals. Abraham Krzepicki, one of Treblinka's very few escapees, reported that "selection was a constant threat, like a drawn sword over our heads."[19]

Geography determined transport patterns. Jews from the Lublin district were sent primarily to Bełżec and Sobibór. So were Jews from the Galicia district, including Lvov, which Hitler added to the General Government in August 1941 to show Ukrainian nationalists in the Organization of Ukrainian Nationalists (OUN) that Ukraine would not become independent. Jews from the Kraków district were sent mainly to Bełżec or Auschwitz. Jews of the Warsaw and Radom districts went primarily to Treblinka.

But matters were never this neat. When rail transport was unavailable or when the camps were overloaded, other camps took the surplus. In the summer of 1942, when Sobibór was inaccessible thanks to swampy rail bed foundations, more went to Treblinka, which could not handle the daily arrivals expeditiously. German and Ukrainian police also resorted to mass shooting, particularly in the Galicia district, where shooting had been common since Operation Barbarossa. The *Reinhard* camps also murdered Jews from beyond the General Government. Nearly 188,000 from the Białystok district east of the General Government were sent to Treblinka, as were nearly 10,000 from Thrace and Macedonia and 8,000 from the Theresienstadt ghetto in the Protectorate

---

[16]Quoted in Musial, "The Origins of 'Operation Reinhard,'" p. 144.

[17]Figure in Yitzhak Arad, *Belzec, Sobibor, Treblinka: The Operation Reinhard Death Camps* (Bloomington, IN, 1987), pp. 97, 377.

[18]Quote and figures from Peter Black, "Foot Soldiers of the Final Solution: The Trawniki Training Camp and Operation Reinhard," *Holocaust and Genocide Studies*, 25, no.1 (Spring 2001), pp. 1–99.

[19]Quote and figures from Arad, *Belzec, Sobibor, Treblinka*, pp. 97, 377.

MAP 11.1 Death camps in occupied Poland. *Source:* Caplan, Jane, and Nikolaus Wachsmann, eds. *Concentration Camps in Nazi Germany: The New Histories,* (New York: Routledge, 2010).

of Bohemia and Moravia. Nearly 14,000 Jews from Lida, Minsk, and Vilna were shipped to Sobibór after Himmler ordered these ghettos liquidated in June 1943. Thirty-four thousand Jews from the Netherlands were also sent to Sobibór during backups at Auschwitz.[20]

Deportation Procedures

Deportation from ghettos depended on surprise, deceit, and terror. It began when large police units surrounded a ghetto in the early morning hours to prevent escapes. Jewish councilmen were informed of the immediate resettlement of certain numbers of Jews further east where they would, the Germans said, engage in productive labor. Jewish Councils were to inform the ghetto of the resettlement and the items that deportees could take, from luggage (12 to 15 kilograms), to food for the journey, to money and jewelry. Jews were to report voluntarily.

In theory, the Germans first demanded nonproductive or asocial persons and spared those with valid work passes. In practice, German and Ukrainian, Polish, Belarusian, or Baltic police sealed off ghetto blocks and took whomever they could grab to reach their daily quota. Jews who resisted, Jews caught hiding, and Jewish invalids were often shot on the spot. Jewish policemen, though unarmed, were to help in roundups. Their performance varied. In Łódź and Warsaw, they ruthlessly did their jobs to protect themselves and their families from deportation. In Białystok, they provided no help to the Germans despite dire threats and beatings.

Rail transports were nightmares. The Reich Ministry of Transport prioritized the army's needs in the east, providing *Aktion Reinhard* with a limited number of locomotives and boxcars. Each could reasonably accommodate sixty persons, but police forced as many Jews as they could into each, sometimes up to 200. Jews were practically atop one another. Boxcars had a single bucket for bodily functions. Because transports with Jews had lower priority on the German rail net, they were constantly shunted onto on rail sidings and delayed. Even when moving they traveled slowly. Trips that should have taken hours took days.[21] Rail spurs within the *Reinhard* camps, meanwhile, could not accommodate entire transports. Treblinka's could hold but twenty boxcars at a time, Sobibór's only seven. The rest sat outside, locked and guarded, until they were rehitched and hauled in.

Jews suffocated amidst excrement and vomit. "The lack of air," remembered Zvi Baumrin of Lvov, "caused people to cry out loud." Zofia Pollack remembered that on her train to Bełżec, there was "absolutely no air to breathe . . . whoever has hairpins, nails, fasteners starts to bore between the boards to get a little bit of air. . . . People behind us are in much worse plight. . . they are hawking, choking, and driven into utmost despair." Thirst drove Jews mad. "Mothers," Pollack remembered, "hand their children urine to still their thirst."[22] In the winter when the trains were stopped, Poles sold snow to Jews for hundreds of złoty. "I later learned," remembered Abraham Krzepicki, "that there were transports to Treblinka from which only corpses were removed."[23]

Trawniki guards seized valuables as trains waited. En route to Sobibór from Chełm, Kalmen Wewryk recalled that the guards "said openly that we were all being taken to be gassed. . . . They ordered us to hand over to them all gold, money, jewelry."[24] "They told us," remembered

---

[20]For deportation figures to the *Reinhard* camps, see Arad, *Belzec, Sobibor, Treblinka*, pp. 138–49, 383–398.

[21]Alfred Mierzejewski, *The Most Valuable Asset of the Reich: A History of the German National Railway*, vol. 2 (Chapel Hill, NC, 2000), pp. 119–122.

[22]Quoted in Simone Gigliotti, ed., *The Train Journey: Transit, Captivity, and Witnessing in the Holocaust* (New York, 2009), pp. 98–99, 106.

[23]Quoted in Arad, *Belzec, Sobibor, Treblinka*, p. 64.

[24]Kalmen Wewryk, *To Sobibor and Back: An Eyewitness Account* (Montreal, 1999), p. 19.

Ada Lichtman, who was sent to Sobibór from Jarosław, "that we would not be needing them anymore . . . 'because you are all going to die.' We did not believe them. . . . [W]e thought it was just one of their tricks to take everything from us. We could not believe we were going to die; not in our wildest imagination. . . ."[25]

Murder Procedures

Most camp records were destroyed. Our information comes mainly from the very few Jewish camp escapees and from SS officers later tried by postwar West German courts. Camp personnel used deception to kill arrivals immediately. As boxcars entered the camp, Ukrainian guards emptied disoriented arrivals, ranging from children to the elderly, onto platforms using whips, rifle butts, and sporadic shootings. The prisoners, counted at their embarkation points, were never registered in the camps. Work Jews removed the corpses of those who had suffocated, sorted luggage, then washed feces and urine from the cars for their subsequent use.

In the reception area, arrivals learned that they were in a transit camp en route to another destination. No gas chambers were visible—they were isolated from the rest of the camp and surrounded by barbed wire fences camouflaged with thick branches. "The camp looked quite friendly," recalled Jozef Wins, the sole survivor from his transport to Sobibór. "There were red roofs and gravel paths."[26] Treblinka's reception area had a fake railway station with a fake clock, fake ticket office, and flowerbeds. "You will be taken to a place where you will prosper," announced SS Sergeant Hermann Michel to arrivals in Sobibór:

> You must keep yourselves clean. . . . [It is] desirable that hygiene precautions are taken. This is why you will shortly undress and shower. Your clothes and luggage will be guarded. . . . Valuables such as gold, money and watches must be handed in at the counter over there. You must remember carefully the number the man behind the counter calls out, so that you will be able to retrieve your possessions more easily afterwards. . . . There is no need to bring a towel and soap; everything will be provided. . . .[27]

Such announcements after horrible rail journeys sometimes brought relieved applause. Invalids unable to walk were offered medical care in the camp infirmary. They were placed on carts, moved to the rear of the camp, and shot.

After bundling their clothes and shoes, Jews proceeded naked to a "tube"—a fenced, camouflaged passage linking the camp reception area with the extermination area. Sobibór's tube was 150 meters long. Treblinka's was decorated with flowers. Men and women with children proceeded separately to preserve the deception of shower baths. A detail of work Jews sheared hair from female arrivals. It was packed in bales for use as industrial filters or yarn for winter socks. Ukrainian guards hurried Jews through the tube, often with beatings. "Faster, faster," one guard in Treblinka yelled, "the water is getting cold and others have to use the showers too."[28]

Gas chamber buildings were disguised as showers with signs, pleasant-colored paint, exterior flower boxes, interior tiles, water pipes, and showerheads. Once they crammed the multiple chambers full, the guards bolted the doors. A combustion engine outside the building pumped carbon monoxide in through separate pipes. Final realization triggered screaming. Within twenty

---

[25]Jules Schelvis, *Sobibor: A History of a Nazi Death Camp* (New York, 2007), p. 49.

[26]Quoted in Schelvis, *Sobibor*, p. 76.

[27]Quoted in Schelvis, *Sobibor*, p. 70.

[28]Quoted in Arad, *Belzec, Sobibor, Treblinka*, p. 86.

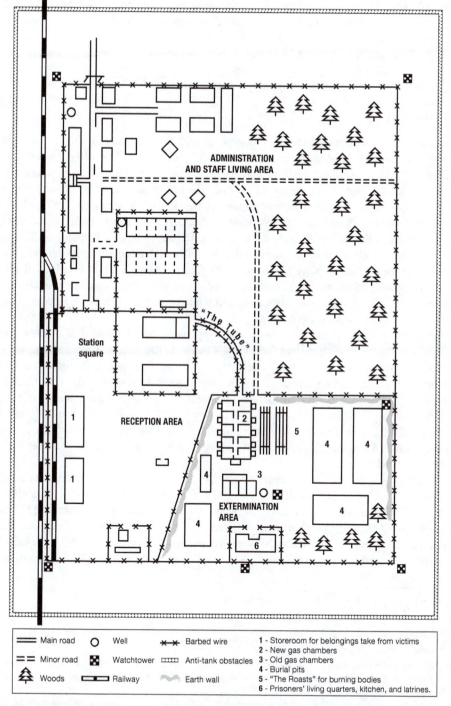

ADMINISTRATION
AND STAFF LIVING AREA

"The Tube"

Station
square

RECEPTION AREA

EXTERMINATION
AREA

═══ Main road	○ Well	✕—✕ Barbed wire
══ Minor road	◼ Watchtower	▭ Anti-tank obstacles
🌲 Woods	▭◼▭ Railway	〰 Earth wall

1 - Storeroom for belongings take from victims
2 - New gas chambers
3 - Old gas chambers
4 - Burial pits
5 - "The Roasts" for burning bodies
6 - Prisoners' living quarters, kitchen, and latrines.

MAP 11.2   Diagram of Treblinka.   *Source:* Arad, Yitzhak, and *Belzec, Sobibor, Treblinka: The Operation Reinhard Death Camps* (Bloomington, IN: Indiana University Press,1987), p. 39. Reprinted with permission of Indiana University Press.

minutes all in the chambers were dead. "It is quite amazing," remembered Sobibór gas technician Erich Bauer, "how oblivious the Jews were that they were going to die. There was hardly ever any resistance. The Jews became suspicious only after they had entered the gas chamber. But at that point, there was no way back."[29] Kalmen Wewryk, a Jew who served on a work detail in Sobibór, explained it similarly. "You could tell most Jews one thousand times what was really going on there," he remembered, "and they wouldn't believe you."[30]

After the Killing

Separate Jewish work details removed the bodies, cleaned the chambers of filth, and dragged the dead to burial pits. "The chambers," remembered Rudolf Reder, one of two Jews in Bełżec to survive the war, "were so crammed full of people that even after they had died, they were still upright." SS-Sergeant Karl Schluch from Bełżec added that "the bodies were at least partially covered in excrement and urine. . . . Some had their eyes closed, others still opened, their eyes rolled upward."[31]

Other Jewish workers removed gold teeth with tongs and searched body cavities for other valuables. Back in the reception area, work Jews sorted mountains of belongings. They separated bed linens, clothing, watches, pens, toiletries, cash, and small valuables hidden in clothing seams. In theory, all property belonged to the German state. Freight cars hauled it to the Trawniki camp. Yet SS officers and auxiliary guards stole what they could. SS officers sent full suitcases home. Auxiliaries, flush with cash and trinkets, traded with nearby Poles. The area around Treblinka experienced a gold rush.

Aktion Reinhard was hurried. Camps began operating before construction was complete. The initial gas chamber buildings had timber walls and were too small to accommodate the transports. Combustion engines sometimes stalled, prolonging victims' agony. Treblinka was so overwhelmed by transports in the summer of 1942—some days in August saw 10,000 to 12,000 Jews arrive—that decomposing bodies, clothes, and belongings were strewn throughout the reception area. Himmler insisted on speed regardless. "I hereby order," he commanded in mid-July 1942, "that the resettlement of the entire Jewish population of the General Government be carried out and completed by December 31, 1942."[32] In all three camps, larger brick gas chamber buildings replaced the wooden ones.

Death tolls from *Aktion Reinhard* remain in dispute, but all estimates defy imagination. Bełżec killed between 434,000 and 600,000 Jews between March 1942 and its closure in December.[33] Sobibor was operational from May 1942 to October 1943. Over 213,000 might have been gassed there; its death toll would have been higher save for suspended rail travel.[34] Treblinka killed at least 713,000 Jews between its opening in July 1942 and the end of that year. By the time it ceased operating in August 1943, it killed as many as 900,000.[35] These figures do

---

[29]Quoted in Schelvis, *Sobibor*, p. 102.

[30]Kalmen Wewryk, *To Sobibor and Back*, p. 22.

[31]Quoted in Schelvis, *Sobibor*, pp. 105, 106.

[32]Noakes and Pridham, eds., *Nazism, 1919–1945*, vol. 3, p. 566.

[33]Competing figures in Peter Witte and Stephen Tyas, "A New Document on the Deportation and Murder of Jews During 'Einsatz Reinhardt' 1942," *Holocaust and Genocide Studies*, 15, no. 3 (Winter 2001), p. 472, and Arad, *Belzec, Sobibor, Treblinka*, pp. 127, 383–389.

[34]Competing figures in Witte and Tyas, "A New Document," p. 472; Arad, *Belzec, Sobibor, Treblinka*, pp. 148, 390–1; and Schelvis, *Sobibor*, pp. 1, 28.

[35]Competing figures in Witte and Tyas, "A New Document," p. 472; Arad, *Belzec, Sobibor, Treblinka*, pp. 392–7, 141–6; and Witold Chrostowski, *Extermination Camp Treblinka* (Portland, OR, 2004), pp. 100–1.

not count Jews killed in ghetto roundups and mass shootings, or Jews who died in work camps like Majdanek, where in 1942 alone, at least 25,000 were killed.[36] In January 1942, the Germans counted nearly 2.3 million Jews in the General Government. By the end of the year they counted fewer than 300,000.[37] By June 1943, no ghettos in the General Government remained.

Aktion 1005

The *Aktion Reinhard* camps lacked crematoria to dispose of victims' bodies. They used burial pits. Initially Sobibór had a single pit, sixty meters long and some seven meters deep. By June 1942, it was filled and covered in sand. Horribly, the heat caused the bodies to bloat and break through the surface. More pits were dug. In Treblinka, which did not begin functioning until July 1942, the Germans had multiple pits excavated from the start. But by October, army officers based miles away complained that "the air is saturated with the unbearable stench of bodies."[38]

In June 1942, the Germans began destroying the physical evidence. Gestapo chief Heinrich Müller code-named the obliteration of mass graves *Aktion 1005*. He assigned the task to SS-Colonel Paul Blobel, an *Einsatzgruppe* officer who oversaw mass shootings at Babi Yar months earlier. Blobel developed a disposal system at Chełmno. Work Jews exhumed bodies and piled them on "grilles" made of crisscrossed railroad track with dried wood soaked in gasoline underneath. Beginning in the fall of 1942, Blobel's team supervised exhumations and cremations at Bełżec and Sobibór. In early 1943, they began work at Treblinka. In June 1943, they moved east to excavate mass graves and incinerate bodies in the USSR.

At Bełżec and Sobibór, the cremation of well over 500,000 bodies proceeded around the clock from November 1942 to March 1943. Teams burned 2,000 bodies in a twenty-four-hour period.[39] Fires could be seen and smelled miles away. Grinding machines pulverized the remaining bits of bone; work Jews sifted through pulverized bone and ash for hidden gold and jewels. Leon Weliczker of Lvov was one of very few work Jews who escaped. "After grinding the bones," he testified later, "we used to throw the ashes up in the air so that they would disappear, replace the earth on the graves, and plant seeds, so that nobody could recognize that there ever was a grave there."[40]

The Work Camps

Jews who survived *Aktion Reinhard* by the end of 1942 did so because they were able to work in their ghettos with special permits or because they were sent to SS work camps in the General Government. It was Himmler's concession to the army, which needed the production, especially with nearly 1.7 million Polish laborers sent to the Reich by 1944.[41] Frank's deputy Bühler wrote on May 5, 1942, that "there are plans to dissolve the Jewish ghettos, keep the Jews capable of work, and to deport the rest further east. The Jews capable of work are to be lodged in numerous large concentration camps that are now in the process of being constructed."[42]

---

[36]Witte and Tyas, "A New Document," p. 471.

[37]Arad, *Belzec, Sobibor, Treblinka*, pp. 129–30.

[38]Quoted in Shmuel Spector, "*Aktion 1005*: Effacing the Murder of Millions," *Holocaust and Genocide Studies*, 5, no. 2 (1990), p. 161.

[39]Figure in Spector, "*Aktion 1005*," pp. 161–2.

[40]Israel, Ministry of Justice, *The Trial of Adolf Eichmann: Record of Proceedings in the District Court of Jerusalem*, vol. 1 (Jerusalem, 1992), p. 370.

[41]Figures in Ulrich Herbert, *Hitler's Foreign Workers: Enforced Labor in Germany Under the Third Reich* (New York, 1997), pp. 1, 61–92, 198, 278–82.

[42]Quoted in Browning, *Nazi Policy, Jewish Workers, German Killers*, p. 75.

The General Government's work camps were notorious even by SS standards. Majdanek was the largest of many in the Lublin district. Himmler ordered it built in July 1941 as part of *Generalplan Ost* for Soviet POWs and Polish and Ukrainian civilians, but after January 1942, Jews comprised most prisoners sent there, mostly from the General Government but also from Białystok, the Reich, and western Europe. They worked in SS and private enterprises, from clothing to armaments. By the summer of 1942, 17,000 Jews reached Majdanek, and by the summer of 1943, Globocnik boasted 45,000 Jewish workers in the Lublin district. Inadequate facilities made the camp breeding grounds for typhus. By October 1942, Majdanek had gas chambers to kill those incapable of work, and indeed the camp served as a murder site for some 24,000 arriving Jews in November and December after Bełżec was closed.[43]

The Płazów camp near Kraków, built in 1942 was equally notorious. Its sadistic commandant, Amon Göth, served under Globocnik in *Aktion Reinhard* and took control of Płazów in February 1943. The camp held 25,000 prisoners at its peak. Surviving inmates said that Göth personally shot inmates at random, that he had entire work groups murdered for sport, and that his dogs were trained to kill inmates. Under his command, 8,000 to 12,000 were killed in Płazów, up to 500 by Göth personally. Living under Göth, remembered his Jewish maid Helen Hirsch, was "almost like living under the gallows twenty-four hours a day."[44]

11.3 WORD LEAKS: FROM THE GHETTOS TO THE ALLIES

What Jews Understood

Aktion Reinhard began when German and auxiliary police surrounded the Lublin ghetto the night of March 16, 1942. SS Lieutenant Josef Worthoff, the Gestapo chief in Lublin, told the Jewish Council that 1,600 Jews would be evacuated each day for work in the east. The first trainload left the next day. On March 31, Worthoff ordered half of the Jewish Council, including Chairman Henryk Bekker, deported. They were, Worthoff said, needed in the new location. Bekker brought no luggage. He wore his prayer shawl instead. Did he know of Bełżec? Probably not. But he demonstrated the grim fear that accompanied deportation. Many ghettos in the General Government, though miserable, had achieved some stasis by 1942. However tenuous, they provided shelter. The violence and uncertainty of deportation were terrifying. Many did not expect a happy end.

Seventeen-year-old Halina Nelken survived hard labor and hunger in the Kraków ghetto. But contemplating the fate of Kraków's first 5,000 evacuees was worse. She wrote in her diary for June 4, 1942,

> At seven o'clock, we heard screams and weeping on the streets, and from the corner window we saw these unfortunate people with bundles on their back and children in their arms being pushed and beaten with rifle butts. . . . Rifle fire was heard throughout the night. . . . No news of the transport except that the train left the station for the East, the people in the overcrowded, locked boxcars were fainting for lack of water and air. . . . In Mszana Dolna [southeast of Kraków] people were . . . forced to dig a mass grave before being shot on the spot. And this was supposedly just a resettlement to Russia or the Ukraine for work![45]

---

[43]On workers, see Barbara Schwindt, *Das Konzentrations- und Vernichtungslager Majdanek: Funktionswandel im Kontext der "Endlösung"* (Würzburg, 2005), pp. 156, 291. On gassing, see Black, "Foot Soldiers of the Final Solution," p. 22.

[44]David M. Crowe, *Oskar Schindler: The Untold Account of His Life, Wartime Activities and the True Story Behind The List* (Cambridge, MA, 2004), pp. 237, 256–60.

[45]Halina Nelken, *And Yet, I Am Here!* (Amherst, 1999), June 1, 1942, June 4, 1942, and June 8, 1942.

In Lvov, the initial roundup of March 1942 took 15,000 Jews. Officially, only "asocials" were to be evacuated, but German and Ukrainian police seized orphans, the elderly, and many with work permits. By July, word reached Lvov about deportations from Kraków and its environs to a place called Bełżec. "For the first time," remembered Rabbi David Kahane, "we heard about towns declared as *Judenrein* [Jew-free]. . . . Stories circulated about endless trains packed with Jews pulling up daily at the Bełżec station and disappearing. . . ."[46] In August, German and Ukrainian police seized 60,000 Jews from Lvov in a lethal three-week rampage. They killed hospital patients; reverted to mass shootings; and hanged Dr. Henryk Landesberg, the Jewish Council chairman, along with numerous Jewish policemen. "By then," Kahane wrote, everyone saw the fate . . . intended for us."[47]

Deportations from Łódź

The terror was most sickening in the Łódź ghetto because of Jewish cooperation there. Łódź was not part of *Aktion Reinhard*. Located in the *Warthegau*, most of its Jews died in Chełmno. Jewish Elder Chaim Rumkowski obliged the Germans more than other Jewish leaders in hopes of preserving what he could of his working ghetto. The Germans told him of pending deportations in December 1941. He created a resettlement commission to determine who would go.

In the first half of 1942, welfare recipients, recently arrived German Jews, and those who had violated the ghetto criminal code were deported. By Rumkowski's orders, Jews hiding other Jews—even relatives—would be deported as well. Jews not appearing voluntarily would be deported without luggage. The Germans cut food supplies to starve Jews from hiding places. Łódź's Jewish police provided quotas of Jews without German police having to enter the ghetto. Mournful scenes ensued as starving families trudged to the assembly point. German Jews, who had never seen squalor like that in Łódź, often reported voluntarily, assuming that nothing could be worse.

Łódź's Jews hoped that each wave of deportation in 1942 would be the last. Yet it also became apparent that something was wrong. On September 1, 1942, German police entered the ghetto to take hospital patients. "The fashion in which the Germans took away the patients," wrote Dr. Leon Szykier, "left no doubt at all. . . . They threw them down steps, they took them off operating tables, they beat them and laid the patients on top of one another in the trucks. No one knew where they were being taken, but for everyone it was clear that they were being taken to death."[48]

Clearer still was the September deportation of children up to ten years old and adults over sixty-five. Chaim Rumkowski's infamous public appeal of September 4 for the ghetto's children and elderly is one of humanity's most infamous speeches:

> The ghetto has been dealt a grievous blow. They demand that we give them . . . the children and old people. . . . [A]s difficult as it will be, we must make ourselves responsible for implementing the decree. I must carry out the grim, bloody surgery. I must amputate limbs to save the body! I must take away children, and if I do not, others too may be taken. . . . When a decree has been imposed, one must weigh and measure who should be saved and who can be saved. . . . I raise my broken, trembling hands to you and beg: give me the sacrifices in order to prevent further sacrifices, in order to protect this community of a hundred thousand Jews.[49]

---

[46]David Kahane, *Lvov Ghetto Diary* (Amherst, 1990), p. 54.

[47]Kahane, *Lvov Ghetto Diary,* p. 73.

[48]Quoted in Trunk, ed., *Łódź Ghetto*, p. 240.

[49]Rumkowski's speech recounted in Josef Zelkowicz, *In Those Terrible Days: Writings from the Łódź Ghetto* (Jerusalem, 2002), pp. 280–3.

Mordechai Chaim Rumkowksi making a speech in the Łódź ghetto, date unknown.   *Source*: United States Holocaust Memorial Museum.

Mothers holding children wailed. In the days ahead, parents spoiled their children with extra food. Some discussed killing them with their own hands. Mothers hid with their children in attics and cellars. Jewish police, whose own children were exempt, moved building to building, tearing children from parents. German police entered the ghetto, publicly shooting one mother and her four-year-old daughter as an example. Some mothers boarded trains with their children. "Now the ghetto is no longer taut. . .," wrote Josef Zelkowicz. "Now it convulses. The whole ghetto is one huge convulsion. . . . Everyone is prepared to die then and there, as the terror and horror are beyond bearing. . . . They do not want to die, but staying alive is so, so difficult." Of the 162,680 Jews in the Łódź ghetto in January 1942, 89,446 remained by October. The Germans used it as a textile-producing labor camp until mid-1944. Then they deported the rest.[50]

Alerting the World

Because of delays in Treblinka's construction, deportations from the Warsaw ghetto began late—not until July 1942. Zionists and Bundists there maintained contacts with other ghettos. The arrival in Warsaw in January of an Orthodox Jew named "Szlamek" (Yakov Grojanowski), an escapee from Chełmno, provided detailed evidence of extermination. So did steady news—from March through May 1942—of evacuations from Lublin, Lvov, and other ghettos, and the disappearance of these Jews at Bełżec. *Oyneg Shabes*, Emanuel Ringelblum's underground archiving team, collected news as it arrived. Warsaw's underground Yiddish press reported the findings. Would Warsaw's Jews suffer the same fate? "Everyone is terrified," wrote Abraham Lewin of *Oyneg Shabes* in May 1942. "Rumors have been circulating. . . . The abyss is getting closer to each one of us. . . ."[51]

---

[50]Quote in Zelkowicz, *In Those Terrible Days*, pp. 304–5. Population figures in Trunk, ed., *Łódź Ghetto*, p. 267.

[51]Abraham Lewin, *A Cup of Tears: A Diary of the Warsaw Ghetto* (Cambridge, MA, 1989), May 17, 1942.

Oyneg Shabes hoped to alert the world. It could only do so through its contacts in the Polish Home Army, which maintained contact with the Polish government-in-exile in London under General Władysław Sikorski. The Home Army's Bureau of Information had a Jewish Affairs section that collected intelligence from Jewish groups and on its own. Almost as soon as *Aktion Reinhard* began, it sent news to the government-in-exile. The Sikorski government initially shared this news with representatives of Poland's Jewish parties in London and with British intelligence. It also used the information for its own publications and broadcasts back to Poland.

On learning of mass shootings in the USSR in 1941, the British publicized nothing. Now on June 2, 1942, the British Broadcasting Corporation (BBC) broadcast news of mass murder in Poland, mentioned Chełmno and Bełżec, and promised retribution. Ringelblum felt vindicated. "They told about everything we know so well," he wrote. "[We have] fulfilled a great historical mission. [We have] alarmed the world to our fate and perhaps saved hundreds of thousands of Polish Jews from extermination. . . . We have struck the enemy a hard blow. We have revealed his satanic plan to annihilate Polish Jewry, a plan he wished to complete in silence. . . . And if England keeps its word and turns to formidable massive attacks . . . then perhaps we shall be saved."[52]

But would they? *The Daily Telegraph* and other British newspapers reported in June 1942 that more than 1 million Jews in Europe had been murdered and that the Nazis' aim was to "wipe the [Jewish] race from the European continent."[53] Other papers including the *New York Times* followed but buried the story in the middle of the paper, assuming that it may be exaggerated. Dignitaries, mostly Jewish, spoke out in Britain and the United States, culminating on July 21 with a rally in New York's Madison Square Garden organized by Rabbi Stephen Wise's American Jewish Congress. Twenty thousand attended. But senior government figures were circumspect. President Roosevelt sent a message to the rally promising nothing more concrete than "a day of reckoning" for the perpetrators.[54]

The war went badly for the Allies in mid-1942. The Battle of Midway in early June was the first Allied victory in the Pacific after a string of defeats. The Allies had no forces in Europe. In the USSR, the Germans drove toward the Caucuses. And in North Africa, the German capture of Tobruk on June 21 opened Egypt to invasion. The Grand Mufti of Jerusalem, in Berlin since November 1941, incited Arabs to rise against the British. "Do you not know," said broadcasts via German radio, "that the British are the servants of the Jews?"[55] Now was not the time to aggravate the Jewish question. Victor Cavendish-Bentinck, who oversaw British intelligence, later said that the stories from Poland were exaggerations designed "to stoke us up." "I feel certain," he wrote, "that we are making a mistake in publicly giving credence to this gas chamber story."[56] Press coverage of the Jews' fate in Poland slowed to a trickle.

The Polish government-in-exile never pressed matters. The fate of Poland's Jews was a small part of its broader narrative of Polish suffering, which included the killing of Polish intelligentsia and resistors, the mass displacement of Poles, the use of Poles for forced labor, and the

---

[52]Jacob Sloan, ed., *Notes from the Warsaw Ghetto: The Journal of Emanuel Ringelblum* (New York, 1958), pp. 295–6.

[53]Quoted in Walter Laqueur, *The Terrible Secret: Suppression of the Truth About Hitler's "Final Solution"* (New York, 1980), p. 74.

[54]Quoted in Robert N. Rosen, *Saving the Jews: Franklin D. Roosevelt and the Holocaust* (New York, 2006), p. 229.

[55]Quoted in Jeffrey Herf, *Nazi Propaganda for the Arab World* (New Haven, CT, 2009), p. 126.

[56]Quoted in Laqueur, *The Terrible Secret*, p. 83; Richard Breitman, *Official Secrets: What the Nazis Planned, What the British and Americans Knew* (New York, 1998), p. 120.

destruction of Poland itself. Many in Sikorski's government still maintained grudges dating to World War I. "The Polish nation," said one official in May 1942, "will never forgive the Jews for the 'neutrality' they demonstrated with regard to [Lvov] in 1918."[57] Five percent of a major June 9 radio broadcast by Sikorski dealt with Poland's Jews. He mentioned nothing of deportations or death camps and reduced the Jewish death toll to "tens of thousands."[58] Nor did this broadcast call on Poles to help. Once deportations began from Warsaw, the Sikorski government actively suppressed arriving news.

11.4 WARSAW: FROM DEPORTATION TO UPRISING

The Great Deportation

Meanwhile, the older Jewish establishment in Warsaw could not imagine impending doom. Yitzhak Schipper, a prominent Jewish historian, argued in April 1942 that it was "impossible to wipe out a population of a half million."[59] Jewish Council Chairman Adam Czerniaków worked tirelessly to preserve the ghetto. He intervened for arrested Jews, improved sanitary conditions, provided quarters for arriving German Jews, and found food for orphans. As late as May 1942, he began a playground construction project. "These are tragic times," he noted in a June 7 speech, "but we must stand firm. Whenever we hear children laughing and singing our windows will be open to let in the sound. This will give us hope and courage to go and fight for the future."[60]

Treblinka was complete in mid-July. Rumors of waiting trains brought panic. "A day full of foreboding," Czerniaków wrote in his diary on Saturday, July 18. "Rumors that the deportations will start on Monday evening. . . ." He asked German authorities for clarity. On July 20, Gestapo officials denied to Czerniaków that deportations were even considered.[61] Two days later, at 10:00 a.m., Globocnik's deputy Hermann Höfle entered Czerniaków's office. All Jews regardless of age, Höfle ordered, would be deported to the east, 6,000 per day, seven days a week, starting that very afternoon. Czerniaków was to post the order. Czerniaków took cyanide the next day. "They are demanding of me," he wrote to his wife, "that I kill the children of my people with my own hands. Nothing is left for me but to die." "My act," he wrote to the Jewish Council, "will show the truth to all and will perhaps lead them to the right path of action."[62]

But Czerniaków's act could not stop the horrifying whirlwind known as the Great Deportation. From July 22 to September 21, 1942, the Germans deported 265,000 Jewish men, women, and children from Warsaw to Treblinka. Street by street, house by house, shop by shop, thousands per day were forced toward an assembly point, known as the *Umschlagplatz*, where they were guarded and packed into boxcars. Police minimized resistance with terror, shooting

---

[57]Quoted in David Engel, "Lwów, 1918: The Transmutation of a Symbol and Its Legacy in the Holocaust," in *Contested Memories: Poles and Jews During the Holocaust and Its Aftermath*, ed. Joshua D. Zimmerman (East Brunswick, NJ, 2003), pp. 32–46.

[58]Quoted in David Engel, *In the Shadow of Auschwitz: The Polish Government-in-Exile and the Jews, 1939–1942* (Chapel Hill, NC, 1987), p. 180.

[59]Quoted in Yisrael Gutman, *The Jews of Warsaw, 1939–1943: Ghetto, Underground, Revolt* (Bloomington, IN, 1982), p. 167.

[60]Michael Zylberberg, *The Warsaw Diary 1939–1945* (London, 1969), p. 52.

[61]Raul Hilberg et al., eds. *The Warsaw Diary of Adam Czerniaków: Prelude to Doom* (New York, 1999), July 18 and 20, 1942.

[62]Quoted in Barbara Engelking and Jacek Leociak, *The Warsaw Ghetto: A Guide to the Perished City* (New Haven, CT, 2009), p. 164.

10,000 Jews during roundups, and lured starving Jews with promises of bread and jam. Nothing could stop the lethal momentum, not even German businessmen who needed ghetto workers for army contracts. Workshops became traps when police entered. Jews frantically tried to hide or find safe work. "Jewish Warsaw," Chaim Kaplan wrote in his diary, "is in its death throes." "We shall not," he added, "be privileged to witness the downfall of the Nazis."[63] His final entry was on August 4.

Some Jews protected their families, some abandoned them, and most lost them amid the mayhem. Most surrendered themselves to the unknown. In August 1942, Janusz Korczak, a revered children's advocate who ran an orphanage, accompanied his young charges to the trains along with his staff. Such adults, wrote Ringelblum, "knew what awaited them at the *Umschlagplatz*, but held that . . . they could not let the children go alone and must go to their death with them."[64] On the last day, Jewish policemen, most of whom ruthlessly helped round up Jews to preserve their own safety, were taken. "When news of that tragedy reached me," remembered one Jewish resistor, "I didn't shed a tear."[65]

The Jewish Combat Organization

On July 28, after a week of deportations, Zionist youth leaders founded the Jewish Combat Organization, known by its Polish initials, ŻOB. Leaders included Mordechai Anielewicz, a twenty-three-year-old member of *Hashomer Hatza'ir*, and Yitzhak Zuckerman, a twenty-seven-year-old veteran of *He-halutz*. Information arrived from Treblinka in August and September from youth group escapees who returned to warn their brethren. One account, recorded by *Oyneg Shabes*, ran ninety pages.[66]

The ŻOB posted the truth of Treblinka and called on Jews to resist the roundups. Yet events were too relentless for general comprehension. "To our astonishment and bitterness," Zuckerman remembered, "our appeal fell on deaf ears then. They still didn't believe."[67] "Everyone, clung to the hope that perhaps the journey would not end in death," wrote another observer, ". . . and so people took warm clothing, shoes, a towel, soap, a spoon—the absolute basics."[68] But the ŻOB had no plan for resistance either. The youth groups, Anielewicz now understood, wrongly spent the previous years on cultural work instead of procuring weapons. "The entire store of arms in the ghetto at that time," remembered Zuckerman, "consisted of one revolver!"[69]

When the Great Deportation ended in September 1942, 73,000 Jews were left. Worse, 99.1 percent of all children ranging from infants to nine-year-olds—nearly 51,000 in all—had been deported.[70] Agony, anger, and shame pervaded. "Why did everything come so easily to the enemy?" asked Ringelblum. "Why didn't the hangman suffer a single casualty?"[71] The ŻOB debated whether it was better to set the ghetto aflame or to regroup, find weapons, and fight the

---

[63]*Kaplan Diary*, July 26, 1942, August 2, 1942.

[64]Sloan, ed., *Notes from the Warsaw Ghetto*, p. 322.

[65]Yitzhak Zuckerman, *A Surplus of Memory: Chronicle of the Warsaw Ghetto Uprising* (Berkeley, CA, 1993), p. 245.

[66]Gutman, *Jews of Warsaw*, p. 222; Samuel D. Kassow, *Who Will Write Our History? Emanuel Ringelblum, the Warsaw Ghetto, and the Oyneg Shabes Archive* (Bloomington, IN, 2007), pp. 309–10.

[67]Quoted in Gutman, *Jews of Warsaw*, p. 237.

[68]Quoted in Engelking and Leociak, *Warsaw Ghetto*, p. 701.

[69]Quoted in Gutman, *Jews of Warsaw*, p. 238.

[70]Figures in Gutman, *Jews of Warsaw*, pp. 212–13; Kassow, *Who Will Write Our History?* p. 308.

[71]Sloan, ed., *Notes from the Warsaw Ghetto*, p. 310.

Mordechai Anielewicz, probably from 1938 or 1939.   *Source:* Oasis/Photos 12/Alamy.

next deportation to the end. It chose the latter. It soon numbered 600 young men and women, not counting 250 members of *Betar*.[72] In the following weeks, it wrested control of the ghetto, assassinating Jewish collaborators, including Jewish Council members and police as well as informants. It posted manifestos: "Not even one single Jew will ever again perish in Treblinka."[73]

Poles and the Destruction of the Jews

The record of ordinary Poles during the catastrophe is mixed. During the Great Deportation, many were strangely indifferent. Some actually sunbathed on the banks of the Vistula River as Jews were hauled to Treblinka.[74] Yet thousands of Jews during and after the Great Deportation began using Polish underground contacts to flee to the Aryan side and locate hiding places. Families sent children (as well as payments) to Polish families. Adult Jews could leave with work passes and not return. Others procured false papers. One historian estimates that eventually a "secret city" of perhaps 28,000 hidden Jews lived on the Aryan side, helped by Poles who either faced the death penalty by hiding Jews or who knew but kept quiet about Jews in hiding.[75]

Life on the Aryan side remained hazardous. Polish blackmailers—known as *szmalcovniki*—were a small percentage of the Polish population. But they blackmailed the same Jews repeatedly, and once they knew of a hard-found hiding place, it was no longer safe. Ita Dimant referred to them as "a whole cloud of locusts" and noted that shortly after leaving the ghetto, "we no longer had any rings, or watches, or shoes. We already had nothing." In some cases, Polish policemen demanded thousands of złoty for their silence. Many Jews actually returned to the ghetto owing to the stress of denunciation or because they ran out of money. "There

---

[72]Figure in Engelking and Leociak, *Warsaw Ghetto*, pp. 760–2.

[73]Quoted in Gutman, *Jews of Warsaw*, pp. 300, 305.

[74]Barbara Engelking, "Between Poles and Jews in Nazi-Occupied Warsaw," in Zimmerman, ed., *Contested Memories*, p. 49.

[75]Figures in Gunnar S. Paulsson, *Secret City: The Hidden Jews of Warsaw, 1940–1945* (New Haven, CT, 2002), pp. 5, 57ff.

is no way to make it over there," said Eugenia Szajn-Lewin. "People lack money to pay off the blackmailers."[76]

Despite the obstacles, some Poles of conscience worked to save Jews. In October 1942, socialist and democratic members of the Polish underground created Żegota—the Council for Aid to the Jews. Żegota undertook many, albeit belated, functions. Through the Jewish underground, Żegota members made contact with Jewish parents in the larger ghettos; smuggled children; and placed them in convents, orphanages, and private homes. It also printed false identity papers. By the spring of 1943, Żegota might have provided shelter for 4,000 Jews, mostly in Warsaw.[77] Żegota also called for the execution of blackmailers by the Polish underground. As one underground newspaper put it, "[t]he Germans will someday answer . . . for what they have done to the Jews. Let us not suppose, however, that our turn will not also come to give an accounting for our attitude to what happened before our eyes."[78]

Jan Karski's Mission

Jan Karski was a Polish Home Army courier who collected information from underground groups. In October 1942, in the wake of the Great Deportation, he met Leon Feiner of the Bund and Zionist leader Menachem Kirschenbaum. They arranged for Karski to see the Warsaw ghetto. Thirty years later, Karski could barely describe it. "It was not a part of humanity," he remembered, "I never saw such things." "Every day counts," Feiner and Kirschenbaum told him. "The Allies cannot treat this war only from a purely military strategic standpoint. . . . We will not survive. . . . We contributed to humanity—we gave scientists for thousands of years. We originated great religions. We are humans. Do you understand it? Do you understand it? Never happened before in History, what is happening to our people now."[79]

Karski arrived in London in November. His report was searing. "The Polish Jews," he said, "solemnly appeal to the Polish and Allied governments to undertake *extraordinary* measures in an attempt to stop the extermination." They called, he said, for an Allied announcement that their war aims included an end to Jewish extermination, for information on Nazi deeds to be broadcast to Germany, for the bombing of German targets if Germans failed to force their government to cease, for money in the hope that remaining Jews might be ransomed, and for Sikorski's personal intervention with the Home Army so that it would provide weapons to Jewish fighters. "The Jews are Polish citizens," the message said, "They are entitled to have weapons. . . ."[80] Polish leaders were noncommittal.

By now, a report from Gerhart Riegner of the World Jewish Congress in Geneva—that Hitler planned to murder all of Europe's Jews—had reached London and Washington. It was made public in late November (see Chapter 12). Karski was an eyewitness to the crime, and a Pole who could not be accused of exaggeration. Regardless, British Foreign Secretary Anthony Eden politely rejected all requests. In 1943, the Polish government sent Karski to the United States.

---

[76]Quoted in Engelking and Leociak, *Warsaw Ghetto*, pp. 741, 742; Paulssen, *Secret City*, p. 84.

[77]Figure in Paulssen, *Secret City*, pp. 207–8.

[78]Quoted in Gunnar S. Paulssen, "Ringelblum Revisited: Polish-Jewish Relations in Occupied Warsaw, 1940–1945," in Zimmerman, ed., *Contested Memories*, p. 185.

[79]Claude Lanzmann, *Shoah: The Complete Text of the Acclaimed Holocaust Film* (New York, 1995), pp. 154, 156, 161.

[80]Quoted in Laqueur, *The Terrible Secret*, pp. 232–4,

The Initial Rising

The Germans returned to the Warsaw ghetto in mid-January 1943 to deport 8,000 Jews. They achieved surprise, but they faced difficulties. Most Jews hid. The Germans encountered isolated ŻOB fire in ambushes and small skirmishes. In four days, the Germans captured 5,000 Jews, but the boxcars left Warsaw half empty. The ŻOB learned it could draw blood. The morale of Warsaw's Jews, who had expected total liquidation, rose. Beyond the ghetto walls, the Home Army's underground press, which despite the silence of the government-in-exile, published all information on Poland's Jews, called it "a glorious chapter in the history of Polish Jewry."[81]

The ŻOB maintained steady contact with the Polish Home Army, but it could not convince the Poles to provide concrete help beyond forty-nine pistols and fifty hand grenades. Anielewicz was furious. The Polish contribution, he wrote, "impresses [us] as being a bitter mockery of our fate and confirms that the venom of anti-Semitism continues to permeate the ruling circles of Poland. . . ."[82] Zivia Lubetkin, the ŻOB's one female founder and leader, remembered that "[a]ll Jewish youth stood ready to join us. . . . If we had been adequately supplied, we would have had two thousand fighters during the April uprising rather than our five hundred."[83]

Left on its own, the ŻOB confiscated some 10 million złoty from the Jewish Council and remaining well-to-do Jews to purchase weapons on the black market (a handgun cost between 10,000 and 20,000 złoty).[84] It manufactured its own explosives and hundreds of Molotov cocktails. By mid-April, each fighter had at least a handgun, up to fifteen rounds, a few hand grenades and homemade bombs. ŻOB cells were on constant alert. No lines of retreat were prepared. Warsaw's Jews were surrounded and alone. "We saw our job," remembered Zuckerman, "as fighting the Germans, which was to end by being killed in battle. . . . It never occurred to us that any of us would remain alive."[85] In the meantime, ghetto residents completed a network of underground bunkers begun the previous year. The entire population could hide.

The Warsaw Uprising

The Germans massed for the final *Aktion* on the night of April 18 to 19, 1943—the eve of Passover. This time they brought combat soldiers from the SS and army—over 2,000 troops—plus armor, artillery, heavy machine guns, and flamethrowers. "They look," said one ŻOB fighter, "like they are going to war."[86] At 6:00 a.m., German infantry entered the ghetto, expecting trouble but unaware of the extent of Jewish advanced knowledge and preparations. As they marched, singing, into the central ghetto, ŻOB units attacked from buildings on either side with grenades and homemade bombs, inflicting casualties and setting tanks aflame. By evening, the Germans retreated from the ghetto.

SS-General Jürgen Stroop, an officer with combat experience, assumed command. In the days ahead, he deployed artillery and heavy machine guns against Jewish defenses and set buildings aflame. The entire ghetto was consumed in fire. Marek Edelman, a Bundist ŻOB commander, described thick black smoke choking his unit and asphalt melting beneath their feet.

---

[81]Quoted in Gutman, *Jews of Warsaw*, p. 320.

[82]Figure and quote in Gutman, *Jews of Warsaw*, pp. 320, 358.

[83]Zivia Lubetkin, *In the Days of Destruction and Revolt* (Tel Aviv, 1981), p. 180.

[84]Figures in Engelking and Leociak, *Warsaw Ghetto*, pp. 771–2.

[85]Zuckerman, *A Surplus of Memory*, p. 230.

[86]Quoted in Kazik, *Memoirs of a Ghetto Fighter* (New Haven, CT, 1994), p. 33.

Complete destruction, reported Stroop, "is the only way to defeat the rabble and scum of the earth. . . ."[87] By now, Polish Home Army detachments in Warsaw tried repeatedly to breach the ghetto walls—to no avail.[88]

The Germans searched for individual bunkers, using explosives and poison gas to kill or drive out those hiding. By day, ŻOB fighters stayed underground with little air and no water. By night, they engaged the enemy. By May 8, Stroop reported that "no bunker is opened up without the Jews inside fighting back with everything they have. . . ."[89] On that day, the Germans located the ŻOB command bunker, which included Anielewicz and 120 fighters. Some were killed by poison gas, some committed suicide, some escaped. Anielewicz was among the dead.

On May 16, in a blazing finale, Stroop detonated Warsaw's Great Synagogue. "The Warsaw ghetto," he reported, "is no more." He reported that his forces liquidated 631 bunkers with over 56,000 Jews. They killed 6,000 in combat, shot 7,000 prisoners, sent about 7,000 to Treblinka, and dispatched 36,000 to work camps. Stroop reported sixteen of his own troops killed and eighty-five wounded.[90] The ŻOB's remnants escaped through tunnels and sewers to fight another day.

Untrained and poorly armed against a battle-hardened foe, the ŻOB held out for six weeks, creating a legacy of military honor from the destruction of Jewry in Poland. In his final letter of April 23, addressed to Zuckerman, Anielewicz reflected. "In our opposition to the Germans we did more than our strength allowed—but now our forces are waning. . . . The last wish of my life has been fulfilled. Jewish self-defense has become a fact. . . . I am happy to have been one of the first Jewish fighters in the ghetto. . . . Where will rescue come from?"[91]

A Final Casualty

While in London in November 1942, Jan Karski met with two Jewish parliamentary leaders from Poland, Shmuel Zygielbojm of the Bund and Ignacy Schwarzbart of the General Zionists. He relayed a message from Leon Feiner (a Bund leader hiding in Warsaw's Aryan side) that Polish Jews in London were not doing enough to save their brethren. Zygielbojm, a courageous politician who had escaped Warsaw in 1939, was crushed. He had tried to move world opinion in every way imaginable. Now he felt guilty for not sharing the fate of Polish Jewry. Feiner contacted Zygielbojm directly in March 1943. "Arouse world opinion," he ordered. "Only you can save us; posterity will hold you responsible."[92]

The burden was too much. Toward the end of the Warsaw ghetto revolt on May 12, 1943, Zygielbojm committed suicide. His final note blamed the murder of Poland's Jews on the killers. "But indirectly," he said, "it falls upon the whole of humanity, on the people of the Allied nations and on their governments, who thus far have not taken any real steps to halt this crime. . . . By my death I wish to express my strongest protest against the inactivity with which the world is looking on and permitting the destruction of the Jewish people."[93]

---

[87]Quoted in Gutman, *Jews of Warsaw*, p. 386.

[88]Timothy Snyder, *Bloodlands: Europe Between Hitler and Stalin* (New York, 2010) p. 291.

[89]Quoted in Gutman, *Jews of Warsaw*, p. 395.

[90]Figures in Engelking and Leociak, *Warsaw Ghetto*, p. 786.

[91]Quoted in Jacob Glatstein et al., ed., *Anthology of Holocaust Literature* (New York, 1982), pp. 334–5.

[92]Quoted in Daniel Blatman, "On a Mission Against All Odds: Samuel Zygielbojm in London (April 1942–May 1943), *Yad Vashem Studies*, 20 (1990), p. 266.

[93]Quoted in Blatman, "On a Mission Against All Odds," pp. 269–70.

11.5 THE END OF *AKTION REINHARD*

The Camp Revolts

In September 1942, a work Jew in Treblinka named Meir Berliner fatally stabbed SS-Sergeant Max Bialas with a homemade knife. In retaliation, the Germans killed Berliner and 160 Jews.[94] Resistance in the *Reinhard* camps was hindered by lack of weapons and fear of such reprisals. Weakness from hunger, rolling selections, lack of trust among Jews because of the presence of informants, and the segregation of Jewish work details also stymied resistance.

But resistance was the only means of escape and survival. In Treblinka, a small group of work Jews revolted in August 2, 1943, when much of the staff left the camp on an outing. They broke into the armory, killed a dozen Trawniki guards, set buildings aflame, cut telephone wires, and cut holes in the fences. Perhaps 200 escaped into the forest. Most were caught and killed with help from Poles, who were threatened with death should they hide Jews. But a Polish Home Army company helped some escapees cross the Bug River, and some civilians pointed other escapees in safe directions. Perhaps eighty-seven survived the escape. Those too terrified or confused to run were killed.[95]

A revolt followed at Sobibór in October 1943. By now rumors swirled of Sobibór's liquidation. A small group coalesced around Lt. Alexander Petsjerski, a Jewish Red Army officer who arrived with other Soviet Jewish soldiers in September. The plan was to kill individual SS officers, hide their bodies, don their uniforms, and lead Jews from the camp. "I was not really all that confident," Petsjerski remembered later. But he hoped that at least some would escape "so that we could tell the world the truth."

On October 14, a number of SS officers, including the commandant Gustav Wagner, were on leave. The plotters killed twelve Germans and two Trawniki guards with axes and knives, and then seized firearms. But the secret emerged prematurely. Understanding that a revolt was in progress, perhaps 365 of the 650 prisoners tried to escape. Some pushed over the fence nearest the roll call area. Others stormed the main gate. Others cut holes in different parts of the fence.

"We ran and crawled as fast as we could," remembered Regina Feldman, "climbing over trees, ducking our heads and hoping not to get hit by bullets." Some were shot. Others tripped land mines. German police hunted down escapees with help from Polish farmers who provided information for payment. Polish Home Army fighters killed some others. Forty-seven escapees survived the war, some in hiding with former Polish friends, some, like Petsjerski and his men, in partisan groups. Bewildered Jews who remained behind in Sobibór were killed. SS men killed at Sobibór were buried with full military honors.[96]

At Treblinka, everything from the gas chambers to the fences was dissembled and transported following the August revolt. Remaining prisoners were shot or sent to Sobibór. The land was ploughed, and a farmhouse was built and given to one of the Ukrainian guards, who was ordered to say that he had lived there for years. After the Sobibór revolt, work Jews there demolished the camp buildings, planted trees, prepared crates of stolen Jewish property for shipment to Berlin, and were then murdered.

---

[94]Arad, *Belzec, Sobibor, Treblinka*, pp. 98–9.

[95]Figure in Chrostowski, *Treblinka*, p. 93.

[96]Quotes and figures in Schelvis, *Sobibor*, pp. 154, 168, 186.

Operation Harvest Festival

The risings in Warsaw, Treblinka, and Sobibór confirmed Himmler's long-standing fears that Jews left alive in the General Government were security risks. He quickly gave orders to kill the remaining Jews in the Lublin district. Waffen SS and police units converged from throughout the General Government. On November 3 and 4, 1943, the Germans launched Operation Harvest Festival—the murder of up to 42,000 Jewish prisoners in the Lublin work camps. Most of the victims, including women, children, and sick Jews from camp infirmaries, were taken to open areas and machine-gunned. It is unlikely that the Jews were planning a revolt. One prisoner in Majdanek attacked an SS man with a knife and wounded him before being shot. Others tried to hide before they were located and killed. The killers were drunk. One fired so many automatic rounds that he fused the parts of his gun. It was one of the Final Solution's largest massacres.

Jews in other labor camps nearby were also liquidated. On November 5, the day after Harvest Festival, all 4,000 workers in the Szebnia camp in the Kraków district were sent to Auschwitz. On November 19, the work camp at Janowska near Lvov was also liquidated, with all 4,000 killed on the spot. In March 1943, the Security Police guessed that 300,000 work Jews were still alive in various ghettos and camps of the General Government. By the end of November 1943, they counted some 25,000.[97] The Gestapo continued to search for Jews in hiding. In March 1944, in Warsaw, they located the hiding place of a number of families, including Emanuel Ringelblum, his wife, and his thirteen-year-old boy. They shot them all.

Oskar Schindler

The near complete murder of Poland's Jews makes the story of Oskar Schindler, an unlikely German hero, all the more remarkable. A womanizing businessman and Nazi Party member, Schindler migrated to Kraków in 1939. He attained three formerly Jewish-owned firms, the most important of which, Emalia, produced crockery and limited armaments. He quickly obtained military contracts, cheap Polish labor, and cheaper Jewish labor. His dependence on Jewish labor for production grew as the Germans deported more Polish workers to Germany.

Emalia was located just outside the Kraków ghetto. Schindler thus understood the terrible fate of Kraków's Jews through the brutal roundups of June and October 1942, which included shootings and mass deportations to Bełżec. He and other German industrialists intervened to protect their workers. When the Germans liquidated the ghetto in March 1943, Schindler kept his Jewish workers in the Emalia factory to protect them. He then steadily bribed the commandant at Płazów, Amon Göth, to allow his and other Jewish workers, perhaps up to 1,450, to live in a separate subcamp, which Schindler built at his own expense. They received adequate food, which Schindler procured through black market contacts, and protection from Göth's guards.[98]

In part, Schindler was protecting his investment. The workers were trained, cheap, and part of his primary industrial enterprise. In part, he was motivated by humanitarian concerns. He helped convince the army to keep Płazów open even after Operation Harvest Festival by arguing that it was more important to armament production than it really was. He also voluntarily provided information to the Joint Distribution Committee (JDC) in 1943 on the state of Jewry in Poland. When Płazów was closed down in the fall of 1944, Schindler managed—through more

---

[97]Figures in Browning, *Nazi Policy, Jewish Workers, German Killers*, p. 86.

[98]Figure in Crowe, *Oskar Schindler*, p. 284.

bribes—to have some 1,000 male and female workers transferred to a new armaments enterprise in the Sudetenland, where they survived the war through more black market purchases of food and medicines.

The Final Inventory

But most Jews in Poland were murdered. Already on October 19, 1943, after the Sobibór revolt, Odilo Globocnik declared *Aktion Reinhard* complete. Only the Jews in the work camps, he said, remained. Reassigned to anti–partisan operations in Trieste near the Adriatic, Globocnik wrote Himmler on November 4, asking if his men from *Aktion Reinhard* might receive Iron Crosses—German military decorations—for their "achievements involved in this difficult task." He added in closing, "I like to see the hard work of my men rewarded."[99]

The following January 1944, Globocnik sent an inventory of what was seized in the *Reinhard* camps for the Reich. It included 54 million marks in currency; 1,800 kilos of gold bars; 10,000 kilos of silver bars; 1,000 freight car–loads of textiles; and other items including wedding rings, necklaces, brooches, pocket watches, pen and pencil sets, cigarette cases, pocket knives, eyeglass frames, flashlights, shaving kits, and alarm clocks. These items, many of them personal gifts of a sentimental nature, were the terrible detritus of the Holocaust's most terrible operation.[100] The victims' most valuable memories—their birth certificates, school diplomas, personal letters, and family photographs—were all thrown into the garbage.

---

[99]Noakes and Pridham, eds., *Nazism, 1919–1945*, vol. 3, p. 578.

[100]Document PS-4024 in Office of United States Chief of Council for Prosecution of Axis Criminality, *Nazi Conspiracy and Aggression. Supplement A* (Washington, DC, 1947). pp. 744–770.

12

Auschwitz
The Final Solution in Europe, 1941–1943

The very name *Auschwitz* symbolizes Nazi Germany's destruction of humanity. Most Jews in the USSR were shot. Most Jews from Poland were murdered in the temporary *Reinhard* camps. But most Jewish victims from other European states were sent to Auschwitz, a massive and permanent factory of death whose perfected methods of murder distinguish it even from other Nazi horrors. Most Jewish arrivals to Auschwitz were gassed immediately. Others were worked to death in a universe of atrocity. Deportations to Auschwitz occurred simultaneously with the second wave of killing in the USSR and with *Aktion Reinhard*. But deportations to Auschwitz continued long after the other operations ended. This chapter describes the camp's evolution, the dynamics of deportation in western Europe, and the Allied responses on learning of the scope of the Final Solution in Europe.

12.1 AUSCHWITZ

Adolf Eichmann and Deportations: An Overview

Deportations from most of German-controlled Europe centered on the Gestapo's Office of Jewish Affairs (Office IV-B-4 of the Reich Security Main Office [RSHA]) under Adolf Eichmann. Eichmann had staff members in occupied states and in states allied to Germany. They worked with local authorities to arrest, detain, and deport Jews. They also worked with the German National Railroad to coordinate timetables, departure points, and rolling stock. After the war, Eichmann described the coordination of transports throughout Europe as "a science in itself," occurring as it did while the army's need for trains was prioritized.[1]

In Poland and the USSR, German police generally used ghettos as bases for roundups and transports. In western Europe Jewish populations were smaller and more assimilated. The Germans did not use closed ghettos, often out of concern for public opinion. Instead they used the subterfuge of transit camps—intermediate enclosures where Jews from Germany, Belgium, France, the Netherlands, Italy and elsewhere were detained. Ranging from infants to the elderly, Jews awaited transport, allegedly for work, as trains became available. Days after embarkation, most were murdered.

---

[1]Quoted in Raul Hilberg, *The Destruction of the European Jews*, 3rd ed., vol. 2 (New Haven, CT, 2003), p. 433.

Adolf Eichmann, 1942. *Source:*
World History Archive/Alamy.

Deportations began in October 1941 from Germany, Austria, and the Protectorate of Bohemia and Moravia, which altogether had perhaps 297,000 Jews.[2] In March 1942, Eichmann's staff began deporting Slovakia's nearly 89,000 Jews, mostly to Auschwitz. Perhaps 18,000 of them survived. Systematic deportations from France, Belgium, and the Netherlands began in July 1942. Up to 206,000 Jews from these countries perished. Starting in November 1942, nearly 750 of Norway's 1,700 Jews were sent to Stettin by ship, then to Auschwitz by train.[3] Hitler's war in mid-1942 was at high tide; he even expected that German units would soon kill the Jews of Palestine.

The Jewish question in prewar Yugoslavia, which had 80,000 Jews in 1941, was solved locally. The Ustaša government in Croatia killed two-thirds of Croatia's Jews in its camp at Jasenovać and handed over an additional 9,000 Jews for deportation to Auschwitz after August 1942. Of Croatia's 39,000 Jews, 29,000 were killed. German military and police authorities began shooting Jewish men in Serbia in August 1941 in reprisal for Serb resistance. In December, they turned to Jewish women and children, using rifles and mobile gas vans. By mid-1942, German officials in Serbia claimed that the Jewish question had been solved there, meaning that some 15,000 of 16,000 Jews were dead.[4]

Germany suffered military reverses in 1943. The Sixth Army surrendered at Stalingrad in February. The Soviets won a great armored victory at Kursk in July. The Allies' captured Tunisia in May and invaded southern Italy in September. But deportations continued. In March 1943, the Germans began deporting some 54,000 Jews to Auschwitz from German-occupied Greece, particularly Salonika, where Sephardic Jews had lived since the fifteenth century. The same month, Eichmann's subordinates arranged the deportation to Treblinka of over 11,000 Jews from Greek and Serb territories (Thrace and Macedonia) occupied by

---

[2]Figures are derived from Israel Gutman, gen. ed., *Encyclopedia of the Holocaust* (New York, 1990), vol. 1, pp. 131, 229–30; vol. 2, p. 574.

[3]Figure in Gutman, gen. ed., *Encyclopedia*, vol. 4, pp. 1799–1802.

[4]Figures in Gutman, gen. ed., *Encyclopedia*, vol. 4, pp. 1716–22.

Bulgaria, which had joined Hitler's war two years earlier.[5] German troops moved into Italy in August 1943 and took control in September 1943 after a new Italian government surrendered to the Allies. Most of Italy's 45,000 Jews hid, but the Germans still deported nearly 6,800 Jews, mostly to Auschwitz.[6]

Origins of Auschwitz

Auschwitz began as a response to German labor needs. In 1939, the German concentration camp system had some 25,000 potential slave laborers. War and conquest increased the need for slave labor, but it had also increased the number of political enemies interned. The number of camps expanded, and major camps developed satellite camps near industrial works. Firms needing laborers for quarrying, mining, and the like, contracted with the SS for prisoners.

East Upper Silesia was a coal-rich region in western interwar Poland, annexed by Germany after Poland's defeat. Oświęcim, a town there, sat near key road, rail, and river junctions. The Germans renamed it Auschwitz. In April 1940, Himmler approved a new concentration camp built at a nearby Polish army barracks. By March 1941, the camp, later designated Auschwitz I, held nearly 11,000 inmates, mostly Polish political prisoners. Himmler hoped to lure German industry to the region. Auschwitz would become a thriving German town, and the camp, which he ordered expanded to a 30,000-prisoner capacity, would provide endless labor.

Himmler also ordered built, as part of *Generalplan Ost*, a much larger camp a mile to the west in the village of Brzezinka (Birkenau). The Auschwitz-Birkenau camp, later designated Auschwitz II, was to hold 100,000 prisoners. Himmler thought most inmates would be Soviet POWs, and in October 1941, 10,000 Soviet prisoners arrived to build the Auschwitz-Birkenau camp. With no tools and almost no food, most died during construction.[7] Auschwitz-Birkenau's designers viewed future prisoners similarly. Their availability mattered. Their health did not. There was no fresh water and no sanitation. Dirt-floor barracks designed with 180 sleeping surfaces on three-tiered bunks were expected to hold 700 prisoners and often held more.[8]

Auschwitz eventually had about fifty additional subcamps. The most prominent industrial concern in the region was chemical giant IG Farben. In 1941, it began building a synthetic rubber plant near Auschwitz to take advantage of plentiful raw materials, good transport, tax breaks, and slave labor. Monowitz, the second largest Auschwitz subcamp, served as the source of labor for the plant's construction. Thirty-five thousand inmates passed through the Monowitz camp in 1943 and 1944. Twenty-three thousand died.[9] The plant was never completed. No synthetic rubber was ever produced.

Auschwitz-Birkenau: The Extermination Camp

Himmler first thought of Auschwitz-Birkenau as a storehouse of Soviet slave labor, but in October 1941, Soviet POWs were dying too quickly in Wehrmacht camps. Jews were a second

---

[5]Gutman, gen. ed., *Encyclopedia*, vol. 1, p. 268; vol. 2, pp. 612–15.

[6]Susan Zuccotti, *The Italians and the Holocaust: Persecution, Rescue and Survival* (Lincoln, NE, 1996), pp. 116–23, 189–200.

[7]Yisrael Gutman and Michal Berenbaum, eds., *Anatomy of the Auschwitz Death Camp* (Bloomington, IN, 1994), pp. 138–9.

[8]Figures in Wacław Długoborski and Franciszek Piper, gen. eds., *Auschwitz 1940–1945: Central Issues in the History of the Camp* (Oświęcim, 2000), vol. 2, p. 54.

[9]Figure in Peter Hayes, *Industry and Ideology: IG Farben in the Nazi Era*, 2nd ed. (New York, 2001), p. 359.

choice. The Nazi leadership decided in 1941 to kill them anyway and, as Heydrich later mentioned at the Wannsee Conference, the fittest Jews could be put to work within the context of the Final Solution. Jews began arriving in March 1942.

Arrivals at Auschwitz-Birkenau who could not work were murdered. Roughly 1.1 million Jews were deported to Auschwitz out of 1.3 million prisoners as a whole.[10] Forced from trains amid shouts and blows after nightmare journeys, they were separated by gender. SS doctors undertook a "selection" process. Those deemed fit for work, generally 20 percent of any given transport, were directed to the right. The unfit went to the left. Selections were perfunctory. Mothers with children; children alone; pregnant women; and the elderly, sick, and the disabled were declared unfit as a rule. Family members generally never saw one another again. Those selected for death walked or were driven to the rear of the camp to gas chambers hidden from the rest of the complex.

Work details moved belongings to the rear of the camp for sorting. It was now state property, but camp personnel helped themselves to what they could. Special detachments made up mostly of Jews known as *Sonderkommandos* handled the dead. They sheared hair, knocked loose gold dental work, and incinerated the bodies. Hair was shipped to Germany, where it was used to make socks for the navy. Ash was dumped into the Vistula River, used as farm compost or insulation for camp buildings, or to fill ruts in roads and pathways. Very few of the 2,000 who served in *Sonderkommandos* survived the war.[11]

Killing at Auschwitz was streamlined with time. Beginning in August 1941, prisoners who could no longer work at the Auschwitz I camp were murdered in the infirmary with phenol injections to the heart. An extension of the 14 f 13 euthanasia program, lethal injections killed thousands but also gave way to poison gas. Auschwitz used prussic acid, or Zyklon B, a solid fumigant developed by Degesch, a German chemical firm. Zyklon B pellets vaporized once introduced through vents. It was tested initially in September 1941 on 850 Soviet POWs and ruined Polish workers in Auschwitz I.

Gassing was extended to Auschwitz-Birkenau in March 1942, just as deported Jews arrived there. The camp initially used two converted farmhouses, which together could kill about 2,000 persons at a time. The bodies, buried in mass graves, were exhumed and burned after September 1942. Inadequate equipment slowed the process so that, by the end of 1942, Auschwitz killed "only" 175,000 Jews.[12] Four permanent structures called crematoria were planned for Auschwitz-Birkenau in February 1942 and were completed by March 1943.

The new crematoria were self-contained buildings with undressing rooms, underground gas chambers disguised as disinfectant baths, and elevators to move bodies to multiple ovens feeding into common chimneys. Their permanence, as opposed to the makeshift structures of the *Reinhard* camps, owed to Auschwitz's function as a permanent slave labor camp. Together with a fifth crematorium in Auschwitz I, the units could kill and incinerate 4,756 victims in a twenty-four-hour period, according to J. A. Topf and Sons, the German engineering firm that built them. In fact, they processed twice that number when the camp authorities sped the incineration process.[13]

---

[10]Figure in Robert Jan Van Pelt, *The Case for Auschwitz: Evidence from the Irving Trial* (Bloomington, IN, 2002), p. 115.

[11]Sybille Steinbacher, *Auschwitz: A History* (New York, 2006), p. 103; Gutman and Berenbaum, eds., *Anatomy of the Auschwitz Death Camp*, p. 171.

[12]Figures and timing in Gutman and Berenbaum, eds., *Anatomy of the Auschwitz Death Camp*, pp. 162–3.

[13]Gutman and Berenbaum, eds., *Anatomy of the Auschwitz Death Camp*, pp. 87–8, 164–6.

The crematoria were secret only to disoriented new arrivals. Jan Hartman, a Czech Jew, remembered: "[W]hat struck me about the camp was the smell. . . . The air was not clean; you were breathing the dead." "I was with a friend," remembered Anna Bergman, another Czech Jew, "whose parents were in the same transport but had been sent to the other side of the selection. . . . When we got into our barrack, she asked the women already there, 'Where are my parents? When will I see them again?' And they all started screaming with laughter, 'You stupid idiot, they are in the chimney by now.'"[14]

Those taken straight to the gas chambers were never registered in the camp. But the accepted numbers are these: Of the 1.1 million Jews who moved through the Auschwitz complex from all over Europe, only 205,000 were registered. The rest—some 865,000—were killed on arrival. The next largest classification of victims killed on arrival was comprised of 10,000 Poles, many of who were sent to Auschwitz by the Gestapo for execution as political prisoners.[15]

The Concentration Camp

Auschwitz's 400,000 *registered* inmates included everyone from Germans to Frenchmen, to Poles, to Roma, to Soviet POWs, to Jews. Jews were the largest group of registered inmates (205,000) and the largest number of dead among registered prisoners (100,000). Along with registered Roma, a higher percentage of whom were killed at Auschwitz (19,000), Jews were at the bottom of the prisoner hierarchy. Registered Poles and Soviet POWs also fared poorly, suffering 64,000 and 12,000 deaths, respectively.[16]

Men and women who arrived at Auschwitz and were selected for work entered a universe designed to dehumanize and kill. Amid shouting and physical abuse, their possessions and clothing were taken. Their heads, armpits, and genitals were shaved. They were disinfected. Registration numbers were tattooed on their left arms. They received the camp uniform—ill-fitting, coarse, striped fatigues—and shoes that were really wood slabs with straps across the top. The initial transformation was shock. "Some naked headed monster," remembered Hungarian Jew Isabella Leitner as she described her sister, "is standing next to me. Some naked-headed monster is standing next to her."[17]

Each prisoner was assigned to a barrack bloc so crowded that one could hardly lie down. The blocks had no ventilation, crawled with vermin, and stank of refuse. Food, provided daily, was insufficient—a slice of moldy bread, foul soup with potato peels or parsnips, and some substitute coffee or tea. There was no clean water for drinking or washing. Toilet facilities were open trenches in latrine barracks. "There was one latrine for thirty-two thousand women," said Gisella Perl of the women's camp at Birkenau, "and we were permitted to use it only at certain hours of the day. We stood in line to get in to this tiny building, knee deep in human excrement. As we all suffered from dysentery, we . . . soiled our ragged clothes . . . thus adding to the horror of our existence. . . ."[18]

The workday began at 4:30 a.m. with an outdoor roll call. It ended at sundown with another. Rain or shine, cold or hot, prisoners stood at attention for hours to be counted, particularly if a

---

[14]Both quoted in Lyn Smith, ed., *Remembering: Voices of the Holocaust—A New History in the Words of the Men and Women Who Survived* (New York, 2006), p. 162.

[15]Van Pelt, *The Case for Auschwitz*, p. 115.

[16]Van Pelt, *The Case for Auschwitz*, p. 116.

[17]Isabella Leitner, *Isabella: From Auschwitz to Freedom* (New York, 1994), p. 39.

[18]Quoted in Debórah Dwork and Robert Jan van Pelt, *Auschwitz, 1270 to the Present* (New York, 1996), p. 268.

prisoner had disappeared. They worked through daylight hours, some within the camp, some several miles outside the camp in mines, quarries, roads, construction sites, or farms. There was no protection from injury or the elements. "The sun," one recalled, "was never life to me. It was destruction. It was never beautiful."[19]

Prisoners endured constant beatings from "prominents" assigned by the SS to control inmates. A *Blockführer*, together with his or her assistants, kept order in each barrack and was responsible for roll call. A *Kapo* was responsible for work details. They tended to be ethnic Germans from the criminal ranks and received better rations and sleeping quarters. To satisfy their sadistic impulses and to keep their jobs, they beat prisoners for moving too slowly, for slouching, or for not understanding orders. Beating was the camp's unspoken language.

Injuries were common, and poor diet, poor hygiene, cold, and exposure caused illness, from typhus to dysentery. Prisoners who could no longer work were killed on the spot by the SS or sent to the gas chambers after rolling selections aimed at making room for new arrivals. A trip to the infirmary could result in a few days away from work. But it carried the risk of death should a selection take place. In the meantime, one became less human. "My belly is swollen," wrote Primo Levi, an Italian Jew who survived Monowitz, "my limbs emaciated, my face is thick in the morning and hollow in the evening; some of us have yellow skin, others grey. When we do not meet for a few days we hardly recognize each other."[20]

Prisoners referred to those descending quickly toward death as *Musselmänner*—Muslims— in reference to their submission. "To sink," wrote Levi, "is the easiest of matters. . . . All the [*Musselmänner*] who finished in the gas chambers have the same story, or more exactly, have no story . . . they are overcome before they can adapt themselves. . . . Nothing can save them from selections or from death by exhaustion. Their life is short, but their number is endless. . . . One hesitates to call them living: one hesitates to call their death death . . . as they are too tired to understand."[21] Eighty percent of registered prisoners died within months of their arrival.[22]

Prisoners who survived needed luck. Gender mattered. Unsuited to the heavy construction work of Auschwitz's early years, women were often selected for death on arrival even if they had no children. The SS carried out subsequent selections of female workers often and ruthlessly. Women made up just 30 percent of all registered prisoners, and of 28,000 women brought into Auschwitz in 1942, just 5,400 were still alive at the end of the year. In the camp's later history, women were able to find more work opportunities, on assembly lines, for example, producing artillery shell fuses, and within the camp itself. Their chances of living longer thereby increased.[23]

Language also mattered. The camp functioned in German. Polish and Yiddish were also common. "The misfortune of the Greek girls," recalled Maria Ossowoski, a Pole, "was that they didn't know any other language than Greek . . . that made their life a double misery because you had to understand what all the shouting was about, and the shouting was all in German. I remember that they were still quite lovely because they were fresh arrivals in May 1943 and they were singing beautiful songs. They didn't last long. . . ."[24]

---

[19]Quoted in Lawrence Langer, *Holocaust Testimonies: The Ruins of Memory* (New Haven, CT, 1991), p. 105.

[20]Primo Levi, *Survival in Auschwitz: The Nazi Assault on Humanity* (New York, 1993), p. 37.

[21]Levi, *Survival in Auschwitz*, p. 90.

[22]Figure in Długoborski and Piper, gen. eds., *Auschwitz 1940–1945*, vol. 2, p. 40.

[23]Długoborski and Piper, gen. eds., *Auschwitz 1940–1945*, vol. 2, p. 185.

[24]Smith, ed., *Voices of the Holocaust*, p. 173.

Prisoners might survive by accepting Auschwitz's moral ambiguity, whereby the Germans pitted prisoners against each other. Some, despite being Jews, managed to ingratiate themselves with "prominents," and in this way, through the web of influence and favors by which the camp functioned, secured better jobs as cooks, tailors, or infirmary staff, with access to more food. A few became block leaders or *Kapos* who beat their charges. "I have lost so many relatives here," said block leader Sara Meisels, a Jew from Slovakia, "that I know no pity."[25] Some Jewish prominents managed to preserve their humanity. Jewish doctors working in infirmaries, for instance, gave false diagnoses that saved patients from the gas chambers.

Others learned to "organize"—camp slang for attaining ordinary goods by any means possible. "We have learnt," said Levi, "that everything is useful: the wire to tie up our shoes, the rags to wrap around our feet, waste paper to (illegally) pad our jacket against the cold. We have learnt, on the other hand, that everything can be stolen, in fact is automatically stolen as soon as attention is relaxed. . . ."[26] "Organization," wrote Kitty Hart of Lublin, "was the key to survival." She took necessities from the dead. "What use," she asked, "had the dead for their clothes or their pitiful rations?"[27] Anything taken could be traded for other items, from extra food to better fitting shoes. "Death," wrote Levi in reference to swollen and infected feet, "begins with the shoes."[28]

Easier labor was essential for survival. "It was of the utmost importance to get the right *Kommando*," remembered Samuel Don of Ostrykol. "To get the wrong *Kapo* and the wrong job could mean that you survived for only two or three weeks."[29] Kitty Hart initially worked lifting rocks while being beaten. She eventually managed to clean latrine trenches, which were partly indoors. In 1944, as hundreds of thousands of Hungarian Jews were gassed, she was assigned to the *Kanadakommando*. "Kanada" was camp slang for the warehouses near the crematoria where Jewish property was sorted. It had food, clothing, and more spacious barracks. But Hart also came face to face with the crematoria and Auschwitz's ethical impossibilities. "Of course we had known, had whispered about it, and had been terrified of it from a distance," she later wrote, "but now I was *seeing* it, right there in front of me." She adjusted:

> To preserve your sanity you had to tell yourself that whatever was happening . . . was not in fact happening at all. . . . We laughed and sang with . . . reeking hell all round us; I even had books to read, found while sorting the bundles. . . . Ought we to have shouted out and warned those children, and the stumbling sick and older men and women? We would have been shot out of hand. . . . And we might have caused unnecessary suffering to those who still did not quite appreciate what was in store. . . .[30]

Medical Atrocities

Concentration camp prisoners were used for medical experiments. In Dachau, they were subjected to pressure chamber experiments to benefit German pilots. At Ravensbrück, doctors inflicted and infected wounds on female prisoners to study bacteria. Physicians in Auschwitz studied sterilization and genetics to serve Nazism's racial utopia. Auschwitz's most notorious SS

---

[25]Quoted in Hermann Langbein, *People in Auschwitz* (Chapel Hill, NC, 2004), p. 172.

[26]Levi, *Survival in Auschwitz*, p. 33.

[27]Kitty Hart, *Return to Auschwitz: The Remarkable Story of a Girl Who Survived the Holocaust* (New York, 1982), pp. 63, 71–2.

[28]Levi, *Survival in Auschwitz*, p. 34.

[29]Samuel Don, *Prisoner 83571* (Huntington, WV, 1991), p. 41.

[30]Hart, *Return to Auschwitz*, pp. 112, 116–17.

doctor was Josef Mengele, Auschwitz's chief physician after November 1943. He studied genetics partly by dissecting Jewish and Roma twins after killing them with phenol injections.

Yet sterilization experiments were more urgent given Himmler's worries about mixed German Jewish children. It was politically impossible to kill mixed children (each had a German family), but they could not be allowed to procreate. At Himmler's behest, SS doctors Carl Clauberg and Horst Schumann experimented in Auschwitz with over 1,000 prisoners in search of quick, nonsurgical mass sterilization methods. Fewer than a hundred survived.[31] Schumann subjected patients to high radiation doses, then had their reproductive organs removed (without anesthetic) for study. Clauberg had the uteruses of Jewish women from the Netherlands and Greece repeatedly injected with chemicals including formaldehyde, which closed the fallopian tubes.

Sylvia Friedman, a tall, Aryan-looking Jewish prisoner-nurse from Slovakia, assisted Clauberg and perhaps had a sexual relationship with him. She thus secured privileged status for herself and her mother. "Sylvia," remembered Schewa Meltzer, one of Clauberg's surviving victims, "undertook the injection herself. . . . [I had] the feeling that my abdomen was coming apart. . . . I was screaming. . . ."[32] Meltzer suffered debilitating fevers and repeated procedures. But Clauberg reported to Himmler in June 1943 that "[i]n a short time it will be possible for one trained physician . . . with the help of ten assistants to carry out in one day . . . the sterilization of several hundred or even a thousand women."[33]

12.2 THE DESTRUCTION OF THE REICH'S JEWS

Deportation from the Reich

With the decision for the Final Solution, Hitler was determined to rid the Reich of Jews first. By the autumn of 1941, there were still roughly 157,000 Jews in the *Altreich* (pre-1938 Germany), 48,000 in Austria, and 92,000 in the Protectorate of Bohemia and Moravia.[34] Eichmann began deportations in October 1941—before the death camps in Poland were even begun. His staff arranged transports of 1,000 Jews each from German, Austrian, and Czech cities. Jews slated for deportation received notification several days in advance ordering them to appear at collection points for work-related relocation. They could take fifty kilograms of luggage and fifty marks cash. Other property, from furniture to china, remained behind.

Starting in October 1941, some 70,000 Reich Jews were sent to the ghettos in Łódź, Kovno, Riga, and Minsk. Nearly all were murdered, some immediately, some after laboring or deteriorating. From March to October 1942, at least twenty-five more transports went to the General Government, where ghettos and the *Reinhard* camps awaited. Most Jews in these transports were murdered. Transports to Auschwitz began in the summer of 1942 when gassing facilities became ready; in January 1943, Auschwitz replaced other destinations.[35] Throughout the war, about 137,000 Jews were deported from Germany's pre-1938 borders. Nine thousand survived. All but a thousand of the Jews living in Austria in 1941 were deported, and just 1,747 returned. More than

---

[31]Figure in Długoborski and Piper, gen. eds., *Auschwitz 1940–1945*, vol. 2, p. 356.

[32]Quoted in Jane M. Georges and Susan Benedict, "An Ethics of Testimony: Prisoner Nurses at Auschwitz," *Advances in Nursing Science*, 29, no. 2 (April/June 2006), pp. 161–9.

[33]Quoted in Długoborski and Piper, gen. eds., *Auschwitz 1940–1945*, vol. 2, p. 352.

[34]Figures derived from Gutman, gen. ed., *Encyclopedia*, vol. 1, pp. 131, 229–30; vol. 2, p. 574.

[35]Figures derived from Henry Friedlander, "The Deportation of German Jews: Post-War West German Trials of Nazi Criminals," *Leo Baeck Institute Yearbook*, vol. 29 (1984), pp. 201–26.

78,000 Jews from the Protectorate were killed.[36] Eichmann was promoted to SS Lt. Colonel in November 1941 for what his superiors called "commendable initiative and necessary firmness."[37]

What Reich Jews Understood

German Jews did not initially comprehend their fate. An SS reporter in Riga quipped that arriving German Jews "actually considered themselves pioneers about to be employed in the coloniza-tion of the East."[38] Most broke under the weight of the eastern ghettos. Their language and cul-ture made them strangers even to local Jews. In Minsk, they lacked smuggling connections and traded their winter clothes for food. In Łódź, they were paralyzed by squalor. Oskar Rosenfeld, a Vienna-educated Jewish writer sent to Łódź, described the "pools of sewage . . . stinking refuse . . . countless tired, crooked creatures . . . [and] the smell of things unknown in the West." Trained in professions, they could find no work, and they starved on pitiful rations. "Every day, somebody died here and there in his bed," wrote Rosenfeld. "Those from Vienna and Frankfurt are falling victim in quick succession." By June 1942, German Jews in Łódź volunteered for resettlement only to die in Chełmno. "Hunger hallucination," said Rosenfeld, "drives them there."[39]

Early misperception among German Jews stemmed from the Final Solution's newness. Later it stemmed from the lies surrounding Theresienstadt, a walled fortress town sixty-five kilometers from Prague. Theresienstadt opened in November 1941 as a transit camp for Czech Jews. In June 1942, it also became a publicized destination for German Jews over age sixty-five; disabled German Jewish war veterans; and prominent German Jews with social connections, including artists, musicians, and academics. Represented as a spa town, it allowed the Nazis to maintain that able-bodied Jews would indeed work while the old would receive care. It even had concerts and theater thanks to talented inmates. "Theresienstadt," wrote Victor Klemperer in his diary, "is considered a privilege and probably is one compared to Poland."[40] But German rule was similar everywhere. Of the 141,000 Jews who entered Theresienstadt, more than 33,000 died of hunger or disease, and over 88,000 were transported to eastern ghettos, Treblinka, and ultimately Auschwitz.[41]

Nazi deception wore thinner with time. Already by the autumn of 1942, German Jews came to know Auschwitz as a place where friends and acquaintances died of causes ranging from "escape attempts" to "stroke" to "heart failure."[42] Theresienstadt also triggered suspicion. "Whether people starve and die there," Klemperer wrote, "or whether they exist in a halfway human state, no one really knows."[43] Three thousand to four thousand older German Jews facing deportation chose suicide. Demand for Veronal, a sleeping drug, drove the price to a thousand

---

[36]Gutman, gen. ed., *Encyclopedia*, vol. 1, pp. 132, 230; vol. 2, p. 574; Wolfgang Benz, ed., *Die Juden in Deutschland 1933–1945: Leben unter nationalsozialistischer Herrschaft* (Munich, 1989), p. 651.

[37]Quoted in David Cesarani, *Becoming Eichmann: Rethinking the Life, Crimes, and Trial of a "Desk Murderer"* (Cambridge, MA, 2004), p. 97.

[38]Quoted in Hans Safrian, *Eichmann's Men* (New York, 2010), p. 122.

[39]Oskar Rosenfeld, *In the Beginning Was the Ghetto: Notebooks from Lodz* (Evanston, IL, 2002), pp. 12, 13, 23, 24, 71.

[40]Victor Klemperer, *I Will Bear Witness: A Diary of the Nazi Years, 1942–1945* (New York, 1999), July 12, 1943.

[41]Figures in H. G. Adler, *Theresienstadt 1941–1945: Das Antlitz einer Zwangsgemeinschaft*, 2nd ed. (Tübingen, 1960), pp. 48, 53–4, 701–2.

[42]Klemperer, *I Will Bear Witness, 1942–1945*, October 30, 1942, January 8, 1943, April 25, 1943, August 23, 1943, August 14, 1944.

[43]Klemperer, *I Will Bear Witness, 1942–1945*, June 13, 1943.

marks for thirty pills.[44] In her final note of July 1942, Helene Waldeck said, "I voluntarily leave this life that I can no longer bear. For a person of eighty it is too much. . . ."[45]

Increasingly the Gestapo dragged Jews from their homes and off the streets. Eichmann's most notorious deputy was SS-Captain Aloïs Brunner, who in 1942 developed methods in Vienna that included cordoning off buildings, beating arrestees, shooting hostages to deter hiding, and ignoring deportation exemptions. "He was unbelievably brutal," one victim remembered. In February 1942, Brunner personally tortured and killed a Jewish banker named Sigmund Bosel on the last train from Vienna to Riga. Brunner next moved to Berlin, where he promised to show "those Prussian pigs how to deal with those *Schweinehunde* Jews." In 1943, he was in Salonika, where he wrote a friend that "our work is progressing terrifically."[46] Eichmann referred to Brunner as "one of my best men."[47]

What Germans Knew

Nazi leaders spoke openly—in general terms—of the Final Solution. Hitler repeated his 1939 prophecy of Jewish annihilation so often that even German housewives living abroad knew it by heart.[48] Robert Ley, head of the German Labor Front, proclaimed on the radio in May 1942 that "[t]he Jew is the greatest danger to humanity. If we don't succeed in exterminating him, then we will lose the war. It is not enough to take him someplace. . . . You have to annihilate them, you have to exterminate them. . . ." Joseph Goebbels wrote publically in June 1942 that Jews were responsible for the Allied bombing of German cities and that "they will pay for it with the extermination of their race in Europe and perhaps even beyond Europe as well."[49]

Germans knew of deportations. Berlin alone had 188 of them.[50] Some Germans were surely engulfed in fear, or at least self-preservation. Housewives watched roundups from behind their curtains. German bishops maintained silence for fear of retaliation against churches. Others were too involved in their own lives to consider the implications, especially as Allied bombs fell on German cities in 1942 and 1943. Others still, following state propaganda, blamed the Jews for Allied bombing and were openly pleased. Police reports from other cities noted popular "satisfaction" or "approval" of deportations.[51] "Everybody saw it," remembered Herta Rosenthal from Leipzig, "and they were happy, a lot of them. They were standing there laughing."[52] In Hamburg, some 100,000 German buyers purchased property formerly owned by Jews at auction.[53]

---

[44]Figures in Konrad Kwiet, "The Ultimate Refuge: Suicide in the Jewish Community Under the Nazis," *Leo Baeck Institute Yearbook*, vol. 29 (1984), p. 155.

[45]Quoted in Benz, ed., *Die Juden in Deutschland*, p. 653.

[46]Safrian, *Eichmann's Men*, pp. 7, 120, 122–3, 130.

[47]Mary Felstiner, "Alois Brunner: Eichmann's Best Tool," *Simon Wiesenthal Annual,* vol. 3 (1986), pp. 1–41.

[48]Norman J. W. Goda, "True Confessions: Allied Intelligence, German Prisoners, Nazi Murders," in *Secret Intelligence and the Holocaust*, eds. David Bankier and Shlomo Aronson (New York, 2006), pp. 157–70.

[49]Quoted in Jeffrey Herf, *The Jewish Enemy: Nazi Propaganda During World War II and the Holocaust* (Cambridge, MA, 2006), pp. 144, 155, 156, 167.

[50]All listed in Beate Mayer, et al., eds., *Jews in Nazi Berlin: From Kristallnacht to Liberation* (Chicago, IL, 2009), pp. 177–83ff.

[51]Ian Kershaw, *Hitler, Germans and the Final Solution* (New Haven, CT, 2008), pp. 220–23.

[52]Eric A. Johnson and Karl-Heinz Reuband, eds., *What We Knew: Terror, Mass Murder and Everyday Life in Nazi Germany* (New York, 2005), p. 68.

[53]Frank Bajohr, *Aryanization in Hamburg: The Economic Exclusion of the Jews and the Confiscation of Their Property in Nazi Germany* (New York, 2002), p. 291.

Rumors and occasional statements suggested the terrible truth. Soldiers home on leave spoke of mass shootings. A leaflet distributed in June 1942 by the White Rose, a student resistance group in Munich whose leaders were eventually beheaded for treason, mentioned 300,000 Jews murdered in Poland. A priest in Franconia sermonized in February 1943 against the extermination of the Jews. A few were arrested for calling Hitler a mass murderer.[54] But very few took direct action.

Margarete Sommer was an assistant to Bishop Konrad Preysing of Berlin. From the start of the deportations, she was determined to learn the Jews' fate, garnering some information from Hans Globke, a Catholic official in the Interior Ministry. She told German bishops, one of whom wrote in his diary as early as February 1942 that "[t]he plan surely exists to exterminate the Jews completely."[55] With Bishop Preysing's approval, Sommer developed a network to hide Jews. Operating without written records for fear of the Gestapo, she was unsure how many she saved. Scholars estimate that she and others acting independently might have hidden 10,000 Jews.[56]

The Rosenstrasse Protest

The one open protest in Germany against deportations involved intermarried couples. The Nuremberg Laws of 1935 banned Aryan–Jewish unions but stopped short of requiring divorces in existing marriages. State and society used different pressures. Aryans married to Jews often lost their jobs and suffered police harassment. Neighbors taunted mixed couples and referred to the women, whether Jewish or not, as "Jew-sows." Friends often turned away.

Complaints after *Kristallnacht* from German spouses induced the state to divide mixed marriages into "privileged" and "unprivileged" categories. Privileged marriages had German husbands and baptized children. Reflecting the belief that husbands determined household character, privileged marriages were exempt from measures such as residence in Jew-houses and reduced rations. Marriages with Jewish husbands and German wives were unprivileged. The wives could obtain easy divorces. Few did so, however, and mixed marriages numbered about 28,000 by January 1943.[57]

By December 1942, most German Jews had been deported. Most remaining Jews, about 51,000, worked in factory jobs vital to the war effort. Himmler wanted them killed along with the Jewish husbands from unprivileged marriages. On February 27, 1943, with Hitler's approval, the Gestapo launched the so-called *Factory-Aktion*, locating Jews in their places of work. By March 7, nearly 11,000 German Jews—workers and their families—were shipped to Auschwitz where most were gassed.[58] In Berlin, where 7,000 Jews were deported, Eichmann tried to deceive Aryan wives as to the fate of their Jewish husbands by routing the husbands, numbering roughly 1,800, through a different assembly point, a Jewish community building on *Rosenstrasse* in central Berlin. When their husbands failed to return from work on the afternoon of February 27, the wives frantically looked for them. In small groups, they converged on

---

[54]Kershaw, *Hitler, Germans and the Final Solution*, pp. 202–4.

[55]Quoted in Saul Friedländer, *Nazi Germany and the Jews, 1939–1945: The Years of Extermination* (New York, 2007), p. 303.

[56]Michael Phayer, *The Catholic Church and the Holocaust, 1930–1965* (Bloomington, IN, 2001), pp. 122–4; Benz, ed., *Die Juden in Deutschland*, p. 660.

[57]Figure in Nathan Stoltzfus, *Resistance of the Heart: Intermarriage and the Rosenstrasse Protest in Nazi Germany* (New York, 1996), p. xxvii.

[58]Figures in Wolf Grüner, "The Factory Action and the Events at the Rosenstrasse in Berlin: Facts and Fictions About 27 February 1943 Sixty Years Later," *Central European History*, 36, no. 2 (2003), pp. 184–5, 192.

Rosenstrasse. Aryan family members joined them along with a few unrelated Germans. There they stood in the cold.

Over the next week the crowd grew. The wives shouted, "We want our husbands," defying warning shots from police. "The street was full," remembered Elsa Holzer. "It was," remembered Ursula Braun, "the most urgent sense of emergency that drove us." By March 6, the crowd became bolder. "Now we couldn't care less," remembered Charlotte Israel, "We yelled 'Murderer, murderer, murderer, murderer.' We didn't scream it once, but again and again, until we lost our breath."[59] The government had to decide whether to shoot German housewives and risk spreading further unrest.

Goebbels, sensitive to public opinion, ordered the *Rosenstrasse* Jews released in his capacity as Gauleiter of Berlin. Thirty-five more intermarried Jewish husbands routed to Auschwitz were returned. Hitler and Himmler agreed with the step, thinking it but a temporary delay. But a solution to the question of mixed marriages was not tried again. In September 1944, only 13,217 registered Jews (plus those in hiding) were left in Germany. Ninety-eight percent had Aryan spouses. The success of the *Rosenstrasse* protest, meanwhile, raises the question as to whether other Germans might have done more to save their once-fellow citizens.[60]

12.3 THE DESTRUCTION OF THE JEWS OF THE NETHERLANDS

The Pace of Deportation

On June 11, 1942, Eichmann summoned his subordinates from France, the Netherlands, and Belgium to Berlin. He ordered that Jews of both sexes in western Europe between age sixteen and forty be sent to Auschwitz "for labor." From mid-July forward, he added, trains would leave daily from western Europe.[61] The death toll in different parts of western Europe varied thereafter. Of the 330,000 Jews in France, the Germans murdered 26 percent. The Germans killed 44 percent of the 55,600 Jews registered in Belgium. But they killed 73 percent of the 140,547 Jews registered in the Netherlands. How to explain the death toll in the Netherlands? Assimilated Dutch Jews could not imagine the truth. Amsterdam, where most Jews lived, had a high police presence. The Netherlands had no forests in which to hide, no government to act as even a reluctant buffer between the Germans and Jews, and few willing to risk their lives to hide Jews.

Eichmann's key subordinate in Amsterdam was SS-Captain Ferdinand aus der Fünten. On June 26, 1942, he informed the *Joodse Raad*—the Jewish Council in Amsterdam—that all Jews age sixteen to forty would register for work call-ups and travel to central Europe to serve German labor needs. The *Joodse Raad* since 1940 had worked to minimize German demands rather than reject them. Co-chairmen Abraham Asscher and David Cohen also thought initially that only German Jewish refugees would be deported. They raised no protest, believing further that Jews, if needed for work, would be treated decently.

Aus der Fünten's staff initially sent notices to individual Jews to report for work transports. The initial call-up was for 4,000 Amsterdam Jews to report by July 17. Some appeared willingly. The first and only girls' graduating class from Amsterdam's Jewish Lyceum reported in order to save their parents from punishment. "Very few," remembered one teacher, "had the sense to go

---

[59]Quoted in Stoltzfus, *Resistance of the Heart*, pp. 224, 228, 243.

[60]Figure in Stoltzfus, *Resistance of the Heart*, pp. 304, n. 46.

[61]Cesarani, *Becoming Eichmann*, pp. 139–40.

into hiding."[62] But as of July 14, enough Jews disobeyed their notices that the Germans arrested 700 Jews and threatened to send them to the Mauthausen concentration camp—which for Dutch Jews meant certain death—unless all 4,000 appeared for the work transports. "Think carefully," the *Joodse Raad* advised those who disobeyed their notices. "The fate of 700 fellow Jews is at stake."[63] But only 962 appeared for the first trains on July 15 and 16.

The Germans resorted to more extreme measures. An announcement of August 7, 1942, threatened Jews avoiding call-up, Jews not wearing yellow stars, and Jews changing address without permission with transport to Mauthausen. German and Dutch police also dragged Jews from their homes at night. They quickly ignored age limits, seizing the elderly and children. "[A]s night approached," remembered one survivor, "the pressure became unbearable. Food stuck in our throats."[64] "In the evenings . . .," wrote thirteen-year-old Anne Frank in her diary, "I often see rows of good, innocent people accompanied by crying children walking on and on . . . bullied and knocked about until they almost drop. . . . No one is spared."[65] The *Joodse Raad* could do little more than advise Jews to have their bags packed when police arrived. By September 1943, the Germans declared Amsterdam, where Jews from other cities had been forced to move, free of Jews. Jewish property was inventoried, sent to Germany, or sold locally.

As they awaited transport to the east, Jews were interned at Westerbork, a camp in northern Holland built in 1939 as a Dutch government enclosure for up to 3,000 German Jewish refugees. In July 1942, the Germans assumed control of Westerbork and turned it into a transit camp. A miserable half-square kilometer surrounded by barbed wire, guard towers, and Dutch police, the camp was beset with mud, vermin, and sandstorms. As more Jews crammed in during 1943, creating a standing population of up to 13,000, its barracks were overcrowded with people and baggage. Westerbork had a post office that received food parcels and a well-staffed hospital with nearly 1,800 beds. But many left thinking nothing could be worse. "Westerbork," wrote Abel Herzberg, "was another word for purgatory. . . ."[66]

By September 1944, the Germans deported between 100,000 and 105,000 Jews to the east. Over 61,000 went to Auschwitz, where 1.75 percent survived. From March until July 1943, when Auschwitz was occupied with gassing Salonika's Jews as well as a typhus epidemic, the Germans sent 34,313 Dutch Jews to Sobibór, only nineteen of whom survived. Nearly 5,000 more were sent to Theresienstadt because they were in the "privileged" categories for which Theresienstandt was supposedly built, but fewer than 1,500 of them survived.[67] On March 21, 1943, the Jewish holiday of Purim, which commemorates a failed scheme in ancient Persia to kill local Jews, Himmler's Higher SS and Police Leader in the Netherlands, Hanns Rauter, told a group of Dutch SS officers that the Dutch people "demand to be cleansed of this plague and to have the Jewish question solved once and for all." He complained about Dutch churches' opposition, then noted amid general laughter that "I shall gladly answer with my soul for what crimes

---

[62]Quoted in Jakob Presser, *The Destruction of the Dutch Jews* (New York, 1969), p. 142.

[63]Quoted in Bob Moore, *Victims and Survivors: The Nazi Persecution of the Jews in the Netherlands 1940–1945* (New York, 1997), p. 93.

[64]Quoted in Presser, *Destruction of the Dutch Jews*, p. 162.

[65]Entry from November 19, 1942, quoted in Alvin H. Rosenfeld, *The End of the Holocaust* (Bloomington, IN, 2011), p. 110.

[66]Quoted in Presser, *Destruction of the Dutch Jews*, p. 406.

[67]Figures in Moore, *Victims and Survivors*, pp. 102–3; Gutman and Berenbaum, eds., *Anatomy of the Auschwitz Death Camp*, pp. 86–9; Adler, *Theresienstadt 1941–1945*, pp. 39–60.

I have committed against the Jews."[68] After the war, a Dutch court put Rauter on trial. Before hearing his death sentence, he denied everything.

Jews in the Netherlands

From London on July 29, 1942, Dutch-language radio repeated the British Broadcasting Corporation (BBC) story that Jews were being gassed in Poland.[69] But Dutch Jews, who had not experienced pogroms or anti-Jewish legislation until 1940, could not imagine the worst. Some even felt duty-bound to share the work burden. Twenty-eight-year-old Etty Hillesum filled out the required forms. "I shall take the few steps I have to," she wrote in her diary. "My turn might not come for a long time." Later she argued that Jews in hiding "may say they're doing it because they don't want to work for the [Germans], but it's not nearly as heroic and revolutionary as that. All they're doing is using a high-sounding excuse to dodge a fate that they ought to be sharing with everyone else."[70]

Elements of the *Joodse Raad* worked tirelessly to sustain Dutch Jews while also failing to comprehend. Gertrud van Tijn, a veteran Jewish social worker, headed the council's Displaced Persons' Aid Bureau, which collected clothes, blankets, and food for those facing deportation. "Most of those needing your help," she told her 400 volunteers, "are in a state of great nervous agitation; be prepared, therefore, to *serve* selflessly. . . ."[71] Asscher and Cohen, meanwhile, continued disastrous mitigation tactics. In September 1942, they asked to issue exemption stamps on the papers of Jews deemed indispensable to the Jewish community. Aus der Fünten agreed, knowing that exemptions would hinder any united Jewish opposition. Van Tijn remembered frantic Jews rushing *Joodse Raad* offices, breaking doors down, and attacking council members to attain stamps. Favoritism and corruption influenced who received the 17,500 exemptions. By May 1943, most Jews remaining in Amsterdam had the coveted stamps, but with fewer Jews left, fewer still were indispensable. Eventually no stamps were honored.[72]

The official *Joodse Raad* newspaper *Joodse Weekblad* published letters from deported Jews who surely wrote under duress. "The food is good," said one letter, "with hot lunches, cheese and jam sandwiches in the evening. . . . We have central heating and sleep under two blankets. There are magnificent shower arrangements. . . ."[73] Such reportage only added to the shock later. Dutch Jews arriving in Poland simply could not comprehend. Kalman Wewryk, a work-Jew in Sobibór, revealed the truth to a group of Dutch Jewish women who insisted on knowing their fate. He remembered afterward that, "They kept yelling . . . in some cases semi-hysterically, 'It's impossible! It's impossible! It can't be! It can't be!'" One man in Sobibór kept trying to show the guards his round-trip ticket.[74]

Meanwhile, trains left Westerbork each Tuesday. Etty Hillesum volunteered on the *Joodse Raad*'s Westerbork reception team once transferred there in June 1943. She comforted distraught

---

[68]Quoted in Presser, *Destruction of the Dutch Jews*, p. 191.

[69]Presser, *Destruction of the Dutch Jews*, p. 147.

[70]Klaas A. D. Smelik, ed., *Etty: The Letters and Diaries of Etty Hillesum* (New York, 1983), July 28, 1942, July 29, 1942, pp. 508, 523.

[71]Quoted in Dan Michman, "The Committee for Jewish Refugees in Holland, 1933–1940", *Yad Vashem Studies*, XIV (1981), 205–32.

[72]Friedländer, *Years of Extermination*, pp. 407–8.

[73]Quoted in Presser, *Destruction of the Dutch Jews*, p. 176.

[74]Kalmen Wewryk, *To Sobibor and Back: An Eyewitness Account* (Montreal, 1999), pp. 26–7.

Members of the Jewish police supervise deportations from the Westerbork transit camp, 1943 or 1944.
Source: United States Holocaust Memorial Museum.

new arrivals. The plight of the elderly disturbed her most. "A woman of eighty-seven," she wrote, "clung to my hand with so much strength that I thought she would never let go. She told me how the steps in front of her little house had always gleamed. . . ." Others, like Etty's father Levie, who gave Greek and Latin lessons to sick children, remained stoic. "What all those thousands before us have borne," he said, "we can also bear." In time, Etty suspected the worst. In August 1943, she wrote, "a hundred thousand Dutch members of our race are toiling away under an unknown sky or lie rotting in some unknown soil. We know nothing of their fate."[75] The next month she and her family were sent to Auschwitz. By November, she was dead.

The Germans set Westerbork's weekly deportation quotas. But Westerbork's leadership, comprised of German Jews who had been interned there since 1939, compiled the lists. They overwhelmingly selected Dutch Jews while exempting their own. Kurt Schlesinger, a German Jew interned in Westerbork since February 1940, ran Westerbork's Jewish administration. Bald, bullnecked, and wearing a Hitler mustache, Schlesinger identified more with German Nazis than Dutch Jews. Arthur Pisk, a former Jewish officer in the Austrian army, commanded—in riding breeches and boots—the Jewish camp police who helped shove deportees onto waiting trains. Pisk's men also aided with roundups outside the camp.[76]

As they fearfully waited for their names to appear on transport lists, Dutch Jews in Westerbork seethed at their German brethren. Philip Mechanicus, a Dutch Jewish journalist, noted that "German Jews here play the leader just as the German Aryans play the leader wherever they are. . . ." They also settled scores. Mechanicus noted that "[many German Jews] ask

---

[75]Smelik, ed., *Etty*, pp. 587–90, 624, 654.

[76]Jacob Boas, *Boulevard des Misères, The Story of Camp Westerbork* (Hamden, CT, 1985), pp. 33–54.

their Dutch fellow Jews, 'What did you do to make our lot easier when we were flung in here by fate before you were ever subjected to the blight of the National Socialist regime?'"[77]

Schlesinger even hosted camp commandant Albert Gemmeker at Westerbork's cabaret, reputed to be one of the Netherlands' best owing to talented Jews held there. Thanks to Gemmeker's indulgence, the cabaret featured elaborate costumes and performers like Max Ehrlich, once a celebrated Berlin comic who now wore a yellow star as he entertained inmates and police alike. In September 1944, Ehrlich boarded the last train to Auschwitz, where he was gassed. One hundred thousand Jews passed through Westerbork. When Canadian troops liberated it on April 12, 1945, nine hundred were left.[78] Among them were Schlesinger and Pisk, who disappeared after the war.

The Dutch and the Jews

Might more Dutch Jews have been saved? Dutch reactions once deportations commenced ranged from collaboration with the Germans to open protest, to hiding Jews. On the first deportation announcement in July 1942, Catholic and Protestant leaders sent a telegram to *Reichskommissar* Arthur Seyss-Inquart, insisting that deportations "contradict the deepest moral conscience of the Dutch people." Seyss-Inquart exempted Jews baptized before 1941. Having won freedom for converts, Protestant clerics desisted from further protest. Catholic leaders pressed on. During Sunday services on July 26, 1942, they read a pastoral letter that included the text of the telegram sent to Seyss-Inquart.

The Germans retaliated by deporting Jewish converts to Catholicism, including Edith Stein, the German Jewish philosopher who became a Carmelite nun, pressured Pope Pius XI to speak against Nazi brutality in 1933, and moved with her convent to the Netherlands in 1934. She was gassed at Auschwitz on August 9, 1942. Protestants of Jewish descent were not safe either. Seyss-Inquart told subordinates that he made the concession "to keep the Christian churches silent about the evacuation of the Dutch Jews." Protestant Jews, he said, "will be deported at the first politically favorable occasion."[79] In September 1944, 500 Protestant Jews were sent to Theresienstadt, where most perished.

Church protests led to German caution regarding the roughly 20,000 mixed marriages in the Netherlands. For a year, Jews in mixed marriages were exempt from deportation. In May 1943, the Germans offered them the "option" of sterilization. Eligible Jews in Westerbork readily chose the option, which allowed them to return to Amsterdam, rather than face the unknown. "For young men in the full prime of life," wrote Mechanicus, "it was horrible."[80] In Amsterdam, Jewish and Dutch doctors performed surgeries on about 3,000 Jews amid church protests. Eight thousand to nine thousand Dutch Jews in mixed marriages, mostly women without children, survived the war. Most of the men were eventually killed.[81]

Only 25,000 Jews in the Netherlands, about one in seven, hid. Of those, some 17,000 survived the war.[82] Why did so few Dutch Jews go underground? Fear was one factor. Dispatch

---

[77]Philip Mechanicus, *Year of Fear: A Jewish Prisoner Waits for Auschwitz* (New York, 1964), June 3, 1943.

[78]Figure in Boas, *Boulevard des Misères*, pp. 3, 153.

[79]Quoted in Father Paul Hamans, *Edith Stein and Companions on the Way to Auschwitz* (San Francisco, CA, 2010), pp. 14–22.

[80]Mechanicus, *Year of Fear*, June 10, 1943.

[81]Figures in Moore, *Victims and Survivors*, p. 125.

[82]Figure in Moore, *Victims and Survivors*, p. 146.

to Mauthausen was the punishment for hiding, and this seemed worse than the possibility of labor call-up. The obligation to help one's family members, especially if they were already in Westerbork, was also strong. Jews wishing to go underground also needed an "address"—a place with people willing to hide them—as well as money to pay for their upkeep. Otto Frank, a German Jewish businessman, moved his family to the Netherlands in the 1930s. He hid his family—including his famous daughter Anne—in a secret annex of his Amsterdam factory in July 1942 once Anne's elder sister Margot received her labor call-up. His gentile business contacts provided support. But most Jews in the Netherlands lacked such resources or contacts.

Jews in hiding also needed new identity papers, which were especially hard to forge in the Netherlands. Dutch identity cards used watermarks, special inks, and fingerprints. Ration cards, moreover, were tied to identity cards. The police presence was also formidable. The Germans had 5,000 police in the Netherlands as opposed to only 3,000 in France. Most Dutch police followed German orders during the arrests and deportations either out of conviction or because they would lose their salaries and pensions otherwise. The Gestapo placed bounties on Jews in hiding, which attracted informants and even professional Jew hunters. Jews hiding in Amsterdam were especially vulnerable. The Frank family was discovered in August 1944 and deported on the last train from Westerbork to Auschwitz in September.

Most Jews in hiding depended on Dutch networks that emerged over the course of 1943 to help the Dutch underground more generally. The networks provided addresses, identification papers, and support. Archbishop Jan de Jong, who protested the initial deportation of Dutch Jews, financed one network. Also involved was Walter Süskind, a German Jew who had fled to the Netherlands in March 1938. In July 1942, Süskind became the *Joodse Raad* official charged with overseeing the *Hollandsche Schouwburg*, an Amsterdam theater used as a holding center for Jews bound for Westerbork. Over eighteen months he smuggled perhaps 1,000 Jewish children through the Dutch underground to safe addresses. Süskind himself did not survive the war. His wife and daughter died in Auschwitz in 1944, and he died in February 1945 during a death march after Auschwitz's evacuation.

Rural Dutch Calvinists saved a disproportionate number of Jews. Forming but 8 percent of the Dutch population, they helped rescue perhaps one-quarter of all who went into hiding.[83] Calvinist pastors arranged transit homes and long-term addresses in sparsely populated farming communities in northern Holland. The most determined Dutch rescuer might have been Johannes Bogaard, a devout Calvinist farmer. After July 1942, he began retrieving Jews from urban areas. Using his family's three farms and those of neighbors, Bogaard managed a network that hid 200 Jewish children and adults. He continued despite police raids and the arrest and murder of his father, brother, and daughter. Bogaard saw himself as fulfilling God's task. Yet he risked so much because many of his neighbors risked so little. "Not for a million, Bogaard," one said, "will I risk my family." Bogaard had asked him to hide a Jewish child for a few days.[84]

12.4 VICHY, THE FRENCH, AND THE JEWS

Vichy Collaborates

On June 11, 1942, Eichmann's representative in Paris, Theodor Dannecker, promised to deport 100,000 Jews from France over the next eighteen months. On June 30, Eichmann arrived in Paris

---

[83]Figures in Moore, *Victims and Survivors*, p. 165.

[84]Quoted in Moore, *Victims and Survivors*, p. 180.

with a directive from Himmler that all Jews were to be deported from France. But would Vichy cooperate? Since 1940, Vichy's leaders tried to mitigate high German occupation costs; the internment of 1.5 million French POWs; constant shortages; and after May 1942, the conscription of French workers for German factories. The French public grew impatient with Vichy's failure to alleviate the occupation. The handover of French citizens—even Jews—to the Germans would sit poorly with many.

The Germans understood the problem. In June 1942, when they issued the yellow star decree in France, they applied it to the occupied zone only. Jews there also faced other restrictions regarding public transit, shopping hours, and the like. Fearing negative public reaction, Vichy refused to issue the star decree in the unoccupied zone. Indeed German police reported "lively and unanimous indignation" among the French. "Even anti-Semites condemn the measure," said one report, "especially because children have to wear the star."[85] In the unoccupied zone, Jews carried a "*Juif*" stamp on their identification papers. It carried dangers but was less overt.

Dannecker placed his hopes in Pierre Laval, a politician with a long record of unprincipled opportunism. In April 1942, Laval became Vichy's premier, minister of foreign affairs, and minister of the interior. In July 1942, he agreed that French police would arrest and deliver, ostensibly for work details in the east, *stateless and foreign* Jews from both zones. It was politically expedient. Foreign Jews were a contentious issue even before the war and thousands were still in detention camps. Laval wanted them out as a matter of "national health and hygiene."[86] Meanwhile, he would build confidence in his government while sparing French Jewish citizens. To ensure that foreign Jews were available for handover, he cancelled all exit visas, even those already issued to foreign Jews.

Did Vichy know what awaited the deportees? At the very least, it knew that deportation meant terrible hardship and death for many. Jewish groups and the US government told them as much. Laval remained indifferent. In July, he suggested to the Germans that children born in France to foreign Jews—who were French citizens by law—would "be allowed to accompany their parents" in what he called "the interest of humanity."[87] Later in the year, he rejected an initiative from the Joint Distribution Committee (JDC) and the US State Department to send thousands of Jewish children to the United States, Argentina, Canada, and the Dominican Republic.[88]

The Paris Roundup and After

Jews in Paris felt the terror first. On July 16, 1942, at 4:00 a.m., 9,000 French policemen with index cards fanned out across Paris, targeting Jews from Germany, Austria, Poland, Czechoslovakia, and the USSR. Some were zealous, even removing hospital patients. Although foreign Jews lived in distinct neighborhoods, Paris had no walled ghetto and many could hide, sometimes after warnings from more sympathetic policemen. By 5 p.m. the next day, French police arrested 12,884, including 5,165 women and 4,051 children under age sixteen. The Germans were disappointed. The objective was 28,000 Jews.[89]

---

[85]Quoted in Susan Zuccotti, *The Holocaust, the French and the Jews* (New York, 1993), p. 94.

[86]Quoted in Renée Poznanski, *Jews in France During World War II* (Hanover, NH, 2001), p. 256.

[87]Quoted in Zuccotti, *The Holocaust, the French, and the Jews*, p. 99.

[88]Figures in Tuvia Friling, *Arrows in the Dark: David Ben-Gurion, the Yishuv, and Rescue Attempts During the Holocaust* (Madison, WI, 2005), vol. 1, p. 144.

[89]Figures in Serge Klarsfeld, ed., *Memorial to the Jews Deported from France 1942–1944* (New York, 1983), pp. 57–8.

Arrestees were initially detained in holding facilities. The main transit camp was a half-finished apartment complex in the Paris suburb of Drancy. For Jews with children, the French temporarily used a covered cycling stadium called the *Vélodrome d'Hiver*. Conditions were abominable. There was no clean water and no facilities for the aged, sick, handicapped, pregnant, or children. A Jewish social worker in the *Vélodrome* recorded that prisoners lay packed together amid heat, filth, and stench. Many went mad. "Kill us!" some screamed. "Don't leave us here. . . . An injection so we can die."[90]

Eichmann did not approve deportation of the children until August 13. In the meantime, French police tore children under age thirteen from their parents, often beating the mothers to do so. Adult deportations from the Paris roundup began on July 19. From August 13 to August 25, 3,082 children age two to twelve arrived in Drancy alone, covered in filth, insects, and sores. The youngest did not know their names. "We were cowards," said Odette Daltroff-Baticie, a Jewish volunteer. "We told them they were going to be reunited with their parents. . . . They show us their most precious possessions: the pictures of their parents, which their mothers gave them at the moment of separation. . . ." "Every night," remembered survivor George Wellers, "one heard . . . the wailing of children who had lost all control." French police boarded the children piecemeal on trains with adults to avoid images of children's transports. None returned. "Don't let them take her away from me," cried one eight-year-old boy covering his younger sister. "She's all I have left."[91]

In the unoccupied zone, French police in August began deporting Jews already in French detention camps. But there were not enough Jews in the camps to please the Germans. Laval's police chief René Bousquet ordered regional police prefects to carry out "extremely severe checks and identity verifications in order to liberate your region totally of all the foreign Jews." By October, French police in the unoccupied zone arrested over 11,000 Jews, who were marched—sometimes for miles in the summer heat—to railroad stations from which they were shipped to Drancy.[92] Raymond-Raoul Lambert, who tried to help Jews at the Les Milles detention camp, could not believe his eyes. "There are children, old people, war veterans, women, disabled people, old men. . . . We lose count of those who fall and must be carried. . . . To think that none of these unfortunates has committed any crime except to be born non-Aryan!"[93]

The French and the Jews

For the rest of 1942, French police targeted Jews in Paris from the Netherlands, the Baltic States, Bulgaria, Yugoslavia, Romania, Belgium, and Greece. In November 1942, in response to the Allied landings in French North Africa, Axis forces occupied the Vichy zone. German police authorities applied greater pressure in southern France thereafter and took part in raids. By year's end, some 42,500 Jews were deported from France. But in all of 1943, the Germans deported roughly 17,000 Jews.[94] Though appalling, the numbers, even from 1942, were far short of targets. What happened?

---

[90]Richard I. Cohen, ed., *Diary of a Witness 1940–1943* (hereafter *Lambert Diary*) (Chicago, IL, 2007), October 15, 1942.

[91]Figures and quote in Serge Klarsfeld, ed., *French Children of the Holocaust—A Memorial* (New York, 1996), pp. 48, 51; Michael R. Marrus and Robert O. Paxton, *Vichy France and the Jews* (New York, 1981), p. 264.

[92]Quote and figures in Zuccotti, *The Holocaust, the French, and the Jews*, pp. 126–8.

[93]*Lambert Diary*, October 11, 1942.

[94]Figures in Marrus and Paxton, *Vichy France and the Jews*, p. 261; Zuccotti, *The Holocaust, the French, and the Jews*, p. 189.

Many French citizens were ambivalent about Jewish refugees. But their handover to the Germans was another matter. Even during the July 1942 Paris roundup, some Parisians opened their homes to Jews. The aftermath of the initial mass arrests caused broader indignation. One letter to the French police prefect in Nice from August 1942 showed that a line had been crossed. "I have just learned," said the writer, "that the refugee Jews are being handed over to Hitler for [deportation to] Poland—even the old, the women and children. I do not like the Jews . . . [but] this is inhuman! As a Frenchman of old stock, as a veteran of the front, as a Catholic, I implore you to stop this immediately!"[95]

Catholic clergy supported the conservative Vichy regime. But numerous Catholic prelates also spoke openly against the deportations. In a letter read by priests throughout his diocese in August 1942, Cardinal Jules-Gérard Saliège, the seventy-two-year-old archbishop of Toulouse, registered his outrage "that children, that women, fathers and mothers should be treated like cattle, that members of a family separated and dispatched to an unknown destination. . . . The Jews," he continued, "are real men and women. . . . They cannot be abused without limit. They are part of the human species."[96] This and many other such pastoral letters were read, printed, distributed, and later included in resistance pamphlets and BBC broadcasts to France. Laval asked the Vatican to retire Saliège. The SS spoke of "unparalleled resistance within the Church."[97]

Foreign Jews remained vulnerable. "I don't take Jews," said the head of the Red Cross nursing school in Montpellier when Marthe Cohn, a young Jewish woman from Lorraine, tried to enroll.[98] But others provided help. A most notable network was that of Father Pierre-Marie Benoît, a Capuchin monk in Marseille whose monastery produced thousands of fake baptismal certificates and who helped hundreds of Jews reach the Swiss and Spanish borders. "What I did for the Jewish people," Benoît later said, "was but an infinitesimal contribution to what ought to have been done. . . ."[99]

Although 11,400 Jewish children were ultimately deported, some 72,000 escaped this fate because of concerted efforts. Most were French Jewish children who remained with their parents or foreign Jewish children placed directly by their parents with non-Jewish families. About 10,000 Jewish children whose parents could no longer protect them were hidden in monasteries, convents, private homes, schools, and farms scattered throughout France. Networks that hid them and provided false identities involved the Zionist underground and France's main Jewish children's relief agency, the *Oeuvre de Secours aux Enfants* (OSE), but also church figures, private citizens, and French charities.[100]

The Germans increased pressure on Vichy. But the political winds had shifted. In September 1942, Dannecker's successor, SS-Lieutenant Heinz Röthke, insisted that French police arrest over 5,000 prominent French Jews in Paris. SS-Colonel Helmut Knochen, who was responsible for security in Paris, rejected the idea for fear of a Franco-German police rupture. In

[95]Quoted in Asher Cohen, *New Approaches to French Public Opinion Under Vichy, 1940–1942*, in *Studies in Contemporary Jewry*, vol. 5, ed., Peter Meding (New York, 1989), p. 223.

[96]Quoted in Marrus and Paxton, *Vichy France and the Jews*, p. 271.

[97]Quoted in Lucien Lazare, *Rescue as Resistance: How Jewish Organizations Fought the Holocaust in France* (New York, 1996), p. 163.

[98]Marthe Cohn, *Behind Enemy Lines: The True Story of a French Jewish Spy in Nazi Germany* (New York, 2002), p. 89.

[99]Quoted in Mordechai Padiel, *The Path of the Righteous: Gentile Rescuers of Jews During the Holocaust* (Hoboken, NJ, 1993), p. 58.

[100]Figure in Lazare, *Rescue as Resistance*, pp. 154, 203–4.

July 1943, Röthke pressed Vichy to strip citizenship from all Jews naturalized since 1927. Laval refused to risk public backlash over the measure. French and German police launched numerous smaller operations, targeting the most vulnerable. In January 1943, they raided Marseille's old port region and arrested nearly 2,500 Jews for deportation. Victims included North African Jews lacking French citizenship and prostitutes. On February 10 and 11, 1943, French police arrested over 1,500 Jews in Paris, mostly old people in nursing homes and hospitals. The Germans also gradually began arresting French Jews.[101]

In June 1943, Eichmann dispatched the ruthless Aloïs Brunner from Salonika to Paris. Brunner took control of Drancy from the French police and began deporting French Jews held there for "criminal violations," ranging from covering their stars to shopping at the wrong time of day. The Gestapo also depended increasingly on the *Milice*—Vichy's political police—who were more reliable than regular police officers. Manhunts left few stones unturned. In April 1944, forty-four Jewish children hidden by the OSE in the remote farming village of Izieu were captured and deported. The Allies invaded France in June and liberated Paris in August. But the Germans deported 14,833 Jews in 1944, more per month than in 1943. Seventy percent of Jews deported to the east were foreigners. Thirty percent were French citizens.[102]

The Jews and the Deportations

On August 2, 1942, as foreign Jews awaited deportation in Drancy, Jacques Heilbronner, the French Jewish president of the *Consistoire Israélite*, noted, "I am going on holiday from August 8 until September, and nothing in the world can persuade me to come back."[103] Other *Consistoire* members became less indifferent to the foreign Jews' plight. Chief Rabbi Jacob Kaplan informed senior Catholic clergy of atrocities in the USSR and Poland. The *Consistoire* protested to Vichy on August 25, 1942, that the deportation of the sick, the elderly, the pregnant, and children from France "confirms . . . that the German government demands them . . . with the unmistakable intention of exterminating them. . . ."[104]

The *Union Générale des Israélites de France* (UGIF) was created in November 1941 as a French Jewish welfare organization for all Jews in France. The Germans expected to use it as a Jewish Council. UGIF leaders were no resistors. They refused to jeopardize their extensive relief work by provoking the Germans. In keeping with their French bourgeois traditions, they instead protested the legality of deportations to Vichy authorities. "My country," wrote UGIF leader Raymond-Raoul Lambert in September 1942, "has dishonored itself with these inhuman perse-cutions. . . . We cannot allow such a crime."[105] At the same time, some UGIF officials sanctioned careful clandestine work. In Paris, the UGIF created orphanages for the children of deported parents. The orphanages were under German surveillance, but with help from underground contacts, UGIF officials smuggled up to 1,600 orphans into hiding by mid-1943.[106]

---

[101]Figures in Donna F. Ryan, *The Holocaust and the Jews of Marseille: The Enforcement of Anti-Semitic Policies in Vichy France* (Urbana, IL, 1996), p. 186; Zuccotti, *The Holocaust, the French, and the Jews*, p. 169.

[102]Figures in Zuccotti, *The Holocaust, the French, and the Jews*, pp. 190–209.

[103]*Lambert Diary*, September 6, 1942.

[104]Quoted in Lazare, *Rescue as Resistance*, p. 159.

[105]*Lambert Diary*, September 6, 1942.

[106]Richard I. Cohen, *The Burden of Conscience: French Jewish Leadership During the Holocaust* (Bloomington, IN, 1987), p. 96.

The Gestapo demanded UGIF cooperation in 1943. Brunner insisted that it help move Jewish families to Drancy, that it scotch Jewish escape networks, and that it hand over lists of children's homes and welfare lists. Refusals by UGIF leaders and continued protests against deportations resulted in UGIF leaders' deportations, including that of Lambert and his entire family in August 1943. As the Allies approached Paris in late July 1944, UGIF leaders reacted too slowly. Brunner raided the UGIF orphanages in Paris, arresting 250 children—"terrorists of the future" as he called them—along with fifty UGIF staff members. Most were on the last train from Drancy to Auschwitz on July 31.[107]

East European Jews in France, especially those on the political left, had fewer illusions than French Jews, who hoped that in France, justice would somehow prevail. Jewish communists in Paris, under their organization *Solidarité*, called for resistance when Germany attacked the USSR in June 1941. They pressured Jewish workshops to engage in sabotage and strikes, and by May 1942, they formed Jewish communist partisan units that launched sabotage attacks.[108] They believed broadcasts from the USSR concerning the extermination of Jews there. On hearing rumors of the Paris roundup in early July 1942, *Solidarité* published the following pamphlet in Yiddish: "Do not wait for these bandits in your home. Take all necessary measures to hide. Not one Jew should fall victim to the bloodthirsty Nazi beast. . . . We must not, we may not, we will not allow ourselves to be exterminated."[109]

Jewish communists did not know everything. "We knew," remembered Henri Krasucki, who was sent to Auschwitz in 1943, "that terrible camps existed. . . . What we did not know was the degree of savagery and especially the existence of the gas chambers. It was necessary to arrive to know that."[110] But they followed available news on the fate of Jews in Europe, and in Yiddish- and French-language underground newspapers, they warned the Jewish and French populations against complacency. Vichy thought that such information was dangerous enough that it amplified its own propaganda, arguing that the Jews it "had decided to send back [to eastern Europe] were all instigators of revolution. The greatest danger to the world at present is the threat posed by the Jews."[111]

Solidarité also understood after the Paris roundup that they were at war with the Germans. Young foreign Jews demanded guns and made bombs. *Solidarité* combatants in Paris, who were part of the general communist resistance, attacked hotels, restaurants, and theaters frequented by the Germans as well as German troop trucks. In 1943 and 1944, they even attacked UGIF offices to destroy files that had locations of Jews in hiding. The consequences of capture were grim. French communist resistors were political enemies, to be tortured, sent to a work camp, and possibly killed. Jewish communist resistors were Jews, to be tortured, killed on the spot, or sent to Auschwitz as Jews.

Zionists in France created an underground "Jewish army" in the south, which assassinated collaborators. They also created networks for tens of thousands of false identity documents, for escape from Paris, and for hiding children, all with the help of French underground and church networks. Most Jews aided by such groups survived the war. Meanwhile, the Zionist underground

---

[107]Klarsfeld, ed., *French Children of the Holocaust*, pp. 89–91; Cohen, *Burden of Conscience*, p. 98.

[108]Jacques Adler, *The Jews of Paris and the Final Solution: Communal Responses and Internal Conflicts, 1940–44* (New York, 1987), pp. 201, 212.

[109]Quoted in Poznanski, *Jews in France*, p. 260.

[110]Quoted in Zuccotti, *The Holocaust, the French, and the Jews*, p. 153.

[111]Quoted in Poznanski, *Jews in France*, pp. 301, 378.

retained Jewish distinctiveness. Moishe Brycman was a Jewish refugee from Poland and part of the Zionist resistance. He and his wife placed their boy in a convent near Grenoble. "He'll make a fine little priest," the Mother Superior said. Many Jewish children sheltered in convents were indeed converted if their parents were deported. "Since he was born a Jew," Brycman told the Mother Superior, "let him remain a Jew." He offered to remove the child from the convent. She allowed the boy to stay. His parents retrieved him after the war.[112]

12.5 THE ALLIES AND THE BERMUDA CONFERENCE

The Riegner Report

Did the Allies understand the connection between deportations in western Europe and the comprehensive murder of all of Europe's Jews? In mid-1942, word leaked, not only of individual massacres or ghetto clearings, but also of the Final Solution as a state-directed, all-inclusive whole. Eduard Schulte was the general director of a leading mining company operating near Auschwitz. He had high contacts in the Nazi Party and the army. Regardless, Schulte viewed the Nazis as criminals. He gathered sensitive intelligence on everything, from German strategy to gasoline stocks, and passed it to contacts in Switzerland, whom he knew would pass it to the Allies. Schulte's most notable report arrived in Zurich on July 30, 1942. In Hitler's headquarters, he said, a comprehensive plan was afoot to concentrate all Jews from German-occupied Europe in the east and to murder them with prussic acid. The plan involved some 4 million Jews. The intelligence was absolutely reliable, and Schulte wanted it forwarded to the Allies.

The messenger was Gerhart Riegner, a thirty-year-old Berlin Jew who had fled Germany in 1933. Now the World Jewish Congress's representative in Geneva, Riegner received Schulte's information on August 1. Years later Riegner recalled that "[d]espite everything we already knew about what was happening in Germany itself and in occupied Europe—and we knew a great deal—this seemed extraordinary to us." But Riegner's experience with Nazi criminality; Hitler's public statements about the Jews' annihilation; and recent reports of mass arrests and deportations of Jews from transit camps in France, Belgium, and the Netherlands all convinced him. "The message," Riegner remembered, "finally gave meaning to everything that was happening."[113]

Riegner went to the Allied consulates in Geneva requesting that they send a telegram with the news to World Jewish Congress (WJC) leaders in Washington and London. "My personal opinion," reported Howard Elting of the US consulate, "is that Riegner is a serious and balanced individual . . . he never would have come to the consulate if he did not have confidence in the informant's reliability." But the State Department balked, characterizing the news as "[w]ild rumor inspired by Jewish fears." It did not forward the telegram as Riegner requested, and further ordered US diplomats not to send such "fantastic" reports unless they touched US interests.[114] The British Foreign Office was also skeptical. Yet as Riegner requested, the British government shared the news with Sidney Silverman, a member of Parliament and the head of the WJC's British section. Silverman telegrammed Rabbi Stephen Wise, the President of the WJC in New York, on August 29.

---

[112]Quoted in Jonathan Boyarin, *Polish Jews in Paris: The Ethnography of Memory* (Bloomington, IN, 1991), pp. 60–1.

[113]Gerhart M. Riegner, *Never Despair: Sixty Years in the Service of the Jewish People and the Cause of Human Rights* (Chicago, IL, 2006), pp. 36–7.

[114]Quotes in Walter Lacquer and Richard Breitman, *Breaking the Silence: The German Who Exposed the Final Solution* (New York, 1986), pp. 148–51.

Gerhart Riegner in Switzerland, 1948.   *Source:*
United States Holocaust Memorial Museum.

Wise contacted Undersecretary of State Sumner Welles, a friend of President Roosevelt who was not part of the State Department's culture. Welles asked Wise to remain silent until the information could be confirmed. He then ordered Leland Harrison, the US minister in Bern, to meet with Riegner and Richard Lichtheim, the Jewish Agency Executive's representative in Geneva. Meanwhile, more information from all over Europe reached Geneva. On October 22, Riegner and Lichtheim presented Harrison with a thirty-page report. To stress its reliability, they included Schulte's name and a country-by-country breakdown of German deportations.

More intelligence reached Harrison from Carl Burckhardt, a Swiss diplomat who worked with the International Red Cross. Burckhardt had high contacts in the German army and foreign ministry from whom he also learned the Final Solution's outlines. He hoped the Red Cross would make a public appeal for Europe's Jews, but the Red Cross Executive Committee refused on October 14, arguing that it "would jeopardize all the work undertaken for the prisoners of war and civil internees—the real task of the Red Cross."[115] Instead, Burckhardt went to the Americans in November.

Welles summoned Wise to confirm the worst on November 23. Until now, Jewish organizations in the United States worried that repeated published stories of Jewish suffering might confirm Nazi propaganda that the Allies were fighting for the Jews and even trigger an American antisemitic backlash. Now, however, Wise called a press conference. The *New York Herald Tribune*'s headline of November 25 read: "Wise says Hitler has ordered 4,000,000 Jews Slain."

---

[115]Interview with Burckhardt, November 7, 1942, in *The Red Cross and the Holocaust*, ed. Jean-Claude Favez (New York, 1988), p. 293.

It was the first major US newspaper account of the Final Solution as a whole, and even this story lacked official government imprimatur.[116] In the State Department, Robert Borden Reams, a refugee specialist for whom no amount of confirmation sufficed, was livid. He wrote:

> All of these reports are unconfirmed. [The] Jewish people of Europe are oppressed and it is certain that considerable numbers of them have died in one way or another since the war started. Whether the number of dead amounts to tens of thousands, or, as these reports state, to millions is not material to the main problem. . . . Our main purpose is the winning of the war and other considerations must be subordinate thereto.[117]

On December 8, Rabbi Wise and a delegation of representatives from the major Jewish organizations in the United States met with Roosevelt. They presented a memorandum on what Wise called "the most overwhelming disaster of Jewish history" and asked the president to "do all in your power to bring this to the attention of the world and to do all in your power to make an effort to stop it." Roosevelt confirmed that he knew of the reports. But with wars raging on two fronts and the outcome in doubt, he was vague. "We shall do all in our power to be of service to your people in this tragic moment," he said.[118]

For now, this meant an official statement. After weeks of domestic pressure in Britain from Jewish and Christian leaders, including the Archbishop of Canterbury, Foreign Secretary Anthony Eden read a statement on December 17 in Parliament in the name of eleven allied governments, including the United States and the Soviet Union. The Germans, he said, "are now carrying into effect Hitler's oft-repeated intention to exterminate the Jewish people in Europe. . . . In Poland, which has been made the principal Nazi slaughterhouse, the ghettos established by the German invaders are being systematically emptied of all Jews. . . . None of those taken away are ever heard of again. . . ." Eden added that "those responsible for these crimes shall not escape retribution. . . ." But when questioned about what might be done immediately, Eden said, "I fear that what we can do at this stage must inevitably be slight."[119]

It was slight indeed. Eden already intimated to Jan Karski, the Polish army courier who arrived with Jewish pleas from Warsaw in November, that London would do nothing to divert from the war effort. The British cabinet established a committee on Jewish refugees under Eden, which quickly rejected the notion that Jewish refugees were in a separate class from Polish, Czech, or other refugees who had governments in exile working from London. "Allied criticism would probably result," the committee reported in January 1943, "if any marked preference were shown in removing Jews from territories in enemy occupation." And what if Germany agreed to release the Jews? Eden's committee worried that Hitler would "embarrass other countries by flooding them with alien immigrants."[120] In fact, Jews were not refugees at all by 1942. They were imprisoned victims of impending mass murder.

Other Allied politicians understood as much. In September 1942, US Secretary of State Cordell Hull pressed Vichy to halt deportations, telling the French ambassador that the Germans would "mistreat, enslave, and eventually exterminate these unhappy human beings in conditions

---

[116]Meredith Hindley, "Constructing Allied Humanitarian Policy," in *Bystanders to the Holocaust: A Reappraisal*, eds. David Cesarani and Paul A. Levine (London, 2002), p. 93.

[117]Quoted in Richard Breitman et al., *US Intelligence and the Nazis* (New York, 2005), p. 26.

[118]Quoted in David Wyman, *The Abandonment of the Jews: America and the Holocaust, 1941–1945* (New York, 1984), pp. 72–3.

[119]*Hansard—House of Commons*, Series 5, vol. 385, c. 2082–84.

[120]Bernard Wasserstein, *Britain and the Jews of Europe, 1939–1945* (New York, 1979), p. 184.

of extreme cruelty."[121] When Spain closed its border to Jews fleeing France in March 1943, Winston Churchill warned its ambassador that "the destruction of good relations" would result if Spain turned Jews away or handed Jews over to the Nazis.[122] But after deciding that neither Britain nor any of its Dominion countries could take more Jews—and that Palestine would take none over the assigned quota—Eden's committee punted the issue to Washington.

The Bermuda Conference

American Jews became more vocal in 1943. Wise held a mass rally at Madison Square Garden under the call "Stop Hitler Now!" on March 1, 1943, which drew 75,000. It called for several steps aimed at rescuing Europe's Jews and moving them to the United States, Palestine, Latin America, and elsewhere. Newspapers were sympathetic. "The shame of the world," wrote the *New York Times*, "filled the Garden Monday night."[123] *The Nation* claimed that "you and I and the President and the Congress and the State Department are accessories to the crime and share Hitler's guilt."[124] The White House and State Department were flooded with mail.

Soon after Wise's rally, an elaborate pageant entitled *We Will Never Die!* was staged at Madison Square Garden and other major cities. Financed by the Bergson Group, an argumentative Revisionist Zionist association in the United States, the pageant memorialized the first 2 million Jewish victims while calling for safe havens and intensified rescue efforts. "There will be no Jews left in Europe," said the narration, "when the peace comes."[125] The show received positive reviews, including one from Eleanor Roosevelt, and thus dramatized the Holocaust for hundreds of thousands.

In March 1943, Eden arrived in Washington to discuss strategic issues. Reluctantly he spared thirty minutes on March 27 to speak with Rabbi Wise and Joseph M. Proskauer of the American Jewish Committee. He dismissed their idea of an appeal to Hitler to release Europe's Jews as "fantastically impossible." As for the movement of Bulgarian Jews through Turkey to Palestine, Eden countered, "Turkey does not want any more of your people."[126] Later that day he met with Roosevelt, Welles, and Hull. Eden agreed to accept Jews in Palestine up to the White Paper quota, but noted that they would have to get there on their own and complained that the Germans could slip agents among the refugees. To Hull's worry about Bulgaria's Jews, who, he said, "are threatened with extermination if we do not get them out," Eden replied, "If we do that, then the Jews of the world will be wanting us to make similar offers in Poland and Germany."[127]

Rescue advocates placed their hopes on the Bermuda Conference, a joint Anglo-American meeting on refugees in April 1943. But the conference was calibrated in advance for limited results. Richard K. Law, one of Eden's undersecretaries, headed Britain's delegation. Princeton University President Harold Dodds, a kindred spirit of Breckenridge Long, headed the US

---

[121]Quoted in Zuccotti, *The Holocaust, the French, and the Jews*, pp. 100–1.

[122]Quoted in Wasserstein, *Britain and the Jews of Europe*, p. 206.

[123]Quoted in Max Fraenkel, *The Times of My Life and My Life with The Times* (New York, 1999), p. 49.

[124]Quoted in Wyman, *The Abandonment of the Jews*, pp. 89–90.

[125]Quoted in Atay Citron, "Ben Hecht's Pageant-Drama *A Flag is Born*," in *Staging the Holocaust: The Shoah in Drama and Performance*, ed. Claude Schumacher (New York, 1998), p. 76.

[126]Quoted in Richard Breitman, *Official Secrets: What the Nazis Planned, What the British and Americans Knew* (New York, 1998), p. 182.

[127]Department of State, *Foreign Relations of the United States: Diplomatic Papers 1943*, vol. 3 (Washington, DC, 1963), pp. 38–9.

delegation. It was determined in advance that neither Palestine immigration quotas nor US immigration laws would be challenged, that nothing could be done to divert Allied shipping, and that Jewish refugees would not receive precedence over other refugees.

The twelve-day conference opened on April 19, 1943, the day Jews in the Warsaw ghetto launched their revolt against the Germans. Sol Bloom, a congressman from Brooklyn, was the one Jewish member of either delegation. He was not the choice of American Jews. Long sent him thinking he would be easy to handle. But Bloom irritated both delegations by pressing for a broad rescue policy. It was "preferable," he insisted, "to negotiate so that we could determine what the Germans [are] willing to do."[128] Both Law and Dodds insisted that negotiating with Hitler was out of the question and that millions of Jews could not be accepted. Bloom was outnumbered.

What did the Bermuda conference accomplish? Discussions on non-Jewish refugees, who would return to their countries after the war, were easy. Thus 40,000 Polish refugees in Persia, it was decided, could go to Kenya and India for the war's duration.[129] Jews were another matter. The delegations discussed temporary destinations for Jews stuck in neutral countries, particularly Spain, so that Spain and other neutrals might take more Jews. French North Africa seemed a feasible destination, but it took the United States until May 1944 to establish two small camps in French Morocco, one of which received but 630 Jews. US diplomats and military officers feared Arab reaction should more Jews arrive there, and Roosevelt agreed that moving large numbers to Morocco would be "extremely unwise." Churchill had to press the president personally.[130]

What of Palestine? The British agreed at Bermuda that Palestine could take 29,000 Jews from Bulgaria, a German ally. They fit under the White Paper. Roosevelt afterward agreed to pay for their transport out of emergency funds. But the Nazis scotched the idea after learning of it. To please the Grand Mufti of Jerusalem and perhaps kill the idea altogether, Himmler insisted that these Jews could go to England, not Palestine, and that four Aryan prisoners must be received for each Jew sent. Hitler had no intention of allowing this many Jews to escape.

Law summed up Bermuda's meager results for Eden. Washington, he said, was willing to play a part in the refugee problem. But it was worried about the large slice of public opinion that was

> without being purely anti-Semitic . . . jealous and fearful of an alien immigration. . . . The Americans, therefore, while they must do their utmost to placate Jewish opinion, dare not offend 'American' opinion. . . . If it came to a showdown, Jew and Gentile, I am convinced that their internal position is such that they would have to tell the Jewish organizations to go to hell."[131]

Jewish organizations and other sympathizers understood. Wise called the Bermuda Conference "sad and sordid." *The New York Times* called it a "cruel mockery." "And so," reported the *Jewish Chronicle* in May 1943, "the greatest tragedy in modern history must go on."[132]

---

[128]Morning Conference, April 20, 1943: Confidential Memorandum for the Chairman, National Archives and Records Administration (College Park, MD), RG 59, Lot File 52 D 408, Box 3.

[129]Wasserstein, *Britain and the Jews of Europe*, p. 193.

[130]Richard Breitman, "The Allied War Effort and the Jews, 1942–1943," *Journal of Contemporary History*, 20, no. 1 (January 1985), p. 149.

[131]Quoted in Wasserstein, *Britain and the Jews of Europe*, pp. 201–2.

[132]Quotes in Wyman, *The Abandonment of the Jews*, p. 120; Wasserstein, *Britain and the Jews of Europe*, p. 202.

13

Rescue
The Final Solution Interrupted, 1942–1943

In March 1942, 75 to 80 percent of the Holocaust's victims were still alive; 20 to 25 percent had perished. After a furious eleven months of killing that accompanied the start of *Aktion Reinhard*, deportations to Auschwitz-Birkenau, and the second wave of killing in the USSR, the situation reversed. In February 1943, 75 to 80 percent of the Jews who would perish in the Holocaust were dead; 20 to 25 percent were still alive.[1] But as more throughout Europe understood what deportation meant, the Final Solution became more difficult. Resistance became more common, as shown by the Warsaw ghetto uprising in Poland and the growing activity of rescue networks in France. Even in Germany, a group of Aryan housewives protested their Jewish husbands' deportation.

Governments also helped to interrupt German planning. The Bermuda Conference showed that the Allies would not place rescue operations above the war itself. But Allied military victories saved large numbers of Jews—more than rescue operations would have accomplished. Other European states, meanwhile, from Sweden in the north to Italy in the south, began to save those who could be saved. Indeed this trend became the de facto condition of rescue. The Allies fought the battles. It was up to European states to withstand Germany's war against the Jews.

13.1 THE NAZIS AND THE JEWS OF THE MIDDLE EAST

Palestine

Roughly 425,000 Jews lived officially in Palestine when the war began. The Grand Mufti of Jerusalem, Haj Amin al-Husseini, spoke for Arab nationalists and Muslim fundamentalists who rejected *any* Jewish presence. In February 1941, from his exile in Baghdad, he offered Hitler the Arab world's support against the British and the Jews, describing the latter as "that dangerous enemy whose secret weapons are finance, corruption, and intrigue."[2] He arrived in Berlin in November, after a failed anti-British coup in Iraq, where he met Hitler.

---

[1]Christopher R. Browning, "One Day at Jozefow: Initiation to Mass Murder," in *Lessons and Legacies: The Meaning of the Holocaust in a Changing World*, ed. Peter Hayes (Evanston, IL, 1991), pp. 196–209.

[2]Klaus-Michael Mallmann and Martin Cüppers, *Nazi Palestine: The Plans for the Extermination of the Jews of Palestine* (New York, 2010), p. 64.

Grand Mufti Haj Amin
al-Husseini, in Berlin, 1942
Source: Scherl/DIZ München GmbH,
Süddeutsche Zeitung Photo/Alamy.

The Grand Mufti hoped Hitler would support Arab independence and eliminate the Jewish national home in Palestine. By now killing operations against Jews were unway in the USSR. German Jews had been deported to Riga and Minsk. *Aktion Reinhard* was in its planning stages. Hitler talked around Arab independence but was pleased to grant the Mufti's second wish:

> Germany [stands] for uncompromising war against the Jews. . . . This naturally [includes] . . . the Jewish national home in Palestine, which [is] nothing other than a center . . . for the . . . destructive influence by Jewish interests. . . . Germany [is] resolved. . . . to ask one European nation after the other to solve its Jewish problem, and at the proper time to direct a similar appeal to non-European nations as well. . . . It [goes] without saying that Germany [will] furnish positive and practical aid to the Arabs involved in the same struggle. . . .

When German forces reached Palestine, he continued, "Germany's objective would then be solely the destruction of the Jewish element residing in the Arab sphere. . . ."[3] The German Foreign Ministry provided the Mufti with generous funding and accommodations in Berlin. Heinrich Himmler visited him several times, referring to "the fellowship of our common struggle." Adolf Eichmann agreed to have his staff aid the Mufti when German forces reached Jerusalem.[4]

General Erwin Rommel commanded German and Italian forces in Libya. He hoped to drive eastward through Egypt to the Suez Canal, cutting Britain's lifeline to India. In June 1942, Rommel finally captured Tobruk, the eastern Libyan port that he needed to advance. An elated Hitler crowed to Mussolini that "the British Eighth Army is virtually destroyed," while in London, Parliament debated whether Churchill should be replaced.[5] Rommel pressed to Britain's defensive position at El Alamein outside Alexandria, just three days' march to the Suez Canal and Palestine.

---

[3]Germany, Auswärtiges Amt, *Akten zur deutschen auswärtigen Politik 1918–1945*, Series D, vol. 13 (Baden-Baden, 1956), doc. 515.

[4]Quoted in Mallmann and Cüppers, *Nazi Palestine,* pp. 100, 128.

[5]*Völkischer Beobachter*, June 22, 1942; Santi Corvaja, ed., *Hitler and Mussolini The Secret Meetings* (New York, 2008), p. 205.

On July 1, 1942, Himmler and Hitler agreed to create an *Einsatzkommando* to murder the Jews of Egypt and Palestine. SS-Colonel Walter Rauff, a protégé of Reinhard Heydrich who helped developed the gas vans used in 1941 and after, commanded the unit. By late July, Rauff's group moved to Athens and awaited transport to Africa. The unit, named *Einsatzkommando Egypt*, was small. Rauff expected help from the Arabs.

Haj Amin al-Husseini and his followers in Berlin called Arabs to action through radio broadcasts originating from Berlin. "All over the country," said a June 1942 broadcast, "the Jews should be watched. Every Jew's name should be written down, together with his address. . . . The Jews must be watched carefully so that they can be wiped out at the earliest opportunity. . . ." A broadcast in July was more explicit:

> You must kill the Jews before they open fire on you. Kill the Jews, who have appropriated your wealth. . . . Arabs of Syria, Iraq and Palestine, what are you waiting for? The Jews are planning to violate your women, to kill your children, and to destroy you. According to the Muslim religion, the defense of your life is a duty, which can only be fulfilled by annihilating the Jews. This is your best opportunity to get rid of this dirty race. . . . Kill the Jews, burn their property, destroy their stores. . . . Your sole hope of salvation lies in annihilating the Jews. . . .[6]

The Germans never passed El Alamein. The Royal Navy sunk Axis supply ships headed for Africa. The United States sent tanks to the British in Egypt. Repeated German assaults failed, and in the second half of October, General Bernard Law Montgomery attacked with a three-to-one advantage in troops and full air superiority. By February 1943, he drove Rommel through Libya into Tunisia. With its main theater in the USSR, Germany could not reinforce Rommel. The Mufti remained in Berlin.

What if Rommel had triumphed? Despite Churchill's argument that the Jews "are our only friends in Palestine," Britain's War Office refused the offer of a Jewish army division from the Jewish Agency Executive (JAE) in Jerusalem.[7] Over 22,000 Jewish volunteers from Palestine served in the British army by late 1942, but they were deployed throughout the Mediterranean theater.[8] The British formed a small, poorly outfitted Jewish-Arab Palestinian regiment between June and September 1942, to which three Jewish battalions were transferred. But they would be pulled out in a British retreat. Another 19,000 Jewish policemen could serve as auxiliaries, but the British provided less than one-third with weapons. The JAE expanded its own militia, the *Hagana*. But the *Palmach*—the *Hagana*'s elite force—had but 1,300 trained members by August 1942.[9]

The JAE depended on moderate Arabs. "All of us, Jews and Arabs," remembered Aharon Danin of the Jewish National Fund, "were convinced that the Mufti's men would arrive at the head of the German forces and would do their best to destroy their Arab opponents as well as the Jews." Prominent Arab moderates established "peace brigades" that rooted radicals from villages in return for payments from the JAE. *Shai*, the *Hagana's* intelligence arm, used former followers of the Mufti as informants, often in return for benefits such as construction jobs. "Cut off

---

[6]Quoted in Jeffrey Herf, *Nazi Propaganda for the Arab World* (New Haven, CT, 2009), pp. 112, 126.

[7]Quoted in Morris Beckman, *The Jewish Brigade: An Army with Two Masters 1944–1945* (Rockville Center, NY, 1998), p. 14.

[8]Figure in *American Jewish Yearbook*, vol. 45, p. 334.

[9]Figures in Yehuda Bauer, "Cooperation to Resistance: The Hagana 1938–1946," *Middle Eastern Studies*, 2, no. 3 (April 1966), p. 198; Ronald W. Zweig, "British Plans for the Evacuation of Palestine in 1941–1942," *Studies in Zionism*, 4, no. 2 (Autumn 1983), p. 299; Beckman, *The Jewish Brigade*, p. 24.

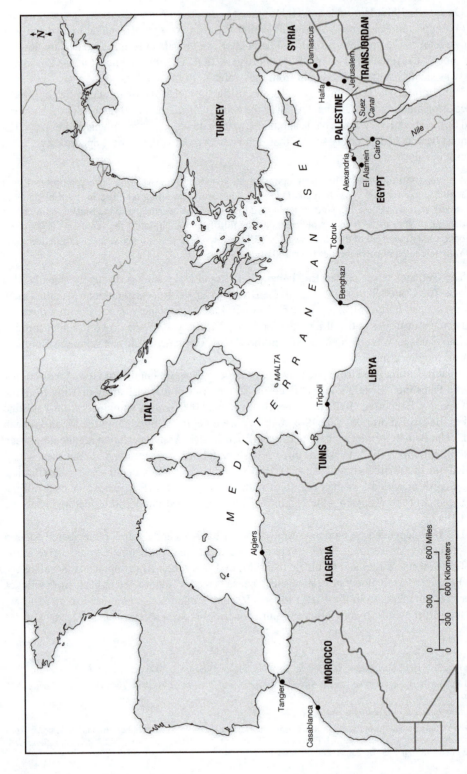

MAP 13.1 North Africa and the Middle East. *Source:* Based on a map from the History Department Atlas database of the United States Military Academy.

my hand," said one, "if I repeat my foolish actions."[10] This intelligence led to arrests of radical imams and seizure of weapons caches.

Still, Palestine sat on a knife's edge. Yitzhak Tebenkin of the labor movement *Histadrut* called for partisan warfare. "Every man on the spot," he said, "with every kind of weapon, must be ready for self defense, because the Arabs will also attack us."[11] Jews prepared to replay the last ditch battle of 73 CE at Masada against the Romans. "To perish honorably," said *Palmach* commander Yitzhak Sadeh, "has some value."[12]

French North Africa

French Morocco, Algeria, and Tunisia fell under Vichy control with France's 1940 defeat. Jews in French North Africa numbered some 280,000, mostly concentrated in the coastal cities. Vichy's anti-Jewish laws, starting with the October 1940 *Statut des Juifs*, applied across North Africa. The Germans expected to include North Africa's Jews in the Final Solution. The Wannsee Conference estimated 700,000 Jews in unoccupied France even though only 330,000 at most lived in the entire country. Many scholars agree that Jews in French North Africa were part of the German estimate.[13]

Vichy laws were applied most stringently in Algeria, the north of which was administratively part of France and where French pro-Vichy, antisemitic, and anti-Muslim elements were strong. In August 1940, Algeria's republican Governor General Georges Le Beau was retired. "Jewish friends," he warned, "you are going to suffer. Stay courageous. . . ."[14] Vichy stripped Algeria's 115,000 Jews of their citizenship, seized their property, fired them from state jobs, prohibited them from professional practice, and expelled their children from public schools. Anti-Jewish violence was common. Algerian Jews were pro–de Gaulle, anti-Vichy, and on their guard. "They wish us to die simply because we are Jews," proclaimed underground leader José Aboulker in 1941, "but I will die because I am an anti-Nazi, and it will be in a manner of my own choosing."[15]

French Morocco and Algeria also had some sixty work camps of varying size and duration.[16] Primarily they held Spanish republican refugees and foreign Jews stranded in the midst of their flight from Europe. Some had joined the French Foreign Legion to fight Hitler and were now demobilized. The camps had insufficient food, water, and shelter as well as lice, scorpions, and poisonous snakes. Disciplinary methods included *tombier*—burial up to one's neck and stoning by guards if one moved.[17]

---

[10]Quotes from Hillel Cohen, *Army of Shadows: Palestinian Collaboration with Zionism, 1917–1948* (Berkeley, CA, 2009), pp. 144, 176, 181.

[11]Quoted in Yehuda Bauer, *From Diplomacy to Resistance: A History of Jewish Palestine, 1939–1945* (New York, 1973), p. 181.

[12]Quoted in Yoav Gelber, "The Defense of Palestine in World War II," *Studies in Zionism*, 8, no. 1 (Spring 1987), pp. 78–9.

[13]Dan Michman, "Waren die Juden Nordafrikas im Visier der Planungen zur 'Endlösung'? Die 'Schoah' und die Zahl 700.000 in Eichmanns Tabelle am 20. Januar 1942," in *Besprechung mit anschließendem Frühstück: Die Wannsee-Konferenz am 20. Januar 1942*, eds., Norbert Kampe and Peter Klein (Vienna, 2013, forthcoming).

[14]Quoted in Gitta Amipaz-Silber, *The Role of the Jewish Underground in the American Landing in Algiers, 1940–1942* (Jerusalem, 1992), p. 64.

[15]Quoted in Geoffrey Adams, *Political Ecumenism: Catholics, Jews and Protestants in de Gaulle's Free France, 1940–1945* (Montreal, 2006), p. 245.

[16]Figure in Robert Satloff, *Among the Righteous: Lost Stories from the Holocaust's Long Reach into the Arab Lands* (New York, 2006), pp. 60–1.

[17]Figures, which range from 2,000 Jewish legionnaires, are in Zosa Szajkowski, *Jews and the French Foreign Legion* (New York, 1975), p. 84. For the camps, see pp. 87–190.

Vichy's chief labor project in Africa was the Trans-Sahara Railroad, a 1,300-mile link between French North and West Africa. Work paid a half penny a day and included clearing rocks, leveling dunes, mining coal along the route, and laying track in 125-degree heat. Harry Alexander, a German Jew interned in the Algerian desert, remembered a French commandant's announcement: "You all came here to die. You are the scum of Europe . . . the garbage of the world. My job is to see that you all die here. . . . And I'm good at what I'm doing."[18]

Allied troops landed in French Morocco and Algeria in November 1942. Of the 377 French resistance fighters who took control of Algiers the night before US troops arrived, 315 were Jews.[19] But to attain a quick cease-fire with Vichy troops that would enable advance against the Germans, the United States allowed Vichy loyalists to remain in power. French authorities arrested Jewish resistors after the Allied invasion. Antisemitic laws remained in force, labor camps stayed open, and Vichy propaganda blamed Jews for the Allied invasion. The French maintained that they could not afford to upset the European or Muslim populations.

US authorities did not argue. General George Patton warned, "If we get orders to favor the Jews we will precipitate trouble and possibly civil war."[20] North African Jewish groups and the World Jewish Congress pressed for restoration of Jewish rights and closure of the camps. *The New Republic* wrote in February 1943 that "[w]e can either have [camp prisoners] released immediately, or else acknowledge ourselves as accomplices."[21] Not until March and April 1943 did French authorities, under Allied pressure, repeal anti-Jewish laws and close the camps. Jews' citizenship in Algeria was restored in October 1943 thanks to General de Gaulle, who ousted the Vichy leaders after arriving in Algiers in May.

The Germans in Tunisia

When Allied troops landed in French Morocco and Algeria, Germans troops landed in Tunisia to stem Allied advances. Rauff's *Einsatzkommando*, once slated for Palestine, arrived on November 24, 1942 to launch an assault on Tunisia's 66,000 Jews, half of whom lived in the capital of Tunis. Rauff remained for six months but could not organize mass murder. The local French governor, Admiral Jean-Pierre Estéva, opposed even Vichy's measures, and the Italian government protected the 5,000 Jews in Tunisia who held Italian citizenship. The Germans deported several dozen Jewish notables to their deaths in Europe. If this was the start of a larger plan, Allied advances thwarted it.

Tunisian Jews were terrorized nonetheless. Rauff's unit demanded tens of millions of francs in cash and gold and plundered Jewish property owing to Jewish "responsibility" for the Allied invasion. He ordered Tunis's leading Jews to form a Jewish Council to provide slave labor for army projects. When too few Jews turned up for work, Rauff's police and German soldiers arrested Jews in synagogues and community centers and took hostages to ensure the council's obedience. The Jewish Council raised some 5,000 Tunisian Jews from poorer families. They filled over forty slave labor camps in Tunisia. Jewish contributions kept them fed, but miserable conditions and the proximity of Allied forces emboldened many to escape and hide. By May 1943, only

---

[18]Quoted in Satloff, *Among the Righteous*, pp. 60–61.

[19]Figure in Israel Gutman, gen. ed., *Encyclopedia of the Holocaust* (New York, 1990), vol. 1, p. 21.

[20]Quoted in Richard Breitman, "The Allied War Effort and the Jews, 1942–1943," *Journal of Contemporary History*, 20, no. 1 (January 1985), p. 142.

[21]Quoted in Szajkowski, *Jews and the French Foreign Legion*, p. 117.

1,500 remained in work camps. Hitler acknowledged in March that North Africa was lost. Rauff's unit was extracted from Tunis on May 9, four days before 250,000 Axis soldiers surrendered. It was redeployed in Italy. Over 2,500 Tunisian Jews were killed during the German occupation.[22]

"The North Africans know," said the Grand Mufti, ". . . that Jews were the champions of imperialism that has mistreated North Africa for so long."[23] Still, Muslim bystanders mirrored their European counterparts. Some jeered at Jews, some stole Jewish property, some were informants or sadistic camp guards. Others took fleeing Jews into their homes, risked their lives by confronting assailants, and showed humanity to Jewish laborers. In Algiers, Muslim imams instructed followers not to enrich themselves by buying stolen Jewish property. One Jewish resistor noted that, with regard to the struggle against Vichy, "The Arabs do not participate. . . . It is not their war. But, as regards the Jews, they are perfect."[24]

13.2 THE GERMANS, THE JAPANESE, AND THE SHANGHAI GHETTO

The Germans and Shanghai

Japan's war in Asia was criminal. Its troops killed roughly 260,000 noncombatants when they captured Nanking in 1937. Japan's murder of Allied prisoners of war on death marches and in prison camps led to numerous trials after 1945. Japan's Unit 731 in Manchuria conducted biological experiments on up to 10,000—mostly Chinese—prisoners. But most of the 18,000 Jewish refugees in Shanghai survived. Japanese troops occupied Shanghai's International Settlement on December 8, 1941. Enemy nationals—from Britain and the United States, for example—had their bank accounts frozen, had to register with the Japanese authorities, and had to wear red armbands. The Japanese censored news and arrested enemy journalists. But they took no special measures against Jewish refugees save for halting Jewish immigration in March 1942. Most Jews were not from Allied countries.

Germany and Japan fought common enemies but never coordinated their war efforts. Irritated with Japan's reticence on the Jewish question, Berlin acted where it could. Through intelligence contacts, Germany's general consulate in Shanghai kept itself informed regarding émigré Jews, particularly journalists who wrote anti-Nazi stories. The consulate insisted that children born in Shanghai to mixed German-Jewish couples not receive German names. After November 25, 1941, the consulate stripped *Mischlinge* (half or quarter Jews) in Shanghai of German citizenship and threatened to void the citizenship of Aryans in mixed marriages who would not divorce their Jewish spouses. "In view of their marriage," said a missive in June 1940, "[they] have lost all connection to their former homeland."[25]

In June 1942, as the killing of Europe's Jews reached a crescendo, SS-Colonel Joseph Meisinger travelled to Shanghai. From 1939 to 1941, Meisinger earned the name "Butcher of Warsaw" as the police chief of the General Government's Warsaw District. There he ordered over 3,000 Poles sent to Auschwitz and conducted reprisal shootings against both Poles and Jews.[26]

---

[22]Figures in Michael Abitbol, *The Jews of North Africa During the Second World War* (Detroit, MI, 1989), p. 134; Satloff, *Among the Righteous*, p. 55.

[23]Quoted in Mallmann and Cüppers, *Nazi Palestine*, p. 177.

[24]Quoted in Satloff, *Among the Righteous*, p. 108.

[25]Quoted in Astrid Freyeisen, *Shanghai und die Politik des dritten Reiches* (Würzburg, 2000), p. 456.

[26]Figures in Freyeisen, *Shanghai*, pp. 465–6.

Himmler transferred him to Tokyo, where he served as the German embassy's police attaché, visiting Shanghai several times.

In July, Meisinger met with a Japanese delegation in Shanghai that included Japan's vice consul Shibata Mitsugi. Years later, Shibata remembered Meisinger's proposal: "For the sake of our alliance we believe that the Jewish plague in Shanghai must be erased. You needn't trouble yourselves at all over carrying it through; we will manage all of the details. . . ."[27] Meisinger suggested rounding up Shanghai's Jews on Rosh Hashanah, when they would be easy to catch, and then placing them in a camp at the mouth of the Yangtze River. He proposed several extermination methods, including starvation, death through work, or medical experiments.

Shibata was horrified. Fearing that other Japanese officials might approve these proposals, he informed leading Jews of German intentions. He might have had other motives. Some Japanese authorities saw Shanghai Jews—some of whom had connections to Chinese forces—as a security threat. But some leading Jews served as Japanese spies and even business partners in Shanghai, and Shibata fared well from these connections.[28] Japan never followed Meisinger's suggestions.

The Shanghai Ghetto

Japan's military authorities took measures on February 18, 1943, however, to segregate suspicious Jews. They announced the formation of a one-square-mile designated area in the Hongkou district to which all stateless refugees had to move by May 18. The decree avoided the words *Jews* and *ghetto*, but it proclaimed East Asia's first ghetto nonetheless. The Japanese saw it as a security measure. Jews who were not refugees, namely Jews of Middle Eastern and Russian descent who arrived before 1937, were not affected. Aryan women married to German Jews who arrived after 1937, on the other hand, had to enter the restricted area with their husbands. The German consulate counted 517 such spouses and offered to protect and support them financially if they divorced.[29]

In all, perhaps 10,000—most stateless refugees—had to move. The ghetto had no barbed wire or walls, but Japanese troops guarded the perimeter and Jews could not leave without permission. It was the most crowded part of the International Settlement. Food and sanitation were insufficient, lice and mosquitoes were everywhere. Some 6,000 central European Jews were said to be near starvation, and between 1943 and 1945, several hundred children and elderly people died of malnutrition and disease.[30] The Japanese were occasionally magnanimous. They provided passes in September and October 1943 so that Rosh Hashanah and Yom Kippur services could be held in two theaters outside the ghetto. In 1944, the Japanese allowed the American Jewish Joint Distribution Committee (JDC) to transfer funds to the ghetto for food, which the US government also allowed.[31]

The Germans surrendered on May 8, 1945. Japan did not surrender until September 2. The Americans inadvertently bombed the ghetto in July 1945, killing several hundred Chinese and thirty-one Jewish refugees.[32] The ghetto was not opened until September 1945, when US and

---

[27]Quoted in Freyseisen, *Shanghai*, p. 470.

[28]Pan Guang, "The Relations Between Jewish Refugees and Chinese in Shanghai During Wartime," in *Exil Shangai 1938–1947*, eds., Georg Armbrüster et al. (Teetz, 2000), pp. 77–83.

[29]Christiane Hoss, "Der lange Arm des Deutschen Reiches: Zu den Ausbürgerungen von Emigrantinnen und Emigranten in Shanghai," in Armbrüster et al., eds., *Exil Shanghai*, p. 178.

[30]Figure in Ernst Heppner, *Shanghai Refuge: A Memoir of the World War II Jewish Ghetto* (Lincoln, NE, 1993), p. 99.

[31]Evelyn Pike Rubin, *Ghetto Shanghai* (New York, 1993), p. 136.

[32]Figure in David Kranzler, "The Miracle of Shanghai," in Armbrüster et al., eds., *Exil Shanghai*, p. 43.

Chinese troops liberated Shanghai. "Europe," said one Jewish refugee, "would have been much safer for us."[33] Only as more news arrived did they realize how fortunate they were.

13.3 RESCUE IN THE NORTH

The Northern Theater

Germany's occupation of Denmark and Norway in 1940 also guaranteed the pliability of neighboring Sweden, now cut off from the western powers. Officially neutral, the Swedes exported strategic minerals to Germany, and German forces used Sweden's railways and coastal waters. Finland, meanwhile, was a natural German ally, having fought the Soviets alone in 1939 and then again on the German side after 1941 to recover final territory it lost earlier. The northern theater increased in importance. Germany used Norwegian bases to attack British convoys to the Soviets after 1941, Swedish iron ore became more critical, Denmark supplied one-twelfth of Germany's food, and Germany stationed 200,000 troops in Finland. All of these factors affected German steps against Jews in these states.

The Jewish populations were small and assimilated. The northern states had few German Jewish refugees because they restricted the number who entered before the war. As Denmark's Justice Minister Karl Steinke put it in 1938, his country could not "contribute . . . to solving the so-called Jewish problem."[34] Yet no state, left to its own, was willing to hand Jews over to the Germans. At the Wannsee Conference of January 1942, Foreign Ministry representative Martin Luther surmised as much. "In some countries" he said, "such as the Scandinavian states, difficulties will arise . . . it will therefore be advisable to defer actions in these countries."[35]

Finland

Finland's 2,300 Jews were included in the Wannsee discussions, and Finland was a German ally. But Finland was a democracy and not antisemitic. In June 1942, Himmler visited Helsinki. Prime Minister Johann Wilhelm Rangell claimed later to have told him that "[w]e have no Jewish question," and Finland placed no restrictions on its Jews, many of whom were fighting at the front. Himmler offered to take the 200 or so Jewish refugees who had come from Germany and Austria and who were now in refugee camps. He might also have threatened to curtail German food imports if Helsinki did not cooperate.

The Finnish State Police, whose leaders were antisemetic, prepared lists of foreign Jews for deportation. In November 1942, it began handing Jewish refugees to the Germans. But the initial transport became public thanks to a postcard sent en route by Dr. Walter Cohen, an Austrian Jewish refugee, to the head of Helsinki's Jewish community. An outcry resulted. Eight Jewish refugees were handed over to the Germans, seven of whom were killed, but Finnish police sent the rest to Sweden, which accepted the refugees in 1944.

Finland protected other Jews under its control. Most Jewish Red Army prisoners held by the Finns were kept in separate work camps because Helsinki's Jewish community intervened. None were handed to the Germans. Finnish Jewish soldiers prayed in the Eastern Front's only

---

[33]Quoted in Rubin, *Ghetto Shanghai*, p. 140.

[34]Quoted in Lone Rünitz, "The Politics of Asylum in Denmark in the Wake of *Kristallnacht*: A Case Study," in *Denmark and the Holocaust*, eds. Mette Bastholm Jensen and Steven L. B. Jensen (Copenhagen, 2003), p. 31.

[35]Protocol in Mark Roseman, *The Wannsee Conference and the Final Solution: A Reconsideration* (New York, 2002), p. 166.

field synagogue and Jewish medics, whatever their feelings, treated wounded German soldiers. In January 1943, Wippert von Blücher, Germany's representative in Helsinki, warned that Germany should not press the Jewish question in Finland. Berlin followed his advice. On Finland's independence day, December 6, 1944, Marshal Carl Gustav Emil Mannerheim, Finland's president and the commander of its armed forces, visited Helsinki's main synagogue to show appreciation to his Jewish officers, who expressed their own appreciation in return.[36]

Sweden and Norway

Sweden's prewar Jewish population was 6,000. The Swedish public condemned prewar Nazi violence against Jews. But Europe's Jewish problem, as Swedish diplomats said at the Evian conference, was not Sweden's to solve. Sweden tightened restrictions on visas for Jews in 1939 so that, while the Netherlands had some 20,000 Jewish refugees from Germany by war's outbreak, Sweden had 2,000.[37] "No matter how great the sympathy for the Jews may be in Sweden," reported the US embassy in Stockholm, "no one really wants to take the risk of creating a Jewish problem by the liberal admission of Jewish refugees."[38]

But Sweden's neutrality meant that it had well-informed diplomats in Germany and the lands Germany occupied. They reported to Stockholm in 1941 about the pogroms in the USSR, the conditions for Jews in Poland, and deportations of German Jews. In 1942, they reported on deportations of French and Dutch Jews. In September 1942, an SS colonel named Kurt Gerstein approached a Swedish diplomat in Warsaw named Göran von Otter. A horrified Gerstein had witnessed gassings of women and children in Bełżec and was determined that the truth be known. His information reached Stockholm, confirming similar reports from other sources. Gösta Engzell was in charge of the legal division that controlled visas. Unlike his counterparts in Washington, he did not dismiss the reports as wild rumors.[39]

A shift in Sweden's refugee policy began with the deportation of Norway's tiny Jewish population of 1,700 Jews, which was concentrated in Oslo and Trondheim. When the Germans occupied Norway, King Haakon VII and the government fled to London. The Germans used an unpopular collaborationist Norwegian government under Vidkun Quisling that issued official laws, but in truth, the Germans ruled directly through reliable Norwegian police. Arrests of Jews and the seizure of their property began with the invasion of the USSR. Brutal deportations under Eichmann's staff began in November 1942. Ships carried Jews from Oslo to Stettin; trains took them to Auschwitz. By March 1943, the Germans transported 759 Jews. Twenty-five survived. In all, the Germans killed 40 percent of the Jews in Norway, two-thirds of whom were Norwegian citizens.[40]

[36]Figures and quotes on Finland's Jews in William B. Cohen and Jörgen Svensson, "Finland and the Holocaust," *Holocaust and Genocide Studies*, 9, no. 1 (Spring 1995), pp. 70–92; Antero Homila, "Finland and the Holocaust: A Reassessment," *Holocaust and Genocide Studies*, 23, no. 3 (Winter 2009), pp. 413–40; Hannu Rautkallio, "Cast into the Lion's Den: Finnish Jewish Soldiers in the Second World War," *Journal of Contemporary History*, 29 (January 1994), pp. 53–94.

[37]Figure in Paul Levine, *From Indifference to Activism: Swedish Diplomacy and the Holocaust, 1938–1944* (Uppsala, 1996), p. 103.

[38]Sterling to Secretary of State, November 18, 1938, in *The Holocaust: Selected Documents in Eighteen Volumes*, vol. 3, gen. eds. John Mendelsohn and Donald S. Detwiler (New York, 1982), doc. 30.

[39]Levine, *From Indifference to Activism*, pp. 127–9.

[40]Figures in Oskar Mendelsohn, "Norwegen," in *Dimensionen des Völkermordes: Die Zahl der jüdischen Opfer des Nationalsozialismus,* ed., Wolfgang Benz (Munich, 1991), p. 187–96.

What of the other 60 percent? Swedish diplomats witnessed the deportations and reported to Stockholm. The Swedish newspaper *Dagens Nyheter* reported in November 1942 that "these measures are . . . completely incomprehensible" and that "[o]ur neutrality must not become an unfeeling indifference." In Stockholm, Engzell noted on November 27 that "[i]f these Jews are transported into Poland's interior, we fear that nothing more can be done." On December 3, the Swedish legation in Berlin received orders from Sweden's Prime Minister Albin Per Hannsson. The German Foreign Ministry was to be told: "Sweden is prepared to accept all remaining Jews in Norway. . . ."

The German Foreign Ministry helped to implement the Final Solution. But to avoid diplomatic problems, they allowed foreign governments to claim—and thus save—their small numbers of Jews living abroad by certain deadlines. Denmark, Finland, and Sweden all claimed their Jews. But on orders from Foreign Minister Joachim von Ribbentrop, German diplomats repeatedly rejected Swedish offers to claim non-Swedish Jews. They complained instead about the Swedish press's hostility to the deportations and warned that Sweden's offers should not be made public lest relations between the two countries suffer. Eric von Post of Sweden's legation in Berlin cabled, "German authorities completely disregard representations and requests from outsiders."[41]

Stockholm undertook alternatives without public announcement. Its general consulate in Olso issued Swedish passports to arrested foreign Jews, which in turn entitled them to the protection of the Swedish government. This procedure did not always work with suspicious German authorities who issued exit visas from Norway. Swedish police also allowed the 900 Norwegian Jews who reached the Swedish border in 1942 and 1943 into the country. The Norwegian underground provided Jews with escape routes, escort, and food. Despite the 1,100-mile border, escape was difficult, especially in the winter months. Elderly Jews were carried over the border in stretchers.[42]

Denmark

Home to 8,000 Jews when the war broke out, Denmark has a heroic legacy. It was the only Nazi-occupied country where most of the Jewish population—95 percent—was saved. One cannot draw general conclusions regarding nationality and heroism. Denmark's Jewish population also benefited from a more benign German occupation; an oddly executed deportation plan; and Danish geography, which allowed escape to Sweden. But the story remains remarkable.

Denmark, like everyplace else, restricted the arrival of Jewish refugees before the war. Yet Nazism was not popular in Denmark, and the Germans stepped carefully. Denmark remained theoretically sovereign under a light occupation presence. King Christian X remained in Copenhagen, the elected government remained intact, and the German government negotiated for base rights, ship sales, roughly 100,000 Danish workers, and substantial food imports to Germany amounting to a twelfth of annual rations.[43]

Most Danes saw Jewish citizens as full members of the community, and despite German pressure, the government refused to implement anti-Jewish legislation. When a German diplomat told King Christian in November 1941 that Denmark needed to initiate anti-Jewish measures, the king sarcastically responded, "We Danes don't need to do anything in this matter because

---

[41]Quotes from Levine, *From Indifference to Activism*, pp. 136–9, 144.

[42]Figures in Mendelsohn, "Norwegen," in Benz, ed., *Dimensionen*, p. 197.

[43]Figure in Gerhard L. Weinberg, *A World at Arms: A Global History of World War II* (New York, 2005) p. 509.

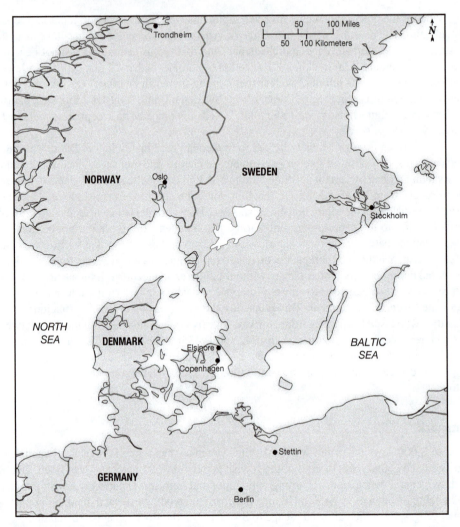

MAP 13.2   The northern theater in World War II.   *Source:* Based on Gilbert, Martin, *The Righteous: The Unsung Heroes of the Holocaust* (Henry Holt & Company, 2003), p. 460.

we don't feel inferior to Jews."[44] In the same month in Berlin, Foreign Minister Eric Scavenius told Hermann Göring that there was "no Jewish question in Denmark." On Scavenius's return to Copenhagen, Denmark's chief rabbi Max Friediger was told, "as long as the Danish government has anything to say . . . the Jews have no grounds for fear."[45]

In August 1943, German military defeats in the USSR and North Africa, combined with the lengthening occupation in Denmark, triggered Danish strikes and sabotage. On August 29, following the bombing of a German military barracks by Danish resistors, the Germans declared martial law. The king was placed under house arrest; Danish soldiers were interned; and leading Danes, including Rabbi Friediger, were taken hostage.

---

[44]Quoted in Levine, *From Indifference to Activism*, p. 231.

[45]Quotes in Leni Yahil, *The Rescue of Danish Jewry: Test of a Democracy* (Philadelphia, PA, 1969), pp. 47, 50.

SS-General Dr. Werner Best was Germany's plenipotentiary in Denmark. Up to this point, he had resisted the idea of Jewish roundups for fear of Danish reactions. The delay caused irritation in Berlin. Best understood that the imposition of martial law intensified the Jewish question. "It is my opinion," he cabled the German Foreign Ministry on September 8, "that measures should now be taken toward a solution of the problem of the Jews. . . ."[46] Hitler approved the deportation by September 16.

How serious Best was is a matter of dispute. To arrest and deport Denmark's Jews in one sweep and to keep order afterward, Best requested a larger-than-possible influx of German police. Only 1,800 German policemen, mostly Order Police, began arriving in Denmark in mid-September. Himmler could not send more thanks to Germany's occupation of Italy, which had just quit the war. And unlike his counterparts elsewhere, Best could not depend on local police who, with their own government suddenly pushed aside, would not take German orders. Germany's military commander in Denmark, Lt. General Hermann von Hannecken, refused to have German troops help and warned that deportations would result in a halt of imports.

Best chose a route between obedience and self-preservation. On September 11, 1943, he leaked information regarding the deportation to Georg Ferdinand Duckwitz, Germany's shipping attaché in Copenhagen. Duckwitz had many contacts among Danish government officials and businessmen. On September 17, Best had German police seize lists of Jewish addresses from Jewish community organizations. The seizure predictably fed rumors of impending trouble and triggered protests from Danish officials. Best reported to Berlin on September 18 that the "deportation of the Jews will undoubtedly cause a sharp deterioration of the situation in Denmark."[47] Himmler rebuffed the warning.

Matters moved to a head at the end of the month. The transport ship *Wartheland* arrived in Copenhagen, ordered by Eichmann's office to take Denmark's Jews to Stettin en route to Auschwitz. By September 28, it was decided that the Jewish roundup would take place on the night of October 1–2. Duckwitz informed his contacts in the Danish government, who in turn informed Jewish leaders. "The dreaded action against the Jews is coming," said Hans-Hedoff Hansen, the chairman of the Danish Social Democratic Party, to C. B. Henriques, the chairman of Denmark's Jewish community. "On the night between 1st and 2nd October the Gestapo will search for all Jews in their homes and then transport them to ships in the harbor. You must . . . warn every single Jew. . . ."[48]

Henriques, like other Jewish leaders who received this warning, did not believe it at first. But as word spread through friends and family members, the worst was understood. Most Jews fled their homes within hours, hurriedly entrusting their property and businesses with friends and neighbors. They fled to the countryside or hid with sympathetic Danes. Some stayed in hospitals under false names. Danish churches were vocal. "Wherever Jews are persecuted for racial or religious reasons," all pastors read on October 3, "it is the duty of the Christian church to protest. . . . We shall fight for the right of our Jewish brothers and sisters to keep the freedom that we ourselves value more highly than life."[49] One bishop hid 150 refugees in his palace at Nykøbing.[50]

---

[46]Document in Yahil, *The Rescue of Danish Jewry*, pp. 138–9.

[47]Quoted in Yahil, *The Rescue of Danish* Jewry, p. 156.

[48]Quoted in Hans Sode-Madsen, "The Perfect Deception: The Danish Jews and Theresienstadt 1940–1945," *Leo Baeck Institute Yearbook*, 38 (1993), pp. 263–290.

[49]Quoted in Michael Morgensen, "October 1943—The Rescue of the Danish Jews," in *Denmark and the Holocaust*, Jensen and Jensen, eds., p. 44.

[50]Figure in Marcus Melchior, *A Rabbi Remembers* (New York, 1968), pp. 181–2.

Jewish refugees ferried out of Denmark en route for Sweden, October 1, 1943. *Source:* United States Holocaust Memorial Museum.

But where could Jews go afterward? The safest haven was in Sweden, across the narrow sound (Øresund) that separated the two countries. The Swedish government understood when the Germans implemented martial law in Denmark that deportations were not far behind. In early September 1943, the Foreign Ministry prepared to issue entry visas to all Danish Jews. But the Germans would have to approve the exit visas from Denmark. Stockholm remembered its attempts on behalf of Norway's Jews in December 1942 and understood that there was no time to lose. Arrests of Jews began in Copenhagen on the night of October 1. On October 2, the Swedish Foreign Ministry announced publicly that Sweden would accept all Danish Jews. Stockholm was calling Berlin's bluff. There was a place to send arrested Jews besides Poland.

In fact, Danish Jews were already fleeing to Sweden. From various points, 7,000 Jews made it across the sound between September 28 and mid-October, in small to medium Danish vessels in up to 700 trips. The first Jews arranged their own transport with local skippers, paying high prices. Jews fleeing later had fewer means. They were hidden by friends or the Danish underground, which arranged transport after negotiating prices. Some captains acted from altruism. Others charged substantial fees because of the risk of losing one's boat. Danish resistors complained that "many . . . Danish skippers have used the opportunity to amass money in a distasteful manner."[51] The Swedes, meanwhile, provided more than harbors. They deployed patrol boats by night to guide Danish boats to safety. Swedish working vessels also took Jewish passengers from small, overloaded Danish boats.

The Germans managed to arrest 190 Danish Jews on the night of October 1. Subsequent captures brought the total to 481. Hans Juhl, a zealous Gestapo officer whose command post was near Elsinore at the sound's narrowest point, arrested more than half. Though Juhl's men shot

---

[51]Quoted in Morgensen, "October 1943," p. 47.

at embarking boats, the German navy did not have the ships to patrol the sound and the Danish coast guard did not help them. To Berlin, Best reported the glass half full. Denmark was free of Jews, and proper relations with the Danish government had been reestablished.

Thanks to intervention by Danish officials the arrested Danish Jews were sent not to Poland but to Theresienstadt, described by Best, as "a town where the Jews are self-governing and lived under appropriate conditions."[52] When they arrived there, 45,000 Jews were already crammed into the hungry, lice-infested camp. Allowed to write back to Denmark, Jews found ways, despite German censors, to convey the conditions and lack of food.

Danish officials intervened. Eichmann and Best agreed that Danish Jews would remain in Theresienstadt, that Danish authorities could visit, and that clothing (but not food) parcels could be sent through the Danish Red Cross. Danish church and underground political organizations assembled parcels, which eventually numbered up to 240 per week and which, despite Gestapo orders, contained food.[53] On June 23, 1944, Eichmann also allowed Danish government and Red Cross members to visit the well-fed and well-clothed Danish internees.

Eichmann hoped to use the tour to show the world that the mass murder reports, which were rampant by mid-1944, were false. Danish Jewish internees were placed in decent quarters and warned not to reveal Theresienstadt's truth. Thousands of inmates were moved to alleviate overcrowding. Flowers and grass adorned Theresienstadt's market square. "Their state of health," remembered Danish diplomat Frants Hvass, "was better than we had dared expect."[54] With Theresienstadt spruced for the visit, the Germans even made a propaganda film showing the humane conditions there.

As the June 23 tour was in progress, Auschwitz-Birkenau was in the midst of its most terrible period—the murder of over 400,000 Hungarian Jews. In September 1944, mass deportations from Theresienstadt to Auschwitz resumed. Yet Denmark's Jews were relatively safe. The Danish government was determined that they remain so. German officials used the safekeeping of Danish Jews in Theresienstadt to maintain quiet on Germany's northern border, and later, with the war ending, to solicit goodwill from the Allies. In April 1945, the Danish Jews were transported from Theresienstadt to Sweden.

13.4 ITALY AND THE FINAL SOLUTION

Italy's Occupation Zones

Fascist Italy entered the war to attain long-coveted territories. In Italy's Mediterranean sphere, it occupied these lands jointly with the Germans. With the destruction of Yugoslavia, Italy annexed part of neighboring Slovenia and much of the Dalmatian coast as payment for backing the Ustaša before the war. Later in the year, Italy occupied additional territory in Croatia (Map 8.2). With the Axis conquest of Greece in April 1941, Italy occupied most of peninsular Greece, including Athens, and a number of Greek islands. Bulgaria, which joined the attack on Greece to acquire long-coveted territory, occupied much of Thrace, and the Germans kept the port city of Salonika and its hinterland (Map 14.1). In November 1942, when German troops occupied most of France's free zone, Italy occupied France east of the Rhône River, including the coastal city of Nice (Map 7.1).

---

[52]Quoted in Sode-Madsen, "The Perfect Deception," p. 273.

[53]Figure in Sode-Madsen, "The Perfect Deception," pp. 279–80.

[54]Quoted in Sode-Madsen, "The Perfect Deception," pp. 283–4.

Italy never handed over Jews from these occupation zones. As junior partners who needed German help with each military campaign, Italian officials resented Berlin's high-handedness, and as the war turned against the Axis, Rome refused to be dragged into German criminality. Antisemitism was not fundamental to Italian fascism. "In spite of all the disasters that have struck the Germans," wrote Count Luca Pietromarchi from the Italian Foreign Ministry in February 1943, "they confirm that by the end of 1943 there will not be a single Jew alive in Europe. Evidently they want to involve us in the brutality of their policies."[55]

As the Ustaša killed some 20,000 of Croatia's 39,000 Jews in 1941, perhaps 4,000 Croatian Jews fled into Italian-controlled territory.[56] The Croatian government was incensed. A German officer complained in December 1941 that in Mostar, "the Italians simply revoke all Croatian orders and let the city overflow with Jews."[57] In August 1942, as the Germans planned to deport Croatia's remaining Jews to Auschwitz, Berlin pressed the Italians to hand over Jews under their protection. Mussolini had no objection. "With regard to the Jews," he joked, the Germans were "letting them emigrate . . . to another world."[58] Yet his subordinates refused. They protected Jews in detention facilities near the Dalmatian coast. "Our entire activity," said an Italian officer in August 1942, "has been designed to let the Jews live in a human way . . . [handing them over] would not be true to the obligations we assumed . . . they have given us no trouble of any sort."[59]

The Germans killed roughly 85 percent of Greece's 77,000 Jews in 1943 and 1944. Greece's largest Jewish population, in Salonika, was also the world's largest community of Sephardic Jews. Descended from the Spanish expellees of 1492, it numbered roughly 56,000. The Germans specifically targeted Salonika's Jews, and after using them for forced labor, ghettoizing them, and extorting their funds, the Gestapo deported more than 48,000 to Auschwitz, most in two months between March and May 1943. Salonika's Jews were told that they were being moved to Kraków. "Courage," said Greek bystanders watching the deportations, "You'll be back." Most deportees, however, were gassed immediately.[60]

The country in the best position to help Greece's Jews was Spain. In 1924, Madrid offered extraterritorial citizenship to Salonika's Jews, most of whom spoke Spanish, as a way to enhance its influence abroad. Most of Salonika's Jews never did the paperwork. After he arrived in Salonika in April 1943, Spanish consul Sebastián Romero Radigales tried to use this solution but was thwarted by his own government, which felt Spain had enough refugees. Only Sephardim with current passports, Madrid decided, were eligible for repatriation. They numbered 367. Other Spanish diplomats were furious. Deportation, said one, "automatically condemns them to death. . . . I cannot believe there exists no possibility of saving them from the horrible fate that awaits them."[61]

---

[55]Quoted in Jonathan Steinberg, *All or Nothing: The Axis and the Holocaust 1941–1943* (London, 1990), p. 93.

[56]Figure in Susan Zuccotti, *Under His Very Windows: The Vatican and the Holocaust in Italy* (New Haven, CT, 2002), pp. 113–4.

[57]Quoted in Steinberg, *All or Nothing*, p. 46.

[58]Quoted in Zuccotti, *Under His Very Windows*, p. 106.

[59]Quoted in Steinberg, *All or Nothing*, p. 59.

[60]Quote in Steven B. Bowman, ed., *The Holocaust in Salonika: Eyewitness Accounts* (New York, 2002), p. 192. Figures in Steven B. Bowman, *The Agony of the Greek Jews, 1940–1945* (Stanford, CA, 2009), pp. 61, 85–6.

[61]Quote and figure in Stanley Payne, *Franco and Hitler: Germany and Spain in World War II* (New Haven, CT, 2009), pp. 226–8.

Deportation scenes in Salonika also disturbed Italy's consul there, Guelfo Zamboni. He tried to grant Italian citizenship to Jews with any connection with Italy. "You are," Zamboni's superiors told him, "empowered to act . . . with criteria of generosity."[62] Here, however, the road-block was Berlin. "Only Italian Jews who incontestably possess Italian citizenship," the German Foreign Ministry ordered, "may be released for repatriation to Italy."[63] Zamboni still saved 350 Jews from Salonika. Meanwhile, however, the Italians refused to surrender the 18,000 Jews in their zone of occupation in Greece, 5,000 of whom had fled there from Salonika and Thrace. "The German authorities," Italian officials in Greece noted, "accuse us of not following . . . as the Bulgarians were anxious to do. The day will come, however, when our humane attitude will be acknowledged as being right." One Italian official suggested moving Greek Jews to one of Greece's islands.[64]

Italian forces also refused to hand over Jews in France. After Axis forces occupied southern France in November 1942, thousands of panicked Jews fled to Italy's new occupation zone there. Italian army officers protected synagogues, allowed Jews to print new identification papers, kept no records of Jewish addresses, and repeatedly prohibited Vichy police from arresting Jews. Vichy officials, who aimed to deliver foreign Jews to the Germans, were livid, one prefect calling Italy's zone the "promised land." Jews in Nice, meanwhile, held their breath. "We are," said one, "like survivors on the high sea. The sea is still stormy."[65]

The Germans, who estimated that 30,000 Jews were in Nice alone, were beside themselves.[66] Eichmann's man in France, Heinz Röthke, described Italian policy as "incomprehensible" and "revolting."[67] Ambassador to Rome Hans-Georg von Mackensen complained that the Italians succumbed to a "misguided humanitarian sentimentality . . . inappropriate to our harsh times."[68] Von Ribbentrop labeled the Italian foreign minister, Giuseppe Bastianini, "an honorary Jew."[69] Himmler worried about the example set to other governments when "even our Axis partner is not prepared to follow our lead in the Jewish question."[70] Berlin applied pressure. The evacuation of Jews, German officials told their Italian counterparts, was vital to the war. Though Mussolini wavered, his subordinates did not budge.

In the meantime, Italy's military fortunes plunged. Italian troops were routed outside Stalingrad in January 1943, and they surrendered with the Germans in Tunisia in May. In July, the Allies invaded Sicily and bombed Rome itself. Italy lay open to Allied invasion. King Victor Emmanuel III exercised his royal prerogative, removed Mussolini from power, and had him arrested on July 23. Fascist rule was over. The new prime minister was military chief Marshal Pietro Badoglio. To keep the Germans at bay while negotiating a cease-fire with the

---

[62]Venturini to Zamboni, April 3, 1943, Daniel Carpi, ed., *Italian Diplomatic Documents on the History of the Holocaust in Greece (1941–1943)* (Jerusalem, 1999), p. 150.

[63]Zamboni to Foreign Ministry, April 11, 1943, Carpi, ed., *Italian Diplomatic Documents*, p. 157.

[64]Pièche to Foreign Ministry, April 28, 1943, Carpi, ed., *Italian Diplomatic Documents*, pp. 178 and 179.

[65]Quoted in Daniel Carpi, *Between Mussolini and Hitler: The Jews and the Italian Authorities in France and Tunisia* (Hanover, NH, 1994), p. 144.

[66]Figure in Susan Zuccotti, *The Holocaust, the French, and the Jews* (New York, 1993), p. 166.

[67]Quoted in Zuccotti, *The Holocaust, the French, and the Jews*, p. 168; Michael R. Marrus and Robert O. Paxton, *Vichy France and the Jews* (New York, 1981), p. 317.

[68]Quoted in Carpi, *Between Mussolini and Hitler*, p. 128.

[69]Quoted in Steinberg, *All or Nothing*, p. 118.

[70]Quoted in Carpi, *Between Mussolini and Hitler*, p. 105.

Allies, Badoglio promised Berlin he would continue the war. Hitler sent German troops into Italy regardless. In early September, US and British forces invaded southern Italy, thus starting a hard fight up the peninsula against German counterattacks and rugged terrain. On the September 8, 1943, Badoglio surrendered to the Allies.

During the forty-five days between Mussolini's fall and Italy's surrender, the fate of Jews in Italy's occupation zones was in doubt. Angelo Donati, a Jewish Italian financier who had lived in Paris since 1919 and fled to Nice in 1940, hatched the most ambitious rescue scheme. Donati's idea was to move 30,000 Jews from Nice through Italy to Allied-controlled North Africa. He attained Allied support through the US and British representatives to the Vatican, promises of financing from the JDC, and Italian support in the form of passports. Everything hinged on Italy's surrender not being announced until October. Yet Allied commander General Dwight D. Eisenhower announced it on September 8. Overnight, Italian rule in Croatia, Greece, and France collapsed. German police arrived quickly.

Still, Italian delays might have helped to save 50,000 Jews in their occupation zones.[71] In Croatia, before Mussolini's fall, Italian troops moved up to 3,600 Jews to the Adriatic island of Arbe. Most went into hiding or joined the Yugoslav partisan fight against the Germans. On arriving in Arbe in March 1944, the Germans deported the 200 remaining sick and elderly. After the Germans occupied the remainder of Greece, the Gestapo destroyed a number of smaller Jewish communities, even on the Greek island of Corfu. But significant percentages of Jews in Athens and elsewhere were saved either with false papers and baptismal certificates provided by Greek officials and clerics, or by joining or finding protection with Greek resistors in the mountains.

The most dramatic scenes were in Nice, where Eichmann's brutal henchman Aloïs Brunner arrived two days after the announcement of Italy's surrender. His staff arrested Jews in synagogues; people with Jewish-sounding names; and those who "looked" Jewish in hotels, apartment houses, and on sidewalks. Brunner tortured arrested Jews in order to find Jews in hiding and paid non-Jewish informants handsomely for such information. His staff deported 1,800 Jews during his three-month stay, from September to December 1943. Yet it was but 6 percent of the Jews in the former Italian zone. The Italians left no lists, and by now the French police provided no help.

The Holocaust in Italy

Hitler's fury at Italy's surrender in September 1943 led him to order Mussolini's rescue and the creation of an Italian puppet government called the Republic of Salò. Germany annexed Italian areas to which it had ethnic claim (the South Tyrol and Trieste) and began deporting Jews from these areas immediately. They ruled northern and central Italy (Mussolini's so-called republic) through their police organs. SS-General Karl Wolff, Himmler's former chief of staff, now became the Higher SS and Police Leader in northern Italy. Eichmann's staff arrived in October.

At the time, Italy held roughly 37,000 Italian Jews and 8,100 foreign Jews. Most lived in the northern cities and Rome. Since 1938, Italian Jews functioned under legal disabilities but they had not been surrendered to the Germans. The German occupation put them in immediate danger. On September 25, 1943, Himmler cabled his Security Police chief in Rome, SS-Colonel Herbert Kappler: "All Jews, regardless of nationality, age, sex, and personal conditions must be transferred to Germany and liquidated. . . ." But Himmler tried to create an atmosphere of complacency among Rome's Jews. "The success of this undertaking," he continued, "will have to be

---

[71]Figure in Steinberg, *All or Nothing*, p. 5.

ensured by a surprise action and for that reason it is strictly necessary to suspend the application of any anti-Jewish measures . . . likely to stir up . . . suspicion of an imminent action."[72]

Some Jewish leaders understood the danger regardless. When the surrender was announced in Florence, Rabbi Nathan Cassuto, who later died in the Gross-Rosen concentration camp, told the small Jewish community there to hide. "My brother," remembered Cassuto's sister after the war, "went from house to house to warn them."[73] But Rome's leading Jews, including Dante Almansi (the president of the Union of Italian Jewish Communities) and Ugo Foà (the president of Rome's Jewish community) failed to act, perhaps for fear of provoking the Germans or of spreading panic.

On September 26, 1943, Kappler demanded fifty kilograms of gold from Almansi and Foà as a ransom for the safety of Rome's Jews. "It is your gold we want," said Kappler. "If you [raise it], nothing will happen to you."[74] As Almansi and Foà organized the collection, they allowed Rome's main synagogue to remain open with its membership lists inside. The Germans took the files on September 29. By now, many of Rome's Jews were hiding, including Almansi and Foà themselves. But neither issued a warning to the full Jewish community even when Rome's chief rabbi Israel Zolli asked them to do so. Zolli, meanwhile, hid on Rosh Hashanah without warning his congregation. They were told that he was ill.

The Germans struck in Rome on October 16. In nine hours, they arrested 1,259 Jews, most in their homes. Almost all were sent to Auschwitz and killed. The victims included poor Jews from the old Roman ghetto neighborhood but also Lionello Alatri, a department store owner, together with his wife and her ninety-year-old mother. The Germans conducted similar roundups in Milan, Turin, Florence, Genoa, and Venice. In each city, they arrested but a fraction of the Jewish population. To help locate Jews, the Germans increasingly depended on paid informants and on Italian police who continued to serve Mussolini's republic. On December 1, 1943, Italian police received orders from Salò that all Jews were to be arrested as enemy aliens. They detained arrested Jews, along with other political enemies, in camps in northern Italy. After February 1944, the SS took over the camps. They used some prisoners for target practice and deported most interned Jews to Auschwitz. In all, they deported 4,439 Italian Jews, 1,915 foreign Jews, and perhaps 500 more of undetermined origin. More than half were arrested after December 1943. Few had any idea of the terrible fate that awaited them.[75]

Still, these were not the figures for which the Germans hoped. Whether warned or not, many Jews understood instinctively to hide. Those with means rented alternate apartments or took residence in the countryside. Some made it to the Swiss border (this necessitated a guide) or to Allied lines to the south. Many more lived on the run, taking refuge with Italians who were simply determined to defy the Germans. At times, even the former fascist bureaucracy helped. Giovanni Palatucci, the police commissioner in Fiume, destroyed all of his Jewish files when the Germans occupied the city, warned Jews about impending searches, and even helped Jews move by boat to the Allied lines. Other bureaucrats behaved similarly. "Every time we needed help," remembered Elena Minervi, "we always found somebody who would help us, somebody who would warn us to escape at the right moment, and someone who would . . . give us shelter."[76]

---

[72]Quoted in Susan Zuccotti, *The Italians and the Holocaust: Persecution, Rescue and Survival* (Lincoln, NE, 1996), p. 109.

[73]Quoted in Zuccotti, *The Italians and the Holocaust*, pp. 157–8.

[74]Quoted in Zuccotti, *Under His Very Windows*, p. 153.

[75]Figures in Zuccotti, *The Italians and the Holocaust*, pp. 116–23, 189–200.

[76]Quoted in Nicola Caracciolo, ed., *Uncertain Refuge: Italy and the Jews During the Holocaust* (Urbana, IL, 1995), pp. 27–8.

Roman Catholic institutions, including monasteries, convents, hospitals, and boarding schools, were at the front of rescue efforts. In the countryside, these institutions had extra room and extra food, and could disguise even foreign Jews as members. Urban Catholic institutions developed larger networks. Most noteworthy was Father Maria Benedetto. Living in Marseille in 1942 under his French name, Father Pierre-Marie Benoît, he used an underground network to save thousands of Jews in France. Moving to Rome in 1943, he used his monastery there to provide false papers and locate rooms for perhaps 4,000 Jews, native and foreign, none of whom were arrested during the German roundup on October 16, 1943. As in France, he funded his work partly with money and pledges from the JDC. Even for some clerics still loyal to Mussolini, politics came second. Father Umberto Loiacono of Florence was a chaplain to the local fascist militia. But he also sheltered Jews.

Heroism carried lethal risk. The Germans quickly began fighting a partisan war in Italy that included mass reprisal shootings. Among the 10,000 Italians killed in reprisal shootings were up to 170 priests, often for helping Jews. Benedetto remembered that "the risk . . . was enormous and constant . . . there was no lack of threatening letters, denunciations and spies against us and our centers." In August 1944, a fascist spy in Turin betrayed a Dominican monk named Giuseppe Girotti, who had hidden many Jews in his monastery. Girotti was arrested, sent to Dachau, and murdered by lethal injection on the eve of liberation there.[77]

13.5 THE SILENCE OF THE VATICAN

Pope Pius XII

Few subjects are as controversial as the Vatican's behavior during the Holocaust. Uncritical scholarship from Catholic presses argues that Pope Pius XII did all he could reasonably have done to rescue Jews. Although the Vatican published eleven volumes of selected documents in the 1960s, it has not opened its wartime archives to independent scholars, who have tried over the years to piece Vatican policy together from other records. It is an overstatement to say that Pius was indifferent to the Holocaust because of his traditional antisemitism. But one can safely argue that his policy was tragically limited and cautious at a time when courageous moral leadership was needed.

Before he became Pope Pius XII in February 1939, Eugenio Pacelli served as Vatican secretary of state. He advocated a parochial policy that emphasized uninterrupted pastoral care of Catholics and opposed the atheistic scourge of communism, which unabashedly closed and destroyed churches, from the USSR to Spain. Pacelli deplored Hitler's barbarism and the Nazis' violations of the 1933 concordat. But he valued Berlin's anticommunism and understood that German churches at least remained open. He preferred to avoid grand protest gestures that could trigger retaliation against German Catholics, preferring the quiet diplomacy to which he had grown accustomed.

When war erupted, Pius was confronted immediately with Germany's brutal treatment of Catholic Poles. German police shot or arrested thousands of Polish leaders, including priests. Of Poland's forty-six prewar dioceses, bishops from thirty-nine fled or were arrested. The Germans killed up to 2,300 clerics, from priests to nuns, and imprisoned 5,400 more. They used churches as barracks and stole church property.[78] On Rome's instructions, the nuncio in Berlin, Monsignor Cesare Orsenigo, made private protests to the German government. He was ignored.

---

[77]Zuccotti, *Under His Very Windows*, pp. 182, 243.

[78]Figures in Zuccotti, *Under His Very Windows*, p. 96.

Pius XII never protested publicly, fearing that open statements could make matters worse. The Nazis allowed churches to remain open for ethnic Germans in the areas of Poland that it annexed, and with Poland having vanished, Germany also formed a bulwark to the expansion of the Soviet Union, which annexed eastern Poland and closed *all* churches while deporting tens of thousands of Poles to Siberia. Polish Catholics, Pius lamented, were tragically condemned to suffer between Hitler and Stalin. Criticism of the pope arose within the church itself. Cardinal August Hlond, a Polish bishop who justified antisemitism before the war, now registered doubt that "it was the will of God that the atrocities and anti-Christian programs . . . be passed over in silence."[79] But by 1942, the worst for Poles was over. The Germans needed their labor and had shifted to the mass killing of Jews.

Vatican Knowledge and Silence

How much did the Vatican know about the Final Solution? Pius XII and his secretary of state, Cardinal Luigi Maglione, had more information by late 1942 than any government save Germany. The Vatican had nuncios in European capitals, from Berlin to Bratislava, to Budapest. It had clerics throughout Hitler's Europe. Many of them relayed information on mass shootings, ghettos, and deportations. Informed Jews such as Gerhart Riegner and the Allied governments also communicated reliable information to Vatican officials. Information even came from within Germany itself. Although most German bishops were silent concerning the Final Solution and tried at the very most to protect Catholic converts from Judaism, Bishop Konrad von Preysing of Berlin relayed information from several sources, including SS-Colonel Kurt Gerstein, who had seen gassings in Bełżec in August 1942. Repeatedly, von Preysing urged the pope to break relations with Germany and to openly condemn German actions.

Astonishingly, the Vatican did not disseminate the information it received, either to other governments or even to its own bishops. It was a dead end for intelligence. Vatican information in 1942 was crucial. Dutch, French, and Belgian clerics spoke against Jewish deportations and worked to hide Jews. Had they known the exact fate of deported Jews, they might have recruited more would-be rescuers. It may be that the Vatican doubted the veracity of the information at first. In September 1942, Roosevelt's personal envoy to the Vatican, Myron Taylor, urgently asked Maglione if he could confirm the information Washington had received from Gerhart Riegner. Maglione said he could not. But by May 1943, a memorandum written in the Vatican State Secretariat noted that Germany was systematically gassing Jews and that "there is no doubt that the majority [of Jews in Poland] have been killed." The report placed the death toll in the millions.[80]

The pope was indeed troubled by the news. But he would undertake nothing that might endanger his institution. As his nuncio in Berlin put it to von Preysing, "Charity is well and good, but the greatest charity is not to make problems for the Church."[81] And by late 1942 and early 1943, Pius found other matters more pressing. One was the Allied policy, announced by Roosevelt in January 1943, for Germany's unconditional surrender. The pope preferred a negotiated peace that would leave Germany intact as a barrier against Bolshevism—whatever this might mean for Jews under German control. Pius XII thus openly condemned the Allied bombing of

---

[79]Quoted in Michael Phayer, *Pius XII, the Holocaust, and the Cold War* (Bloomington, IN, 2007), p. 30.

[80]Quoted in Zuccotti, *Under His Very Windows*, pp 109–10.

[81]Quoted in Saul Friedländer, *Nazi Germany and the Jews, 1939–1945: The Years of Extermination* (New York, 2007), p. 516.

German cities. Myron Taylor noted with irony that the pope had kept silent when the Germans bombed Warsaw, Rotterdam, and London.

Pius also feared that the Allies would bomb Rome, the center of Catholicism, damaging Vatican properties and treasures. The British bombed Genoa, Turin, and Milan in September 1942. Pius never pressured the Germans to stop killing Jews. But he tried dozens of times to secure Allied promises not to bomb Rome, threatening "vehement protest" while having US and British bishops intercede in London and Washington. These representations only irritated the Allies. "We should not hesitate to bomb Rome," said British Foreign Secretary Anthony Eden in June 1943, "if the course of the war rendered such action convenient and helpful."[82]

The Allied governments meanwhile pressed the pope in 1942 and afterward to condemn German crimes. Allied hesitance to speak out against mass murder was conditioned by their fear of augmented pressure to rescue millions of Jews. Germany could also discredit Allied statements as Jewish propaganda. Yet the Vatican could speak without such handicaps and with unquestioned moral authority. Allied diplomats became exasperated. "I'm not asking the pope to speak out against Hitler," said Taylor, "just the atrocities." "The Vatican," Britain's minister told Maglione on December 14, 1942, "instead of thinking but nothing but the bombing of Rome should consider their duties in respect to the unprecedented crime against humanity of Hitler's campaign of extermination of the Jews. . . ."[83]

The Allied statement in Parliament of December 17, 1942, explicitly acknowledged a Nazi program of mass murder of Jews thorough deportation and gassing. It promised retribution. The closest thing to a Vatican statement came in the pope's Christmas address that year. It consciously avoided anything that might upset Berlin. One sentence in the forty-eighth paragraph of a fifty-two-paragraph speech mentioned "hundreds of thousands of persons who, without any fault on their part, sometimes only because of their nationality or race, have been consigned to death or slow decline." The pope strongly condemned Marxism in the Christmas address, but he mentioned neither Nazis nor Jews. British and US representatives to the Vatican were mildly pleased with the address, but surely it might have done more.[84]

Urged by its own clergy abroad and by the Allies, the Vatican occasionally tried diplomacy. In 1943, Vatican officials urged the Italians not to hand over the Jews from their occupation zones in Croatia and France. It reinforced the independent Italian decision to resist German pressure. "We do not want to be butchers," Italian Foreign Minister Bastianini assured the nuncio in Rome.[85] Vatican efforts were less influential elsewhere. Slovakia, a Catholic state, suspended handovers of Jews to the Germans in July 1942 after 52,000 had already been deported. The Vatican weakly suggested to Slovak officials in the spring that the deportations stop, but domestic objections in Slovakia might have been more decisive.

The pope made no representations in Berlin at all. An appeal of March 6, 1943, by von Preysing for Pius to speak publicly on behalf of Berlin's remaining Jews is poignant. "Would it not be possible," von Preysing asked, "for Your Holiness to try once again to intervene for these many unfortunate innocents? It is the last hope. . . ." The pope answered nearly two months later

---

[82]Quoted in Harold H. Tittmann, Jr., *Inside the Vatican of Pope Pius XII: The Memoir of an American Diplomat During World War II* (New York, 2004), p. 155.

[83]Quoted in Owen Chadwick, *Britain and the Vatican During the Second World War* (New York, 1986), p. 216.

[84]Quote and analysis of the address in Michael Phayer, "Helping the Jews Is Not an Easy Thing to Do. Vatican Holocaust Policy: Continuity or Change?" *Holocaust and Genocide Studies*, 21, no. 3 (Winter 2007), pp. 421–53.

[85]Quoted in Zuccotti, *Under His Very Windows*, p. 125.

on April 30. By then more than 5,000 additional Jews were sent from Berlin to Auschwitz and Theresienstadt. "It was a consolation for Us to learn," Pius wrote, "that Catholics, notably in Berlin, had manifested great Christian charity toward the sufferings of 'non-Aryans.'" He gave local bishops latitude to speak, but preferred "restraint—despite the reasons that may exist for intervention—in order to avoid greater evils." As for Vatican action on behalf of the Jews, he said, "We cannot offer them effective help other than through Our prayers."[86]

The Roundup of Rome's Jews

On October 16, 1943, German police in Rome arrested 1,259 Jews and detained them only blocks from the Vatican. On October 18, trains took 1,023 of them to Auschwitz. Even in the eternal city, Pius XII remained silent. If he was prepared to protest the Allied bombing of Rome, why could he not protest the murder of its Jewish citizens? Did he understand that such a protest might have had the effect of the Rosenstrasse wives, who eight months earlier stared down the SS in Berlin? Or was he afraid that, as in the Netherlands, the Germans would retaliate with anti-Catholic actions? Without access to Vatican records, all we have are clues.

Even before the roundup, the Vatican was oddly miserly toward Rome's Jews. Jewish leaders asked for Vatican help as they scrambled to raise Herbert Kappler's ransom of fifty kilograms of gold. The Vatican held $20,000,000 worth of gold in the United States alone, to say nothing of stocks and bonds. The ransom amounted to less than $16,000. The pope offered a *loan*, not a gift, amounting to whatever Rome's Jews could not raise themselves. Rome's Jews scraped together enough jewelry and coins to reach the target. Had the Vatican simply paid the ransom, the gesture would have established solidarity with Rome's Jews that the Germans could not have ignored. Jews, meanwhile, had been more generous. In 1940, American Jews donated $125,000 to help Catholic war refugees. In 1943, Jews in Nice raised money to care for Italian bombing victims.[87]

The Vatican learned of the Rome roundup in advance through the German ambassador, Ernst von Weizsäcker. Several German officials in Rome opposed the roundup for fear of possible political repercussions. A seasoned diplomat, Weizsäcker hedged against a Vatican protest by giving it a chance to warn Rome's Jews. There was cause for optimism. Pius had not raised the Jewish question with Weizsäcker before, and as Weizsäcker reported earlier, "hostility toward Bolshevism is, in fact, the most stable component of Vatican foreign policy."[88] To guarantee Pius's goodwill, Weizsäcker provided "letters of protection" to Vatican properties throughout Rome to ensure that they would not be entered. Jews hiding in these properties would thus be safe for the moment.

The pope knew that church officials on their own had hidden Jews all over Rome, some in Vatican properties. He never gave orders for them to do so, and there is evidence that high Vatican officials strongly disapproved of Jews hiding in Vatican buildings. Even when asked for financial help by clerics such as Father Benedetto, the Vatican refused. One senior Vatican official complained that Benedetto took too many risks. The Vatican would not even allow its bank to convert dollars donated by the JDC for Benedetto into Italian lire so that Benedetto could pay for hiding places.[89] Perhaps Pius, ever risk-averse, feared provoking the Germans. In any event,

---

[86]Quotes in Friedländer, *Years of Extermination*, pp. 570–2; figures in Beate Meyer et al., *Jews in Nazi Berlin: From Kristallnacht to Liberation* (Chicago, IL, 2009), pp. 177–82.

[87]Phayer, *Pius XII, the Holocaust, and the Cold War*, p. 121.

[88]Quoted in Michael Phayer, *The Catholic Church and the Holocaust, 1930–1965* (Bloomington, IN, 2001), p. 195.

[89]Susan Zuccotti, "Pius XII and the Rescue of Jews in Italy: 'Evidence of a Papal Directive?'" in *Jews in Italy Under Fascist and Nazi Rule 1922–1945*, ed. Joshua D. Zimmerman (New York, 2005), pp. 287–311.

the pope, despite knowing of the impending roundup in Rome, neither warned Rome's Jews nor called on clerics in Rome to hide them. They were either on their own or dependent on more courageous Italians.

When arrests began on the morning of October 16, 1943, Pius XII was informed immediately. Surely a line had been crossed that, if nothing else, made Pius look bad. Cardinal Maglione called Weizsäcker for a meeting. Maglione's notes read as follows: "I asked [Weizsäcker] to intervene in favor of those poor people. I spoke to him as best I could in the name of humanity, of Christian charity. . . . I told him simply: try to save these many innocent people. It is painful for the Holy Father, painful beyond words that here in Rome, under the eye of the Common Father, so many people are made to suffer simply because of their particular descent. . . ." The cardinal added, "The Holy See would not want to be obliged to express its disapproval." It was the first time such a threat had been made.

Weizsäcker knew there was no stopping the roundup. He simply hoped to stop a papal reaction. He expressed his admiration for the pope's ability during the war to maintain "a perfect equilibrium." "I ask myself now," he told Maglione, "if . . . it is appropriate to put everything at risk. . . . I am thinking of the consequences that a step by the Holy See would provoke. . . . The [German] directives come from the highest level." It was a veiled warning that a reaction from the pope would trigger grave consequences, possibly the German occupation of the Vatican, possibly the abduction of the pope himself. There were no German directives for such a step. But rumors to this effect were circulating. Allied diplomats to the Vatican were already burning their documents.

The next day Weizsäcker wrote Berlin. To forestall a papal protest, he suggested that no more Jews be rounded up and that those in custody be put to work rather than deported. His warning was ignored, but he need not have worried. Pius XII made no public condemnation, and Vatican publications the following week only vaguely mentioned the pope's efforts to alleviate suffering based on one's religion or descent. Pius did not mention Germans, Jews, or the Rome roundup. "By all accounts," Weizsäcker reported, "the Pope, although harassed from various quarters, has not allowed himself to be stampeded into making any demonstrative pronouncement against the removal of the Jews from Rome. . . . [He] has done everything he could, even in this delicate matter, not to injure the relationship between the Vatican and the German Government or the German authorities in Rome."[90]

Might public action from the Vatican have slowed the Final Solution? We will never know for certain. Local objections, where it reached critical mass, tempered the pace of deportation. Yet what constituted critical mass varied from place to place, depending on German policies, the level of German police presence, local reactions, and even geographic factors. Pius, meanwhile, had objectives of his own that weighed more heavily, from the pastoral care of Catholics to the stemming of Bolshevism in Europe and even to the preservation of the Vatican from German occupiers, Allied bombers, and Italian communists. In the end, Vatican actions and nonactions must be measured against those of every other government in Europe that furthered or hindered the destruction of Europe's Jews. By this gauge, the Vatican could have done better.

---

[90]Exchanges in Zuccotti, *Under His Very Windows*, pp. 158–61, 164.

14

Hitler's Southeastern Allies and the Hungarian Jewish Catastrophe, 1941–1944

When implementing the Final Solution the Germans encountered difficulties with their allies in southeast Europe. Romania and Bulgaria pursued murderous policies in the regions they occupied but balked at deporting their own Jews to Poland. Hungary was more ambivalent. By 1943, it had the largest Jewish population left in Europe—roughly 800,000. It pursued brutal anti-Jewish policies but refused to hand its Jews to the Germans. Hitler and Foreign Minister Joachim von Ribbentrop personally pressed the heads of all three states on the Jewish question in April 1943. But recent Soviet and Allied military successes put Germany in a quandary. Too much pressure from Berlin could trigger friction over its allies' war contributions.

Matters boiled over in March 1944 when Hungary tried to quit the war. Already incensed that Hungary had not cooperated with the Final Solution, Hitler ordered its occupation. The Germans installed a new government in Budapest—a government that would stay in the war and hand over Hungary's Jews. With Soviet forces approaching Hungary, the transport and murder of so many had to be swift. Thus began one of the Holocaust's most terrible chapters—the destruction of over 400,000 Jews in less than two months, in full sight of the world as Germany was losing the war.

14.1 ROMANIA RECONSIDERS

Romania's Jews and Deportation

With the invasion of the USSR in 1941, Marshal Ion Antonescu's government pursued bloody pogroms in the Regat and murdered Jews in Bessarabia, Bukovina, and Transnistria, eventually killing between 280,000 and 380,000, a figure second only to Germany. In the Regat and in southern Transylvania (acquired in 1940), there were roughly 300,000 more Jews. Antonescu's government reduced most to poverty through various taxes, forced some 60,000 Jews into labor squads, and expelled tens of thousands from villages and townships. There was no reason to think in 1942 that Romania's Jews would not be included in the Final Solution.

In July 22, 1942, Adolf Eichmann's deputy in Bucharest, Gustav Richter, secured Antonescu's agreement to deliver the roughly 300,000 Jews from Romania's pre-1941 borders. "Evacuation transports," Eichmann reported on July 26, "will be able to roll in a short time."[1]

---

[1] Quoted in Raul Hilberg, *The Destruction of the European Jews*, 3rd ed., vol. 2 (New Haven, CT, 2003), p. 840.

Railroad officials expected transports of 2,000 Jews to leave every two days for Bełżec, the death camp closest to Romania's border.[2] But Antonescu wavered by the fall. In part, Romania could not appear subservient to Berlin at a time when Hungary, Romania's chief rival within the German-led alliance, had not delivered its own Jews. Romanian officials increasingly worried that in the eyes of the world, Hungary would look more deserving of the divided and bitterly disputed region of Transylvania because it had not yet handed over its Jews there.[3]

But there were other reasons as well. In 1942, German-language newspapers in Romania noted that Romania's Jews would be resettled. Readers assumed that resettlements would be in Transnistria, the dreadfulness of which was known. "The rumors that reach us from Transnistria," wrote Emil Dorian in June 1942, "are horrifying. . . . A graveyard from which an agonized voice rises. . . ."[4] Leading Romanian Jews desperately lobbied Romanian officials. Romania's chief rabbi, Alexandru Şafran, spoke to the Swedish, Swiss, and Turkish ministers, and to the papal nuncio Andreas Cassulo, who until this time worried only for converts. All intervened with Antonescu, as did Queen Mother Elena, the mother of King Michael. Romanian intellectuals also asked publicly how far Romania would go to please the Germans.

Antonescu himself had also become irritated by German high-handedness. Berlin ignored his complaints that Romanian troops were scattered in support of German operations and short on supplies. The Germans also snubbed Romania's commissar for Jewish affairs, Radu Lecca, by discussing Romania's Jewish problem without him during his August 1942 visit to Berlin. "Deep inside," remembered one Romanian official, Antonescu "was offended, irritated by German demands regarding 'his' Jews. . . . Why were the Germans meddling in the question of the Jews of Romania, which remained an internal matter?"[5] In August 1942, Antonescu waived diplomatic protection for several thousand Romanian Jews in occupied countries abroad—3,000 in France alone—abandoning them to deportation. But in October, he cancelled the first scheduled deportation of 40,000 Jews, ostensibly due to bad weather.[6]

In theory, deportations were postponed until spring. But the massive Soviet defeat of the Romanian Third and Fourth armies outside Stalingrad between November 1942 and January 1943 meant that they were never rescheduled. Berlin had little room for protest. Romania supplied over one-third of Germany's oil. When Ribbentrop met Antonescu in April 1943, the discussion centered on oil deliveries, with Jews coming up only afterward. Antonescu was the only ally Hitler trusted to fight the Soviets until the end. "As for Romania," Hitler once said, "she has only one man, Antonescu."[7]

[2]Figure in Jean Ancel, "The German-Romanian Relationship and the Final Solution," *Holocaust and Genocide Studies*, 19, no. 2 (Fall 2005), pp. 262–3.

[3]Holly Case, *Between States: The Transylvanian Question and the European Idea During World War II* (Stanford, CA, 2009), p. 188.

[4]Marguerite Dorian, ed., *The Quality of Witness: A Romanian Diary 1937–1944* (hereafter *Dorian Diary*) (Philadelphia, PA, 1982), June 7, 1942.

[5]Quoted in Radu Ioanid, *The Holocaust in Romania: The Destruction of Jews and Gypsies Under the Antonescu Regime, 1940–1944* (Chicago, IL, 2000), p. 248.

[6]For trends and figures, see Ioanid, *The Holocaust in Romania*, pp. 238–48, 264.

[7]Germany, Auswärtiges Amt, *Akten zur deutschen auswärtigen Politik 1918–1945* (hereafter *ADAP*), Series E, vol. 5 (Göttingen, 1978), doc. 300; Hugh R. Trevor-Roper, et al., eds., *Hitler's Table Talk 1941–1944: His Private Conversations* (New York, 2000), January 4–5, 1942; Ian Kershaw, *Hitler, 1936–1941: Nemesis* (New York, 2000), p. 582.

The Transnistrian Rescue Scheme

In Romanian-occupied Transnistria, native Jews and Jewish deportees from Bessarabia and Bukovina died by the tens of thousands in 1941 and 1942. In Bucharest, protests by Wilhelm Filderman, Romania's chief Jewish advocate, left Antonescu apoplectic. The deportees, Antonescu replied in February 1942, "are getting what's coming to them for their actions and their unspeakable behavior. . . . Those who identify with them," he warned, "will meet a similar fate."[8]

But the Romanian defeat at Stalingrad triggered reconsideration. In late 1942, as the catastrophe unfolded, Filderman discussed with senior Romanian officials a scheme to return from Transnistria roughly 70,000 surviving Jews, after which they would go to third countries, including Palestine. The Romanian government would receive a cash payment of some 200,000 Romanian lei for each Jew. German Minister Manfred von Killinger learned of the scheme in December. "On the one hand," he reported, "[Antonescu] wants to get hold of the 16 billion lei he desperately needs, and on the other, he is looking for a convenient way of getting rid of a large part of the Jews. He rejects a radical solution."[9] Filderman sent word of the talks to Joseph Goldin, the Jewish Agency Executive (JAE) representative in Istanbul. Goldin relayed the scheme to the JAE chairman in Jerusalem, David Ben-Gurion.

Throughout 1942, Jewish organizations in Romania—despite their own state-imposed financial troubles—sent cash, medicine, clothing, and other goods to Transnistrian ghettos and camps. In 1943 and 1944, food and clothing also came from the JAE in Palestine and from the American Jewish Joint Distribution Committee (JDC) via the Red Cross. The aid saved thousands despite Romanian government tariffs on goods entering Transnistria, local officials helping themselves to incoming money and goods, and some Jewish Council heads taking care of friends and family first.

But could deportees be rescued entirely? When the JAE learned of Nazi extermination plans in the autumn of 1942, Ben-Gurion prioritized the rescue of children. "Five hundred thousand Palestinian Jews," he said, "would be happy to adopt the children of the ghetto."[10] In December 1942, Churchill's cabinet agreed to issue immigration certificates (within White Paper limits) for 4,000 Jewish children from Bulgaria. Ben-Gurion hoped that it would lead to a larger program. But even small operations were formidable. Although the JDC offered to pay for ships, neutrals were unwilling to provide them. Berlin in 1943 prohibited children's emigration schemes, denied safe conduct even for Red Cross ships carrying Jews, and pressed its allies and neutrals to prohibit land passage. Turkey agreed to allow just fifty Jewish children to pass through at a time, with one group entering only as another left. Saving 10,000 children at this rate would take over four years. [11]

The much larger Transnistrian scheme thus had no chance of success. Irrespective of German policies, the British dismissed anything that threatened the White Paper and smacked of "Romanian blackmail." As one British official warned, "The Jewish problem is not the only problem." The United States, meanwhile, had been at war with Romania since December 1941

---

[8]Quoted in Jean Ancel, *Transnistria, 1941–1942: The Romanian Mass Murder Campaigns*, vol. 1 (Tel Aviv, 2003), p. 374.

[9]*ADAP*, Series E, vol. 4, doc. 279.

[10]Quoted in Tuvia Friling, *Arrows in the Dark: David Ben-Gurion, the Yishuv, and Rescue Attempts During the Holocaust*, vol. 1 (Madison, WI, 2005), p. 145.

[11]Dalia Ofer, *Escaping the Holocaust: Illegal Immigration to the Land of Israel, 1939–1944* (New York, 1990), pp. 191–3; Friling, *Arrows in the Dark*, vol. 1, pp. 151, 168, 174.

and was bombing Romanian oil refineries by August 1943. As JAE treasurer Eliezer Kaplan put it, "On our part everything has been done in order to rescue the refugees. We are knocking on every open and closed door, but it does not depend on us."[12]

Jewish groups fought for time. Filderman pressed the Romanian government to allow orphans and then Jews in other categories to return from Transnistria to Romania. Through agents in Turkey and Switzerland, the JAE and JDC pledged funds. Between December 1943 and March 1944, the Romanian government allowed the return of nearly 24,000 deportees. The rescue of the rest came a month later when the Red Army crossed into Transnistria.[13] As Romanian troops retreated, German detachments arrived in order to kill what Jews they could. But the Soviet advance thwarted their efforts.

As Romania neared surrender in the spring and summer of 1944, Antonescu—in defiance of Berlin—allowed 9 Mossad-chartered Turkish ships with over 3,000 Jewish refugees to sail. A German submarine sank one, the *Mefkura*, on August 4. Five of the 320 refugees on board survived.[14] But Romania's war was nearing its end. On August 23, King Michael dismissed Antonescu, announced a cease-fire with the Soviets, and declared war on Germany. Soviet troops pushed through Romania. The scheme of ridding Romania of Jews in return for payment was left to Antonescu's communist successors.

14.2 THE SURVIVAL OF BULGARIA'S JEWS

Bulgaria and the Reich

In World War I, Bulgaria fought on Germany's side and lost territory to its neighbors. It began World War II as a neutral, but King Boris III moved into Germany's orbit hoping to reacquire the lost lands. In 1941, Bulgaria allowed German troops to move through the country, and it participated in the attacks on Greece (thus acquiring most of Thrace) and Yugoslavia (thus acquiring Macedonia). A traditional Russian ally with a significant communist movement, Bulgaria did not declare war on the USSR when Germany attacked in June 1941, but it did declare war on the United States and Great Britain in December.

Bulgaria's Jews came mostly from Sephardic exiles from Spain. Numbering 48,398 in 1934, they were less than 1 percent of the population and concentrated in cities like the capital of Sofia.[15] Though many Bulgarian writers insisted that the country had no Jewish question, the government in September 1939 worked to expel 4,000 foreign Jews who had come to Bulgaria to find passage to Palestine. The next month, King Boris appointed German-educated Bogdan Filov as prime minister. Filov in turn made Petur Gabrovsky his interior minister, who in turn made Alexander Belev his top legal official. Belev was a leader of the Ratnitsi, an antisemitic party with ties to Germany, and he brought similar types into his department.

In January 1941, Filov's government enacted the Law for the Protection of the Nation. Modeled on the Nuremberg Laws, it defined who was a Jew, banned Jews from public office and state jobs, outlawed mixed marriages, set Jewish quotas for professions, and imposed new taxes on Jews. Belev implemented the law thereafter, traveling periodically to Berlin to study German

---

[12]Quoted in Friling, *Arrows in the Dark*, vol. 1, pp. 172, 209.

[13]Figures in Ioanid, *The Holocaust in Romania*, pp. 255–7.

[14]Ofer, *Escaping the Holocaust*, pp. 195–8, 256–66, 326–7.

[15]Figure in Frederick B. Chary, *The Bulgarian Jews and the Final Solution, 1940–1944* (Pittsburgh, PA, 1972), p. 29.

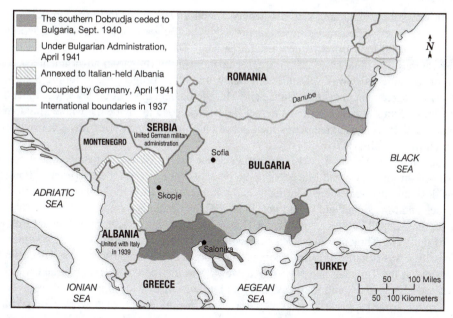

MAP 14.1   Bulgarian expansion, 1940–1941.   *Source:* Based on Crampton, R. J. *Bulgaria* (Oxford University Press, 2007), p. 257; and United States Department of State, *Documents on German Foreign Policy 1918–1945,* Series D, vol. XIII (Washington, DC: USGPO, 1962).

measures against Jews. He was in Berlin during the Wannsee Conference in January 1942, and by June he called for "the radical solution of the Jewish problem in our country," which he explained as "the deportation of the Jews and simultaneous confiscation of their property."[16] In August 1942, he became Bulgaria's Commissioner for Jewish Questions, a new position that created and implemented new anti-Jewish legislation. Aided by a growing staff, Belev required that Jews wear yellow stars, confiscated Jewish property and businesses either directly or though augmented taxation, confined Jews to ghettoized urban districts, and had perhaps 9,000 Jewish men in labor battalions working on highway and railroad construction under frightful conditions.

Bulgaria's Deportations

Despite Belev's policies, Berlin had grounds for concern. Professional groups and Orthodox Church leaders in Bulgaria protested state Jewish policies from the start. The Law for the Defense of the Nation, Bulgaria's leading Orthodox bishops argued to Prime Minister Filov, "cannot be considered just or useful. . . ."[17] German representatives in Sofia noted local opposition to the government's Jewish policies. In November 1942, Bulgaria's Foreign Ministry told the Germans that though it favored the idea of deportations, Bulgaria's Jews were needed for labor. German Ambassador Adolf-Heinz Beckerle lamented in January 1943 that "Bulgarian society doesn't understand the real meaning of the Jewish question."[18]

---

[16]Quoted in Chary, *The Bulgarian Jews*, p. 52.

[17]Grand Vicar Neofit of Vidin to Filov, November 15, 1940, Tzvetan Todorov, ed., *The Fragility of Goodness: Why Bulgaria's Jews Survived the Holocaust* (Princeton, NJ, 2001), pp. 54–7.

[18]Quoted in Michael Bar-Zohar, *Beyond Hitler's Grasp: The Heroic Rescue of Bulgaria's Jews* (Holbrook, MA, 1998), p. 60.

In December, Eichmann sent his deputy Theodor Dannecker to Sofia. On February 22, 1943, he and Belev signed an agreement, approved by the Bulgarian cabinet, "for the deportation of the first 20,000 Jews from the new Bulgarian lands Thrace and Macedonia into the German eastern regions. . . . In no case," said the agreement, "will the Bulgarian government ask for the return of the deported Jews."[19] Dannecker, Belev, and other Bulgarians, including King Boris, who saw the agreement knew that Thrace and Macedonia held but 12,000 Jews. The other 8,000 had to come from Bulgaria itself, and in fact Belev proceeded to divide the whole kingdom into deportation districts. The agreement's mention of only the new territories was a convenient fiction regarding its full extent.

Beginning on March 4, 1943, Bulgarian police quickly arrested, detained, and deported 11,393 Jews from Thrace and Macedonia—96 percent of the Jews in these regions.[20] Politically it was desirable and expedient. Germany had not agreed to Bulgaria's permanent annexation of Thrace and Macedonia and would not do so if Bulgaria did not solve the Jewish problem in these regions. Legally it was easy. Jews in Thrace and Macedonia were never granted Bulgarian citizenship. "The Thracian and Macedonian Jews," Belev said, "are Germany's subjects."[21] Financially it was beneficial. Belev's commissariat sold Jewish property that was left behind.

Most of the Thracian and Macedonian Jews were murdered at Treblinka and Auschwitz after dreadful detentions and journeys. They had no idea of their destination. "Transports were now arriving from Bulgaria," remembered Yankiel Wiernick, a Jewish worker in Treblinka, "comprising well-to-do people who brought with them large supplies of food. . . . They were killed off just like all the others. . . . The Bulgarian [sic] Jews were strong and husky specimens. Looking at them, it was hard to believe that in twenty minutes they would be dead. . . ."[22]

Peshev's Protest

In keeping with the figure of 20,000 Jews in the agreement with Dannecker, Belev's commissariat compiled lists of Bulgarian Jews who were "rich, prominent, and generally well-known" and "defenders of the Jewish spirit." From these lists, Belev personally selected 8,400 especially dangerous Jews and their families.[23] Bulgarian police began gathering these Bulgarian Jews in early March, even as they arrested Jews in Thrace and Macedonia. Belev wanted to move quickly to avoid popular reaction.

He could not do so thanks to leaks from his own office. Belev's secretary Liliana Panitsa informed one of Belev's prime targets, Dr. Nissim Levi, a Jewish consistory officer in Sofia, that Jews in Macedonia and Thrace were being deported and that Bulgaria's Jews were next. "She knew I was Vice-President of the Consistory," Levi remembered, "and by informing me she would do us a great service."[24] Other leaks reached Iako Baruh, a Jewish Agency Executive official in Sofia. Levi, Baruh, and other Jewish leaders quickly contacted sympathetic officials, including Dimitar Peshev from Kyustendil, the first Bulgarian town from which deportations were to occur.

---

[19]Agreement printed in Chary, *The Bulgarian Jews*, pp. 208–10.

[20]Figure in Chary, *The Bulgarian Jews*, p. 127.

[21]Quoted in Bar-Zohar, *Beyond Hitler's Grasp*, p. 72.

[22]Quoted in Alexander Donat, ed., *The Death Camp Treblinka: A Documentary* (New York, 1979), p. 172.

[23]Quotes and figures in Chary, *The Bulgarian Jews*, pp. 86–7.

[24]Quoted in Bar-Zohar, *Beyond Hitler's Grasp*, p. 84.

Peshev was no rebel. A forty-nine-year-old lawyer who served as the parliamentary vice president, he backed the alliance with Germany, the annexation of Thrace and Macedonia, and earlier government measures against Jews. But murder was something else. On March 9, 1943, Peshev met with Jewish leaders in Sofia and then with Interior Minister Gabrovski, flanked by a parliamentary delegation. Peshev's group threatened to raise the deportation publicly. Gabrovski consulted with Filov and then postponed deportation orders for Bulgaria. Bulgarian Jews already detained were released, perhaps, as the Germans believed, on the king's personal orders.

"I had grounds to believe," Peshev wrote after the war, "that the deportation measures [in Bulgaria] had only been temporarily suspended, and could be revived, especially under pressure from the Germans."[25] Dannecker was indeed furious with the delay. Thus, on March 19, Peshev delivered a letter to Prime Minister Filov, signed by forty-three parliamentary deputies. It noted that the deportation of Bulgarian citizens, particularly women and children, constituted "exceptional and cruel measures . . . that may expose the government and the entire nation to accusations of mass murder." "Our nation's reputation," it continued, "would be stained forever."[26] Filov was incensed. "Now," he wrote in his diary, "I truly realize the extent of Jewish influence and how harmful these people really are."[27] Filov had Peshev removed from his vice president's post and politically ostracized.

The Halt of Deportations

But the die was already cast. Britain publicly announced in February 1943 that 4,000 Palestine certificates could be distributed to Jewish children in Bulgaria. In March, US Secretary of State Cordell Hull, through channels in Switzerland, urged Filov to allow general Jewish emigration to neutral countries, and US Ambassador Laurence Steinhardt in Ankara pressed Turkey to allow passage to 30,000 Bulgarian Jewish refugees. Swiss chargé d'affaires Charles Rédard bluntly told Filov on March 11 that evacuated Jews "are being sent to their death." If Romania had cancelled deportations, why did Bulgaria have to carry them through?[28] Berlin countered with its own diplomatic pressure. An irritated Ribbentrop told King Boris in early April, "Our opinion on the Jewish question [is that] the most radical solution is the only correct one."[29] Filov indeed rejected the children's immigration certificates for Palestine, citing a shortage of trains (though plenty had been allocated for deportations) and his supposed reluctance to separate children from their parents.[30]

The Bulgarian government maintained local anti-Jewish policies. In April 1943, King Boris insisted to Ribbentrop that Bulgaria needed Jewish workers for road construction in Bulgaria and indeed forced labor continued.[31] The king also argued to Orthodox Church leaders in April regarding "the enormous harm inflicted on humanity for centuries by the profiteering spirit of the Jews." Mature nations, he continued, "understand that the sooner they rid themselves of Jewish influence and exploitation, the sooner they will be able to strengthen and consolidate their sense of nationhood. . . ."[32] In May, Belev's commissariat, over vocal church objections, expelled over

[25]Quoted in Bar-Zohar, *Beyond Hitler's Grasp*, p. 146.

[26]Letter in Todorov, ed., *The Fragility of Goodness*, pp. 78–80.

[27]Excerpt from Filov Diary, March 19, 1943, Todorov, ed., *The Fragility of Goodness*, p. 87.

[28]Excerpt from Filov Diary, March 11, 1943 and Rédard report of March 11, 1943 in Todorov, ed., *The Fragility of Goodness,* pp. 86, 92.

[29]*ADAP*, Series E, vol. 5, doc. 273.

[30]Chary, *The Bulgarian Jews*, p. 132.

[31]*ADAP*, Series E, vol. 5, doc. 273; Rédard report of March 11, 1943, Todorov, ed., *The Fragility of Goodness*, pp. 92–3.

[32]Meeting of April 15, 1943, Todorov, ed., *The Fragility of Goodness*, pp. 102–3.

19,000 of Sofia's Jews to designated houses in twenty provincial towns. Jewish leaders viewed the expulsions as a prelude to resumed deportations, and indeed Belev intended them as such. "We are not leaving the country," Sofia's chief rabbi Asher Hananel told Metropolitan Stephen of Sofia. "We are ready to die. Please tell His Majesty that we are ready to give our blood, but here in Bulgaria."[33]

But deportations were not resumed. Beckerle blamed the recent course of the war and Bulgarian fears of Allied bombing. "For the moment," he reported in August 1943, "it is absolutely senseless to insist on deportation. . . . [W]e shall be able to solve the Jewish problem completely when German successes again come to the fore. Then the time will come for an intervention."[34] The time never came. King Boris unexpectedly died the same month, and Belev lost influence thereafter. The Germans kept killing Jews it could reach in occupied areas. In Poland, Operation Harvest Festival killed nearly as many Jews on November 3 and 4—43,000—as lived in Bulgaria. But reluctant allies were another matter.

Increased partisan fighting in the Balkans made Bulgaria's military and economic contributions more important. In August 1944, a new Bulgarian cabinet initiated peace feelers with the Allies, professed regret for past actions, and repealed anti-Jewish laws. In September, the Soviets crossed into Bulgaria, which, like Romania, changed sides and declared war on Germany. A combination of domestic protest, Allied and neutral diplomatic pressure, and German defeat saved Bulgaria's Jews. Most Jews, however, did not forget the experience. They left Bulgaria for Israel after 1948.

14.3 HUNGARY, THE JEWS, AND THE WAR

Hungary and Its Jews

No Jewish population in Europe was more acculturated than Hungary's. Once emancipated in 1868, Hungary's Jews fully backed Hungary's conservative ruling gentry. They adopted a reformed (Neolog) Judaism to minimize Judaism's foreignness, adopted the Hungarian language, and even changed their names to accommodate Hungary's campaign of national homogeneity. In return, they prospered in the growing urban economy in Budapest and elsewhere. But the Hungary's landed aristocracy never fully accepted Hungary's bourgeois Jews. They were seasonal allies subject to changes in the political landscape.

Seismic shifts came after World War I. The first trauma was the 100-day communist dictatorship of Béla Kun in 1919. The fact that Kun and most of his ministers were of Jewish origin proved for many the link between Jews and Bolshevism. An army-led counterrevolution and "white" terror swept through Hungary after Kun's ouster and included 5,000 executions. It targeted communists but also killed Jews in many locales. Business-minded Jews were as appalled by the Kun government as were Hungary's conservative rulers. "For every single communist," said the Jewish congregation in Pest, "there are at least a thousand Hungarian citizens of the Jewish faith who . . . faithfully served the Hungarian fatherland. . . ."[35]

---

[33]Quoted in Bar-Zohar, *Beyond Hitler's Grasp*, p. 193.

[34]Quoted in Haim Oliver, *We Were Saved: How the Jews of Bulgaria Were Kept from the Death Camps* (Sofia, 1978), pp. 207–8.

[35]Quoted in Raphael Patai, *The Jews of Hungary: History, Culture, Psychology* (Detroit, MI, 1996), p. 469.

The second trauma was the Treaty of Trianon in 1920, by which Hungary paid for the lost war. Hungary lost two-thirds of its territories, including Slovakia and Carpatho-Ruthenia (which went to Czechoslovakia), Croatia and the Banat (which went to Yugoslavia), and Transylvania (which went to Romania). The lost lands contained national minorities but they also contained one-third of Hungary's Hungarians. Once a powerful multinational kingdom, Hungary was now a rump state. Ten thousand Hungarian Jewish soldiers died in the war, and Hungary's Jews were as outraged as anyone by the treaty.[36] Yet as the sole minority left in Hungary, they were blamed as disloyal profiteers—all the more because almost half of Hungary's 473,355 Jews in 1920 lived in Budapest, forming nearly one-quarter of the capital's population.[37]

The conservative magnates hoped to restore Hungarian power while preserving the old political system. They reinstated the monarchy in 1920, and because the Allies would not approve the return of exiled Habsburg King Charles IV, they appointed one of their own, Admiral Miklós Horthy, as the regent. Like a king, Horthy appointed and dismissed governing cabinets from the conservative, landed ranks. Horthy and other conservatives, including senior church leaders who hoped to restore a "Christian Hungary," distinguished between "good Jews" and "bad Jews," but they were convinced that Hungary had a Jewish question. In 1920, the government initiated a solution by limiting Jewish university enrollment. Jewish leaders emphasized their loyalty and openly rejected Zionism as confirming Jewish national separateness. "We cannot," argued Neolog spokesman Mór Mezei, "have two fatherlands!"[38] Zionists made up but 5 percent of Hungarian Jews.[39]

In the 1930s, successive Hungarian cabinets backed Hitler diplomatically as a means by which to recover the lost lands. Because Hungary bordered the Reich after Germany's annexation of Austria, Hitler used Hungary's revisionism to geopolitical advantage. When Germany dismembered Czechoslovakia in 1938 and 1939, Hungary received southern Slovakia and Carpatho-Ruthenia. In 1940, the Germans transferred northern Transylvania from Romania to Hungary, much to the fury of the Romanians. In 1941, when Hitler invaded southeast Europe, Hungary joined the Axis, helped with the invasion of Yugoslavia, and occupied the Banat. Riding a white horse and wearing his royal naval uniform, Horthy made ceremonial entrance into each recovered region. On June 27, 1941, Hungary joined Germany's invasion of the USSR.

Alignment with Germany did not come free. Berlin pressed Budapest to address its Jewish problem, especially because the Hungarian-annexed lands contained some 325,000 more Jews and up to 35,000 more Jewish refugees had fled to Hungary from Austria, Czechoslovakia, and Poland.[40] Additional pressure came from Hungary's radical right, which in the depressed 1930s coalesced in a movement called the Arrow Cross (*Nyilas*). It called for Hungarian racial purity and the end of all Jewish influence in Hungary. Yet it also called for an end to rule by the Hungarian aristocracy and agrarian reform. To steal Arrow Cross thunder—the party gained one-third of the parliamentary seats in 1939—Hungarian cabinets enacted their own

---

[36]Figure in Nicholas M. Nagy-Talavera, "László Endre, Frontrunner of the Final Solution in Hungary," in *The Holocaust in Hungary Fifty Years Later*, eds. Randolph L. Braham and Attila Pók (New York, 1997), p. 361.

[37]Figures in Ezra Mendelsohn, *The Jews of East Central Europe Between the World Wars* (Bloomington, IN, 1983), pp. 99–101.

[38]Quoted in Patai, *The Jews of Hungary*, pp. 480–1.

[39]Figure in Yehuda Bauer, *Jews for Sale: Nazi-Jewish Negotiations, 1933–1945* (New Haven, CT, 1994), p. 151.

[40]Figures in Randolph L. Braham, *The Politics of Genocide: The Holocaust in Hungary* (New York, 1981), vol. 1, p. 200; vol. 2, p. 1143.

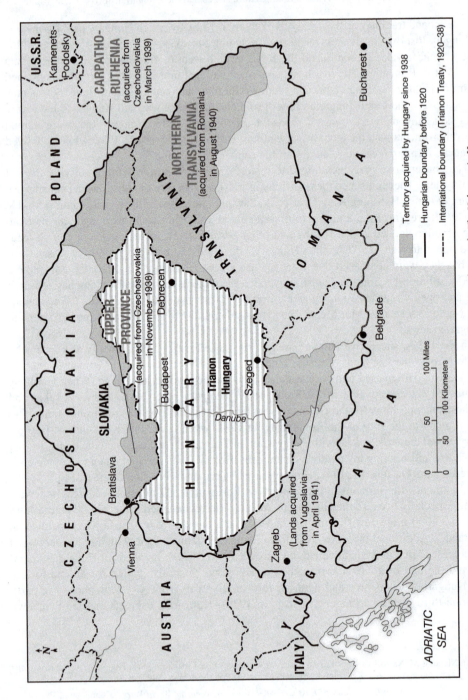

MAP 14.2 *Source:* Adapted from Braham, Randolph L., *The Politics of Genocide: The Holocaust in Hungary*

Hungary, 1944.

Legend:
- Territory acquired by Hungary since 1938
- Hungarian boundary before 1920
- International boundary (Trianon Treaty, 1920–38)

U.S.S.R.
Kamenets-Podolsky

CARPATHO-RUTHENIA
(acquired from Czechoslovakia in March 1939)

POLAND

NORTHERN TRANSYLVANIA
(acquired from Romania in August 1940)

TRANSYLVANIA

Bucharest

ROMANIA

CZECHOSLOVAKIA

SLOVAKIA

UPPER PROVINCE
(acquired from Czechoslovakia in November 1938)

Debrecen

Bratislava

Vienna

Budapest

HUNGARY

Trianon Hungary

Szeged

Danube

Belgrade

Zagreb

(Lands acquired from Yugoslavia in April 1941)

AUSTRIA

YUGOSLAVIA

ITALY

ADRIATIC SEA

100 Miles

100 Kilometers

50

50

0

0

N

anti-Jewish laws between 1938 and 1941. The laws restricted Jews in professions and commercial enterprises to 6 percent, defined Jews by their parentage, and prohibited marriage between Jews and non-Jews.

The laws, though applied unevenly, drove thousands of Hungarian Jews into poverty. "The expansion of Jews," read the Jewish law of 1938, "is as detrimental to the nation as it is dangerous. We must take steps to defend ourselves."[41] Hungarian Jewish leaders, meanwhile, fully misread their position. Unlike acculturated Jews in Germany, Austria, Poland, and Romania, who were under no illusions by 1938, Hungarian Jews looked to the conservative government for protection from even worse measures while maintaining their loyalty for fear of provoking worse. "[T]he homeland must be loved," said Samu Stern, the leader of the Pest Jewish community in 1938, "even when it does not bestow on us the totality of its love."[42] Hungarian Jewish tradition allowed no other response. And given the trials of Jews elsewhere in eastern Europe, Hungarian Jews viewed themselves as fortunate.

Kamenets-Podolsky: The Initial Massacre

Hungary joined Germany's war against the USSR for fear that its recovered territories would otherwise be returned to Slovakia and Romania, both of which joined the German attack. Hungarian forces accompanied German advances in Ukraine, eventually flanking the German attack north of Stalingrad on the Don River at Voronezh. They were lightly equipped, poorly trained, and undermanned. Hungary's Second Army, its main force, was destroyed when Soviet armored forces attacked in January 1943. A 40,000-man remnant of the original 209,000-man force returned to Hungary in May.

Hungary's war on the Eastern Front initiated participation in genocide. The first mass crime concerned a scheme by Hungary's Alien Control Office to dump eastern Jews living in the newly acquired northern and eastern regions of Hungary into German-occupied Ukraine. On July 12, 1941, roughly two weeks after Hungary entered the war, the government decreed "the deportation of the recently infiltrated Polish and Russian Jews in the largest possible number and as fast as possible."[43] Hungarian police rounded up foreign Jews from refugee camps as well as entire Jewish communities in Carpatho-Ruthenia on the Ukrainian border. Some Hungarian Jews who could not find their identity papers were also arrested. By August, some 16,000 Jews were crammed into freight cars and turned over to the Germans, who moved them to the old fortress city of Kamenets-Podolsky across the Dniester.

German army officers complained that they "could not cope with all these Jews."[44] But Hungary refused their return. The question was left to Himmler's Higher SS and Police Leader in Ukraine, Friedrich Jeckeln, who promised to liquidate the Jews by September 1. True to his word, Jeckeln had them marched into bomb craters beyond city limits. Standing atop the craters with machine guns, German, Ukrainian, and Hungarian policemen murdered the deportees as well as local Jews over two days, burying many alive. It was the single largest massacre—23,600—up to

---

[41]Quoted in Judith Magyar Isaacson, *Seed of Sarah: Memoirs of a Survivor* (Urbana, IL, 1991), p. 12.

[42]Quoted in Ezra Mendelsohn, "Trianon Hungary, Jews and Politics," in *Hostages of Modernization: Studies on Modern Antisemitism 1870–1933/39*, ed. Herbert A. Strauss (New York, 1993), vol. 2, p. 909.

[43]Quoted in Braham, *The Politics of Genocide*, vol. 1, p. 202.

[44]Quoted in Richard Rhodes, *Masters of Death: The SS Einsatzgruppen and the Invention of the Holocaust* (New York, 2002), p. 129.

that time. Witnesses were aghast. "I felt," remembered Gábor Mermelstein, a Hungarian Jewish driver who had moved Jews to Kamenets-Podolsky, "[that] I had been banished forever from the ranks of humanity and condemned to eternal hell."[45]

Ferenc Keresztes-Fischer, Hungary's anti-Nazi minister of the interior, had allowed Jewish refugees into Hungary at the request of the Jewish Agency Executive in Jerusalem, and he opposed the deportations of Jews to Ukraine. On learning of the massacre, he halted deportations and recalled seven trains of deportees. But contrary trends were also at work. The army promulgated steady antisemitic indoctrination. "Only the Jews," said one army publication referring to the Soviet system, "are capable of perpetrating such a constant rule of terror."[46] Various schemes within the army and government in 1942 discussed deporting 100,000 Jews. Eichmann declined, noting that this would not solve Hungary's Jewish problem in its entirety.

Labor Service

As Hungary prepared for war in 1939, the government conscripted politically unreliable men of military age into labor service companies rather than combat units. Jews of military age were thus placed in labor companies attached to regular army units. The initial requirement was three months. Workers received uniforms and the same pay as other servicemen. Conditions changed with the war against the USSR. The requirement jumped to two years and the Ministry of Defense deliberately conscripted Jewish professionals, businessmen, and community leaders, often ignoring the age limit of forty-two and even fitness for service. Labor service became Hungary's ad hoc solution to the Jewish question.

Jewish laborers wore their civilian clothes (which wore out quickly) with yellow armbands. Officers overseeing labor companies, particularly Arrow Cross sympathizers, became more sadistic as the war progressed. Some 50,000 poorly equipped Jewish labor servicemen were sent into Ukraine as part of the Hungarian Second Army. They had no winter provisions, ate insufficient rations, dug anti-tank ditches in frozen ground, cleared minefields, and slept in snow-huts. "The fate of our relatives in the labor battalions was a constant anxiety," remembered Hermann Gruenwald, who was fifteen when Hungary entered the war. "We became preoccupied with trying to help them, sending blankets and other necessities. When these men were sent east, they often disappeared."[47]

The Soviet destruction of Hungary's Second Army in January 1943, in which labor companies also came under fire, revealed true valor. "I've heard," wrote one Hungarian officer, "that the Jewish companies act bravely on the front line and do not leave anyone behind, neither the wounded nor the dead Hungarians. We may live to see that they are regarded as heroes, while our infantry is constantly routed."[48] Such appreciation was rare. Hungarian troops and marauding SS killed thousands of retreating Jews. Lacking everything from food to boots, thousands died of hunger, cold, and disease. Fear that one group of labor servicemen would spread typhoid to the troops led to 800 being burned alive in a barn in the Ukrainian village of Doroshich in April 1943. In all, some 7,000 of the 50,000 Jews attached to the Second Army returned to Hungary.[49]

---

[45]Gábor Mermelstein, "A Jew in a Motorized Unit of the Hungarian Army," in *The Wartime System of Labor Service in Hungary: Varieties of Experience*, ed. Randolph L. Braham (New York, 1995), pp. 5–6.

[46]Judit Pihurik, "Hungarian Soldiers and Jews in the Eastern Front, *Yad Vashem Studies*, 35, pt. 2 (2007), p. 77.

[47]Hermann Gruenwald, *After Auschwitz: One Man's Story* (Montreal, 2007), p. 39.

[48]Quoted in Pihurik, "Hungarian Soldiers and Jews," p. 87.

[49]Figure in Braham, *The Politics of Genocide*, vol. 1, p. 318.

14.4 THE GERMAN OCCUPATION AND THE HOLOCAUST IN HUNGARY

The Occupation

Miklós Kállay became prime minister in March 1942. Kállay was a long-time aristocratic opponent of the alignment with Germany and of the Arrow Cross's fixation on the Jewish question, which struck him as insanity. He repeatedly refused German requests to hand over Hungary's Jews. After the military disaster at Voronezh, Kállay worked in earnest to extricate Hungary from the war. He relaxed censorship so that newspapers could call for peace, he purged the Hungarian Foreign Ministry of Nazi sympathizers, and his government established contact with Allied intelligence in Istanbul. German intelligence quickly learned of Kállay's treachery.

Hitler had long considered Hungary a fair weather ally and predicted that it would be the last country to hand over its Jews. In April 1943, he summoned Admiral Horthy to Germany. Recent trends in Budapest, Hitler seethed, threatened Europe's very existence, and Hungary's refusal to solve its Jewish problem was to blame. Hitler continued that the Jews, as in 1918, would destroy the war effort from within and open Europe to Bolshevism. In Germany, Hitler said, "Jewish decomposition has been made impossible." It was now Hungary's time to act. "There can," he said, "be no hesitation. . . . Whoever believes in compromise on this question is fundamentally mistaken." Nor should the Jews "be treated with kid gloves." They instigated the global war and were "therefore responsible for millions of victims," including women and children. Horthy agreed that Hungary had "substantial difficulties" with its money-obsessed Jews. But he also noted that Hungary would handle its own Jewish problem.[50]

Berlin continued to watch Hungary closely while fuming at its refusal to take part in the Final Solution. The last straw came in March 1944. With Soviet troops 100 miles from Hungary, Kalláy insisted on pulling Hungarian troops back to the border. Hitler signed the order to occupy Hungary on March 12. "The Jews," he explained, "who control everything in Hungary . . . have brought the Hungarian people, who were well disposed to us, to this situation."[51] When explaining the impending occupation to Horthy on March 17, at Klessheim Palace in Austria, he repeated that Horthy had done nothing to solve the Jewish problem. By the time Horthy returned to Budapest, the country was occupied.

The Sztójay Government

Berlin occupied Hungary on March 19 to keep Hungary in the war while deporting its Jews as quickly as possible. Along with the troops came a special detachment of 150 to 200 men under Eichmann. "I remember the date," Eichmann said years later, "because it was my birthday."[52] The week before, he and his staff planned the liquidation of Hungary's Jews. But they could not execute the task alone, particularly with the Soviets now forty miles from Carpatho-Ruthenia. The failures in Denmark, Italy, Romania, and Bulgaria made clear that a new Hungarian government was needed. An Arrow Cross government was out of the question because any new government had to maintain stability and general Hungarian support. Horthy thus remained regent. But the new cabinet was chosen by the German Foreign Ministry and the Security Service (SD), once under Reinhard Heydrich and now under the equally ruthless Austrian SS-General, Ernst Kaltenbrunner.

---

[50]*ADAP*, Series E, vol. 5, doc. 315.

[51]Quoted in Braham, *The Politics of Genocide*, vol. 1, p. 363.

[52]Quoted in David Cesarani, *Becoming Eichmann: Rethinking the Life, Crimes, and Trial of a "Desk Murderer"* (Cambridge, MA, 2004), p. 163.

The new prime minister and minister of foreign affairs was Döme Sztójay, who had been Hungary's minister in Berlin since 1935. Four members of Kalláy's cabinet remained in place for continuity. But the Ministry of the Interior—which controlled the police—was filled with Hungarian SD protégés. Andor Jaross, the new minister, was an extreme antisemite, as were his two state secretaries: László Baky, a member of the officer corps, and László Endre, a police prefect. Both clearly understood German expectations. "I make my job dependent," Baky announced, "on the final and total liquidation of left-wing and Jewish mischief in this country. I am sure that the government will be able to accomplish this overwhelming task which is of enormous historical importance."[53] Endre was more direct, stating, "The time of experiments and halfway solutions has passed."[54] "Endre," Eichmann joked, "wants to devour the Jews with sweet peppers."[55]

Deportation depended on the Hungarian police and the local civil service. Both were purged of unreliable members. Most, however, were pleased to cooperate. The cabinet's first public statement noted that the German occupation was by mutual agreement for warfare against the common enemy and that "the German Reich considered the unrestricted presence of some 1 million Jews and another 1 million socialists and refugees on Hungarian soil as a concrete threat to the safety of German arms in the Balkan peninsula."[56] On trial in Jerusalem in 1961, Eichmann noted that, despite the formidable numbers of Jews and the small timeframe available to transport and kill them, "everything went like a dream."[57]

Deportations

Drawing on nearly five years of experience, Eichmann's staff went to work. They immediately ordered Jewish communities to create Jewish Councils, beginning with a central council in Budapest. These were officially under Endre's control. Lies prevailed. Amid arrests of thousands of prominent Jews listed by the SD as security threats, Eichmann told Budapest's Jewish leaders, "After the war, the Jews would be free to do whatever they wanted."[58] Most Jewish leaders, including seventy-year-old Samu Stern, the central Jewish Council chairman, believed him. Aside from the terrible casualties in the labor companies, Hungary's Jews had survived thus far under Hungarian cabinets, Horthy was still regent, and Allied victory seemed near. Like Jewish Councils elsewhere, they tried to serve Jewish community needs while mitigating the severity of anti-Jewish measures.

But the concentration and deportation of Hungary's Jews moved with terrible speed. By Hungarian state decrees in April 1944, what was left of Jewish property—ranging from bedding to rugs, to silverware, to paintings, to apartments, to business inventories—was expropriated. Jews were banned from professions, barred from public places like bakeries, forbidden to have radios and telephones, and marked with yellow stars. Meanwhile, Jews in the provinces were registered, brutally rounded up, moved to larger towns, and held in isolated ghettos that often, for lack of space, included outdoor brickyards. These ghettos often lasted a matter of weeks. Ghettoized Jews suffered from overcrowding, hunger, and torture by Hungarian police determined to find their hidden valuables.

---

[53]Quoted in Braham, *The Politics of Genocide*, vol. 1, p. 404.

[54]Quoted in Nagy-Talavera, "László Endre," p. 367.

[55]Rudolf Kasztner, *Der Kasztner-Bericht über Eichmanns Menschenhandel in Ungarn* (Munich, 1961), p. 109.

[56]Quoted in Braham, *The Politics of Genocide*, vol. 1, p. 404.

[57]Quoted in Nagy-Talavera, "László Endre," p. 367.

[58]Quoted in Braham, *The Politics of Genocide*, vol. 1, p. 439.

Was help available? Was resistance possible? The first Jewish response was to approach the Hungarian government. Intervention had been effective in Romania and in Bulgaria. Provincial Jewish Councils got word to the central council in Budapest, which in turn tried to contact the Interior Ministry. But Endre simply denied all wrongdoing. He told the Hungarian press that concentration was "a self-defense [measure] that will end Jewish predominance," but that measures were "always carried out humanely. . . . Really, no harm is befalling them."[59] Zionist youth group members were well informed about German intentions. Their emissaries tried to warn the provincial Jewish leaders and encourage resistance. But Jewish leaders could not comprehend the worst. Most healthy young men, meanwhile, were in labor service details. Hungarian bystanders or clergymen provided no appreciable help. Many wanted Jewish property. Only 4,500 Jews at most managed to escape, mostly over the Romanian border.[60]

For deportation purposes, Hungary was divided into six administrative zones to be emptied sequentially, beginning with the easternmost portion of the country. Thus Zone I consisted of Carpatho-Ruthenia and northeastern Hungary, Zone II was northern Transylvania, and so on. Budapest was the sixth and final zone. The system ensured that a Soviet breakthrough into eastern Hungary would be too late to save Jews living there. It also ensured that Budapest Jews would not be able to flee to the countryside when their turn came. By early May 1944, Eichmann's staff worked out the railroad schedules and routes through Slovakia to Auschwitz-Birkenau.

The Killing Frenzy

Deportations began May 14, less than two months after the occupation. Four trains left Hungary daily for Auschwitz carrying an average of 12,056 Jews between them.[61] "We shall remove every Jew from the country," said Baky in an official statement. "Not a single one is going to stay here."[62] Within ten days, Eichmann reported that 116,000 Jews had been deported—nearly 40 percent more than the number deported from France in two years.[63] And the daily total was climbing. By the time Horthy definitively halted deportations on July 8, 1944, the Germans counted 437,402 Jews sent to Auschwitz in just eight weeks. Ninety percent were murdered on arrival. Only the Jews of Budapest remained alive.[64]

Auschwitz-Birkenau's extermination facilities were refitted to prepare for the arrivals. The system whereby arrivals selected for death were marched to the gas chambers at the rear of the camp was not fast enough, so the Germans added a half-mile railway spur leading from the camp entrance straight to the crematoria. They also installed new elevators and aeration systems in the crematoria and relined the chimneys. To handle excess bodies, they ordered large burning pits fifty meters in length near the crematoria and expanded the Jewish *Sonderkommando* detachments, which burned the bodies, by 700 men. "From this day on," said one German officer, you'll work hard but you won't lack for food and clothing."[65] Indeed the Hungarian Jews brought plenty of

---

[59]Quoted in Braham, *The Politics of Genocide*, vol. 1, p. 132.

[60]Figure in Bauer, *Jews for Sale*, p. 160.

[61]Figures in Braham, *The Politics of Genocide*, vol. 2, pp. 606–7.

[62]Quoted in Braham, *The Politics of Genocide*, vol. 2, p. 613.

[63]Figure in Hans Safrian, *Eichmann's Men* (New York, 2009), p. 203.

[64]Figures in Braham, *The Politics of Genocide*, vol. 2, pp. 607, 676.

[65]Gideon Greif, ed., *We Wept Without Tears: Testimony of the Jewish Sonderkommando from Auschwitz* (New Haven, CT, 2005), p. 185.

Jews from Carpatho-Ruthenia, who have been selected for death at Auschwitz, wait to be taken to the gas chambers, May 1944. *Source:* United States Holocaust Memorial Museum, courtesy of Yad Vashem.

food, including delicacies. "All we had to do," said Leon Cohen of Salonika, "was reach out and gorge ourselves."[66]

Hungarian Jews had been spared the worst for so long and the deportations were so rapid that most remained unaware of their fate. Judith Isaacson, then nineteen, thought she was headed for labor service at the front. After four days, she saw the station sign: "'AUSCHWITZ,' I read, turning to the others. 'Auschwitz?' said mother. 'I've never heard of it.'" When the cattle car doors were thrown open, Judith's friend Magda whispered, "It smells like burning skin." Judith remembered seeing giant flames reaching into the night, thinking that it was a forest fire. Dying of thirst, her transport obediently lined up when guards led them to the showers. "We queued up," she remembered, "anxious to bathe and drink at last."[67] She was selected for work at the last moment.

"All the crematoria," remembered *Sonderkommando* member Shlomo Dragon, "worked in two shifts . . . from six in the morning, to six in the evening and from six in the evening to six in the morning." He remembered, "There were women, men, and children of all ages among them. . . . Most of them didn't know that they were going to their deaths. When we told them, they didn't believe us."[68] The fat were burned with the skinny to keep the fires burning. "You wouldn't believe it," said Saul Chazan, of the *Sonderkommando*. "Thousands of people were turned into a heap of dust."[69] Though some committed suicide, most *Sonderkommando*

---

[66]Greif, ed., *We Wept Without Tears*, p. 304.

[67]Isaacson, *Seed of Sarah*, pp. 61–4.

[68]Greif, ed., *We Wept Without Tears*, pp. 163–4.

[69]Greif, ed., *We Wept Without Tears*, p. 275.

members simply lost themselves, unable to feel and unable to weep. "Whenever people got hungry," remembered Ya'akov Silberberg, "they sat down on the bodies and ate."[70]

14.5 JEWISH LEADERS AND THE HUNGARIAN CATASTROPHE

The Vrba-Wetzler Report

An important Jewish channel of information on the Final Solution was a group of Jewish leaders in Slovakia's capital of Bratislava known as the Working Group, which functioned within the Jewish Council there. Its most important figures were Gisi Fleischmann, a Zionist women's leader and JDC representative who was involved with *Aliyah Bet*, and Michael Dov Weissmandel, an Orthodox rabbi. The Working Group assembled information from Jews escaping to Slovakia from Poland. By 1943, they determined numerous details of the German extermination program, including the names of the camps. Through a network of couriers, they got word to Jewish leaders in Geneva, Istanbul, and Budapest.

In early 1944, the Working Group warned Hungary's Jewish leaders of impending catastrophe. The most important intelligence came from Alfred Wetzler and Rudolf Vrba, two Slovakian Jews in Auschwitz who had become clerks and saw the preparations for the arrival of Hungary's Jews. "I thought that if this would be made known," remembered Vrba, "especially within Hungary, from where a million Jews were to be transported . . . this might . . . stir up the Resistance outside and bring help. . . ."[71] After planning with the camp underground they escaped Auschwitz on April 7 and reached Slovakia by April 21; in Slovakia, they provided a full report on the camp to the Working Group. The written Vrba-Wetzler Report, also known as the Auschwitz Protocol, was the most detailed report on Auschwitz to date, with layouts of the camp, details on selections, and estimated numbers of the Jews murdered there. It also became the most public.

The report was forwarded to many destinations, including Budapest, where it reached the Jewish Council. By now—Vrba later said the report went to Hungary in late April—Hungary's Jews were being ghettoized and robbed. Yet central Jewish Council leaders miscalculated. They handled the report confidentially to prevent panic, wasted time having it translated into Hungarian, and sent the report to members of the Hungarian government—including Horthy's son—and senior church officials. Samu Stern and others believed that the government—*their* government—would halt the deportations if they knew German intentions. By June, the documents had some impact on Admiral Horthy. But in the meantime, Hungary's government was not the place to turn to for help.

Ransom: The Europa Plan

Might the Germans have been bribed? The idea originated in 1942 with Fleischmann and Weissmandel in Bratislava. Slovakia's Jews were the first outside the Reich deported to Poland, starting in March 1942. Eichmann's deputy Dieter Wisliceny was in charge of the operation. From August to October 1942, the Working Group raised substantial sums (up to $50,000) to bribe Wisliceny and additional amounts for key Slovak officials. In July 1942, a halt in deportations occurred, which, for the moment, spared 24,000 Jews. The Slovak government insisted on

---

[70]Greif, ed., *We Wept Without Tears*, p. 322.

[71]Claude Lanzmann, *Shoah: The Complete Text of the Acclaimed Holocaust Film* (New York, 1995), p. 153.

the halt, and the bribery of Slovak officials might have helped, along with intervention by Slovak clerics. But Fleischmann and Weissmandel believed that the money had a decisive effect on German officials as well.

Thus, in November 1942, the Working Group devised a larger scheme, called the Europa Plan, by which killing in Poland might be halted altogether. Wisliceny insisted that he could halt the deportations for a price—namely, $3,000,000, to be raised by Jews abroad. The Working Group's pleas for money reached the Jewish Agency Executive (JAE) in Jerusalem as well as Saly Mayer, the representative of the Joint Distribution Committee (JDC) in Switzerland. The JAE, already occupied with Transnistria, could not raise more funds. Senior JDC officials thought the scheme was a ruse. Mayer still raised some money, but Swiss exchange rules made transfer difficult and only $200,000 was moved. Wisliceny considered it an installment. The Germans did not stop killing Jews and did not intend to. But Fleischmann and Weissmandel believed that more money arriving sooner would have had a positive effect. This idea was soon applied in Hungary.

Ransom: Manfréd Weiss

During the destruction process, Hungary became a "wild west" of stolen Jewish property. Theft ranged from individual Hungarian policemen stealing jewelry to the notorious Gold Train—twenty-four wagons packed with rings, watches, candlesticks, silverware, stamp collections, furs, and rugs seized by the Hungarian government and moved to Austria toward the end of the war.[72] If substantial enough, Jewish wealth could ransom lives. The Manfréd Weiss Works was Hungary's most important heavy industrial and weapons producer. Acting for Himmler in May 1944, an SS-Colonel named Kurt Becher acquired controlling shares in Manfréd Weiss, in part by allowing the top Jewish owners and their families (forty-eight in all) to flee to Switzerland and Portugal, with five remaining in Vienna as hostages to ensure good behavior from the others. For the price of a few Jews, the SS obtained a windfall. The deal infuriated the Hungarian government—Jewish property of this type was to pass to Hungary—but it pleased Hitler, who followed the acquisition personally.

Ransom: The Kasztner Transport

Ransoms could not have halted the deportations. Hitler would at most approve tiny numbers and even then, against substantial assets.[73] But desperate Jewish leaders hoped otherwise. Rezső (Rudolf) Kasztner was a thirty-eight-year-old journalist from northern Transylvania who had moved to Budapest. He was chief officer of the *Va'adah*—the Committee for Assistance and Rescue—a Zionist organization formed in 1943 under the auspices of agents sent by the Jewish Agency Executive to Istanbul. Initially created to prepare armed resistance, the *Va'adah* also helped eastern European Jews escape into Hungary before that country was occupied.

In 1944 Kasztner understood German intentions because of his connections with the Working Group, JAE representatives, and even German and Hungarian intelligence officers. Before the occupation, he warned Zionist youth group members to procure arms, but they numbered only a few hundred persons and were unable to convince provincial Jews of the lethal danger.[74] Ransom

---

[72]Ronald W. Zweig, *The Gold Train: The Destruction of the Jews and the Looting of Hungary* (New York, 2001).

[73]Richard Breitman and Shlomo Aronson, "The End of the 'Final Solution'? Nazi Plans to Ransom Jews in 1944," *Central European History*, 25, no. 2 (June 1992): p. 181.

[74]Figure in Bauer, *Jews for Sale*, pp. 160–1.

seemed the only option, and Kasztner viewed his ransom efforts as an extension of those of the Working Group and the JAE itself.

On April 5, 1944, Kasztner and Joel Brand, another *Va'adah* leader, met Wisliceny. Wisliceny demanded an advance of $2,000,000, with $200,000 (6.5 million Hungarian pengő) due immediately as a show of good faith and of the *Va'adah's* ability to raise large sums. In return, Wisliceny said that he would intervene so that a number of Jews could leave Hungary safely. Samu Stern of the Jewish Council helped raise the amount by April 21. Kasztner viewed it as the start of a broader rescue enterprise. Wisliceny, however, was already overseeing Jewish ghettoization in Carpatho-Ruthenia. By dealing with Kasztner, he removed the *Va'adah* as an opposition center while accumulating funds.

By May and June, deportations were fully underway. Kasztner and Brand bargained with Eichmann directly. There were various intertwined plans in the works. Brand was sent to Palestine on a failed mission (described below) to convey Eichmann's offer to halt deportations entirely in return for 10,000 trucks. After Brand left, Kasztner repeatedly pressed his Jewish Agency contacts to help Brand while imploring Eichmann to halt the deportations and release a number of Jews as an initial show of good faith. "You must supply proof," Kasztner remembered telling Eichmann, "that you are serious about your offer."[75] Eichmann allowed Kasztner to assemble a small number of Jews for potential emigration to a special camp in Budapest. But he never slowed the deportations.

As these ideas were considered, Eichmann offered to place 30,000 Hungarian Jews "on ice," thus exempting them from deportation to Poland. But this offer was coincidental and hardly geared toward rescue. Ernst Kaltenbrunner in his capacity as head of the Reich Security Main Office had called for more slave labor in Austria. In the last week of June, 1944, 15,011 Jews were sent to the Strasshof labor camp near Vienna. Despite miserable conditions, some 12,000 survived the war, partly due to the generosity of local Austrians. It was the largest number of Jews actually removed from Hungary to relative safety, it served German labor needs, and Eichmann demanded ransoms from Kasztner for these transports.[76]

In mid-June, Kasztner continued working on the initial good-faith rescue transport. By now, he noted privately that "there can be no more talk of cessation of deportations in general. What can be negotiated is the rescue of a small part. . . ."[77] What Kasztner hoped would be the first of several such transports left on June 30 with 1,684 Jews, in return for substantial payments. It was a Noah's Ark of sorts, with Jews ranging from Zionists to rabbis, to orphans, to doctors. They were told they were going to Spain. Instead they went to a holding camp in Bergen-Belsen in northern Germany, where they were held as hostages. Not until much later were they sent to Switzerland, where they survived the war.

Considered in isolation, the so-called "Kasztner train" had the air of impropriety. To raise additional ransom funds, the *Va'adah* sold 150 places to wealthier Jews. Kasztner and Hansi Brand (Joel Brand's wife and a *Va'adah* member) also placed family members on the transport. In 1954, Israeli judge Benjamin Halevi opined that, by negotiating with Eichmann to save family members while allowing others to perish, Kasztner "sold his soul to the devil."[78] This sentiment encouraged Kasztner's murder by right-wingers in Israel in 1957. But in fact,

[75]Kasztner, *Kasztner-Bericht*, p. 104.

[76]Figures in Bauer, *Jews for Sale*, p. 201.

[77]Quoted in Breitman and Aronson, "The End of the 'Final Solution'?" p.188.

[78]Quoted in Tom Segev, *The Seventh Million: The Israelis and the Holocaust* (New York, 1991), p. 283.

Kasztner remained in Budapest to negotiate for the transport's continued safety. He could not know whether Eichmann would send it to Auschwitz and indeed Eichmann threatened to do so. In the meantime, Kasztner tried to arrange more transports and negotiated for more lives with the unscrupulous Kurt Becher, all in the shadow of mass deportations from Budapest and the Soviet advance.

14.6 THE ALLIES AND THE HUNGARIAN JEWS

The War Refugee Board (WRB)

By the autumn of 1942, the Allies were aware of the Final Solution. But the war itself, combined with Britain's Palestine policy and US immigration laws, blocked broad rescue activity. The Bermuda Conference of April 1943 rejected deals with Hitler and provided no general rescue plan. The Allies rejected ransom schemes such as that for Jews in Transnistria. By 1943, the US State Department tried to block further information on the Final Solution emerging from Geneva for fear that it would trigger more public calls for rescue. Threats of retribution, pressure on Hitler's allies, and pressure on neutrals was the best that would be done.

The State Department's obstruction of even some modest ideas especially upset President Roosevelt's secretary of the treasury, Henry Morgenthau, Jr. One of Roosevelt's close friends, Morgenthau was the sole Jewish cabinet member and familiar with humanitarian disaster. As ambassador to Turkey in 1916, his father had reported on the Armenian genocide. State Department sabotage of Treasury procedures to transfer private funds to help Europe's Jews fanned the growing feud between the two agencies in 1943. Increased impatience from Jewish groups, criticism in the press, and Morgenthau's intervention led Roosevelt to establish the War Refugee Board (WRB) in January 1944.

The president established the WRB by executive order, bypassing Congress. Under John W. Pehle, one of Morgenthau's subordinates, the WRB removed refugee questions from State Department purview. By Roosevelt's order, it was to "take all measures within its power to rescue the victims of enemy oppression who are in imminent danger of death." To stay on safe political ground, the order did not mention Jews and noted that WRB actions had to be "consistent with the successful prosecution of the war."[79] In addition, the WRB's administrative budget came from the president's emergency funds, and the WRB's operating money came from private Jewish organizations such as the JDC, thus avoiding politicization of rescue. As Pehle noted to his new staff, "The last thing I want you to do is go to Congress."[80]

Partly for public consumption, the WRB established in June 1944 a refugee camp in Oswego, New York. It held but 983 refugees from southern Italy, 913 of whom were Jews. All of them, Roosevelt assured the public, would return home after the war. Behind the scenes, the WRB's work was more substantial. Pehle immediately alerted US embassies and foreign governments that refugee safety was now part of US policy, and he sent WRB attachés to neutral capitals. Ira Hirschmann, the WRB representative in Istanbul, worked tirelessly with Ambassador Lawrence Steinhardt to procure ships to move Jews from Romania to Turkey, then to Palestine. The WRB was soon involved in larger rescue efforts from German occupied territories.

---

[79]Roosevelt Executive Order Number 9417, quoted in Richard Breitman and Alan Kraut, *American Refugee Policy and European Jewry, 1933–1945* (Bloomington, IN, 1987), p. 191.

[80]Quoted in Breitman and Kraut, *American Refugee Policy*, p. 191.

The Brand Mission

Yet the war came first, and it is in this context that the mission of Joel Brand should be understood. In late April 1944, as the *Va'adah* negotiated with Eichmann's deputies, Eichmann personally made a startling offer to Brand, a member of Kasztner's group. Brand's underground connections and well-placed bribes had rescued a number of Jews from Kamenets-Podolsky in 1941. Now Eichmann told him he would spare 1 million Jews in return for items later revealed to feature 10,000 winterized trucks, which would only—Eichmann said—be used against the Soviets. At the time of Eichmann's offer, Hungarian Jews had been ghettoized but not yet deported. Eichmann said that the Jews would be delivered to the Allies. Brand, he continued, could go to Palestine to make contact with world Jewish organizations and the Allies.

Was the offer legitimate? Nazi leaders never understood how Great Britain and the United States could support the Soviet war against Germany. They explained the riddle by arguing that Jews controlled the Allied governments. The Allied delivery of trucks to Germany might split the alliance, allowing Germany to shift all forces to the Eastern Front, while also "revealing" that the Allies were fighting for the Jews. The Nazis also believed that world Jewry had unlimited funds to finance such a scheme. Yet they never slowed the process of murder. Indeed, Brand left for Istanbul on May 17, three days after deportations began from eastern Hungary.

The Allies viewed all ransom schemes with skepticism, and the Brand mission was no different. Palestine, as always, was out of the question as a destination for Jewish refugees. Lord Walter Moyne, Britain's resident minister in Cairo, laconically put it thus: "And what shall I do with a million Jews?"[81] Allied intelligence also smelled a rat. Along with Brand, the Germans sent a Catholicized Jewish smuggler named Andor (Bandi) Grosz, ostensibly to initiate peace feelers. A rogue of the lowest order, Grosz was an agent in Hungary for the Jewish Agency Executive, and the Office of Strategic Services (OSS), the primary US intelligence agency. But he also worked for German and Hungarian military intelligence as well as the Gestapo. By May 1944, the Americans knew that Grosz was a double agent who gave the Germans Allied secrets while planting false information with the Allies. Allied counterintelligence officers further argued that "to help Jews in Europe, [Jewish agents] . . . deal with Nazi Party officials and the German Intelligence Service, sometimes 'selling out' Allied contacts, agencies and operations."[82]

The British arrested Brand and Grosz in Syria in early June, quickly informed the Soviets, and vetoed any negotiation with Berlin. On June 19, London publicly exposed the Brand mission as a German ploy to split the Allies. The announcement's timing was key. Allied forces landed in France on June 6, 1944, and the Soviets launched a massive offensive from Belarus on June 22. The British theory was also correct. In 1945, a British interrogation of a German intelligence agent revealed that Walter Schellenberg, Himmler's intelligence chief, approved the Brand mission as a means to split the alliance against Germany.[83]

Might the Brand mission have borne some fruit? The Jewish Agency Executive and the War Refugee Board both understood that trucks could not be sent to the Germans and that relations with Moscow could not be risked. But negotiations, they thought, could buy time and save lives. As Moshe Shertok of the JAE put it to Eden, "We fully appreciate [that] Gestapo offers [to

---

[81]Quoted in Shlomo Aronson, *Hitler, the Allies, and the Jews* (New York, 2004), p. 229.

[82]Quoted in Aronson, *Hitler, the Allies, and the Jews*, p. 256. On Grosz and the Brand mission, see Friling, *Arrows in the Dark*, vol. 1, pp. 300–331; vol. 2, pp. 3–69.

[83]Richard Breitman et al., *US Intelligence and the Nazis* (New York, 2005), p. 57.

release Jews must have ulterior motives but [we] consider [it] not improbable that in [the] false hope [of] achieving those ends they would be prepared to let out [a] certain number of Jews large or small."[84]

Roosevelt too wondered if negotiations might be kept open. Ira Hirschmann, the WRB's representative in Turkey, was sent to meet Brand in Syria. "President Roosevelt," Hirschmann remembered, "was interested in using these possible discussions as a means of saving lives and obtaining information." Pehle told Hirschmann, "As long as you can keep talking, there is hope. . . . Negotiate as long as you can." Hirschmann was impressed by Brand's sincerity. "They need things," Brand told Hirschmann. "Besides, I know from years of work that every one of them can be bought."[85] "It was a hideous proposal," Brand remembered years later. "Eichmann put a million human lives on my back."[86] But, in fact, Eichmann never slowed deportations during Brand's mission.

The Halt of Deportations

With great difficulty, the Jewish underground smuggled the Vrba-Wetzler report along with supporting documentation to Switzerland. It arrived in mid-June. Newspaper reports thereafter ignited global interest. German intentions toward Jews had been publicly known since late 1942, but the eyewitness report from within Auschwitz-Birkenau itself provided stark, undeniable, and unimaginable detail. All governments knew that pressure on Berlin meant nothing. The Allies were already bombing German targets heavily and regularly. Pressure had to go on Hungary.

Already on March 24, 1944, shortly after the German occupation of Hungary, Roosevelt publicly condemned "the wholesale systematic murder of the Jews of Europe" as "one of the blackest crimes of all history." He further warned that "none who participate in these acts of savagery shall go unpunished." Secretary of State Cordell Hull added that "firm resistance to the hated invader" was Hungary's "hope to regain the respect and friendship of free nations."[87] More statements came from Congress and religious leaders. WRB representatives issued warnings to Hungarian diplomats in neutral capitals. From London, the British Broadcasting Corporation (BBC) threatened even Hungarian railway workers with retribution should they continue in their jobs. "I am in accord," said Churchill, "with making the biggest outcry possible."[88] Attempts to have Moscow issue statements failed, but warnings from Stalin would likely have been counterproductive.

Global efforts intensified when the deportations began in May 1944. Angelo Rotta, the papal nuncio in Budapest, wrote Hungarian Prime Minister Döme Sztójay on May 15: "The whole world knows what deportation means in practice."[89] Rotta prioritized converts to Catholicism, but he also insisted that the Hungarian government not "continue its war against the Jews beyond the limits prescribed by nature and God's commandments."[90] He urged Hungarian bishops to

---

[84]Shertok to David Ben-Gurion and Nahum Goldmann, July 6, 1944, in *The Bombing of Auschwitz: Should the Allies Have Attempted It?* eds., Michael J. Neufeld and Michael Berenbaum (New York, 2000), p. 265.

[85]Ira Hirschmann, *Lifeline to a Promised Land* (New York, 1946), pp. 109, 121.

[86]State of Israel, Ministry of Justice, *The Trial of Adolf Eichmann: Record of Proceedings in the District Court of Jerusalem*, vol. 3 (Jerusalem, 1992), p. 1035.

[87]Quoted in Braham, *The Politics of Genocide*, vol. 2, p. 1102.

[88]Quoted in Martin Gilbert, *Churchill and the Jews: A Lifelong Friendship* (New York, 2007), p. 213.

[89]Quoted in Michael Phayer, *The Catholic Church and the Holocaust, 1930–1965* (Bloomington, IN, 2001), p. 106.

[90]Quoted in Braham, *The Politics of Genocide*, vol. 2, pp. 1068, 1071.

speak. Most remained quiet, but a minority gave graphic statements that equated deportation with the murder of children and the elderly. More effective was Pope Pius XII's public telegram to Horthy on June 25. Coming after months of US prodding, it was Pius's first personal intervention with a head of state concerning the Final Solution. Typically, Pius did not mention the Jews, but he urged Horthy to "do everything in your power to save as many unfortunate people from further pain and sorrow."[91] The pope's cable triggered a flood of messages, the sternest of which was from Roosevelt on June 26. "Hungary's fate," he said, "will not be like that of any other civilized nations . . . unless the deportations are stopped."[92]

The Sztójay government as a rule ignored international pressure. In cabinet meetings in late June 1944, Minister of Interior Andor Jaross insisted that the atrocity stories were enemy propaganda. Endre insisted that "[i]n the transfer to the camps and during the resettlement in general, the prevailing principle is that they are to take place in a humane and humanitarian manner in accord with the Christian spirit." Hungary, Endre continued, was already benefiting. "One no longer sees on the streets whispering Jews. . . . One can notice everywhere the feeling of liberation."[93] As late as June 30, Sztójay told Rotta that deported Hungarian Jews were sent for labor. They were allowed to take their families, he said, "since greater performance can be expected from Jews when relaxed in the presence of their families." Sztójay continued, "Hungarian Jews are not slated for deportation" and that the government "has prescribed humane and equitable treatment."[94] By now, deportations from all zones save Budapest were completed.

Initially Admiral Horthy allowed the Sztójay cabinet a free hand with the Jewish question. By June 1944, he was deeply disturbed. Partly he was bothered by the wanton brutality, which came to his attention from the central Jewish Council via his son. Hungarian nobles were also uneasy. Count István Bethlen wrote Horthy that Hungary needed a new government "to put an end to the inhuman, stupid, and cruel persecution of the Jews . . . with which the current government has besmirched the Hungarian name before the eyes of the world." Surely the personal appeals from the pope and others also had their effect. Horthy answered Pius's appeal personally, pledging to "do everything in my power to enforce the claims of Christian and humane principles."[95]

On July 2, 1944, 620 bombers from the Fifteenth US Army Air Force based in Foggia, Italy, attacked Budapest, hitting the main railroad marshaling yard there. Government offices were hit inadvertently. The attack was purely strategic, but the Hungarians had reason to think that it was related to the deportations. Elizabeth Wiskeman, a British diplomat in Bern, suggested in an uncoded telegram that the Allies bomb the Hungarian ministries responsible for the deportations. She even included the residences of Hungarian ministers. As intended, Hungarian intelligence intercepted the telegram and might have understood the bombing as Allied retribution.[96]

Horthy began to act at the Crown Council meeting on June 26. After several ministers resisted the truth of the atrocity stories and the international reaction, Horthy interjected, "I shall not tolerate this any further! I shall not permit the deportations to bring further shame on the Hungarians!"[97] Baky and Endre were to be removed, and the deportations were to stop. The

---

[91]Quoted in Phayer, *The Catholic Church*, p. 107.

[92]Quoted in Braham, *The Politics of Genocide,* vol. 2, p. 754.

[93]Quoted in Braham, *The Politics of Genocide,* vol. 2, pp. 750–1.

[94]Quoted in Braham, *The Politics of Genocide,* vol. 2, p. 1071.

[95]Quotes in Braham, *The Politics of Genocide,* vol. 2, pp. 753, 1072.

[96]Gilbert, *Churchill and the Jews,* p. 212.

[97]Quoted in Braham, *The Politics of Genocide,* vol. 2, p. 755.

Interior Ministry defied Horthy at first, continuing deportations from Budapest's environs. Word that Baky was planning a coup against Horthy, however, forced the regent's hand on July 7, when he formally announced a halt. The Germans were infuriated. Without Hungarian help, they could not deport Budapest's Jews. Eichmann surreptitiously deported over 1,000 Jewish detainees after the ban, and Berlin pressed for the formal resumption of deportations. The Hungarian government tried to find a way between German and Allied threats. Budapest's Jews, meanwhile, hung in the balance. The final phase of the war would determine their fate, as well as that of other Jews still under German control.

The Bombing of Auschwitz

With the dissemination of the Vrba-Wetzler report in June 1944, Allied officials discussed the bombing of railways between Hungary and Poland as well as the Auschwitz-Birkenau camp itself. Bombing individual railways would do little. The Germans repaired them quickly and by 1944, the Allies focused on marshaling yards where locomotives and rolling stock assembled. Bombing Birkenau, moreover, would kill Jewish victims. But Chaim Weizmann, still president of the Zionist Organization, and Moshe Shertok of the Jewish Agency Executive both requested that British bomb the railways and the camp.[98] Churchill seemed to favor the idea and suggested to Eden, "Get anything out of the Air Force you can."[99] But Air Minister Archibald Sinclair was negative. The distance from British bases (2000 miles) together with the need for the Royal Air Force to support the Allied invasion of France, he said, was prohibitive. He suggested raising it with the Americans.

Jewish groups indeed raised the question in Washington. Jacob Rosenheim, the president of the Orthodox Agudas Israel organization in the United States, focused on key railroad junctions. Bombing them, he said, would "*slow down, at least*, the process of annihilation and thus . . . preserve a greater number of Jewish lives for the day of liberation." "Every day of delay," he continued, "means a very heavy responsibility for the human lives at stake."[100] In late June 1944, WRB chief John Pehle forwarded to Assistant Secretary of War John J. McCloy calls from his representatives in Switzerland to bomb the Birkenau camp. The Germans would need time and scarce resources to devise another extermination method, and "[s]ome saving of lives would be the most likely result." Bombing, moreover, would serve "as the most tangible—and perhaps only tangible evidence of the indignation aroused by the existence of these charnel-houses."[101]

McCloy's official reply, to be repeated many times, came on July 4. Focusing on "certain sections of railway lines between Hungary and Poland," he replied that "[t]he War Department is of the opinion that the suggested air operation is impracticable. It could be executed only by the diversion of considerable air support essential to the success of our forces now engaged in decisive operations and would in any case be of such doubtful efficacy that it would not amount to a practical project."[102] McCloy sidestepped Auschwitz-Birkenau as a prospective target.

Logistically, the US Army Air Force (USAAF) could have bombed railroad junctions or the camp. By June 1944, the Fifteenth Army Air Force in Foggia contained five bomber wings

---

[98]Shertok to Ben-Gurion and Goldmann, July 6, 1944, Neufeld and Berenbaum, eds, *The Bombing of Auschwitz*, p. 265.

[99]Quoted in Michael Makovsky, *Churchill's Promised Land: Zionism and Statecraft* (New Haven, CT, 2007), p. 182.

[100]Rosenheim to Henry Morgenthau, June 18, 1944, in Neufeld and Berenbaum, eds., *The Bombing of Auschwitz*, p. 254.

[101]Pehle to McCloy and enclosure, June 29, 1944, Neufeld and Berenbaum, eds, *The Bombing of Auschwitz*, p. 265.

[102]McCloy to Pehle, July 4, 1944, in *The Holocaust: Selected Documents in Eighteen Volumes*, vol. 14, gen. eds. John Mendelsohn and Donald S. Detwiler (New York, 1982), p. 118.

amounting to 1,146 aircraft, plus a fighter escort wing.[103] In the summer of 1944, it flew numerous missions against strategic targets near Auschwitz-Birkenau, including the Blechhammer camp that serviced German oil production, 10 miles to the northwest, and IG Farben's synthetic rubber plant, less than 4 miles to the east. In September, US aircraft inadvertently dropped bombs on the Birkenau camp. But it was not a strategic target that affected German war-making capabilities and did not fall under USAAF priorities.

Would an operation have saved Jews? Hungary never resumed deportations after Horthy halted them on July 7, 1944. But there was no guarantee that they would not start anew, and the Germans deported other Jews to Auschwitz-Birkenau while continuing gassing operations there until November. Hitler, according to postwar statements by his Armaments Minister Albert Speer, "would have ordered the return of mass shooting" had the Allies bombed the crematoria.[104] No one knew better than Pehle Germany's determination to kill as many Jews as quickly as possible. "I had several doubts," he told McCloy in June, "whether it would be difficult to put the railroad line out of commission for a long enough period to do any good."[105] But "long enough" and "any good" are relative terms. The point was to *slow* the killing machinery, a point Pehle made subsequently.

US military authorities, in any event, never studied the problem. There was but a single request—this not until early October—from USAAF commander Hap Arnold to General Carl Spaatz, his subordinate in Europe. It came with the caveat, "THIS IS ENTIRELY YOUR AFFAIR. WE HAVE NOT MODIFIED MILITARY NECESSITY. . . ." Spaatz's staff dismissed it within a day.[106] McCloy's staff meanwhile argued that "the bombing of Polish extermination centers should be within the operational responsibility of the Russian forces."[107] The Soviets were indeed 300 miles from Auschwitz by April 1944 and could have undertaken bombing with ease. Although Stalin was willing to use the murder of Jews in 1941 for political effect, he would not promote what he saw as a separate Jewish agenda. Instead the Soviets in 1944 monitored surviving Yiddish writers in liberated Kiev for traces of Zionism.[108]

In the summer of 1944, with Allied troops pushing through France and with the Red Army fighting its way into Poland, humanitarian targets were not considered. The Allied liberation of Paris in August 1944 and the Soviet liberation of Auschwitz in January 1945 indeed saved many thousands of Jews. Nonetheless, a sortie over Auschwitz-Birkenau in the summer of 1944 would have made an important statement to Germans, to Jews, and to the future generations of the world.

---

[103]Figures in Rondall R. Rice, "Bombing Auschwitz: US Fifteenth Air Force and the Military Aspects of a Possible Attack," in Neufeld and Berenbaum, eds., *The Bombing of Auschwitz*, pp. 163–4.

[104]Aronson, *Hitler, the Allies, and the Jews,* p. 290.

[105]Memorandum by Pehle, June 24, 1944, in Neufeld and Berenbaum, eds., *The Bombing of Auschwitz,* p. 256.

[106]Quoted in Joseph W. Bendersky, *The Jewish Threat: Anti-Semitic Politics of the US Army* (New York, 2000), p. 341.

[107]Gerhardt to McCloy, October 5, 1944, eds. Neufeld and Berenbaum, *The Bombing of Auschwitz,* p. 277.

[108]Vladimir Khanin, ed., *Documents on Ukrainian Jewish Identity and Emigration 1944–1990* (London, 2003), pp. 44–58.

15

The Reich's Destruction and the Jews, 1944–1945

From June 1944 to May 1945, Soviet and Allied forces ground the Third Reich to defeat. German losses were staggering. In these eleven months, an average of 8,000 German soldiers were killed daily.[1] Millions of German civilians fled advancing Soviet armies. Allied and Soviet airpower and artillery pulverized German cities. Yet Hitler insisted that Germany would fight to the last bullet. There would be no repeat of 1918. The Reich would prevail, either through miracle weapons such as V-2 rockets and jet-powered aircraft or through an eleventh-hour crack in the alliance between the western Allies and the Soviet Union.

Caught between Germany's murderous policies and debilitating Allied and Soviet offensives, Jews under German control suffered the Final Solution's *denouement*. Auschwitz remained open until 1945. Fanatical German allies such as the Arrow Cross in Hungary continued killing Jews as long as they could. "Death marches" from liberated camps to overflowing camps in Germany killed thousands upon thousands in the war's twilight. On entering German concentration camps at wars' end, Allied troops could not believe their eyes.

In the midst of it all, many tried to rescue Jews. In Budapest, neutral diplomats devised daring schemes to protect Jews until the Soviets' arrival. Jewish representatives of the Joint Distribution Committee and the World Jewish Congress tried to save whatever Jews they could, even negotiating with German officials. The War Refugee Board encouraged these efforts and engaged in its own talks. Loyal to Hitler until the end, German negotiators used Jewish prisoners as a means by which to attain better terms for the ruined Reich and for themselves. But the horror ended only when the war did.

15.1 AUSCHWITZ: THE FINAL ACT

Operation Bagration and the Halt at the Vistula

By June 1944, the Red Army reconquered most Soviet territory save Belarus, the Baltic States, and western Ukraine. On June 22, 1944—three years to the day after Germany's invasion of

---

[1]Figures from Rüdiger Overmanns, *Deutsche militärische Verluste im zweiten Weltkrieg* (Munich, 2004), p. 239.

the USSR and two weeks after the Allied invasion of France—the Soviets launched Operation *Bagration* into the teeth of German defenses. It was a crushing, relentless offensive. The Soviets held a 5,200 to 900 advantage in tanks and an aircraft advantage of 5,300 to 1,350. Advancing through Minsk, Lvov, Białystok, and Lublin, they inflicted 500,000 German casualties.[2]

Conspirators within the German army led by Colonel Claus von Stauffenberg tried to assassinate Hitler on July 20, 1944, with a suitcase bomb in his East Prussian headquarters. Code-named Operation *Valkyrie*, it was the last of many attempts to kill Hitler and ended with the arrest, trial, and execution of the conspirators. Convinced that Providence had spared him, Hitler intended a fight to the finish. Military commanders, determined to preserve what was left of their careers, followed his orders, and the SS continued to kill internal enemies.

The Red Army reached the Vistula River just east of Warsaw by July 28. To the south, the Soviets also liberated western Ukraine, retook Bessarabia, and pushed into Romania. On August 23, King Michael removed Marshal Antonescu from power, and Romania quickly changed sides. It now attacked Hungary to recover northern Transylvania. In September, the Soviets invaded Bulgaria, which also changed sides. Meanwhile, German losses mounted, numbering some 1.35 million killed on all fronts between June and December 1944. By October, 1.79 million German troops stood against 6.4 million Soviet soldiers.[3]

But the Soviets did not cross the Vistula and take Warsaw until January 1945. They sustained heavy casualties while outrunning their supplies, and the Germans redeployed forces from northern and western Europe to stem the Soviet advance. But Stalin also had political reasons. In London, the Polish government-in-exile hoped to renew its claim to prewar Poland. Stalin aimed to keep the parts of Poland that Hitler gave him in 1939 while creating a Polish government friendly to Moscow. As the Red Army reached the Vistula, the Polish Home Army rose against the Germans in Warsaw. Himmler ordered bloody reprisals against Polish fighters and civilians alike. By early October, SS troops smashed the Home Army and killed some 150,000 noncombatants, including hospital patients. The Soviets provided no help. As Stalin told exiled Polish leader Stanisław Mikołajczyk, "I cannot trust the Poles."[4]

The four-month Soviet delay at the Vistula had lethal consequences for Jews still under German control. Auschwitz, fewer than 200 miles from Warsaw, remained open. The Germans, even as they fought Allied and Soviet advances, kept deporting all Jews they could reach to Auschwitz-Birkenau. The final Auschwitz transports from France, Belgium, the Netherlands, and Italy came in this period. Perhaps most telling of the German desire to kill all Jews within reach was the deportation on July 24—on Adolf Eichmann's order—of 2,500 Jews from the Greek-speaking island of Rhodes off the coast of Turkey. Moved on coal barges to Athens and then by rail to Auschwitz, all but 600 were killed on arrival.[5]

The Łódź Ghetto

The final destruction of the Łódź ghetto was especially dreadful. In June 1944, it had one of the largest Jewish populations—nearly 76,000—left in Nazi Europe. Chaim Rumkowski, the ghetto's Jewish Elder, hoped that the ghetto would survive because of its textile production. The German army valued the ghetto but Himmler forced the issue. In April and May 1944, as

---

[2]Figures in Chris Bellamy, *Absolute War: Soviet Russia in the Second World War* (New York, 2007), pp. 613–15.

[3]Figures in Overmans, *Deutsche militärische Verluste*, p. 239; Bellamy, *Absolute War*, p. 635.

[4]Quoted in Stanisłław Mikołajczyk, *The Pattern of Soviet Domination* (London, 1948), p. 81.

[5]Figure in Danuta Czech, *Auschwitz Chronicle, 1939–1945* (New York, 1990), p. 688.

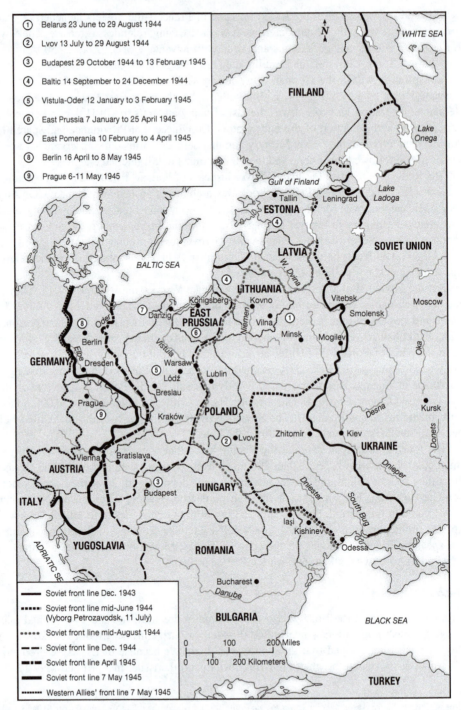

① Belarus 23 June to 29 August 1944

② Lvov 13 July to 29 August 1944

③ Budapest 29 October 1944 to 13 February 1945

④ Baltic 14 September to 24 December 1944

⑤ Vistula-Oder 12 January to 3 February 1945

⑥ East Prussia 7 January to 25 April 1945

⑦ East Pomerania 10 February to 4 April 1945

⑧ Berlin 16 April to 8 May 1945

⑨ Prague 6-11 May 1945

—— Soviet front line Dec. 1943

■■■■■ Soviet front line mid-June 1944
(Vyborg Petrozavodsk, 11 July)

••••• Soviet front line mid-August 1944

— · — Soviet front line Dec. 1944

■·■·■ Soviet front line April 1945

—— Soviet front line 7 May 1945

········ Western Allies' front line 7 May 1945

MAP 15.1 Soviet offensives, June 1944–May 1945. *Source:* Bellamy, Chris. *Absolute War: Soviet Russia in the Second World War* (New York: Vintage, 2008), p. 620. Courtesy Martin Lubikowski.

German civilians in Łódź enjoyed theater and circuses, work Jews built outdoor crematoria at the Chełmno death camp. Deportations to Chełmno had stopped in March 1943 but now, in June 1944, Himmler ordered the liquidation of the Łódź ghetto.

Rumkowski announced that Łódź's Jews were to work in Germany. To preserve illusions, the Gestapo provided them with German money, allowed families to travel together, and ensured that their baggage was carefully loaded. Some starving Jews volunteered. Ten transports totaling 7,196 Jews from June 23 to July 14 went straight to Chełmno.[6] Others hid once they learned that trains supposedly bound for Germany returned to Łódź the next day. Rumkowski's police hunted them down. "A shameful and shocking image," read the Łódź ghetto chronicle. "Jews are hunting Jews as if after wild beasts."[7]

Deportations stopped on July 14, 1944, leaving 68,516 in the ghetto.[8] Air raid sirens, the passage of German troops to the front, and the distant sound of Soviet artillery raised hopes. "We are facing either the apocalypse or redemption," wrote Oskar Rosenfeld in his diary. "The chest dares breathe more freely already."[9] By August 1, the Red Army reached the Vistula, just 70 miles from Łódź. "It's coming to an end," one German sentry said. "The Jews will be freed . . . ."[10] "It would be impossible," agreed Jakub Poznański in his diary, "to evacuate such a large city in a few days."[11]

The Germans closed Chełmno for good. But now they intended to send Łódź's Jews to Auschwitz, presumably because those not killed were needed for labor. On August 2, Hans Biebow, the German overseer of the Łódź ghetto, announced that the entire Jewish population would be moved to Germany at the rate of 5,000 per day for the Jews' own safety. German companies needed their skills and they would be spared Moscow's wrath for having served the Reich. "Come with your families," he implored Jewish tailors, "I assure you that you will be take care of."[12]

Neither this appeal nor Rumkowski's own produced volunteers. The Gestapo entered the ghetto, blockaded streets, removed Jews at gunpoint, and reduced the ghetto's boundaries. Panic reigned. "People were running in every direction," wrote Poznański in his diary, "The entire ghetto is like an insane asylum."[13] "Gunfire can be heard close by" he added, "first a single shot, then another, a third, a fourth, ever more frequently."[14] By the end of August 1944, when the deportation ceased permanently, the Germans with Łódź's Jewish police removed over 67,000 Jews, leaving 1,500 for work tasks. Sixty-seven percent of those sent to Auschwitz were gassed on arrival or soon after. The rest were assigned to other work camps, many swept up in the death marches of 1945.[15]

Rumkowski's turn came on August 30. When the Germans refused to spare his family from the final transport, the Elder of the Jews boarded it. Back in July, he congratulated himself. "There are 78,000 Jews in the ghetto," he said. "And the Russians are advancing!"[16] Now his last

---

[6]Figure in Andrzej Strzelecki, *The Deportation of Jews from the Łódź Ghetto to KL Auschwitz and Their Extermination: A Description of the Events and the Presentation of Historical Sources* (Oświęcim, 2006), p. 25.

[7]Isaiah Trunk, ed., *Łódź Ghetto: A History* (Bloomington, IN, 2006), p. 256.

[8]Figure in Trunk, ed., *Łódź Ghetto*, p. 267.

[9]Quoted in Gordon Horwitz, *Gettostadt: Łódź and the Making of a Nazi City* (Cambridge, MA, 2008), pp. 285–86.

[10]Trunk, ed., *Łódź Ghetto*, p. 260.

[11]Quoted in Horwitz, *Gettostadt*, pp. 286–7.

[12]Trunk, ed., *Łódź Ghetto*, p. 291.

[13]Quoted in Horwitz, *Gettostadt*, p. 290.

[14]Quoted in Strzelecki, *The Deportation of Jews from the Łódź Ghetto*, p. 45.

[15]Figure in Strzelecki, *The Deportation of Jews from the Łódź Ghetto*, pp. 37, 48, 56–118; Trunk, ed., *Łódź Ghetto*, p. 267.

[16]Quoted in Horwitz, *Gettostadt*, p. 295.

order was for remaining ghetto inmates to extinguish the lights, lest the authorities punish them for providing Soviet aircraft with a target. He vanished into Auschwitz, a final victim of his failed strategy. The Soviets captured Łódź on January 19, 1945. Two days earlier, Hans Biebow, who had spent the previous months raping Jewish women at gunpoint, commanded Łódź's remaining Jews to appear for roll call. Burial pits awaited them. Most ignored the order.

Slovakia

From March to October 1942, the Germans deported 58,000 Jews from Slovakia with the help of Jozef Tiso's collaborationist government. Appeals from local clergy and objections from within the Slovak government brought a suspension of deportations, and most of Slovakia's remaining 24,000 Jews survived into 1944. Berlin pressured the Slovaks to resume arrests and deportations, and many Slovak officials, including Prime Minister Vojtech Tuka and Interior Minister Alexander Mach, wanted to oblige. But protests from clerics and other cabinet ministers gave them pause, particularly as the war turned against Germany. On July 30, 1944, as the Soviets reached the Vistula, Mach proclaimed publicly, "[I]f the Jews do not provoke and force us with their behavior, we will not deport them."[17]

On August 29, 1944, with Romania having changed sides and Soviet forces nearing Slovakia, Slovak rebels, ranging from dissident army factions to communists, rose against the collaborationist government. The insurgents freed Jews from Slovak work camps and some 2,500 Jews joined the rebellion. Other Jews left the capital of Bratislava in western Slovakia for rebel-controlled areas in the east. As with Warsaw, however, the Soviets provided no help. German army and SS forces quickly moved into Slovakia to crush the revolt and gradually did so by late October.

Himmler explained the uprising as the work of the Jews and blamed the Slovaks for not solving the Jewish problem sooner. Slovakia's embassy in Berlin agreed with the Germans that "the Jewish problem in Slovakia must be solved radically," with Jews "gathered together and removed without any humanitarian dementia."[18] But the work was left to the Germans. As US forces approached Paris in mid-August 1944, Eichmann's most brutal deputy Aloïs Brunner left. Eichmann reassigned him to Bratislava. Brunner promised to "tackle the [Jewish] problem radically" through the "total concentration of all Jews still at large . . . ."[19]

The Slovak government wanted to place Jews in the work camp at Sered, east of Bratislava, and use them for labor. But Brunner turned Sered into a transit camp. To locate Jews still hiding in Bratislava, he seized Jewish administrative records, cordoned off streets, conducted manhunts, and had Jews in Sered tortured to learn their relatives' hiding places. Jews in Sered were also systematically robbed; they were told that they could remain if they handed over their valuables and cash. Eleven transports between September and November 1944 took roughly 8,000 Jews from Sered to Auschwitz. Four thousand more Jews were sent to Sachsenhausen and Theresienstadt afterward.[20] The Soviets liberated Sered on April 1, 1945.

The fate of Gisi Fleischmann, the leader of the Working Group in Bratislava, is of particular note. Before the uprising in 1944, she hid Jewish fugitives, bribed officials in the Slovak Interior Ministry, and worked with Slovak partisans to sabotage transports of Hungarian Jews

---

[17]Quoted in Ivan Kamenec, *On the Trail of Tragedy: The Holocaust in Slovakia* (Bratislava, 2007), p. 300.

[18]Quoted in Kamenec, *On the Trail of Tragedy*, p. 331.

[19]Quoted in Hans Safrian, *Eichmann's Men* (New York, 2009), p. 208.

[20]Figure in Safrian, *Eichmann's Men*, p. 210.

through Slovakia. As the Germans crushed the Slovak revolt, friends urged her to flee to Palestine where her children awaited. Fleischmann refused. "My whole being," she said, "is bound up with saving the Jews. I must do what my conscience tells me. . . . I am remaining with you, whatever may come." Like Kasztner in Hungary, she was sure that bribery could save Jews. She approached Brunner when he arrived in Bratislava. Brunner moved her to Sered. He interrogated her at length, offering to spare her life if she revealed Jewish hiding places. She refused. Brunner had her sent to Auschwitz on October 17 and murdered on her arrival. On Bratislava's liberation on April 4, 1945, 5,000 Jews emerged from hiding.[21]

Theresienstadt

In June 1944, a Red Cross delegation visited Theresienstadt thanks to Denmark's insistence on maintaining the wellbeing of the Danish Jews sent there in October 1943. The Germans dressed up parts of the camp with walkways and gardens. In August 1944, to counter "atrocity propaganda" that accompanied the recent Soviet liberation of Majdanek, the SS made a film entitled *Theresienstadt: A Documentary Film from the Jewish Settlement Area.* As cameras rolled, hopeful Jews looked content at work and leisure. By now 27,475 Jews, mostly from Germany, Austria, the Protectorate, and the Netherlands, were in Theresienstadt.[22] But the uprising in neighboring Slovakia put them in danger. The Germans would not risk the camp's liberation by rebels or the escape of its healthier inmates.

On September 23, 1944, Dr. Paul Eppstein, the German Jewish chairman of Theresienstadt's Jewish Council, was told that production in Theresienstadt was inadequate and that 5,000 able-bodied men would move to a new camp. The Germans executed him four days later, and from September 29 to October 1, they moved 5,501 Jews straight to Auschwitz; only 740 survived.[23] Deportees remained remarkably unaware of their fate. Zdenka Fantlová's older brother told his family, "There are plenty of us, we're young, and we can stand a lot. Anyway the war will be over soon. . . . We'll all meet again at home when the war's finished."[24]

By October 28, 1944, an additional 12,903 Jewish men were sent from Theresienstadt to Auschwitz. October 30 saw the final selection on the Birkenau train ramp. Eighty-three percent of the last transport from Theresienstadt was sent to the gas chambers.[25] Among the dead were the musicians, actors, and other artists who had given Theresienstadt its cultural character. Back in Theresienstadt, Fantlová remembered that "[c]rowds of women besieged the registration department for permission to travel voluntarily in the wake of their menfolk . . . the cynics were dismissed as prophets of doom and no one took their warnings seriously."[26]

On April 6, 1945, a month before the German surrender, another Red Cross delegation visited Theresienstadt. They viewed the beautified parts of the camp as well as the recently completed German "documentary" film. By now most of the Jews in the film were dead. "The overall impression made by the camp," wrote Dr. Otto Lehner of the Red Cross delegation, "is very favorable."[27]

---

[21]Quote and figure in Joan Campion, *In the Lion's Mouth: Gisi Fleischmann and the Jewish Fight for Survival* (Lanham, MD, 2006), pp. 111, 112, 117.

[22]Figure in H. G. Adler, *Theresienstadt 1941–1945: Das Antlitz einer Zwangsgemeinschaft*, 2nd ed. (Tübingen, 1960), p. 699.

[23]Figures in Adler, *Theresienstadt*, pp. 699–700.

[24]Zdenka Fantlová, *My Lucky Star* (New York, 2001), p. 120.

[25]Figures in Adler, *Theresienstadt*, p. 700; Czech, *Auschwitz Chronicle*, pp. 741–4.

[26]Fantlová, *My Lucky Star*, pp. 120–1.

[27]Quoted in Livia Rothkirchen, *The Jews of Bohemia and Moravia: Facing the Holocaust* (Lincoln, NE, 2005), p. 262.

After the commission left, the camp was flooded with some 15,000 refugees from death marches, swelling the population to over 30,000.[28] A typhus epidemic broke out. The Germans surrendered Theresienstadt to Red Cross jurisdiction on May 2. Soviet troops arrived nine days later.

Auschwitz's Only Revolt

Underground activity in Auschwitz mostly involved the political prisoners in the Auschwitz I camp. Jews in the Birkenau camp either did not last long enough or were too debilitated by hunger and exhaustion to think past the next day. An exception lay with the *Sonderkommandos*—the detachments of Jewish prisoners who burned bodies. The Germans expanded the *Sonderkommandos* to 952 men to incinerate Hungary's Jews in the spring of 1944. In September, 200 *Sonderkommando* Jews were gassed, and word leaked. Zalman Lewenthal, a Jew from Poland, had been in Auschwitz since 1942. He was assigned to *Sonderkommando* duty in 1943 and survived until October 1944. His notes were discovered in 1962 in a jar buried near one of the crematoria. "We believed," Lewenthal recorded, "that the Germans would erase every trace of their crime. . . . The only way they could do this was through the extermination of our detachments. . . . We could see that the Russians were drawing nearer."[29]

The revolt was planned by a small group of Polish, Greek, and Soviet Jews on *Sonderkommando* detail. They fashioned knives and made simple bombs from food cans filled with rocks, bits of metal from barbed wire fences, and smuggled gunpowder with fuses. "The *Sonderkommando* men," remembered survivor Leon Cohen, "were to kill as many SS men as possible." "We wanted the hand grenades," remembered Eliezer Eisenschmidt, "to scatter as much shrapnel as possible. . . ." "There are eighty thousand prisoners in the camp," said one Soviet Jewish army major who helped plan the revolt. "Even if the Germans shoot half of them, forty thousand will survive. That's a horde. These people have nothing to lose."[30]

But the SS acted first. On October 7, members of the 300-man detachment from Crematorium IV learned they were to be gassed. The SS came to take them away. "They raised a loud cry," wrote Lewenthal, "and threw themselves on the guards with hammers and axes."[31] In the melee, they set Crematorium IV on fire. Seeing the flames, other *Sonderkommandos* joined the revolt, killing several SS guards. But the Germans reacted. "The Germans called for reinforcements," remembered Leon Cohen, "and began to fire automatic weapons in every direction."[32] Some escapees barricaded themselves in a nearby barn, which the Germans set on fire. In all, 451 rebels were killed, including all of the 300 who rebelled initially; 212 remained alive. Non-Jews in the Auschwitz underground did not join Auschwitz's only revolt. With the Soviets near and death less imminent for them, they waited for liberation.

Birkenau's final gassing was on November 2, 1944. Himmler ordered a cessation because of the proximity of the Soviets. As the Red Army approached, the Germans destroyed as much evidence as they could. They burned files in giant bonfires. They shut down the medical experimentation facilities. Burning pits and human ash were covered with grass. All four

---

[28]Figures in Adler, *Theresienstadt*, p. 701.

[29]Quoted in Hermann Langbein, "The Auschwitz Underground," in *Anatomy of the Auschwitz Death Camp*, eds. Yisrael Gutman and Michael Berenbaum (Bloomington, IN, 1994), p. 500.

[30]Quotes from Gideon Greif, ed., *We Wept Without Tears: Testimony of the Jewish Sonderkommando from Auschwitz* (New Haven, CT, 2005), pp. 253, 305.

[31]Quoted in Langbein, "The Auschwitz Underground," p. 501.

[32]Greif, ed., *We Wept Without Tears*, p. 307.

crematoria were dynamited, the ovens and ventilators removed beforehand and shipped west to be used again. "The Germans," remembered Shaul Chazan, "didn't want any evidence of their existence to remain . . . we piled up the bricks and hauled them away so as not to leave evidence."[33] On January 27, 1945, with the last crematoria still smoldering, the Soviets liberated Auschwitz-Birkenau.

15.2 BUDAPEST UNDER THE ARROW CROSS

The Arrow Cross Coup

When Admiral Miklós Horthy halted Jewish deportations from Hungary on July 7, 1944, the Hungarian government had just begun deporting Budapest's 200,000 Jews to Auschwitz. It had already confined Jews to 1,948 designated yellow star houses, much like Germany's own Jew houses from 1939.[34] Mass deportations from Budapest did not occur, but Jews there suffered a different sort of terror in the fall and winter of 1944.

Soviet units reached the Hungarian frontier soon after Romania changed sides in August 1944. On October 6, they launched an offensive into the Hungarian plain, pressing north toward Budapest. On October 14, the Soviets took Debrecen, just sixty miles from the capital. Through secret contacts with Moscow, Horthy negotiated a cease-fire that he hoped would preserve Hungary's autonomy and spare Budapest. "It is obvious to any sober person," he said in a crown council meeting on October 15, "that the German Reich has lost the war."[35] Government radio read his cease-fire proclamation later the same day.

Horthy's cease-fire negotiations, which German agents followed, were the last straw for Berlin. SS commandos stormed the royal palace and captured Horthy. The Gestapo arrested his son, an instrumental figure in the cease-fire planning, and held him hostage. To save his son, Horthy authorized a new government dominated by Ferenc Szálasi's ultraright Arrow Cross (*Nyilas*) party. He then left Hungary in German custody. The monarchy in Hungary was no more. Hitler, meanwhile, was determined to defend Budapest to the last stone. The city underwent a three-month siege and, because no effort was made to evacuate civilians, some 38,000 noncombatants, Jews and non-Jews, were killed.[36]

The brief Jewish euphoria that followed Horthy's cease-fire proclamation—many Jews tore off their yellow markings—turned quickly to fear. On the night of the October 15, 1944, coup, Arrow Cross radio broadcasts decried Jewish treachery. Arrow Cross youth gangs engaged in revenge killings in yellow star houses and in Jewish labor units. They dragged hundreds of Jews to bridges over the Danube and shot them. The government could not tolerate vigilantism and reestablished order. "Let no one," proclaimed Interior Minister Gábor Vanja on October 18, "be an arbitrary or self-appointed judge of the Jews." But Vanja also noted that the state would solve the Jewish question and that "[t]his solution—even if ruthless—will be what the Jews deserve by reason of their previous and present conduct."[37] Eichmann met with Vanja the same day and pressed for the transfer of Jews to the Reich. By now, Germany truly needed the workers.

---

[33]Greif, ed., *We Wept Without Tears*, p. 281.

[34]Figure in Tim Cole, *Holocaust City: The Making of a Jewish Ghetto* (New York, 2003), pp. 156–62.

[35]Miklós Horthy, *Memoirs* (New York, 1957), p. 259.

[36]Figure in Krisztián Ungváry, *The Siege of Budapest: One Hundred Days in World War II* (New Haven, CT, 2005), p. 372.

[37]Quoted in Randolph L. Braham, *The Politics of Genocide: The Holocaust in Hungary* (New York, 1981), vol. 2, p. 833.

Labor and Ghetto

Starting on October 20, Arrow Cross units entered yellow star houses, rounded up Jewish males regardless of health or age, and placed them in open detention centers with no food or shelter. Captured Jews, even those over age 60, were pressed into labor companies, which dug fortifications outside Budapest. Arrow Cross guards shot stragglers. They beat and killed other Jews as they worked. After October 22, Arrow Cross gangs also took women for labor. When the Soviets launched their offensive against Budapest on November 2, Jewish trench diggers, now numbering about 35,000 men and women, were pulled back to the city.[38] For sport, Arrow Cross gangs shot individual Jews as they trudged over the Danube bridges.

Szálasi also agreed to "lend" Germany another 25,000 Jewish men and women to build fortifications around Vienna. These Jews were taken from trench-digging details and from within Budapest and held in open detention centers. Beginning November 8, 2,000 Jews left Budapest daily to march west toward the checkpoint of Hegyashalom, where they were handed over to Eichmann's deputy Dieter Wisliceny. These marches, which covered up to 125 miles in a week, were deadly. Stragglers were shot or left to die. Convinced that they were being marched to gas chambers, some Jews committed suicide. Even SS officers noted of the marchers that "all human appearances and human dignity have left them."[39]

In late November 1944, as the Soviets advanced on Budapest, the Szálasi government forced most of Budapest's remaining Jews into a contiguous ghetto amounting to one-tenth of a square mile. By January 1945, the Budapest ghetto contained 70,000 Jews.[40] Even after the Soviets encircled Budapest in late December 1944, the Szálasi government continued to issue anti-Jewish decrees, and vengeful Arrow Cross gangs raided the ghetto. They massacred Jews nightly, shooting them on the spot or drowning them in the Danube. The ghetto suffered from a food allocation of about 750 calories per day, per person and rampant illness. Somehow, the Jewish Council kept a semblance of order, which included public kitchens and dreadfully overcrowded hospitals. Some evidence exists that a contingent of SS and Arrow Cross formations planned to kill the ghetto's inhabitants before the Soviets arrived. On January 17, however, the Soviets liberated the ghetto, which had been in existence for seven weeks. Three thousand bodies awaited burial.

International Protection

Neutral diplomats understood the fate of Hungary's Jews in 1944. From Washington, the War Refugee Board pressed neutral governments to intervene with the Hungarian government and to expand their diplomatic staffs in Budapest. By mid-1944, neutral diplomats intervened more often, partly because of their revulsion concerning events in Hungary and partly to win favor with the United States, whose victory by now was assured.

Foreign protests meant nothing to Berlin. Szálasi, however, was less cavalier with neutral opinion. He achieved power through a coup and understood that full international recognition—in the form of raising foreign legations to full embassy status—added legitimacy to his state and its wartime borders that might carry over into the postwar period. Open diplomatic protests angered Szálasi, and indeed neutrals could not halt Arrow Cross policy. But mitigation was

---

[38]Figure in Braham, *The Politics of Genocide*, vol. 2, p. 836.

[39]Quoted in Braham, *The Politics of Genocide*, vol. 2, p. 842.

[40]Figure in Braham, *The Politics of Genocide*, vol. 2, p. 854.

possible and neutral diplomats used imaginative diplomatic prerogatives to protect individual Jews from shooting or deadly work details.

The key to saving Jews lay in foreign citizenship, which the Hungarian government might recognize even if the Germans would not. There were limits to how many actual passports neutral countries could issue. Passports conveyed actual citizenship, took time to process, and would trigger suspicion if too many suddenly appeared. Another answer lay in "certificates of protection"—emergency passports that could be issued on the spot. Theoretically, they provided diplomatic protection until proper passports could be issued either by the state that issued the certificate or by another state whose interests it represented.

In reality, certificates of protection were a bluff that could be called by any policeman or guard. Their only validity lay in the fact that the pre-Arrow Cross Hungarian government, to curry favor with important neutral countries, recognized a limited number of them. Thus Papal Nuncio Angelo Rotta was allowed 2,500 for baptized converts. Swiss Vice Consul Carl Lutz was allowed to issue 7,800 to cover Jews approved for emigration to Palestine (Switzerland represented British interests in Hungary). The Swedish legation was allowed to issue 4,500; Portugal, 698; and Spain, 100 for Jews who could show family connections to those countries.[41] After initial irritation, the Szálasi government honored these figures.

As Arrow Cross violence became more horrible and as the Soviets drew closer, neutral legations, often without approval from their capitals, ignored these limits in the hopes that certificates of protection would buy time until the Soviets took Budapest. Rotta turned a blind eye toward counterfeit baptismal certificates and issued some 15,000 of them. Lutz interpreted his 7,800 passes for Palestine immigrants to mean 7,800 families rather than individuals.[42] Angel Sans-Briz, Spain's chargé d'affaires in Budapest, protected some 3,500 Jews. After his recall to Madrid in November, his assistant, an Italian adventurer named Giorgio Perlasca, convinced Hungarian authorities that he was a Spanish diplomat and continued to issue forms.[43] Jewish *Hehalutz* volunteers from Poland helped consulates print and distribute certificates. After the Arrow Cross coup, they printed counterfeit passes as well—125,000 allegedly from Switzerland alone. These numbers frightened Lutz, who feared correctly that the counterfeit documents would render genuine ones suspect.[44]

Raoul Wallenberg and the International Ghetto

As a neutral capital sympathetic to rescue, Stockholm in 1944 became an important post for the War Refugee Board (WRB). Together with the Swedish Foreign Ministry, US officials in Stockholm chose thirty-two-year-old Raoul Wallenberg as a special attaché to the Swedish legation in Budapest. A member of one of Sweden's leading business families, Wallenberg was travelled, energetic, and familiar with the city. His exact mission was vague, but as Herschel Johnson of the US legation wrote WRB director John Pehle, "I was told by Wallenberg that he wanted to help effectively and save lives, and that he was not interested in going to Budapest merely to write reports. . . ."[45]

---

[41]Eugene Levai, *The Black Book on the Martyrdom of Hungarian Jewry* (Zurich, 1948), p. 366.

[42]Meir Wagner, *The Righteous of Switzerland: Heroes of the Holocaust* (Hoboken, NJ, 2001), pp. 175–180.

[43]Bernd Rother, *Spanien und die Holocaust* (Tübingen, 2001), pp. 313–18.

[44]Figure in Asher Cohen, *The Halutz Resistance in Hungary* (New York, 1986), p. 193.

[45]Quoted in Paul Levine, *Raoul Wallenberg in Budapest: Myth, History, and Holocaust* (London, 2010), p. 143.

A Swedish legation letter of protection issued to Lili Katz. It is signed by Raoul Wallenberg (W) at the bottom.   *Source:* United States Holocaust Memorial Museum.

Wallenberg arrived in Budapest in July. "We are," he wrote, "surrounded by a tragedy of immeasurable proportions."[46] He quickly understood that money was everything. It procured food and medicine, bribed key Hungarian officials, and provided the funds to print convincing Swedish certificates of protection as well as other documents like fake baptismal certificates. WRB officials in Stockholm funneled large donations from the American Jewish Joint Distribution Committee (JDC) to Wallenberg to help finance his work.

In November 1944, as Budapest's Jews were forced to move into the government-decreed ghetto there, internationally protected Jews were ordered into a so-called international ghetto—a collection of 122 designated buildings under neutral protection in Budapest's fifth district. The

---

[46]Quoted in Levine, *Raoul Wallenberg*, p. 175.

international ghetto held 15,600 Jews with genuine certificates, and an unknown number of Jews with unauthorized or counterfeit documents, in a space that had previously held 3,969 Jews.[47] It never provided fully reliable protection. The Szálasi government demanded full diplomatic recognition as a price for properly guarding the buildings, and neutrals never conveyed it. Foreign Minister Gábor Kemény even threatened the Swedish legation in late November that "if no form of recognition is obtained . . . then all Jews under Swedish protection will be drowned in the Danube."[48]

Arrow Cross gangs raided the international ghetto to look for counterfeit protection documents. Often they ignored or destroyed genuine documents and removed Jews to labor columns or to the Danube for execution. Protection thus had to be maintained constantly under dangerous circumstances. Wallenberg and Carl Lutz of Switzerland went into the international ghetto and to detention centers to rescue Jews holding their consulates' documents. Hundreds of Jews also lived in Wallenberg's and Lutz's offices, and Wallenberg continued to purchase stores of food and maintain relationships with senior Hungarian figures. "The situation is risky and tense," Wallenberg wrote his mother on December 8, "and my workload almost superhuman."[49]

In late December 1944 and January 1945, with Budapest surrounded by Soviet troops, neutral diplomats urged protected Jews to move to the main ghetto for their own safety from vengeful Arrow Cross thugs. There they remained until the Soviets liberated the ghetto on January 17, 1945. The Soviets ordered Lutz home, where his superiors disciplined him for exceeding his authority. Wallenberg intended to stay in Budapest to help Jews there recover their property. Instead he was arrested by Soviets for reasons that have never been determined. He died in Soviet captivity in 1947. How many Jews he saved in Budapest is impossible to say. Clearly he infuriated the Germans. On December 15, 1944, the Swedish legation reported, "The head of the SS-Kommando for the solution of the Jewish problem here, . . . Eichmann, has [said] that he intended to have the Jew-dog Wallenberg shot."[50]

15.3 FROM EVACUATIONS TO DEATH MARCHES

Evacuations in 1944

Beginning in 1944, the Germans evacuated countless concentration and slave labor camps that lay in the path of advancing Soviet and Allied armies. The camps held Jews used for labor and also political prisoners, including resistors and communists from Germany and occupied countries. Partly, evacuation was a security issue. Political prisoners could launch revolts as enemy armies approached. By September 1944, some 13,000 Polish and Soviet prisoners were thus moved from Auschwitz to camps in Germany. The Germans similarly evacuated some 36,000 west European prisoners in the Natzweiler-Struthof camps in eastern France.

Evacuation also stemmed from labor needs. Hitler's armament experts used slave labor for everything from arms production to digging fortifications. In the summer of 1944, up to one-quarter of all Jews sent to Auschwitz from Hungary, Slovakia, and Poland were selected for labor, and many were shipped to various other concentration camps. Jews now became a majority of prisoners at certain camps that had previously held mostly political prisoners. From April to October 1944, 47,000 Jews were evacuated from the Baltic States and from Auschwitz to

---

[47]Figures in Cole, *Holocaust City*, pp. 205–10.

[48]Quoted in Levine, *Raoul Wallenberg*, p. 350.

[49]Quoted in Levine, *Raoul Wallenberg*, p. 343.

[50]Quoted in Levine, *Raoul Wallenberg*, p. 363.

Stutthof, near Danzig. The Jewish population at Gross-Rosen camp in Lower Silesia increased to 60,000 in the second half of 1944.[51]

Extermination and labor remained complementary aims. The Mittelbau-Dora camp complex in central Germany is a case in point. When it was built in 1943, non-Jewish laborers, including Soviet prisoners of war (POWs) and French resistors, dug and maintained tunnels in the Harz Mountains where rocket and aircraft construction was sheltered from Allied bombs. From mid-1944 until March 1945, the complex received slave laborers, including Hungarian and other Jews from Auschwitz, thanks to Hitler's conviction that so-called miracle weapons could still win the war. State enemies, Jews included, would be killed through work, and if the Reich were to be defeated, they would not live to see its demise. Indeed, Mittelbau-Dora survivors remembered burning countless Auschwitz prisoners who arrived dead.[52]

The first mass evacuations of Jews—perhaps 23,000 in all—were in the Baltic States in the summer of 1944 as the Soviets approached. The Germans moved them west on cattle cars and cargo ships. But German and local police also killed up to 11,000 Jews who could not work or who had hidden. They did not trouble themselves to cover evidence. Thus, when clearing Vilna on July 2, 1944, just two weeks before the Soviets reached the city, police dragged a final 2,000 Jews to Ponary and shot them. When simultaneously clearing Kovno, they killed some 1,500 Jews by tossing grenades in *malines*—Jewish hiding places—and by setting Jewish buildings on fire.[53]

Perhaps 9,000 Lithuanian Jews still labored in work camps in Estonia building fortifications, wavering between dreams of liberation and the fear that the Germans would never allow it. "Any minute," wrote Vilna's Hermann Kruk in the Klooga camp in Estonia in late July 1944, "we may get out of hell. When I write about it I can hardly believe it." Yet in the same entry, he registered apprehension of mass shootings.[54] The Germans evacuated but half of the Jews in Estonia before the Soviets arrived. Sensing doom on September 17, Kruk buried his manuscripts. Two days later, German and Estonian police murdered Kruk along with some 3,000 remaining Jews. They quickly poured gasoline on the bodies, set them on fire, and left.[55] When the Soviets arrived at Klooga five days later, the bodies were still smoldering.

Further south in Poland Soviet forces in July 1944 approached Majdanek, which continued to operate as a work and extermination complex. A very conservative estimate is that some 60,000 Jews were murdered in Majdanek's main camp along with perhaps 19,000 others, mostly Poles and Soviet POWs.[56] The Germans evacuated the camp for good by July 22, hurriedly moving most prisoners by rail to other camps. They left 500 sick prisoners behind, mostly Soviet POWs, and the entire camp remained intact, including the crematoria and the storehouses. The Soviets arrived the next day.

Soviet troops were no strangers to atrocity, but Majdanek was the first death camp they encountered. Ordinary soldiers and war correspondents viewed gas chambers, ovens with

---

[51]Figures in Daniel Blatman, *The Death Marches: The Final Phase of the Holocaust* (Cambridge, MA, 2011), p. 48.

[52]André Sellier, *A History of the Dora Camp* (Chicago, IL, 2003), pp. 274–6.

[53]Figures in Yitzhak Arad, "The Murder of the Jews in German Occupied Lithuania," in *The Vanished World of Lithuanian Jews*, eds. Alvydas Nitzentaitas et al. (Amsterdam, 1994), p. 198.

[54]Hermann Kruk, *The Last Days of the Jerusalem of Lithuania: Chronicle from the Vilna Ghetto and the Camps, 1939–1944*, ed. Benjamin Harshav (New Haven, CT, 2002), July 23, 1944.

[55]Figure in Yitzhak Arad, *The Holocaust in the Soviet Union* (Lincoln, NE, 2009), pp. 331–2.

[56]Figures in Tomasz Kranz, "Lublin-Majdanek: Stammlager," in *Der Ort des Terrors: Geschichte des nationalsozialistischen Konzentrationslagers*, vol. 7, eds. Wolfgang Benz and Barbara Distel (Munich, 2008), pp. 72–3.

half-burned bodies, and warehouses teeming with clothing and shoes, including those of children. "During the German occupation," wrote one Soviet soldier, "I witnessed their crimes, but such horrifying atrocities as I saw with my own eyes at Majdanek I had yet to see." Western journalists, despite everything they knew, remained skeptical of Soviet reports thanks to Moscow's penchant for propaganda. "Maybe we should wait," said one American correspondent in London, "for further corroboration of the horror story that comes from Lublin."[57]

Death Marches

The final Soviet offensive commenced on January 12, 1945. Facing tremendous disadvantages in men, artillery, and aircraft, the German East collapsed. The Soviets liberated Polish cities from Warsaw to Kraków to Łódź within days. They also pressed into the eastern German regions of East Prussia, Pomerania, and Silesia. Certain "fortress cities" commanded by ruthless Nazi Party officials held out until the end. Thus, the Red Army surrounded Breslau in February and shelled it until it surrendered in May with 20,000 civilians dead. In the meantime, millions of German civilians in eastern cities, towns, and villages fled west. In the dead of winter, women, children, and the elderly clogged roads along with retreating troops, whose discipline now broke. Roughly half a million German refugees died during flight and expulsions.[58]

The Allies, meanwhile, tried to end the war through the air. With German fighter defenses virtually gone in 1945, Allied bombers targeted city after city, dropping more than twice as many bombs—471,000 tons—as in all of 1943, when they targeted the industrial Ruhr valley. On average, bombing raids killed more than 1,000 German civilians per day in 1945 while reducing cities to rubble.[59] One Berliner, after devastating raids in February, noted a terrible irony: "The dead are all cremated together and a share of the ashes are put into each urn. Whoever wants one can take one."[60] In early March, Allied forces assaulted the Rhine and pressed into western Germany.

The war's severe final stage also marked the final stage of the Holocaust, both for Jews and for other prisoners in Germany's concentration camps. Having misjudged the strength of their own defenses and thus the speed with which the Soviets would advance, the Germans now hurriedly evacuated masses of prisoners. Initially, prisoners from Auschwitz trudged to Gross-Rosen and Stutthof. Afterward they were forced from these camps to others in the German interior such as Buchenwald, Ravensbrück, Sachsenhausen, Bergen-Belsen, Mauthausen, Flossenburg, and Dachau. There was no advance planning. Columns of ragged, starving prisoners crisscrossed Germany in a lethal tangle of death marches that lasted until the end of the war.

In January 1945, Germany's concentration camps held 714,211 inmates, 202,647 of whom were women. By the end of the war in May, up to 250,000 inmates died, a figure also representing one-fourth of all deaths in the Nazi concentration camp system since 1933. Record keeping eroded toward the end of the war, so the death totals could be much higher.[61] Lack of central direction augmented the final tragedy. Himmler's orders were vague. Camp commandants left

---

[57]Quotes in Anita Kondoyanidi, "The Liberating Experience: War Correspondents, Red Army Soldiers, and the Nazi Extermination Camps," *The Russian Review*, 69, no. 3 (July 2010), pp. 438–62.

[58]Figures in Alastair Noble, *Nazi Rule and the Soviet Offensive in Eastern Germany, 1944–1945: The Darkest Hour* (Brighton, 2009), pp. 191, 198; Richard Bessel, *Germany 1945: From War to Peace* (New York, 2009), pp. 68–9ff.

[59]Figures in Ian Kershaw, *The End: The Defiance and Destruction of Hitler's Germany* (New York, 2011), pp. 236–9; Peter Fritzsche, *Life and Death in the Third Reich* (Cambridge, MA, 2008), p. 291.

[60]Quoted in Jörg Friedrich, *The Fire: The Bombing of Germany, 1940–1945* (New York, 2006), p. 321.

[61]Figure in Yehuda Bauer, "The Death Marches, January–May 1945," *Modern Judaism*, 3, no. 1 (February 1983), p. 2.

MAP 15.2   German camps, 1944–1945.   *Source:* Caplan, Jane, and Nikolaus Wachsmann, eds. *Concentration Camps in Nazi Germany: The New Histories* (New York: Routledge, 2010), p. x.

prisoners to the mercies of guards once they left the camp gates. Brutal to begin with, guards had no tolerance for stragglers, particularly when their columns had to share roads with troop transports and fleeing civilians. Destination camps had no capacity for arrivals. All the while, Allied and Soviet forces closed in on roads, bridges, and marching columns, adding to the chaos all the more.

These disastrous movements began with the Auschwitz complex. With the Soviet offensive in January, Himmler ordered that no healthy prisoners were to be left behind. They would work for the Reich until they died. He said nothing about the sick. Despite its proximity to Soviet forces since mid-1944, Auschwitz had no evacuation plan. Thus, on January 18 it hastily began to assemble and move 56,000 relatively healthy prisoners.[62] The pandemonium allowed *Sonderkommando* members, whom the Germans intended to kill, to mix in with other prisoners. But prisoners also feared that evacuation was now the preferred method of annihilation. "We

---

[62]Figure in Blatman, *The Death Marches*, p. 81.

were afraid to leave," remembered Anna Heilman, "we knew what we had in Auschwitz, but we were not sure what dangers awaited down the road."[63]

The wisdom of sick prisoners' decision to leave or stay depended on luck. In the main Auschwitz camps, the Germans simply abandoned 7,600 prisoners.[64] Some died before the Soviet liberation on January 27, but most lived to see it after an eerie period of quiet. "The Germans," Primo Levi thought in disbelief from the Monowitz camp, "were no longer there. The towers were empty. . . ."[65] But in the subcamps of Gross-Rosen, guards made a point of killing prisoners who remained when the Germans evacuated these camps in February.[66]

Marches became interminable. The Soviets cut off escape routes, and temperatures dropped to five degrees Fahrenheit in the brutal winter of 1945. Their feet and bodies bound in rags, prisoners slogged through snow, ice, and mud in columns that stretched for miles. Though many received extra bread to begin evacuations, they received nothing during the marches, which could last many days. Guards shot those unable to keep up. If laborers were assets of the Reich, then those who could not manage were not worth keeping.

Examples are endless. One column of 2,500 to 3,000 Jews from Hungary, the Netherlands, and Poland left Auschwitz-Birkenau on January 18 and followed a circuitous 175-mile march to Gross-Rosen. A third died within a week. A column of 4,000 prisoners from Blechhammer, a subcamp of Auschwitz, took from January 21 to February 2 to reach Gross-Rosen. Eight hundred died or were killed en route. One column of eight hundred women marched some 400 miles from one of the Gross-Rosen subcamps to Bergen-Belsen, foraging en route for grass and sleeping, when fortunate, in barns. Up to half died en route.[67]

The dead littered the roads. "[E]veryone who would fall on the road," remembered Jürgen Bassfreund, "was shot, no difference whether it was a man or woman." "We saw the blood on the white snow," remembered Yitzhak Grabowsky, "and we walked on."[68] Escape was possible but few managed it. Only fourteen prisoners from Elisabeth Herz's column of 2,000 got away, this during the confusion caused by an Allied air raid. "Fear of death is so great," remembered Halina Klein after the war, "that . . . you are not particularly brave. . . . [T]here is always hope that tomorrow you will be saved."[69]

German bystanders, moreover, could not be gauged. Would they help or not? Aliza Besser recalled that Hitler Youth in Silesia pelted her column of Jewish girls with rocks and that German peasants would not allow the prisoners to sleep in their stables. The girls slept in the snow. A female guard stopped one German woman who tried to give the girls bread. "What are you doing, pitying Jews?" she demanded.[70] Other survivors recall Germans and Poles handing food to marchers. Guards often shooed the compassionate away because they slowed the column. Others recalled that guards allowed gifts of food and the hospitality of farmers who allowed the use of their barns at night.

---

[63]Quoted in Blatman, *The Death Marches*, p. 85.

[64]Figure in Harold Marcuse, "The Afterlife of the Camps," in *Concentration Camps in Nazi Germany: The New Histories*, eds. Jane Caplan and Nikolaus Wachsman (London, 2010), p. 186.

[65]Primo Levi, *Survival in Auschwitz: The Nazi Assault on Humanity* (New York, 1993), pp. 157, 159.

[66]Blatman, *The Death Marches*, pp. 114–15.

[67]Figure in Blatman, *The Death Marches*, pp. 88, 92–3, 109–10.

[68]Quotes in Blatman, *The Death Marches*, pp. 87, 96.

[69]Bauer, "The Death Marches," p. 8; Blatman, *The Death Marches*, p. 111.

[70]Quoted in Bauer, "The Death Marches," pp.10–11.

Rail travel was similarly lethal. The suffocating cattle cars or freezing open flatbeds were packed with prisoners. There was no food, water, or protection from the elements. Passing supply or troop transports necessitated long delays. "In every wagon," remembered Alexander Gertner, "there were every morning from ten to fifteen dead. . . . We slept on the dead. We lay on top of the dead."[71] After moving from Auschwitz with 2,000 women to dig anti-tank ditches, Elisabeth Herz and her fellow prisoners were transported on open cars for three days and three nights. It was, she said, "worse than death by shooting. . . . On the way 75% of us were frozen."[72]

In destination camps, shelter and food were stretched past all limits. Prisoners huddled in the mud, emaciated from hunger and disease. The Germans responded with selections, the victims killed with Zyklon B, phenol injections, shooting, or neglect. Gross-Rosen's population grew from 76,728 in January 1945 to well over 97,000 in February, when it too was evacuated. Sixty-five thousand prisoners died in Stutthof from 1939 to 1945, but nearly the entire Jewish death toll of 28,000 there occurred between July 1944 and May 1945.[73] At the women's camp at Ravensbrück, nearly 6,000 were gassed toward the end of the war. "I recognized the terrible stench that hung in the air," remembered one Jewish survivor who arrived, ". . . bodies were burning; the overwhelming fear of dying in the ovens left me trembling."[74] Doctors in Neuengamme killed 6,224 sick prisoners by lethal injection between January and March 1945. At Dachau, the death toll in 1945 varied between 2,625 and 3,977 per month.[75]

But nothing quite matched Bergen-Belsen, originally conceived as a camp for several thousand "privileged" Jews held for international exchange. In December 1944, the camp, now designated for sick prisoners, held 15,257. In mid-April 1945, it held 67,000. In 1945, roughly 37,000, almost all of them Jews, died of hunger, disease, and exposure; 18,000 died in March alone. Prisoners resorted to cannibalism.[76] To camp commandant Josef Kramer, Bergen-Belsen's problems were a case of arithmetic. It had been agreed, he complained to his superiors in March, "that the camp could not hold more than 35,000 detainees. In the meantime the number has been exceeded. . . . As a result all barracks are overcrowded by 30 percent. . . ."[77] To others, the victims were more than numbers. Among the dead in March 1945 were Margot and Anne Frank, aged 19 and 15, who were sent to Bergen-Belsen from Auschwitz. An eyewitness remembered: "The Frank girls were so emaciated. . . . They had those hollowed out faces, skin over bone. They were terribly cold. . . . They showed the recognizable symptoms of dying—that gradual wasting away. . . ."[78]

Liberation

On liberating the camps, Allied units were dumbstruck. British troops found 10,000 unburied corpses at Bergen-Belsen. "I can give no adequate description," reported British medical officer

---

[71] Quoted in Blatman, *The Death Marches*, p. 105.

[72] Quoted in Bauer, "The Death Marches," p. 8.

[73] Figures in Benz and Distel, eds., *Der Ort des Terrors*, vol. 6, pp. 203–4, 520.

[74] Quoted in Sabine Kittel, "Liberation—Survival—Freedom: Jewish Women of Ravensbrück Concentration Camp Recall Their Liberation," in *A Holocaust Crossroads: Jewish Women and Children in Ravensbrück*, ed. Irith Dublon-Knebel (London, 2010), p. 245.

[75] Figures in Blatman, *The Death Marches*, pp. 129, 130–1; Harold Marcuse, *Legacies of Dachau: The Uses and Abuses of a Concentration Camp, 1933–2001* (New York, 2001), p. 49.

[76] Figures in Benz and Distel, eds., *Der Ort des Terrors*, vol. 7, pp. 204–5.

[77] Quoted in Marcuse, *Legacies of Dachau*, p. 48.

[78] Quoted in Alvin H. Rosenfeld, *The End of the Holocaust* (Bloomington, IN, 2011), p. 146.

A mass grave in the Bergen-Belsen camp after liberation, May 1945.   *Source:* United States Holocaust Memorial Museum.

M. W. Gonin. "Corpses lay everywhere, some in huge piles."[79] The impression of Dachau was similar when the Americans reached it on April 29. Troops first came across boxcars spilling over with expired prisoners who had been moved from Buchenwald. General Dwight D. Eisenhower, commander of the Allied forces in Europe, urged Washington to send members of Congress and reporters. "We are told," he said, "that the American soldier does not know what he is fighting for. Now at least, he will know what he is fighting *against*."[80]

The living presented insurmountable challenges. At Bergen-Belsen, Gonin reported "at least 20,000 sick suffering from the most virulent diseases known to man, all of whom required urgent hospital treatment, and 30,000 men and women who might die if they were not treated but who certainly would die if they weren't fed and removed from the horror camp." Medical students shipped in to help wondered, "Where do we start?" Twelve thousand prisoners in Bergen-Belsen—one-fifth of those liberated—died in the ten weeks *after* liberation.[81] To stem the further spread of disease, the British buried the dead with bulldozers in giant pits. At Dachau, 35,000 prisoners were alive when the Americans arrived, but more than 125 continued to die each day.[82]

---

[79]Quoted in Paul Kemp, "The British Army and the Liberation of Bergen-Belsen, April 1945," in *Belsen in History and Memory*, eds. Jo Reilly et al. (London, 1997), pp. 136–7.

[80]Quoted in Marcuse, *Legacies of Dachau*, p. 54.

[81]Quotes in Paul Kemp, "The British Army and the Liberation of Bergen-Belsen, April 1945," in Reilly et al., *Belsen in History*, pp. 137, 142. Figures in Christine Lattek, "Bergen-Belsen: From Privileged Camp to Death Camp," in Reilly et al., *Belsen in History*, p. 37.

[82]Figure in Marcuse, *Legacies of Dachau*, p. 51, 54.

Journalists and photographers followed the troops. American photographer Margaret Bourke-White accompanied General George Patton's men into Buchenwald. Her photos, all snapped from aesthetically effective angles, became iconic images. "I have to work with a veil over my mind," she remembered. "In photographing the murder camps, the protective veil was so tightly drawn that I hardly knew what I had taken until I saw prints of my own photographs."[83] Others, like British photographer George Rodger, found their limits more quickly. "When I discovered that I could look at the horror of Belsen," Rodger said, "and think only of a nice photographic composition, I knew something had happened to me and I had to stop. . . . I said this is where I quit." Rodger could not look at his own photographs for decades.[84]

15.4 HIMMLER'S BARGAINS AND THE REICH'S DESTRUCTION

The Problem of Negotiations in 1945

In the war's last phase, several senior German officials tried to reinvent themselves as humanitarians. They included Luftwaffe Commander-in-Chief Hermann Göring; Foreign Minister Joachim von Ribbentrop; Reich Security Main Office (RSHA) Chief Ernst Kaltenbrunner; and, most important, Reichsführer-SS Heinrich Himmler. Their contacts with Allied and neutral diplomats were extremely convoluted, but in essence, they offered prisoners' lives in return for various concessions that might save something of the Reich. They also hoped to erase the indelible stain of their own criminality.

To Jewish, Allied, and neutral negotiators, these talks became more urgent with each liberated camp. Hitler refused to hand over camp prisoners alive, and many camp commandants had inchoate plans for evacuations or mass killing. But German negotiators also triggered suspicion. They lacked Hitler's approval, and the Allies wondered what authority they really had. They also demanded ransoms or pressed separate peace proposals, making them all the more suspect. Senior Nazis, moreover, could not suddenly change themselves into decent men. They still believed that Jews were behind Germany's destruction. Thus, while arbitration saved thousands of lives, only Germany's surrender could halt the horrors.

The Kasztner-Becher Connection

Small, effective rescues included the Kasztner train (discussed in Chapter 14), which left Budapest for Bergen-Belsen on June 30, 1944, with 1,684 Jews. Here German and Jewish negotiators found some common ground. Resző Kasztner headed the *Va'adah* in Budapest. He conceived of the initial transport and hoped to rescue many more Jews. Saly Mayer, the JDC representative in Switzerland, who the Germans thought represented "world Jewry," tried to procure and transfer ransom funds. SS-Colonel Kurt Becher, Himmler's procurement agent in Budapest, knew how to extort treasure from desperate Jews.

In August 1944, Kasztner, Mayer, Becher, and their representatives began talking on the Swiss-German frontier. Becher convinced Himmler to transport 318 of the Kasztner Jews from Bergen-Belsen to Switzerland. A sign of goodwill, Becher thought, would keep talks alive and procure trucks or other goods for the Reich. In September, Mayer promised the Nazis

---

[83]Quoted in Robert H. Abzug, *Inside the Vicious Heart: Americans and the Liberation of Nazi Concentration Camps* (New York, 1985), p. 58.

[84]Quoted in Barbie Zelizer, *Remembering to Forget: Holocaust Memory Through the Camera's Eye* (Chicago, IL, 1998), pp. 88–9.

$5,000,000 in credit in Switzerland. It was a bluff—neither the Americans nor the Swiss would allow actual ransom payments. But Mayer hoped to buy time for Jews still facing deportation. Becher demanded more funds from Mayer while urging Himmler to continue the discussions. The remaining 1,366 Jews of the Kasztner train reached Switzerland on December 7. It was a small price for the Germans to pay if benefits could be derived.

In March 1945, Kasztner hoped Becher might use his influence to save Jews in the camps from a final spasm of mass murder. By now, Becher needed to strengthen his newfound humanitarian credentials and Kasztner promised to vouch for him after the war. Himmler—in connection with his Swedish negotiations (see below)—gave Becher authority to intervene at Bergen-Belsen so that the camp would pass to the Allies without an SS massacre. This Becher did by April 11. The British reached the camp four days later.

Becher next went to Mauthausen, arriving on April 20. There he rescued Moshe Schweiger, an associate of Kasztner's from Budapest, and placed him in a nearby hunting lodge to recuperate. He then made his way to Dachau. After the war, Becher testified that he saved more than 80,000 Jews in Mauthausen and more than 26,000 in Dachau from evacuation and death. The figure is surely an exaggeration, and, of course Becher would have done nothing for Jewish prisoners without the approach of the Allies. Regardless, Becher told Kasztner, "I hope the Allies will have enough discretion to honor my effort and achievements."[85]

Becher had left Schweiger with several cases of stolen gold, jewelry, and cash—a portion of the ransoms that he had collected in Budapest. Understanding that the treasure could purchase goodwill, he told Schweiger to give the cases to the Jewish Agency. Becher likely hid the greater portion of his loot and retrieved it later.[86] Kasztner, as promised, vouched for him when the time came. "Becher," he testified in 1947, "was one of the very few SS leaders brave enough to resist plans of extermination and who tried to save human lives."[87] Becher avoided prison and became one of postwar Germany's wealthiest businessmen. He died in 1995. Kasztner was not so lucky. Believing him a collaborator, Israeli right-wingers assassinated him in Tel Aviv in 1957.

The Swiss Connection

Jean-Marie Musy was a prominent right-wing Swiss politician and former Swiss president who had met Himmler in 1941. In October 1944, Swiss rabbi Isaac Sternbuch, approached Musy on behalf of the Union of Orthodox Rabbis in the United States and Canada. Musy traveled to Germany with his son Benoit, a bobsled champion from the 1936 Olympics in Germany. According to Roswell McClelland, the War Refugee Board representative in Switzerland, Musy was motivated by "the desire for personal gain, the hope to play a prominent humanitarian role, and the conviction that he could obtain peace conditions favorable to the Nazis."[88]

Through Himmler's opportunistic intelligence chief Walter Schellenberg, Musy and his son met with Himmler in the Reichsführer's private railway car in November 1944. According to his own postwar statements, Musy told Himmler that Germany could not win the war and called for the

---

[85]Quoted in Gábor Kádár and Zoltán Vági, *Self-Financing Genocide: The Gold Train, the Becher Case, and the Wealth of the Hungarian Jews* (Budapest, 2004), p. 243.

[86]Yehuda Bauer, *Jews for Sale: Nazi-Jewish Negotiations, 1933–1945* (New Haven, CT, 1994), pp. 196–251; Ronald W. Zweig, *The Gold Train: The Destruction of the Jews and the Looting of Hungary* (New York, 2003), pp. 223–32; Kádár and Vági, *Self-Financing Genocide*, pp. 249–56.

[87]Quoted in Kádár and Vági, *Self-Financing Genocide*, p. 244.

[88]Quoted in Alain Dieckhoff, "Une Action de Sauvetage des Juifs Européens en 1944–45: L'affaire Musy," *Revue d'histoire modern et contemporaine*, 34, no. 2 (April–June 1989), p. 292.

release of all Jews and their movement to the United States via Switzerland. Himmler's tone, remembered Musy, "was that he had had enough of the Jewish question. . . ." But Himmler insisted on compensation; first trucks, then cash, then "that the press in the United States comment favorably."[89]

Further meetings among Musy, Schellenberg, and Himmler brought a single transport—the arrival of 1,200 Jews from Theresienstadt to Switzerland on February 7, 1945. Musy extracted agreement on a second transport of 1,800 Jews from Bergen-Belsen, but the arrangement broke down.[90] The problem was the very publicity that Himmler said he wanted. The Swiss press reported the arrival of the 1,200 Theresienstadt Jews. Hitler was furious, and Himmler later commented that Hitler "forbade that any other Jews be handed over."[91] "Schellenberg," remembered Musy, "told me that Hitler did not wish this to happen." Transports of Jews to safety, in other words, were to cease.[92]

Despite his frustration, Musy continued to press. In April 1945, he proposed to Himmler a four-day truce during which prisoners could be moved to safety. Himmler, according to Schellenberg, "did not have the courage to present [the idea] to Hitler.[93] Musy thus called for a promise that all camp evacuations cease and that the camps be handed over to the Allies. On April 7 Himmler consented to Musy's request with the proviso that Musy quietly inform the Allies of his decision.[94] By now, Himmler was engaged in more extensive negotiations with Swedish representatives, which revealed the full extent of his expectations.

The Swedish Connection

The Swedish government also engaged in efforts to rescue prisoners in 1945. The personalities were many. Hillel Storch was a Latvian Jewish refugee in Stockholm and a member of the World Jewish Congress. The Nazis killed Storch's entire family, and he thereafter made rescue his primary cause. Felix Kersten was Himmler's personal masseur. His primary residence was in Stockholm, and he became a conduit between the Swedish Foreign Ministry and Himmler. Count Folke Bernadotte was a Swedish nobleman, seasoned diplomat, and nephew of King Gustav V. In 1945, he was the vice president of the Swedish Red Cross and undertook missions to save camp prisoners. Iver Olsen was the representative of the War Refugee Board in Stockholm as well as a member of the Office of Strategic Services (OSS). He reported to Washington all possibilities of rescuing Jews and provided funds for rescue.

Initial negotiations were tentative. In June 1944, German agents led by Bruno Peter Kleist, a former member of the Ministry for the Eastern Territories, approached Storch. Kleist offered to send 2,000 Jews from camps in Latvia to Sweden. Storch introduced the Germans to Olsen. Olsen and Herschel Johnson, the head of the US legation in Stockholm, were suspicious. "[N]ot for a thousand years," Olsen wrote, "should anyone forget what these murderous Nazis have done. . . ."[95] And the Germans wanted cash and materials. "If the government of Germany is

---

[89]Testimony of Jean-Marie Musy, October 26, 1945, further Testimony of Jean-Marie Musy, October 29, 1945, in *The Holocaust: Selected Documents in Eighteen Volumes*, vol. 16, eds. John Mendelsohn and Donald S. Detwiler (New York, 1982), pp. 11, 18.

[90]Figures in Reinhard R. Doerries, ed., *Hitler's Last Chief of Foreign Intelligence: Allied Interrogations of Walter Schellenberg* (London, 2005), pp. 33–4.

[91]Interrogation of Kurt Becher, June 22, 1948, Mendelsohn and Detwiler, eds., *The Holocaust*, vol. 16, p. 2.

[92]"Further testimony of Jean-Marie Musy," October 29, 1945, Mendelsohn and Detwiler, eds., *The Holocaust*, vol. 16, p. 23.

[93]Doerries, ed., *Hitler's Last Chief of Foreign Intelligence*, p. 171.

[94]Doerries, ed., *Hitler's Last Chief of Foreign Intelligence*, p. 172.

[95]Quoted in Meredith Hindley, "The Strategy of Rescue and Relief: The Use of OSS Intelligence by the War Refugee Board in Sweden," *Intelligence and National Security*, 12, no. 3 (July 1997), p. 145.

behind these feelers," Johnson reported, "it becomes a simple ransom proposition from which they would hope to trap us into a series of extortions of a much larger scale."[96] Olsen used OSS connections, Swedish intelligence, and teams of Baltic refugees to rescue 1,200 persons in numerous, very hazardous missions by sea, but negotiations with the Germans fizzled.[97]

As Soviet and Allied forces drove into Germany in 1945, the Swedes undertook their own efforts. Musy's success in liberating 1,200 Jews from Theresienstadt in February inspired the Swedes. Norwegian and Danish leaders, as well as members of the World Jewish Congress, pressed Stockholm. Using Kersten as his intermediary, Bernadotte flew to Berlin. After meeting with Kaltenbrunner, Ribbentrop, and Schellenberg, he sat with Himmler on February 19. The mission was hazardous. Berlin was under bombardment, Himmler's mood could not be gauged, rumors circulated that all prisoners might be killed, and Hitler was not informed of the meetings. The Swedes mitigated the danger by reporting nothing to the press.

Bernadotte asked Himmler to move Danish and Norwegian political prisoners—numbering some 9,000—to a single camp where the Red Cross could care for them. Himmler complained about the Swedish press's treatment of Germany but agreed that the Swedish Red Cross could move the prisoners to Neuengamme near Hamburg. In Stockholm, the Red Cross arranged white-painted buses together with medical personnel. The busses arrived in Germany in mid-March and by early April, some 7,000 Norwegian and Danish prisoners were at Neuengamme under Red Cross care. On April 18, the Swedish Red Cross mission removed the 423 Scandinavian Jews from Theresienstadt.

Storch, meanwhile, undertook parallel efforts on behalf of Jewish prisoners. He contacted Kersten in late February with proposals for Himmler that included the freeing of 5,000 to 10,000 Jews and the placement of all remaining Jews under International Red Cross protection.[98] Himmler viewed the effort as a chance for back-channel negotiation with the United States. In a letter carried back to Stockholm by Kersten in mid-March, Himmler claimed that Jewish emigration "in conjunction with Jewish-American organizations" had always been his preferred solution "until the war and the unreason unleashed by it in the world made it impossible to carry through." He hoped that "wisdom and reason, along with humane sentiments and the willingness to help, will inevitably, notwithstanding the bloodiest wounds, come to the fore among all parties."[99]

The German Foreign Ministry undertook similar efforts. At midnight on March 9, 1945, Fritz Hesse, a senior German diplomat, visited Olsen and Johnson in Stockholm. Hesse claimed to speak for "the top officials . . . the very top, in the German government." The Allies, he warned, had "very little time to realize their fatal mistake in setting Russia up as the ruler of Europe." He called on the Allies to "humanize the war" by sparing German civilians from bombing, which was "nothing short of murder." In return, Hesse said, the Germans "would permit all Jews to leave Germany, as soon as technical details could be worked out."[100]

The shamelessness of these statements seems not to have occurred to the Germans, but Himmler became more persistent in the days ahead. On March 21, he told Kersten that he would free 10,000 Jews, but that he wished to negotiate with Storch, who he thought carried enormous

[96]Quoted in Meredith Hindley, "Negotiating the Boundary of Unconditional Surrender: The War Refugee Board in Sweden and Nazi Proposals to Ransom Jews, 1944–1945," *Holocaust and Genocide Studies*, 10, no. 1 (Spring 1996), p. 56.

[97]Figure in Hindley, "The Strategy of Rescue and Relief," p. 154.

[98]Steven Koblik, *The Stones Cry Out: Sweden's Response to the Persecution of the Jews, 1933–1945* (New York, 1988), pp. 128–9.

[99]Quoted in Peter Longerich, *Heinrich Himmler: A Life* (New York, 2012), p. 725.

[100]Herschel Johnson to Secretary of State, PEM-33, March 9, 1945, National Archives and Records Administration, RG 226, Microfilm Publication M1642, roll 113, frames 824–835.

weight with the Allies. The Swedes were hopeful, but the British were skeptical. Eden argued from London that the proposal "may be a Himmler plant and it may have entangling consequences." Churchill agreed: "No truck with Himmler." British diplomats in Stockholm, meanwhile, described Storch as "self-important and very nearly lunatic in some respects." "[I]n no circumstances," they said, "must Storch be allowed to go to Germany. . . ."[101]

Determined to follow up, US and Swedish diplomats found a substitute for Storch in Norbert Masur, a Swedish delegate of the World Jewish Congress. On April 21, he accompanied Kersten to meet Himmler near Berlin. By now, the Soviets and Allies had liberated numerous camps, from Gross-Rosen to Buchenwald, to Bergen-Belsen, to Dachau. The Germans controlled a narrowing strip of territory reaching from the coasts in the north through Hamburg, Berlin, and Dresden. Travel through the region was hazardous, and the German behavior toward remaining camp prisoners was unpredictable.

At about 3:00 a.m. Himmler sat with Masur against the surreal backdrop of Allied bombardment, fleeing German troops, and terrified German civilians. Masur pressed for assurance that no more Jews would be murdered or evacuated, that they receive Red Cross aid, that they be handed over to the Allies, and that a number of Jewish and non-Jewish prisoners be freed immediately. Himmler agreed on the proviso that nothing be made public. But his discourse was worrisome. In a lengthy harangue, Himmler blamed German Jews for the defeat in 1918 and blamed eastern Jews for helping partisans, firing on the Germans from their ghettos, and spreading epidemics. The crematoria, he insisted, were built only to prevent epidemics from spreading further. The Allies, he argued, should have taken more Jews before the war. Now, Himmler complained, they rewarded Germany for the handover of Bergen-Belsen with "atrocity tales" in the press.[102] "And now because of this," Himmler said, "they want to put a rope around our necks."[103] Masur reported afterwards that "it is not inconceivable that Himmler . . . at the last moment, would give orders for the murder of all Jews."[104]

At 6:00 a.m., an exhausted Himmler met again with Count Bernadotte, who raised the women's camp at Ravensbrück. Himmler laconically agreed that he could take all women from that camp. Transports began the following day, and within a week, Bernadotte's mission evacuated over 7,000 women—half of whom were Jews. The Soviets occupied the camp on April 30. In all, Bernadotte's missions rescued 20,937 prisoners of various nationalities, beginning with Scandinavians and finishing with the women from Ravensbrück. Perhaps 6,500 of those rescued were Jews.[105]

And the remaining Jewish prisoners? Years later Storch wrote that on the morning of April 21, Himmler told Bernadotte to "[t]ake all the Jews you want."[106] Two days later, Himmler asked Bernadotte to convey to Eisenhower his hope for a separate peace—an end, he said, to "any further senseless fighting and bloodshed. . . ." Regarding the Soviets, Himmler added that "it is impossible for us Germans, and above all for me, to capitulate."[107] Bernadotte conveyed the message. The answer from Eisenhower, relayed on April 27, was negative. Himmler, who tied

---

[101]Quoted in Koblik, *The Stones Cry Out*, pp. 133, 284.

[102]Quoted in Koblik, *The Stones Cry Out*, p. 291.

[103]Quoted in Bauer, *Jews for Sale*, pp. 246–7.

[104]Quoted in Koblik, *The Stones Cry Out*, p. 291.

[105]Figures in Sune Persson, *Escape from the Third Reich: The Harrowing True Story of the Largest Rescue Effort Inside Nazi Germany* (New York, 2009), pp. 216–17; Koblik, *The Stones Cry Out*, pp. 138–9.

[106]Quoted in Gerald Fleming, "Die Herkunft des 'Bernadotte-Briefs' an Himmler vom 10. März 1945, *Vierteljahrshefte für Zeitgeschichte*, 26, no. 4 (October 1978), p. 586.

[107]Doerries, ed., *Hitler's Last Chief of Foreign Intelligence*, p. 160.

his generosity toward the Jews to a separate peace, was stunned at Allied ingratitude. But within three days, Hitler was dead, and Himmler, according to Hitler's last will, was out of a job.

The Bunker

In January 1945, Hitler retreated to his underground command bunker beneath the bomb-damaged Reich Chancellery in Berlin. Suffering from Parkinson's disease, stomach cramps, growing dependence on pills, and visible aging, he became increasingly separated from reality. He spoke wistfully of miracle weapons and the impending breakup of the Allied-Soviet alliance. He studied make-believe plans for the rebuilding of German cities.

On learning of President Roosevelt's death on April 12, 1945, Hitler was elated. It had been Roosevelt who, owing to his Jewish sponsors, made a European war a world war. "Fate," Hitler proclaimed in his April 16 Order of the Day, "has removed the greatest war criminal of all times from this earth." With Roosevelt dead, he continued, "the turning point of this war will be decided." But defeat, should it come, would be heroic. "I will continue to fight," Hitler told General Alfred Jodl on April 21, "as long as I have a single soldier left."[108] As Germany went down to defeat, thousands of soldiers were executed for desertion and hundreds of civilians, including women, were shot or hanged for defeatist attitudes.[109]

April 20 was Hitler's fifty-sixth birthday. After an awkward celebration, most of his ministers fled Berlin while time remained. Hitler stayed. On April 22, he berated his staff officers, then ordered them to leave the city. He decided on suicide rather than capture. The fate of Mussolini, who was captured by partisans, shot, and then displayed as a trophy with his mistress, strengthened Hitler's resolve. On April 25, the encirclement of Berlin by 2 million Soviet troops was complete. Fighting moved to the boulevards and buildings. Civilians took cover. By April 29, the Soviets were a quarter mile from the Chancellery.

On the same day, Hitler dictated his last will and his political testament. He expelled Hermann Göring and Heinrich Himmler from the government and the Nazi Party for their peace feelers to the enemy. He passed supreme power to naval commander Karl Dönitz, whose admiration of Hitler meant that he would fight until the end. The new government—such as it was—was moved to Dönitz's headquarters in the north German city of Flensburg.

Most notably, Hitler used his last testament to justify the mass murder of Europe's Jews. He insisted that it was not he, but "international statesmen who are either of Jewish origin or work for Jewish interests" who instigated the world war. He recalled his oft-repeated prophecy of 1939. "I made it perfectly clear," he said, "that this time it would not happen that millions of grown men die and hundreds of thousands of women and children burn in the cities or die under the rain of bombs without a punishment being inflicted on the actually guilty one, although by more humane means."[110]

On April 30, Hitler committed suicide with his companion Eva Braun by biting a cyanide capsule and firing a bullet into his head. In accordance with his wishes, his staff carried the bodies to a crater in the Chancellery courtyard, doused them in gasoline, and burned them. On May 8, the Reich surrendered. Though the war in the Pacific continued until September, the war in Europe was over. Understanding the war's greatest crime, however, would take decades.

---

[108]Quoted in Anton Joachimsthaler, *The Last Days of Hitler: The Legends—The Evidence—The Truth* (London, 1996), pp. 92, 100.

[109]Bessel, *Germany 1945*, pp. 61–63; Kershaw, *The End*, pp. 321–9.

[110]Max Domarus, ed., *Hitler: Speeches and Proclamations*, vol. 3 (Wauconda, IL, 1997), pp. 3055–57.

16

Legacies: 1945 to the Present

How the Holocaust is remembered is its own field of study. This book's final chapter samples ways in which Holocaust memory, postwar justice, and politics have intersected since 1945. Forgetting was the initial trend. Amid the war's wreckage, non-Jews insisted that their own claims to memory be addressed first. The Cold War, which lasted from 1947 to 1989 and included Soviet control of eastern Europe, the division of Germany into two states, and the creation of rival European alliances, also created conditions for mass forgetting. In the immediate postwar years, Jews were alone in their understanding that the Holocaust was different than other wartime catastrophes, and even for Jews, the political needs of the new Israeli state affected memory. The rest of the world followed later, making its greatest strides in most recent years. Yet to this day and beyond, the memory of history's greatest crime remain impossible to grasp fully. It is a wound in Jewish and world history that will never heal.

16.1 REFUGEES

Renewed Violence

After the war, surviving Jews sought some remnant of their prewar lives. In eastern Europe, they faced severe difficulties. By the summer of 1946, Poland had but 240,000 Jews out of a prewar population of 3.1 million, 195,000 of whom were recently returned from the USSR.[1] Some were Bundists determined to rebuild in Poland. Others were Zionists determined to go to Palestine. Others were not political at all. "Maybe someone survived," remembered Ewa Koźmińska-Frejlak, "maybe I will find somebody. . . . Such was that irrational, subconscious hope."[2] She was disappointed. "This was no longer Poland, but one big cemetery," remembered

---

[1] Figures in Natalia Aleksiun, "Jewish Responses to Antisemitism in Poland, 1944–1947," in *Contested Memories: Poles and Jews During the Holocaust and Its Aftermath*, ed. Joshua D. Zimmerman (East Brunswick, NJ, 2003), pp. 248–49; Zeev W. Mankowitz, *Life Between Memory and Hope: The Survivors of the Holocaust in Occupied Germany* (New York, 2002), p. 18.

[2] Quoted in Bożena Szaynok, "The Impact of the Holocaust on Jewish Attitudes in Postwar Poland," in Zimmerman, ed., *Contested Memories*, pp. 240–41.

Yitzhak Zuckerman, a commander from the Warsaw ghetto uprising now working to help Jewish refugees.[3]

Ordinary Poles who took Jewish property during the war or who blamed Jews for the Soviet imposition of communist rule were hostile. Even Poles who saved Jews during the war were afraid. "I know this nation," said one rescuer, "they would never forgive us for sheltering two Jews."[4] New ritual murder accusations triggered pogroms in Kraków (August 1945) and Kielce (July 1946), the latter resulting in forty-two Jewish deaths.[5] Polish police, aided by Soviet troops, dispersed crowds, restored order, arrested perpetrators, and executed some after trial. The communist press pilloried "reactionary" elements, including the Catholic Church. Cardinal August Hlond, Poland's chief prelate who promoted antisemitism before the war, blamed Jewish communists for the violence. The Vatican remained silent. As one Polish participant put it, "Everybody around said that the Jews were murdering children . . . the old hatred of Jews started boiling within me so I simply let it out."[6] By the summer of 1947, Polish hoodlums and mobs killed over 1,500 Jews and injured many more.[7]

Jews in Romania had it no better. Some 430,000 were in Romania when it surrendered to the Soviets, 150,000 of them repatriates from Transnistria and refugees from Hungary, Poland, and Slovakia.[8] Romanian nationalists, bitter at the imposition of communist rule, saw another Jewish invasion. "We still have a score to settle with those bastards," was an oft-heard comment.[9] Hundreds of Jews returning to their homes were murdered. Those not killed, according to government reports, "found nothing left. All their property had been expropriated. . . ." A *Hashomer Hatza'ir* representative in 1946 described one-third of the Jews in Iaşi as "the living dead." "Dimmed eyes," "swollen bellies," and poorly stocked Joint Distribution Committee (JDC) soup kitchens defined their lives.[10] Soviet requisitions as well as a famine after the 1946 harvest were also blamed on Jews. Romania's pro-Soviet government did little for fear of a pro-Jewish label.

The Allies and the Displaced Person (DP) Question

After the war, the Soviets kept the Baltic States and the Polish lands received from Hitler in 1939 and 1940, as well as Bessarabia and other border areas. Poland was compensated with prewar German lands east of the Oder and Neisse rivers. Romania recovered northern Transylvania. Czechoslovakia recovered the Sudetenland. Austria was separated from Germany. This time, unlike in 1918, ethnic groups on the wrong side of the border were forced to move. Among them were millions of Germans, expelled from Poland, Czechoslovakia, and elsewhere. It was tough medicine, ironically based on Hitler's old argument that ethnic Germans could not live under the rule of others.

---

[3]Yitzhak Zuckerman, *A Surplus of Memory: Chronicle of the Warsaw Ghetto Uprising* (Berkeley, CA, 1993), p. 656.

[4]Quoted in Jan Gross, *Fear: Antisemitism in Poland After Auschwitz* (New York, 2006), p. x.

[5]Figure in Gross, *Fear*, p. 93.

[6]Quoted in Anna Cichopek, "The Cracow Pogrom of August 1945: A Narrative Reconstruction," in *Contested Memories*, ed. Zimmerman, p. 234.

[7]Figure in Mankowitz, *Life Between Memory and Hope*, p. 18.

[8]Figure in Arieh Kochavi, *Post-Holocaust Politics: Britain, the United States, and Jewish Refugees, 1945–1948* (Chapel Hill, NC, 2001), pp. 202–3.

[9]Quoted in Special Agent John V. Lapurke, Memorandum for the Officer in Charge, September 17, 1947, National Archives and Records Administration (hereafter NARA), College Park, MD, RG 319, Entry ZZ-7, File MSN 45806.

[10]Quotes from Jean Ancel, "'The New Jewish Invasion': The Return of Survivors from Transnistria," in *The Jews Are Coming Back: The Return of Jews to Their Countries of Origin After World War II*, ed., David Bankier (Jerusalem, 2005), pp. 241, 251.

Germany and Austria were each divided into four occupation zones administered by the United States, Great Britain, France, and the USSR. Allied zones teemed with refugees. More than 12 million were ethnic Germans who had either fled their homes in the war's last phase or were expelled afterward. The Allies were content to have them integrate within Germany's new borders. The others were known administratively as displaced persons (DPs). They included 7 million east Europeans, many of whom had been forced laborers. They gravitated to DP camps supervised by the Allies. In 1945, some 6 million DPs went home, and by May 1946, DPs in Germany's western occupation zones numbered 716,000. Most were Lithuanians, Latvians, Estonians, and Ukrainians, whose regions now sat within the USSR and who qualified as "stateless" persons. Some had collaborated with the Nazis and knew better than to go home and face retribution.

Eventually some 300,000 DPs were Jews, the minority liberated from German camps, the majority arriving in 1946 and 1947 from eastern Europe, mostly Poland and Romania. They called themselves *She'erith Hapleitah* ("the saved remnant").[11] A clandestine Zionist network known as the *Bricha* ("Escape"), aided their movement west, with the ultimate aim of moving them to Palestine whether Britain approved or not. Zionist leaders reached agreements with Soviet and new east European authorities not to require exit visas for emigrating Jews.

Bricha-smuggled groups made their way to the US and British occupation zones of Germany and Austria. When one crossing point shut down, *Bricha* operatives found another. The trek was arduous. One refugee wrote a loved one: "Monday we left Bucharest and arrived in Satu Mare at 5 o'clock, Thursday in Carci . . . 20 kilometers on foot . . . crossed [Hungarian] border at 4 o'clock and proceeded 50 km. . . . On Saturday we started for Budapest . . . then we went by car to Sopron and with 200 more people crossed the Austrian border and finally reached Vienna by car."[12] Vienna served as *Bricha* headquarters. Arthur Pier, a Viennese Jew who fled to Palestine in 1938 and returned after the war posing as a news correspondent, coordinated operations. From July to November 1946 alone, 70,000 Jews arrived, supported by JDC funds. "We had people's lives in our hands," Pier remembered, "and no less, the fate of the Jewish people as a whole."[13] On leaving Austria in 1947, Pier took the name Asher Ben-Natan, and in 1956 became Israeli minister of defense.

In August 1945, the Jewish Agency Executive (JAE) for Palestine demanded 100,000 immigration certificates for Jewish DPs. The British government, now under Prime Minister Clement Attlee, held to the 1939 White Paper, according to which fewer than 11,000 immigration certificates remained. British officials in the Middle East feared that even this number would trigger "a wave of hostility throughout the Arab countries . . . threatening Great Britain's whole position in the Middle East."[14] London refused even to classify Jewish DPs as a separate nationality for fear it would strengthen Zionist claims to Palestine. The British argued that they were Poles, Romanians, and others who should return home like all DPs. The exodus from eastern Europe, Attlee argued, was a Zionist plot "engineered largely with a view to forcing our hand over Palestine."[15] At one point, British authorities withheld food rations from new arrivals at

---

[11]Figures in Atina Grossmann, *Jews, Germans and Allies: Close Encounters in Occupied Germany* (Chapel Hill, NC, 2007), pp. 131–32, 134.

[12]Excerpt from letter from Jean Schreiber, May 8, 1947, Civil Censorship Group in Austria, Report May 22, 1947, NARA, RG 260, Entry ZZ-19, Project Symphony, vol. 2, box 61.

[13]Asher Ben-Natan, *The Audacity to Live* (Jerusalem, 2007), p. 31.

[14]Quoted in Kochavi, *Post-Holocaust Politics*, p. 61.

[15]Quoted in Kochavi, *Post-Holocaust Politics*, p. 52.

the Bergen-Belsen DP camp to dissuade more from coming. "The best British propaganda for Zionism," said JAE Chairman David Ben-Gurion, "is the [DP] camp at Bergen-Belsen. They behave like Nazis there."[16]

Washington developed a different mind-set. On urging from Jewish groups in the United States, President Harry Truman sent a fact-finding mission to Germany under Earl G. Harrison, a member of Roosevelt's Inter-Governmental Committee on Refugees. In August 1945, Harrison reported that Jewish DPs should be considered as Jews first and foremost. "Jews as Jews," he said, "have been more severely victimized than non-Jewish members of the same or other nationalities." The British, he added, should provide the 100,000 certificates. "The civilized world," Harrison said, "owes it to this handful of survivors to provide them with a home where they can again settle down and begin to live as human beings."[17]

Truman approved these recommendations. US authorities winked at *Bricha* activity, accepted Jewish arrivals, and allowed Jewish DP camps with self-governing institutions. With US approval, the Central Committee of Liberated Jews formed in Munich. It coordinated politics, medical care, and schooling within the camps and worked to trace lost relatives. Mostly, it formed the narrative of the Jews as a separate nation whose home was Palestine. Zalman Grinberg was a physician from Lithuania who became chairman of the Central Committee after his liberation from Dachau. His address to the opening congress of *She'erith Hapleitah* in January 1946 received wide press coverage. "We are not Poles or Lithuanians or Latvians," he said, "nor do we belong to any other nation which possesses states in Europe. We have nothing in common with these peoples. The best proof of that has been given by these people themselves. . . . We are Jews, the descendants of these people who 2,000 years ago were driven from their country, the country of their ancestors, *Eretz Israel*, and now we want to return there."[18]

Toward a Jewish State

From 1945 to 1948, 140 ships with 70,000 illegal Jewish immigrants left European ports.[19] Initially they sailed from Romania, Bulgaria, and Yugoslavia. Later they left from France and from Italy. Thanks to *Bricha* smuggling through the Alpine passes, Italy had more Jewish refugees by 1947 than any other Mediterranean country. "The Jews today fear Europe," a *Bricha* leader in Italy told US agents. "In every country that has been under German occupation, anti-Jewish feeling is running high. . . . Centuries of cruel persecutions have taught the Jews their lesson. They all believe that only a free Palestine can give them . . . full security and they are determined to reach their goal at any cost."[20]

London pressured European governments to prohibit sailings. British authorities also intercepted immigrant ships, moving 51,000 refugees to stark holding camps in Cyprus.[21] Palestine, meanwhile, came apart at the seams. Dissident Zionist groups such as the *Irgun* under Menachem Begin launched terror attacks against the British, most notably bombing British headquarters at

---

[16]Quoted in Tom Segev, *The Seventh Million: The Israelis and the Holocaust* (New York, 1991), p. 130.

[17]Quoted in Grossmann, *Jews, Germans and Allies*, pp. 138, 140.

[18]Report of Dr. Z. Grinberg, January 27, 1946, NARA, RG 319, Entry ZZ-7, File XE169385.

[19]Figure in Segev, *The Seventh Million*, p. 132.

[20]"Jewish Clandestine Emigration to Palestine," June 10, 1946, NARA, RG 260, Entry ZZ-19, Project Symphony, vol. 2, box 61.

[21]Figure in Dalia Ofer, "Holocaust Survivors As Immigrants: The Case of Israel and the Cyprus Detainees," *Modern Judaism*, 16, no. 1 (February 1996), pp. 1–23.

Jerusalem's King David Hotel in July 1946. Arab leaders from Palestine, Egypt, Iraq, Syria and elsewhere complained that Zionists exaggerated Jewish suffering in Europe, that Palestine was "already saturated with Jews," and that they would never accept a Jewish homeland in Palestine.[22]

The climax came in July 1947 when the refitted ship *Exodus* approached Palestine with 4,530 passengers, many of them children. British warships surrounded and rammed the ship. Troops boarded. Jews resisted with bottles and cans. Three Jews were killed, 200 injured, and most of the rest taken to occupied Germany. International outcry was instantaneous. Completely frustrated, London had already transferred the search for a solution to the newly founded United Nations, which in November 1947 voted for a scheme to partition Palestine between Arabs and Jews. Angry at Jewish ingratitude, worried about inflaming Arab opinion, and beset with financial troubles, Britain cut its losses in Palestine.

At midnight on May 15, 1948, as the British mandate officially ended, David Ben-Gurion publicly proclaimed the independence of the new State of Israel and became its first prime minister. Armies from Transjordan, Iraq, Egypt, and Syria, attacked. Israel's victorious War of Independence, the flight and expulsion of hundreds of thousands of Palestinian Arab refugees, Jewish immigration to Israel from Europe and elsewhere, the military and cultural triumphs of the Jewish state, and Israel's turbulent relationship with its Arab neighbors are all subjects for another book. In the meantime, Jewish refugees had what they lacked before—a state dedicated to their safety.

16.2 JUSTICE IN OCCUPIED GERMANY

The Problem of Postwar Justice

In October 1943, the Allies and Soviets jointly issued the Moscow Declaration, part of which promised that German perpetrators would face justice in the countries where they committed their crimes or, if their crimes were in multiple locations, by the victorious powers. With the end of the war, the victors arrested hundreds of thousands of German officials, particularly members of the SS and Gestapo. The victors also seized mountains of files from various German agencies, including the Reich Security Main Office (RSHA), the Foreign Ministry, the Nazi Party, and the armed forces. Together with interrogations and witness statements, these were the bases for trial.

Several major figures escaped justice through suicide. The day after Hitler's suicide in the bunker, Joseph and Magda Goebbels killed their six children and then themselves. "The world that is coming after the Führer and National Socialism," Magda wrote on April 28, 1945, "is not worth living in. . . ."[23] Heinrich Himmler bit a cyanide capsule after the British captured him in May. Odilo Globocnik, the director of *Aktion Reinhard*, did the same. In December, Eichmann's deputy Theodor Dannecker hanged himself in jail after US authorities arrested him. His wife was already under arrest for poisoning their children.[24]

Perhaps 1,000 SS officers and thousands more collaborators escaped Europe by using false identities. The most common escape route was through Italy. Former Nazi contacts arranged hideouts, and sympathetic Catholic officials in Rome procured false identity documents with which fugitives could flee for safe countries. Notorious fugitives, including Adolf Eichmann in

[22]Quoted in Kochavi, *Post-Holocaust Politics*, p. 73.

[23]Joseph Goebbels, *Tagebücher 1945: Die letzte Aufzeichningen* (Hamburg, 1977), pp. 549–50.

[24]NARA, RG 319, Entry ZZ-6, File XE 099228.

Argentina and Treblinka commandant Franz Stangl in Brazil, were eventually discovered and captured. Others, such as Auschwitz doctor Joseph Mengele, gassing specialist Walter Rauff, Eichmann deputy Aloïs Brunner, and Ustaša chief Ante Pavelić died free men. Mengele died of a heart attack on a Brazilian beach in 1979. Brunner worked for Syrian intelligence after the war and died in 1992.[25]

Still, some 95,000 Germans and Austrians were convicted of Nazi crimes, either by the occupying powers, in states the Germans had occupied, or by postwar German authorities.[26] They included camp commandants and guards, *Einsatzgruppen* officers, administrators, and businessmen. Tens of thousands of collaborators were also tried and convicted in countries formerly occupied or allied to Germany. Many early trials provided speedy, rough justice that ended in hanging. Later trials followed more rigid procedure and often resulted in prison sentences. The Holocaust, meanwhile, formed the centerpiece only in later trials. In initial proceedings, it was subsumed in different narratives of the war.[27]

Nuremberg

The Trial of the Major War Criminals in Nuremberg, from November 1945 to October 1946, was the signature postwar trial. Held by a temporary court known as the International Military Tribunal, which consisted of judges and prosecutors from the four occupying powers, it was Europe's only international postwar trial. The twenty-two defendants were the top surviving Nazi leaders, including RSHA Chief Ernst Kaltenbrunner, Foreign Minister Joachim von Ribbentrop, Armaments Minister Albert Speer, Supreme Armed Forces Chief Wilhelm Keitel, Governor General Hans Frank, and Nazi jack-of-all-trades Hermann Göring.

It was a mixed success. In 1945, the victors were sorting through the wreckage of the war as a whole. They thus tried the Nuremberg defendants for everything Germany did—violating treaties, attacking neutrals, bombing civilians, plundering property, sinking merchant ships, and killing prisoners. The defendants faced several broad counts including crimes against peace (planning and starting a war of conquest), war crimes (legally established crimes against prisoners and civilians), and the new legal innovation of crimes against humanity (crimes based on religion, race, or political affiliation even against one's own citizens). The trial established a broad narrative of the Nazi years, with the war itself as the primary transgression.

The Holocaust emerged at Nuremberg. Testifying as a witness in the case against Kaltenbrunner, Otto Ohlendorf described his command of *Einsatzgruppe D* in Ukraine. "In the year between June 1941 to June 1942," he said, [my] *Einsatzkommandos* reported 90,000 people liquidated. . . . The figures which I saw of other *Einsatzgruppen*," he added, "were considerably larger."[28] Eichmann's subordinate Dieter Wisliceny, also called as a witness, testified that "it was perfectly clear to me that [the orders for deportations] spelled death to millions of people. . . ."

---

[25]The best study of escape networks is Gerald Steinacher, *Nazis on the Run: How Hitler's Henchmen Fled Justice* (New York, 2011).

[26]Figure in Devin Pendas, "Putting the Holocaust on Trial in the Two Germanies, 1945–1989," in *The Routledge History of the Holocaust*, ed. Jonathan C. Friedman (London, 2011), p. 425.

[27]Up-to-date essays are in Patricia Heberer and Jürgen Matthäus, eds., *Atrocities on Trial: Historical Perspectives on the Politics of Prosecuting War Crimes*, (Lincoln, NE, 2008); Nathan Stoltzfus and Henry Friedlander, eds., *Nazi Crimes and the Law* (New York, 2008); István Deák et al., eds., *The Politics of Retribution in Europe: World War II and Its Aftermath* (Princeton, NJ, 2000).

[28]International Military Tribunal, *Trial of the Major War Criminals Before the International Military Tribunal, Nuremberg, 14 November 1945–1 October 1946* (hereafter *TMWC*), vol. 4 (Nuremberg, 1946), p. 319.

Eichmann, said Wisliceny, boasted that "he would leap laughing into his grave because the . . . five million people on his conscience would be for him a source of extraordinary satisfaction."[29] Auschwitz commandant Rudolf Höss testified that "we executed about 400,000 Hungarian Jews alone in the summer of 1944." He admitted, "We built our gas chambers to accommodate 2,000 people at one time. . . ."[30] The Soviets found Jewish themes internationally useful and brought a few Jewish witnesses to Nuremberg. Treblinka survivor Samuel Rajzman thus testified, "My work was to load the clothes of the murdered persons. . . . When I was loading clothes on the freight cars, my comrades found my wife's documents and a photograph of my wife and child. That is all I have left of my family, only a photograph."[31]

The defendants blamed their dead superiors. "I immediately went to see [Hitler and Himmler]," Kaltenbrunner said on describing his reaction on 'learning' of the Final Solution, "and complained to both of them saying that I could not for one single minute support any such action."[32] Hans Frank claimed ignorance even though his bailiwick—the General Government— housed the *Reinhard* camps. "In answer to my repeated questions as to what happened to Jews who were deported," Frank testified, "I was always told that they were to be sent to the East . . . to work there."[33] "Himmler," Göring insisted, "kept all of these matters very secret."[34] Prosecutors shredded denials by introducing documents and by showing a gruesome US army film of the liberated camps. The verdicts were severe. There were no appeals. Half of the defendants, including Göring, Kaltenbrunner, and Frank, were dead two weeks after the trial ended.

Still, the Trial of the Major War Criminals obscured the Holocaust. It was but one crime among many for which the defendants answered. Unable so soon after the war to understand Hitler's war against the Jews as Nazi Germany's *raison d'être*, prosecutors explained it as a particularly depraved component within a much broader theme of German conquest and human degradation. The year-long proceeding also lacked drama for long stretches. It hinged on reading documents into evidence, lengthy legal motions, and tedious translations into different languages. The Palace of Justice in Nuremberg, wrote reporter Rebecca West, "was a citadel of boredom." "The symbol of Nuremberg," she continued, "was a yawn."[35]

Nuremberg's Successor Trials

Because joint trials were cumbersome, especially with the Soviets, US military tribunals at Nuremberg held twelve subsequent trials between 1946 and 1948. They examined a variety of German crimes. One case against German physicians examined the systematic killing of the disabled and human medical experiments. Three trials prosecuted German industrialists, including those from IG Farben, for their use of slave labor and for the plunder of property. SS officers were tried for exploiting concentration camp labor and for the expulsion of racial inferiors. Senior military officers were tried for offenses ranging from crimes against peace to war crimes against prisoners. One trial prosecuted German judges, and another tried a collection of diplomats and

---

[29]*TMWC*, vol. 4, pp. 317, 366, 371.

[30]*TMWC*, vol. 11, pp. 414, 416.

[31]*TMWC*, vol. 8, p. 327.

[32]*TMWC*, vol. 11, p. 304.

[33]*TMWC*, vol. 12, p. 18.

[34]*TMWC*, vol. 9, p. 610.

[35]Quoted in Ravit Pe'er-Lamo Reichman, "Committed to Memory: Rebecca West's Nuremberg," in *Law and Catastrophe*, eds. Austin Sarat et al. (Stanford, CA, 2007), pp. 12, 97.

other senior state officials. Of the 185 defendants in these trials, 142 were convicted, and thirteen were executed.

All of the subsequent Nuremberg trials included the persecution of Jews on one level or another. But only one—the *Einsatzgruppen* trial—confronted the Holocaust specifically, after prosecutors fortuitously discovered the *Einsatzgruppen* reports. Twenty-two *Einsatzgruppen* officers, including the notorious Ohlendorf, stood trial. They blamed superior orders and the need for legitimate antipartisan measures. Werner Braune, who served under Ohlendorf, argued that "the Jews of the East were the decisive bearers of communism and its illegal manner of fighting."[36] The number of murdered women and children made hay of this argument. But US prosecutors, confident that documents alone would render the desired guilty verdicts, did not call Jewish witnesses. The trial revealed the story of the mass murder of Jews in the USSR, but the opportunity for more dramatic testimony that might have captured the world's attention was lost, particularly due to the escalating Cold War between the United States and the USSR.

Allied and Soviet military courts in the occupied zones carried out hundreds of other trials that convicted nearly 9,000 perpetrators.[37] They dispensed swift justice, mostly to camp personnel and Germans accused of killing prisoners of war. Crimes against Jews were handled ambiguously. In 1946, British authorities convicted and executed two managers of the German firm Tesch and Stabenow, which distributed Zyklon B to Auschwitz, Majdanek, and other camps.[38] But they skirted the Jewish question when convenient. In 1945, they tried forty-five defendants from the Bergen-Belsen and Auschwitz camps. Despite all the British knew of Germany's war against the Jews, and despite the number of Jews discovered at Bergen-Belsen, British prosecutors indicted the defendants for mistreating Allied nationals. Jews from Poland and Russia (though not Axis countries) were technically included in this group, but Jews as such were not even mentioned in the indictment.[39]

16.3 JUSTICE, POLITICS, AND HOLOCAUST NARRATIVE IN EUROPE

The immediate purpose of Allied trials in Germany lay in dispensing justice while laying bare Nazi crimes to the Germans. Countries once occupied by or allied with the Germans had a more complicated task. Trials, combined with general memorialization, aimed to create a narrative of the war within a general process of redefining postwar society. In eastern Europe, the wartime narrative had to suit newly imposed communist regimes. In western Europe, it had to fit within the reestablishment of liberal democratic consensus. Everywhere, wartime narratives had to consider local national feeling. Collaboration and the Holocaust were confronted to a point. But recent history was also skewed to accommodate local politics.

The Soviet Union

Moscow understood that the Nazis targeted Jews for total extinction. To exploit Jewish sentiment abroad, Stalin in 1942 created the Jewish Anti-Fascist Committee (JAC), a collection of Jewish intellectuals under Solomon Mikhoels that delivered news on Jewish suffering to Allied states.

---

[36]Quoted in Hillary Earl, *The Nuremberg SS-Einsatzgruppen Trial, 1945–1958: Atrocity, Law, Theory* (New York, 2009), p. 202.

[37]Pendas, "Putting the Holocaust on Trial," p. 426.

[38]Peter Hayes, *From Cooperation to Complicity: Degussa in the Third Reich* (New York, 2004), pp. 297–98.

[39]Donald Bloxham, *Genocide on Trial: War Crimes Trials and the Formation of Holocaust History and Memory* (New York, 2001), pp. 97–101.

But the USSR was an empire of over 100 nationalities held together by the ideology of international proletarian equality. Nazism's singular crimes against Jews were deliberately subsumed into a broader Soviet narrative of Nazi murders and Soviet resilience.

Politically, this strategy was practical. During the war, Soviet citizens from Lithuania to Belarus to Ukraine had turned against Jews. And given the millions of Russian, Belarusian, and Ukrainian war dead, few were interested in exclusively Jewish stories. As the Red Army liberated territory in 1943 and 1944 and as Jews returned to claim their homes, local antisemitic incidents erupted. Local communist officials reported the episodes to Moscow but also suppressed Jewish memory. Thus, they forbade David Hofshteyn, a Yiddish poet and member of the JAC, to organize a memorial at Babi Yar when he returned to Kiev in 1944. In fact, they warned Hofshteyn against Jewish chauvinism that could promote antisemitic violence.[40]

These tendencies carried over into Soviet trials of thousands of German criminals. The most notable postwar proceedings occurred in 1945 and 1946 in eight liberated cities, including Riga, Leningrad, Minsk, and Kiev. Each had multiple German defendants, the most important being Friedrich Jeckeln, one of Himmler's Higher SS and Police Leaders in the occupied USSR. Show trial atmospheres prevailed. Defendants underwent rough pretrial interrogations, they offered little defense beyond confessions, and executions by hanging were immediate and public. Although witnesses mentioned mass killings of Jews at Babi Yar and elsewhere, the official reportage of the trials referred to all victims as "Soviet citizens."[41] This terminology was to unite all Soviets behind the memory of the war.

At the same time Moscow silenced a JAC project called *The Black Book*, a collection of witness statements of Nazi crimes against Jews compiled initially by Jewish writer Ilya Ehrenburg. Ehrenburg argued that *The Black Book* must be published. "The main task of the [JAC]," he said, "must consist of fighting antisemitism in our country."[42] It was also essential, Ehrenburg added, "to show that Jews died bravely, highlighting all the instances of active or passive resistance. . . ."[43] A Soviet-sanctioned English-language version of *The Black Book* was published in the United States in 1946. But it never appeared in the USSR. Communist authorities argued that "the book contains serious political errors" and that "Hitler's ruthless slaughters were carried out equally against Russians, Jews, Belorussians, Ukrainians, Latvians, Lithuanians and other peoples of the Soviet Union."[44]

Stalin, meanwhile, became increasingly convinced that Soviet Jews were disloyal. Mikhoels, for instance, insisted on commemorating the Holocaust. In September 1945, the former actor lifted a vase with dirt from Babi Yar, beseeching an audience to see "laces from a child's shoes . . . the tears of an old Jewish woman . . . [and] your fathers who are crying *Sh'ma Yisroel*. . . ."[45] Mikhoels also pressed for *The Black Book*'s publication and openly supported the

---

[40]Mordechai Altschuler, "Antisemitism in Ukraine Toward the End of World War II," in *Bitter Legacy: Confronting the Holocaust in the USSR*, ed. Zvi Gitelman (Bloomington, IN, 1997), pp. 80, 81.

[41]Vladimir Prusin, "Fascist Criminals to the Gallows: The Holocaust and Soviet War Crimes Trials, December 1945–February 1946," *Holocaust and Genocide Studies*, 17, no. 1 (Spring 2003), p. 9.

[42]Quoted in Shimon Redlich, *War, Holocaust, and Stalinism: A Documented Study of the Jewish Anti-Fascist Committee in the USSR* (Luxembourg, 1995), p. 414.

[43]Quoted in Ilya Altman, "The History and Fate of *The Black Book* and *The Unknown Black Book*," in *The Unknown Black Book: The Holocaust in the German-Occupied Soviet Territories*, eds. Joshua Rubenstein and Ilya Altman (Bloomington, IN, 2008), p. xxv.

[44]Quoted in Altman, "History and Fate of *The Black Book*," p. xxxiii.

[45]Quoted in Joshua Rubenstein and Vladimir Naumov, eds., *Stalin's Secret Pogrom: The Postwar Inquisition of the Jewish Anti-Fascist Committee* (New Haven, CT, 2001), p. 38.

Jewish home in Palestine. A secret police report to Stalin in 1946 conceded that the JAC "played a certain positive role [during the war with] the mobilization of Jews abroad," but warned that the JAC now assumed "an increasingly nationalistic, Zionist character."[46] In January 1948, Stalin's secret police murdered Mikhoels. The official story blamed a car accident.

"Hitler," said Yiddish poet Peretz Markish, "wanted to destroy us physically. Stalin wants to do it spiritually."[47] After Mikhoels's murder, Stalin shut down the JAC and Yiddish publications. In September 1948, the police arrested JAC members, including prominent Yiddish writers. Brutal interrogations followed to show, in the words of one police interrogator, that "Jews all over the Soviet Union are conducting an anti-Soviet whisper campaign."[48] In 1952, fifteen JAC members stood trial. Thirteen were executed, including Yiddish writer Yitzhak Fefer, who, though on trial for his life, still testified, "You will not find another people that has suffered as much as the Jewish people. . . . We have a right to our tears."[49]

Stalin's campaign continued with a trial of Jewish physicians and possible plans to deport all Jews from Soviet cities to remote regions. "Every Jew," Stalin said in December 1952, "is a nationalist."[50] The persecution might have escalated if Stalin had not died in March 1953. But his successors continued to bury the Holocaust. In 1976, the Soviets unveiled a heroic memorial at Babi Yar. The inscription memorialized the "citizens and Kiev and prisoners of war," who were—by this narrative—the main victims there. The communist newspaper *Pravda* explained that, at the end of September 1941, "tens of thousands of totally blameless, peaceful residents of Kiev including many children, women and old people, were shot to death."[51] Jews were not mentioned. Only with the USSR's breakup in 1991 did Jewish victims receive acknowledgment. The Ukrainian government allowed a Jewish memorial at Babi Yar in the shape of a menorah. It was vandalized in 2006.

Poland

The Holocaust claimed 90 percent of Poland's Jews. Yet 10 percent of Poland's Catholic population was also dead. The new Polish regime's national and pro-Soviet credentials were tied to painting Germans as killers of Poles and enemies of socialism. Poland's Jews were not forgotten. They represented half of Poland's dead. But they were integrated into a more useful narrative of Polish and socialist martyrdom.

Between 1946 and 1949, Polish tribunals tried over a thousand defendants from Axis countries, including major Holocaust perpetrators handed over by the United States.[52] They included Arthur Greiser (the Gauleiter of the *Warthegau*), Amon Göth (the liquidator of the Kraków ghetto and commandant of the Płazów labor camp), Rudolf Höss (Auschwitz's most important commandant), Joseph Bühler (Hans Frank's deputy governor), Hans Biebow (the administrator of the Łódź ghetto), and later Jürgen Stroop (destroyer of the Warsaw ghetto). The Poles hoped to impress foreign observers with their evenhandedness. Evidence came from Nuremberg and

---

[46]Quoted in Rubenstein and Naumov, *Stalin's Secret Pogrom*, pp. 31–32.

[47]Quoted in Arkady Vaksberg, *Stalin Against the Jews* (New York, 1994), p. 182.

[48]Quoted in Rubenstein and Naumov, *Stalin's Secret Pogrom*, p. 52.

[49]Quoted in Altman, "History and Fate of *The Black Book*," p. xxxv.

[50]Quoted in Rubenstein and Naumov, *Stalin's Secret Pogrom*, p. 62.

[51]"Monument at Babi Yar," *Pravda*, June 23, 1976.

[52]For a summary, see Alexander Prusin, "Poland's Nuremberg: The Seven Court Cases of the Supreme National Tribunal," *Holocaust and Genocide Studies*, 24, no. 1 (Spring 2010), pp. 1–25.

The Warsaw Ghetto Monument.   *Source:* Bjorn Svensson/Alamy.

from Polish authorities but also from the Central Jewish Historical Committee in Poland, which was documenting the Holocaust. "The full might of these cruel German measures," said prosecutor Mieczysław Siewierski in the case against Göth, "were directed against the Jewish population. No other nation has been subjected to such crimes. . . ." Still, the final judgment melded the victims. "The policy of extermination," it said, "was in the first place directed against the Jewish and Polish nations."[53]

Permanent memory in Poland raised other questions. Auschwitz became a state memorial in 1947. The site's planners emphasized "biological destruction of the Poles," while noting that "Jewish victims must be designated . . . as citizens of particular states." The state turned Auschwitz I, the concentration camp for political prisoners, into a museum emphasizing slavery, torture, and death. They neglected Auschwitz-Birkenau, the death camp where nearly 1 million

---

[53]United Nations War Crimes Commission, *Law Reports of Trials of War Criminals*, vol. 7 (London, 1947–9), p. 9.

Memorial site at Treblinka.   *Source:* Hadj/Sipa/Newscom.

Jews were murdered, save for the erection of a Christian cross on the crematoria ruins. Only in 1967 did Birkenau receive a memorial, the Monument to the Victims of Fascism, which included plaques in nineteen languages. With no further explanation, they read: "Four million [sic] people suffered and died here at the hands of the Nazi murderers between the years 1940 and 1945."[54]

Other memorials in Poland commemorated the Holocaust more directly. In April 1948, on the fifth anniversary of the Warsaw ghetto uprising, state authorities unveiled the Warsaw Ghetto Monument by Nathan Rapoport, a Jewish sculptor born in Warsaw. Still one of Warsaw's great landmarks, it follows Rapoport's heroic style of socialist realism, casting Warsaw's Jewish resistors as muscular proletarians. In this way, it also told a story of more general Polish resistance, especially because the authorities would not allow a memorial to the Polish Home Army revolt of 1944. Such a memorial would have praised the anticommunist government-in-exile. "Everyone," writes James E. Young, the foremost expert on Holocaust monuments, "memorializes something different here."[55]

The most solemn memorial in Poland is at the remote site of Treblinka. Nothing of the death camp remained after the Germans demolished it in 1943. Built in the 1960s, the memorial on the site reflects the giant Jewish cemetery that Treblinka became, with 17,000 shards of stone representing Jewish communities murdered there. At the center, where the gas chamber once sat, stands a giant obelisk, cracked down the middle. At its base, a slice of granite reads, in Yiddish, Polish, and four other languages, "Never Again."

But the creation of Jewish memorials did not mean that Poland had reconciled with the 25,000 to 30,000 Jews that still lived there. Israel's stunning military victory over its Soviet-sponsored Arab

---

[54]Quotes in Jonathan Huener, *Auschwitz, Poland and the Politics of Commemoration, 1945–1979* (Athens, OH, 2003), pp. 74–75, 161.

[55]James E. Young, "The Biography of a Memorial Icon: Nathan Rapoport's Warsaw Ghetto Monument," *Representations*, no. 26 (Spring 1989), p. 70.

neighbors in the Six-Day War (1967) embarrassed Moscow and triggered an anti-Zionist campaign in Poland. "Among Polish citizens of Jewish ethnicity," said Premier Józef Cyrankiewicz, "there is a certain number . . . with nationalist convictions, Zionist and thus pro-Israeli. . . . Loyalty to socialist Poland and imperialist Israel is not possible simultaneously." Jews were purged from government and communist party posts as well as positions in the press and higher education. Communist Party leader Władysław Gomułka noted, "I presume that Jews [more loyal to Israel] will leave the country." Nearly 13,000 did so by 1971, leaving but a tiny remnant behind.[56]

Since the end of the Cold War, Poland has sought to depoliticize the Holocaust. New plaques at Auschwitz-Birkenau, installed in 1990, read: "Forever let this place be a cry of despair and a warning to humanity, where the Nazis murdered about one and a half million men, women, and children, mainly Jews, from the various countries of Europe." Yet Holocaust memory remains turbulent. Historian Jan Gross's book *Neighbors* (2000), which describes the massacre of 1,600 Jews by local Poles in Jedwabne in 1941, triggered a bitter public debate about the role of ordinary Poles in the Holocaust. A flood of scholarship creating a new narrative of Polish-Jewish relations during the Holocaust is now emerging.

Hungary and Romania

Both Hungary and Romania were allied to Nazi Germany and together were complicit in the murder of close to 1 million Jews. The Soviets imposed new regimes, and local communists purged the old leaders. But remembering the genocidal crimes of each state was another issue.

Hungary's "people's tribunals" punished 400,000 and executed 146 after the war, but the trials had a very political nature.[57] Döme Sztójay and many of his ministers were hanged for their collaboration with Berlin, as were leading members of the radical Arrow Cross, including Ferenc Szálazi. Chief anti-Jewish officials such as deportation experts László Baky and László Endre were also tried and hanged. But so were numerous political enemies of the communists who had nothing to do with the Holocaust, including, by 1949, suspected enemies within Hungary's communist party itself. The Holocaust was quickly subsumed in communist rhetoric. As historian Randolph Braham puts it, "[T]he Holocaust was virtually sunk into the Orwellian black hole of history."[58]

After the fall of communism in 1989, Hungary did better. Budapest is the only east-central European capital with a sizable Jewish population, numbering some 80,000. Its Holocaust Memorial and Documentation Center, which chronicles the deprivation of Jewish rights and the destruction of Hungary's Jews, opened in 2004. "It was a heinous crime," said Prime Minister Péter Medgyessy on the museum's opening, "committed by Hungarian people against Hungarian people. There is no excuse, no explanation, only reconciliation."[59] The names of Hungary's Jewish victims shall be inscribed on the wall surrounding the museum. The following year (2005) brought one of Europe's most powerful memorials—sixty pairs of shoes, made of bronze, stretching forty meters along the Danube in central Budapest. The work boots, ladies shoes, and children's slippers memorialize the hundreds of Jews shot and drowned each day by the Arrow Cross during the Soviet siege.

---

[56]Quotes and figures in Dariusz Stola, "The Anti-Zionist Campaign in Poland," Jewish Studies at the Central European University, Public Lecture, 2000, http://web.ceu.hu/jewishstudies/lectures.htm.

[57]Figures in István Deák, "Retribution or Revenge: War Crimes Trials in Post World War II Hungary," in *Hungary and the Holocaust: Confrontation with the Past-Symposium Proceedings* (Washington, DC, 2001), p. 34.

[58]Randolph L. Braham, "The Assault on Historical Memory: Hungarian Nationalists and the Holocaust," *East European Quarterly*, 33, no. 4 (January 2000), p. 415.

[59]"Katsav Inaugurates Hungary's First Holocaust Museum," *Ha'aretz*, April 15, 2004.

Yet communism's fall also triggered broad efforts to obscure Hungary's role in the Holocaust. One narrative of the 1990s was that the Germans, with a few Arrow Cross thugs, perpetrated crimes against Jews in Hungary. Thus, in 1997, students in a Jewish school in Budapest learned of Raoul Wallenberg's heroism but nothing of how Hungarian officials arranged mass deportations.[60] A subsequent narrative was that Hungary's chief victims of the twentieth century were those persecuted under communism after 1945. The House of Terror in Budapest, opened in 2002 as a museum of the Arrow Cross and the communist secret police, emphasizes the brutality of the latter, which tormented a greater cross section of Hungarians but did not kill anything close to 500,000 of them. Far more disturbing trends emerged in 2010, with the return of Hungarian nationalists to power. Efforts to rehabilitate Admiral Horthy and even figures of the Arrow Cross with statues and ceremonial reburials have been accompanied by the defacement of Jewish memorials and cemeteries.

Romania's relationship with the Holocaust is even more difficult. "People's tribunals," as in Hungary, launched postwar purges. Marshal Ion Antonescu was executed, as was his Foreign Minister Mihai Antonescu. But King Michael commuted most death sentences before the communists deposed him at gunpoint in 1947. Radu Lecca, Antonescu's Jewish expert, and General Nicolae Macici, Romania's commander in Odessa, were among those spared. The king knew that many Romanians believed that Moscow provoked the war in 1940 by annexing Bessarabia, and that few cared about crimes in far-off Transnistria. What mattered were Romanian military casualties after Stalingrad. Antisemitism in Romania persisted despite a 1948 trial of policemen who participated in the Iaşi pogrom and the court's following conclusion: "Not only Jews were murdered at Iaşi, morality was murdered [and] the country's good name was murdered."[61]

After Israeli independence in 1948, Romanian communists swallowed Stalin's paranoia concerning Jewish disloyalty. "The Zionists," argued Prime Minister Petru Groza in 1949, "are the perfect candidates for the fifth column. . . ."[62] The Israeli government insisted that Romania's 350,000 Jews be allowed to emigrate to Israel and, by the fall of the communist regime in 1989, most did. But Romania's government exacted a price. Jews were first traded against goods such as oil-drilling equipment and livestock. After the advent of corrupt communist party chief Nicolae Ceaucescu in 1965, they were simply sold for cash. Ceaucescu used the money to develop Romanian trade in everything from synthetic diamonds to cocaine while filling his personal slush fund. Jews, he once said, were among "our best export commodities."[63]

Romania's communist bosses thus succeeded where interwar governments failed. This time, however, Jews had someplace to go and a government that would pay for their safety. In the meantime, Romania's export of its Jewish question prevented an honest look at its wartime past, even after communism collapsed. Victimization by the Soviets remained the theme. In the 1990s, many Romanian writers denied Romanian involvement in the Holocaust, and in 1991, Romania's parliament observed a moment of silence for Antonescu. Not until 2004 did the Romanian government formally acknowledge Romanian participation in the Holocaust, thanks to the work of an international research commission that presented its report to Romania's president that year.[64]

---

[60]Braham, "The Assault on Historical Memory," pp. 419–20.

[61]Quoted in Radu Ioanid, "The Holocaust in Romania: The Iaşi Pogrom of June 1941," *Contemporary European History*, 2, no. 2 (July 1993), p. 148.

[62]Quoted in Radu Ioanid, *The Ransom of the Jews: The Story of the Extraordinary Secret Bargain Between Romania and Israel* (Chicago, IL, 2005), p. 52.

[63]Figures and quote in Ioanid, *Ransom of the Jews*, pp. 104, 125, 135, 147.

[64]See International Commission on the Holocaust in Romania, *Final Report of the International Commission on the Holocaust in Romania* (Bucharest, 2004).

France

Some 206,000 Jews from western Europe were murdered between 1942 and 1944. Here, delays in memory owed not to communism but to democracy, which demanded a livable national consensus on the recent past. After the war, western European democracies developed a public consciousness that emphasized German guilt and national resistance while downplaying complicity and apathy during the Holocaust.

French memory is a poignant example. General Charles de Gaulle headed France's postwar provisional government. Following a period of vigilantism against local collaborators, he implemented legal proceedings against Vichy officials for treason against the nation. Three wartime leaders, including Pierre Laval, were executed, as were 1,500 lesser state officials. This process suggested that most Frenchmen remained patriots during the war. It also glossed over crimes against the Jews. Amnesty laws were passed in 1951 and 1953, and those imprisoned for treason were released. The past was seemingly buried.[65]

Unpleasant memories boiled to the surface in the 1980s thanks partly to the efforts of Serge Klarsfeld, a Romanian Jew who survived the war in France as a hidden child. With his wife Beate, he became a Nazi hunter and advocate for justice. The signature trial was that of Klaus Barbie, the Gestapo chief in Lyon who tortured and killed French resistors and deported hidden Jews, including forty-four children from the farming village of Izieu. In a case of remarkably bad judgment, US Army intelligence officials hired Barbie in 1947 to set up anticommunist networks in Germany. When the French demanded his extradition, US officials had him smuggled to South America. He resurfaced in Bolivia. Thanks to the Klarsfelds' efforts, he was extradited in 1983. But Barbie's highly publicized trial in Lyon in 1987 revealed the extent to which the Gestapo depended on French collaborators to implement the Final Solution.

The heated public discourse of the 1980s led to the first indictments of Vichy police officials for crimes against humanity rather than for simple treason. The most notorious was René Bousquet, Laval's police chief who spearheaded the arrest of foreign Jews in 1942 and 1943. Bousquet never made it to trial. In 1993, at age eighty-four, he was shot and killed in his Paris apartment. His assassin, a self-important publicity seeker named Christian Didier, compared his act to "killing a serpent." The press condemned Didier for robbing the world of an important legal proceeding. Despite Bousquet's death, the French, amid great public interest, tried and convicted lower-ranking Vichy police figures, most notably, Paul Touvier in 1994 and Maurice Papon in 1998. Touvier had worked closely with Barbie in Lyon. Papon had deported Jews from the Bordeaux region.[66]

In 1993, France established a National Day of Commemoration of Racist and Anti-Semitic Persecutions. It occurs annually on July 16, the day of the 1942 Paris roundup, and centers on the site of the *Vélodrome d'Hiver*, from which thousands of Jewish children were deported to their deaths. The site, which already had historical markers, received a new monument in 1994, which depicts women and children awaiting deportation. Repeated speeches at the site by French leaders have acknowledged postwar France's responsibility to remember the Vichy regime's crimes. As a result, the *Vélodrome d'Hiver*, though demolished after the war, has become integrated into French history and culture as a symbol of bitter historical truth.[67]

---

[65]Figures in Henri Rousso, "Did the Purge Achieve Its Goals?" in *Memory, the Holocaust and French Justice: The Bosquet and Touvier Affairs*, eds. Richard J. Golsan et al. (Hanover, NH, 1996), pp. 100–4.

[66]Richard J. Golsan, *Vichy's Afterlife: History and Counterhistory in Postwar France* (Lincoln, NE, 2000).

[67]Peter Carrier, *Holocaust Monuments and National Memory Cultures in France and Germany Since 1989* (New York, 2005), pp. 49–98.

The Vatican

The Cold War also delayed the Roman Catholic Church's reckoning with the Holocaust. Pius XII remained pope and an ardent anticommunist until his death in 1958. He called for leniency for even the worst German war criminals and surely knew of the help Catholic officials in Rome provided for Nazi fugitives. He displayed an almost willful misunderstanding of the Holocaust, arguing that all German Catholics were martyrs who opposed Nazism. His representatives in Germany blamed continued German antisemitism on Jewish DPs, who, they complained, were treated better than German expellees. Meanwhile there was no effort to reconcile with Jewry. On the contrary, Pius discouraged efforts by Catholic scholars to rethink canards about the Jews killing Christ. He also refused diplomatic recognition of Israel after 1948, convinced that the Jewish state would desecrate Catholic holy places in Jerusalem, Nazareth, and elsewhere.[68]

Only after Pius XII's death did the Vatican accept that antisemitism was partly a Catholic responsibility. The Second Vatican Council in 1965 instituted the statement *Nostra Aetate* ("In Our Time"), which proclaimed that "what happened in [Christ's] passion cannot be charged against all the Jews, without distinction, then alive, nor against the Jews of today." The statement continued: "[T]he Church, mindful of the patrimony [it] shares with the Jews . . . decries hatred, persecution, displays of antisemitism, directed against Jews at any time and by anyone."[69] The German bishops' delegation to the Vatican Council apologized publicly for the "inhumane extermination of the Jewish people," while others noted that "[a] truly Christian declaration cannot omit the fact that Jewish people have been subjected to centuries of injustices and atrocities by Christians."[70] It was a start. Whatever missteps the Vatican has made in the years since the Second Vatican Council—and there have been plenty—the church has not returned to the darkness of its medieval heritage.

16.4 GERMANY AND THE NAZI PAST

Nazi Germany was the author of the Holocaust. Thus, postwar Germany's reckoning with the past has taken decades and has been painful. Many Germans preferred to emphasize Germany's own suffering at the hands of Hitler and his wartime enemies. During the war, over 5.3 million German military personnel died, as did 642,000 civilians. Millions of German refugees fled their homes and most German cities were destroyed.[71] The division of Germany into two states from 1949 to 1991 left East Germany (the German Democratic Republic) under Soviet domination, while West Germany (the Federal Republic of Germany) was a truncated country on the Cold War's front line. It was easy for Germans to feel victimized.

East Germany conducted anti-Nazi purge trials but in general accepted no responsibility for the Nazi past because communism was Nazism's antithesis. On the contrary, East Germany spent much of its lifespan likening West Germany and its allies in the North Atlantic Treaty Organization (NATO) to the Nazis as a threat to world peace. Thus, it was left to the Federal Republic to face the Nazi past. With pressure from the Allies, Nazism was indeed discredited in the immediate postwar

[68]In general, see Michael Phayer, *The Catholic Church and the Holocaust, 1930–1965* (Bloomington, IN, 2001), p. 176.

[69]Geoffrey Wigoder, *Jewish-Christian Relations Since the Second World War* (Manchester, 1988), pp. 143–4.

[70]Quoted in Phayer, *The Catholic Church*, p. 214.

[71]Military casualties can be found in Rüdiger Overmanns, *Deutsche militärische Verluste im zweiten Weltkrieg* (Munich, 2004), p. 233, and in Richard Bessel, *Germany 1945: From War to Peace* (New York, 2009), p. 11; civilian casualties can be found in Militargeschichtliches Forschungsamt, gen. eds., *Das deutsche Reich und der zweite Weltkrieg*, vol. 9/1 (Stuttgart, 2004), p. 460.

years. Senior Nazis never returned to power. But a true national soul searching did not occur either. It took time, and really generational change, for most Germans to face their nation's crimes.

Denazification and Allied Trials

Denazification, the attempt to remove Nazis from all positions of public influence, illustrates the initial difficulties for Germans to face the recent past. One German male in five was a member of the Nazi Party in 1945, with the ratio higher in the educated middle class. In 1946, the Allies entrusted denazification to German panels known as *Spruchkammer* made up of non-Nazis. In the western occupation zones, the panels considered over 3.6 million cases. But they depended on questionnaires filled out by the accused, could not make detailed investigations, and faced social pressure for lenience. The panels thus placed only 4.8 percent of all defendants in the top categories of complicity. Twenty-seven percent of all defendants paid a fine as nominal followers, 33 percent of all defendants were acquitted, and 21 percent were never formally charged. Most Germans viewed denazification as vindictive, and the program ended in 1950.[72] Lower-level Nazis returned to work in local government, business, and even higher education.

The West German government also worked to liquidate the residue of Allied war crimes trials. To many Germans, the trials represented invalid "victor's justice," especially because seemingly respectable military officers and businessmen were among those imprisoned. In the early 1950s, West German chancellor Konrad Adenauer pressured the United States, Britain, and France for releases. Meanwhile, anticommunist groups in Allied countries argued that the Germans had been punished enough because West German goodwill was needed to stem Soviet expansion. Of the 1,315 German perpetrators imprisoned by the Allies on West German soil in 1950, none remained imprisoned by 1958, despite numerous life and twenty-year sentences.[73] These political winds even benefited *Einsatzgruppen* officers. Four of the most notorious, including Ohlendorf, were hanged amid loud opposition in 1951. The rest had their sentences commuted. Convicted military figures even managed to rebuild their reputations after their release.

West German Criminal Trials

West German courts placed some 4,000 Nazis on trial during the occupation. Most of these trials in the late 1940s and early 1950s concerned Nazi crimes against other Germans, such as denunciations, euthanasia, or late-war executions for treason. Trials resulted from individual complaints forwarded to state authorities. Thus, prosecutions for killing Jews were extremely rare. Conservative judges who had also served during the Nazi period also treated defendants leniently. In 1949, Benno Martin, Himmler's Higher SS and Police Leader in Nuremberg, received a three-year sentence for deporting 4,754 German Jews—most of whom died—to Riga, Lublin, Auschwitz, and Theresienstadt. An appellate ruling accepted Martin's defense that he acted under duress, and he walked free thereafter.[74]

Matters changed in 1958, when a West German court in Ulm heard a case against ten defendants from an *Einsatzkommando* that killed over 5,000 Jews immediately after Germany invaded the USSR. The sentences were predictably light. But the Ulm trial revealed that such perpetrators were at large and that state governments on their own lacked the resources to investigate

---

[72]Konrad H. Jarausch, *After Hitler: Recivilizing Germans, 1945–1995* (New York, 2008), pp. 50–6.

[73]Frank Buscher, *The US War Crimes Trial Program in Germany, 1946–1955* (New York, 1989), Appendix B.

[74]Henry Friedlander, "The Deportation of German Jews: Postwar German Trials of Nazi Criminals," *Leo Baeck Institute Yearbook*, vol. 29 (1984), pp. 220–1.

them. West Germany's international standing, meanwhile, now demanded concerted action. The result was the creation of the Central Office for the Investigation of National Socialist Crimes in Ludwigsburg. The Central Office initiated investigations of potential defendants and assembled evidence for homicide trials in state courts.

The Federal Republic employed prewar German homicide statutes rather than the Allied innovation of crimes against humanity, which most Germans regarded as ex post facto law. Murder convictions thus remained difficult. Prosecutors had to prove "base intent" by which a defendant initiated the idea of killing based on his own depravity. Killing by superior orders brought conviction only as an accomplice to murder. Prosecutors also had to show a direct tie between the defendant and the act, not simply that a defendant's unit engaged in killings. Because Nazi defendants were frequently liars, investigations also involved lengthy searches for documents and eyewitnesses. Regardless, the Central Office investigated over 120,000 individuals between 1958 and 2005, and trials led to 563 homicide convictions over that period.[75]

West German trials after 1958 included important proceedings against defendants from Bełżec, Treblinka, Sobibór, Auschwitz, and Majdanek. They ended in acquittals for defendants such as drivers and assistants who argued that they served under duress. More important defendants received stiff prison sentences (the Federal Republic has no death penalty). Wilhelm Boger, a Gestapo official, and Josef Klehr, a medical orderly, received life sentences in 1965 for sadistic murders at Auschwitz that included torture and phenol injections happily administered to varieties of prisoners. Treblinka Commandant Franz Stangl received a life sentence in 1970 for the co-responsibility for the murder of 900,000 Jews. Simon Wiesenthal, the Nazi hunter who located Stangl in Brazil, argued, "The Stangl case provided West Germany with its most important criminal case of the century."[76]

Prosecutions did not sit well with everyone. In the 1960s and 1970s, the West German parliament (Bundestag) held contentious debates over the extension and then the elimination of the statute of limitations on Nazi murders. German conservatives held that further trials damaged German honor. But statutory extensions were necessary because of the time needed for investigations. And as Social Democrats argued, the damage to German honor was done by Nazi criminals, not their prosecutors. In 1979, the Bundestag narrowly voted to abolish the statute of limitations on Nazi murders. "We all belong," said Social Democrat Fritz Erler, "to all of German history."[77] All Germans, he meant, had to confront the terrible past in order to master it.

Restitution

The restitution of stolen property and financial compensation for wartime suffering is an extremely tangled thicket of moral, legal, and financial issues that extends to the present day. It involves all countries touched by the Holocaust, even neutrals such as Switzerland, whose banks hid unclaimed Jewish accounts as well as substantial Nazi loot.[78] Since 1949, the efforts of the Federal Republic and West German businesses have been substantial, though necessarily short of the Holocaust's magnitude and, unfortunately, rather grudging on the part of those making restitution. Steady Allied pressure, the Federal Republic's need to build and maintain a positive image abroad, and the moral convictions of certain German leaders have made restitution possible.

---

[75]Figures in Andreas Eichmüller, "Die Strafverfolgung von NS-Verbrechen durch westdeutsche Justizbehörden seit 1945: Eine Zahlenbilanz," *Vierteljahrshefte für Zeitgeschichte*, 56, no. 4 (October 2008), pp. 621–40.

[76]Gitta Sereny, *The Healing Wound: Experiences and Reflections on Germany, 1938–2001* (New York, 2001), p. 94.

[77]Quoted in Jeffrey Herf, *Divided Memory: The Nazi Past in the Two Germanys* (Cambridge, MA, 1996), p. 339.

[78]An excellent summary is in Peter Hayes, "Plunder and Restitution," in *The Oxford Handbook of Holocaust Studies*, eds., Peter Hayes and John K. Roth (New York, 2010), pp. 540–59.

The restitution of Jewish-owned real estate and businesses in West Germany initially occurred at the insistence of the US occupation government, which in 1947 issued Germany's first restitution law. Restitution courts settled most existing property disputes between Jews who fled Germany and subsequent German owners by the mid-1950s, either with the return of property or monetary settlements, totaling DM (Deutschmarks) 3.5 billion in all. Disputes were sometimes bitter, and settlements were often less than original value. As lawyers from the German chemical firm Degussa complained, the law "gives every emigrant a hunting license, and when he cannot shoot a stag, the courts try to give him at least a rabbit."[79] West German businessmen further griped that Jewish émigrés had benefited during the war while they themselves had suffered the real loss. Walter Roland, a Nazi steel magnate whose enterprises used slave labor, returned to business prominence after the war. Referring to his estate, which sustained Allied bomb damage, he noted that, as far as he was concerned, "the account with the Jews is settled."[80]

The Allies insisted on broader restitution after formal West German independence in 1955. Germany's Federal Restitution Law of 1957 theoretically assumed liability for property stolen in all German-occupied territories. By 1971, 128,000 rulings resulted in DM 4 billion in settlements. Still, the state implemented the law stringently to limit exposure. Most would-be claimants were dead. Live claimants had to meet high standards of proof. Claimants living in countries with which West Germany had no diplomatic relations, namely, most communist states of eastern Europe, could not receive compensation. Thus, a group of Jews in Czechoslovakia whose property was stolen before their deportation to Auschwitz received a positive decision but no compensation. As West German officials put it, the inclusion of eastern Europe would have made restitution "barely calculable."[81]

The most dramatic form of German payment came under the 1952 Luxembourg Accords. Here the West German government agreed to make payments to the State of Israel and to the Conference on Jewish Material Claims against Germany—also known as the Claims Conference—an umbrella organization representing twenty-three international Jewish organizations. Payments were not for stolen property but rather to support social welfare efforts for Holocaust survivors. The accords were controversial among Germans, who pointed to their own refugees and rebuilding efforts. "We have to state quite openly," said one parliamentarian, "that in our society *Wiedergutmachung* [compensation] has no popular appeal."[82] Adenauer, however, remained firm. "Unspeakable crimes," he argued, "were committed in the name of the German people, calling for moral and material indemnity."[83] To date, the Claims Conference has received and disbursed over DM 100 billion to individuals and organizations dedicated to their welfare.[84]

German Memorialization

Germany's most singular memorial to Holocaust victims is the Memorial to the Murdered Jews of Europe designed by the architect Peter Eisenman. It opened in central Berlin in 2005, sixty years

---

[79]Quoted in Hayes, *From Cooperation to Complicity*, p. 106.

[80]Quoted in S. Jonathan Wiesen, *West German Industry and the Challenge of the Nazi Past, 1945–1955* (Chapel Hill, NC, 2001), p. 224.

[81]Figures and quote in Jürgen Lillteicher, "West Germany and the Restitution of Jewish Property in Europe," in *Robbery and Restitution: The Conflict over Jewish Property in Europe*, eds. Martin Dean et al. (New York, 2007), pp. 99–106.

[82]Quoted in Hans Günter Hockerts, "*Wiedergutmachung* in Germany: Balancing Historical Accounts, 1945–2000," in *Restitution and Memory: Material Restoration in Europe*, eds. Dan Diner and Gotthard Wunberg (New York, 2007), p. 337.

[83]Quoted in Robert G. Moeller, *War Stories: The Search for a Usable Past in the Federal Republic of Germany* (Berkeley, CA, 2001), p. 25.

[84]Figure in Marilyn Henry, *Confronting the Perpetrators: A History of the Claims Conference* (London, 2007), pp. 215–6.

Memorial to the Murdered Jews of Europe, opened in Berlin, May 2005.   *Source:* Muhs/Caro/Alamy.

after the war and fifteen years after the unification of East and West Germany, which enabled Berlin to become Germany's capital once more. What took so long? Postwar West Germany had many memorials commemorating Nazism's victims, ranging from the villa at Wannsee to concentration camp sites at Dachau and Buchenwald, to plaques marking deportation sites. But it lacked a single all-encompassing memorial to the nearly 6 million murdered Jews.

The debate on whether to build such a memorial lasted from 1989 to 1999. Writer Martin Walser acknowledged Germany's historical burden but argued that such a memorial would be a "monumentalization of shame," which would define German history by guilt alone. Yet as Ignatz Bubis, the Holocaust survivor who now spoke for Germany's small Jewish community said, the memorial was a necessary measure of the degree to which Germany now faced its past.[85] Put

---

[85]Quoted in Bill Niven, *Facing the Nazi Past: Unified Germany and the Legacy of the Third Reich* (London, 2002), pp. 178, 194.

this way, the memorial had to be built, but what would it look like? "How," asked scholar James Young, "would a nation of former perpetrators mourn its victims? How would a divided nation reunite itself on the bedrock memory of its crimes?"[86]

Public debate over the design was so acrimonious that some openly wondered whether tortured German discourse was itself the best form of remembrance. More than 500 ideas were submitted, many of which were too unoriginal to appeal to postmodern sensibilities. On joining the commission in 1997 that decided on the final design after a new round of submissions, James Young (the only non-German and the only Jew on the commission) insisted that the memorial incorporate modern artistic skepticism, meaning that the memorial itself "reflect . . . the insufficiency of memorials," thus suggesting permanent loss rather than redemption through construction.[87]

The Memorial to the Murdered Jews of Europe is a vast five-acre space with 2,711 unmarked sandstone pillars, ranging from a half meter to three meters high, climbing and falling as an undulating wave. Visitors move among the pillars, disoriented, overwhelmed, and even somewhat lost, near the sites of the very buildings in which the Nazis determined the fate of Europe's Jews. To some, the field of pillars reflects the variety of victims, to others the claustrophobia of freight cars, to others still a more abstract maze in which discomfort meets fresh air and the present can never fully escape the past. One gazes not upon a static memorial so much as one becomes part of remembrance and retains the experience afterward. The memorial is too vast and ambiguous to give closure. Though the guilt belongs to past generations, post-Cold War Germany, with the monument, accepts the Holocaust as part of a permanently damaged national identity. As James Young says, it "will always remind Germany and the world at large of the self-inflicted void at the heart of German culture and consciousness."[88]

16.5 JEWISH MEMORIALIZATION

The Problem of Jewish Remembrance

When Moshe Maltz returned to the East Galician town of Sokal in 1944, most of the Jewish community was dead. Synagogues and shops were now empty shells. Jewish cemeteries were desecrated, the tombstones removed and used for roadways, the grass used to graze cattle. "I stand in silence, unable to speak," he wrote, "I can almost see them before my eyes, my relatives and friends. . . ." On finding Sokal's mass burial pit, Maltz lamented, "[B]eneath this ground lies a community of Jews that began hundreds of years ago. Here the history of the community has come to an abrupt end. . . ."[89] Most of the dead would never be found. Their bones were mixed together in thousands of pits. Their ashes had been strewn over fields and into rivers.

Funerary rituals and memorials are central components of Judaism. They range from the Mourner's *Kaddish,* the sanctification of God by the deceased's family members on his or her behalf, to *Yahrzeit,* the remembrance of family members on the anniversary of their passing, to the physical memorialization of one's dead in Jewish cemeteries. But how, with entire families destroyed with no physical trace and no date of death, would the memory of the dead be preserved and honored? And how would memorialization contribute to a Jewish understanding of

---

[86]James E. Young, "Germany's Holocaust Memorial Problem—And Mine," *The Public Historian,* 24, no. 4 (Fall 2002), p. 80.

[87]Young, "Germany's Holocaust Memorial Problem," p. 72.

[88]Young, "Germany's Holocaust Memorial Problem," p. 80.

[89]Moshe Maltz, *Years of Horror—Glimpse of Hope: The Diary of a Family in Hiding* (New York, 1993), August 1944, pp. 130, 133.

the Holocaust as a whole? These impossible questions have found many answers in the past decades, ranging from the religious to the secular and from the personal to the national.

Local Remembrance

Those still alive from the annihilated *shtetlach* of eastern Europe were determined to maintain communal memory of their towns and their traditions. After the war, they established mutual aid societies known in Yiddish as *Landsmanschaftn* that kept contact with surviving town members, first in Poland, then in DP camps in Germany, then throughout the world. *Landsmanschaftn* commemorated the dead, often with annual memorial meetings on the anniversary of the day when the Germans liquidated their ghettos. It was the closest they could get to the anniversary of death. They also created communal tombstones in cemeteries in Israel, the United States, or wherever else they lived after the war.

Such religious remembrance went beyond *Landsmanschaftn*. In Germany, Jewish DPs constructed plaques imploring God Himself to "[r]emember . . . the six million Jews who perished for the sanctification of Your name. . . ."[90] In the United States, Jews incorporated into their Passover seders a prayer "for the six million Jews who perished at the hands of the Nazis and for the heroes of the ghetto uprisings," and they built small memorials in their synagogues, in some cases, including pieces of Torah scrolls and other artifacts recovered from Europe.[91] In Latin America, Jews created markers in their cemeteries for the millions who perished. Such remembrance was not overly demonstrative, leading scholars to believe for years that Jews psychologically suppressed the Holocaust until the 1960s. But in fact, they mourned within their own traditions.

But the most poignant memorials to destroyed Jewish communities were hundreds of memorial (Yizkor) books, financed by *Landsmanschaftn*, with written memories from those who wished to participate in communal remembrance. Painfully conscious that their town was gone forever, compilers often included maps and town layouts. Each Yizkor book tells community history, with details ranging from synagogue interiors to holiday traditions, to market days, to the memorable town characters. They also include meticulous, harrowing memories of the destruction. "We are not professional writers," began the Yizkor book from Ryki near Lublin. "Only the shocking pain in the face of the horrible death opened our silent lips. . . . Every individual record, every line, every recollection of the former life in our *shtetl* has its place and great value in this book to the memory of our close and dear ones."[92] Hundreds of Yizkor books appeared in the 1950s and 1960s. Survivor and scholar Nachman Blumenthal called them "paper tombstones" that serve as "a guarantee of directness and sincerity."[93]

The Eichmann Trial

After years of looking, Israeli agents located Adolf Eichmann in Argentina in 1960. They kidnapped him and brought him to Israel for trial. Eichmann's stunning capture was a transformative moment for the small Jewish state of 2 million in its twelfth year of existence, and for Jews everywhere. Not

---

[90]Quoted in Gabriel N. Finder, "*Yizkor!* Commemoration of the Dead by Jewish Displaced Persons in Postwar Germany," in *Between Mass Death and Individual Loss: The Place of the Dead in Twentieth Century Germany*, ed. Alon Confino et al. (New York, 2008), p. 234.

[91]Hasia Diner, *We Remember with Reverence and Love: American Jews and the Myth of Silence After the Holocaust* (New York, 2009), pp. 18–85.

[92]Quoted in Jack Kugelmass and Jonathan Boyer, eds., *From a Ruined Garden: The Memorial Books of Polish Jewry*, 2nd ed. (Bloomington, IN, 1998), p. 38.

[93]Anat Livneh, "'The Cry of the Desperate and the Fortitude of the Remaining Will Suffice': Commemorative Literature, Documentation, and the Study of the Holocaust," *Dapim: Studies on the Shoah*, vol. 24 (2010), p. 182.

the Soviets, not the Americans, and not the British, but rather the Jews seized one of Nazi Germany's most notorious criminals, and they would try him themselves. "We are no longer waiting like the poor man at the door, begging for the generosity of the nations and the pity of the gentile" wrote Israeli Rivka Gruber to Prime Minister David Ben-Gurion. "We have taken our fate in our hands."[94]

Eichmann's 1961 trial in Jerusalem placed the Holocaust at its center. His conviction for crimes against the Jewish people was assured through an ample documentary record. But to make the trial resonate, prosecutors called over 100 diverse witnesses who provided riveting testimony. They included armed resistors such as Abba Kovner of Vilna and Yitzhak Zuckerman of Warsaw. They included survivors such as Ada Lichtman of Sobibór, Eliahu Rosenberg of Treblinka, Perla Mark of Transnistria, and Yehiel Dinur of Auschwitz. They also included *Va'adah* leaders Joel and Hansi Brand, who in 1944 bargained with Eichmann for Jewish lives. Burdened by everything, from survivor's guilt to shame, many had never spoken publicly before. Now their stories became part of a collective catharsis.

In her famous *Eichmann in Jerusalem* (1963), the German Jewish émigré Hannah Arendt criticized the trial. Israel, she said, lacked legal standing to try Eichmann. It kidnapped the defendant, and neither the State of Israel nor the laws under which Eichmann was tried existed at the time of his crimes. There were also show trial elements. The defendant sat in a bulletproof booth in a theater converted into a courtroom, and most witnesses had no dealings with Eichmann. An international trial, Arendt argued, would have been more appropriate. But other tribunals, from Nuremberg to Belsen, to Kiev, to Iași had their chances after the war. Repeatedly they failed to address the Holocaust's immensity. And if the Jewish State could not try Eichmann, whose entire job was the destruction of Jewry, then who could?

Yet the Eichmann trial also served as a public memorial. Conscious of his duty to the dead as well as to the law, lead prosecutor Gideon Hausner opened the state's case thus:

> When I stand before you here, judges of Israel, to lead the prosecution of Adolf Eichmann, I am not standing alone. With me are six million accusers. But they cannot rise to their feet and point an accusing finger. . . . For their ashes are piled up on the hills of Auschwitz and the fields of Treblinka, and are strewn in the forests of Poland. Their graves are scattered throughout the length and breadth of Europe. Their blood cries out, but their voice is not heard. Therefore I will be their spokesman, and in their name I will unfold the awesome indictment."[95]

Witness after witness, meanwhile, remembered the dead—from family members to fallen comrades, to complete strangers. "Our watchword," remembered Adolf Berman of the Warsaw ghetto, "was naturally to save our children from hunger and death. We did not save them. We did not succeed. . . ."[96] Yehiel Dinur, a survivor of Auschwitz, could not testify at all. "I see them," he said. ". . . they are staring at me, I see them, I saw them standing in the queue. . . ."[97] He then collapsed on the witness stand.

Eichmann argued that he was a reluctant cog in the Nazi machine—a timetable specialist carrying out superior orders, the consequences of which he did not understand. "I did not take any initiative at all," he insisted. "I was not someone who liked or tended to take decisions. . . ."[98] The

---

[94]Quoted in Hanna Yablonka, *The State of Israel vs. Adolf Eichmann* (New York, 2004), p. 34.

[95]Israel, Ministry of Justice, *The Trial of Adolf Eichmann: Record of Proceeding in the District Court of Jerusalem*, vol. 1 (Jerusalem, 1992), p. 62.

[96]*Trial of Adolf Eichmann*, vol. 1, p. 426.

[97]*Trial of Adolf Eichmann*, vol. 3, p. 1298.

[98]*Trial of Adolf Eichmann*, vol. 4, pp. 1698–99.

defense failed under a blizzard of documentary evidence. He was hanged in June 1962, his ashes scattered offshore. The trial was more important than the punishment, for the scale of Eichmann's crimes and the drama of the trial outweighed any sentence that he could receive. As historian Shabai Teveth noted at the time, "[T]he human hand will achieve what it can. Justice cannot be measured."[99]

Yom Ha'Shoah

For better or worse, Israel's identity is closely linked with the Holocaust. Israeli memorialization initially aimed to stress, amid the unimaginable loss, heroic Jewish resistance and the danger of weakness. The emphasis was based on the perception among many Zionists that historic Jewish passivity in the Diaspora contributed to catastrophe. "Complacency," said historian Benzion Dinur, "plays a role in the destruction."[100] With the new country surrounded by hostile Arab states, the legacy of the armed Jewish fighter rather than the Diaspora Jew had to form the national narrative even amid sorrow over the unarmed victims.

Israel's initial national memorial came in the form of Holocaust Remembrance Day (*Yom Ha'Shoah*), which emerged by act of the Israeli Knesset in 1951. It is based on the recognition that, while nothing can replace individual religious mourning, collective, secular remembrance is also essential. Starting in 1958, official state ceremonies were held in Jerusalem, and after 1959, the entire state observed two minutes' silence. Even traffic comes to a stop. But the date, the 27th of Nissan, is significant. It coincides with the Warsaw ghetto uprising and sits between Passover, which commemorates the exodus from Egypt, and Israel's Day of Independence. The date thus honors ghetto fighters while linking them to the hard-won state. Ceremonies have connected ghetto fighters to contemporary Israeli soldiers while imploring Jews never to be complacent before their enemies. "If you wish to know the source from which the Israeli Army draws its strength," said Army Chief of Staff Mordechai Gur during *Yom Ha'Shoah* ceremonies in 1976, "go to the holy martyrs of the Holocaust and the heroes of the revolt. . . . The Holocaust . . . is the root and legitimization of our enterprise."[101]

Yad Vashem

At the center of Israeli Holocaust memory is Yad Vashem, the Holocaust Martyrs' and Heroes' Remembrance Authority in Jerusalem. Established in 1953 by the Knesset, it is Israel's preeminent Holocaust memorial site, museum, and research center. It was conceived during the war on the assumption that such a memorial could only be in Palestine. But its charter was daunting. On one hand, Yad Vashem was to commemorate all Jews who perished. On the other, it was to honor "the mighty courage of a few, desperate, empty-handed men who went to face the enemy. . . ."[102]

From the start, Yad Vashem struggled to reconcile this dual mission. Initial plans for a Holocaust Hall (to commemorate the murdered) and a Shrine of Heroism (to commemorate fallen Jewish fighters) foundered on objections from Jewish groups abroad who helped finance the site. Moshe Carmel, who moved to Palestine in 1924 and led a brigade in Israel's War of

---

[99]Quoted in Yablonka, *State of Israel vs. Adolf Eichmann*, p. 146.

[100]Dalia Ofer, "The Strength of Remembrance: Commemorating the Holocaust During the First Decade of Israel," *Jewish Social Studies*, 6, no. 2 (Winter 2000), p. 39.

[101]Quoted in James E. Young, *The Texture of Memory: Holocaust Memorials and Meaning* (New Haven, CT, 1993), p. 275.

[102]Quoted in Roni Stauber, *The Holocaust in Israeli Public Debate in the 1950s: Ideology and Memory* (London, 2007), p. 119.

Independence, argued that pity for those who simply hoped to survive must have limits. Where would Israel be with such attitudes? Scholar and survivor Nachman Blumenthal differed. "Death," he said, "should not be a matter of discrimination."[103] The passage of time—and particularly the Eichmann trial—increased understanding that Jews were not so neatly divided between a few armed resistors and a mass of passive victims.

Yad Vashem's memorial landscape thus includes the solemn Hall of Remembrance (1961) with the names of Nazi murder sites, ashes of the dead, and an eternal flame; a memorial to Janusz Korczak and the orphans of Warsaw (1978); the Children's Monument, for the 1.5 million children who perished in the Holocaust (1988); and the Valley of the Communities (1992), in which 5,000 names of lost Jewish communities are carved in stone. Yet it also includes the heroic broadly defined—a reproduction of Rapoport's Warsaw Ghetto Monument (1976); the Memorial to Jewish Soldiers, in which a giant sword reaches for the heavens through six massive blocks resembling tombstones (1985); and the Pillar of Heroism (1974), a twenty-one-meter column towering over the entire site, which commemorates all Jewish heroes, from ghetto fighters to all who risked and gave their lives for others.

During the early arguments over Yad Vashem in 1954, a different kind of memorial was begun in the Judean Hills near Jerusalem—the Holocaust Martyrs' Forest. For early Zionist settlers, the planting of trees connected Jews to the homeland both physically and spiritually. It symbolized return to the land, described in the Hebrew Bible as green and abundant. Yet the planting of trees is also a way to redeem the dead. The Holocaust Martyrs' Forest will soon have 6 million trees. With 7,500 acres, it is the largest of all commemorative spaces. It also claims the memory of the 6 million lost as Israel's own. "The memory of our six million holy ones," read the official announcement, "will be eternalized in the trees which will be planted in the earth closest to the heart of each and every Jew."[104]

America's Holocaust Museum

A broad Holocaust consciousness emerged in the United States in the late 1960s and 1970s. The Six Day War of 1967 and the Yom Kippur War of 1972 reminded American Jews of Israel's vulnerability. A 1978 neo-Nazi march in Skokie, Illinois—the home to many Holocaust survivors—raised the specter of antisemitism. The realization in the 1970s that several thousand low-level Nazi collaborators immigrated to the United States after the war posing as legitimate refugees was an affront to what the United States represented. A highly successful 1978 television miniseries entitled *Holocaust* brought the murder of Europe's Jews into American living rooms.

Perhaps as an act of reconciliation for his difficult relationship with Israel and American Jewish groups, President Jimmy Carter in 1978 created a Presidential Commission on the Holocaust. It was made up of Jewish survivors, scholars, and advocates as well as non-Jewish elected officials. Its charge was to recommend "an appropriate memorial to those who perished in the Holocaust." The next year, the commission proposed a "living memorial . . . that can transform the living by transmitting the legacy of the Holocaust."[105] The result was the United

---

[103]Carmel paraphrased in Ofer, "The Strength of Remembrance," p. 42; Blumenthal quoted in Stauber, *The Holocaust in Israeli Public Debate*, pp. 125, 126.

[104]Quote from Shaul Ephraim Cohen, *The Politics of Planting: Israeli-Palestinian Competition for Control of Land in the Jerusalem Periphery* (Chicago, IL, 1993), p. 65.

[105]Quoted in David Linenthal, *Preserving Memory: The Struggle to Create America's Holocaust Museum* (New York, 1995), pp. 23, 36.

States Holocaust Memorial Museum, built adjacent to the national mall in Washington, DC, and completed in 1993. It serves as a memorial, museum, research center, and educational resource.

The museum's conceptual process triggered impassioned debate among Jews and gentiles in the United States and elsewhere. One issue was the definition of the Holocaust in an increasingly pluralistic American society. Was it defined by Hitler's singular war against the Jews? Or should it be understood to encompass all of Hitler's victims, thus risking a dilution of its uniqueness and its Jewish core? How to memorialize a foreign catastrophe in a landscape that included soaring memorials to Washington, Jefferson, and Lincoln? And how to represent the terrible events? Should displays, like the Holocaust itself, contain no satisfying ending? Or should they draw out a far-reaching message based on the American insistence on broader lessons and redemption?

These debates brought some scholars, including Israel's Yehuda Bauer, to worry about an "Americanization of the Holocaust." But American Jewish scholar Michael Berenbaum, who helped to shape the museum in a number of leadership roles, understood the careful balance. For American Jews, he wrote, the Holocaust acted less to discredit the Diaspora than it did to "reinforce their commitment to pluralism by recalling the atrocities that sprang from intolerance." And while maintaining its Jewish center, Berenbaum continued, the Holocaust had to be explained to all Americans in a way that would resonate with them. If successful, such an explanation could "provide insights that have universal import for the destiny of all humanity."[106]

Indeed America's Holocaust museum succeeds. With its austere structure that recalls ghettos and camps yet still allows sunlight, with its Jewish yet inclusive themes that embrace diverse individual testimonies, with its deeply personal exhibitions that include family photographs and tactile artifacts painstakingly collected from all over Europe, and with its contemplative yet secular spaces, the museum attracted 30 million visitors as of March 2010.[107] It leaves a mark on all who visit. It also provides a warning, not against Jewish weakness, but against ignorance and, above all, against indifference to the fate of one's fellow human beings, whoever they may be, wherever they may live.

***

But we end in Jerusalem. In 1962, Yad Vashem inaugurated the Avenue of the Righteous Among Nations. It is a shady, peaceful walkway lined with trees and plaques honoring non-Jews who saved Jews from destruction. Nearby is the Garden of the Righteous with more trees, plants, and a wall containing the engraved names of the Righteous Among Nations whose names are known.

Numbering some 23,000 from all countries of Europe and from a few beyond, they include many that we have met: Portuguese Consul Aristides de Sousa Mendes, who lost his career and his fortune for writing visas for desperate Jews in Bordeaux; Swedish businessman Raoul Wallenberg, who lost his life by remaining in Budapest to protect Jews; German entrepreneur Oskar Schindler, who protected over 1,000 Jews in the shadow of the death camps; French monk Father Pierre-Marie Benoît, whose networks in France and Italy saved thousands of Jews; and Francisca Halamajowa, a simple Polish woman who, despite hostile neighbors and her own hardships, hid half of the Jews who survived in her East Galician town.

The avenue and garden symbolize flickers of redemption amid unimaginable darkness. Heroes, it would seem, are very few in number. But however difficult they may be to find, they walk somewhere among the rest of us.

---

[106]Michael Berenbaum, *After Tragedy and Triumph: Essays in Modern Jewish Thought and the American Experience* (New York, 1990), pp. 3, 22.

[107]Figure in Alvin H. Rosenfeld, *The End of the Holocaust* (Bloomington, IN, 2011), p. 66.

STARTING POINTS FOR FURTHER READING—WORKS IN ENGLISH

Reference, Overviews, and Documents

Reference works on Jewish history include the magisterial *Encyclopaedia Judaica*, 2nd ed., 22 vols. (Farmington Hills, MI, 2007). The standard reference on anti-semitism is Richard S. Levy, ed., *Anti-semitism: A Historical Encyclopedia of Prejudice and Persecution* (Santa Barbara, CA, 2005). Reference for the Holocaust in general is Yisrael Gutman et al., eds., *Encyclopedia of the Holocaust*, 4 vols. (Jerusalem, 1990). Detailed reference for eastern European Jewish localities include Gershon David Hundert, ed., *The YIVO Encyclopedia of Jews in Eastern Europe*, 2 vols. (New Haven, CT, 2007), which also has an online version at http://www.yivoencyclopedia.org.

For camps and ghettos, see Guy Miron, gen. ed., *The Yad Vashem Encyclopedia of the Ghettos During the Holocaust*, 2 vols. (Jerusalem, 2009), and the excellent, still-emerging Geoffrey P. Megargee, gen. ed., *The United States Holocaust Memorial Museum Encyclopedia of Camps and Ghettos, 1933–1945*, 7 vols. (Bloomington, IN, 2009–). Online resources for the Holocaust, including encyclopedia entries and standard documents, are at the sites of the United States Holocaust Memorial Museum (www.ushmm.org) and Yad Vashem in Israel (www.yadvashem.org). All of the reference works include extensive bibliography.

Exceptional up-to-date reference volumes with topical essays and bibliography include Peter Hayes and John Roth, eds., *The Oxford Handbook of Holocaust Studies* (New York, 2010), and Jonathan C. Friedman, ed., *The Routledge History of the Holocaust* (London, 2011). Recent research and approaches to understanding the Holocaust are discussed in Dan Stone, *Histories of the Holocaust* (New York, 2011), which supplements Michael R. Marrus, *The Holocaust in History* (New York, 1993). The classic overview of German administration of the Holocaust is Raul Hilberg, *The Destruction of the European Jews*, 3rd ed. (New Haven, CT, 2003), and the best integrated account with German, Jewish, and bystander narratives is Saul Friedländer's masterful *Nazi Germany and the Jews*, vol. 1: *Years of Persecution 1933–1939*, and vol. 2: *The Years of Extermination: Nazi Germany and the Jews, 1939–1945* (New York, 1998–2007).

For published documents on Nazi Germany, see Jeremy Noakes and Geoffrey Pridham, *Nazism, 1919–1945: A Documentary Reader*, 4 vols. (Exeter, 1998–2001). For Jewish reactions in Germany and elsewhere, see the emerging series from the United States Holocaust Memorial Museum, *Jewish Responses to Persecution*, 5 vols. (Lanham, MD, 2010–). Very useful sets of international documents include John Mendelsohn and Donald S. Detwiler, eds., *The Holocaust: Selected Documents in Eighteen Volumes* (Clark, NJ, 1982), and Henry Friedlander and Sybil Milton, gen. eds., *Archives of the Holocaust: An International Collection of Selected Documents*, 18 vols. (New York, 1985–1995). New research and current bibliographical information is in the journal of the United States Holocaust Memorial Museum, *Holocaust and Genocide Studies*. Students should also know the English-language Israeli journals *Yad Vashem Studies* and *Dapim: Studies on the Shoah*, published by Yad Vashem and The Institute for Holocaust Research at the University of Haifa, respectively.

The Jews, Emancipation, Antisemitism

General histories of the Jews include John Effron et al., *The Jews: A History* (Upper Saddle River, NJ, 2009), and Michael Brenner's *A Short History of the Jews* (Princeton, NJ, 2010). For modern Jewry, see Howard Morley Sachar, *A History of the Jews in the Modern World* (New York, 2005), and Paul Mendes-Flohr and Jehuda Reinharz, *The Jew in the Modern World: A Documentary History*, 3rd ed. (New York, 2011). For emancipation's mixed legacy, see Jacob Katz, *Out of the Ghetto: The Social Background of Jewish Emancipation, 1770–1880* (Syracuse, NY, 1998), and David Vital's darker *A People Apart: A Political History of the Jews in Europe, 1789–1939* (New York, 1999).

For emancipation in western Europe, see Paula E. Hyman, *The Jews of Modern France* (Berkeley, CA, 1998); David Sorkin, *The Transformation of German Jewry, 1780–1840* (New York, 1987); and Marion A. Kaplan, *The Making of the Jewish Middle Class: Women, Family and Identity in Imperial Germany* (New York, 1991). The essays in Pierre Birnbaum and

Ira Katznelson, *Paths of Emancipation: Jews, States, and Citizenship* (Princeton, NJ, 1995), and Jonathan Frankel and Steven J. Zipperstein, eds., *Assimilation and Community: The Jews in Nineteenth Century Europe* (New York, 1992), are excellent.

For Poland and the Pale of Settlement, see Antony Polonsky, *The Jews in Russia and Poland*, 3 vols. (Portland, OR, 2010–2012). On pogroms in the Russian Empire before and during the Russian Civil War, see John D. Klier and Shlomo Lambroza, eds., *Pogroms: Anti-Jewish Violence in Modern Russian History* (New York, 1992), and the more recent Oleg Budnitskii, *Russian Jews Between the Reds and the Whites 1917–1920* (Philadelphia, PA, 2012). The best one-volume treatments of Jews in interwar Europe are Ezra Mendelsohn, *The Jews of East Central Europe Between the World Wars* (Bloomington, IN, 1983), and Bernard Wasserstein, *On the Eve: The Jews of Europe Before the Second World War* (New York, 2012). On the international problem of Jewish rights, see Carole Fink, *Defending the Rights of Others: The Great Powers, the Jews, and International Minority Protection, 1878–1938* (New York, 2004).

Analyses of modern antisemitism are too numerous to list. A good starting point is George Mosse, *Toward the Final Solution: A History of European Racism* (New York, 1985). History and contemporary implications are in Albert S. Lindeman and Richard S. Levy, eds., *Antisemitism: A History* (New York, 2010), and Robert S. Wistrich, *A Lethal Obsession: Anti-Semitism from Antiquity to the Global Jihad* (New York, 2010). For the development of Zionism as a response to antisemitism, the best primer is Walter Laqueur, *A History of Zionism: From the French Revolution to the Establishment of the State of Israel* (New York, 2003). More in-depth essays are in Zvi Gitelman, ed., *The Emergence of Modern Jewish Politics: Bundism and Zionism in Eastern Europe* (Pittsburgh, PA, 2003).

Germany and the Rise of the Nazis

On interwar Germany in general, see Eric D. Weitz, *Weimar Germany: Promise and Tragedy* (Princeton, NJ, 2007), and Anton Kaes et al., eds., *The Weimar Republic Sourcebook* (Berkeley, CA, 1994), which has important entries on the stab-in-the-back myth. For German Jews in the Weimar period, see Donald Niewyk, *The Jews in Weimar Germany* (Baton Rouge, LA, 1980), and Michael Brenner, *The Renaissance of Jewish Culture in Weimar Germany* (New Haven, CT, 1996). Important essays are in Wolfgang Benz et al., eds., *Jews in the Weimar Republic* (London, 1998), and articles on Jewish culture and politics in Germany are throughout the annual *Leo Baeck Institute Yearbook: The Journal for German-Jewish History and Culture* (New York, 1956–).

For Nazi Germany in general, one should start with Richard J. Evans, *The Coming of the Third Reich* (New York, 2003), *The Third Reich in Power* (New York, 2005), and *The Third Reich at War* (New York, 2009). The best of many Hitler biographies is the two-volume work by Ian Kershaw, *Hitler, 1889–1936: Hubris* (New York, 1998), and *Hitler, 1936–1945: Nemesis* (New York, 2000). The best studies of Hitler's most important henchmen include Ralf Georg Reuth, *Goebbels* (New York, 1993); Richard Overy, *Goering: The "Iron Man"* (Boston, 1984); Peter Longerich, *Heinrich Himmler: A Life* (New York, 2012); Robert Gerwarth, *Hitler's Hangman: The Life of Heydrich* (New Haven, CT, 2011); and Peter R. Black, *Ernst Kaltenbrunner: Ideological Soldier of the Third Reich* (Princeton, NJ, 1984). The best studies of Adolf Eichmann and his subordinates are David Cesarani, *Becoming Eichmann: Rethinking the Life, Crimes, and Trial of a "Desk Murderer* (Cambridge, MA, 2006), and Hans Safrian, *Eichmann's Men* (New York, 2009).

Standard essays on the police state and concentration camps are in Helmut Krausnick, et al., eds., *Anatomy of the SS State* (London, 1965). New research is in Jane Caplan and Nikolaus Wachsmann, eds., *Concentration Camps in Nazi Germany: The New Histories* (London, 2010). For Nazi policies toward Jews in the 1930s, see Karl Schleunes, *The Twisted Road to Auschwitz: Nazi Policy Toward German Jews, 1933–1939* (Urbana, IL, 1970), as well as Saul Friedländer's volumes listed under Reference, Overviews, and Documents. More particular aspects include Gregory Paul Wegner, *Anti-Semitism and Schooling Under the Third Reich* (New York, 2002); Alan E. Steinweis, *Studying the Jew: Scholarly Antisemitism in Nazi Germany* (Cambridge, MA, 2006); and Avraham Barkai, *From Boycott to Annihilation: The Economic Struggle of German Jews, 1933–1943* (Hanover, NH, 1989). Alan E. Steinweis, *Kristallnacht 1938* (Cambridge, MA, 2009), is the most up-to-date treatment of that subject.

On levels of popular German support for the Nazis, see Peter Fritzsche, *Life and Death in the Third Reich* (Cambridge, MA, 2009); Robert Gellately, *Backing Hitler: Consent and Coercion in Nazi Germany*

(New York, 2001); Claudia Koonz, *The Nazi Conscience* (New York, 2003); and the essays in David Bankier, ed., *Probing the Depths of German Antisemitism: German Society and the Persecution of the Jews, 1933–1941* (New York, 2000). On the attitudes of German churches, see the essays in Robert P. Ericksen and Susannah Heschel, *Betrayal: The German Churches and the Holocaust* (Minneapolis, MN, 1999), and in Kevin P. Spicer, ed., *Antisemitism, Christian Ambivalence, and the Holocaust* (Bloomington, IN, 2007). Particular theological aspects are in Susannah Heschel, *The Aryan Jesus: Christian Theologians and the Bible in Nazi Germany* (Princeton, NJ, 2008), and Doris L. Bergen, *Twisted Cross: The Germanic Christian Movement in the Third Reich* (Chapel Hill, NC, 1996). For Austria, one should start with Bruce Pauley, *From Prejudice to Persecution: A History of Austrian Anti-Semitism* (Chapel Hill, NC, 1992), and Evan Burr Bukey, *Hitler's Austria: Popular Sentiment in the Nazi Era, 1938–1945* (Chapel Hill, NC, 2000).

For important essays on the Nazi treatment of non-Jewish social outsiders, see Robert Gellately and Nathan Stoltzfus, eds., *Social Outsiders in Nazi Germany* (Princeton, NJ, 2001), and Dagmar Herzog, ed., *Sexuality and German Fascism* (New York, 2005). The best works on the so-called euthanasia program are Henry Friedlander, *The Origins of Nazi Genocide: From Euthanasia to the Final Solution* (Chapel Hill, NC, 1987), and Michael Burleigh, *Death and Deliverance: "Euthanasia" in Germany c. 1900–1945* (New York, 1995). On the persecution of Roma, see Günther Lewy, *The Nazi Persecution of the Gypsies* (New York, 2000).

For the Jewish struggle for survival in Germany, see Marion A. Kaplan, *Between Dignity and Despair: Jewish Life in Nazi Germany* (New York, 1998) and Francis R. Nicosia, *Zionism and Anti-Semitism in Nazi Germany* (New York, 2010). On German Jewish refugees in Europe, one should start with Debórah Dwork and Robert Jan van Pelt, *Flight from the Reich: Refugee Jews, 1933–1946* (New York, 2009), and the essays in Frank Caestecker and Bob Moore, eds., *Refugees from Nazi Germany and the Liberal European States* (New York, 2010). Two of the best accounts of Jewish families unable to leave Germany are David Clay Large, *And the World Closed Its Doors: The Story of One Family Abandoned to the Holocaust* (New York, 2003), and Rebecca Boehling and Uta Larkey, *Life and Loss in the Shadow of the Holocaust: A Jewish Family's Untold Story* (New York, 2011).

War and Mentalities of Mass Murder

The Holocaust cannot be understood without a background in World War II, and the best one-volume history of the war is Gerhard L. Weinberg, *A World at Arms: A Global History of World War II* (New York, 2005). More particular military and economic aspects are in the ten-volume study by the Germany's Office of Military History, *Germany and the Second World War* (London; 1997–2008). Economic factors of Germany's war are in Adam Tooze, *The Wages of Destruction: The Making and Breaking of the Nazi Economy* (New York, 2006). German treatment of enemy civilians and prisoners is a broad subject, but crucial works include Rafael Scheck, *Hitler's African Victims: The German Army Massacres of Black French Soldiers in 1940* (New York, 2006); Ulrich Herbert, *Hitler's Foreign Workers: Enforced Foreign Labor in Germany Under the Third Reich* (New York, 1997); Ben Shepherd, *War in the Wild East: The German Army and Soviet Partisans* (Cambridge, MA, 2004); and Karel C. Berkhoff, *Harvest of Despair: Life and Death in Ukraine Under Nazi Rule* (Cambridge, MA, 2004).

Alternate interpretations regarding the evolution of the Final Solution of the Jewish Question in German thinking are Richard Breitman, *The Architect of Genocide: Himmler and the Final Solution* (New York, 1991); Christopher R. Browning, *The Origins of the Final Solution: The Evolution of Nazi Jewish Policy, September 1939–March 1942* (Lincoln, NE, 2004); Philippe Burrin, *Hitler and the Jews: The Genesis of the Holocaust* (London, 1994); and Peter Longerich, *Holocaust: The Nazi Persecution and Murder of the Jews* (New York, 2010). Essays on these and other interpretations are in Christopher R. Browning, *Nazi Policy, Jewish Workers, German Killers* (New York, 2000), and Ulrich Herbert, ed., *Nazi Extermination Policies: Contemporary German Perspectives and Controversies* (New York, 2000).

There is a great deal of work on the mentalities of the perpetrators. On policemen, the work begins with Christopher R. Browning's classic *Ordinary Men: Reserve Police Battalion 101 and the Final Solution in Poland* (New York, 1998); Ernst Klee, ed., *"The Good Old Days": The Holocaust as Seen by Its Perpetrators and Bystanders* (Old Saybrook, CT, 1996); and Edward B. Westermann, *Hitler's Police Battalions: Enforcing Racial War in the East* (Lawrence, KS, 2005). On command positions, see Michael Wildt, *An Uncompromising Generation: The Nazi Leadership of the Reich Security Main Office* (Madison, WI, 2010). On the army's complicity, see Hannes Heer and Klaus Naumann, eds., *War of Extermination: The German Military in World War II* (New York, 2000). The public Nazi rhetoric concerning the global war against the Jews is discussed in Jeffrey Herf, *The Jewish Enemy: Nazi Propaganda During World War II and the Holocaust* (Cambridge, MA, 2006).

On the plunder of Jewish property before and during the war, see Martin Dean, *Robbing the Jews: The Confiscation of Jewish Property in the Holocaust, 1933–1945* (New York, 2010), and Frank Bajohr, *Aryanization in Hamburg* (New York, 2002). On German business mentalities toward slave labor and mass murder, starting points include Peter Hayes, *Industry and Ideology: IG Farben and the Nazi Era* (New York, 2000); Peter Hayes, *From Cooperation to Complicity: Degussa in the Third Reich* (New York, 2007); Harold James, *The Deutsche Bank and the Nazi Economic War Against the Jews* (New York, 2001); and Michael Thad Allen, *The Business of Genocide: The SS, Slave Labor and the Concentration Camps* (Chapel Hill, NC, 2005).

Ghettos and Camps in Poland

Libraries of work discuss the Holocaust in Nazi-occupied Poland, particularly the major ghettos. Jewish Councils are the subject of Isaiah Trunk, *Judenrat: The Jewish Councils in Eastern Europe Under Nazi Occupation* (New York, 1972). Records from Łódź are in Isaiah Trunk, ed., *Łódź Ghetto: A History* (Bloomington, IN, 2006), and German plans for the city are discussed in Gordon Horwitz, *Ghettostadt: Łódź and the Making of a Nazi City* (Cambridge, MA, 2008). An exhaustive treatment of Warsaw can be found in Barbara Engelking and Jacek Leociak, *The Warsaw Ghetto: A Guide to the Perished City* (New Haven, CT, 2009). Israel Gutman, *The Jews of Warsaw, 1939–1943: Ghetto, Underground, Revolt* (Bloomington, IN, 1982) remains a classic. Samuel D. Kassow, *Who Will Write Our History? Emanuel Ringelblum, the Warsaw Ghetto, and the Oyneg Shabes Archive* (Bloomington, IN, 2007), is an almost miraculous account because it is based on the archive that Ringelblum and his followers painstakingly collected and then hid in the hope that someone would write this very history. The best of several firsthand accounts of the Warsaw uprising is Yitzhak Zuckerman, *A Surplus of Memory: Chronicle of the Warsaw Ghetto Uprising* (Berkeley, CA, 1993).

Official Polish reactions to the murder of Poland's Jews is explained in David Engel, *In the Shadow of Auschwitz: The Polish Government-in-Exile and the Jews, 1939–1942* (Chapel Hill, NC, 1987), and *Facing a Holocaust: The Polish Government-in-Exile and the Jews, 1942–1945* (Chapel Hill, NC, 1993). The current discussion over ordinary Polish bystanders currently begins with Jan T. Gross, *Neighbors: The Destruction of the Jewish Community in Jedwabne, Poland* (New York, 2001), and continues with the essays in Joshua D. Zimmerman, ed., *Contested Memories: Poles and Jews During the Holocaust and Its Aftermath* (New Brunswick, NJ, 2003). An excellent gendered approach to Jews and Poles is Nechama Tec, *Resilience and Courage: Women, Men, and the Holocaust* (New Haven, CT, 2003). A new, general history of Jewish resistance in the Polish context is Nechama Tec, *Resistance: How Jews and Christians Fought Back Against the Nazis* (New York, 2013). Also important is Gunnar S. Paulsson, *Secret City: The Hidden Jews of Warsaw, 1940–1945* (New Haven, CT, 2002).

There is not as much scholarship on the *Aktion Reinhard* camps as one might think. For the Chełmno death camp, see Patrick Montague, *Chełmno and the Holocaust: A History of Hitler's First Death Camp* (Chapel Hill, NC, 2012). On the Reinhard camps themselves, see Yitzhak Arad, *Belzec, Sobibor, Treblinka: The Operation Reinhard Death Camps* (Bloomington, IN, 1999). The best study of a single *Reinhard* camp is Jules Schelvis, *Sobibor: A History of a Nazi Death Camp* (New York, 2007). Gitta Sereny, *Into That Darkness: An Examination of Conscience* (New York, 1983) provides in-depth discussions with Franz Stangl, who served as Commandant at Sobibór and Treblinka. Dick de Mildt, *In the Name of the People: The Euthanasia and "Aktion Reinhard Cases"* (The Hague, 1996) examines postwar trials of camp staff. A searing survivor's account is Chil Rajchman, *The Last Jew of Treblinka: A Memoir* (New York, 2011).

An immense amount of research has been done on Auschwitz, beginning with Wacław Długoborski and Franciszek Piper, gen. eds., *Auschwitz 1940–1945: Central Issues in the History of the Camp*, 4 vols. (Oświęcim, 2000); Yisrael Gutman and Michael Berenbaum, eds., *Anatomy of the Auschwitz Death Camp* (Bloomington, IN, 1994); Debórah Dwork and Robert Jan Van Pelt, *Auschwitz* (New York, 2002); and Sybille Steinbacher's very concise *Auschwitz: A History* (New York, 2006). All deal with the construction of the camp, how the camp functioned, and prisoners' lives and deaths. There are many published firsthand survivor accounts and anthologies of such accounts. The classic is Primo Levi, *Survival in Auschwitz: The Nazi Assault on Humanity* (New York, 1986). Extraordinary accounts of women's experiences are Rena Kornreich Gelissen, *Rena's Promise: A Story of Sisters in Auschwitz* (Boston, MA, 1995), and Judith Magyar Isaacson, *Seed of Sarah: Memoirs of a Survivor* (Urbana, IL, 1992).

The USSR

Scholarship on the Holocaust in the USSR has expanded in the past twenty-five years thanks to the opening of Soviet-captured German records and Soviet records themselves. Yitzhak Arad, *The Holocaust in the Soviet Union* (Lincoln, NE, 2009) is an encyclopedic treatment. The place of Jews before the German invasion is the subject of Dov Levin, *The Lesser of Two Evils: Eastern European Jewry Under Soviet Rule* (Philadelphia, PA, 1995). On the Holocaust in the context of nationality struggles, see Timothy Snyder, *Bloodlands: Europe Between Hitler and Stalin* (New York, 2010). The most balanced of many recent studies of German policy on the local level is Wendy Lower, *Nazi Empire Building and the Holocaust in Ukraine* (Chapel Hill, NC, 2007). On collaborators in the USSR, see Martin Dean, *Collaboration in the Holocaust: Crimes of the Local Police in Belorussia and Ukraine, 1941–1944* (New York, 2000). A fine set of essays is Ray Brandon and Wendy Lower, eds., *The Shoah In Ukraine: History, Testimony, Memorialization* (Bloomington, IN, 2008).

Accounts of major ghettos, their leaders, and resistors in the USSR include Yitzhak Arad, *Ghetto in Flames: The Struggle and Destruction of the Jews in Vilna in the Holocaust* (Jerusalem, 1981); Sara Bender, *The Jews of Białystok During World War II and the Holocaust* (Lebanon, NH, 2008); and Barbara Epstein, *The Minsk Ghetto 1941–1943: Jewish Resistance and Soviet Internationalism* (Berkeley, CA, 2008). An exceptional study of Jews in *shtetlach* in the Soviet borderlands is Yehuda Bauer, *The Death of the Shtetl* (New Haven, CT, 2009). On the issue of rape in the USSR and elsewhere, see the essays in Sonja M. Hedgepeth and Rochelle G. Saidel, eds., *Sexual Violence Against Jewish Women During the Holocaust* (Waltham, MA, 2010). Nechama Tec, *Defiance: The Bielski Partisans* (New York, 1994), is a fine oral history of this Jewish partisan group.

For the Soviet government and the Holocaust, see Shimon Redlich, ed., *War, Holocaust and Stalinism: A Documented Study of the Jewish Anti-Fascist Committee in the USSR* (Luxembourg, 1995). See also the accounts on Soviet Jews and bystanders collected in Ilya Ehrenburg and Vasily Grossman, eds., *The Complete Black Book of Russian Jewry* (New Brunswick, NJ, 2002), and Joshua Rubenstein and Ilya Altman, eds., *The Unknown Black Book: The Holocaust in the German-Occupied Soviet Territories* (Bloomington, IN, 2008). Important essays on the Holocaust in the USSR and its legacies are in Zvi Gitelman, *Bitter Legacy: Confronting the Holocaust in the USSR* (Bloomington, IN, 1997).

Central and Western Europe

For Jews in Germany during the war, see the books listed in Germany and the Rise of the Nazis. See also the essays in Beate Meyer, ed., *Jews in Nazi Berlin: From Kristallnacht to Liberation* (Chicago, IL, 2009), and the personal accounts in Eric A. Johnson and Karl-Heinz Reuband, eds., *What We Knew: Terror, Mass Murder, and Everyday Life in Nazi Germany* (New York, 2005). Nathan Stoltzfus, *Resistance of the Hearst: Intermarriage and the Rosenstrasse Protest in Nazi Germany* (New York, 1996), is a powerful treatment. On the Protectorate of Bohemia and Moravia, as well as Theresienstadt, see Livia Rothkirchen, *The Jews of Bohemia and Moravia: Facing the Holocaust* (Lincoln, NE, 2005). The best account of the death marches at the war's end, all of which ended in Germany, see Daniel Blatman, *The Death Marches: The Final Phase of Nazi Genocide* (Cambridge, MA, 2010).

For the Netherlands, the most recent synthesis is Bob Moore, *Victims and Survivors: The Nazi Persecution of Jews in the Netherlands, 1940–1945* (London, 1997). An informative set of essays on Belgium is Dan Michman, ed., *Belgium and the Holocaust: Jews, Belgians, Germans* (Jerusalem, 1998). Writing on the Holocaust in France begins with Michael R. Marrus and Robert O. Paxton, *Vichy France and the Jews* (New York, 1981), and continues with Renée Poznanski, *Jews in France During World War II* (Hanover, NH, 2001). On the rescue of Denmark's Jews, see the essays in Mette Bastholm Jensen and Steven L. B. Jensen, eds., *Denmark and the Holocaust*, eds., (Copenhagen, 2003), which supplement Leni Yahil, *The Rescue of Danish Jewry: Test of a Democracy* (Philadelphia, PA, 1969). On rescue networks in general, see Bob Moore, *Survivors: Jewish Self-Help and Rescue in Nazi-Occupied Western Europe* (New York, 2010).

For Italy and its occupation zones, see Susan Zuccotti, *The Italians, the Jews, and the Holocaust: Persecution, Rescue and Survival* (Lincoln, NE, 1996); Jonathan Steinberg, *All or Nothing: The Axis and the Holocaust 1941–1943* (London, 1990); and Daniel Carpi, *Between Hitler and Mussolini: The Jews and the Italian Authorities in France and Tunisia* (Hanover, NH, 1994). Research on the Vatican and the Holocaust is vast and much of it is polemical. An extremely important treatment of Pius XI's policies is Hubert Wolf, *Pope and Devil: The Vatican's Archives and the Third Reich* (Cambridge, MA, 2010). Michael Phayer, *Pius XII, the Holocaust, and the Cold War* (Bloomington, IN, 2007) supplements his earlier, very balanced, *The Catholic Church and the Holocaust, 1930–1965* (Bloomington, IN, 2001). Susan Zuccotti, *Under His Very Windows: The Vatican and the Holocaust in Italy* (New Haven, CT, 2002) is also excellent.

Germany's Allies in Southeast Europe

For Romania one should begin with Radu Ioanid, *The Holocaust in Romania: The Destruction of Jews and Gypsies Under the Antonescu Regime, 1940–1944* (Chicago, IL, 2000), and Tuvia Friling, Radu Ioanid, and Mihail E. Ionescu, eds., *Final Report: International Commission on the Holocaust in Romania* (Bucharest, 2004). The most comprehensive treatment is Jean Ancel, *The History of the Holocaust in Romania* (Lincoln, NE, 2012). The most reliable treatment of atrocities in Yugoslavia is Jozo Tomasevich, *War and Revolution in Yugoslavia, 1941–1945: Occupation and Collaboration* (Stanford, CA, 2001).

The primary authority on the Holocaust in Hungary is Randolph L. Braham, *The Politics of Genocide: The Holocaust in Hungary*, 2 vols. (New York, 1981), and his many edited volumes of essays. Ronald W. Zweig, *The Gold Train: The Destruction of the Jews and the Looting of Hungary* (New York, 2003) is an important account of the fate of Jewish property there. For Slovakia, the best starting point is Ivan Kamenec, *On the Trail of Tragedy: The Holocaust in Slovakia* (Bratislava, 2007). The best overview of Bulgaria is Frederick B. Chary, *Bulgaria and the Final Solution, 1940–1944* (Pittsburgh, PA, 1972). Related documents are in Tzvetan Todorov, ed., *The Fragility of Goodness: Why Bulgaria's Jews Survived the Holocaust* (Princeton, NJ, 2003).

The Wider World and Rescue

On the Jewish Agency Executive in Palestine and its rescue attempts, see Dalia Ofer, *Escaping the Holocaust: Illegal Immigration to the Land of Israel, 1939–1944* (New York, 1990); Dina Porat, *The Blue and Yellow Stars of David: The Zionist Leadership in Palestine and the Holocaust 1939–1945* (Cambridge, MA, 1990); and Tuvia Friling, *Arrows in the Dark: David Ben-Gurion, the Yishuv Leadership, and Rescue Attempts During the Holocaust*, 2 vols. (Madison, WI, 2005). On German plans for the Middle East, see Klaus-Michael Mallmann and Martin Cüppers, *Nazi Palestine: The Plans for the Extermination of the Jews of Palestine* (New York, 2010); Jeffrey Herf, *Nazi Propaganda for the Arab World* (New Haven, CT, 2009); and Klaus Gensicke, *The Mufti of Jerusalem and the Nazis: The Berlin Years* (London, 2011).

On the rescue of Jews through diplomatic means in 1940, see José-Alain Fralon, *A Good Man in Evil Times: The Story of Aristides de Sousa Mendes* (London, 2000); Pamela Rotner Sakamoto, *Japanese Diplomats and Jewish Refugees: A World War II Dilemma* (Westport, CT, 1998); and the newer Gao Bei, *Shanghai Sanctuary: Chinese and Japanese Policy Toward European Jewish Refugees During World War II* (New York, 2012). For Swedish efforts in northern Europe and Hungary, see Paul A. Levine, *From Indifference to Activism: Swedish Diplomacy and the Holocaust, 1938–1944* (Uppsalla, 1996), and Paul A. Levine, *Raoul Wallenberg in Budapest: Myth, History, and Holocaust* (London, 2010). Spanish efforts and lack of effort are included in Stanley Payne, *Franco and Hitler: Spain, Germany and World War II* (New Haven, CT, 2009).

The research on Allied policy and the Jews is vast and constantly expanding. On what the Allies knew at any given time, the best place to start is Walter Laqueur, *The Terrible Secret: Suppression of the Truth About Hitler's "Final Solution"* (New York, 1998). Mainstream press coverage in the United States is discussed in Laurel Leff, *Buried by the Times: The Holocaust and America's Most Important Newspaper* (New York, 2005). Standard studies on Great Britain are Bernard Wasserstein, *Britain and the Jews of Europe, 1939–1945* (London, 1979); Louise London, *Whitehall and the Jews, 1933–1948: British Immigration Policy, Jewish Refugees and the Holocaust* (New York, 2000); and Sir Martin Gilbert, *Churchill and the Jews: A Lifelong Friendship* (New York, 2007).

The role of the United States and Franklin Roosevelt had been strongly influenced by David Wyman's somewhat polemical *The Abandonment of the Jews: America and the Holocaust* (New York, 1984). More balanced accounts are Richard Breitman and Alan Kraut, *American Refugee Policy and European Jewry, 1933–1945* (Bloomington, IN, 1984), and Richard Breitman and Allan Lichtman, *FDR and the Jews* (Cambridge, MA, 2013, forthcoming). On Allied intelligence and ransom/rescue schemes, see Yehuda Bauer, *Jews for Sale? Nazi-Jewish Negotiations* (New Haven, CT, 2009), and Shlomo Aronson, *Hitler, the Allies, and the Jews* (New York, 2006). For controversy regarding the bombing of Auschwitz, see the essays and documents in Michael J. Neufeld and Michael Berenbaum, eds., *The Bombing of Auschwitz: Should the Allies Have Attempted It?* (Lawrence, KS, 2003). For the actions of Jews in the United States, one should begin with Yehuda Bauer, *American Jewry and the Holocaust: The American Joint Distribution Committee, 1939–1945* (Detroit, MI, 1981), and Henry L. Feingold, *Bearing Witness: How America and Its Jews Responded to the Holocaust* (Syracuse, NY, 1998).

Books on the Latin American role in the Holocaust are not as numerous, but the research is slowly growing. Argentina's policy toward Jewish immigration is the subject of Haim Avni, *Argentina and the Jews: A History of Jewish Immigration* (Tuscaloosa, AL, 1991). For Brazil, see Jeffrey Lesser, *Welcoming the Undesirables: Brazil and the Jewish Question* (Berkeley, CA, 1995). Allen Wells, *Tropical Zion: General Trujillo, FDR and the Jews of Sosúa* (Durham, NC, 2008) is a thorough international account, as is recent research on Cuba and the voyage of the *St. Louis* in C. Paul Vincent, "The Voyage of the *St. Louis* Revisited," in *Holocaust and Genocide Studies*, 25, no. 2 (Fall 2011), pp. 252–89.

Refugees, Justice, Remembrance

The fate of Jewish refugees in Europe after the war is an expanding area of inquiry. The political and social aspects of displaced persons camps is treated in Zeev W. Mankowitz, *Life Between Memory and Hope: The Survivors of the Holocaust in Occupied Germany* (New York, 2002), and Atina Grossmann, *Jews, Germans and Allies: Close Encounters In Occupied Germany* (Princeton, NJ, 2007). The politics of returning Jews is the subject of the essays in David Bankier, ed., *The Jews Are Coming Back: The Return of Jews to Their Countries of Origin After World War II* (Jerusalem, 2005), and Jan Gross, *Fear: Anti-Semitism in Poland After Auschwitz* (New York, 2006). The geopolitical problem of Jewish emigration to Palestine after the war is discussed in Arieh Kochavi, *Post-Holocaust Politics: Britain, the United States, and Jewish Refugees, 1945–1948* (Chapel Hill, NC, 2001).

There is an increasing number of books regarding the trials of Nazi perpetrators and their collaborators simply because there were so many trials. The best overview of how the Holocaust fits into judicial reckoning is Lawrence Douglas, *The Memory of Judgment: Making Law and History in the Trials of the Holocaust* (New Haven, CT, 2001). One can find many analyses of the Nuremberg trials and the Holocaust; the better ones include Donald Bloxham, *Genocide on Trial: War Crimes Trials and the Formation of Holocaust History and Memory* (New York, 2001), and Hilary Earl, *The Nuremberg SS-Einsatzgruppen Trial, 1945–1958: Atrocity, Law, and History* (New York, 2009). An excellent study of Nazi escapees is Gerald Steinacher, *Nazis on the Run: How Hitler's Henchmen Escaped Justice* (New York, 2011).

Current essays on postwar justice in Europe are in Patricia Heberer and Jürgen Matthäus, eds., *Atrocities on Trial: Historical Perspectives on the Politics of Prosecuting War Crimes* (Lincoln, NE, 2008); Nathan Stoltzfus and Henry Friedlander, eds., *Nazi Crimes and the Law* (New York, 2008); and István Deak et al., eds., *The Politics of Retribution in Europe* (Princeton, NJ, 2000). Fine accounts of the Eichmann trial are Hanna Yablonka, *The State of Israel vs. Adolf Eichmann* (New York, 2004), and Deborah E. Lipstadt *The Eichmann Trial* (Omaha, NE, 2011). A very helpful overview of the controversial issue of postwar financial restitution and in the United States, Germany, Switzerland, and elsewhere is Michael R. Marrus, *Some Measure of Justice: The Holocaust Era Restitution Campaign of the 1990s* (Madison, WI, 2009).

Germany's national identity struggle with the Nazi past is a field almost without end. The standards are Jeffrey Herf, *Divided Memory: The Nazi Past in the Two Germanys* (Cambridge, MA, 1996); Norbert Frei, *Adenauer's Germany and the Nazi Past: The Politics of Amnesty and Integration* (New York, 2002); and Bill Niven, *Facing the Nazi Past: United Germany and the Legacy of the Third Reich* (London, 2002). Important essays on a variety of topics are in Philipp Gassert and Alan E. Steinweis, *Coping with the Nazi Past: West German Debates on Nazism* and Generational Conflict, 1955–1975 (New York, 2006). For West German trials in the 1960s within the context of German memory and the Cold War, see Rebecca Wittmann, *Beyond Justice: The Auschwitz Trial* (Cambridge, MA, 2005), and Devin O. Pendas, *The Frankfurt Auschwitz Trial, 1963–1965: Genocide, History, and the Limits of the Law* (New York, 2005).

Different approaches to the politics of memory elsewhere in Europe include Richard J. Golsan, *Vichy's Afterlife: History and Counterhistory in Postwar France* (Lincoln, NE, 2007); Joan B. Wolf, *Harnessing the Holocaust: The Politics of Memory in France* (Stanford, CA, 2003); Jonathan Huener, *Auschwitz, Poland, and the Politics of Commemoration, 1945– 1969* (Athens, OH, 2003); and Omer Bartov, *Erased: Vanishing Traces of Jewish Galicia in Present-Day Ukraine* (Princeton, NJ, 2007). An important assessment on the understanding of the Holocaust in the Arab world is Meir Litvak and Esther Webman, *From Empathy to Denial: Arab Responses to the Holocaust* (New York, 2009). The disturbing features of Holocaust denial are explained in Deborah Lipstadt, *Denying the Holocaust: The Growing Assault on Truth and Memory* (New York, 1993).

Jewish remembrance of the Holocaust is a field coming into its own. Hasia Diner, *We Remember with Reverence and Love: American Jews and the Myth of Silence After the Holocaust* (New York, 2009) corrects a number of misconceptions, as its title suggests. A fine introduction to the politics of memory in Israel is Tom Segev, *The Seventh Million: Israelis and the Holocaust* (New York, 2000). The problem of the Holocaust in U.S. culture is best discussed in Alvin H. Rosenfeld, *The End of the Holocaust* (Bloomington, IN, 2011). The aesthetic challenges of physical and cultural memorialization of the Jews in Germany, Poland, Israel, and the United States are the subjects of James E. Young, *The Texture of Memory: Holocaust Memorials and Their Meaning* (New Haven, CT, 1994). Finally, powerful and moving samples of memorial testimony from Yizkor books can be found in Jack Kugelmass and Jonathan Boyer, eds., *From a Ruined Garden: The Memorial Books of Polish Jewry* (Bloomington, IN, 1998).

INDEX

CPSIA information can be obtained
at www.ICGtesting.com
Printed in the USA
FFHW01n0738280818
48034500-51748FF